PARTNERS FOR DEMOCRACY

Partners for Democracy

CRAFTING THE NEW JAPANESE STATE UNDER MACARTHUR

RAY A. MOORE

DONALD L. ROBINSON

OXFORD

UNIVERSITY PRESS

2002

OXFORD
UNIVERSITY PRESS

Oxford   New York
Auckland   Bangkok   Buenos Aires   Cape Town   Chennai
Dar es Salaam   Delhi   Hong Kong   Istanbul   Karachi   Kolkata
Kuala Lumpur   Madrid   Melbourne   Mexico City   Mumbai   Nairobi
São Paulo   Shanghai   Singapore   Taipei   Tokyo   Toronto

Copyright © 2002 by Oxford University Press, Inc.

Published by Oxford University Press, Inc.
198 Madison Avenue, New York, New York 10016

www.oup.com

Oxford is a registered trademark of Oxford University Press

Library of Congress Cataloging-in-Publication Data
Moore, Ray A., 1933–
    Partners for democracy : crafting the new Japanese state under MacArthur / by Ray A.
Moore and Donald L. Robinson
        p. cm.
    Includes bibliographical references and index.
    ISBN 0-19-515116-X
    1. Constitutional history—Japan.   2. Japan, Kenpō (1946)   3. Japan—History—Allied
occupation, 1945–1952.   I. Robinson, Donald L., 1936–   II. Title.
KNX2201 .M66 2002
342.52'029—dc21   2001051153

9 8 7 6 5 4 3 2 1

Printed in the United States of America
on acid-free paper

Preface

On February 17, 1941, the eve of America's entry into World War II, Henry R. Luce published an essay in *Life* magazine: "The American Century." It was a call to arms, but it was far more than that. Luce declared that the fundamental trouble with America was a reluctance to face its duty and opportunity as the most powerful nation on earth, to exert the "full impact of our influence." It was not America's duty "to police the whole world nor to impose its democratic institutions on all mankind." America was, however, the bearer of ideals that could light the way to an "international moral order." We must share with all peoples "our Bill of Rights, our Declaration of Independence, our Constitution, our magnificent industrial products, our technical skills." This nation, "conceived in adventure and dedicated to the progress of mankind," must now commit itself to the "triumphal purpose of freedom." It must become, not a "sanctuary" of civilization (as former President Hoover had recently said), but the "powerhouse from which the ideals spread throughout the world and do their mysterious work of lifting the life of mankind from the level of the beasts to what the Psalmist called a little lower than the angels."

Luce had a special interest in Asia. When the war was over and won, he dedicated himself and his vast publishing empire to the defense of "freedom" in China, the land of his own birth to missionary parents. But the spirit he articulated in his famous essay was very much present in the soldiers who led the occupation of Japan as well.

The decisive period of the century, the time when America made a commitment to individual liberty, the constitutional state and the rule of law, came in 1945–1946. With much of Europe and Asia in ruin, a victorious America had the unique opportunity to convert Luce's vision into reality in the defeated nations of Germany and Japan.

In this book we study American idealism at work as it imposed constitutional democracy during the military occupation of Japan. As Americans ourselves, we confess ambivalence about the Occupation's project. On the one hand, it is pleasing to observe American soldiers passing on to a conquered foe our nation's foremost contribution to human governance. It is less gratifying to encounter an irritating combination of arrogance, ignorance, and stubborn willfulness in many of those who represented America in this episode. The challenge in telling this story has been to strike the right balance: to recognize the achievement while acknowledging the shortcomings of those who accomplished it. As scholars we have tried to tell it as it really happened, with sympathy and fairness toward all who took part.

Democratization is the process by which nations come to affirm a form of governance that respects human rights and empowers a democratic electorate. Japan is one of the great successes of the democratization process in the twentieth century. Scholars who study democratization have tended to ignore or slight the case of Japan, apparently believing that its circumstances are unique and unlikely ever to be replicated. To us, for reasons we will explain, this seems a mistake. To be sure, Japan in 1945–1946 was a nation under military occupation. Accepting a new liberal constitution was necessary to end the Occupation. Of course, Japan accepted it. The larger point, however, is that constitutional democracy has been stable in Japan for more than half a century. Apparently Japan did something more than accept alien forms under duress.

This book shows how and why the Japanese in 1946 embraced constitutional democracy. It shows how badly we mislead ourselves if we assume that it was simply imposed upon them. Japan was ready for what was being proffered. Japan's affirmation of democracy in 1946 was not cynical or merely tactical.

Acknowledgments

When we began this book in 1998, we had just finished five years of collaboration on *The Constitution of Japan: A Documentary History of Its Framing and Adoption, 1945–1947* (Princeton University Press, 1998). Having edited thousands of pages of documents on the making of Japan's constitution, we felt the strong urge to offer our own interpretation of the historic circumstances in which its American and Japanese authors had struggled to produce this remarkable document. As specialists on modern Japanese history (R. A. Moore) and American constitutional development (D. L. Robinson), we have sought to blend our perspectives into a fresh account of how the Japanese constitution was written and adopted.

Moore's interest in this topic began in earnest 20 years ago, when he organized in 1980 the Amherst Conference on the U.S. Occupation of Japan. His greatest thanks are reserved for several Japanese and American scholars who participated in that conference. John Dower, who gave the keynote address, has been Moore's friend and critic for 30 years. His outstanding scholarship has been an inspiration. After the conference, Moore spent a year on a Fulbright fellowship at the law faculty of Tokyo University, where he enjoyed the warm hospitality of Saitō Makoto and Igarashi Takeshi. Takemae Eiji, Sodei Rinjirō, Amakawa Akira, and Yoda Seiichi welcomed him to the monthly seminars of the association of specialists on the Occupation of Japan. The late Etō Jun and Hatano Sumio introduced him to Japan's Foreign Ministry archives, which had recently been opened to scholars of this period, and to important documents of the Legislation Bureau of the Japanese cabinet. His acquaintance with a young scholar, Koseki Shōichi, which began at this time, led to his translation of Koseki's prize-winning *Birth of Japan's Postwar Constitution* (Westview Press, 1997). We are especially grateful for Koseki's help in locating document collections in the National Diet Library and securing copyright permissions. The influence of Koseki's book will be evident in many chapters of our own study. Wada Takehiro called our attention to documents in the Hussey Papers and to recent articles in regional journals in Japan, which we would have missed without his alert assistance.

vii

Oyama Tsunao told Moore of YWCA activist Kawai Michiko, founder of Keisen Girls School in Tokyo. Through him, we came to know of her friendship with MacArthur's aide, Brigadier General Bonner Fellers, and imperial adviser, Sekiya Teisaburō. Moore's long-time friend and Doshisha University colleague, Uda Yoshitada, arranged for him to see and copy parts of the diary of William Merrill Vories at the Omi Brotherhood. Uda has always responded with alacrity to our requests for help with translations and finding obscure publications. We also wish to thank Sekiyama Ichiro of Kōdansha for his grace and patience and Takagi Kikurō, senior editor of *Yomiuri Shinbun*, for sending us *Yomiuri's* proposals for revising the Japanese constitution.

Robinson's path to the writing of this book began during the bicentennial of the American Constitution, when Shepard Forman, of The Ford Foundation, invited him to suggest ways of enriching understanding of constitutional principles. The project brought him in closer contact with others interested in the comparative study of constitutions, particularly Walter J. Murphy and Stanley Katz, both at Princeton University, and A. E. Dick Howard of the University of Virginia School of Law. Also in the late 1980s, he attended a summer seminar at Harvard on "Japan's Nineteenth-Century Transformation," led by Albert Craig and Hal Bolitho. He had the temerity to send a paper written for that seminar to George Akita, who responded with his usual kindness, initiating what has become a treasured friendship. Robinson's interest in Japan was further stimulated by an opportunity to teach in the Associated Kyoto Program at Doshisha University in Kyoto, during the fall semester of 1989, where Kamata Taisake became a valued friend.

It is a pleasure for us to acknowledge the contributions of other friends in the United States. We would especially like to thank Theodore McNelly, whose knowledge of Japan's Shōwa Constitution saved us from errors; John M. Maki, for publications of the Commission on the Constitution, for translating a transcript of a House of Peers subcommittee, and for sharing his memories of service in the Government Section of the Supreme Commander of the Allied Powers in 1946; Kyoko Inoue for help in understanding linguistic problems arising from constitutional drafts translated between English and Japanese; and Dale Hellegers for allowing us to quote from her 1973 interview with Charles Kades.

We are indebted to the staff at the National Diet Library in Tokyo, and the National Archives of the United States, particularly the branch at College Park, Maryland. We benefited as well from the assistance of the Douglas MacArthur Memorial in Norfolk, Virginia, and especially James Zobel, archivist. Closer to home, we are grateful for the excellent libraries and able staffs that serve our own institutions: Amherst College's Robert Frost Library and Smith College's William Allan Neilson Library. We would like especially to thank Christine Hannon, Pamela Skinner, and Robin Kinder at Smith, and Willis Bridegam and Susan Sheridan at Amherst.

Our earlier collaboration produced a collection of more than 500 documents, to which we refer frequently in this book. That work was generously funded by grants from the Japan Foundation, the Japan–United States Friendship Commission, and research grants from our own institutions. Those grants provided the foundation on which this current work rests.

We owe a special personal debt to the late Colonel Charles L. Kades. From the time he retired from the practice of law in New York City until his death in 1996 at the age of 90, Colonel Kades lived in the western Massachusetts village of Heath, about 30 miles from Amherst and Smith colleges. Throughout our labors on the documentary project, Colonel Kades's generosity knew no bounds. He loaned us all his documents, including his invaluable copies of the translations of the Diet debates (they are now on deposit at the Robert Frost Library, at Amherst College). He met with us frequently to discuss questions of dating, sequence, and identification. Above all, he communicated an intense interest in inviting scholars to examine and assess the project to which he had given such skillful attention, and he took no personal offense when our interpretations of its meaning differed from his own.

Our editor at Oxford University Press, Dedi Felman, contributed greatly to this project through her gentle wisdom in helping us to clarify our intentions. We also benefited from the criticism of several anonymous readers procured by Oxford University Press, who reviewed an early version of the manuscript. Their candid reactions and thoughtful comments persuaded us to make several changes in our approach, to tighten our argument, and to abandon an earlier title we had chosen for the book.

We are especially grateful to John S. Bowman for his careful reading of the manuscript. His sharp eye and balanced judgment have made this a better book, as well as a considerably shorter one! Liane Hartman, of Smith College's Computer Center, also made a crucial contribution. In the final stages of our project, she helped to transform various versions of our typescript into the language of a single word-processing program. We would have been sunk without her.

For assistance with research, fact checking, and word processing, we thank Amanda Stevens, Christina Gosack, Julia Oestreich, Mona Syed, and George Solt. For assistance with the index, we thank Leila Cohan and Stephanie Solywoda.

Finally, we dedicate this work to our beloved wives, Ilga Moore and Molly Robinson. Their patience, encouragement, and confidence have sustained us through a very long process.

Contents

Abbreviations and Japanese Terms

CIE   Civil Information and Education. A section of General MacArthur's headquarters.

CLO   Central Liaison Office. An office in the Japanese Foreign Ministry responsible for maintaining official contact between the Japanese government and MacArthur's headquarters.

FEC   Far Eastern Commission. A group of nations formed in December 1945 by the Moscow Agreement; created to oversee the Allied Occupation of Japan.

FRUS   *Foreign Relations of the United States.* Official series of U.S. State Department documents.

GHQ   General Headquarters. MacArthur's headquarters, located in the Daiichi Seimei building in central Tokyo from 1945 to 1952.

GS   Government Section. A section of MacArthur's headquarters that directed the revision of Japan's constitution and other political reforms.

JCS   Joint Chiefs of Staff. A council consisting of leaders of the American military services.

LB   Legislation Bureau. A bureau of the Japanese cabinet responsible for drafting laws; worked closely with GS in framing the 1946 draft constitution.

NKSRS   *Nihonkoku kenpō seiritsushi.* A four-volume collection of Satō Tatsuo's writings on the making of Japan's 1946 Constitution.

PRJ   *Political Reorientation of Japan.* SCAP's official, two-volume history of the Occupation.

RM   *The Constitution of Japan: A Documentary History of Its Framing and Adoption, 1945–1949,* edited by Ray A. Moore and Donald L. Robinson (CD-ROM).

SCAP   Supreme Commander of the Allied Powers. MacArthur's official title during the Occupation; sometimes used to refer generally to the officers of the American Occupation.

SFE   Subcommittee of the Far East. A committee of SWNCC that formulated U.S. policy for the occupation of Japan.

SWNCC   State, War, and Navy Coordinating Committee. An interdepartmental committee that advised the president on foreign
policy during and after World War II. Created in 1944, it
was replaced by the National Security Council in 1947.

Japanese Terms

We have, in every practical case, provided English translations of Japanese terms,
even when the discussion is about varying ways of expressing an idea in Japanese.
The modified Hepburn system has been used in romanizing Japanese words. Style
in the use of Japanese words follows the standard practice of leading journals in
the field. We have used macrons to indicate long vowels except in the case of
common place names such as Tokyo and Kyushu. We have italicized all Japanese
words that do not appear in *Webster's International Dictionary.* Japanese names
in the text are given in the Japanese order, that is, surname first, followed by the
given name.

PARTNERS FOR DEMOCRACY

Introduction

"A NEW ORDER OF THINGS"

The year following the cataclysmic end of World War II in Japan witnessed one of the great turning points in modern history. Wars often have winners and losers, though rarely on the scale found in East Asia in 1945 when Japan surrendered to the United States and its allies. What truly distinguished the outcome of this war in the Pacific was that it led to Japan's transformation into a stable constitutional democracy.

In the first year of the American Occupation, a victorious American general and a conquered Japanese government cooperated to set Japan on a course toward constitutional democracy and peaceful integration into an international system dominated by competing American and Soviet empires. Their achievement ought not to be underestimated in a world in which democratization is often pursued but rarely accomplished.

It is often said that the United States "imposed" a constitution on Japan.[1] As this book will amply demonstrate, there is substantial truth in this contention. It is one thing, however, to impose a constitutional text and quite another to establish constitutional democracy.[2] On this larger and vastly more important point, this volume demonstrates that the conventional wisdom is a misleading oversimplification, standing in the way of understanding how Japan achieved something that is the envy of many other nations.

How could it not be so? If constitutional democracy could so easily be imposed, why did it not happen in other countries where American soldiers, diplomats and professors have attempted to transplant Western institutions? Many countries in Africa, Latin America, and Asia have adopted Anglo-American constitutions but have failed to achieve stable democratic practice.[3] It is apparently not so easy to "impose" constitutional democracy.

A Special Case?

What made the Japanese case different? First and foremost, although the American military under MacArthur exercised, for almost seven years, total control over Japanese government and political activities, the Americans were not solely responsible for this historic achievement. It was accomplished by collaboration between Americans and Japanese, mostly in Tokyo, and with the connivance of a few military and civilian leaders in Washington, D.C. The cooperation between these leaders was often unspoken, implicit. Sometimes it involved heavy-handed American demands and formal directives, to which the Japanese acceded slowly and with great reluctance. Sometimes agreement was achieved by successful deceptions, as when ambiguities in translation were allowed to remain unresolved.[4]

The special nature of this collaboration has led us at times to employ the word "conspiracy." It should be kept in mind that this word carries two basic meanings. One emphasizes an agreement to perform unlawful, reprehensible acts, especially in relation to treason, sedition, or murder. Clearly, we do not mean to suggest anything like that here. The second meaning speaks of harmonious action or effort, as in the expression "circumstances conspired to produce the result." That is perhaps a bit bland for what we intend. Secrecy, plus a willingness to skirt the law and to ignore others in authority, is very much a part of the picture we are presenting. The end, promoting democracy, may be deemed ultimately to justify such means, but the leading actors in our story did not hesitate to employ them.

Whether labeled "conspiracy" or not, the process that resulted in the new constitution was a special case, based on shared political and security interests, commitment on both sides to constitutional democracy, and hard-won trust between leaders of the two camps, General of the Army Douglas MacArthur and Prime Ministers Shidehara Kijūrō and Yoshida Shigeru, and their principal collaborators. The major objective of both sides was to devise institutional arrangements that could accommodate MacArthur's commitment to American values and practices, on the one hand, and the Japanese leaders' devotion to Japan's mores and its ancient imperial institution on the other.

The first thing to realize about these leaders is that despite their peremptory leadership styles, their hold on power in 1946 was somewhat tenuous. Douglas MacArthur, with his corncob pipe and soft hat, was a dramatic figure. As the senior commander of the Allied Pacific campaign that finally subdued Japan, he was perhaps an inevitable, if fateful, choice to direct the Occupation. It was a role MacArthur greatly coveted. He fancied that he had deep understanding of "Asiatic" people and their culture. He had definite ideas about how Japan ought to be "reoriented."[5] When speaking of democracy's formal framework of basic freedoms, universal suffrage, and representative government, he often used grandiose language. He spoke of the need for "spiritual changes" in Japan's national life; "democracy," he said, "is a thing largely of the spirit." To a visiting American religious leader, he described the problem facing him and defeated Japan as "fundamentally theological." Democracy, he said, must have a "spiritual core" of Christian principles. It was "the American experience" that had given meaning and strength to its formal political institutions. He hoped to be able to instill enough of that to provide a foundation for the spiritual revolution required in Japan. He urged American churches and the Vatican to send missionaries to help fill the defeated nation's "spiritual vacuum."

MacArthur also professed admiration for President McKinley's dictum, justi-fying his annexation of the Philippines, that the "free can conquer but to save." He wrote of the profound impression McKinley's speech had on him, how it had guided his conduct in the occupation of Japan. Like McKinley and his own father, Arthur, who had been military governor of the Philippines (1900–1901), Mac-Arthur cast himself in the role of emancipator of an Asian people. He spoke in Lincolnian cadences of liberating the Japanese people from their "condition of slavery." In short, MacArthur, the Supreme Commander of the Allied Powers (SCAP), had a powerful sense that this mission was a fulfillment of his own, and America's, destiny in Asia.[6]

When the 65-year-old general entered Yokohama, near Tokyo, on August 29, to accept Japan's surrender and inaugurate his regime, he was characteristically unarmed. Churchill called it the most courageous act he had ever encountered: a commander exposing himself, personally defenseless, in the citadel of his only recently defeated enemy. It mightily impressed the Japanese, as did MacArthur's dramatic invitation to the beleaguered Emperor Hirohito to visit him at his head-quarters. The photograph of the two men taken at their meeting on September 27 became an instant icon of the occupation. MacArthur ordered it printed in newspapers throughout Japan. It graphically illustrated his dominance of Japan: the casually dressed, relaxed American commander, standing at a slight remove and leaning away from the formally attired monarch, a much shorter man but erect and dignified.

MacArthur's principal collaborators on constitutional reform were Shidehara and Yoshida. Shidehara played a crucial role in the fall, when he received Mac-Arthur's notice that Japan's Constitution would have to be revised, and in the spring, when he led his reluctant cabinet to accept the SCAP draft as the basis for the project. Later Yoshida became the key figure on the Japanese side. He had served as foreign minister in the postwar cabinets. After the April 1946 elections, he formed a coalition cabinet and then during the summer shepherded the re-vision through the Diet. A diplomat by training and temperament, Yoshida had served as ambassador in England during the 1930s. He had resisted military control of the nation and its drift toward war and was sidelined politically during the terrible struggle against the West. He emerged vindicated after the surrender, a firm and undoubted patriot, a steadfast defender of the imperial institution. Taciturn and scornful of those who disagreed with him, he was utterly inexpe-rienced in, even disdainful of, the small arts of democratic politics.

Yet, to the amazement of many observers in postwar Japan, Yoshida proved to be superbly suited to the demands of leadership in this period. He was a consummate realist and a rock of integrity. He never ducked responsibility for the policies he adopted, even when they went awry. An Anglophile like many of his fellow countrymen, he was unusual in his steady confidence that the Japanese people were perfectly capable of operating the Westminster model of constitu-tional democracy. Without reservation, he would embrace the opportunity to set it in motion.

Three strong men—but somewhat precarious in their hold on power.

The Principal Players

As Supreme Commander in Japan, MacArthur was the agent of an American government in turmoil. Harry Truman had only recently assumed a position for which most observers thought him ill prepared. The new American president was a doughty, strongly partisan Democrat; MacArthur was a conservative Republican who was widely suspected of harboring exalted political ambitions, indeed, of coveting Truman's job. Truman was somewhat uncertain of himself in foreign relations, particularly where the Pacific region was concerned, but he had a lively sense of his responsibilities and he did not intend to shirk them. The rivalry between these two men would later explode over differences about how to wage the war in Korea, but regarding Japan, Truman supported the Supreme Commander to the hilt, whatever his misgivings may have been.

The Truman administration was staffed by vigorous men whose disagreement over treatment of Japan's imperial institution gave MacArthur some room for maneuver. On one side was Joseph Grew, Acting Secretary of State in 1945 and former ambassador to Japan, who saw the emperor as vital to Japan's cohesion and a potential ally in reforming his country's social and political institutions. On the other side were James F. Byrnes, Secretary of State, and Dean Acheson, Undersecretary of State, the latter especially an unsentimental man who did not trust Japan and was determined to make it and its leaders pay dearly for cruelty and aggression in Asia and the Pacific. The conflict between these factions, plus preoccupation with problems in Europe, left openings that MacArthur did not hesitate to exploit. Another factor was that many senior military leaders in Washington—Marshall, Eisenhower—had been MacArthur's subordinates and remained deferential in their attitudes toward him. To resist MacArthur would have required great determination. These men could not easily summon it.

More threatening to the SCAP were the Allied countries themselves. Some of them had definite ideas for the reform of Japan and a firm intention to see them implemented. Stalin, for example, who had seized on Roosevelt's urging to join the war against Japan, was interested in restoring the old Russian empire's influence in northeastern Asia, influence that had been set back when Japan defeated Russia in 1905.

The United States attempted to confine Allied nations strictly to an advisory capacity in the Occupation of Japan, but the Soviet Union and Great Britain were bent on establishing multilateral bodies, with Soviet, British, and Chinese vetoes, having authority to set guidelines for the Occupation and to monitor its performance closely. To MacArthur, these commissions and councils were irritants. He treated them with diplomatic cordiality, at best. When they sought to interfere with his prerogatives, he administered a dose of arch disdain or defiance, as the occasion required.

MacArthur's staff was an extension of himself. His top aide, Major General Courtney Whitney, shared his superior's grandiose vision and bombastic rhetorical style, if not his heroic military record. Educated for a legal career, Whitney had joined the Army Reserves and met MacArthur in the Philippines in the mid-

1920s. He had gained MacArthur's confidence as his attorney in Manila. Admitted to the inner circle of confidantes, he demonstrated perfect loyalty and useful administrative skills. After thirteen years in the Philippines, Whitney returned to Washington for active service in army intelligence. In early 1943 he got word that MacArthur, then marshaling his forces in Australia, needed him to take charge of the guerrilla army in the Philippines. In August 1945 he accompanied Mac-Arthur to Japan, where he served as chief deputy in charge of Government Section.

Whitney, like MacArthur, was a conservative Republican in politics, but in assembling and organizing the staff for the Occupation, he looked for just two qualities: unflagging loyalty and useful skills. He found them, by great good fortune, in a 40-year-old colonel named Charles L. Kades. Trained at Cornell and Harvard Law School, Kades had gone to Washington in 1933 with the New Deal, serving initially as assistant general counsel in the Public Works Administration (1933–1937) and in the same capacity at the Treasury Department (1937–1942). An officer in the Army Reserve, he entered on active duty in 1942, graduated from Command and General Staff School and was assigned to the War Department's Civil Affairs Division, an agency with responsibility to reestablish civil institutions in liberated and conquered areas.

Brilliant and convivial, Kades made a strong impression on people, such as General John Hilldring, who would later be in a position to recommend personnel for postwar occupation regimes. Kades was stationed in Europe in early 1945. When word came that MacArthur was recruiting a staff for the occupation of Japan, Hilldring recommended Kades. He was quickly promoted to the rank of colonel, given a few weeks of training about Japan, and hurried off to join Mac-Arthur's contingent, about to leave Manila for Tokyo.

Kades was in some ways well qualified for the awesome responsibility he would inherit as director of the revision project. Although not a specialist in constitutional law, he had considerable experience in the complex bureaucratic procedures of democratic governance. His temperament was ideal. Clear and confident in his understanding of constitutional principles, he was a lion for hard work. He was also completely comfortable with military discipline. When told, for example, to assemble a small staff and produce a draft of the Japanese Constitution in one week's time, he did not hesitate or raise objections. He simply saw that it was done.

His main drawback was that he knew almost nothing about Japan, its language, or legal traditions, steeped as they were in nineteenth-century European continental, particularly Prussian, forms and procedures.[7] In a way, it was appalling that this assignment fell to someone so ignorant about the history and culture of the nation whose Solon he was about to become. He was not devoid of opinions about Japan. They were the conventional doctrines of American wartime propaganda: that Japanese culture was layered with feudal remnants, chauvinistic, prone to militarism and imperialism, imitative, and mystical—not a promising set of qualities for constitutional democracy. On the other hand, Kades was profoundly confident of the universal appeal, relevance, and efficacy of constitutional liberty and democratic equality. Moreover, he had none of the political scientist's prejudice that a constitution, to be successful, must grow organically from the cultural soil whose governance it seeks to organize. This was to prove deeply frustrating for the Japanese officials and scholars with whom he dealt, for they were more familiar with the European style of constitutionalism than with the American.

Fortunately for the American revision project, Japan did not conform well to the American stereotype. It had constitutional experience, a tradition of self-rule, and some outstanding scholars of constitutional law. What was needed was politically savvy Japanese leadership fully conscious of the nation's total defeat and cognizant of the imperative to adjust to American demands. After a couple of false starts during Shidehara's premiership, Yoshida, as soon as he became prime minister, would sack the inflexible Matsumoto Jōji and name Kanamori Tokujirō to head the Japanese team on constitutional revision.

As Kades's counterpart, Kanamori was perfectly suited for this responsibility. At 58, he was both an experienced bureaucrat and a respected scholar of constitutional law. In the early 1930s, Kanamori had held one of the highest legal positions in the Japanese bureaucracy: director of the cabinet's Legislation Bureau, but he became a target of right-wing critics and was forced, in 1936, to resign from public office. As the author of several books about the Meiji Constitution, Kanamori had an excellent reputation among legal scholars in Japan.

Kanamori was profoundly liberal in his constitutional values. He believed deeply in the rule of law and in human rights. Without reservation, he affirmed the central tenets of constitutionalism: that power must be held accountable, checked, and balanced. On the role of the emperor in the new order, he walked a precarious tightrope. In the marrow of his bones, he shared the Japanese people's profound reverence for the emperor's dignity. Yet partly for that very reason, he thought it imperative to protect the emperor from engagement in politics.

Kanamori's stamina during the Diet debates in the summer of 1946 would be impressive. Day after day, he stood in the well and answered parliamentary inquiries and challenges. His expertise ranged from grand themes to the minutiae of legislation. One moment he would be expounding on the doctrine of checks and balances or the roots of the Anglo-American concept of habeas corpus or the theory of rights in Germany's Weimar Constitution. The next interrogation would draw his attention to some obscure passage in the Japanese Civil Code. He was frequently assailed for defending a draft that sounded to Japanese ears like a crude translation. His retreat from his own prewar writings drew ridicule. Yet he seldom lost his temper or took offense.

He also had to endure harsh criticism from Kades, who did not understand why Kanamori kept insisting that *kokutai*, a unique Japanese form of patriotism that centered on the emperor, had not changed with Japan's acceptance of the Allied terms for surrender. At one awful point in mid-July, Kades would come close to accusing Kanamori of deliberate deception, and Kanamori in anguished protest nearly resigned his post. It was a genuine crisis. Kades himself was on thin ice in this confrontation. MacArthur had taken the public position that the Diet was free to amend the draft in any way it saw fit and that the Occupation would not interfere with its deliberations. If Kanamori had quit over the dispute with Kades, it would have exposed the American heavy-handedness. As Machiavelli remarked, there is nothing more dangerous, more doubtful of success, than to initiate a "new order of things." Constitutional reform in Japan faced many perils over the fifteen months of its gestation, but none more portentous than this struggle over *kokutai*.

The Goals of the Occupation

What were the goals of the Occupation, and what part was constitutional reform given in the Occupation's plans for achieving those goals?

The goals were outlined early[8] and often.[9] In their simplest form they were (1) to ensure as far as possible that Japan would never again become a "menace to the peace and security of the world" and (2) to encourage the establishment in Japan of a peaceful, democratic government.

The achievement of the first goal obviously entailed the dismantling of Japanese armed forces, destruction of related industries, and creation of a compliant ruling class by a massive purge. But in American eyes, it also required an ideological conversion of society—what Secretary of State James F. Byrnes called the "spiritual disarmament" of Japanese culture (in MacArthur's terms, "filling a spiritual vacuum"). This meant, in the words of an American policy document, the elimination of "ultra-nationalistic and totalitarian teachings, in the schools and among the people," to make the Japanese people "want peace instead of wanting war." It also meant the elimination of "oppressive laws and practices, which in the past have closed the door to truth and have stifled the free development of democracy in Japan."[10]

On its face, this understanding involved a potential conflict with the second major, stated goal: encouraging the Japanese people to establish democratic government according to their own "freely expressed will." What if it turned out that the Japanese people preferred imperial government, even with its martial accoutrements? The apparent contradiction was resolved, in American eyes, by the doctrine that the Japanese people shared the universal desire for political liberty and peace, and that these instincts, once they were released from the grip of oppression, would lead them to democracy, American style.

This tension between benign universalism and stern paternalism in the outlook of the American Occupation was no light matter. The Americans had definite ideas, drawn from the American experience, about the requirements of democratic culture and government, and they would make no bones about imposing them on Japan.

They intended, first of all, to repeal the repressive policies of the past. That was substantially accomplished on October 4, 1945, by MacArthur's order to the Japanese government to "abrogate and immediately suspend" all laws and decrees that restricted "freedom of thought, of religion, of assembly and of speech, including the unrestricted discussion of the Emperor, the imperial institution and the imperial Japanese government"; to release all political prisoners held under these oppressive laws; to abolish all organizations that had participated in the suppression of political and civil freedom; and to remove all bureaucrats and police officials who had participated in enforcing these laws. These demands, dropped suddenly and peremptorily on the hapless postwar cabinet of Prince Higashikuni, the emperor's uncle, caused the cabinet to resign. However, the political crisis was short-lived. Baron Shidehara Kijūrō, a respected politician of long experience, quickly agreed to form a cabinet and carry out MacArthur's order.

A week later (October 11), the officers of the Occupation gave indication of a more far-reaching ambition. Beyond the abrogation of oppressive laws, the release of communist political prisoners, and the purge of wartime civil administrators, they now demanded that "the traditional social order under which the Japanese people for centuries have been subjugated be corrected."[11] The directive listed "five fundamental reforms": enfranchisement of women,[12] encouragement of labor unions, introduction of "liberal" principles into education, reform of the judicial system, and "democratization" of economic institutions.[13] MacArthur's directive added that these "reforms in the social order of Japan" were to be accomplished "as rapidly as they can be assimilated."

Where did constitutional revision stand in this picture of reform? From the beginning, the Americans saw it as absolutely fundamental. The opening paragraph of the Five Fundamental Reforms directive makes this quite clear. Before listing specific reforms, it states that "the achievement of the Potsdam Declaration ... will unquestionably involve a liberalization of the constitution."[14] Why then was this item not included among the specific demands listed in the October 11 directive? It is not clear. Perhaps MacArthur felt that he did not have clear authority to impose constitutional reform. He was certainly aware that a policy directive, SWNCC 228, was being prepared in Washington to address the issue.

Several early pronouncements of American policy reflect a similar hesitation to tackle constitutional revision head-on. In speaking of the broad goals of the Occupation, the Initial Post-Surrender Policy cites the imperative of establishing a "peaceful and responsible government." The next sentence affirms that "this government should conform as closely as may be to principles of democratic self-government," but quickly adds that "it is not the responsibility of the Allied Powers to impose upon Japan any form of government not supported by the freely expressed will of the people."[15]

In truth, the American confidence in written constitutions was a bit peculiar. Its principal World War II ally, Great Britain, did not even have one. France had had several; it was currently setting up its Fourth Republic. Latin American nations were veritable laboratories for constitutional experimentation; few observers expected written charters of government to make much difference there.

To citizens of the United States, however, the Constitution was a solemn undertaking, a bulwark of liberty. They believed that their own act of constitution making was normative, that other nations, if they could get it right, might also establish forms of government that would conduce to their happiness.

The American View of Japan

As Americans approached the occupation of Japan, these beliefs, conditioned by their own wartime view of Japan, were central. They lacked the perspective that historians have today on East Asia between the wars: China's collapse into civil war, the continuation of American and European colonial dominance in much of Asia, Stalin's resolve to spread communism in the area, the failure of the Washington Conference's system of international security for China and Manchuria, the worldwide economic depression of the 1930s, the collapse of the League of Nations.

Rather, as Americans viewed the matter, it was simply madness that led Japanese "warlords" to embark on an aggressive quest for regional dominance in the 1930s. No democratically self-governed people could ever have conceived or sought to execute such a grandiose, self-destructive scheme. From the American perspective of the 1940s, the basic problem of Japan's prewar regime was its lack of transparency. The Meiji Constitution of 1889 proclaimed that the emperor ruled Japan. He was commander of the armed forces. He had power to declare war and peace and to enter into treaties. He appointed ministers of the government, who were responsible to him individually. Legislation, including taxes and budgeted expenditures, required the consent of the Diet, but there were various explicit provisions enabling the emperor to govern by ordinance or to spend money in emergencies of his own declaring. As for the judiciary, it too operated in the name of the emperor.

The government of Japan never operated in strict accordance with these provisions. Formally the emperor declared war, but he could not do so arbitrarily. He had full constitutional power to appoint ministers, but in fact his authority to do so was constrained by political factors. In fact, during the early decades of the twentieth century, these formal arrangements—not unlike Britain's—provided a framework for government that seemed to be increasingly democratic. By the mid-1920s, Japan had universal male suffrage. Political parties flourished. A succession of cabinets rose and fell in reflex to the varying political fortunes of factions in the lower house of the Diet. It appeared to many observers that Japan was on the road to parliamentary democracy on the Westminster model.[16]

Then came civil war in China, the collapse of the Washington Conference agreement on East Asian security arrangements in the late 1920s, conflict in Manchuria, and worldwide economic collapse and social strains of the 1930s. Japan's cabinet was threatened by a succession of political assassinations and near-coups d'etat. From the mid-1930s the military gained leverage in government councils and effective control of national security policy. Cabinets were installed that pursued military solutions to problems on the Asian continent. All this happened with no changes at all in the constitutional text.

To American eyes, this kaleidoscopic picture indicated that the Meiji Constitution was seriously defective. It was a screen behind which military officers could concoct schemes and impose them by manipulating the authority of the emperor.

It was a recipe for irresponsibility. It provided no means for holding governmental power accountable. It offered no defense against cabals.

One question divided the Americans: To what extent was the emperor himself to blame for the catastrophe of Japan's course before and during World War II? Was Hirohito a war criminal, an active agent of vicious policies? Or was he the hapless victim of arrogant soldiers and weak politicians?[17] Much turned on the answer to this question. If Hirohito orchestrated the policy that led Japan to disaster, he deserved to be sacked. That did not necessarily mean that the imperial institution itself would have to go, though, practically speaking, it would be hard to make the case for the institution if the incumbent had used its powers so badly. On the other hand, if the military could be blamed and Hirohito personally exonerated, his authority might be used to promote postwar reforms, and he might assume a position comparable to the British monarch.

This issue was fought out in Washington for many months before and after Japan's surrender, and it was never resolved there. In the U.S. Congress, powerful voices called for Hirohito's scalp. Senators Richard B. Russell (D-Ga.) and J. William Fulbright (D-Ark.) introduced a resolution calling on their government to demand that Hirohito be tried as a war criminal. Many officials in the State and War departments agreed. One officer said that the emperor should be called to the dock, asked his name and position, and summarily pronounced guilty. Several Allied governments (the Soviet Union and Australia) were also strong in the belief that Hirohito should be made to pay for the sins of his government.

Others, however, urged caution. There were several reasons. First, the Occupation forces would need help in ruling 80 million Japanese. Cooperation was vital unless war-weary Allied nations were prepared to commit vast forces to pacification, for an extended period. (They were not.) Then there was the Potsdam Declaration of July 1945, outlining the Allies' conditions for ending the war, including the promise that the Occupation would be terminated as soon as there had been established in Japan, "in accordance with the freely expressed will of the Japanese people, a peacefully inclined and responsible government." Many Japanese believed that their acceptance of the Potsdam Declaration had been conditional on their being allowed to retain the emperor as sovereign. Most American and Allied leaders, however, denied that this provision was intended to protect Hirohito from justice. According to this view, the Occupation had every right to tell the Japanese that the imperial institution was inconsistent with democracy and must therefore be abolished.

Summing up the implications of American thinking about the emperor for constitutional form, a State Department aide had written, "If [the Japanese] were to scrap their old governmental system, being wise men, they would adopt the U.S. form of government. If, on the other hand, they were to decide to retain the emperor institution and to democratize it, then they would follow the model of the British government."[18] Taking advantage of the inability of Washington's wise men to reach a consensus, MacArthur unilaterally directed Japan toward the second option. But he could not do it alone. The Allies were getting organized, through a body called the Far Eastern Commission (FEC), to exercise their superintending authority over the Occupation. For SCAP to evade the meddling of

America's allies, it would be essential to present constitutional revision as a project of the Japanese government. To do that, MacArthur would need the cooperation of Japanese authorities. This book explains how it was accomplished.

Japan as a Case Study

This book sheds light on two important sets of questions. We introduced one of them in the preceding section: we will tell how, in the year following the end of World War II, the American Occupation, working with the Japanese government, framed a new constitution, laying a strong foundation for liberal democracy in Japan. How was this collaboration achieved? What ideas did the Japanese have about constitutional revision? Why did the Americans decide to impose their own notions of constitutional form? How did they gain Japanese cooperation? How were hostile forces—on the American side, erstwhile Allies (Soviet Union, Australia), and repeatedly astonished officials in Washington; on the Japanese side, diehard defenders of traditional ideas about the emperor, leftists who wanted simpler democratic forms and more extensive social rights, and the Japanese Communist Party—kept at bay?

The bulk of the book that follows is devoted to this first set of questions.

Japan's Readiness Questioned

There is, however, a second set of questions raised by what happened in Tokyo in 1946. It turns on Japan's place among the many nations that sought to establish constitutional democracy in the aftermath of the world wars of the twentieth century. How does Japan's transition to constitutional democracy compare with these other cases? What does the Japanese case contribute to our knowledge of the conditions, procedures and commitments that make democratic government stable and durable?

This book cannot provide a through analysis of this second set of questions. It is nevertheless in the back of our minds continually as we move through our account of the events of 1946. We believe that theory about democratic transitions ought to take the Japanese case into account. It is wrong to treat the Japanese case as aberrant and thus irrelevant to these broader questions.

Many scholars who study democratic transitions seem to believe that there is little to be learned from the Japanese case.[19] Its circumstances seem so unique. An industrialized Asian nation, under intense pressure, adopted a Western-style constitution. How likely are these circumstances ever to be repeated?

This view, however, is superficial. It is based on a simplification—ultimately a falsification—of the cultures that met in Tokyo after the war. It greatly exaggerates, or miscasts, the tension between them. Specifically, it ignores Japan's readiness to give sympathetic consideration to the model of constitutionalism that Americans were seeking to impose upon them. It also ignores other factors that helped to make Japan ready to make the transition to constitutional democracy in 1946. One of our hopes for this book is that it will encourage an effort to draw the case of Japan into this conversation.

How then does Japan in 1946 compare with other nations attempting a conversion to constitutional democracy? When the case of Japan is noticed at all in this context, it is usually treated in glib, superficial, even stereotypical terms. Japan after the war, it is said, was a chastened nation, broken-spirited, demoralized, utterly unable to resist American dominance. Overborne and dazzled by occupying American armed forces, it quickly converted to Western materialism and commercialism, not to mention pop music and Hollywood movies. Japan, according to this stereotype, is a docile, imitative country, skillful at "mimicry."[20] It was happy to allow American armed forces to protect it from its enemies, concentrating its own resources on economic development. After its defeat in World War II, it affirmed liberal-democratic ways as quickly and thoroughly as it had adopted Western-style modernization at the time of the Meiji Restoration in 1868, or Prussian-style constitutionalism in 1889. Largely eschewing Asian values[21] and even its own traditions, it once again transformed itself, this time into a diminutive clone of Anglo-American democracy. It follows from this line of thinking that Japan is hardly worth studying for lessons about the transition to democracy. What other nation, besides Japan, could or would ever attempt to do such a thing?

We believe these explanations are unsatisfactory, for two reasons. First, old ways persist in Japan. It has not abandoned "Asian" values. Japanese culture is not notably religious, but it is still deeply rooted in a mentality bearing Confucian, Buddhist and Shintō-ist marks. Japanese people still look to the imperial family as a source of cohesion.[22] Second, its commitment to democratic constitutionalism was not altogether new in 1946. It rested on deep cultural foundations that heavily affected the way "democracy" was appropriated.

Perhaps, then, Japan should not be treated as a "case" after all. Perhaps it is wholly exceptional, its own unique blend of factors making the transition to constitutional democracy possible. This sense of bafflement may help to explain the tendency to ignore Japan when speaking of transitions to democracy.

This approach, however, is regrettable. It deprives students of democratic transitions of an important example. Viewed as a case, Japan shows how changing the rules (enfranchising women, granting freedom to the press within tightly controlled limits, purging many rightwing politicians, releasing leftwing activists from prison and allowing others to return from exile, disgracing military officers and conducting war crimes trials, secularizing the emperor's authority) decisively altered the political environment, creating space and liberating energy for radical changes in the constitution of government. It shows the contribution made by a foreign military occupation, committed to liberal values, in helping to ease the transition from authoritarian rule to parliamentary democracy and, ultimately, a successful consolidation of democratic practices.

How did these things happen? What can we learn from Japan's experience about the conditions, possibilities and limits on the transition to democracy?

Conditions for Transition

Recent writers on this subject have focused particularly on nations in the Third World (Latin American, African, South Asian) and on recent experience in the post-communist countries of Central and Eastern Europe. They have identified several conditions that have attended successful transitions to democracy, features whose absence seems to doom the effort to inaugurate democratic government.[23] We mention a few items common to these lists and consider how Japan, in the years immediately following the end of World War II, measured up against these criteria.

Economic Well-being

Most countries that have made successful transitions to constitutional democracy have been relatively prosperous. Necessitous people are unlikely to wait patiently while politicians weigh the merits of different forms of government and debate competing lists of human rights. They demand public order, food, and shelter, immediately, and they tend not to be fastidious about how it comes to them. On the other hand, if the citizenry, most of them middle class, shares a sense of well-being, prospects for embarking on constitutional, democratic governance, and of sticking with it until it stabilizes, are greatly enhanced.

There are exceptions. The case of India suggests that a nation with a staggeringly low annual per capita income may be able to sustain a constitutional system and conduct a succession of democratic elections. As a rule, however, there is a strong correlation between widely shared prosperity and democratic prospects.

How did Japan appear in 1946 in light of this rubric? Surprisingly, perhaps, less well than one might think. It is difficult for observers, a half century after the fact, to develop an accurate picture of Japan's economic condition in 1946.[24] We know that the war shattered its industries, ruined its transportation system, cut off its access to critical raw materials, decimated its labor force, caused epidemic disease and hunger, and eroded morale and confidence. All this was true, but the problem was even deeper. Achieving the standards set by recent analysts as minimal for the consolidation of democracy would require more than repairing the war's damages. Despite several decades of strenuous effort, Japan had still not attained these standards, even before the war.

Another factor inhibited Japan's prospects. It is not well endowed in natural resources for industrial development. There is virtually no petroleum, iron ore, coking coal, or bauxite in the Japanese archipelago, nor are its climate and geography conducive to producing adequate quantities of rubber, cotton, or wool. As for food, Japan has always grown plenty of rice, but in 1946 it relied on imports for 70 percent of other essential grains, such as wheat and soybeans, not to mention other foodstuffs.

These circumstances presented a dire challenge. If Japan were to become a major power, it could not rely on resources at home. Before the war, it sought to deal with this problem by gaining control over raw materials abroad. That drive led to conflict with China and eventually to war with the colonial powers of Europe and North America, with calamitous consequences. After the war, a new mentality would develop. If Japan could develop steady access to outside sources, it was thought, the absence of indigenous supplies would not necessarily inhibit Japanese development. (The corollary, of course, was that any substantial disruption in trade relations with the outside world could be disastrous.)

As Japan shifted toward this new internationalist perspective, there was great uncertainty. How radical a conversion to openness would the world demand? How would the Japanese people react to these demands? Because these questions had no clear answers, Japan's prospects for economic prosperity, and thus for a smooth transition to democracy, were highly uncertain in 1946.

Literacy

Another factor identified in recent studies as critical for democratic prospects is widespread literacy. Literacy may not be sufficient for democratic participation, but it is nearly essential. Reading is both an indicator of mental training and a gateway to vicarious experience. People cannot hold leaders of a populous nation accountable unless they can read.

Japan's population in 1946 was strongly positive by this indicator. At least since the middle of the nineteenth century, Japan has had a population that was highly literate by world standards. Ronald Dore estimated that in 1850, 50 percent of men and 20 percent of women were literate, levels that exceeded Britain's at that time.[25] Since 1872, leaders who understood the relationship between economic growth and popular education made primary schooling universal and compulsory. Since the 1870s, Japan has had few illiterate peasants. By 1950, Japan was close to American standards in the amount of schooling for boys (an average of 8.15 years vs. 9.68 in 1950) and girls (7.22 vs. 10.01).[26]

Ethnic Homogeneity

Another factor found by scholars to be conducive to democratic stability is ethnic homogeneity among the constituent population.[27] Some Americans are surprised and troubled to confront this finding. They ascribe the strength and stability of the United States to the waves of immigration that have contributed so much to the nation's labor force, as well as social and political leadership. What they forget is that, at the founding in the late eighteenth century, men of mainly British descent controlled the politics of the emerging nation. Once established, as David Hume pointed out, republics tend to be quite durable.[28] They can endure even waves of immigration—though not always easily, as urban and nativist conflicts in nineteenth-century America dramatically demonstrate. But ethnic pluralism does not facilitate constitutional foundings. It raises an obstacle to trust, and some trust is essential.

Japan's prospects were bright by this measure. Japan is ethnically homogeneous, although it continues to have difficulty absorbing Korean immigrants, even those who have lived in Japan for several generations, and is unwelcoming to the notion of naturalization. It thinks of itself as a huge community of blood-related people, with the imperial family at its nucleus. These conditions may raise problems for the realization of human rights, but for a smooth transition to democracy, they were auspicious.

Attractive Models

Another propitious factor is the presence of positive, attractive models. The late-to-middle-1930s, for example, would not have been a good time for Japan to attempt a transition to democracy. Advocates of constitutional democracy were on the defensive. The leading democracies—Great Britain, France, and the United States—were not coping very well with worldwide economic depression, and the menace of Hitler's Germany was unnerving them as well. To many people, it seemed that modern governance required central direction and disciplined obedience. Defenders of liberty and democracy assumed a defensive and uncertain tone in these years.[29]

The events of the 1940s changed all that. Though slow to organize, the Western democracies eventually brought overwhelming force to bear on their enemies and turned the tide against the fascist powers. Roosevelt and Churchill used methods that were sometimes hard to distinguish from authoritarian dictatorship,[30] but their nations quickly reverted to constitutional form after the war. By 1946, constitutional democracy basked in the warm glow of success. In the half decade after World War II, democratic governance had no explicit critics, and the blending of democracy and constitutionalism seemed completely natural and untroubled.[31]

In Japan, once the military leadership was disgraced and removed and extreme nationalists "purged" from the arena, political leaders, with few exceptions, were quite ready and willing to affirm the model of constitutional democracy.

Benign International Circumstances

Freedom from acute foreign threats is another factor that tends to be favorable in the transition to democracy. When a nation must maintain virtually a perpetual state of emergency and military readiness, constitutional guarantees (both democratic political processes and the rights of citizens) tend to be fragile and vulnerable to demands for harsh measures and repression. Think of central Europe (Germany and Italy) between the world wars of the twentieth century.

Japan's commitment to constitutionalism succumbed to similar strains between the great wars, though perhaps less egregiously than her allies in the Tripartite Pact of 1940. However, during the period following World War II, Japan was less vulnerable to exploitation by those concerned about "national security." Russia and China, Japan's ancient enemies, certainly hungered for revenge, but the American Occupation prevented either nation from acting on these emotions.

A Supportive Culture

In all these conditions, Japan's situation in 1946 was auspicious for making the transition to democracy. Nevertheless, there were deep misgivings, both within Japan and among the world's observers, about the readiness of Japanese culture for a transition to democracy. Were Japan's fundamental values (Confucian order, blood loyalty, honor, deference, martial spirit) compatible or congruent with norms that support constitutionalism (liberty, equality, tolerance, respect for human rights, widespread inclination to take part actively in political life)? Did Japan's values support a sustainable will to abide by democratic forms of governance?

This book will show Japan's political system struggling, under trying circumstances, to understand what constitutional democracy required and to decide whether it could commit itself to democratic governance without losing its national soul. Here it may be useful, by way of introduction, to touch on some of the cultural prerequisites identified in the literature on democratic transitions and suggest how they may pertain to Japan in 1946.

Success Breeds Success

Analysts note that success with democratic forms of governance tends to feed on itself. Samuel Huntington suggests that once a democratic regime successfully navigates two transitions affecting the political parties in power, it may be considered to have good prospects for stability.[32] The other side of the coin has been emphasized by Robert Dahl, who has found that once democracy is overthrown, succeeding efforts at establishing democratic regimes in that nation become increasingly problematic.[33]

Japan's prospects, in the light of these findings, were decidedly mixed. Certainly by 1946 Japan's political leaders had had considerable experience with governance in the style of constitutional democracy. It had held competitive elections for seats in the parliament (Diet) regularly since 1890, even during World War II. Since 1925, there had been universal manhood suffrage. Under the Meiji Constitution, cabinets had had to deal with parliamentary majorities and were dependent on them for national budgets. The vicissitudes of electoral campaigns and the arts of coalition building in the Diet were well known to Japanese politicians during the first three decades of the twentieth century. Japan certainly qualified as experienced in democratic politics and a good bet for stability by Huntington's two-changeover rule.

By Dahl's standard, however, the challenge to those who would bring democracy to Japan was steep. Since the mid-1930s, the perceived exigencies of national security had wrenched and frayed Japan's fledgling democratic processes. The will to put Japan back on course was as strong among Japanese leaders as in the camp of the victorious Allies, but some bad habits had developed. They would now have to be rooted out and strong constitutional safeguards erected to prevent their recurrence.

Compatible Ideology

Some writers on democratic transitions have suggested that Confucian culture is inhospitable to democracy, whereas others believe that because Confucianism is so diluted in Japan, this problem is less severe in Japan than elsewhere in Asia.[34] More immediately relevant than Confucianism in 1946 was reverence for the *tennō* (imperfectly translated into English as "emperor"). Was this spirituality compatible with Western ideas of sovereignty and secular rule?

Though treated by official Japanese opinion before the war as if it were ancient, the ideology of emperor worship was actually of fairly recent invention. Between 1600 and the middle of the nineteenth century, while the Tokugawa shogunate presided over national administration from Edo (present-day Tokyo), the emperor and his extended family lived in seclusion at a palace in Kyoto, 250 miles to the west. When a band of feudal barons overthrew the shogunate, they grounded the legitimacy of their revolutionary regime on the sovereign will of the emperor. Twenty years after their coup, they dressed their rule in a Prussian-style constitution, proclaimed by the emperor in 1889.

The ideology that supported the regime grew to feverish intensity during the 1930s. The term *kokutai*, expressing Japan's unique spirit and centering on reverence for the emperor, came to have mystical meaning. Anyone who questioned it was deemed to have committed the crime of lese majesty and faced ostracism and serious punishment. In the period following the war, perhaps the greatest challenge facing Japan's framers was to transform this imperial ideology into something compatible with liberal constitutionalism. Much of the story in the pages that follow relates to this theme.

Individualism

Another central aspect of this cultural challenge centers on the place of the individual in the social order. Theorists of liberal constitutionalism put this point in various ways. Some emphasize its roots in Western religious conceptions that see human beings as created in God's image. Others stress the importance of a legal culture that posits rights (to liberty and property) in individuals and empowers courts to protect these rights, even in the face of the government's claims. For Japanese culture, both the theological and secular variants of this emphasis on individuality were highly problematic. Japan's people had evolved a culture that placed the claims of the group before those of individuals. Order and social discipline were valued ahead of autonomy and individual expression.

Indeed, deep misgivings about the individualistic bias of liberalism are one of the bright threads through the debates of 1946. We will encounter it frequently in the pages ahead. Balancing it was the notion that liberal constitutionalism was not a recent American invention. It had roots going back to the Magna Carta.

A Readiness to Adapt

Moreover, there was in Japan a powerful tradition of stateways altering folkways, in service of a common ideal or national aspiration. Toshio Nishi has written an account of "how, between 1945 and 1952, the American occupation forces deliberately used education as an instrument to transform Japanese culture from an imperialistic society into a democratic nation." During his youth, as a school and college student in Japan, Nishi experienced firsthand the revolution his book describes. The book's foreword notes: "Few examples from history equal the Japanese experience in the intentional use of education to change a people's basic values and behavior. In the middle of the nineteenth century the Meiji Emperor designed an educational system to catapult Japan into the modern world. A generation ago General Douglas MacArthur . . . employed education to inculcate democratic values and institutions."[35] Like most authors on the Occupation, Nishi devotes little space (just two short paragraphs) to the debates in the Diet during the summer of 1946.[36] Nevertheless, he does offer a penetrating critique of the analyses set forth by Robert Ward and Kazuo Kawai, leading proponents of the view that the constitution was simply "imposed." Concerning Ward's argument that the constitution was "hopelessly unsuited to Japanese political ideals," Nishi suggests that Japan's traditions were not so rigidly set. He agrees that the Japanese people had been "well conditioned to perpetuate its own subjugation in the name of loyalty and patriotism." But he insists that, after the surrender, "the disillusioned people abruptly rejected hierarchy and the bureaucracy that supported it."

In the pages that follow, we will observe Diet members, throughout the summer of 1946, calling on the Ministry of Education to conduct a vigorous national campaign to teach people the virtues of democracy and constitutionalism. Clearly the decision to "mold" the Japanese mind in attitudes supportive of democracy was one in which many elected Japanese leaders heartily concurred.

How Constitutionalism Takes Root

As the following pages show, the consolidation of democracy in Japan after the war was no accident, no "miracle." The victorious Allies prepared the way at Potsdam in July 1945. In Tokyo, General MacArthur and his staff officers, in close, if tacit, collaboration with the cabinets of Shidehara and Yoshida, worked through the fall and winter of 1945 and the spring and summer of 1946 to lay a strong and durable foundation for constitutional democracy.

The framing of a new constitution was a critical event in the consolidation of democracy in Japan. By closely studying how it came to pass, we can deepen understanding of how constitutionalism took durable root in an Asian nation. Though there are aspects of this story that are indeed unique to Japan, we hope to show that it has many features that are comparable to other cases.

FALL 1945

"Negotiated Surrender"

• AMERICAN PLANNING AND OCCUPATION

•

The dramatic events that produced a new constitution for Japan did not spring suddenly into being with the arrival of the Occupation forces in September 1945. In fact, during the war, government planners in Washington envisioned constitutional revision and other major reforms that would be carried out during the American Occupation of Japan, 1945–1952. A brief review of the planning that took place in 1944–1945 will help to establish the source and nature of the ideas that influenced constitutional reform in postwar Japan.

The View from Washington

From May 1942 until early 1944, a small group of Japan specialists in the State Department—including Hugh Borton, George Blakeslee, and Cabot Coville—began working on plans to reform a defeated Japan. Borton and Blakeslee were scholars with experience in Japan and international affairs. Coville had served in the 1930s in the U.S. embassy in Tokyo under Ambassador Joseph Grew.

The State Department's planning proceeded on the belief that militarism in Japan constituted an aberration in the normal pattern of that nation's promising domestic development and peaceful international relations of the 1920s. By September 1943, several State and War Department committees had defined the first objective of postsurrender policy as creating "a government in Japan that would fulfill Japan's international obligations and respect the rights of other states." Constitutional and administrative changes would be needed to "strengthen moderate political elements" and deprive the military of its special political privileges.[1]

A specific, continuing concern of these early planners was whether the retention of Emperor Hirohito as Japan's sovereign ruler would help, or hinder, plans to achieve this objective. A State Department study drafted by Coville in March 1943 was the first serious effort to confront the problem of imperial sovereignty.[2] He warned of the risks of allowing the institution to survive. He thought

23

the emperor was an easily manipulated tool of political groups, especially the Japanese military. Once removed from their control, however, the emperor could be "an instrument of change which the United Nations might wish to bring about." Coville was optimistic about the role the imperial institution could play after the war. On balance, he thought a limited constitutional monarch would be a positive force for liberal political development in postwar Japan.

The influence of Japan specialists in the State Department expanded greatly in May 1944, when Grew assumed control of the Office of Far Eastern Affairs, replacing Stanley Hornbeck, the leader of the pro-China group in the department. Grew appointed his former assistants in Tokyo to key positions: Joseph Ballantine as his deputy, Earle Dickover as head of the Japan Section, and Eugene Dooman as his special assistant. When Edward Stettinius succeeded Cordell Hull as secretary of state in November 1944, he chose Grew as his under secretary, strengthening his hold on the planning of postwar policy for Japan. Grew in turn appointed Dooman as chairman of the Subcommittee for the Far East in the newly formed State, War, and Navy Coordinating Committee. Dooman, former counselor of the Tokyo embassy under Grew, had been born in Japan, was fluent in Japanese, and was Grew's righthand man in Tokyo and Washington. Grew's views on the Japanese emperor as a positive and useful "liberal" force would influence American official thinking and planning for the occupation of Japan after the war.

Throughout 1944, Grew's followers (the "Japan crowd," as their critics labeled them) struggled to formulate a policy for the American military occupation of Japan. American objectives would be to root out extreme military influences from the government and to undertake institutional reforms, freeing moderate and liberal forces that they believed existed in Japanese society. Plans for accomplishing these objectives included destroying the military, punishing war criminals, and reforming political institutions to establish civil liberties and encourage democratic tendencies among the Japanese people. Believing that the emperor could be useful in achieving these objectives, Allied propaganda broadcasts in late 1944 avoided direct criticism of the emperor while debunking "emperor worship," the doctrines of State Shintō, and the kokutai myth.[3]

In February 1944 Major General John L. Hilldring, chief of the civil affairs division of the War Department, submitted a list of questions to the State Department, requesting guidance on policy issues that would arise during a military occupation. The State Department's planning committees responded with papers on such matters as control of the Japanese government, the role of the emperor, and terms of surrender.[4] But Hilldring's staff was looking well beyond political reform and the emperor as they drafted directives and prepared handbooks to provide guidance for military occupation forces in Germany and Japan. Hilldring had already sought the help of officials in the Treasury Department, the Office of Strategic Services, and the Office of War Information. As Hilldring's staff developed an Army policy directive for the occupation of Japan (later JCS 1380), the scope widened to include reforms of Japanese society never contemplated by Japan specialists in the State Department. Even some of the policy directives for the occupation of Germany were included in this directive.[5]

By December 1944 the State Department's committee on postwar programs had begun to flesh out the argument for using the emperor to serve occupation policy. He could announce Japan's unconditional surrender, sign the surrender document, and order his officials to continue in office under the Allied military government. The committee thought that the emperor and his family should be placed in protective custody, that he should be kept in seclusion while permitting his advisers access to him, and that he should be treated "with the courtesy normally extended . . . to a head of state." Nothing was said at this point about the ultimate disposition of the Japanese imperial institution or its occupant.[6]

In December, the cabinet created the interdepartmental State, War, and Navy Coordinating Committee (SWNCC), bringing together civilian and military planners in the three departments. SWNCC provided a forum for examining the State Department's analysis of Japan's political system and plans for reform then emerging from the War Department. SWNCC's Subcommittee on the Far East (SFE) assumed responsibility for drafting a comprehensive statement of U.S. postwar policy for Japan to guide the military commander who would lead the Allied Occupation, and a policy statement on "treatment of the emperor."

The State Department's views on Japan's constitutional system came under close scrutiny. Officials in the War Department challenged Grew's assumption that the emperor, supported by prewar liberal political elements, should be part of the postwar political system. For example, Herbert Feis, special consultant to Secretary of War Henry Stimson, complained that the State Department's plan for ruling Japan during a period of military occupation would reinforce the Japanese people's sense of loyalty to the emperor. "I think we should not take any steps," he wrote, "to make it easier for the present system to continue into the future fundamentally unchanged. Fifty years of aggression should be sufficient proof of its inevitable tendencies."[7] However, preoccupied as it was with drafting the Potsdam Declaration and a statement of American policy for postwar Japan, SWNCC made little progress on defining U.S. policy for treatment of Hirohito until late September, well after Japan's surrender.

Meanwhile, in the wake of Germany's defeat and intensive American fire-bomb raids on Japanese cities in the spring of 1945,[8] Grew came to believe that Japan could be persuaded to surrender without an invasion. His belief was reinforced when, in April 1945, he learned from the War Department's psychological warfare section that high-ranking Japanese prisoners of war thought Japan might capitulate if the Allies would ensure the safety of the emperor. The American policy of "unconditional surrender" stood in the way of such assurance. Roosevelt and Churchill had agreed on the unconditional surrender formula at the Casablanca conference in January 1943. Any assurance to Japan would violate that policy. Critics faulted the phrase as too vague. Even the SFE reasoned that if unconditional surrender were defined in specific terms and announced to Japan, it might surrender.[9] In late May, Grew decided to urge President Truman to issue a statement clarifying what the policy of unconditional surrender would mean for Japan.[10]

Grew had Dooman draft a statement aimed at Japan for the president to include in his report to Congress on the progress of the war. In a meeting with

Truman on May 28, Grew presented his case, arguing that Japan might surrender "now" if the United States would assure Japan that surrender would not "entail the destruction or permanent removal of the Emperor."[11] While the president considered the proposal, Grew began to encounter strong opposition in his own department. Elmer Davis, director of war information, denounced the plan as a "negotiated surrender."[12] Assistant secretaries Dean Acheson and Archibald Mac-Leish objected to any wording that would imply U.S. support for the reigning dynasty. Acheson's unhappiness with Grew became personal, as he scathingly referred to his immediate superior as "the Prince of Appeasers."[13]

Nevertheless, Grew's initiative won the support, in principle, of Secretary of War Stimson and Secretary of Navy James Forrestal, though both thought the timing was wrong—the battle of Okinawa, April to June 1945, was in progress. The Joint Chiefs of Staff (JCS), however, had misgivings about offering any hard and fast presurrender commitments to the enemy. After consulting them, Truman told Grew in mid-June that he would postpone issuing a statement to Japan until his meeting with the Allies at Potsdam, Germany, which was scheduled for late July. During the intervening five weeks, Grew and Stimson came to agreement on the major provisions of the Potsdam Declaration.[14]

Working Out the Potsdam Declaration

Truman's conference with Churchill and Stalin at Potsdam almost ended without a declaration calling on Japan to surrender. Only Grew's persistence and Stimson's unwavering support kept the idea alive. By late June, Stimson, and his assistant secretary, John J. McCloy, had taken the lead in stressing to President Truman the importance of issuing an ultimatum to Japan. In a memorandum to the president, Stimson revealed the War Department's plans for an invasion of Japan's main islands. He stressed the possibility of heavy American casualties and then asked:

> Is there any alternative to such a forceful occupation of Japan? I am inclined to think that there is enough such chance to make it well worthwhile our giving them a warning . . . and a definite opportunity to capitulate. I believe Japan is susceptible to reason. Japan is not a nation composed wholly of mad fanatics. She has shown herself to possess extremely intelligent people. Her advance during the short period of sixty or seventy years has been one of the most astounding feats of national progress in history.[15]

Stimson discussed the draft proclamation that had been prepared for the conference at Potsdam. Concerning the emperor, he argued that Japan was more likely to accept an ultimatum if "we add that we do not exclude a constitutional monarchy under her present dynasty." Paragraph twelve of the draft proclamation read:

> The Occupying forces of the Allies shall be withdrawn from Japan as soon as our objectives are accomplished and there has been established beyond

doubt a peacefully inclined, responsible government of a character representative of the Japanese people. *This may include a constitutional monarchy
under the present dynasty if it be shown to the complete satisfaction of the
world that such a government will never again aspire to aggression.* [emphasis
in original][16]

Grew and his Japan specialists in the State Department distinguished between
the emperor, the imperial institution, and the "cult of emperor worship." They
agreed that "emperor worship" was pernicious and must go. But they argued that
the emperor himself had not wanted the war with the United States, and that
"Japanese liberals" close to the emperor wished to end the war. As for the future,
as long as the Japanese people supported the monarchy, they believed that any
attempt to abolish the institution or to legislate it out of existence would require
an indefinite period of military occupation. Therefore, the United States ought
to use the emperor to gain a surrender and then have him order his officials to
obey and enforce all occupation orders.[17]

Meanwhile, however, Acheson and MacLeish in the State Department and
Hilldring, Hull, and Feis in the War Department viewed the emperor and the
imperial institution as a major cause of Japan's militarism. They saw no difference
between the "pernicious doctrine of emperor worship" and the emperor himself
or the imperial institution. They believed the existence of one would necessarily
lead to the other. They saw no reason why the U.S. government should defy
American public opinion on the question (and public opinion was strongly on
their side) by retaining the emperor and treating Japan differently from Germany.
They did not, however, counter Grew's argument that Japanese advocates for
surrender could only prevail if the United States would permit the emperor to
remain.

Acheson and MacLeish proposed that all of paragraph twelve be struck from
the draft proclamation. They told Secretary Byrnes that Japan's imperial institution must be abolished because "it is an anachronistic, feudal institution" and
the "Japanese cult of emperor worship" is dangerous. On July 6, the day Byrnes
departed for Berlin, MacLeish made a last appeal to remove the whole paragraph
or, failing that, to have the U.S. government admit publicly that it was dropping
its demand for Japan's unconditional surrender. But such a change, he argued,
was inconsistent with policy for Germany; it was unsound and dangerous because
"the Japanese cult of emperor worship" gave the ruling group control over the
Japanese people. He agreed with Acheson's argument that "the usefulness of the
emperor in arranging surrender must be weighed against the long-term dangers
of the institution."[18]

The last sentence of Stimson's draft, allowing the Japanese to keep their em-
peror, underwent several changes in the U.S. delegation's working paper as the
Potsdam conference drew near. On July 16, former Secretary of State Hull, whom
Byrnes had consulted, stated his opposition to the provision. Two days later the
Joint Chiefs added their objections.[19] Responding to this pressure, Truman and
Byrnes had the offending sentence struck out shortly before the document was
approved and released in Potsdam on July 26, 1945.[20]

Arriving at an Ultimatum

The elimination of this provision signaled the defeat of Grew's view of Japan and his hope for a negotiated surrender. As we have seen, Grew wished to abandon the unconditional surrender formula and assure Japan it could keep a reformed imperial institution in return for a quick surrender. In this way the war could end without a massive American invasion of Japan's main islands and before an expansionist Soviet Union could get involved. The existing imperial Japanese government, shorn of its military and refitted with democratic institutions, could then lead Japan toward an era of peace and cooperation with the United States. Grew and his Japan specialists believed that democracy in Japan could be revived and nourished through political reform under the reigning emperor.

Stimson, though willing to compromise on the imperial institution, doubted negotiations would end the war. He favored an ultimatum backed by the atomic bomb and, if that failed to induce capitulation, an invasion of the main islands. In this case, he thought Soviet assistance was vital. Byrnes, Acheson, and the JCS refused to concede on the emperor. In their view, Japanese militarism was not a recent aberration but a product of forces deep in Japanese society and culture. The war was a basic conflict of cultures, not simply national interests, with militarism dominating Japan and representing anti-Western values. They perceived the emperor institution as a "feudal" system of government inconsistent with democracy and urged its abolition. This interpretation of Japan's modern history, along with a strategic view of how to defeat Japan, prevailed in the struggle over policy in the summer of 1945.

The Potsdam Declaration promised complete destruction of the Japanese armed forces and utter devastation of the homeland unless Japan accepted the following terms: Allied military occupation, elimination of the "military's authority and influence" and destruction of "Japan's war-making power," limiting Japan's sovereignty to its four main islands and a few minor ones, payment of reparations, and punishment of war criminals. The Japanese government was to declare and guarantee the unconditional surrender of its armed forces, retain sovereignty over its territory, revive democratic tendencies, undertake reforms to assure basic freedoms and human rights, and establish a peacefully inclined and responsible government "in accordance with the freely expressed wishes of the Japanese people."

To the Americans, the final words of the declaration meant a commitment to achieving democratic government in defeated Japan. They represented a compromise with Grew's position. His followers in the State Department would use them to advance a strategy of preserving and using the imperial institution to democratize Japan. To the Japanese, they signified that and more: an opportunity to preserve the imperial institution while ending the devastating war. As we shall see, these words inspired hope, even confidence, among Japan's ruling elite that Japan could achieve, through statutory reform or limited constitutional revision, the democratization of the country, under the emperor, that the Allies demanded.

Yet the Potsdam Declaration's unstable compromises were particularly hard for the Japanese to interpret. The Allies' ultimatum failed to persuade Japan's political and military leaders to surrender immediately. Although Foreign Minister Tōgō Shigenori felt "the document left considerable room for interpretation,"[21] no point-by-point discussion occurred at the cabinet level until August 9. It is impossible to know whether a provision allowing Japan to retain its imperial institution would have made a difference. In any event, on July 28 Prime Minister Suzuki told the press in a prepared statement that the government would "ignore" the ultimatum.

The Allies unanimously concluded that Suzuki's statement was indeed a rejection. President Truman quickly authorized the dropping of atomic bombs on two Japanese cities: Hiroshima on August 6 and Nagasaki three days later. Meanwhile, on August 8 the Soviet Union, violating its April 1941 neutrality pact, declared war on Japan and swiftly occupied Manchuria, the north of Korea, southern Sakhalin Island, and the Kurile Islands north of Hokkaidō.

Countdown to Surrender

On August 9, following the bombing of Nagasaki, Japan's Supreme Council (consisting of the army and navy chiefs, army and navy ministers, foreign minister, and prime minister) met to reconsider the Allied declaration of July 26.[22] In a heated debate, the military leaders resisted three of the Potsdam demands: Allied military occupation, demobilization of armed forces, and trial of war criminals. Foreign Minister Tōgō criticized the military's stand as unreasonable and warned that Japan had no alternative but to sue for peace. His sole concern, in the end, was "to obtain an Allied guarantee to respect and maintain the welfare of Japan's imperial house."[23] Unable to reach agreement, the supreme council met with the cabinet and rehashed the same arguments. When, after almost seven hours, the cabinet found itself stalemated, the prime minister and foreign minister decided to take the highly unusual step of reconvening the group in the presence of the emperor and seeking the emperor's decision.

Emperor Hirohito met with his advisers at midnight on August 9 in an underground bomb shelter attached to his library, where he and his family had been living since American fire bombs burned the main imperial residence four months earlier. All advisers favored a conditional acceptance of the Allied ultimatum. But a stalemate continued over what the condition(s) would be. A group led by Foreign Minister Tōgō insisted on only one condition: that the Allies guarantee the preservation of the imperial institution. The three military leaders agreed with this but demanded that Japan also be permitted to demobilize and disarm its own troops and to arrest and try any Japanese accused of war crimes and that Allied military occupation troops be restricted to certain locations in Japan.

After three hours of fruitless debate, Prime Minister Suzuki turned to Emperor Hirohito and announced: "Your Imperial Majesty's decision is requested as to which proposal should be adopted—the one by the Foreign Minister or the one containing the four conditions."[24] The emperor rose to his feet at the head of the table and spoke emotionally of the destruction and bloodshed caused by the war, especially the deaths of many young men who had faithfully served their nation. He spoke of the personal pain of seeing "the brave and loyal fighting men of Japan disarmed" and the punishment as instigators of the war of those "who have rendered me devoted service." But, he continued, the time has come to "bear the unbearable." "I swallow my own tears and give my sanction to the proposal to accept the Allied proclamation on the basis outlined by the Foreign Minister."[25]

At Foreign Minister Tōgō's temporary offices on the fourth floor of the Ministry of Education building,[26] Vice Minister Matsumoto Shun'ichi and his staff were drafting Japan's reply to the Allies—and anxiously awaiting word from the foreign minister. Tōgō finally returned from the imperial conference at 4:00 A.M. on August 10. He informed his staff of the decision of the conference: Japan would accept the Potsdam Declaration with the sole condition that the emperor's authority as sovereign be preserved. Matsumoto and his staff revised the Japanese text in accordance with that decision, making changes in the sentence concerning the emperor's authority as sovereign.[27]

The essence of Japan's one condition for accepting the Potsdam ultimatum and ending the war was that the emperor must retain his sovereign authority. The statement read: "The Japanese Government are ready to accept the terms enumerated in the joint declaration . . . with the understanding that the said declaration does not comprise any demand which prejudices the prerogatives of His Majesty as a Sovereign Ruler." The message was cabled to the Allied powers via Japanese consulates in Switzerland and Sweden.[28] Later that same morning American carrier-based planes and wave after wave of General Curtis LeMay's B-29s hit Tokyo and other Japanese cities with one of the largest fire-bomb raids of the war.[29]

The Japanese surrender offer officially reached Washington on August 10; it immediately posed a dilemma for Byrnes and Truman.[30] The Potsdam strategy, hinting that Japan might be able to preserve the imperial institution by surrendering, was the product of a compromise. Now Japan was asking for explicit assurances from the Allied powers regarding the emperor's prerogatives as sovereign. To accede to the Japanese request, in the face of strong anti-emperor public feelings, would be politically dangerous for the president.[31] Byrnes said accepting Japan's terms would lead to the "crucifixion of the President."[32] The American government would have to finesse the response.

The opinions of the president's senior advisers, conferring at the White House the morning of August 10, were divided. Leahy and Stimson favored giving the assurance Japan wanted. Byrnes resisted. Truman directed Byrnes to draft a reply and then return to get approval before sending it. Byrnes's wording did not deny Emperor Hirohito's prerogatives as sovereign ruler but said they would be subordinate to the Supreme Commander's own authority. The operative sentence said: "From the moment of surrender the authority of the Emperor and the Japanese Government to rule the state shall be subject to the Supreme Commander of the Allied Powers." The last sentence in Byrnes's note restated more emphatically the Allies' pledge of July 26: "The ultimate form of government in Japan shall, in accordance with the Potsdam Declaration, be established by the freely expressed will of the Japanese people."[33]

As Japanese Foreign Ministry officials examined Byrnes's note on August 12 and 13, they puzzled over the words "subject to" and consulted their English dictionaries. What did it mean to be "subject to" the authority of the Supreme Commander of the Allied Powers? Japanese leaders disagreed vehemently over both the words "subject to" and the "freely expressed will" clause. Could the emperor and the government be subject to MacArthur's control while preserving the "prerogatives" of the emperor as a sovereign ruler? Or would such an arrangement suspend, temporarily, Emperor Hirohito's sovereignty, even end it completely?

The second sentence regarding the "ultimate form of government in Japan" seemed to make the Japanese people the final arbiters of the emperor's authority. That seemed promising, at first glance; at least it could be interpreted as a pledge to take the matter out of the hands of the Allied powers. But on second thought, to subject the emperor's authority to the freely expressed will of the people—to make the people the ultimate authority—would violate their constitution. Did the word "government" in the sentence mean only the executive and legislative branches of government (seifu), or did it also include the imperial institution? If the latter, the American position would change the basis of the traditional national polity (kokutai), denying imperial sovereignty in favor of popular sovereignty.

Meanwhile, the Japanese military was doing its own translation and analysis of the Byrnes message. War Minister General Anami Korechika told Privy Seal Kido Kōichi on August 13 that it would be impossible to protect Japan's kokutai if the fourth clause (freely expressed will) were accepted.[34] Japan could not accept the note as it was; it would destroy the nation. Kido disagreed with Anami; he supported the foreign ministry's interpretation and argued that Japan could not possibly reject the note at this final stage of negotiation. At a meeting of the Supreme Council in the morning of August 13, Navy Minister Admiral Toyoda attacked the Allied intention of making the emperor "subject to" the Allies' supreme commander. He interpreted the words to mean that the emperor would be directly under the command of the Allied occupation. And to have the ultimate form of government determined by the freely expressed will of the Japanese people, he argued, would completely deny the traditional "sacred nature of kokutai" and replace it with a new form of government.[35] The military leaders stood their ground, forcing Prime Minister Suzuki to ask the emperor again to convene an imperial conference. When the emperor met his ministers, in the same air raid shelter he had used at their first meeting on August 9, he wasted little time reaffirming his wish to "accept the Allied reply as it stands." He told them: "It is my desire that you, my Ministers of State, accede to my wishes and forthwith accept the Allied reply."[36]

These were the final words of the conference. The cabinet prepared an imperial rescript containing the decision and approved and promulgated it late that night, August 14. The foreign ministry transmitted the imperial decision to the Allied powers. At approximately 4 A.M. on August 15, General Anami committed suicide in his office. In Washington, a smiling President Truman announced to waiting reporters that Japan had capitulated.[37] In Tokyo, palace officials recorded an imperial statement informing the Japanese people of their nation's surrender. A small group of soldiers serving as palace guards staged a putsch and attempted but failed to seize the recorded surrender message.[38] On August 15, Hirohito's message was broadcast to the nation.

Ambiguities and Ambivalences

Japan surrendered believing the imperial institution would be saved. There was evidence to support this. In late summer and fall of 1945, Washington's early policy directives to MacArthur stated what had only been implied in the Potsdam Declaration in July. The "United States Initial Postsurrender Policy for Japan," signed by Truman on September 6 (and published in Washington on September 22 and in Tokyo the next day), said that it "was not the responsibility of the occupation forces to impose on Japan any form of government not supported by the freely expressed will of the Japanese people."[39] This was a strong, clear statement. It was thus not unreasonable for the Japanese leaders to believe that the issue would be left in their hands.

However, the statement was ambiguous, the result of an unstable compromise. That compromise—between Grew and his opponents—was reached by saying that the final form of Japan's government would be determined in a democratic fashion, by "the freely expressed will of the Japanese people." But Japan's acceptance of the Potsdam Declaration did not end the debate in Washington over the emperor. Byrnes's reply to Japan on August 11, saying the emperor would be "subject to the Supreme Commander of the Allied Powers," meant, to Acheson at least, that MacArthur or the Allies could still eliminate the Japanese monarchy.[40] And the SFE of SWNCC began efforts in early September to determine U.S. policy on treatment of the emperor after Japan's surrender.[41] These two developments suggested that this central issue would not be left to the wishes of the Japanese people.

The "freely expressed will" phrase of the Potsdam Declaration appeared in several important directives Washington sent to MacArthur. In addition to SWNCC 150, a confidential State Department paper titled "Reform of the Japanese Governmental System" (SWNCC 228), sent in draft to MacArthur in early October 1945,[42] repeated the phrase several times and said the Japanese could keep the imperial institution—appropriately reformed—if they wished. The Joint Chiefs' more detailed directive on occupation policy, sent to MacArthur in November, repeated that it was not his responsibility to "impose on Japan any form of government not supported by the freely expressed will of the Japanese people."[43]

But Truman's statement to the press on August 15 that the surrender was "unconditional," coupled with personnel changes in the government, raised doubts about the future of the imperial institution. The influence of Grew and his "Japan hands" was already in decline before August 15. Truman's appointment of James Byrnes as Secretary of State on July 3 undermined Grew's influence. Secretary of War Stimson retired as the war ended. Grew submitted his resignation on August 15, and Dooman retired later in the month. By the end of August, Grew's acerbic opponent Dean Acheson replaced Grew as under secretary. And John Carter Vincent, a China specialist and critic of Hirohito, succeeded Dooman as chairman of the SFE of SWNCC. George Atcheson, Jr., another China specialist, joined MacArthur's staff as the chief political adviser.

Underlying this shift was the statement in SWNCC 150 that U.S. policy "does not commit the Supreme Commander to support the Emperor or any other Japanese governmental authority. The policy is to use the existing form of Government in Japan, not to support it." This meant allowing changes initiated by the Japanese people to modify the government's "feudal and authoritarian tendencies" even if such changes involved the use of force.[44] None of this augured well for Hirohito.

The Occupation of Japan

With Japan's acceptance of the Potsdam Declaration, events in Japan moved swiftly. In his radio broadcast of August 15, Hirohito called on the people of Japan to accept his decision and "bear the unbearable." A member of the imperial family, Prince Higashikuni Naruhiko, formed a new national unity cabinet on August 17. The government dispatched imperial princes to the commanders of major military commands abroad to ensure compliance with the emperor's decision. Following American instructions, Japanese military representatives flew to Manila to hear from MacArthur the details of the surrender and occupation. American troops began arriving on Japanese soil a few days later, followed by MacArthur himself on August 30. On September 2, Japanese representatives signed the formal surrender in the presence of MacArthur and representatives of the Allied Powers. The Occupation of Japan that began on that day would last until April 28, 1952.

In theory, the Occupation was undertaken and directed by the Allied powers that had fought Japan.[45] In fact, it was almost entirely an American operation, dominated by the personality of MacArthur. As SCAP, MacArthur's mission was to implement American policy as defined by the Potsdam Declaration and Washington's policy directives.[46] But seldom did MacArthur simply implement orders from Washington; if he disagreed, he would interpret, protest, or simply ignore them. When he saw the final version of SWNCC 150/4 on September 3,[47] he cabled a strong protest to the chairman of the JCS, General George C. Marshall, complaining that the document went well beyond the surrender terms and the Potsdam Declaration. Implementation of it would, he said, require revision of his occupation plans and a greater military force than he had contemplated. Marshall hastened to assure him that he could exercise "reasonable discretion normally permitted a field commander" and treat the document as a guide for his actions rather than a directive.[48] Thus from the outset MacArthur extracted

an understanding from the JCS that permitted him to act with considerable freedom in political matters of great importance to the United States, its Allies, and
Japan.

To rule Japan during the Occupation, MacArthur used two government structures. His general headquarters (GHQ) in Tokyo, with roughly 5,000 American
personnel, issued orders and policy directives to the Japanese government, which
implemented them. GHQ special sections (Government Section, Economic and
Social Section, Civil Information and Education Section, Civil Intelligence Section, Office of the Political Adviser, to name the major ones) were roughly equivalent to Japan's principal government ministries.[49] In addition, the U.S. Eighth
Army, with headquarters in Yokohama and units based near all major cities of
Japan, constituted the real occupying forces.

In late August 1945, Japan established a new bureau in the foreign ministry
to serve as liaison with MacArthur's headquarters. This group of former diplomats
was known to the Americans as the Central Liaison Office (CLO).[50] The CLO
opened special regional offices in Yokohama, near Eighth Army headquarters,
and in seventeen major cities around the country to maintain contact with lower
levels of the occupation forces.[51]

The Occupation rested on two broad assumptions. The first was that Japanese
leaders since the early 1930s had engaged in a conspiracy to wage aggressive war
due less to national interests than to the nature of their society and political
system. Both SWNCC 150/4 and JCS 1380/15 assumed that Japan's military aggression grew from a certain social structure, from a "feudal" society in which
the emperor was worshipped as a living god, reactionary politicians ruled the
nation, and a small but powerful group of corporations (*zaibatsu*) formed an
economic monopoly that controlled Japan's economy and supported expansion
abroad. Moreover, the Japanese people shared a national character that was so
imbued with emperor mythology that radical reform in every sphere of society
would be required to demilitarize and democratize the nation so that it would
no longer pose a threat to American interests.

Acheson stated the guiding proposition clearly: "The present economic and
social system in Japan which makes for a will to war will be changed so that the
will to war will not continue."[52] From this followed certain goals of the Occupation, as the Potsdam Declaration had indicated: destruction of the military;
trial of leaders accused of war crimes; a massive purge of Japan's ruling class; and
basic political, economic, and social reforms.

The second assumption was that democratizing Japan according to Western
values and institutions was the best way to create a peaceful Japan. Washington's
policy directives to MacArthur formed part of the Occupation's blueprint: Political reform was essential to guarantee basic freedoms, universal suffrage, free
elections, representative government, and a responsible executive. The "American
experience" provided another part of MacArthur's blueprint for reform. He had
complete faith in the superiority and universal applicability of that experience.
He believed that American values, institutions, and concepts of freedom "have
never [been] equaled in human history" and were "fit for all peoples everywhere."[53] But, he wrote to an admirer, these constituted only the essential frame-

work which could be erected by military fiat and "handled with . . . brusqueness."[54] True democracy required more; it required a "spiritual core." To introduce that to Japan would necessitate "spiritual changes in the national life" that would give meaning to formal institutions and processes, for "democracy . . . is a thing largely of the spirit."[55]

Thus as the military occupation of Japan began, it was clear that MacArthur, both as Commander of U.S. Military Forces in the Pacific and as Supreme Commander of the Allied Powers, would place his indelible imprint on this chapter in American and Japanese history. Wartime planning in Washington had provided an ambiguous policy blueprint for the political reform of Japan and treatment of the emperor. MacArthur would read that blueprint and interpret it according to his own understanding of his dual responsibilities and of his reflection on American and Japanese history. Often the results would be surprising.

2 • • • • • • • •

"This Fundamental Problem"

• ## MacARTHUR SAVES HIROHITO

•

As Japan made its final decision in August to accept the Potsdam
• Declaration, policymakers in Washington were already hammering
out a tougher set of postsurrender policies for Japan than the Allies
• had issued at Potsdam. With support from Dean Acheson and William L. Clayton of the State Department and John J. McCloy of the
• War Department, SWNCC's SFE added provisions for deconcentra-
tion of economic power, purges, and reparations. Only days after
• Truman signed that document on September 6,[1] the committee re-
opened the thorny issue of treatment of the Japanese emperor and
• the imperial system of government.[2]

•

Washington Takes the Lead

•

On September 7, Japan specialists in the State Department—Hugh
• Borton, Robert Fearey, and George Blakeslee—submitted to a meeting of the SFE a draft directive, intended ultimately for MacArthur,
• concerning treatment of the emperor.[3] The basic assumption of the
draft was, in keeping with provisions of the Potsdam Declaration,
• that a reformed monarchy could continue with the support of the
Japanese people. It provided that (1) Hirohito should be permitted
• to retain his throne and be immune from trial as a war criminal,
and (2) General MacArthur should seek advice from the Joint Chiefs
• of Staff before taking any action aimed at punishing the emperor,
such as removing him.

War and Navy departments' members of the subcommittee attacked the State Department's draft proposal, arguing that American
policy was to try war criminals. The United States had made no
specific commitment to the Japanese government to protect the emperor, and American public opinion would certainly demand Hirohito's trial and punishment. Their argument was strengthened by
a congressional resolution of September 25, which was debated but
not acted on, declaring it to be "the policy of the United States that
Emperor Hirohito be tried as a war criminal."[4] The SFE received a
copy of the resolution the same day.

Borton and Fearey, responding to these criticisms, argued that their position (to retain and use the emperor) was the only reasonable interpretation of Secretary Byrnes's August 11 note to the Japanese. Japan had surrendered with that understanding. To put the emperor on trial for war crimes would constitute an act of bad faith that might imperil the Occupation's goals and ultimate American objectives in Japan.

The hard-liners acknowledged the distinction "between the individual and the system" but refused to defer action on treatment of the emperor until a paper on constitutional reform could be completed.[5] Captain Robert Dennison of the Navy and Colonel Mark Howe of the Army pressed for a firm stand immediately: The emperor ought not to be immune from punishment; MacArthur should arrest and try him as a war criminal. Vincent, more moderate, favored encouraging the Japanese themselves to "seek abolition of the institution of the Emperor."[6]

Unable to reach a consensus on the draft, proponents of trying the emperor appealed to the SFE chairman, Vincent. He put the question before the new under secretary of state, Dean Acheson. Acheson quickly rejected immunity for the emperor. The SFE revised the draft to make it conform to the policy, as interpreted by Acheson, that the emperor could be put in the dock for war crimes.

When the new draft reached the parent committee (SWNCC) for adoption as formal American policy, Assistant Secretary of War Robert A. Lovett objected, charging "the paper prejudged the Emperor's guilt."[7] He faulted the injudicious tone of the subcommittee's discussion, called for a "dispassionate appraisal" of the evidence against the emperor, and urged further study of the future of the imperial institution.

The SFE revised the draft, acknowledging that the policy "cannot be divorced from our overall objectives in Japan." These objectives included encouraging the Japanese to establish a democratic government fully responsive to the Japanese people. And this could involve the abolition of the imperial institution by the Japanese themselves or its complete alteration to make it consistent with democratic government.

When the Joint Chiefs transmitted the document to MacArthur on November 30, 1945, they enclosed instructions repeating that the emperor "is not immune from arrest, trial and punishment." The question of his trial might be raised in the future "when the occupation can get along without him." MacArthur was directed to collect evidence Washington needed to make a decision on the emperor's future and to forward it to the Joint Chiefs along with his personal recommendations. Although Washington had not made a decision against trying the emperor, it had, by initiating this process, made a trial less likely. More important, Washington's indecision, coupled with MacArthur's determination to protect the emperor, spelled victory for the Grew faction's position. As Supreme Commander, only MacArthur was in a position to say "when the occupation can get along without Hirohito." By the time the policy directive reached MacArthur in Tokyo,[8] he had already decided.

The Joint Chiefs' directive of November 30 to General MacArthur raised two questions: Was the emperor a war criminal? Would he be useful to the occupation forces in ruling Japan? The two questions were related but different. If compelling evidence surfaced that tied the emperor directly to decisions to wage aggressive war, pressure would mount to try him regardless of his putative usefulness to the occupation. On the other hand, if he proved to be compliant and cooperative, MacArthur might be tempted, in replying to the Joint Chiefs, to ignore or play down evidence that the emperor had supported war against the United States.

MacArthur's Position

What most influenced MacArthur's treatment of the emperor? Three factors appear to have been decisive: MacArthur's interpretation of U.S. policy for Japan, including Grew's arguments regarding the emperor; palace insiders' attempts to present the emperor as a pacifist willing to cooperate; and MacArthur's personal goal of advancing Christianity in Japan and his conviction that the emperor would cooperate in that effort.

MacArthur began his mission inclined to retain and use Emperor Hirohito. In July 1945 he told Chief of Staff General George Marshall that he favored "maximum utilization of the existing Japanese governmental agencies and organization." He remarked that "premature dislocation of governmental machinery would be undesirable."[9] Removing the emperor would have been a major dislocation. This agreed with Washington's initial preference to rule through the Japanese government without necessarily supporting Hirohito and the imperial institution. Despite this, MacArthur's staff had prepared written orders instituting direct military rule, use of U.S. military currency, and adoption of English as the official language. Foreign Minister Shigemitsu Mamoru personally appealed to MacArthur to cancel such orders. In a cable to Marshall shortly after this meeting, MacArthur said he wished to leave much initiative in the hands of the Japanese.[10] MacArthur's decision to rule through the Japanese government made the emperor vital to the Occupation. This was a commitment that went beyond the Potsdam Declaration and the "U.S. Initial Post-Surrender Policy for Japan" (SWNCC 150/4). In effect, MacArthur moved a step closer to Grew's position with respect to the importance of the emperor, and this in turn made him vulnerable to appeals from supporters of Hirohito.

The Japanese Defend the Emperor

In the early days and weeks after surrender, the emperor's palace retinue engaged in a concerted effort to persuade Americans, especially MacArthur, that the emperor was not only innocent of war crimes but had himself been a victim of militarists in his own government; that it was he, personally, who had decided to accept the Potsdam Declaration as the basis of surrender; that he was eager to cooperate to achieve the objectives of the Potsdam Declaration; and that he had widespread public support. As we have seen, the Japanese government was extremely nervous about Truman's insistence that the emperor be "subject to the

authority of the Supreme Commander." No clear international agreement protected the emperor; he was—to put it bluntly—at the mercy of the Americans,
particularly MacArthur.

The Japanese were quite aware of the American public's hatred for Hirohito
and demands that he be tried as a war criminal. But they took heart from reports
of the Japanese delegates summoned to Manila by MacArthur in late August 1945.
The general would not subject the emperor to the personal humiliation of signing
the surrender document at a public ceremony. Yet fear for the emperor's personal
safety remained strong, indeed the primary concern of those near the throne.
Efforts to save the emperor—his throne and perhaps even his life—began early
and took some unusual turns.

On August 24, 1945, the new prime minister, Prince Higashikuni (an army
general and the emperor's uncle), announced the appointment of several special
advisers to his cabinet. One was the noted Christian evangelist and socialist leader
Kagawa Toyohiko.[11] A graduate of Princeton Theological Seminary, Kagawa spoke
English well and had many American friends and admirers. In 1941 he had organized a conference in San Francisco to pray and work for peace between Japan
and the United States. Though often sharply critical of U.S. policy, Kagawa was
essentially pro-American. As a regular visitor to the palace, his name appears
often in the diary of Sekiya Teisaburō, prewar vice minister of the imperial household ministry.[12]

Playing the Christian Card

Although Kagawa's responsibility as special adviser to Higashikuni was to organize
a movement to "restore popular morale," he initially spent much of his time
preparing public statements defending the emperor. In a long open letter to
MacArthur on September 2, he mounted an emotional defense of the emperor
as a pacifist influenced by Christianity.[13] Speaking in language that appealed to
MacArthur, Kagawa admitted Japan's "spiritual flaws" (in his victory speech the
same day on the battleship USS Missouri, MacArthur used the term "spiritual
vacuum"). But, he argued, democratization of Japan, a basic American goal, could
best be achieved under the imperial system and the emperor's personal guidance.
To counteract stories critical of the emperor in the foreign press, Kagawa repeated
this thesis at news conferences attended by foreign journalists. On one occasion
he told American reporters that the emperor was a good man because he had
been influenced by his mother, who was herself interested in Christianity. To
support his argument, he put out a story that Hirohito, while visiting London as
crown prince in 1920, had joined the YMCA.[14]

Imperial advisers encouraged Japanese Christians and long-time American
missionaries in Japan to speak out on behalf of the emperor. On September 10,
the deputy prime minister, Prince Konoe Fumimaro, dispatched an elderly American missionary, William Merrill Vories,[15] to MacArthur's temporary headquarters
in Yokohama to establish contact for Konoe. Vories talked to a young naval
officer, Lt. Commander Samuel Bartlett, an aide to MacArthur and the son of a

missionary family Vories had known before the war at Doshisha University in Kyoto.[16] Through Bartlett, Vories got his "message to the General and some invaluable data for the Prince" and furthered the court's effort to cast the emperor in a positive light. He told Bartlett that the military government had concealed from the emperor the truth about the war, and that the emperor's anger at this deception led him to favor ending the war.[17] Vories assured Bartlett that the emperor was a man of peace and had opposed the war in 1941.[18] He also tried to dispel the widespread American notion that the emperor saw himself as "a living god" and Japan as a divine country. The emperor might be willing to issue a formal statement repudiating the more extreme versions of that myth.

Two days later, on September 12, while awaiting word from Bartlett on an appointment for Konoe, Vories wrote in his diary that he had come up with "the suggested wording for a Rescript or Declaration that would provide the 'Single word from the Emperor' which MacArthur would accept as worth more than anything else in restoring full confidence in Japan." This suggests that Vories was proposing to Konoe something similar to the famous declaration that the emperor did issue on January 1, 1946.[19] Vories soon learned from Bartlett that Mac-Arthur had agreed to meet with Konoe the next day, September 13.

Konoe's first meeting with MacArthur at the general's temporary headquarters in the Yokohama Customs Building had something of mystery about it. He was a senior statesman, despite his relatively young age of forty-six, and had served three times as prime minister before the war. He was also deputy prime minister in the Higashikuni cabinet. Yet his unofficial approach to MacArthur had an air of secret maneuvering for which he was famous. His associates in the cabinet who knew of the visit (Prime Minister Higashikuni apparently did not know in advance) thought that he had requested the meeting to inform MacArthur of conditions in Japan.[20] Yet when he met MacArthur for an hour in the late afternoon of September 13, Konoe was frustrated because he could neither share important information with MacArthur nor solicit much new from him. The reason, according to Konoe, was that MacArthur's American interpreter was unable to perform his duties adequately.[21] Yet Konoe apparently heard MacArthur say quite clearly that the government must revise the constitution to make Japan more democratic, for this is what he reported to Higashikuni.[22]

On September 20, a week after the first Konoe–MacArthur encounter, Prime Minister Higashikuni made his own move to enlist Christians in the effort to save the emperor. Addressing a small gathering of Japanese Christians and American missionaries who had spent the war years in Japan, he thanked them for the good work they had done for Japan and apologized for the military's attack on that work. He then made a remarkable statement to the guests. "We need," he said, "a new standard of ethics, like that of Jesus Christ. Buddhism can never teach us to forgive our enemies, nor can Shintoism. If Japan is to be revived we need Jesus Christ as the basis of our national life."[23] This was only the beginning of numerous episodes designed to demonstrate the imperial family's interest in Christianity. The emperor's brother ostentatiously attended church in Tokyo, while both the emperor and empress had Bible lessons in the palace.[24]

Such private diplomacy to influence MacArthur was not without direction.

One link between the imperial palace and MacArthur's headquarters was forged early by a Christian educator, Kawai Michiko, the founder and president of Keisen (Christian) Girl's High School and Junior College in Tokyo. Kawai was a Bryn Mawr College graduate and ardent admirer of the United States.[25] Her close friend, Isshiki (born Watanabe) Yuriko, had attended Earlham College in Indiana with one of MacArthur's closest advisers, Brigadier General Bonner Fellers. After Earlham, Fellers attended West Point and saw service in the Philippines and as military attache in Tokyo.[26] He visited Japan and kept in touch with Isshiki and Kawai over the years. On his arrival in Japan (on MacArthur's plane) on August 29, Fellers sent food and a message to Kawai and Isshiki and later invited them to dinner at the American Embassy. Kawai recalled: "General Fellers had his quarters in the same [embassy] compound and we saw him very often." By late September, they were discussing Japan's responsibility for Pearl Harbor, the extent of the emperor's advanced knowledge of the attack and his personal responsibility for the war.[27]

Kawai had another friend in a sensitive position on the Japanese side—inside the palace bureaucracy. He was Sekiya Teisaburō,[28] the former vice minister of the imperial household ministry, member of the House of Peers and Privy Council, and a Christian. In August 1945, he returned to the palace as a special adviser. His diary entries show an active calendar of meetings in fall 1945 with ministers, vice ministers, and palace officials.[29] From early September 1945, Sekiya encountered a growing number of Japanese Christian leaders, American Christian missionaries, and SCAP officials.

Then came the famous meeting between Emperor Hirohito and MacArthur on September 27, and its still more famous photograph. It was the latter that alarmed Sekiya and other palace officials. Arranged by Foreign Minister Yoshida Shigeru as a way of ingratiating the emperor with MacArthur, the meeting had apparently produced little for the Japanese but a humiliating photograph in the newspapers showing the American general towering over the small Japanese emperor.[30]

New Efforts Are Made

On October 2 Kawai revealed to Sekiya that she had been meeting with Fellers. He showed great interest in this American general, who, as Sekiya put it, "was not only close to MacArthur but friendly to Japan." Within days he would arrange, with Kawai's help, to meet Fellers face to face and seek to advance the palace campaign on behalf of the emperor.

Like many on the palace staff, Sekiya felt that the foreign press was presenting an "inaccurate view of the emperor and the war." In early October he shared his concern with Tanaka Kōtarō[31] (also a Christian); Major Harold Henderson, a professor of Japanese literature at Columbia University and special SCAP adviser; and Kagawa. They believed that such reports revealed a serious American "misunderstanding" of the emperor's role in the war and his dedication to peace. Could something be done about it? Sekiya asked Kagawa to see the new prime minister, Shidehara Kijūrō,[32] and make sure he was aware of the many distortions contained in the foreign press.

As apprehension grew, palace advisers considered using an imperial rescript, a formal statement from the emperor himself, about his role in Japan's decisions leading to the war. Would such a statement—the ultimate weapon in their diminished arsenal—persuade the Americans, especially MacArthur, that the emperor was not a war criminal? Sekiya got in touch with Kawai on October 12 and asked her to explore this with Fellers. She reported back that, unfortunately, the American side would not consider an imperial rescript sufficient evidence of the emperor's innocence.

The campaign on behalf of the emperor was stalled. Yet the matter was increasingly urgent, for the American government was drawing up lists of war criminals. Two lists had already arrived from Washington in September, one of which was shown informally to a foreign ministry official, who reported that the emperor's name was not on it.[33] This provided little solace, however, for other lists would follow and American opinion polls, editorials, and statements by influential senators favored trying the emperor as a war criminal. The palace's efforts had so far failed, as Sekiya said, "to gain understanding" of the emperor's innocence. What more could be done?

At this point of growing despair, Kawai put forth a personal proposal. Would Sekiya himself meet with Fellers and make the argument of imperial innocence and, perhaps, secure the latest news from Washington on American plans for treatment of the emperor? As a temporary appointee recalled for special service in the palace, Sekiya could not undertake such a sensitive mission on his own authority. He consulted former Minister of the Imperial Household Matsudaira Yoshitami and the current minister, Ishiwata Sōtarō. They now had an opportunity to make their case directly to someone close to MacArthur. It was a chance, they reasoned, that should not be missed. After two days of discussion in the palace, Ishiwata authorized Sekiya to see Fellers and, if it would help the imperial cause, offer to arrange a meeting between Fellers and Emperor Hirohito himself. The emperor's historic meeting with MacArthur on September 27 had not touched on the critical question of the emperor's war guilt. The emperor's advisers now, two weeks later, obviously regretted that missed opportunity. Therefore, the emperor was willing to make the case himself if Fellers wished to see him.

Kawai sprang into action again, not only arranging for Sekiya to meet Fellers at his office on October 16 but accompanying him as his interpreter. The event could not have come at a more auspicious moment. Fellers himself had submitted a brief on the subject to MacArthur a few days earlier, urging that the emperor system be retained and warning of dire consequences if the emperor were put in the docket as a war criminal.[34] His views were reinforced by Washington's draft paper on "Reform of the Japanese Governmental System" (SWNCC 228), a draft copy of which Robert Fearey had brought to Tokyo earlier in the month. The document allowed that the monarchy could continue to exist in a reformed Japanese government. Sekiya noted in his diary on this day, October 16, that "the meeting [with Fellers] was most beneficial." What he apparently heard from Fellers was that the "save-the-emperor" thesis was already circulating on the sixth floor of MacArthur's headquarters.

This was confirmed by Kagawa, who also managed to arrange a meeting with Fellers to discuss the emperor and U.S. policy. In a report to his group, he quoted Fellers to the effect that "today a report from the U.S. has arrived which completely supports General MacArthur's position that the emperor system should continue."[35] The reference was apparently to the draft paper on reform of the Japanese government (SWNCC 228), which Fearey brought from Washington. If so, Fellers's characterization of Washington's policy was overly optimistic. The emperor system as it had existed heretofore could not continue. The SWNCC paper said, "retention of the Emperor institution in its present form is not considered consistent with . . . general objectives [of democratization]." It would have to be reformed along more democratic lines, deprived of all authority, or abolished.[36]

The Christian Line Reinforced

While debate on treatment of the emperor and the imperial institution was going on, public expression of support for both came, quite fortuitously, from four representatives of several American church groups. One of them, Luman J. Schafer, a former missionary in Japan and leader in the Federal Council of Churches, began planning the return of Protestant missionaries to Japan well before the war ended. He had organized a conference of American church leaders in 1943 to discuss postwar American policy for Japan. The conference report warned against overthrowing Japan's imperial institution. In January 1945, Schafer met with Under Secretary of State Grew to propose a role for the Mission Boards of North America in the occupation of Japan.[37]

Shortly after Japan's surrender, Japanese Christian groups in a radio message issued an invitation to American Protestant church leaders to send a delegation to Japan. Schafer, Douglas Horton, and two other prominent leaders[38] in the Federal Council of Churches sought Washington's permission to travel to Japan and a letter of endorsement from President Truman. In his letter of October 16, Truman not only endorsed the project but quoted from MacArthur's statement at the surrender of Japan on September 2 that the "problem [the Occupation faces in Japan] is theological and involves a spiritual recrudescence and improvement of human character."[39] Truman's letter concluded with these words: "Your deputation should in a large measure aid in solving this fundamental problem facing Japan."[40]

The churchmen spent three weeks in late October and November reestablishing contact with Japanese Christians and preparing to renew their prewar missionary effort to bring Japan into the Christian fold. They made courtesy calls on Prime Minister Higashikuni, Prince Konoe Fumimaro, and Emperor Hirohito, and they met twice with MacArthur. Before their meeting with Hirohito, they sent him a copy of President Truman's letter. He expressed sincere appreciation for Christian work in prewar Japan, as Higashikuni had done earlier, and appeared to welcome such work in the postwar period.[41] He complained about American immigration laws that discriminated against Japanese, a matter of special interest to him apparently.[42] The American church leaders assured the emperor that the church in America was working to gain repeal of such laws.

This personal imperial diplomacy paid immediate dividends. Shafer sent a letter to the *Nippon Times* stating that in his opinion, a majority of Americans favored "recognition of the Japanese Imperial Household as an integral part of Japanese culture."[43] This infuriated Secretary of State Byrnes, who fired off a telegram to Schafer warning him to "avoid public discussion of Japan or making public pronouncements that may tend to stir up the Japanese on controversial matters of far-reaching importance."[44] Undeterred, these American Christian leaders continued to defend the emperor. Their report on the visit to Japan praised the emperor as a man of diligence, exemplary morals, and an exponent of "the highest ideals—including the ideal of peace." He had not wanted war, indeed had put his life on the line to end the war, and enjoyed broad popular support.[45]

The imperial advisers' strategy had indeed borne fruit. By pushing their own Christian officials to the fore and by embracing American Christian leaders, they were making a strong appeal to MacArthur. They knew democratization of Japan was one of his major goals. They also knew he believed Christian values were essential to democracy.[46] And although it would take a while longer to make a convincing case, they were trying in October to tempt him to think that saving the emperor from the war crimes tribunal was a first step toward turning "Japan into a Christian democracy."[47]

MacArthur not only welcomed the church leaders publicly but spoke to them in private meetings of Japan's loss of values and of the unprecedented opportunity this offered Christians. They were familiar with MacArthur's public statements about Japan's "spiritual vacuum" and aware of his reputation as a Christian, but were surprised by the strength of his embrace and the urgency of his words. He challenged them to begin at once propagating the Christian faith in Japan. As supreme commander, he promised a warm welcome to all missionaries who wished to come to Japan. He urged them to fill Japan's "spiritual vacuum," and warned "if you do not fill it with Christianity, it will be filled with communism. Send me 1,000 missionaries."[48] Later MacArthur, in the best ecumenical spirit, issued the same appeal to Archbishop Paul Marella, the Apostolic Delegate to Japan. The time had come, he said, for the church to act quickly. "I challenge you and the Church to begin work at once." Then he added: "Tell that to the Holy Father in Rome."[49]

By December MacArthur was not only "telling that to the Holy Father in Rome," he was telling it to the Joint Chiefs in Washington. He cabled them on December 29: "It is my policy to permit the return of missionaries to Japan to the maximum extent practicable." When, in months ahead, the churches complained of delays in getting clearances from Tokyo, MacArthur's headquarters broadened the guidelines in late December 1945: "It is the policy of this theater to increase greatly the Christian influence and every effort will be made here to absorb missionaries as rapidly as the church can send them into the area." The

Joint Chiefs concurred in MacArthur's policy, and later Secretary of Army Kenneth Royall and President Truman endorsed it.[50]

SCAP cleared more than 2,000 missionaries for entry into Japan by 1949. Still MacArthur urged the churches to send more, for he considered this rare historical opportunity to convert an Asian nation would last no more than ten years. He told one missionary that "today there is an opportunity to Christianize Japan never offered before." To another he said: "Democracy, as we interpret it, is the exemplification of the tenets of Christianity." He boasted to visiting American publishers and editors that "the world will remember that America gave to Japan the two major concepts of American civilization—Christianity and democracy."[51]

His ardor never cooled. In 1947, when a Christian socialist, Katayama Tetsu, became prime minister of Japan, MacArthur issued a press release, calling attention to the political and spiritual implications that "three great Oriental countries now have men who embrace the Christian faith as the head of their governments, Chiang Kai-shek in China, Manual Roxas in the Philippines, and Tetsu Katayama in Japan."[52] In 1950, five years into the Occupation, he could still say to an editor of a Christian publication: "Tell the churches of America that the Christian church has never met such an opportunity in 500 years as they now meet in Japan . . . let them lay their plans big enough for this task. . . . Japan cannot be a democracy without Christianity."[53] MacArthur later told a convention of Episcopalians in Los Angeles: "I felt that it became my duty as a Soldier of God to attempt to restore and revive religion in Japan—to fill this moral vacuum—just as it was my duty as a Soldier of the Republic to revitalize the general welfare of the country."[54]

MacArthur's decision to enlist the American churches in his political mission of reforming Japan was the product of several personal and historical factors: his own pious faith, his unprecedented power as the supreme political authority in Japan, his belief that democracy could not exist without Christianity, and his ethnocentric notion that the principles of American democracy were fit for the entire human race, irrespective of geographical delimitations or cultural traditions. MacArthur and his staff acted on his convictions and his policies: authorizing the entrance of foreign missionaries to Japan before any other group, providing logistical support, favoring Christianity in educational and religious reforms, personally encouraging Japanese to embrace Christianity, and supporting the establishment of a new international Christian university in Tokyo.[55]

An Obstacle Remains

However promising the emperor as a partner in ruling Japan and, perhaps, Christianizing its people, MacArthur had still to deal with U.S. policy defined in the Potsdam Declaration and in the instructions he had received from the JCS regarding the emperor. On December 15, SCAP issued the so-called Shinto Directive, which sought to "free the Japanese people from direct or indirect compulsion to believe or profess to believe in a religion or cult officially designated by the state." On December 31, MacArthur ordered Japanese schools to suspend the teaching of all history, geography, and morals education courses until "mytho-logical interpretations" based on the presumed divinity of the emperor could be removed from textbooks.

Meanwhile, the central question of what to do with the emperor gained urgency. The words of the paper, "Treatment of the Emperor," which the JCS had sent to MacArthur, were coldly pragmatic: Retain him as long as he is useful to the goals of the Occupation. But how could MacArthur use the emperor without seeming to support the imperial institution and the *kokutai* myth? Were the emperor and the myth separable? Could the Occupation remove the divine aura that surrounded the emperor without destroying the institution and its utility to U.S. policy?

History suggested that it could be done. One approach might be to strip away the accretions to the institution of the late nineteenth century. This would leave a symbol for the Occupation to manipulate for its own purposes, much as the Meiji government had done. Americans believed that Japanese aggression was fed by "emperor worship," the "god emperor myth" of the Japanese nation. But shorn of its divine aura the imperial institution could be a force for peaceful change and democratization. The answer was to drop the myth but keep the man by demythologizing the emperor, or better yet have him do the deed himself. For MacArthur to order it might arouse powerful conservative forces to resist the occupation. MacArthur and his advisers sensed in their talks with the imperial advisers, and with the emperor himself, a surprising flexibility. He seemed genuinely open to change, even more so than many of his advisers.[56] The idea soon developed in MacArthur's headquarters that an imperial rescript would be useful in stripping away the "pernicious" features of the institution and paving the way for a constitutional monarchy.

The precise origins of the emperor's January 1, 1946, "Declaration of Humanity"[57] are obscure. The idea of such a public pronouncement was widely discussed in the fall of 1945. Palace advisers appear to have coordinated this important document. In November 1945 the staff of MacArthur's Civil Information and Education Section (CIE) discussed the matter in detail with R. H. Blyth, an Englishman who taught at Gakushūin (Peers School), and with Major Harold Henderson, an adviser to CIE. CIE then prepared a draft of the statement, while Japan's Minister of Education, Maeda Tamon, prepared another at the request of Prime Minister Shidehara.[58] MacArthur approved the final English version and issued a press release when the emperor published it.[59]

The rescript invoked, at the emperor's express request, the spirit of Emperor Meiji by repeating in full the 1868 Meiji Charter Oath,[60] and it warned the nation of difficult days ahead. Then in one short paragraph, buried deep in the document, came the expected disclosure: the emperor's relations with the people were grounded in history, not myths and legends. In the statement, the emperor said: "The ties between us and our people have always stood upon mutual trust and affection. They do not depend upon mere legends and myths. They are not predicated on the false conception that the Emperor is divine, and that the Japanese people are superior to other races and fated to rule the world." Whether it was an assertion of his humanity, as the Japanese said, or a denial of his divinity, as the Americans claimed, the statement repudiated the "sacred and inviolable" clause of Article III of the Meiji Constitution. The New Year's rescript thus opened the way for MacArthur to use the emperor in making fundamental changes in the imperial institution and the constitution.

The Debate Becomes International

The timing of the rescript was important. It came on the heels of the foreign ministers' agreement in Moscow on December 26, which permitted the Allies a significant voice in reforming the Japanese government, and while the Allied War Crimes Commission was meeting in London. And it appeared just ten days before MacArthur received from the Joint Chiefs of Staff the final version of "Reform of the Japanese Governmental System" (SWNCC 228). Earlier drafts of this document informed MacArthur that the "State Department was unanimous in believing that the British system of democratic government is better adapted to Japanese conditions than the American."[61] Washington's directive to investigate the emperor as a potential war criminal gave MacArthur a major voice in determining whether the emperor would continue in office. The emperor's New Year's declaration signaled that he himself had rejected the troublesome "sacred and inviolable" clause of the Meiji Constitution and had embraced the rational principles of the Meiji Charter Oath. Whether or not MacArthur understood the historical parallel, he readily grasped the central implication: The Japanese emperor was prepared to accept a limited and symbolic role in a new constitution.

MacArthur's political adviser, George Atcheson, summarized SCAP's options in a memorandum on January 7, 1946.[62] Noting that the emperor was not immune from trial as a war criminal, but that treatment of him could not be divorced from the Occupation's overall objectives in Japan, he posed two choices: "If we are prepared . . . to increase effective forces in Japan to take care of any contingency that might arise—then we can adopt a strongly aggressive political policy, try the Emperor as a war criminal and encourage the complete abolition of the Emperor system." Otherwise, "we may do what we can and continue to proceed cautiously to give the Japanese the framework within which they may work out their own destiny with the aid, if they desire it, of the stabilizing force of the Throne."

Atcheson acknowledged his own preference for the first option: "The Emperor system must disappear if Japan is ever to be really democratic." But he recognized that the United States and its allies were unlikely to "stick with the Japanese problem" long enough to overcome the upheaval this might cause in Japanese society. Therefore, he cautioned, "it would seem unwise to take strong steps striking directly at the Emperor institution." On the positive side, the emperor had been enormously useful to the Occupation: "He is obeyed by the officials and the people at large. He manifests sincerity in wishing to aid in the accomplishment of our general objectives and is seemingly more anxious to be democratic than some of the people around him. His New Year's Rescript was encouraging."[63] Atcheson's memorandum and the arrival of Washington's policy paper on reforming the Japanese government triggered a decision that had been forming in MacArthur's mind: to put an end to the uncertainty surrounding the future of the Japanese emperor and throne.

MacArthur Decides

The immediate occasion was an Australian proposal of January 21, 1946, to the War Crimes Commission in London to charge Hirohito and sixty-one other Japanese leaders as war criminals. The JCS cabled a copy of the Australian proposal to MacArthur the same day. MacArthur replied four days later in a long telegram defending the emperor and warning of the frightful consequences of putting him on trial.[64] He wrote that his investigation had uncovered no evidence that the emperor had made political decisions for the Japanese government and that "his connection with the affairs of state up to the time of the end of the war was largely ministerial." MacArthur's recommendation was clear: The emperor should not be tried. And he clearly stated his reasons for opposing the abolition of the institution: "Practically all Japanese venerate him as the social head of the state and believe rightly or wrongly that the Potsdam Agreements [sic] were intended to maintain him as the emperor of Japan." MacArthur deliberately accepted the Japanese government's contention that the Potsdam Declaration constituted "Agreements" between the Allied powers and Japan. It served his purpose to make this argument, which the Japanese government had made since the surrender. The Allied powers, not he, had accepted a conditional surrender based on a contractual arrangement which left it to the "freely expressed will of the Japanese people" to determine the ultimate form of their government.[65]

These are the only arguments made in the telegram. The rest of it paints in the strongest tones the grave consequences of any move against the emperor. Such an action would be regarded as a "betrayal." "It would engender resentments and hatreds that will unquestionably last for all measurable time. A vendetta for revenge will thereby be initiated whose cycle may well not be complete for centuries if ever." Nor was that enough. MacArthur raised the specter that "civilized practices will largely cease," that government agencies will break down and guerrilla warfare spread across the land. "I believe all hope of introducing modern democratic methods would disappear and that when military control finally ceased some form of intense regimentation probably along communistic lines would arise from the mutilated masses." The JCS and the American government should know the implications: "It would be absolutely essential to greatly increase the occupational forces. It is quite possible that a minimum of a million troops would be required which would have to be maintained for an indefinite number of years."

Such hyperbole was calculated to frighten Washington and stop any further talk of putting the emperor on trial, and it worked. The cost of a million troops, hundreds of thousands of civil servants, and supplies for millions of Japanese for an indefinite period was too much for Washington to contemplate. The Joint Chiefs hurriedly discussed the telegram with Admiral Leahy at the White House, sent a copy to the military attache in London, and urged the State Department to act promptly. The department instructed Ambassador Winant in London to avoid any public mention of such a trial and to put pressure on the British government to block Australia's attempts to press public charges against Emperor Hirohito.[66]

Although the matter continued to be discussed in Washington intermittently for several more weeks, MacArthur's telegram and Washington's actions to block Australia constituted a decision to defend the emperor against Allied threats of trial as a war criminal. MacArthur himself proceeded to move well beyond this policy. Eight days later, on February 3, without informing Washington, he penned a top secret note to General Whitney, Chief of Government Section, ordering him to write a "model constitution" for Japan. Three provisions on the emperor were to be included: He was to be at the head of the state, his succession was to be dynastic, and his duties and powers were to be exercised in accordance with the constitution.[67]

General MacArthur played the key role in saving Emperor Hirohito from forced abdication and a humiliating international trial for war crimes. He preserved the imperial institution, shorn of its powers, by holding the Allies and Washington at bay and by dictating the key provisions of a new constitution for Japan. But the emperor demonstrated a strong will of his own. By ordering Japan's surrender and the orderly manner of its achievement, he demonstrated his effective control over the Japanese nation. By cooperating with the American Occupation, he saved himself from trial as a war criminal and possible execution. He would soon accept MacArthur's dictate on his status as a powerless symbolic head of state. He had indeed demonstrated his willingness to collaborate with MacArthur and the American Occupation.

To rule Japan, MacArthur needed the cooperation of the Japanese government and people. The emperor's willingness to collaborate extended to MacArthur a share of the emperor's authority and legitimacy in the eyes of the Japanese people. The general's personal belief in the power of the Christian faith added a peculiar dimension to his relationship with the emperor. The Occupation's political objective of democratization became linked to MacArthur's personal goal of converting Japan to Christianity. The emperor as a potential Christian convert became doubly useful. Ironically, the imperial mystique, which many Americans saw as the root cause of Japanese militarism, could now serve to advance American interests, political and religious. Imperial endorsement of Christianity and of the foreign missionary movement extended to both of them the highest sanction of Japanese society. The emperor's declaration of his own humanity on New Year's day in 1946 symbolized for MacArthur both the promise of achieving his political goals as a "Soldier of the Republic" and his religious goals as a "Soldier of God."

3 . . . .

"In Good Faith"

• JAPAN CONSIDERS CONSTITUTIONAL REFORM

One of the two major goals of American policy during the occupation of Japan was democratization. In legal terms this meant establishing institutions and prescribing procedures for democracy through a new constitutional order. Initiating the revision of Japan's Constitution in 1946 was perhaps MacArthur's most important and controversial reform. He and his Government Section maintained that they had to act because the Japanese government failed to meet its obligation to carry out thorough political reform on its own.

Some Japanese and foreign scholars have tended to agree with SCAP's criticism of the Japanese government's performance on constitutional reform during the fall of 1945.[1] They point to the failed efforts of the Konoe and Matsumoto committees. They cite the limited revisions proposed by these officials as evidence of a wish to escape basic reform, to try to preserve the prewar constitutional system, shorn only of the military. They conclude that given this Japanese resistance to change, MacArthur had no alternative but to write a model constitution and pressure the Japanese to accept it as their own.

However, neither the Potsdam Declaration nor the U.S. Initial Postsurrender Policy was clear regarding the need or extent of constitutional revision. The victors and the vanquished could, and did, interpret these policy documents in different ways. Did the Japanese understand the meaning of the Potsdam demands that "Japan revive and strengthen democratic tendencies"? Were Japanese proposals consistent with U.S. published policy and MacArthur's private advice to them? Did MacArthur or his staff clearly explain the extent of constitutional reform they expected? To explore these questions, we will consider the Japanese government's perception of U.S. policy, and the extent to which the cabinet and bureaucracy were prepared to comply. We begin with ideas for reform originating in the cabinet's Legislation Bureau and in the Foreign Ministry, and then examine (in chapter 4) proposals from the groups headed by Konoe and Matsumoto.

The Cabinet Confronts Reform

In September and October 1945, Japanese politicians and bureaucrats took the first halting steps towards constitutional reform. In signing the instrument of surrender, the Japanese government had pledged "to accept the provisions set forth in the [Potsdam] declaration," to carry out those provisions in good faith. Within days of Japan's formal surrender on September 2, 1945, talk of political reform was rife in the Higashikuni cabinet. The press reported that the cabinet intended to initiate democratization by amending existing laws, such as the Peace Preservations Law that had restricted basic civil rights since 1925.[2]

MacArthur's conversations with Higashikuni and Konoe in early September and the publication of SWNCC 150/4 defining American policy for postwar Japan[3] put pressure on the cabinet to consider political reform. Higashikuni and Konoe—premier and vice premier respectively—and Foreign Minister Yoshida Shigeru[4] favored a gradualist approach. Their reading of the Potsdam demand that "the Japanese Government shall remove all obstacles to the revival and strengthening of democratic tendencies among the Japanese people" confirmed their conservative inclinations.

Japan's government officials believed that the solution lay with better enforcement of the Meiji Constitution's provisions rather than revision. The Potsdam Declaration did not, in their view, require revision of the constitution.[5] The declaration called for democratic tendencies to be revived and strengthened. The Japanese believed democracy—at least democratic tendencies—had existed before the war. Taishō democracy of the 1920s had been real. The Potsdam statement virtually conceded the point. Lifting restrictions on civil liberties, for example, or reforming the Diet to strengthen the House of Representatives, or extending the right of citizens to participate in politics—such reforms as these, they thought, could satisfy the requirement without the more radical action of revising the constitution.

Their initial understanding derived from their reading of the only two American policy statements available to them.[6] Neither demanded constitutional revision. MacArthur's statement to Konoe on September 13 that the Constitution must be revised to make Japan more democratic seemed to conflict with American policy. In two meetings with Higashikuni, MacArthur said only that Japan's government must be based on democracy and suffrage extended to women. The prime minister's understanding of the issue is clear from what he told foreign newspaper reporters on September 18: He was making every effort to implement various directives from SCAP and had had no time to consider constitutional reform.[7] Yet, by the end of the month he had informed his cabinet secretary that a committee to study constitutional reform would be established and that Konoe would chair it.[8]

The plan that emerged from the September cabinet discussions, reported widely by the Japanese press,[9] was to attempt fairly straightforward reform by amending existing laws. Higashikuni told foreign reporters on September 18 that he was considering extending suffrage to women to enlarge the electorate.

On September 20 and 22 *Yomiuri Hōchi,* a leading Tokyo newspaper, reported cabinet plans to revise the election laws and electoral districts to make them more representative, to reform both houses of the Diet to give preference to the democratically elected House of Representatives, and to lower the voting age from 25 to 20. Once these reforms were in place, the government would dissolve the House of Representatives and hold a general election in January 1946.[10] If this could be achieved in four or five months, especially in light of the chaos of the time, the government thought it would have taken a major step toward democratizing the political system. However, the plan ignored warnings from MacArthur—however ambiguous—that more basic political changes would be required.

Such confusion in the cabinet is understandable given the circumstances. MacArthur's comments to Higashikuni apparently lacked specificity as to timing and content. Moreover, his warning about constitutional reform appeared inconsistent with provisions of the Potsdam demands, the Byrnes note of August 11, and the Initial Post-Surrender Policy statement. The latter said: "The United States desires that this government [Japan's] should conform as closely as may be to principles of democratic self-government, but it is not the responsibility of the Allied Powers to impose upon Japan any form of government not supported by the freely expressed will of the people." This could be read as leaving any constitutional reform to the Japanese themselves. Strengthening democratic tendencies and guaranteeing civil rights might be achieved simply by enacting new legislation, as they thought.[11] But this reading ignored at least one clear demand made by the Allied powers at Potsdam, namely, that the authority and influence of Japan's military would have to be "eliminated for all time." How this could be done without amending the constitution, Higashikuni and Yoshida did not say.

The Legislation Bureau's Role

The key Japanese government office with responsibility for constitutional reform—indeed, all government legislation—was the Legislation Bureau[12] in the prime minister's office. The Diet, having no office or staff to draft bills, also relied on this bureau. Two of the principal figures in the framing of the postwar constitution—Matsumoto Jōji and Kanamori Tokujirō—had served as directors of this office before the war. Indeed, Japan's most knowledgeable and skillful government legal specialists were to be found here. The earliest tentative proposals for constitutional revision originated in this office in September and October 1945.

As the ministers struggled with questions of political reform, officials of the Legislation Bureau, the foreign ministry, and other concerned ministries were meeting daily to sort out the legal changes they believed were required.[13] They scrutinized the Potsdam Declaration and the U.S. Post-Surrender Policy for Japan. By mid-September they were consulting with Japan's leading constitutional scholars and by early October preparing concrete proposals for the cabinet to consider. The conclusions they reached were quite different from those of their political superiors.

Officials of the Legislation Bureau, who were responsible ultimately to the prime minister, worked under the close supervision of the minister in charge of constitutional reform: Matsumoto Jōji, in the Shidehara Cabinet (October 1945–April 1946), and Kanamori Tokujirō, during the first Yoshida Cabinet (May 1946–April 1947). Senior officials in the bureau, notably Irie Toshio and Satō Tatsuo,[14] helped shape government constitutional drafts, initiating proposals in September 1945 and serving on the cabinet (Matsumoto) committee for investigating problems of constitutional reform between October 1945 and February 1946. Besides its own legal specialists, the Legislation Bureau could draw on the expertise of leading constitutional scholars at Tokyo Imperial University and other national universities.

In the wake of Japan's defeat and military occupation, both the Legislation Bureau and the foreign ministry understood that fundamental legal changes would be required by the Potsdam Declaration, whether undertaken voluntarily by Japan or imposed by American military fiat. By September these officials reached two significant conclusions: (1) Japan's imperial system of government, with the emperor at the center, could indeed be democratized through constitutional reform; and (2) reform could be accomplished voluntarily by the Japanese themselves.

In September and October, serious debate centered on a series of discrete but interrelated constitutional questions: to eliminate or modify the role of the House of Peers; to abolish the Privy Council or merge its functions with another body; to have the prime minister appointed by the emperor or elected by the Diet; to supplement existing civil rights with "basic human rights," such as guarantees of artistic, academic, and economic freedoms and the right to work; and to limit or eliminate the military and the state's warmaking powers.

Irie's First Memorandum

On September 18—ironically, the same day Prime Minister Higashikuni told reporters the cabinet had no time to consider revising the constitution—Irie Toshio, chief of the bureau's first section, produced the first government memorandum on constitutional reform, "The Termination of the War and the Constitution."[15] It was brief, more an outline than a proposal for revision, and it was kept secret from all but a chosen few. Yet it was important as a list of topics that needed to be discussed by bureaucrats whose job was to draft legal documents for the cabinet. It is further noteworthy because its author, Irie, would handle so much negotiating with MacArthur's staff during the next year. It offered a first glimpse of the revisions he thought the Potsdam Declaration required.

Irie recognized that Japan's defeat and acceptance of the Allied declaration meant that the military would lose its privileged status in the nation's constitutional order. He made no attempt to interpret the declaration, and Japan's acceptance of it, as a "contract" between Japan and the Allied powers. The Foreign

Ministry had failed in such an effort in August and early September. Acceptance of the unconditional nature of Japan's surrender, although never mentioned, is implicit throughout the document.

Irie knew that the first requirement was to comply with the Allied demand for demilitarization. Assuming that Japan would have no armed forces, he suggested that every article relating to military matters—appointments, organization, command, conscription—would have to be removed from the constitution. He called attention to the emperor's powers to declare war, make peace, declare a state of siege, and issue emergency imperial ordinances with the power of law. In light of the Potsdam Declaration's demand that Japan's warmaking powers (Article VII) be eliminated, these too would have to be removed or amended to eliminate from the nation's basic law any reference to war. Even if the military continued to exist—an issue not yet determined and not discussed—Irie recommended that any provision which associated the emperor in any way with the military should be stricken.

Irie next turned to democratization, the other central issue addressed in the declaration. What constitutional changes might be required by the Allies' demand that Japan establish basic civil rights and "encourage democratic tendencies"? Legal provisions that placed limits on the exercise of personal freedoms would, of course, have to be amended. The powers of the emperor, the Privy Council and the House of Peers, wrote Irie, would have to be limited (he said nothing eliminating any of these bodies). Moreover, the constitutional authority of the legislature, especially the popularly elected House of Representatives, would have to be enhanced.

Irie stamped his memorandum "top secret" in red ink and circulated it only to those above the level of department chiefs in the bureau's hierarchy. He then sent it to Murase Naokai, the director general of the bureau and a member of the cabinet. Although Murase had not requested the document, Irie reasoned that it would be useful to his boss if and when the subject came up at a cabinet meeting. Murase returned it with the comment that it was premature because the cabinet had not yet adopted a policy of revising the constitution.[16]

Miyazawa Lectures at the Foreign Ministry

The Japanese Foreign Ministry, meanwhile, having played a major role in arranging Japan's surrender on the basis of the Potsdam Declaration, began in mid-September to show keen interest in the constitutional implications of that document. By late September two sections of the ministry's treaty bureau, under the direction of Tatsuki Keiichi, were seeking advice from the nation's leading constitutional scholars. On September 28, Professor Miyazawa Toshiyoshi[17] of Tokyo University presented a short lecture on the topic at the Foreign Ministry and responded to questions from his audience.

Miyazawa was a prolific writer and respected authority on constitutional matters. In October 1945 he would become a major figure on the cabinet's Committee to Investigate Constitutional Problems (the Matsumoto committee). In early 1946, Miyazawa would advance the controversial notion that a "revolution" had occurred when Japan surrendered in August 1945. That is, in acceding to the Allied demand that Japan's future form of government would be determined by the freely expressed will of the Japanese people, Japan had already accepted popular sovereignty.

As Miyazawa addressed his Foreign Ministry audience on September 28,[18] he identified three kinds of legal and constitutional changes that, he believed, were required by the Potsdam Declaration. First, all laws relating to Japan's colonial territories would have to be eliminated. Second, the declaration meant abolition of the military, requiring major changes in many articles of the constitution. Third, democratic tendencies could best be "encouraged" by amending provisions on individual rights and the powers of the national legislature.

Modern Japan's founding fathers in the 1880s had given the emperor supreme command of the army and navy. One effect of this was to make the military high command co-equal with the ministers of state. Several generals and admirals had direct access to the throne, giving them a major say in national policy. Their voices were especially important in foreign and national security policies. Miyazawa referred to this constitutional arrangement in his lecture as "dual government." His views on this—and those of many others by this time—were clear: Provisions of the constitution legitimizing the military's governmental role would have to go, along with the military itself. He also addressed the related issue of special imperial powers not only to appoint military leaders and organize the military but to declare a state of siege and issue ordinances having the power of law. Again, he was clear and forceful. These constitutional provisions, he said, provided the legal basis of military domination of government and should be removed from the constitution.

On the question of encouraging democracy, Miyazawa was less specific. He did point to provisions for imperial sovereignty in chapter I as obstacles to democracy, and he favored eliminating the emperor's emergency legislative powers and control over foreign policy. Apparently he had not yet formulated his "August Revolution" thesis, for there is no mention of a shift away from imperial sovereignty. His major emphasis was on encouraging democracy by expanding and strengthening the powers of the national Diet: appointing ministers, direction of foreign policy, controlling the budget, and determining its own organization and work schedule to make it more effective.

In responding to questions after the lecture, Miyazawa reiterated the need to strengthen democratic tendencies and offered comments that cast light on two underlying concerns: Japan's national polity (*kokutai*) and the possibility that the American occupation might impose a new constitution on Japan. Miyazawa attempted to reconcile imperial sovereignty and democracy. He argued that "the Imperial Constitution does not deny democracy" and went on to suggest specific revisions that, he thought, would satisfy the Potsdam demand that Japan take action to "strengthen democracy." He mentioned several measures, among which were reduction or elimination of many imperial powers, including the emperor's exclusive right to initiate amendments to the constitution,[19] and the treatment of "imperial property as state property under management of the Minister of the Imperial Household."

In short, Miyazawa came close to advocating the creation of a monarchy without power or responsibility, who would reign but not rule. Yet he maintained that neither acceptance of the Potsdam Declaration nor his proposed amendments would change Japan's national political structure and imperial sovereignty. As he said in responding to a question, "This structure [kokutai] was not rejected [when Japan accepted the Potsdam Declaration] and can be preserved." This was a debatable proposition, which Miyazawa himself later revised. Could the kokutai be preserved if the emperor were deprived of his sovereign powers? In short, was the kokutai nothing more or less than the imperial institution itself, the emperor, with or without sovereign powers? Was the existence of the emperor, even if powerless or a mere "symbol,"[20] enough to preserve Japan's kokutai? Miyazawa's answer in late September 1945 was affirmative to all these questions. As long as there was an emperor, even under control of a foreign occupation, the kokutai remained intact.

Another Foreign Ministry official wanted to know whether Japan might enact a new constitution with an article providing for "a complete revision of this constitution at some future date." The suggestion seemed to be that Japan might enact an interim constitution that pleased the occupying powers but rewrite it after the occupation ended. Having such a provision in the constitution would have the advantage of creating legal continuity and at the same time requiring, or at least permitting, revisions when the occupiers departed. Perhaps this was an ingenious way of having it both ways: Please the victors while they were in control and allow Japan to reverse course later.

Miyazawa's response, however, pointed to a more benign tactic and historical analogy. "An interim constitution can be considered," he replied. He used as an example "Europe after the revolutions." European countries recovering from the 1848 revolutions had adopted interim constitutions during a period of transition to more stable conditions. Permanent constitutions were enacted only after political stability was restored.

In calling attention to the historical precedent of 1848, Miyazawa seemed to express the hope that constitutional revision under the American Occupation might be limited and temporary, allowing Japan to control the final product of the process. This no doubt appealed to many officials in Miyazawa's audience, for it held out the hope of preserving much of the Meiji constitutional order during what they assumed would be a fairly brief American military occupation.

This was wishful thinking. There was no way of knowing how long the victors would control Japan. The Potsdam Declaration had said military occupation would continue until the goals of demilitarization and democratization were achieved. The wording was, to most objective observers on both sides, vague and open-ended. Accordingly, SCAP's own timetable was never clearly stated. This uncertainty caused the Japanese government to miscalculate the extent of change that the Americans would insist on. And it was one factor contributing to major conflict between Japan and SCAP over constitutional reform.

Yabe's Report to the Cabinet

While the Foreign Ministry engaged Miyazawa to lecture on constitutional reform, members of the Higashikuni cabinet turned to another member of the law and politics faculty of Tokyo Imperial University for guidance on the topic. On October 5, Professor Yabe Teiji submitted an "interim report on constitutional reform" to the cabinet's deputy secretary, Takagi Sōkichi.[21] The report, like Miyazawa's lecture, attempted to clarify constitutional problems arising from Japan's acceptance of the Potsdam Declaration as the basis of surrender.

Yabe had close ties to the prewar ruling elite, especially former Prime Minister Konoe Fumimaro. He was a leading member of the Shōwa Kenkyūkai, which brought together journalists, scholars, politicians, and businessmen of diverse ideological leanings committed to Japan's goals in Asia. Yabe had drafted many statements for Konoe when the latter was prime minister and would assist him again in his failed effort to take control of constitutional reform in October 1945.[22]

The report is in two parts, the first stating general principles and the second listing and discussing amendments to specific articles of the existing constitution. He recognized that reform could occur either by order of the Allied powers or voluntarily. He made no attempt to anticipate what an Allied directive might require. Rather, he presented his provisional plan on the assumption that Japan would do its own revisions, voluntarily. His plan did take into consideration the intention of the Potsdam Declaration. The basic purpose of his plan, he said, was to achieve a "political structure that would resemble a typical form of parliamentary government," doing away with Japan's autocratic system of government. It would be "based as much as possible on the people's will under the Emperor's rule."[23]

Such a government would be based on certain constitutional principles: (1) respect for basic human rights and the will of the people, and (2) respect for the emperor, "the heart of Japan's national unity." Yabe was careful to say that the emperor would not directly exercise sovereign powers. He would, in short, reign but not rule.

Showing sensitivity to foreign concerns with Japan's previous history linking emperor to empire, Yabe proposed removing all wording from the constitution that suggested Japan was an empire and that Japan's *tennō* was a sacred emperor or ruling sovereign. He proposed that the phrase "The Great Empire of Japan" be reduced to "Japan." Both "great" and "empire" should be omitted entirely. The "Imperial Diet" would become the "National Diet," and *tennō* would not be translated as "emperor." The emperor's sacerdotal prerogatives, deriving from the Shintō myth of his descent from the Sun Goddess, should be eliminated from the constitution to avoid any conflict with provisions on freedom of religion.[24]

Despite these changes, Yabe was not proposing to yield on the emperor's status as sovereign. "It should be established [he wrote] that the word 'Government' includes *tennō* and should be made clear that the Government and the National Diet are equal under the *tennō*."

Third, with respect to the military, Yabe rather reluctantly conceded that it probably needed to be abolished. Therefore, he thought that all provisions concerning the army and navy ministries and the organs of Supreme Command should be eliminated in accordance with political circumstances.

Fourth, the national Diet should be strengthened. As a rule, all government business, not just discussion of legislation and budget bills, should be on the agenda of the Diet. The constitution should make the House of Representatives superior to the House of Peers, and the Peers should be reorganized to permit vocational representation.

Yabe offered several proposals for amending specific articles of the constitution. Defining the "spirit of the reform" as emphasizing basic human rights and government based on the will of the people, he stressed their fundamental nature by placing them in the preamble. As for freedom of religion, he warned that in exercising their freedom, people "shall not threaten peace and order or violate their obligations as subjects." This is a far cry from the ringing commitment to human rights that modern constitutionalism requires.

There is little evidence that Yabe's report made much impact in the cabinet. Some cabinet members, including Konoe, probably saw the report and may even have read it. Yabe's biography of Konoe contains details of his patron's activities during this period that only a close adviser would have known. Yabe was well informed of the substance of Konoe's two meetings with MacArthur on constitutional revision, and he talked with Kido and other court officials on the same subject.[25] But Konoe, in preparing his recommendations on constitutional reform to the emperor in November, never mentioned the report or Yabe.

Foreign Ministry Memoranda

The Potsdam Declaration and the Initial Post-Surrender Policy for Japan thoroughly alarmed the foreign ministry. Three ministry memoranda in early October 1945 expressed fear that Japan was on the verge of losing not only its sovereignty but its identity as a nation and proposed prompt though limited revision of the constitution to preempt radical reform by SCAP. But a strategy of safeguarding Japan's national polity (*kokutai*) by removing institutional barriers between the emperor and the Japanese people were dramatically different from the model of reform that SCAP would insist on.

The first memorandum, dated October 9, came from the political affairs bureau of the ministry.[26] It began with a warning: "International conditions are moving in the direction of putting the Empire under international control. [Japan] is in grave danger . . . of being reduced to the condition of post-surrender Germany." The reference is to demands of the Soviet Union, Britain and other Allied powers for a share in the control of Japan during the military occupation.[27] Such an arrangement, the bureau noted, had led to the division of Germany into four zones. At home, the bureau warned of domestic "revolutionary forces outlining a broad policy . . . to control Japan . . . which stresses pacifism and rationalism." Unless Japan acted promptly to adopt policies of political, economic and cultural reform, the occupation forces would issue orders which Japan would have to carry out. Only "voluntary and prompt" action by Japan could preempt more radical demands by SCAP, which would mean complete loss of sovereignty by the state and destruction of *kokutai*.

Two more memoranda from the Foreign Ministry's treaty bureau dated October 11—the day MacArthur told Prime Minister Shidehara that Japan must undertake constitutional reform—outlined both the principles and actions Japan should take on its own.[28] One provided a brief outline of "the guiding principles of constitutional reform," such as preserving the status of the emperor (safeguard *kokutai*), removing impediments between the ruler and the people, and advancing the welfare of citizens based on the people's will.

In taking concrete actions, this memorandum continued, the government should seek to build a new Japan, not simply implement the Potsdam Declaration. Consequently, revision of the constitution and the law codes should not be limited to the provisions demanded by the Potsdam Declaration. Japan should take the initiative and act quickly by revising individual articles of the constitution and laws rather than taking time for complete revision. Immediate action should be directed toward reforming the Diet by abolishing the special privileges of the House of Peers and the special status of the nobility, amending the election law, and extending suffrage to women. And, as both Miyazawa and Yabe had, the treaty bureau proposed eliminating from the constitution all articles relating to the military and conscription.

There is an anxious, disorderly quality to the Foreign Ministry's proposals, suggesting perhaps a panicky reaction to MacArthur's directive of October 4. The usually cautious bureaucrats were willing to risk legal chaos to try to preempt SCAP's initiative, beating the Americans to the punch, to maintain some Japanese government control over the extent and nature of political reforms.

Their assumptions about democracy and how it might be achieved in Japan are surprising. While rejecting Minobe's and Shidehara's argument that the Meiji Constitution could accommodate democratization without amendment, they seemed to embrace the radical "Showa Restoration" argument of Kita Ikki's military followers in the 1930s.[29] That is, the imperial constitutional order worked best when no intermediary institutions separated the will of the emperor from his people. One principle of reform advanced in this Foreign Ministry document was to "remove the impediments that have heretofore come between the ruler and the people." This implied that political reform could begin by abolishing such extraconstitutional bodies as the Privy Seal and other palace officials, and perhaps the Privy Council.[30] These were the major elements of the so-called bamboo curtain surrounding the emperor and separating him from the Japanese people.

Tatsuki's Memorandum

The argument and its assumptions were spelled out in greater detail in the third memorandum of October 11, written by Tatsuki Keiichi, titled "Preliminary

Thoughts on Problems relating to the Revision of the Imperial Constitution."[31] Drawing on discussions going on in the Foreign Ministry since early September, Tatsuki summarized the ministry's analysis of Allied demands on constitutional revision since late July 1945. There was no doubt, he wrote, that U.S. policy "requires revision of the Imperial Constitution." He noted foreign press opinions and statements by U.S. congressmen regarding constitutional reform. He drew hope from Potsdam's emphasis on basing constitutional revision on "the freely expressed will of the Japanese people." This seemed to him to make the Japanese people—loyal subjects of the emperor—the ultimate arbiters of government in Japan. The absence so far of an ultimatum or timetable for revision from MacArthur also raised hope that political reform would be left in Japanese hands.

Because revision of the constitution should be "based on 'the freely expressed will of the [Japanese] people'," Tatsuki concluded that SCAP did not intend to use force to impose it on Japan.[32] Therefore, the government could determine the content of amendments according to Japan's history, customs, social system, cultural standards *and* the will of the Japanese people, not "the coercion of the United Nations."

Tatsuki's judgment that the Americans would rely on the Japanese government to undertake the reform agreed with the assessment by Konoe, Miyazawa, Yabe, and others. In the middle of October 1945, this was a reasonable inference. Tatsuki's conclusion was an accurate reflection of the Japanese official thinking at the time, based on their reading of U.S. policy documents and official statements. His analysis was also right on the mark with regard to timing. "[T]here is no doubt," he wrote, "that they will expect . . . revision as rapidly as possible." MacArthur had already increased the pressure with his directives of October 4 and 11 ordering political reforms and his comments to Konoe and Shidehara. And although MacArthur's comments on constitutional reform emphasized substance rather than timing, Tatsuki read these as powerful indicators that "a reasonable amount of time cannot be expected."

In the second part of the document, Tatsuki set forth proposals to guide constitutional revision, consistent with what he believed U.S. policy would allow. First, "the preservation of the Emperor System" was described as the absolute foundation of Japan's existence. His reading of U.S. documents convinced him that the United States neither affirmed nor opposed it but entrusted a decision on the imperial institution to the Japanese people. In fact, however, official U.S. policy on the future of the emperor was still unresolved. SWNCC's draft paper on the treatment of the emperor (SWNCC 55), which had arrived in Tokyo in early October, ordered MacArthur to investigate the emperor's role in the war and report back to Washington. It would be January 1946 before MacArthur would send his findings and recommendations to the army chief of staff, General Eisenhower, in Washington. Despite rumors coming from the palace's secret liaison with members of MacArthur's staff,[33] foreign ministry officials had no knowledge of this. Their only clue was contained in the two documents to which Tatsuki referred: the Potsdam Declaration and the U.S. Initial Post-Surrender Policy for Japan. Both documents were ambiguous on the issue of the emperor.

Tatsuki's second proposal was to eliminate "the organs [of government] standing between the Emperor and the people." This was becoming a familiar refrain. Irie, Miyazawa, Yabe, and now Tatsuki—all pointed critical fingers at the offices and officials who controlled access to the sovereign ruler with extensive authority to govern Japan. Now that the military had been disbanded, they were speaking of the Privy Seal, the Privy Council, and numerous palace advisers who surrounded the emperor. In Tatsuki's view, "they had neither legal responsibility nor any connection with the people." They inhibited the development of the imperial institution as a constitutional monarchy by blocking the upward transmission of the will of the people via their representatives to the emperor. They represented groups in society with special status and power, not the people.

Implicit in this was a view—often conveyed to MacArthur and his staff—of the emperor as a good and positive force, perverted by court and military officials who manipulated national policy for their own selfish interests. Former Prime Minister Hiranuma Kiichirō offered MacArthur's political advisers a similar idealistic interpretation of Japan's disastrous foreign policy and road to war.[34] The emperor's will and the people's will were in complete accord, and presumably inclined to peace with other nations. As long as a direct link between the two was maintained, peace and prosperity reigned. The military's interruption of that vital relationship, by substituting its judgment for that of civilian leaders, had caused the war. In the future, Hiranuma concluded, the Japanese must prevent any group from disrupting the "direct relationship existing between the Emperor and the people."[35] So common was this view that it must have represented more than a conspiracy to protect the emperor from personal responsibility for the war. It seems likely that many officials truly believed it. Tatsuki's proposals for constitutional revision grew in part from this simplistic view of Japan's modern political history.

Tatsuki's third proposal was to create "a democratic and rational political system." Such a system could best be created by making Japan's parliamentary system clearly responsible to the people. Once constitutional revisions were made to achieve such a system, the sentiments of the people must be sought by a national referendum or a general election following the dissolution of the Diet. Specific revisions would include provisions relating to the military, such as conscription, the military command, martial law and ordinances, and status of the military. Tatsuki was firm on these, as were most other concerned officials. It was easy, of course, to propose such changes, for the Potsdam provisions on the military were clear, and SCAP had already begun arresting Japan's military leaders, disbanding all armed forces, and destroying ammunition dumps, tanks, antiaircraft guns, ships, and submarines.[36]

On the other hand, constitutional amendments relating to imperial sovereignty and autonomy of the imperial household were more sensitive issues, and here Tatsuki tread with care. He began with two broad assertions: that the imperial institution is the spirit behind the founding of Japan and must be preserved no matter what and that the Initial Post-Surrender Policy for Japan had taken a "neutral position on this issue," entrusting it to the freely expressed will of the Japanese people. He referred to the articles of chapter I of the constitution, which not only defined the emperor as sacred and sovereign but granted him broad powers to govern. (In the fall of 1945, few Japanese officials or politicians had the courage to touch these articles.) Perhaps, Tatsuki ventured, provisions permitting imperial ordinances with the force of law (articles VIII and IX) and imperial control of foreign policy (article XIII) should be revised. Moreover, Diet control over the imperial house law seemed advisable and perhaps that law should apply only to the emperor and his immediate family. Cautious words, to be sure, words befitting this midlevel bureaucrat's station.

As regards the Diet and the cabinet, Tatsuki was more outspoken. He advocated changes that would expand the powers of the Diet to take a hand in matters heretofore reserved for the emperor: revising the Imperial House Law, making foreign policy and treaties, drafting constitutional revisions, and determining the organization of the House of Peers and the election law of the House of Representatives. He also proposed making the cabinet primarily responsible for offering advice to the emperor on all policy matters. This would mean, he noted, reducing the authority of both the Privy Seal and the Privy Council, though he did not propose their elimination.

The New Prime Minister and Irie's Second Report

When Shidehara met MacArthur on October 11, two days after he replaced Higashikuni as prime minister, MacArthur mentioned again, as he had to Higashikuni and Konoe in September, the need to revise Japan's constitution. Shidehara was the leading advocate of strengthening democracy by rewriting laws rather than amending the constitution. As foreign minister five times in the teens and 1920s, during the brief ascendancy of civilian ministers over the military, he was the leading proponent of cooperation with the West and was considered a "liberal" by some Americans. Whatever this meant in political terms, in 1945 Shidehara encouraged the cautious approach to constitutional revision adopted by the Matsumoto committee.

Despite Shidehara's caution, the Legislation Bureau in his office had no doubt that constitutional amendments would have to be made "pursuant to the acceptance of the Potsdam Declaration." The bureau's efforts accelerated as word of MacArthur's advice to Konoe, and now Shidehara, reached the bureau. By October 22, Irie and his colleagues had finished a "Memorandum on Constitutional Reform."[37] The document posed questions and offered suggestions on revising all chapters of the constitution. It represented a considerable advance over Irie's September 18 outline in defining how democracy could be achieved in Japan.

Little was said about chapter I, which defined the status of the emperor and his extensive powers. The cabinet had already appointed Matsumoto's committee to study constitutional revision, and it was clear to the bureau that much of chapter I would remain intact. The bureau did recognize that the emperor's authority to issue emergency ordinances with the force of law (article VIII) threatened "the people's rights and benefits" but was reluctant to eliminate it. Under the supplementary provisions (chapter VIII) of the constitution, however, the memorandum questioned whether expenses of the imperial family should require the consent of the Diet and proposed examining the relationship of the imperial house law to the constitution. The Americans and Japanese would clash over both these issues in 1946.

Chapter II of the Meiji Constitution, rights and duties of subjects, was a major focus of the memorandum, running to one-fourth of the total. One striking feature was its frequent reference to foreign constitutions—those of Weimar Germany, the United States, Germany before World War I, Tsarist Russia, and Italy are mentioned. Irie suggested borrowing especially from Weimar Germany and the U.S. Constitution. He argued that strengthening democracy could best be achieved by including "basic human rights," as generally understood, plus the most liberal version of those rights as defined in the 1919 Weimar Constitution of Germany:[38] freedom to pursue arts, research, teaching, and enterprise and the right to work.[39] He also borrowed the "principle of the equality of men and women as citizens" from the Nineteenth Amendment of the U.S. Constitution. While calling for a guarantee of freedom of religion, Irie recognized that the state's administration of certain Shintō shrines might be seen as a violation of the principle of religious freedom. He suggested two possible solutions: Either make the administration of such shrines part of the imperial household ministry or provide a special status for shrines in the constitution, "much as article one of the Italian Constitution does for Roman Catholicism."

The bureau also proposed reform of the legislative body and related institutions and practice. Regarding the House of Peers, it stated bluntly: "The House of Peers as its exists today should be abolished." But what would replace it? A second chamber, yes, but different from the lower chamber, perhaps representatives not of the people or districts but of professions or some other system of limited elections.

On other issues, the memorandum was more tentative. The constitution should guarantee citizens the right to vote and stand for election and provide for normal elections. But nowhere in the discussion of the Diet's powers, organization, and functions was the body defined as supreme or representing the sovereign people. Instead, it spoke of the emperor exercising his "sovereign authority" in foreign affairs, of the Diet petitioning the emperor for extension of sessions, and of the Diet's authority being restricted. Concerning the executive branch of government, the bureau wanted to abolish the Privy Council, which, when consulted, provided advice to the emperor. The cabinet and ministries would be approved by the Diet but "stipulated by the Emperor." Although state ministers would be responsible to the Diet, the prime minister would be selected by the emperor from candidates nominated by the Diet. Clearly, the Legislation Bureau was not straying far from the provisions of the Meiji Constitution: Both the Diet and the cabinet would remain subordinate to imperial authority. This was not likely to meet American requirements for constitutional reform.

These were the efforts, then, of the cabinet, its Legislation Bureau, and the Foreign Ministry between September 2 and October 22, to shape the debate and future of constitutional reform. Even as these activities were under way, however, there were two other important initiatives being undertaken by prominent Japanese politicians at the suggestion of General MacArthur.

4 . . . .

"A Rational Way"

- ## KONOE AND MATSUMOTO ON CONSTITUTIONAL REFORM

-

- During the weeks of September and October while the Legislation
- Bureau and Foreign Ministry were considering constitutional re-
- form, two committees, associated with prominent cabinet members
- and palace insiders, emerged on the scene to take control of the
- issue. One was under the direction of Prince Konoe Fumimaro, a
- palace insider and deputy prime minister in the Higashikuni cabinet.
- The other was led by Matsumoto Jōji, a prominent legal scholar and
- minister in the new Shidehara cabinet, formed after Higashikuni's
- sudden resignation on October 5.

-

- ### Konoe's October 4 Meeting with MacArthur

-

- Konoe took the initiative early in the occupation when he ap-
- proached MacArthur on September 13. The brief meeting left him
- frustrated, but he understood that MacArthur spoke of the urgency
- of political reform, including revision of Japan's 1889 constitution.[1]
- Konoe sought a second meeting on October 4, this time with his
- own interpreter from the Japanese Foreign Ministry.[2] MacArthur's
- headquarters was by this time located in the Daiichi Seimei Building
- across the moat from the imperial palace. At the meeting, MacAr-
- thur was flanked by his chief of staff, Lt. General Richard Suther-
- land, and his political adviser and State Department representative,
George Atcheson, Jr.

Konoe eagerly seized the opportunity to present, as he had apparently wished to do at the earlier meeting, a self-serving interpretation of the causes of the war. The interpreter, Okumura Katsuzō,
records that Konoe launched into a long monologue blaming a
"union of militarists and leftists" for leading "Japan down the path
to destruction." He ended with a statement to MacArthur casting
himself as the representative of the cabinet and the Japanese government: "If you have any suggestions or instructions concerning
the organization of the [Japanese] Government or the composition
of the Diet, I would be pleased to hear them."

64

MacArthur did not respond directly either to the monologue about the war or to the baited question about Japanese politics. Instead, he told Konoe: "First, the Constitution must be revised and liberal elements included in it."[3] He went on to say that the right to vote must be expanded to include women and workers. When Konoe mentioned technical problems of revising the electoral law, MacArthur responded forcefully: "I hope that a rational way can be found so that essential measures can be devised by the Japanese Government itself. And that must be done as quickly as possible. Otherwise, we ourselves are prepared to see that this shall be done, regardless of the friction that it may cause."[4]

MacArthur's statement echoed the words of the Allies in the Potsdam Declaration: "We will brook no delay." When Konoe expressed his desire to "do everything I possibly can for my country," MacArthur said: "You should stand in the forefront of Japan's leaders. If you rally liberal forces around you and present to the public a plan for revising the Constitution, the National Diet will follow you."[5]

Encouraged by the general's words, Konoe said he would like to have MacArthur's "suggestions on such problems from time to time" and asked if there were someone on MacArthur's staff with whom he might have regular discussions. MacArthur replied somewhat ambiguously: "We will be happy to talk to you at any time." It was his political adviser, Atcheson, who would follow up on MacArthur's promise to Konoe.

Konoe Moves Forward

Despite the resignation of the Higashikuni cabinet the following day (October 5) in protest against MacArthur's order on civil liberties[6] and the appointment of elder statesman Shidehara Kijūrō to form a new cabinet on October 9, Konoe secured the palace's agreement that he would undertake the revision effort as a special imperial appointee in the Office of the Privy Seal.[7] This was in accord with the amendment process outlined in article LXXIII of the constitution, which provided that a proposed amendment "shall be submitted to the Imperial Diet by Imperial Order." Konoe then met with his assistants, Takagi Yasaka and Matsumoto Shigeharu, and his private secretaries, Ushiba Tomohiko and (son-in-law) Hosokawa Morisada. He sent the latter to Kyoto to recruit constitutional scholar Sasaki Sōichi. Together they agreed on an approach for revising the constitution. On October 9, Konoe reported to Emperor Hirohito and was appointed special assistant in the Office of the Privy Seal. Sasaki received a similar appointment a few days later. On October 10, the imperial household minister telephoned the new prime minister, Shidehara, to alert him of Konoe's appointment.[8]

Atcheson, who had attended the meeting of October 4 between Konoe and MacArthur, also moved with dispatch. He sent an urgent cable to the State Department asking for Washington's "latest thinking" on the subject of constitutional reform. Meanwhile, at Konoe's request, Atcheson met with Konoe and Takagi on October 8. Without instructions from Washington, he was cautious, emphasizing that the meeting was "informal" and that the opinions he would present were "personal and unofficial."[9]

He did, however, offer some advice. The Japanese constitution fell short in several respects, he said: It did not hold the cabinet responsible to a democratically elected assembly; its bill of rights was "emasculated" by clauses making rights subject to the "limits of the law" and to suspension during government-proclaimed emergencies; the ministries of war and navy were not subject to civilian control; an undemocratic House of Peers had power to veto legislation and block budgets; the judiciary was powerless to protect the people's rights; and neither the people nor their elected representative could initiate constitutional amendments. Oddly, Atcheson made no mention of the status of the emperor during the course of his talk with Konoe and Takagi.

The meeting ended with Konoe asking for future consultation. Atcheson readily agreed to assist as best he could, while emphasizing that the Japanese themselves must take the initiative. He told Konoe that General MacArthur was "fully empowered to abolish . . . provisions of the constitution that were obstacles to the revival and development of democratic tendencies." Konoe replied that timely guidance was important. SCAP's October 4 directive to the Japanese government, issued "without forewarning," worried him greatly. It had caused a "loss of prestige" by Japanese officials that "mitigated against their effectiveness." Atcheson offered no apology. He noted that the directive concerning freedom of speech and the release of political prisoners had come "after the Japanese Government had sufficient time to take action but had not." Konoe said that it would nevertheless be "helpful to have some advance knowledge of the American government's specific desires" on such an important matter as constitutional revision.

Despite his tough talk, Atcheson apparently had some sympathy with Konoe's position. In reporting to Secretary of State Byrnes on this meeting, he ended by renewing his request that the department expedite the directive on constitutional reform.[10] Atcheson also reported to Byrnes Hirohito's formal appointment of Konoe as soon as he heard of it.[11] And he assigned a seasoned Japan specialist on his Tokyo staff, John K. Emmerson, to maintain contact with Konoe's assistant, Professor Takagi Yasaka of Tokyo Imperial University. Takagi, one of Japan's leading authorities on the United States, was fluent in English and a prewar friend of Emmerson.

State Department Guidelines

On October 17, Secretary Byrnes cabled two sets of guidelines on constitutional revision to Atcheson's office.[12] The first would apply if the emperor were not retained. In that case, the Japanese constitution would have to be amended "to provide government responsible to an electorate based upon wide representative suffrage." The executive branch would have to be responsible directly to the electorate or to a legislative body elected directly by the people. The legislature should have "complete control . . . of financial and budgetary matters." And Japan must guarantee "fundamental civil rights to all persons within Japanese jurisdiction, not to Japanese only."

Additional safeguards would be required if the emperor were to be retained.

These included a cabinet to advise and assist the emperor, which would be responsible to a representative legislature; and no veto over actions of the legislature, by such nonrepresentative bodies as the House of Peers or the Privy Council. The emperor must be deprived of his powers to initiate amendments to the constitution and exercise control over the legislature and the military. As for the legislature, it "should be permitted to meet at will." The emperor would no longer have the authority to suspend, dissolve, or otherwise interfere in the legislature's operation. Although no decision had been made about the future of Japan's armed forces, Byrnes was adamant that "any armed forces should be under civilian control and have no direct access to the Emperor." In closing, Secretary Byrnes told Atcheson to "continue your discussions [with Konoe] and keep the Department informed."

On October 25, Emmerson shared Byrnes's guidelines with Takagi.[13] Atcheson later claimed that Konoe had misunderstood MacArthur's comments on October 4 regarding constitutional reform. Even if true, contact between Emmerson and Tagaki contributed to increased clarity between the two sides; it is unlikely that Takagi misunderstood what he heard from Emmerson about American plans for constitutional reform. From his discussion with Atcheson's staff, Takagi reached the significant conclusion that the Americans were not demanding the abolition of the imperial institution. He informed Konoe that "in the final analysis, this should be determined by the will of the Japanese people. It will not be dictated by an outside power."[14]

The basic ideas suggested by Atcheson's office were a representative legislature, wide suffrage, a cabinet responsible to the legislature, and a military (if any) under strict civilian control. The Americans were less than definite about the most important institution of all, the emperor. They would limit his powers, to be sure, but it was not clear that they would make him subordinate to the will of the Japanese people. Many of the American ideas were incorporated into proposals for revising the constitution that Konoe's committee produced in late November.[15] Even before his October 4 meeting with MacArthur, Konoe, like many others in the Japanese government, had come to understand that constitutional revision was among the occupation's requirements. This much is clear from Konoe's discussion with Prime Minister Higashikuni on September 26. Had the Higashikuni cabinet not resigned on October 5, Konoe would likely have headed a cabinet committee to recommend to the emperor amendments to the constitution. Given Konoe's contact with Atcheson and his staff, such changes would likely have hewed closely to SCAP's line and American ideas for reform. With MacArthur's encouragement, the emperor's backing, and assisted by aides who had close ties to political advisers on MacArthur's staff, Konoe was in some ways well positioned to lead the effort to craft a new basic law for a democratic and peaceful Japan. As it was, substantial progress was made, and well before the Soviet Union and other Allies got involved (through the FEC, created by the Moscow Agreement of December 27, 1945).[16] In the final analysis, however, the Japanese government was riven by rivalries, Konoe himself was tainted, and powerful forces hostile to him were rising to challenge his role in the drama.

Differences Among the Japanese

Konoe's appointment was freighted with controversy from the outset, in Japan as well as abroad. The conflict was in part over constitutional procedure, in part over political influence. The new Shidehara cabinet protested the exclusion of government ministers from the process. Experts disagreed over the proper role of the government in amending the constitution. The Meiji Constitution said only that an amendment project must derive from an "Imperial Order." It was silent on the responsibilities of the cabinet and the inner circle of imperial aides in shaping that "Imperial Order." Tension between the cabinet and Konoe's group quickly escalated into a public confrontation as both sides aired their conflicting views. Before long, the Japanese and American press too were harshly criticizing Konoe's involvement in constitutional revision.

Following his meeting with Atcheson on October 6, Konoe informed Privy Seal Kido of the meeting. The next day, he and his aides gathered in Kido's office to discuss American ideas for revision.[17] Konoe warned that unless they moved quickly, "GHQ might impose a plan of revision." Kido related the whole matter to Prime Minister Shidehara the next day, before the cabinet investiture ceremony at the palace, repeating Konoe's argument that SCAP was impatient with delay and might use coercion to impose revision of the constitution. Shidehara's attitude was "very negative," according to Kido, arguing that SCAP was unlikely to use force, but if it did, Japan would have to submit. Kido told Shidehara that because of the unprecedented nature of the issue, the emperor planned to put Konoe in charge of investigating constitutional revision. Shidehara offered no immediate objection to this plan.[18]

Kido then advised Konoe to brief the emperor on the plan. Konoe's assistants, again summoned to the palace, reported that GHQ was "very positive" about the procedure. On October 10, Kido again consulted the emperor and settled the matter of procedure to the satisfaction of this small circle of palace advisers. The next day the emperor issued a brief charge to Konoe: "[To investigate] whether the acceptance of the Potsdam Declaration requires Japan to revise the Imperial Constitution of Japan, and if it is required, to what extent."[19]

When the cabinet learned of the appointment on October 11, Minister Matsumoto Jōji objected, arguing that such an important affair of state should be the responsibility of the cabinet.[20] This position was reinforced when Shidehara met with MacArthur later that same day. MacArthur directed the new prime minister to carry out what came to be known as "the five great reforms": emancipate women, encourage labor unions, democratize education, abolish oppressive organizations, and democratize economic institutions. He added that liberalizing the constitution would also be required to achieve the objectives of the Potsdam Declaration.

But MacArthur did not order it done that day, October 11. Why? First, MacArthur had no directive from Washington to order constitutional revision; the Americans expected the Japanese to take the initiative in this. Also, behind the scenes, the Japanese had "secured an understanding [through MacArthur's aide,

Bonner Fellers] that no demand for constitutional revision" would be joined with the five political reforms. They argued that it could be done in a different way. As Takagi recalled years later, "We . . . were trying to devise a way by which we could independently consider constitutional reform."[21] MacArthur and his staff seemed eager to accommodate the Japanese.

At the cabinet meeting on October 13, Shidehara established the Committee to Investigate Constitutional Problems, with Matsumoto Jōji as its chairman. The action may have been motivated more by a desire to seize the initiative from Konoe than to respond to MacArthur's prompting.[22] Shidehara and Matsumoto then met with Konoe the same day to work out a division of labor: Konoe's group would conduct an investigation and prepare a report and proposals for the imperial court in response to the emperor's charge to Konoe, while the cabinet would assume responsibility for conducting its own investigation for the government. This offered no clear division of responsibility, however; both were to "investigate" and prepare reports, one to the emperor and the other to the cabinet.[23]

Failure to announce a clear delineation of responsibilities was a recipe for bewilderment in the minds of the public and worse in government. Press reports had Konoe in charge of revising the constitution and the Shidehara cabinet carrying out the "five great reforms directive" issued by MacArthur. Matsumoto contradicted such reports on October 15, referring to Konoe's work as preparing the emperor for constitutional amendments that would be drafted by the government. Newspapers carried Matsumoto's comments. Constitutional scholars Miyazawa Toshiyoshi and Rōyama Masamichi, referring to article LXXIII of the 1889 constitution, agreed with Matsumoto. An *Asahi* editorial on October 18 added its support for the cabinet's approach. Indeed, most commentators agreed that authority to draft amendments to the constitution belonged to the cabinet, not to the office of the Privy Seal.

Konoe Becomes an Issue

Konoe provoked his critics further by holding news conferences and giving interviews to reporters.[24] Especially damaging to his cause were interviews with American newsmen, whose reports were read widely in the United States. According to Associated Press correspondent Russell Brines, Konoe said the emperor had ordered him to revise the constitution; a draft of his proposals would be submitted to SCAP for approval before being sent along to the emperor. He also suggested, Brines reported, that the emperor's abdication might be necessary in order for Japan to fulfill its obligations under the Potsdam Declaration. The *New York Times* put its spin on these comments by concluding that Hirohito would probably abdicate as soon as Japan had met the requirements of the Potsdam agreement.[25]

When Brines's interview appeared in the Japanese press, it set off an explosion of criticism in Japan and the United States. Shidehara and Matsumoto demanded that Konoe issue a public clarification, which he did on October 25, claiming that his statement had been distorted by the press. He insisted that he had merely said that the emperor had ordered him to determine whether the constitution needed to be revised and if so how extensively. He claimed Brines had misquoted his statements about seeking SCAP's approval of a draft constitution and also misrepresented his comments on abdication and the Imperial Household Law.[26]

The American press added its own harsh criticism of Konoe's involvement in constitutional reform. The New York Herald Tribune sharply questioned MacArthur's judgment in an editorial on October 26:

> Among the foolish mistakes the United States has made in the Far East, the most egregious was selecting Prince Konoe as the drafter of Japan's new constitution.... If the Prince were already in prison awaiting trial as a war criminal, there would be absolutely no reason to object. For him to be appointed the drafter of Japan's democratic constitution with the formal approval of the American side is foolish in the extreme.[27]

Asian specialist Nathanial Peffer of Columbia University, in a letter carried in the New York Times, denounced the plan for Konoe to preside over constitutional reform as "dangerous," a "blunder" and "grotesque." In an editorial two days later, the Times labeled Konoe a "pseudo-liberal" and called for a constitutional convention to frame a new constitution in the name of the Japanese people and for the emperor to abdicate.[28] Soviet and British criticism added their sting to MacArthur's sensitive skin.[29]

On November 1, MacArthur returned the fire in withering fashion. SCAP's Public Affairs section issued a statement denying that "Allied authorities" had selected Konoe to revise the constitution. MacArthur had told Konoe, as deputy prime minister in the Higashikuni cabinet, that "the Japanese Government would be required to revise the Constitution." Once the cabinet resigned, which it did the following day, "the Prince [Konoe] had no further connection with the matter."[30] At a news conference, Konoe repeated that MacArthur had indeed suggested constitutional reform to him on October 4. He further admitted that he had not received an order or commission from the general and added: "It is due entirely to the decision of the Japanese side that I came to undertake this important task." He vowed to continue his work and report to the emperor by November 20.[31]

By his statement, MacArthur was not only repudiating Konoe but embarrassing Atcheson and the State Department as well. Atcheson had been present at the October 4 meeting, and acting for MacArthur, he had later met with Konoe, shared Washington's thinking on constitutional reform, and assigned members of his staff to work with Konoe's aides. But now MacArthur directed Atcheson to have no further contact, neither with the Konoe group nor with the issue of constitutional revision in any form "until the Japanese Government itself submits something on the matter."[32] Emmerson reflected this new policy in a meeting on November 4 with Takagi and Ushiba. As Tagaki recalled: "Emmerson's attitude ... had undergone a sudden change.... In a matter of minutes the talks were broken off."[33]

Confirming MacArthur's decision, Atcheson received a report on November 5 from E. Herbert Norman, a Canadian member of SCAP's counterintelligence division, denouncing Konoe as a war criminal.[34] Norman argued that Konoe was responsible for Japan's aggression against China and that "a strong prima facie case can be made against Konoe as a war criminal." Norman concluded: "As long as he dominates the Constitutional Drafting Committee, he will block any serious attempt to write a democratic constitution."[35]

On the same day, Atcheson wrote a personal letter to President Truman defending MacArthur in the Konoe matter and generally shifting the blame elsewhere. He reported that MacArthur had *not* encouraged Konoe to lead the movement to revise Japan's constitution; the whole affair, Atcheson assured Truman, was the result of a mistranslation by Konoe's Foreign Ministry interpreter.[36]

Americans Hold Back

Having defended MacArthur, Atcheson obeyed his order to break off all contact with Konoe. But he had serious reservations about the order. In a personal letter letter to the undersecretary of state, Atcheson confessed that he was "very much worried" about the prohibition of contact with the Japanese. "It is obvious to us now," he wrote, cuttingly, "that General MacArthur, or his Chief of Staff and other members of the Bataan Club, who act as his Privy Council or *genrō*, wish, if possible, to keep the State Department out of this matter." Atcheson reported that he had learned "privately" that Konoe's group expected by the end of November to submit its report to the Japanese government in the name of the emperor. That made it a matter of great urgency for the United States to get its ideas abroad, before Konoe's draft was published "with all the trimmings of imperial sanction, etc." The best way to intercede, Atcheson suggested, was for the State Department to release a statement of principles on constitutional revision in Washington. He continued:

> Release will, of course, cause some irritation in [MacArthur's] Headquarters, as does every pronouncement on policy matters by officers of the Department, but such irritation, I believe, is more than offset by the salutary effects such pronouncements have in reminding Headquarters and others that policy is made at home and that, after all, the making of foreign policy is centered in the State Department.

Atcheson closed by saying he would not have bothered his friend if this were not an "extremely important matter."[37]

Atcheson's idea of publishing an outline of American thinking about constitutional revision was never pursued, either in Tokyo or Washington. That is a pity. It would have given Japanese bureaucrats, politicians, and journalists something solid to go on besides the vague words of the Potsdam Declaration and the U.S. Initial Postsurrender Policy for Japan. Instead, they worked in the dark, having to guess what the Americans might insist on. In fact, Americans had formed some fairly definite ideas on constitutional form and content. A draft of SWNCC 228, titled "Reform of the Japanese Government,"[38] was available in Washington in October, though a final version was not sent to MacArthur until the following January. If Americans believed that the Japanese had gone far astray in their understanding of the principles of democratic government during the preceding decades, it would seem all the more important for American ideas to have been communicated as soon and as clearly as possible. Instead MacArthur left not only Konoe but Matsumoto to grope in the dark, then landed on them quite suddenly, without warning. Thus did MacArthur push constitutional revision off the front burner. Throughout the autumn of 1945, he left it for staffers to fret about.

As for Konoe's effort on behalf of the emperor, it continued, albeit fruitlessly. On October 22 the imperial commission repaired to the mountain resort of Hakone in the foothills of Mount Fuji sixty-five miles west of Tokyo to work on a draft. Much as the father of the Meiji Constitution, Itō Hirobumi, had done in 1887, the Konoe drafting committee lived in inns remote from the capital while pursuing their work. Konoe and Sasaki disagreed over how to proceed. Konoe wished to take American ideas for reform into account, and he asked Atcheson for the assistance of an American constitutional lawyer, but nothing came of the request.[39] In the end, Konoe prepared only an outline, along with a statement providing the rationale for revising the Meiji Constitution. In late November, Konoe, assisted by Takagi and others, finished a report to the emperor, defining basic principles and outlining revisions he believed were needed. He told Emperor Hirohito that it was "necessary to revise the Imperial Constitution" to rebuild the nation. He proposed measures for restricting the sovereignty of the emperor, assuring freedom of the people, increasing powers of the Diet, and strictly controlling the armed forces.[40] These ideas accurately reflect American guidelines that Atcheson had passed to Konoe and his staff.

On the other hand, Sasaki prepared a more conventional draft of 100 articles, which adhered closely to the 1889 Meiji Constitution. His chapter on local autonomy was new, and so was his "right to enjoy the necessities of human life." But he proposed no changes in the status and prerogatives of the emperor as sovereign ruler. Indeed, the first four articles, defining the emperor and his powers, were identical to those of the 1889 constitution. He also preserved existing legal restrictions on the freedoms of Japanese subjects.[41] In general, Sasaki's draft "never ventured beyond the basic framework of the Meiji Constitution."[42]

Konoe submitted his written report to the emperor on November 22, and two days later Sasaki submitted his. Both then made their separate recommendations in person. On the very day Sasaki presented his report in the form of a lecture at the palace, MacArthur's headquarters announced the abolition of the office of the Privy Seal. Sasaki returned to his job at Kyoto Imperial University. When Konoe learned a few days later that the Americans had put his name on a list of persons to be arrested and charged with war crimes, he committed suicide, providing a tragic epitaph for the Meiji Constitution and the traditional interpretation of its provision for amendment.

The Matsumoto Committee

With the resignation of Prime Minister Higashikuni on October 5 in protest against MacArthur's edict on civil liberties, a cabinet had been formed by Shidehara Kijūrō. A veteran diplomat, Shidehara, foreign minister in five prewar cabinets, favored cooperation with the United States and Britain during the 1920s.[43] At the first meeting of the new cabinet, on October 10, Matsumoto Jōji and other ministers argued that constitutional revision would soon become a troublesome issue and needed to be addressed. Shidehara showed little interest. The next day MacArthur told him that the reforms Japan must undertake "will unquestionably involve a revision of the Constitution."[44]

Despite the warning, Shidehara dragged his feet. He believed the Meiji Constitution was flexible enough to permit democratization by passing a few new laws. The emperor's appointment of Konoe and further prodding by Matsumoto finally jolted the elderly prime minister out of his torpor.[45] He appointed a cabinet Committee to Study Constitutional Problems, with Matsumoto as its head.

Why Matsumoto? Many have questioned his qualifications and temperament for the position: he was a specialist in commercial law, not the constitution; he was 68 years old and had last served in government in 1934; he was highly opinionated and quick tempered. Appointed professor of law at the Tokyo Imperial University in 1909 at the age of 32, he resigned in 1922 to become a director of the South Manchurian Railway. A specialist in commercial law, he became "the leading legal spokesman of the financial world."[46] He served as a councilor and director general of the Legislation Bureau in the Yamamoto cabinet (1923–1924). In the early 1930s, he accepted appointment as minister of commerce in the Saitō cabinet (1932–1934) and later was appointed to the House of Peers. In 1938, he headed a group that revised Japan's commercial code. Another professor who participated in the work later recalled that the committee's meetings were "a one-man stage" for Professor Matsumoto. "He has been described as having the finest mind of his generation, and I think that is fully justified. Such brilliance! He advanced his own opinion, demolished opposing arguments, drafted provisions. We were always in awe of him."[47] As events would show, the habit and ability to inspire awe may not have been the best quality for a man undertaking to democratize a constitution under foreign military occupation.

When he joined the Shidehara cabinet in October 1945 at Foreign Minister Yoshida Shigeru's urging, Matsumoto became a minister without portfolio. His own account of how he came to head the cabinet committee reveals the fortuitous circumstances of his appointment: "In the cabinet at the time were two legal specialists, Minister of Justice Iwata Chūzō and myself. However, neither one of us was a constitutional specialist. I did not know much about the Constitution. But since I was the one who had been so outspoken, and Mr. Iwata had so much work to do at the Ministry of Justice, I was put in charge of the committee."[48] As Matsumoto told the press, the committee had no mandate to revise the constitution; its assignment was to conduct the research that was needed to support any recommendations the cabinet might make on constitutional revision. It would be working under no imperial order or charge. However, Matsumoto did promise Prime Minister Shidehara that he would stay in touch with Konoe's group while his own work proceeded.[49]

The Matsumoto committee comprised a truly distinguished group of men. They included Minobe Tatsukichi, Japan's most famous constitutional scholar; Shimizu Tōru, vice president of the Privy Council and member of the Imperial Academy; Nomura Junji, professor emeritus of law; Miyazawa Toshiyoshi, a young but already prominent writer on constitutional issues; and three top bureaucrats from the cabinet's Legislation Bureau: Narahashi Wataru, the director general; Irie Toshio, his deputy; and Satō Tatsuo. Most of them had law degrees from Japan's leading university, Tokyo Imperial, and several were, or had been, members of its faculty.[50] The committee's initial goal was "to undertake a scholarly study" of the problem, not to prepare a draft proposing major amendments.

Matsumoto's tentativeness about revision may have been necessary to persuade senior advisers to join the group. Many of them—Minobe, Shimizu, Miyazawa— agreed with Prime Minister Shidehara that democracy could be achieved within the framework of the Meiji Constitution. To them, democracy did not mean popular sovereignty and human rights guaranteed by the constitution. It meant giving all adults the right to vote for representatives in a legislature that was supreme—something along the lines of the British model. They had publicly stated that enhancing the power of the legislature was the best way to assure "the revival and strengthening of democratic tendencies." Minobe, for example, at the first session of the committee, defended the Meiji Constitution's provision that the rights and duties of the people be specified by law.[51]

Matsumoto Committee's Limitations

This committee, with its broad mandate and prestigious membership, was seriously limited from the outset by a volatile leader, weak political support, and conflicted members. Such weaknesses might have been mitigated if American support and advice had been steady and strong. Unfortunately, it was not forthcoming. As we have seen, MacArthur prohibited Atcheson and his Japan specialists in the political adviser's office from having any contact at all with the cabinet committee.[52] Matsumoto and Shidehara were allowed to proceed encumbered by their narrow views of the requirements of the Potsdam Declaration. In such an atmosphere, the promising reform ideas being discussed by officials of the Legislation Bureau and Foreign Ministry had absolutely no chance to gain a hearing.

The Matsumoto committee and its subcommittees met thirty times between October 27, 1945, and January 2, 1946, to study broad policy and assign research topics. MacArthur's repudiation of Konoe on November 1 caused the committee to redefine its objective from "investigating problems of revision" to an examination of "those articles which we cannot avoid revising."[53]

At the group's first meeting on October 27, Nomura asked whether the Potsdam Declaration's language about removing obstacles and strengthening democratic tendencies might not require the committee to "touch on" articles I and IV. (Article I asserted the "eternal," "unbroken" line of emperors. Article IV provided that the emperor "combined in himself" the rights of sovereignty.) Matsumoto rejected the suggestions out of hand: "Since the Potsdam Declaration says that this issue shall be determined by the free will of the Japanese people, even the Americans cannot forcefully order it. The general will of the Japanese people is as unmovable as a mountain. Therefore, there is no need to mention Articles I and IV. Although there are many things that should be revised, I consider this part of the Constitution permanent."[54]

Given this dismissive decision to skirt the issue at the center of constitutional revision, the committee proceeded on its doomed way. With MacArthur's brutal dismissal of Konoe's effort in early November, Matsumoto's committee assumed even greater importance. On November 24, the committee completed its study of the Meiji Constitution and announced its conclusion that articles on imperial sovereignty "require no revision." The committee did endorse amendments that would transfer the emperor's broad ordinance and emergency powers, as well as his administrative control over the armed forces, to the national legislature. Moreover, the committee favored relaxing provisions that restricted the exercise of rights by the Japanese people.

On December 8, Matsumoto was asked in the Diet to outline the general direction of his inquiry. He responded with a statement that became known as "Matsumoto's Four Principles":

1. There will be no change in the principle that the emperor shall exercise the rights of sovereignty (article IV).
2. The authority of the Diet will be expanded and limits put on the emperor's prerogatives.
3. Cabinet ministers will be made responsible for all matters of state and be responsible to the Diet.
4. The rights and freedom of subjects will not be restricted except by laws enacted by the Diet.[55]

A Failure of Communication

The members of this Diet, chosen in a nonpartisan election during the war, offered virtually no response to Matsumoto's statement, nor, with rare exceptions, did the Japanese press comment. But Atcheson saw this as an opportune moment to reopen talks with the Japanese on constitutional reform. He had been reporting to Washington since November 11 on the Matsumoto committee's ideas for revision. He had summarized the committee's ideas in a cable to the State Department, warning that conservatives were in control and that no Americans or Allies were working with the Japanese on this central issue.[56] The time seemed auspicious. Konoe's and Sasaki's reports to the emperor had been released to the press. The State Department had sent Atcheson a full draft of SWNCC 228, including two paragraphs warning against the dangers of forcing constitutional reform on Japan. MacArthur had received a draft of the SWNCC paper, "Treatment of the Emperor," ordering him to investigate Hirohito for possible war crimes and to submit his recommendations on trying him.

In a memo dated December 13, Atcheson urged MacArthur to allow him to share with the Matsumoto committee the American government's latest thinking on constitutional reform. He warned of the danger of allowing the Japanese to proceed too far with their draft ignorant of specific American requirements. He considered this a "dangerous situation" because the Occupation might later be forced to order certain changes in a draft constitution written by the Japanese.[57]

The memo laid bare the tension between the State Department and the Supreme Commander. Atcheson wished to avoid dictating constitutional changes to Japan, thereby provoking a serious confrontation. However, his appeal failed to move MacArthur. In rejecting Atcheson's appeal, MacArthur closed all available avenues of communication with the Japanese on the issue of constitutional reform.

Revisions and Drafts

Over the turn of the year, Matsumoto took his notes and papers to his country home in Kamakura. Secluding himself there for four days, he drew up a list of proposed revisions. He would have changed article III, about the person of the emperor, from "sacred and inviolable" to "supreme and inviolable" or, in another draft, "the Person of the Emperor is inviolable." He proposed reducing the emperor's ordinance powers (articles VIII and IX) and eliminating his control over the command and organization of the armed forces (articles XI and XII). He would have taken away the emperor's power to suspend the bill of rights in times of war or national emergency (article XXXI).

Meanwhile, beginning on January 4, Miyazawa, with assistance from Irie and Satō, aides from the Legislation Bureau, prepared a somewhat more detailed set of proposals. This document, conventionally called Draft B, would have substituted for article I ("The Empire of Japan shall be reigned over and governed by a line of Emperors unbroken for ages eternal") the simple assertion that "Japan is a monarchy." The phrase "unbroken for ages eternal" was displaced to article III. Instead of the phrase "sacred and inviolable," Miyazawa's draft said that the emperor "assumes no responsibility for his actions," or, in another of his versions, "No one shall profane the Emperor's dignity." A revision of article VIII would have made the emperor's power to issue ordinances subject to Diet approval. Both articles on the emperor's authority over the armed forces (XI and XII) were simply deleted, as was article XXXI, which gave the emperor power to suspend liberties during war or emergencies. While more extensive than Matsumoto's draft, Miyazawa's was not markedly different in substance or tone.

How much did SCAP know about what was going on inside the Matsumoto committee? Apparently not much. Matsumoto and Miyazawa sent their drafts to a subcommittee for discussion in early January. In the course of several meetings the subcommittee made further revisions on the two drafts. Though there was no official contact with the Americans, leaks and rumors produced news stories on the commission's work that SCAP's censors read and translated. Also, Narahashi and Shirasu often provided "SCAP officials" with information on the commission's discussions. The Americans knew, for example, that two drafts existed.[58]

The Committee Fails

On January 26, just days before the subcommittee completed its work, Takagi Yasaka, who had assisted Konoe in securing advice from Atcheson, called on Matsumoto and suggested it might be wise to seek SCAP's views on constitutional revision. Matsumoto demurred, commenting that there was no need to "negotiate with the Americans or to seek their views any further, because constitutional revision is something that we are determined to do voluntarily and independently."[59] This was, as it happened, the line that MacArthur and Kades were taking at that time in talks with the FEC. For the Americans, it was disingenuous; for the Japanese, it was dangerously myopic.

On January 29, just three days after he rebuffed Takagi, Matsumoto sent both drafts to the Shidehara cabinet, with a formal proposal to revise the constitution. The cabinet began meeting in special session on January 30 to debate the two drafts.

Then, on Friday, February 1, the roof fell in. The *Mainichi Shinbun*, one of Tokyo's leading daily newspapers, published a document that purported to be a "provisional draft" of the Matsumoto committee's recommendations. A reporter claimed to have purloined it from a desk in the committee's office. The published version was a copy of the Miyazawa draft, and it was immediately disavowed, both by Matsumoto and by the cabinet. Matsumoto insisted that the draft printed by *Mainichi* was only one committee member's ideas.[60]

Such fine distinctions as Matsumoto was attempting to draw were now completely lost in the clamor. A *Mainichi* editorial pronounced itself "disappointed that it is so conservative and does nothing more than preserve the status quo." Other newspapers joined the chorus of disapproval, urging that the circle of those contributing to the revision be widened immediately to include "those outside the government."[61]

SCAP, too, was scornful. Whitney, in a memo to MacArthur, called the published draft "extremely conservative," observing that it left the status of the emperor "substantially unchanged." Whitney reported that Yoshida had earlier scheduled a meeting for Tuesday, February 5, presumably to deliver the cabinet's proposed constitutional revisions, but the Foreign Office had now requested a postponement until Thursday. Whitney said he had rescheduled the meeting for the following Tuesday, February 12, to allow the cabinet more time, he said, to get serious about "genuine constitutional revision which would comply in good faith with the Potsdam Declaration."[62]

The Matsumoto committee failed for several reasons. It ignored the guidance from Washington proffered by Atcheson to Konoe and the ideas advanced by

Japan's own officials. In acting independently, Matsumoto's legendary "self-confidence" had betrayed him. He had desperately needed to know how the Americans were interpreting the Potsdam Declaration, and he was in no position to tell them what he, or Japan, would tolerate in the way of interference. The committee also ignored the thrust and force of SCAP's reforms during the autumn of 1945: expansion of the franchise, encouragement of labor unions, freeing of political prisoners, abolition of repressive organizations, land reform. It misread the significance of Hirohito's repudiations of "false conceptions" about himself on January 1, 1946. It paid too little attention to the efforts of Japanese academics, journalists, politicians, and others who were thinking about possible revisions and beginning to publish ideas. And it disdained to seek ideas from other modern constitutions, such as those of the United States, France, Weimar Germany, or the Soviet Union. In short, Matsumoto's determination to act independently meant that success in this project would require more astute leadership on the Japanese side.

American and Japanese critics have accused Matsumoto of arrogance in assuming that revision of the constitution could take place without direction from the American occupation forces. But he was not alone. As we have seen, top Japanese officials assumed that they were free to proceed with revision according to their understanding of the Potsdam Declaration and American occupation policy. Events would prove that assumption wrong. Indeed, in the circumstances of the first year of the occupation, it was unjustified. However, MacArthur's policy of no contact on the high-priority issue of constitutional reform must also share the blame for this failure in late 1945 and early 1946.

IMPOSING THE AMERICAN MODEL

5 . . . .

"Only as a Last Resort"

. THE AMERICANS TAKE OVER

.

.

.

From the beginning of the American Occupation of Japan, revision
of Japan's constitution was one of General MacArthur's highest priorities. In early meetings, he emphasized that Japan could not satisfy
the terms of the Potsdam Declaration without revising the Meiji
Constitution.[1] At the same time, American policy expected that the
Japanese would take the initiative in bringing about the necessary
constitutional changes.

Separate If Parallel Paths

The Potsdam Declaration indicated that the future government of
Japan must be based on the "freely expressed will of the Japanese
people." Going a step further, American policy statements repeatedly stated that it was "not the responsibility of the Allied Powers
to impose upon Japan any form of government not supported by
the freely expressed will of the people." Everyone believed that if it
appeared that constitutional revisions had been imposed by the Allies, it would "materially reduce the possibility of their acceptance
and support by the Japanese people for the future."[2]

Although MacArthur expected the Japanese to take the initiative
on constitutional revisions, he had the responsibility to ensure that
the revisions met Allied standards. The key to success was close
collaboration between Americans and Japanese. However, that never
really happened, as we have seen in our review of Japanese efforts
in this area. After MacArthur's embarrassment over his apparent
endorsement of Konoe's effort, SCAP had forbidden all contact between his staff and Japanese officials working on constitutional revision.[3] This left two nations working toward the goal on parallel
but quite separate paths. We have recounted Japanese efforts in earlier chapters. As we shall see in this chapter, it had become clear by
the end of January 1946 that neither side had truly come to grips
with the problem.

During the early stages of the Occupation, SCAP's Government

Section (GS) was located near MacArthur's own office on the sixth floor of the Daiichi building. Until December 1945, Brigadier General William Crist was the director of GS. He authorized Colonel Charles Kades to set up an annex in the Mitsui building, nearby. There Kades developed a planning unit, under the leadership of Lt. Colonel Frank Hays, to undertake a preliminary study of constitutional reform. Hays would emerge as one of the leaders of the GS staff. Before the war, he had served as administrative assistant to Senator Joseph C. O'Mahoney (D-Wyo.). Kades had met him as they served together on an important New Deal planning committee. At the start of the occupation, Hays was put in command of the military team in Kyoto, but Kades asked to have him transferred to Tokyo when GS was set up (October 2).[4]

When Whitney replaced Crist as head of GS,[5] he abolished the planning unit. Naming Kades as his deputy, he returned him and Hays to the Daiichi Building. He told Kades he did not expect the occupation to last long enough to justify a planning unit.[6] Given other heavy demands, it was a relief to be able to treat constitutional revision as a task for the Japanese. Whitney and Kades hoped it would be enough for the Occupation to develop a broad clarification of principles—a "tentative checklist," in the words of one covering memo—to serve as a basis for conversations with Japanese authorities, as soon as the Japanese were ready for them.[7] Despite their rather crude, sometimes even naive, character, the memoranda on constitutional issues prepared by GS officials at this stage are important. They reveal the ideas that were forming in the minds of leading Americans just prior to the radical shift into high gear at the beginning of February 1946.

The Rowell Report

Doing the section's main work on constitutional analysis at this stage was Major Milo E. Rowell. Trained in law at Harvard and Stanford, Rowell had represented business associations in their dealings with government agencies. In military service since 1943, he had served as commander of a civil affairs unit in the Philippines after the Battle of Leyte. In early February, Whitney would ask him to serve, with Kades and Hussey, on the drafting group's steering committee. A conservative Republican in politics, he was regarded by his colleagues as a strong, smart, balanced man.[8]

Rowell's initial study, dated December 6, 1945, was titled "Report of Preliminary Studies and Recommendations of Japanese Constitution." He noted in his introduction that it was based on documentary evidence, supplemented by a few personal interviews. He "strongly recommended" that there be further conferences with Japanese authorities on constitutional law, "particularly those of known liberal tendencies."[9]

When Rowell turned from process to substance, his memorandum betrayed some confusion about the relationship between the parliamentary form of government and American ideas about the separation of powers. As it turned out, it would be important for the Americans to understand how the parliamentary system worked. The basic flaw in the Meiji constitutional system had been the lack of connection between the "transcendent" powers explicitly vested in the emperor and the play of democratic politics centering on the Diet. The key to reform lay in fusing the powers of government and the function of representation into an effective parliamentary system.

Rowell was quite clear in his criticism of the Meiji system in this regard. "Democratic tendencies" in Japan were thwarted, he wrote, by the machinations of "extra constitutional bodies."[10] Coupled with the emperor's constitutional control over the armed forces and the bureaucracy, this was a recipe for irresponsibility and eventually opened the way for militaristic autocracy.

To reform this system, Rowell proposed that the Privy Council be abolished and that direct access to the emperor be expressly limited to certain officials "directly responsible to the people."[11] Only elected members of the Diet, he wrote, should hold positions in government with direct access to the emperor on political matters. The cabinet should be composed of "elected representatives . . . answerable to the [lower] house," and it should "dissolve on a vote of no confidence." Governmental powers should be "divided" into legislative, executive and judicial and each branch made "exclusive in its field and . . . prohibited from delegating its powers." However, the Diet could be authorized to "delegate powers to a committee to act in its name," as long as "such authority be limited to matters other than legislation." Meanwhile, the "highest court" was to be the "exclusive representative of the emperor in the interpretation of the constitution and laws" and was to have "jurisdiction over all disputes of any character including administrative matters."[12]

On human rights, Rowell's report reflected the outlook of a contemporary American lawyer. It made a bill of rights, enforceable by an "independent judiciary," a central tenet of constitutional reform. Because the constitution in Japan is a "reasonably permanent document," he wrote, a guarantee of civil liberties without equivocation,[13] as the "expressed will of the emperor," would make it more difficult for "any militaristic or ultra-nationalistic group to limit these freedoms in the future." Rowell seemed untroubled, indeed not to recognize that in a parliamentary system, the representative assembly is supreme, even over the judiciary. The anomaly of judicial review in a parliamentary system would persist, unacknowledged by the Americans (though clearly worrisome to the Japanese in the Diet), throughout the summer. The focus of Rowell's commentary on rights was typically American: on the rights themselves, rather than on the problem of their reconciliation with democracy.

Another typically American prejudice in Rowell's report is that the autonomy of local governments is a bulwark of democracy. The home ministry in Tokyo, he wrote, dominates the daily life of every subject. To counter the weight of this oppression, the constitution must guarantee the independence of local governments (municipalities and prefectures), including the popular election of local assemblies and chief executives.[14] Rowell seemed unworried that local authority too might be abused, or that the superintendence of national courts, enforcing national laws, might sometimes have a positive effect on democracy at the grass roots. Fortunately, not all of his colleagues at GS were so unmindful of the lessons of American experience.

Shortly after the turn of the New Year (1946), Rowell, by then a newly minted lieutenant colonel, had another opportunity to gather his thoughts, in a memorandum of comments on constitutional revisions proposed by Kenpō Kenkyūkai, a nongovernmental group of Japanese scholars and politicians. Most striking this time was Rowell's calm acceptance of several provisions that were far more radical than his own ideas. He listed eight "outstanding liberal provisions" in the Japanese draft, including the abolition of the peerage, a bar to discrimination by "birth, status, sex, race and nationality," a guarantee of benefits for workers, including free hospitalization and old age pensions, and the promise of a "new Constitution . . . in 10 years." In the same list of approved ideas, he cited a proposal that echoed the radical tradition of American democracy: a referendum to enable the people to legislate directly.[15] Rowell's California background may help to explain his sympathy for this idea.

Rowell's report and these comments of January 12 on the private Japanese proposals for constitutional revision added substantially to GS's expanding files on the issue. But SCAP's thinking on the subject would soon be enriched by an official document that arrived from Washington in mid-January.

SWNCC 228

The best indication of American thinking about Japan's constitutional revision, prior to the cascade of events at the end of January, was a thoroughly vetted document from the SWNCC, that bore the title "Reform of the Japanese Governmental System." It came commonly to be known by its bureaucratic tag, SWNCC 228. Forwarded to MacArthur by the JCS, its principal drafter was Hugh Borton, a prominent scholar of modern Japanese history who had spent several years in Japan in the late 1920s and early 1930s. In 1942, he had taught at the School of Military Government at the University of Virginia in Charlottesville. From 1942 to 1948, he held various positions in the Department of State, including chief of the division of Japanese affairs.[16] Later he would become director of the East Asian Institute at Columbia University and president of Haverford College. He knew Japan well, and he was an unusually careful thinker.

SWNCC 228 represented a distinct advance over previous thinking about the constitutional reform of Japan, in two fundamental respects. It presented a penetrating analysis of the development of Japanese governance since the Meiji period, at just the right level of detail, and it gave directions, again in appropriate but not excessive detail, regarding the constitutional reforms needed to accomplish the goals of the Potsdam Declaration. Its guidance on constitutional form was generally consistent with earlier Allied and American pronouncements, though far more subtle and precise.

It began by listing six basic objectives of constitutional reform: (1) wide suffrage; (2) an executive branch responsible either to the electorate (as in a presidential system) or to the legislature (parliamentary); (3) a fully representative legislature, with untrammeled power to shape the government's budget; (4) civil rights, guaranteed to the Japanese people and to all within Japanese jurisdiction; (5) local election or appointment of local officials; and (6) drafting and adoption of constitutional amendments, or of a revised constitution, "in a manner which will express the free will of the Japanese people."[17]

Apart from the second item, this was a recipe for parliamentary government, pure and simple. The allowance, as an alternative, of an "executive branch . . . responsible to the electorate" was anomalous. If the framers in Tokyo had attempted to blend the other guidelines with a directly elected chief executive, it might have produced something like the hybrid Fifth French Republic, with its parliamentary government and its independently elected president. But it is clear, from the rest of this document, that the planners in Washington intended nothing of the kind. The basic model here was the classic British version of parliamentary government, commonly identified as the Westminster model.

It is worth noting, however, that some elements here are *not* intrinsic to the Westminster model: specifically, the implication of a constitutionally entrenched bill of rights and the emphasis on local government. Both had American origins. Note also two significant omissions: no mention, here or elsewhere in the directive, of an independent judiciary, with power to declare legislation "unconstitutional,"[18] and no mention of political parties.[19] Again, these conform to American ideas about what belongs explicitly in a constitution and what does not.

As for the emperor, the paper stated flatly that retention of the imperial institution "in its present form" was inconsistent with the objectives of the Potsdam Declaration. Although the ultimate form of the Japanese government would depend on the freely expressed will of Japanese people, Japan should be "encouraged" to abolish the imperial institution "or to reform it along more democratic lines."[20]

If Japan decided to give up the emperor, the Supreme Commander should tell the Japanese that other bodies possess at most only a "temporary veto" over legislative enactments, especially constitutional amendments and public finance[21]; the parliament must be able to meet at its own will; and all ministers must be civilians. If Japan decided to retain the emperor, there would be additional requirements. The emperor must be stripped of all military authority and constitutionally bound to accept the "advice" of the government "in all important matters." Also, ministers of state, chosen with the "advice and consent of the representative legislative body," were to form a cabinet "collectively responsible" to the parliament.[22] The collective responsibility of the cabinet is part of the essence of the Westminster model, though the formal consent of the legislature to ministerial appointments is more American than British.

Having laid out these requirements, SWNCC 228 proceeded to set forth the understanding of recent Japanese history on which it rested. The Meiji Constitution, it said, was drafted with two purposes in mind: to still the clamor for representative institutions and to fortify the kind of government—centralized, autocratic—that Japanese leaders at the time deemed necessary for their program of modernization. In this system, power was retained by the elder statesmen (the *genrō*) and their successors, mostly former prime ministers, rather than the leaders of the Diet's majority party.[23] The result was that power lay with the balance of forces around the throne, not with those in the majority in the Lower House.

This constitutional system vested the powers of war and peace with the emperor, leaving the Diet little influence in these vital matters. The Diet was barred from initiating amendments and revising the imperial house law. It could not convene of its own accord, and the emperor could prorogue it for fifteen days, repeatedly, if necessary. In practice, most bills originated with the ministers, in whose selection the Diet had no part.[24] In addition, the Diet had limited powers over the budget; article LXXI enabled the government to carry on under the budget of the preceding year if the Diet was unwilling to pass the government's plan for the present year.[25]

Worst of all, as the system lurched toward military dictatorship in the 1930s, was the "dual nature" of the government. By virtue of the emperor's prerogative, military leaders were independent of the cabinet and often able to control national security policy. An imperial ordinance of 1898 established that the ministers of the army and navy had to be military officers in active service.[26] By this provision, military leaders were able to thwart the formation of cabinets or deflect them from fulfilling international obligations.

SWNCC 228 noted other flaws that interfered with the realization of responsible parliamentary government. The House of Peers, a full partner in the legislative process, was composed one-half of nobility, one-quarter of men appointed by the emperor, and one-quarter of members elected by those who paid the highest taxes. This gave undue influence to the wealthy. The constitution also established a Privy Council, an "important barrier to the development of a sound parliamentary system."[27] Using the emperor's prerogatives to control the government, the council had several times forced the overthrow of cabinets that had the confidence of the Lower House.

SWNCC concluded by reiterating its strong advice on matters of procedure. For constitutional reform to have lasting value and be effective, Japan must initiate it. "Only as a last resort" should MacArthur "specify in some detail the reforms to be effected."[28]

Early drafts of SWNCC 228 had been available at SCAP at least since mid-October, when the State Department sent a summary to George Atcheson.[29] On January 11, the JCS dispatched a fully approved version by cable from Washington.[30] SWNCC 228 had a huge, though perhaps indirect, influence on the thinking of the men and women of GS as they assembled to prepare the SCAP model. Arriving as it did in early January, it strongly fortified their sense that constitutional change was imperative, and it guided their sense of what it must entail.[31] The steering committee told the GS drafters to use it as "a control document,"[32] and, from minutes of the committee's work, we know that arguments between the steering committee and other drafters were often settled by references to it.[33] Indeed, from the close conformity of the SCAP model with the SWNCC 228 outline, one can deduce that Robert E. Ward was not exaggerating when he wrote that the latter was "clearly a model for the Japanese constitution."[34]

The Far Eastern Commission

Nevertheless, despite the arrival of SWNCC 228 on January 11, SCAP still hesitated to grasp the nettle of constitutional revision. To understand why, we must review the Moscow Agreement, signed on December 26 of the previous year, creating the Far Eastern Commission (FEC). As the war with Japan drew to its end in 1945, plans for an international Far Eastern Advisory Commission (FEAC) for Japan began to take shape. The United States was determined to retain for itself a dominant position and a deciding voice in the military occupation and control of Japan, while offering the United Kingdom, China, and the Soviet Union an advisory role. In addition, other nations—Australia, New Zealand, the Netherlands, France, and the Philippines—would be invited to sit with the commission when their particular interests were involved.[35] The United States had consulted the United Kingdom and China (and informed Stalin) at the last moment before issuing the Potsdam Declaration in their names on July 26, 1945. The Soviet Union, after declaring war on Japan August 8, became part of the FEAC. American policy of consulting with its allies while exercising the controlling voice was set forth in the United States Initial Postsurrender Policy for Japan, approved by President Truman on September 6, 1945: "Although every effort will be made . . . to establish policies for the conduct of the occupation and control of Japan which will satisfy the principal allied powers, in the event of any differences of opinion among them, the policies of the United States will govern."[36]

The Allies objected to Washington's appointment of MacArthur as SCAP and plans for exercising unilateral control over Japan. This violated the spirit of their wartime alliance. Both Britain and the Soviet Union wanted an Allied "control council" to give them a voice in defining policies for Japan. There was recent precedent for this in Europe. Stalin preferred a council similar to the one operating in Romania, which gave veto power to each of the three major powers. Before the issue could be resolved, the FEAC began meeting in Washington on October 30, 1945. From the outset, squabbles over which nation would provide the chairman, deputy chairman, and so forth, marred the proceedings.

In an effort to please the other nations without ceding control, Secretary of State James Byrnes informed the advisory commission in December that Mac-Arthur wished to invite them to visit Japan and see for themselves how the occupation was progressing. He cautioned, however, that any "dealings with the Japanese Government would, of course, be entirely through the . . . Supreme Commander."[37] On December 26 the commission left Washington for a six-week visit to Japan.

On the same day, in Moscow, the foreign ministers of the United States, United Kingdom, and the Soviet Union, with China's concurrence, signed an agreement that transformed the advisory commission into the FEC, creating a nightmare for MacArthur.[38] In October and November, Britain and the Soviet Union, frustrated with the American monopoly on the occupation of Japan, had intensified their demands for an Allied control council. Stalin conceded the United States a dominant position in Japan, but he insisted on sharing policymaking and administration of the Occupation of Japan. He proposed a new name for the commission: "Allied Control Council" or "Allied Control Commission." He also demanded a voting arrangement that would, in effect, give him a veto over the commission's decisions. He was unwilling, he said, to have the Russian representative be merely "a piece of furniture."[39]

In the end, both sides compromised. The United States conceded that the new FEC would have authority to formulate policies, not just offer advice; that an Allied Council for Japan for consulting with the Supreme Commander would be established in Tokyo; and that any one of the big four powers could exercise a veto in the commission's and council's proceedings. Britain and the Soviet Union agreed that the United States, in addition to wielding veto power in commission proceedings, could issue interim directives and exercise, through MacArthur, a controlling voice in most matters that came before the commission.[40] Concerning the key issue of constitutional revision, however, the Moscow Agreement said: "Any directives dealing with fundamental changes in the Japanese constitutional structure or in the regime of control, or dealing with a change in the Japanese Government as a whole, will be issued only following consultation and following the attainment of agreement in the Far Eastern Commission."[41] On this point the FEC's terms of reference were unambiguous: "[SCAP] Directives which prescribe fundamental changes in Japan's constitutional structure ... or changes in the Japanese Government as a whole shall be issued only after consultation and agreement has been reached in the Far Eastern Commission."[42]

Though it was not entirely to his liking, Secretary of State Byrnes attempted to put the best face on the agreement. He told an American radio audience: "Our agreement safeguards the efficient administration that has been set up in Japan under the Supreme Allied Commander. It assures that the authority of General MacArthur will not be obstructed."[43]

FEAC or FEC?

Despite the secretary's reassurance, the Moscow Agreement was deeply flawed. Its wording would come back to embarrass the U.S. government and frustrate MacArthur. Numerous disputes would develop over words, phrases, and whole sentences in the agreement.[44] New Zealand's representative, Carl Berendsen, would denounce not only the wording but the "hydra-headed veto monster which had appeared again." There was one particularly egregious flaw: the signatory powers failed to state clearly, in writing, when the agreement would take effect—when the FEAC would become the FEC, with power to order changes in Japan's constitutional structure.

FEAC members themselves were uncertain of their status when they departed for Japan on December 27, the day after the agreement was signed. En route by ship from Honolulu to Japan, they received word that the U.S. government had sent the following message to "all governments concerned with the Far Eastern

Commission": "It is the view of this Government that the Far Eastern Commission succeeded the Far Eastern Advisory Commission on 27 December, the date of the Moscow Communique, and that there is no need to implement this succession by formal dissolution, inauguration or other formalities."[45]

Despite this clear assertion that the FEC was up and running from December 27, 1945, some ambiguity persisted. Commission members continued to refer to themselves as the FEAC during their five weeks in Japan. Washington neither objected to this practice nor repeated its earlier statement. Moscow, meanwhile, told the United States it assumed that the FEC would begin to function as soon as the FEAC returned from Japan to Washington.[46]

MacArthur and his staff initially appeared to accept their government's interpretation of the effective inaugural date of the FEC.[47] When, on January 17, 1946, members of GS gave the visiting commission members a briefing on their activities, the Philippine delegate, Tomas Confesor, asked whether SCAP was "considering amendments to the Constitution?" Kades said no. GS, he said, understood that constitutional revision "is a long range problem concerning fundamental changes in the Japanese constitutional structure which is within the province of your Commission."[48] As Confesor probed further, Kades repeated several times that GS believed revision of the constitution "would constitute a fundamental change in the Japanese constitutional structure, and as such be within the Commission's jurisdiction." There must have been some misunderstanding, he said. SCAP, believing that constitutional revision was a "long-term problem . . . within the terms of reference" of the FEC, had not addressed it. GS advised MacArthur on matters "pertaining to the internal structure of civil government." It did not consider constitutional revision "part of this work."

Kades's answer lacked candor, and it did not satisfy Confesor. However, Sir George Sansom, the British representative (and perhaps the leading scholar of Japanese history in the Western world), joined by A. M. LaCoste, the French representative, suggested that the necessary reforms might well be accomplished by making changes short of formal constitutional amendment, somewhat in the British fashion. There the matter was left until MacArthur himself met the FEC members on January 30, the day before they left Japan.[49]

SCAP's Role

Despite the impression left by MacArthur and Kades, the men at GS were evidently already reconsidering their options. Washington's plan for constitutional revision, SWNCC 228, had arrived on January 11, followed shortly thereafter (January 17) by Confesor's questions. Intelligence indicated, moreover, that Matsumoto and his aides were making unsatisfactory progress. The best evidence of rethinking is a GS memorandum dated February 1, 1946, outlining SCAP's responsibility for constitutional revision.[50]

Besides the explicit prohibition in the Moscow Agreement, the principal difficulty for those seeking to make the case for SCAP's authority to take the initiative was the promise in the Potsdam Declaration that future governance would be in accordance with the "freely expressed will of the Japanese people." To be sure, this was not a simple, straightforward proposition for those who believed that Japanese opinion had been manipulated and molded for over a decade by frenzied propaganda. Still, it was a stretch to argue that the men and women at GHQ were better able to interpret the true will of the Japanese people than their elected representatives in the Diet or a cabinet supported by the coalition that dominated the Diet.

The GS memo on SCAP's authority did not dwell on this point. It simply noted that in the instrument of surrender, Japan had accepted the Potsdam Declaration. The Declaration stated that Japan's aggression had been hatched by "irresponsible militarists" who dominated the Japanese government. It promised that "all obstacles to the revival and strengthening of democratic tendencies among the Japanese people" would be removed and a "peacefully inclined and responsible government" would be established "in accordance with the freely expressed will of the Japanese people." The implication was clear: "Fundamental changes in the Japanese constitutional structure . . . [were] essential to the execution of the Potsdam Declaration."[51]

As for MacArthur's role, it was the same for constitutional revision as it had been for "other matters of substance in the occupation and control of Japan." It was practically unlimited. In accordance with "the agreement [at Potsdam] among the governments of the US, USSR, UK and China," the Supreme Commander served by appointment of the President. His orders came through the JCS. Their controlling directive (JCS 1380) had ordered him to strengthen "democratic tendencies," to eliminate "feudal and authoritarian tendencies," and to lead the Japanese people to develop a "non-militaristic and democratic" nation. These objectives required constitutional revision.[52]

With the Moscow Agreement, the memo acknowledged, a new factor had entered the picture.[53] The Allies had established a Far Eastern Commission, with authority to establish policies for the occupation of Japan. The agreement was explicit in forbidding SCAP from acting on constitutional revision without FEC approval.[54] Regardless, the argument continued, there is a window of opportunity for SCAP, for until the FEC issued its own policy, his authority remained "substantially unimpaired."[55] The FEC might review any policies SCAP issued, and the American Joint Chiefs of Staff could no longer direct SCAP without FEC agreement, but until FEC issued new policies, MacArthur was free to act pursuant to "existing" American directives.

Thus the "sole limitation" on SCAP's authority to pursue constitutional reform was the possibility that an Allied nation might challenge an order from SCAP regarding the implementation of an FEC policy concerning "fundamental changes in the Japanese constitutional structure." In that case, SCAP's order would be referred to the FEC "to determine whether it properly implemented the FEC policy decision." Until SCAP issued such an order, there could be no interference from FEC.

A Conspiracy?

Toward the end of the memo on SCAP's authority over constitutional reform, there is a broad hint of how SCAP intended to deal with this potential challenge to its authority. The tactic was, in fact, the imperative that underlay the conspiracy between SCAP and the Shidehara and Yoshida cabinets. First the memo acknowledged that if the FEC "eventually promulgates" a policy on constitutional reform, an order from SCAP on this subject would not be controlling if any nation of the Allied council objected to it. But if, instead of *ordering* the Japanese to proceed in a certain fashion, SCAP merely *granted its approval* of a measure submitted by the Japanese government, the action would be subject to review by the FEC but not otherwise under FEC control.[56] This was the course eventually followed.

This memorandum was an internal SCAP document. It was submitted neither to the FEC nor to the U.S. government for approval, nor were the Japanese informed of its contents. It was submitted to General MacArthur, the Supreme Commander for the Allied Powers, by lawyers in the GS. It laid out a theory for the role he intended to play on constitutional reform and his strategy for neutralizing the authority of the FEC. It was based on the aims of the occupation, as derived from the Potsdam Declaration, and on the American military's sense of responsibility for "the development of a democratic Japan." It recognized the looming possibility of intrusion by the FEC, particularly the interest of the Soviet Union in taking advantage of Japan's vulnerability in defeat. It proposed to deal with such ambitions by having SCAP pose as the overseer of a *Japanese* effort to reform the constitution. In the matter of constitutional revision, SCAP would not issue orders, as it had during the autumn of 1945. Its formal stance would be to approve the initiative taken by the Japanese cabinet.

The key to this strategy, of course, was to get Japan moving in the right direction. It would have to be done quickly, before the FEC was fully organized. Moreover, it would have to be done in total secrecy. It could not be shared with the U.S. government in Washington, or with the Allies, or with the Japanese public. Even SCAP's Office of Political Adviser (Atcheson) would have to be kept in the dark.[57] The only way to defend against these potentially disastrous intrusions was for the Japanese cabinet to take the lead publicly in sponsoring a liberal constitutional draft. SCAP's effort between February 2 and March 6, 1946, was devoted to achieving that end.

Thus, by the end of January, SCAP had taken two decisive steps toward making a major effort on constitutional reform. One was the reorganization of GS, making it leaner and bringing it closer to the center of SCAP. The other was the preparation of a memo laying out the case for SCAP's authority in this area.

Still, when MacArthur met with delegates from the FEC on Thursday, January 31, the eve of their return to Washington, he went out of his way to say that the matter of constitutional reform had been "taken out of his hands" by the Moscow Agreement.[58] When he first took over as Supreme Commander, he said, his original directive[59] gave him jurisdiction in the matter, and he had "made certain suggestions" to the Japanese. The Japanese cabinet, he reported, had formed a committee to consider reforms of the constitution, but SCAP had "ceased to take any action whatever" in this area. It was his hope, he said, that "whatever might be done about constitutional reform in Japan, it would be done in such a way as to permit the Japanese to look upon the resulting document as a Japanese product." Only so would it be truly effective. It was not yet clear, he admitted, how constitutional reform would be "worked out." But he was absolutely convinced that no constitution, no matter how well written, would survive the end of the occupation if it had been "forced upon the Japanese by bayonet."[60]

At the end of the interview—covering, besides constitutional reform, such highly sensitive topics as reparations, the trial of war criminals, the expected duration of the Occupation, and the peace treaty—the Australian delegate asked if MacArthur's views could be communicated to their several governments. After a moment of silence, MacArthur said that he "of course" had no objection, provided that it be done in confidence and with due respect for the fact that these were his personal views. He wished to treat the commission as part of a team. It would be "tragic," he said, if he were quoted in a way that would force him to take steps "in self-defense" to protect himself.[61]

In interpreting these strange remarks, it is worth noting that the Soviet Union (which had boycotted the predecessor FEAC) was still not present. MacArthur was speaking, presumably, among friends.[62] Nevertheless, here was one of several instances in the long process that seems to support the charge that a conspiracy was at work.

6 . . . .

"A Liberal and Enlightened Constitution"

. THE SCAP MODEL

It is not clear exactly when MacArthur made the decision to prepare a model constitution for Japan. Everything was in place by the end of January: the emperor's disavowal of the "false conception" that he was divine;[1] official guidance from Washington on the basic principles of constitutional revision (SWNCC 228); MacArthur's decision to protect Emperor Hirohito from trial as a war criminal and to retain him as a constitutional monarch in the new order; a strategy for using the Japanese cabinet as co-conspirator, outlined in the memo on SCAP's authority in this area.[2] The plan, having been conceived by SCAP, was ready to be implemented. All that was needed was an occasion.

It came on the morning of Friday, February 1. As the Japanese cabinet was meeting to consider how to proceed with constitutional reform, word came that the *Mainichi*, a daily newspaper, had just published a "scoop": the text of proposals for constitutional revision, allegedly the work of the Matsumoto Committee. For the cabinet, this bombshell was an acute embarrassment. The Japanese press quickly denounced it as a great disappointment and said it showed that Japan's current political leaders were incapable of meeting the challenge of revision.[3]

For SCAP, the "scoop" and the journalistic reaction were a godsend:[4] widely perceived evidence that the Japanese cabinet was not up to the job by itself. The staff at GS immediately sprang into action. The first step, they thought, was to show that the reforms published in *Mainichi* were wholly inadequate. Down the hall at Daiichi, however, MacArthur and Whitney conceived a more radical step. The time had come for SCAP to take the lead. Whitney convened a small group of people from GS and directed them, in utmost secrecy, to prepare a "model" constitution for Japan. It would have to be ready in one week's time! Whitney had an appointment with Yoshida set for Tuesday, February 12, to discuss constitutional reform. He and Whitney agreed that it would be "better strategy" at that meeting if, rather than rejecting an unacceptable draft, they could "orient" the Japanese officials by presenting their own ideas in the form of a concrete draft.[5]

MacArthur's Guidelines

To guide the work, MacArthur prepared a list of basic principles to incorporate in the new draft. The document is brief. (We include a photograph of it in the photo gallery.) We quote it here in full:

I.

Emperor is at the head of the state.

His succession is dynastic.

His duties and powers will be exercised in accordance with the Constitution and responsive to the basic will of the people as provided therein.

II.

War as a sovereign right of the nation is abolished. Japan renounces it as an instrumentality for settling its disputes and even for preserving its own security. It relies upon the higher ideals which are now stirring the world for its defense and its protection.

No Japanese Army, Navy or Air Force will ever be authorized and no rights of belligerency will ever be conferred upon any Japanese force.

The feudal system of Japan will cease.

No rights of peerage except those of the Imperial family will extend beyond the lives of those now existent.

No patent of nobility will from this time forth embody within itself any National or Civic power of government.

Pattern budget after British system.[6]

These guidelines were typed on a single sheet of paper and passed on to Kades, whom Whitney named to chair the drafting project's steering committee. On his copy Kades penciled some notes, probably the very day he got it. His emendations were highly significant, an indication of his own thinking. Before "I" and "II," he wrote the word "Chapter," indicating that provisions on the emperor would be presented in the first chapter and the renunciation of war in the second. Around the word "head" in the first section, he put brackets, and above it he inserted the word, "symbol." Apparently he had already decided to use the word "symbol" to describe the emperor's role in the new constitutional order.

The most substantial of Kades's interlinings occur in the part labeled "II," dealing with the renunciation of war and armed forces. Boldly, he put brackets around the phrase "and even for preserving its own security." (Later in the week, when drafting article 9, he would omit this phrase altogether.) He added "and the threat or use of force" to "war," among the instruments Japan would be renouncing. And he added "or other war potential" to the phrase that foreswore armed forces.

Next to the third set of items, Kades jotted that these pronouncements of doom on traditional Japanese society would have to be expanded into several chapters and sections. They pointed in the right direction, but they gave only a hint of what a modern bill of rights would have to include. MacArthur was leaving the rest to the technicians.

The fourth item in this list ("Pattern budget after British system") was so cryptic that it is hard to tell what MacArthur had in mind. Kades's notes caught the nub of it: The "legislative body," he wrote, would have "control of [the] purse." This would require a marked shift for a country that tended to defer to a highly confident bureaucracy. MacArthur's endorsement provided a solid, if telegraphic, foundation for Kades, Hays, Guy Swope, and others who believed that Japan needed to strengthen its legislative assembly.

It is remarkable that Kades felt able to make these changes in the work of a commander he had not yet met. One wonders whether these notes were made while Whitney was giving him the commission to direct this project. In interviews years later, Kades could not remember.

At any rate, spare though they were, MacArthur's guidelines gave direction on several key points. The emperor would remain "at the head of the state," or at least an important part of the constitutional structure. This was a bold and critically important decision. It would have to be defended against Allied nations that were hostile to the continuation of this institution in any form. On the other hand, the third requirement for chapter I—putting the emperor in a constitutional framework (not as the author of it, as with Meiji, but as subservient to it), and tying his position to the "basic will of the people"—meant that the imperial institution, as every living Japanese person had known it, would now have to change. The renunciation of war would likewise require a fundamental shift in culture. As for the "feudal system," peerage and nobility, they were probably doomed anyway, in the coming egalitarian age.

Calling a "Constitutional Convention"

On Monday, February 4, Whitney called about twenty members of the GS staff together. Solemnly he told them that they would sit that week "as a constitutional convention." General MacArthur had "entrusted [them] with the historically significant task" of drafting a "new constitution for the Japanese people."[7] Whitney said SCAP hoped to lead the Japanese to accept a more "liberal" (Whitney's word) constitution "by persuasive argument," if possible. If not, he is quoted as saying, "General MacArthur has empowered [me] to use not merely the threat of force, but force itself." Whitney then read MacArthur's guiding principles and added that he wanted a completed draft by the end of the week. There was a meeting scheduled with Yoshida for the following week. Yoshida would be told that "the only possibility of retaining the emperor and the remnants of their own power is by their acceptance and approval of a constitution that will force a decisive swing to the left."[8] The model to be drafted by GS would "orient" the Japanese toward such revisions. When Yoshida "and his group" had drafted something "to fit our demand for a liberal constitution," the finished document would be submitted to MacArthur for approval. He would accept it as the work of the Japanese government and so promulgate it to the world.[9]

Whitney added to the drama by directing that the work at GHQ must be done in "absolute secrecy."[10] Only thus could the process of amendment outlined in article LXXIII of the Meiji Constitution be used and the fiction be maintained that constitutional revision was the work of the Japanese government.

The American Framers

To understand SCAP's "model" for Japan's new constitution, we need to look first at the men and women who framed it. We begin with General Courtney A. Whitney, the man who oversaw the entire project and intervened decisively at several crucial points during the week. It is not easy to develop an accurate mental picture of Whitney.[11] Though he was only five feet, six inches tall, he seemed like a giant among these men. He could be brusque of manner, pompous in expression, and self-important, but he was also fiercely loyal to those who served under him, and he was not afraid of their strength. While stationed in Washington as an Army officer during World War I, he earned a law degree at the Columbia National Law School. The Army sent him to the Philippines. In 1927, he resigned his commission, set up a law office in Manila, and began prospecting for minerals and speculating in stocks. Many other men were ruined pursuing such activities during this decade, but not Whitney. He became a millionaire. He returned to Washington a year before Pearl Harbor, reenlisted in the Army Air Corps, and, in 1943, was ordered to report to Australia for assignment. On his arrival in Brisbane, MacArthur asked his old friend (they had belonged to the same Masonic lodge in Manila during the 1930s) to create an underground movement in the Philippines. Whitney oversaw the recruitment of 500 Filipino soldiers and organized their training, in sabotage, radio operations and maintenance, and intelligence, at a camp near Brisbane. Whitney was right behind MacArthur as he waded ashore at Leyte Gulf on October 20, 1944.[12] These experiences forged a strong bond between the two men. Whitney shared MacArthur's staunchly Republican loyalties. Like his mentor, though, he was pragmatic when it came to selecting aides.

The drafting group's "steering committee" consisted of four people: its leader, Colonel Charles L. Kades; Commander A. Rodman Hussey, Jr.; Lt. Colonel Milo E. Rowell; and Miss Ruth Ellerman. We introduced Kades earlier (in our Introduction). As we noted there, his ignorance about Japan made him a strange choice for this assignment. In other ways, however, he was ideally suited. He was well trained in the law. He was entirely comfortable in the company of able men. He accepted without reservation the American faith that people everywhere desire democratic government. Nor did he doubt that the American variant of these ideals was the truest and best. (He would permit an exception for the parliamentary model, as we shall see.) He also had strong faith in written constitutions, another American peculiarity, and he had none of the political scientist's convic-

1. *above.* General MacArthur arrives at Atsugi Airport, outside Tokyo, on August 30, 1945, to assume his duties as Supreme Commander for the Allied Powers. *(National Archives)*

2. *left.* General MacArthur and Emperor Hirohito at their first meeting, September 27, 1945. *(National Archives)*

3. *above* National Diet Building, amidst the ruins of war in 1945. *(Mainichi Photo Bank)*

4. *below* Far Eastern Commission meets with MacArthur's staff, January 14, 1946. At the table, in the center of the picture: Major General Frank McCoy, chairman of the commission. *(National Archives)*

Copy of Pencilled Note of C-in-C handed me on Sunday, 3 Feb. '46 re the terms of draft Constitution. MK.

CCTY   **SECRET**

Chapter I

Emperor is at the *[important]* head of the state.

His succession is dynastic.

His duties and powers will be exercised in accordance with the Constitution and responsible to the basic will of the people as provided therein.

Chapter II.

and the threat or use of force as

War as a sovereign right of the nation is abolished. Japan renounces it as an instrumentality for settling its disputes and even for preserving its own security. It relies upon the higher ideals which are now stirring the world for its defense and its protection.

as China was totally   *with other*

No [Japanese] Army, Navy or Air Force will ever be authorized and no *nations* rights of belligerency will ever be conferred upon any [Japanese] force.

other

The feudal system of Japan will cease.

No rights of peerage except those of the Imperial family will extend beyond the lives of those now existent.

No patent of nobility will from this time forth embody within itself any National or Civic power of government.

Pattern budget after British system.   (?) *Article on budget & appropriations indicated if & control of purse by legislative body*

5. Memo sent by MacArthur to the American drafting committee, February 2, 1946.
Handwritten notes are by Colonel Kades, head of the drafting group. *(Kades Papers, Amherst College Archives)*

6. Shidehara cabinet, April 23, 1946. *Front row, left to right:* Iwata Chūzō minister of justice; Shidehara Kijūrō, prime minister; Mitsuchi Chūzō , minister of interior. *Second row, on the left:* Matsumoto Jōji, minister in charge of constitutional revision; next to him, Ashida Hitoshi, minister of welfare, and later, chair of the Diet's special committee on constitutional revision. *Fourth row, on the left:* Irie Toshio, head of the cabinet's Legislation Bureau. *(National Archives)*

7. *above* General Dwight D. Eisenhower, Chief of Staff, U.S. Army, and General MacArthur, in the latter's car, Tokyo, May 10, 1946. *(National Archives)*

8. *left* General Courtney Whitney, chief of the Occupation's government section. *(Photo provided by Courtney Whitney III)*

9. *top left* Colonel Charles L. Kades, deputy chief of government section and chair of the steering committee that prepared the American draft. *(Photo provided by Phyllis Kades)*

10. *above* Commander A. Rodman Hussey, another member of the steering committee. *(National Archives)*

11. *left* Beate Sirota, 23-year-old Occupation aide, who drafted the clauses that became Articles 14 and 24, granting equal rights to women. *(Photo provided by Beate Sirota Gordon)*

12. *above* Matsumoto Jōji, minister in charge of constitutional revision in the Shidehara cabinet (*Kyōdō News*)

13. *left* Satō Tatsuo, bureaucrat who negotiated with SCAP to transform the American draft into the proposed Japanese government draft. (*National Archives*)

14. *right* Kanamori Tokujirō, minister in Yoshida's cabinet in charge of constitutional revision. (*Kyōdō News*)

15. *above* Katō Shizue, member of the Diet's House of Representatives in 1946 and leading defender of equal rights for women. *(Mainichi Photo Bank)*

16. *below* Prime Minister Yoshida and his predecessor, Shidehara, meet at the Diet Building with a delegation of American congressmen, August 27, 1946. *(National Archives)*

tion that a constitution, to be successful, must grow organically from the cultural soil whose governance it seeks to organize.

"Rod" Hussey was a Phi Beta Kappa graduate of Harvard College. He earned his law degree at the University of Virginia. During the 1930s, he had been a clerk at the Massachusetts Superior Court and held various elective and appointive offices at the local level. Like Rowell and several others at GS, Hussey had trained for civil affairs duty (restoring government in the wake of a conquering army) at the academies set up on various university campuses in the early 1940s. He had attended the Navy's school at Princeton and another at Harvard. Hussey was a vain man,[13] and he could be brusque, but he was a keen lawyer, and he had a sound, if unpracticed, instinct for constitutional form.

Rowell too we have already profiled, in connection with his preliminary work for SCAP on constitutional issues. A lawyer and politically conservative, he had extensive experience in democratic governance at the grassroots level. His brother had been killed in the war, and he would soon leave Tokyo to return to his grieving family, but while he was there, he made an important contribution to the steering committee.

Ruth Ellerman was the drafting group's note taker. It is not clear exactly what influence she had over the drafting process, but she was certainly intelligent and understood what was going on, and she was present when the key decisions were made. She offered the following impression of working conditions during that first week of February:

> There was a small snack bar on the top floor of the Daiichi Seimei Building [where the group worked, in total seclusion]. We ate sandwiches and donuts standing up and worked every day until daybreak. People would return to their quarters at dawn, shower, sleep for about an hour, and then at 8:00 a.m. sharp everybody would gather again and continue working on the draft. As a woman, I did the same thing.[14]

The drafting group included one other woman who made a significant contribution: Beate Sirota. Sirota was born in Vienna in 1923. Her family left Europe in 1929; her father, an internationally acclaimed pianist, took a position at the Tokyo Academy of Music.[15] Sirota lived in Tokyo through her early adolescence. She left for America in the summer of 1939 to attend Mills College, in Oakland, California. During the war, her fluency in Japanese made her valuable. After working for the Office of War Information monitoring Japanese radio broadcasts and a stint with the foreign news division of *Time*, she took a job in Washington at the Foreign Economic Administration. Recruiters for MacArthur's growing staff in Tokyo spotted her and brought her to Tokyo, where she arrived on Christmas Day, 1945.[16] Kades, impressed with her fluency in Japanese, soon grabbed her for GS. When making assignments for his drafting team, he assigned her to the subcommittee for the bill of rights.

We will introduce other members of the drafting group in due course. What can be said to characterize them generally?

First, only a few of them had any real knowledge about Japan. Sirota, as we have noted, lived in Tokyo as a child and teenager. Cyrus H. Peake had a doctorate in East Asian history from Columbia University and had been managing editor and co-editor of the *Far Eastern Quarterly*. Major Cecil G. Tilton had done economic and political research on Japan, China, and Korea and had traveled in those countries. In the fall of 1945, he had taken an intensive tutorial program under the direction of Tanaka Jirō of Tokyo Imperial University, from which Tanaka judged that Tilton had "accumulated considerable knowledge" and become "something of an expert" on local government in Japan.[17] Harry Emerson Wildes had lectured at Keiō University in 1924–1925 and had written a book, *Social Currents in Japan* (1927).[18] He was well informed about Japan, though his temperament limited his influence at GS.

None of the others had deep knowledge about Japan. Several (Hussey, Rowell, Hays, Roest, Rizzo)[19] had attended courses on Japan taught during World War II on university campuses (the School of Military Government at the University of Virginia, or civil affairs training schools at Yale, the University of Michigan, Harvard, or Syracuse, or at the Presidio in Monterey, California).[20] These courses had excellent teachers and many smart, highly motivated students. But the knowledge gained was superficial, measured against the challenge of framing a new constitution for Japan.

Besides this rather spotty training before coming to Japan, most of them had been in Tokyo for several months and had doubtless picked up some impressions. A little learning, though, can be a dangerous thing. Tokyo in the fall and winter of 1945 was hardly typical of Japanese life. As a group these people were not well versed in Japanese affairs, culture, or history.

What they did know was the law as it was taught in several leading American universities and law schools and practiced in the United States at the federal, state, and local levels. Several had experience in and around Congress and in the bureaus of the executive branch. And though several of them (Whitney, Hussey, Rowell) were of a conservative bent ideologically, others (Kades, Roest, Wildes, Esman) were quite liberal. All of them had lived through Franklin Delano Roosevelt's New Deal. To appreciate the weight of that experience, one might imagine a group of Americans at the beginning of the twenty-first century, a broad spectrum of right- and left-leaning types, but all of whom had been in their 20s and 30s during Ronald Reagan's two terms as president. Whatever their individual proclivities, a free-market orientation would seem almost natural to such a group. Similarly, to the men and women of SCAP, New Deal liberalism seemed natural, even to conservative Republicans such as MacArthur and Whitney. Thus Whitney, for example, could tell the Japanese that their new constitution would have to embody "liberal" principles.[21]

The Americans' Principles

As for constitutional principles, they were, first of all, good Madisonians—this despite the fact that they would provide Japan with a parliamentary form of government. They were Madisonian in their belief that constitution making was a matter of distinguishing the functions of government, ensuring that basic institutions had the means and incentive to check one another, and then balancing them properly, securely harnessing those that had gotten out of control in the past, fortifying those that tended to be weak in the Japanese environment, and grounding it all in accountability to the electorate. To their credit, they realized that in framing a constitution for Japan, they would have to depart from some cherished American ideas. There would be no executive veto, for example; the Diet had to be strengthened, and so it was given "decisive and ultimate power over all legislation."[22]

More serious was the decision to make Japan's executive power collective rather than unitary. The American framers in 1787 had vested the executive not in a council but in a single president, to make it more energetic, more decisive, quicker, and more secret when they needed to be, and at the same time more accountable.[23] This preference for a strong, unified executive had a vigorous advocate in Tokyo: Milton J. Esman, a young first lieutenant, who was the best-trained political scientist in the drafting group. Twenty-seven years old, Esman was a newly minted Ph.D. in politics and public administration from Princeton. He had studied in the civil affairs training schools at Charlottesville and Harvard, as well.[24]

Kades appointed Esman to the subcommittee on the executive. In a written dissent to the subcommittee's report, he argued that modern government requires a strong, responsible executive. The best way to ensure sufficient strength in the executive was to vest it in a prime minister and give him authority to dissolve the Diet and to appeal to the people for a verdict on his program. He cited the French and American systems as counterexamples: the French for requiring the executive to resign in cases of disagreement with the Diet; the American for its tendency to deadlock when Congress rejects the administration's program but the president clings to office. The Diet, he said, would no doubt, and quite properly, consist of a multitude of political factions, pulling in many different directions. It would need to be disciplined by a unified executive, for the sake of stability. We should not, he wrote, "saddle the feeble and inexperienced Japanese democracy with devices that have seriously tried the most delicate political skill of veteran democratic peoples." Better to give them "governmental devices which long experience has indicated are most likely to develop stable democratic institutions."[25] Esman made another suggestion, too, for strengthening the executive power: that the prime minister be appointed by an authority "above party politics," namely, the emperor. The steering committee recoiled from Esman's arguments. Kades rejected out of hand the suggestion that the emperor appoint the prime minister. It would not, he thought, be conducive to executive strength and firmness; it would be an invitation to manipulation and meddling by the emperor and his entourage. Furthermore, it was clearly inconsistent with SWNCC 228. As for Esman's appeal for executive power unified in the prime minister, Rowell and Peake contended that it too was inconsistent with SWNCC 228, where the executive is always referred to as the cabinet, not the prime minister. Kades, whose question about the veto indicated some sympathy for Esman's position on executive strength, was willing to compromise, vesting executive power in "the prime minister as the head of the cabinet,"[26] but Hussey insisted that such a formulation was not only "hostile" to SWNCC 228 but "entirely inconsistent with the way things are done in Japan."[27] Hussey carried the day, and the language of the vesting clause mentioned only the cabinet.

The notes on these debates are not entirely clear, but the reasoning behind these provisions seems again to have been Madisonian. Madison had argued that, in balancing the executive and legislative powers, it was wise to check legislative power by dividing it into two chambers, and to fortify executive power by unifying it. For Madisonian reasons, the GS draft went in the opposite direction because, in Japan, the Diet needed to be strengthened and the executive harnessed. Thus the GS draft incorporated a unicameral legislature[28] and a collective executive.[29]

The Emperor's Role

One of the fundamental principles of American constitutionalism is that a constitution is an utterance of "We the people."[30] It ordains the powers that the people commit to the government and the arrangements for doing so. The government has those powers, and no others. This notion, outlined in the Declaration of Independence, is made explicit in the Tenth Amendment to the U.S. Constitution.[31]

In the modern political history of Japan, a different notion—a different myth, if you will—was operative. Japan saw itself as an extended family, with the emperor, a semireligious figure, at its head. In 1889, Emperor Meiji "granted" a constitution and stated that he, his agents, and his successors would rule by its provisions. He kept for himself the power to name and dismiss his ministers, as well as to initiate amendments to the constitution.

Clearly it was fundamental to the American idea of constitutional reform in Japan to force a change in this myth and the governing practices it generated. To do this, the Imperial Throne had to be stripped of some of its mystique and the emperor's pretenses to sovereignty explicitly contradicted. The texts drafted by GS were full of both positive and negative signals of the change. The emperor's position, in the words of the American drafters, derived from the "sovereign will of the people, and from no other source." He was to have "no governmental powers." Succession to the throne was to be "in accordance with such Imperial Household Law as the Diet may enact." His state functions were to be performed on the advice and consent of the cabinet and on behalf of the people. No money or other property was to be given to the Throne, nor expenditures made, unless the Diet authorized.[32]

The tone of this first chapter of the draft was distinctly different from MacArthur's guidelines. He had directed that the emperor be kept "at the head of the state." Contrary to sentiments coming from Washington and from some of the Allies, MacArthur believed it would be a mistake to punish the emperor as a war criminal. He deemed the imperial institution essential to Japan's cohesion as a society. He knew how much the emperor's statement on surrender had contributed to the smooth inauguration of the Occupation, and he believed he could use the same authority to promote his own program of reform.

His staff accepted this assessment, but there were several whose emotional response to the emperor was less sympathetic than their chief's. Kades, for example, told the committee assigned to draft the chapter on the emperor that it should strictly delimit the monarch's power and make it clear that his role was "merely decorative."[33] A clause in chapter I directing that expenditures for the throne be included in the budget was deleted; an appropriate provision would be included elsewhere, in the chapter on finance. Instead, in the first chapter, the steering committee inserted one that emphasized the "complete powerlessness" of the throne either to receive or make gifts without prior authorization of the Diet.[34]

The steering committee also struck the word, "reign," from the opening article, on grounds, as Rowell explained, that the Japanese usage of that term carried the connotation of governing as well. The subcommittee members, Nelson and Poole, had apparently approached their work too timidly. They had, for example, provided for four imperial officers (two Privy Ministers, a Lord Keeper of the Privy Seal, and a Lord Chamberlain), intending thereby to put constitutional limits on the growth of the imperial household. The steering committee directed that the clause be deleted. It gave undue weight to the imperial household.[35]

It was in fact one of the leading goals of this revision of Japanese constitutionalism to take all powers of government from the emperor and his retinue. In the American view, Japan's troubles in the past—its vulnerability to misguided bureaucrats and militarists—stemmed from the failure of the Meiji Constitution to make those who wielded power fully accountable to representatives of the people for their acts. Thus Kades resisted the efforts of his staff to have the emperor "confirm" judicial decrees[36] or "choose" the prime minister.[37] The emperor must not have any powers of governance. Even in ceremonial gestures, he was to act only with the advice and approval of the cabinet.

The Role of the Diet

Throughout the modern period in Japan, the Diet had been the weak stone in the constitutional structure. The elders in the Meiji period had done everything they could to prevent the government from being accountable to political parties in parliament. The Diet, in contrast to the bureaucracy, was seen as a den of hacks, with a penchant for maneuver and a tolerance for corruption that routinely prevailed over dedication to the national interest.

The Americans believed deeply in the rule of law, and that meant an enhanced place for lawmakers and a relative diminution of bureaucrats. How could this revolution in structure be accomplished? Partly, they hoped, by exhortation: The lead article in chapter IV declared mightily that the Diet would be the "highest organ of state power" and the "sole law-making authority of the state."[38] But Madison had taught that lofty sentiments on parchment would have little effect by themselves. The Diet's hand was further strengthened by giving it the power to resolve no confidence in the cabinet, thereby forcing its resignation. Alternatively, the cabinet could dissolve the Diet and call elections, but that would require that the cabinet also resign as soon as the new Diet convened. In the GS draft, the Diet also had power to designate the prime minister and establish ministries and to consent to the appointment of ministers, and it had full power over budgets and new taxes.

Some of the American drafters had misgivings about these arrangements. We have noted Esman's dissent, but he was not the only one with apprehensions about how the Diet might use its power. Kades wondered out loud about the need for an executive veto over legislation. In preliminary discussions on February 5, Frank Rizzo raised the same concern. "If there is no executive veto," he said, "there is no effective hindrance to prevent the legislature from running wild in appropriations; it is conceivable that expensive boondoggling and pork-barrel projects might result." Members of the committee that had framed the chapter on the Diet replied that, once the Diet approved the budget, appropriations could not be increased. If the Diet pressed for unwise distributions within the limits, the cabinet could resign rather than take responsibility for changes of which it disapproved. Commander Swope cited his own experience in Puerto Rico, where as governor (appointed by President Franklin Roosevelt) he had the "practical power" of refusing to spend the money (impounding it, as we would say) if the legislature appropriated it for projects he disapproved of. Kades concluded the discussion of the Diet's powers by pointing out that the parliamentary body would have "all powers not explicitly prohibited to it by the Constitution."[39]

As for the chapter on finance, it was entrusted to Rizzo, one of the stars of GS, then and thereafter.[40] As originally drafted, it included a provision requiring a balanced budget: It forbade the Diet to appropriate money in excess of anticipated income for any given fiscal year. Kades questioned it, noting that it might interfere with long-term planning of public works projects, but Rizzo's argument for fiscal responsibility prevailed at this stage. Another of Rizzo's articles (echoing the Meiji Constitution) provided for a temporary budget in the event that a cabinet was unable to secure parliamentary approval for its budget, to provide funds for a period when the cabinet and Diet were "at loggerheads." Hussey disapproved. He thought the constitution ought not to provide a loophole for an executive budget. If the cabinet could not gain parliamentary approval for its budget, it ought to be forced to resign.[41]

In the end, the drafters placed their confidence in the Diet. The lead article of chapter IV, on the Diet, made this clear: "The Diet shall be the highest organ of state power and shall be the sole law-making authority of the State."[42] This language went far beyond the usual vesting clause. In the early planning sessions, Kades told his staff that SCAP would insist on parliamentary supremacy. When Rizzo asked about the "final source of power," Kades replied that all powers not explicitly vested in the judicial or executive branches of the government reside in the legislative body. Supremacy, he said, must lie with the representative body, itself immediately responsible to the electorate.[43] When the staff sought to add a clause on unenumerated rights being reserved to the people (like the Tenth Amendment to the U.S. Constitution), Hussey objected. "Residual power," he insisted, "is in the Diet, and the people can have no rights against a Diet which is their own creation."[44] Another indication came with the impeachment clause. A drafting subcommittee had produced a version that echoed the American version. Impeachment was to be for all officers and lead to removal from office on conviction for "treason, bribery, or any high crime or misdemeanor." The steering committee threw out that version and directed that impeachment be restricted to members of the judiciary. Impeachment, they said, was "cumbersome and time-consuming." A prime minister could be removed by vote of no confidence, he could remove his own ministers at will, the Diet could make its own rules for removal of members, and all other elected officials could be recalled.[45] The independence of the judiciary was itself an anomalous element in this rendering of parliamentary government,[46] but it was not allowed to compromise the supremacy of the Diet.

Social Issues and Compromises

We have already noted Whitney's contention that those who drafted a constitution for Japan represented a cross-section of American political opinion. From Rizzo's advocacy of a balanced budget to Kades's "red clause" (declaring that all land belongs ultimately to the state),[47]—neither of which, by the way, survived in the draft published by the Japanese government on March 6—we can indeed see a broad spectrum. From the right to work to the guarantee of collective bargaining, from the independence of the judiciary to parliamentary supremacy and the power of dissolution, ideas born of conservatism and radicalism mingled promiscuously.

Even in their approach to the task of constitutional revision, the American framers brought widely varying attitudes to the table. MacArthur had given them a broad invitation, in his third "must," to engage in some social engineering. "The feudal system of Japan will cease," he had written. Waiting to address this challenge was a subcommittee consisting of Lt. Colonel Pieter K. Roest and two civilians, Wildes and Sirota. Roest was a medical doctor (trained in Holland), an anthropologist and a college professor.[48] He was something of a visionary, eager to take up MacArthur's challenge.

As Roest and his fellow members gathered clauses for inclusion in the bill of rights, they soon began to run into stiff resistance from the steering committee. The proposed articles included detailed provisions for social welfare, including public health, free education, child labor laws, and the like. The steering committee contended that such provisions, meritorious though some of them might be, were statutory in character, not constitutional. Roest countered that the inclusion of social welfare provisions was "accepted practice in modern European constitutions" (as indeed it was). It was especially appropriate for Japan, he insisted, because the idea that the state was responsible for the welfare of its people was a new concept here. Women were chattel, he said, bastards took precedence over legitimate children on the whim of a father, and peasants sold their daughters to cover the debts from a bad rice crop. Wildes agreed. We must "force the

Japanese government to go on record for these things." Rowell replied that it was not SCAP's responsibility to set up a system of social welfare. He feared that insistence on these provisions might cause the Japanese government to reject the draft outright. When Wildes answered that SCAP did indeed have the responsibility to produce a "social revolution in Japan" and that the constitution should lay the foundation, Rowell offered the usual conservative rejoinder: "You cannot impose a new mode of social thought upon a country by law."[49]

At this point, Whitney was summoned to resolve a dispute that did not lend itself to compromise. The prospects for the reformers must have seemed hopeless. Whitney perfectly reflected MacArthur's social conservatism. His solution, however, was solomonic: Omit what he called the "minutiae," and include only a general statement that social security must be provided.[50] The reformers had to settle for half of their baby, but it was more than they had any reason to expect.

There is no record, in the minutes of the drafting group, of discussion of the article (eventually article 24) on the family system. Apart from the renunciation of war and armed forces, this was perhaps the most radical provision in the entire draft. Sirota had found models in volumes procured from Tokyo libraries, including the constitutions of the Weimar Republic, the Soviet Union, and various Scandinavian countries. Later she remembered, with anguish, that her drafts were stripped of many valuable details before being incorporated in the draft submitted to the Japanese government on February 13. For example, the first clause in the draft's article on social welfare, the one abbreviated on Whitney's orders, would have called on the Diet to enact legislation to "protect and aid expectant and nursing mothers, promote infant and child welfare, and establish just rights for illegitimate and adopted children, and for the underprivileged."[51] Sirota found the omission of such provisions galling. She was terribly frustrated by her inability to persuade the soldiers in command of the drafting process that the social revolution they sought would never happen unless it were grounded on constitutionally mandated changes in relationships within the Japanese home.

Centralized versus Local Authority

There is one prominent feature of American constitutionalism that fits awkwardly into the picture in Tokyo that winter. Americans call it "federalism." More generally, it is the question of relations between the regime's "center" and "periphery." The United States is a federal republic, created during the last quarter of the eighteenth century out of thirteen semisovereign states. The distribution of power between the states and the national government has varied over time, but state and local governments have always played a major role in American governance. They have taxing power, for example, and other local authorities (e.g., school, water, and sewer districts) exercise real influence in their communities. These arrangements are rooted in a consensus that places a high value on regional particularity and local control. Japan, at least since the Meiji era, had a different tradition, more like France's. Political leaders in the 1870s had to create new systems of local administration for Japan as part of their program for modernization, but the Meiji Constitution contained no provision at all for local governments.

The Americans brought their predisposition in favor of local control to the drafting process, but it was not fully developed. The confusion became apparent when the steering committee rejected a draft prepared by Tilton and two others.[52] Hussey prepared another version, which Tilton in turn found unacceptable.[53] Kades then asked Rowell to draft a compromise, suggesting that it incorporate a clause on the direct popular election of local officials and one on the right of local entities to manage their own properties, within the (national) law. From these elements, the chapter on local government was finally developed.

The draft gave "limited local autonomy" to metropolitan areas, including power to frame their own charters within the limits defined by the Diet. There was one notable feature: a ban on acts applicable to one local community without the assent of the electorate of the community concerned. Ellerman's notes indicate that the draft chapter on local government represented a reconciliation of opposing views: those championed by Rowell, a "strong home rule man" with a background in the Fresno (California) County Taxpayers Association, and those of Kades, a "warm central government man."[54] Kades later contended that Ellerman's characterization of the dispute within GS was inaccurate. It was Hussey, he said, who resisted the idea of grounding local autonomy in the constitution. Tilton was the champion of local autonomy. As for Kades, as an undergraduate at Cornell, he had written a term paper for Professor Robert Cushman, legendary scholar of constitutional law, on "Home Rule in New York." In that paper, he had contended that it was a mistake to provide for home rule in the constitution.[55] Better, he concluded with characteristic prudence, to keep it flexible, giving the state legislature power to adapt home rule statutes to different circumstances and evolving conditions. The terms of the central clause of the chapter on local government—granting the right of cities and towns to manage their property and affairs "within such laws as the Diet may enact"—suggest that Kades's ideas prevailed at this stage.[56]

Disputed Rights

On two other basic issues, Kades also won out, this time with the support of both Rowell and Hussey. One was civil liberties. The drafts prepared by the civil rights committee guaranteed "freedom of person" to "all law-abiding Japanese," barred "ecclesiastics" from all political activity, and qualified freedom of speech and press by prohibiting libel and slander. The steering committee objected to these provisions. Kades insisted that the constitution should be a "bill of rights rather than a bill of restrictions." He noted that the guarantee of free speech in the U.S. Constitution prevented the passage of a criminal libel law. The burden of proving slander or libel should be on the aggrieved individual, he said, not the government. Another clause in the draft provided that legal measures for the suppression of indecent and degrading literature were permissible "for the protection of youth and the maintenance of high public standards." These qualifications were deleted and the clauses rewritten to guarantee freedom of expression without constitutional limitation.[57]

The other issue was whether the Japanese should be permitted to amend the bill of rights, once ratified. The committee's first draft provided that no future constitution, law, or ordinance could limit or cancel the freedoms guaranteed by this new constitution. Kades strongly objected, noting that such a provision implied infallibility and would deny future generations the right to order their own affairs, ensuring that change could come about only through revolution. Roest held his ground, arguing that "the present age has arrived at a certain stage of progress," and we must not allow a future generation to abrogate rights now accepted as inherent in the state of man. Again, Whitney was summoned to resolve the dispute. This time, he sided cleanly with the steering committee; the provision against amendment was dropped.[58] In Jefferson's terms, the "dead hand of the past" would not lie on the living, not even if future generations of Japanese wished to revise the bill of rights.

At issue here was more than whether constitutional liberalism was eternally valid. The framers also had to decide whether they trusted Japan to govern itself in accordance with democratic values. Wildes argued that the omission of a prohibition on amendments would "inevitably open the gates to fascism in Japan."[59] Kades strongly disagreed. Earlier, Roest had discerned a "discrepancy" between American political experience and thinking and the "actions and past expressions of the present Japanese government." Kades granted this discrepancy, but he contended that "no comparable gap exists between American political ideology and the best or most liberal Japanese constitutional thought."[60] Kades, who was overseeing the purge and would monitor the Japanese debates on ratification over the ensuing summer, would have many opportunities to demonstrate his confidence that Japan, once firmly democratized, had the makings of a constitutional democracy. This confidence, firmly backed by MacArthur and Whitney, was an essential ingredient in the constitutional revolution of 1946.

The SCAP Draft

On Sunday, February 10, Whitney delivered the completed draft of SCAP's model to MacArthur. In a covering memorandum, he noted that it represented the "considered and collective view" of a group that included "nearly every form of American political thought." The staff had given "studious attention," he wrote, not only to the historic development of the existing Japanese constitution but to the "constitutional principles governing the lives of our own people and the peoples of the several European nations as well." In the context of Japanese politics, it would bring about a "sharp swing from the extreme right," without yielding anything "to the radical concept of the extreme left."[61]

Whitney was proud of the work his staff had done.[62] It was, indeed, an astonishing achievement. In six days' time, twenty-one Americans[63] had drafted a completely new constitution for Japan. Yoshida, who saw it first on February 13, called it "revolutionary."[64] The word was well chosen. The first thing he noticed were the opening words, "We, the Japanese people," "indicating that it was the people who were framing the constitution, and not the emperor."[65] The draft drove the point home, in the first article, by adding that the emperor's position derived from "no other source" than the people's will. In article III, it added insult both to the emperor and to prospective political leaders by asserting that the emperor "shall have no governmental powers, nor shall he assume nor be granted any." Equally radically, article VIII stripped Japan of the right to wage war "forever" and declared that no armed forces would "ever" be authorized. The repudiation of the Meiji Constitution could not have been stated more emphatically.

The bill of rights, chapter III, was modern and liberal, admirable in many ways, but to Japanese eyes in 1946, it detonated one bombshell after another. Clearly the American framers saw the Japanese people as victims of terrible abuses and themselves as deliverers. Article X stated that the rights "by this Constitution guaranteed to the people of Japan" were the result of an "age-old struggle," implying that the Japanese people had played little part in that struggle. Article XI added that their enjoyment would depend on the people's "eternal vigilance" and admonished them to use these rights "always for the common good." The next article declared that the "feudal system shall cease," and that "all Japanese by virtue of their humanity shall be respected as individuals." Article XIII proclaimed equality before the law and indicated that peerage would end with the current generation. Article XIV held that the people, the "ultimate arbiters of their government"—not the emperor, as in the Meiji system—had an inalienable right to choose public officials. Article XV established a right to peaceful petition, and article XVI granted aliens the right to equal protection of the law. Article XXIII taught that "the family is the basis of human society and its traditions, for good or ill, permeate the nation." It then declared that marriage shall rest on the "indisputable legal and social equality of both sexes," and on "mutual consent instead of parental coercion, and . . . cooperation instead of male domination."

As far as the structure of the government is concerned, the framework SCAP drafted was remarkably democratic. It provided a single-chamber legislature and declared it to be "the highest organ of state power." There was no enumeration, as in the U.S. Constitution, of the powers of the legislature. The model here was parliamentary. The executive power was vested in a cabinet, its ministers appointed by the prime minister with the "advice and consent of the Diet."

The "whole judicial power" was vested in a "strong and independent judiciary," including a supreme court and inferior courts established by the Diet. In an eccentric echo of battles over the judiciary during Franklin Roosevelt's presidency, justices of the supreme court were to hold office during good behavior, "but not after the attainment of the age of 70 years."[66] Judges were to be subject to electoral review every ten years. If a majority of those voting opposed retention of a given justice, he would be removed. The provision for judicial review was peculiar. In cases involving the bill of rights, the supreme court's judgment was final; in all other cases, it was "subject to review by the Diet," where a two-thirds override could restore a law deemed unconstitutional by the court. Also, the

SCAP draft would have authorized trials (except those involving political offenses or rights guaranteed in the bill of rights) to be conducted privately in cases in which the court unanimously determined publicity to be dangerous to public order or morals. The Diet was given full control over public finances (taxes, appropriations, borrowing, the public budget). Article LXXXII decreed that "all property of the Imperial Household, other than the hereditary estates, shall belong to the nation," that all income from imperial properties be paid into the national treasury, and that allowances and expenses of the imperial household be appropriated by the Diet in the annual budget.

Amendments were to be initiated by the Diet, through a two-thirds vote of all its members, a high threshold, and ratified by a popular referendum, requiring the affirmative vote of a majority of voters. The constitution was to be the "supreme law of the nation," and all officials, including the emperor "upon succeeding to his throne," were "bound to uphold and protect this constitution."

Throughout the ensuing six months, critics would insist that the SCAP draft was sloppily crafted. Considering the haste with which it was put together, that was not surprising. Besides, there would be time and opportunity later to correct such defects. In any case, there it was: a constitutional monarchy, parliamentary, unicameral, unitary (not federal)—a system not modeled on that of the United States, closer in form to Britain's. It did have features in the American tradition: It was a written constitution, and it was explicitly "supreme." Its bill of rights incorporated both traditional liberal and modern social–democratic elements. But the most striking feature was its constitutional monarch: an emperor stripped of political power, firmly confined to ceremonial functions, "deriving his position from the sovereign will of the people." Leading Japan to accept its newly designed monarch was the main challenge that lay ahead.

The Fateful Meeting

There was a meeting on the agenda between Whitney and Foreign Minister Yoshida, scheduled for Wednesday, February 13.[67] The Japanese side thought the purpose would be for them to explain and defend their proposals for constitutional revision. In fact, the actions of that dramatic hour would reset the stage of modern Japanese history.

Whitney awoke that morning with a raging fever. Kades had to help him get dressed. He urged Whitney to postpone the meeting, but the general feared that no one would believe he was truly ill. When the American delegation of four (Whitney, Kades, Rowell, and Hussey) arrived at the official residence of the foreign minister, they were ushered to the sun room and took seats, with their backs to the sun. Across a table strewn with papers presumably related to the Japanese proposals were Yoshida, Matsumoto (primed to present his own work), Shirasu (Yoshida's aide), and an interpreter, Hasegawa Motokichi. According to the American account,[68] Whitney began dramatically, saying with great deliberation that the revisions developed by Matsumoto's commission[69] were "wholly unacceptable to the Supreme Commander." Conscious of the "desperate need of the people of Japan for a liberal and enlightened constitution," the Supreme Commander had ordered the preparation of a draft and "directed that I present it to you as one embodying the principles which in his opinion the situation in Japan demands." With that, he handed one copy to Yoshida, one to Matsumoto, one to Hasegawa, and twelve to Shirasu (presumably for other members of the cabinet), and the Americans moved out into the garden, to give a chance for the Japanese to "understand fully the contents of the document." The American report states that the face of the usually impassive Yoshida registered "shock and concern."[70] The physical manifestation may have been in the eye of the beholder, but Yoshida had ample reason for both emotions ascribed to him.

A half hour passed before the Americans were summoned back in.[71] Matsumoto began by saying that he understood the American draft quite well but asked if there were any explanatory notes. Whitney said no, that the draft was "hardly susceptible to misunderstanding" and that it spoke for itself.[72]

Whitney then explained the "spirit and considerations" that had prompted SCAP to submit this draft to them. He noted the pronouncements of various parties calling for constitutional reform, as well as other evidence that the Japanese people were looking in this direction. It was imperative that this impulse be satisfied. He continued: "As you may or may not know," the Supreme Commander has been "unyielding in his defense of your emperor against increasing pressure from the outside to render him subject to war criminal investigation." He had defended the emperor because it was right and just and would continue to do so to the extent of his ability. "But, gentlemen, the Supreme Commander is not omnipotent." By accepting the provisions of this new constitution, the cabinet would render the emperor "practically unassailable"[73] and "bring much closer the day of your freedom from control by the Allied Powers." It would also provide the Japanese people with the "essential freedoms which the Allied Powers demand in their behalf."

Whitney then brought the matter to the level of political survival. Directing himself to Yoshida, he said that MacArthur was presenting this draft to "your government and party" with the hope that they would present it to the Japanese people. He was not requiring them to do this; he could publish it himself. But the cabinet should weigh their actions carefully.

[MacArthur saw this as the] last opportunity for the conservative group, considered by many to be reactionary, to remain in power. [Political survival could only be accomplished by a] sharp swing to the left, [but if they cooperated,] you can be sure that the Supreme Commander will support your position. . . . I cannot emphasize too strongly that the acceptance of the draft constitution is your only hope of survival, and that the Supreme Commander is determined that the people of Japan shall be free to choose between this constitution and any form of constitution which does not embody these principles.[74]

Whitney, who had been speaking slowly and distinctly so that his words would not need to be translated, asked if what he had been saying was clear. Matsumoto said yes but added that the matter would have to be referred to the full cabinet. Whitney said that was understandable, but this matter would have to be given "preferential treatment over all other business." He repeated that SCAP was "prepared . . . to leave sponsorship of the document to your government," but he would lay it before the people himself, if necessary—and would do so before the upcoming general elections (then scheduled for mid-March, later postponed until April 10).

At this point (according to the American account),[75] Yoshida, speaking for just the second time during the meeting, asked that secrecy be preserved in this matter. Whitney replied that it would be, "for your convenience and protection, not for that of the Supreme Commander." Whitney was not being entirely candid here. Both sides needed secrecy: the Japanese cabinet to maintain the appearance of being the initiators, SCAP to avoid the appearance of violating the Moscow Agreement.

The next move belonged to the Japanese. Would they cooperate or resist? The Americans were confident to the point of smugness on February 13, thoroughly enjoying their surprise at the expense of the mortified Japanese officials. But this project could not succeed without Japanese cooperation and that could not be taken for granted.

7 . . . .

"A Very Serious Matter"

• THE CABINET'S INITIAL REACTIONS

•

Foreign Minister Yoshida's first reaction to the SCAP draft on February 13 was to try to negotiate. He sent his protégé, Shirasu Jirō, to talk to General Whitney. A graduate of Cambridge University with an excellent command of English, Shirasu's smooth and frank manner of speaking is said to have captivated Yoshida. Shirasu spent two days talking to Whitney, attempting to convince him of Matsumoto's progressive views and the similarities of the Japanese and American drafts. Far from being charmed by Shirasu, however, Whitney wrote to him on February 16 that "minor changes in the language used or procedure provided" was acceptable, but SCAP would not compromise on "principle or basic form." Unless the Japanese government accepted SCAP's draft, or otherwise satisfied "the opinion of the world," Whitney warned, "a constitution might be forced upon Japan from the outside" that "might sweep away even those traditions and structures" that the SCAP draft would preserve.[1]

Matsumoto himself then tried in a memorandum on February 18 to convince Whitney that the Japanese people would support his more conservative draft.[2] But Whitney summarily dismissed Matsumoto's argument as "a repetitious defense of his draft" and replied that the cabinet must accept "the principles embodied in the draft which I submitted." Minor "variations" would be permitted to "adapt it to the understanding or requirements of the people." Whitney then issued an ultimatum: "Unless I hear from the Cabinet within 48 hours that the principles of the constitution which I submitted are acceptable to the Cabinet and will be sponsored by it before the people," MacArthur would publish it and make it an issue in the forthcoming general election.[3] Faced with this ultimatum, Shidehara called a cabinet meeting for Tuesday, February 19.

The Cabinet Meets

The ministers gathered in the Prime Minister's office at 10:15 A.M.[4] Matsumoto, looking grim and pale, asked for permission to speak

111

about "a very serious matter," and reported on the meeting with Whitney and his staff the preceding Wednesday, February 13. Whitney, he said, had rejected his earlier draft as "far from acceptable." He had then presented a constitution drafted by the Americans with the comment that "MacArthur stands behind the Japanese Emperor and this draft is the only means to protect the person of the Emperor from those who are opposed to him." Only with this constitution, Whitney had stressed, would Japan be able to rejoin the family of nations. Matsumoto had attempted to persuade Whitney of the danger of trying to plant an American constitution in the foreign soil of Japan. But Whitney, Matsumoto told the cabinet, had rejected his argument. When he later sent Shirasu to Whitney to discuss his original draft, Whitney not only refused to discuss it but issued a 48-hour ultimatum: The cabinet must accept the principles and form of SCAP's draft by Wednesday, February 20, or "we will publish the U.S. draft."

After reading a translation of the first two chapters of SCAP's draft, Prime Minister Shidehara, joined by Home Minister Mitsuchi Chūzō and Justice Minister Iwata Chūzō, stated flatly that "we cannot accept this." Welfare Minister Ashida Hitoshi disagreed, warning of the danger of rejecting it. If the SCAP draft were published, he said, the press in Japan would endorse it, the cabinet would be forced to resign, and other politicians would accept it. The result would be an adverse influence on the coming general election, leading to a conservative defeat at the polls and loss of any role in guiding the revision process.

Iwata and Matsumoto agreed with Ashida. The two documents, they reasoned, were not very different. With more time to explain Matusmoto's draft to the Americans, common ground might be found. But Education Minister Abe suggested a different approach. The Matsumoto draft itself was unofficial, he said. Other ministers had had no chance to express their opinions on it,[5] and the cabinet had never approved it. Abe's comments implied criticism of Matsumoto but also suggested another approach: Ask SCAP to allow more time for further work on a Japanese draft. This appealed to Shidehara. He proposed to take up the matter directly with MacArthur, an effort that might get Whitney's deadline extended and perhaps lifted. The cabinet agreed. Ashida suggested that the prime minister make two arguments to MacArthur: (1) the two drafts were not so different in principle, and thus a compromise could probably be worked out; (2) the Japanese side needed more time to study the SCAP draft and to consult with leaders of other political parties.

Shidehara and MacArthur Talk

Shidehara's meeting with MacArthur on Thursday, February 21, lasted three hours.[6] MacArthur welcomed the prime minister and sought to allay his fears by expressing his sympathetic understanding of Japan's concerns. He took the prime minister into his confidence, sharing with him classified reports from Washington on the FEC, and portraying Japan as highly vulnerable and himself as Japan's protector. He spoke of his own "sincerity" in working "for the good of Japan." He reminded Shidehara of his personal concern "with the safety of the Emperor."

He was aware, he said, that Shidehara had also been doing "his best for the sake of his country."

MacArthur subtly implied that he and Shidehara were on the same team, sharing the same goals. And he distanced himself from the other Allied powers. He told Shidehara that the danger to Japan, and especially to the emperor, did not come from him or from the American government. He pointed an accusing finger at the FEC, which, he confided, had said "very unpleasant" things about Japan, things "beyond the Prime Minister's imagination." The real danger to Japan, therefore, came from the FEC, especially the Soviet Union and Australia. As Shidehara weighed this information, MacArthur increased the pressure by confessing his own personal fear: "I don't know how long I can stay at my present position, and I feel great concern when I consider what might happen [to Japan and the emperor] after I leave." Thus even before the SCAP draft was mentioned, MacArthur had skillfully maneuvered Shidehara to his side, where SCAP and the Shidehara cabinet shared a common objective and faced a common foe.

When the conversation turned to the SCAP draft, Shidehara asked what Whitney had meant when he told Matsumoto that Japan must accept certain fundamental principles in the draft. MacArthur's answer was: a monarchy based on popular sovereignty, and the renunciation of war. He assured Shidehara that these two provisions would guarantee the continuity of Japan's monarchy. "I think," he said, "that the American draft is trying to protect the Emperor." The best way to do that is to base the monarchy on popular sovereignty. An emperor who occupies the throne with "the trust of the people" will be stronger, not weaker.

The second key provision was Japan's renunciation of the sovereign right to wage war. MacArthur warned that Japan must respect the views of foreign countries in this matter. A constitutional provision permitting military forces and armaments would convince other countries that Japan was determined to rearm. The trouble with Matsumoto's draft, he continued, is that it would feed the distrust of Japan that exists in other countries. For this reason, the SCAP draft had removed all provisions concerning Japan's armed forces. It was, he concluded, in Japan's own best national interest to renounce war in her constitution.

The Cabinet under Pressure

The next day, Shidehara told the cabinet that "he came away [from the meeting with MacArthur] with the impression that since Article 1 and the renunciation of war were the main points [in the SCAP draft], there was room left for a thorough study of the rest." He expressed no anguish, much less anger, over MacArthur's insistence that SCAP was acting in Japan's best interest. He did not question MacArthur's account of the FEC threat or his fear that he, the emperor's protector, might be removed at any time, leaving Japan completely vulnerable. The prime minister appears to have developed a remarkable trust of MacArthur and seemed willing to accept his argument that, working together, they could fashion a constitution that would protect Japan and its imperial institution.

Shidehara's report drew an immediate skeptical response from Matsumoto, especially his account of MacArthur's description of "basic forms." A few days earlier, Whitney had told Matsumoto the cabinet must accept "the fundamental principles and basic forms" of the SCAP draft and must do so by February 20. Minor changes could be accepted, but nothing more. To Matsumoto, this did not sound as if there were "room left for a thorough study of the rest" of the SCAP draft. Even if Shidehara was correct in his understanding of what MacArthur meant by "basic forms," Matsumoto said it would be prudent to determine if Whitney agreed. His experience with the abrasive "Whitney group" raised doubts in his mind. Moreover, he believed it "impossible in terms of time" to draft a constitution "in the American style" before the Diet opened its next session. Such a draft, even if put before the Diet, had little chance of passing, he predicted, especially in the House of Peers.

Shidehara invited other ministers to express their views. Education Minister Abe Yoshishige thought the two drafts looked very different, particularly the crucial articles on the emperor and renunciation of war. But—and this was the main point—the cabinet should be flexible and avoid giving SCAP the impression that Matsumoto's draft had been approved by the cabinet. Ashida noted the similarities between SCAP's renunciation of war provision and the Kellogg-Briand Pact (1927) and the League of Nation's Covenant, both of which Japan had signed. As for the time Matsumoto needed to rewrite his draft, Ashida expressed confidence that he could do it, "with his scholarship and experience." Had not Germany's Weimar Constitution (1919) been written in three weeks? Mitsuchi and Shidehara shared the view that there was indeed room for compromise. With their support, even without a formal vote, a consensus had emerged: The cabinet would accept the SCAP draft as the basis of Japan's constitution. Prime Minister Shidehara would report to the emperor that afternoon (Friday, February 22), and Matsumoto and Foreign Minister Yoshida would schedule a meeting at GHQ with Whitney and his staff at 2 P.M. that very day. With this understanding, the cabinet "began dealing with ordinary business matters."[7] In just an hour and a half, the cabinet had heard the prime minister's report on his meeting with MacArthur and decided to accept the SCAP draft constitution.

When the cabinet reached this momentous decision, only the first two chapters of the SCAP draft (on the emperor, and renouncing war) had been translated into Japanese. Not until February 26 was a complete translation distributed in mimeograph form to all ministers.[8] In effect, on February 22, Shidehara and his ministers, without a Japanese translation of the whole document or a thorough discussion of it, accepted the "fundamental principles and basic forms" of SCAP's draft as the basis of their own draft.[9] Whitney's ultimatum and Shidehara's reading of MacArthur's plans were the two key elements in the cabinet's decision.

Another Crucial Meeting

Matsumoto and Yoshida went to inform Whitney of the cabinet's decision. The Japanese account of this meeting contains two significant issues: confusion over terminology and disagreement over provisions involving the emperor's sovereign prerogatives, people's rights, composition of the Diet and amendment procedures. This "principles and forms" terminology, used by Whitney and repeated by MacArthur, was never clearly defined. Based on his talk with MacArthur, Shidehara thought it meant only the status of the emperor and renunciation of war. But Matsumoto learned in his meeting with Whitney on February 22 that much more was involved, though not precisely what. This serious misunderstanding was not finally resolved until March 5.

Matsumoto arrived at the meeting with Whitney fully prepared, as he said in an opening comment, to "accept the basic principles of SCAP's draft" based on Shidehara's report of his meeting with MacArthur.[10] He believed, he told Whitney, that these were "not greatly different from our draft." His goal at this meeting was to learn what was required so that he could write a Japanese draft that would incorporate these two fundamental principles. Whitney's first comment was encouraging, apparently confirming the Japanese understanding. He expressed respect for Matsumoto's experience. "I know," he said, "that you can draft an instrument more in tune with Japanese forms than I or my staff can. As General MacArthur told your Prime Minister yesterday [Thursday], it is the basic principles and structure that we are insistent upon." This seemed to confirm Shidehara's report, but, as Matsumoto was shortly to learn, it was misleading.

What Whitney meant by "basic principles and structure" became clear as the questions became specific. Could he not, Matsumoto asked, retain the current constitution and simple amend existing provisions and add new ones? Whitney responded that the SCAP draft "forms a whole" and "we want it understood that appropriate changes of small points will be permitted." This should have been a strong warning to Matsumoto. Whitney had said the same thing before in a variety of ways: Only appropriate changes of small points would be permitted. His statement that the SCAP draft "forms a whole" was another signal that GS would insist on much more than what the Japanese understood by "principles and forms." But Matsumoto pressed ahead with questions about details: the preamble, amendment procedures, the Diet, elections, renunciation of war, the Imperial House Law, rights and duties of the people, and so forth. Whitney's responses revealed the gap between the two: We can't allow that, that would not be acceptable, we can't approve that. Two-thirds of the way through the American transcript of the meeting, we find this exchange as Matsumoto's exasperation began to show:

> *Matsumoto:* How many of the articles in the new [SCAP draft] Constitution do you consider basic and unalterable? I want to advise the Cabinet what and how many of the Articles are absolutely necessary.
> *Whitney:* We feel that the whole Constitution as written is basic. We accept the fact that . . . our language will be subject to modification . . . to make it better understood. But in general, we regard this document as a unit.
> *Col. Rowell:* The new constitution was written as an interwoven unit . . . so there is no section or chapter that can be cut out.

The meaning of Whitney's and Rowell's comments became increasingly clear as they, and Kades, responded to Matsumoto's specific questions. The preamble, for example, made it clear that, as Whitney put it, the constitution "comes up from the people, not down to the people." This meant, as Matsumoto recognized, locating sovereignty in the people rather than the emperor. In the American draft, the Japanese people declared to the world that they were sovereign and wished to live in peace with the peoples of the world. Living in peace was not an issue, but Matsumoto wanted to avoid this bold declaration of popular sovereignty. Whitney told him it was essential because it set forth "fundamental principles that guided the writing of this Constitution." And, he stressed, "we want to present the Constitution to the World in as direct and favorable a fashion as possible."

In addition to making the people sovereign, the American draft would subject the imperial household to control of a popularly elected Diet. Matsumoto expressed serious concern about this provision, pointing to the autonomy the imperial family had enjoyed under the Meiji Constitution. He wanted that feature continued by giving the royal family control over the Imperial House Law. The Americans quickly rejected this, stressing that the emperor and his family are "under the law, as in England," and that "this is a basic principle" of the American draft.

Renunciation of war was another provision that troubled Matsumoto. Although he did not object to it being in the constitution, he would prefer, he said, to have it inserted in the preamble, as a principle, rather than "be given a chapter of its own." Whitney quickly rejected the proposal. He stressed its importance in the "whole scheme for Japan's rehabilitation" and for Hirohito's protection that MacArthur envisioned in the draft constitution. Whitney expanded on the American reasoning: "General MacArthur feels that this principle will do more to attract the favorable attention of the world than anything else." Its larger purpose was to convince the Allied powers that Japan would never again resort to war against them. The provision, Whitney told Matsumoto, "must be stated boldly in order to serve its full purpose." Whitney confessed that he himself would prefer that it be chapter I of the constitution, but he had settled for chapter II out of respect for the emperor.

Matsumoto turned next to problems of "form and translation" in producing a Japanese draft conforming to the SCAP model. This involved the central question of how much slack SCAP would cut the Japanese cabinet in shaping a document in Japanese. Matsumoto was worried because he, as the minister in charge of constitutional revision, would be expected to prepare a draft in strict legal, literary language. A translation of the SCAP draft into colloquial Japanese, even as used in the popular press, could not achieve the dignity demanded by judicial standards of the time. Whitney and his staff seemed to think Matsomoto was stalling. Not knowing Japanese, they failed to understand Matsumoto's concerns about proper constitutional language. They attempted to resolve the issue, or ignore it, by assuring Matsumoto that they had full confidence in his ability to get the job done. Saying that "we are now agreed as to principles," Whitney summarized in highly optimistic fashion the understanding he thought they had reached: "You [Matsumoto] propose, then, merely to put this new Constitution in proper language and phraseology acceptable to the Japanese people, but without working any essential change in the basic principles set forth?" Whitney offered to send some of his staff to the cabinet meeting to help Matsumoto explain what the Americans expected. Matsumoto declined the offer. There then followed this brief exchange:

> *Kades*: Hasn't our draft been translated already?
>
> *Shirasu*: Yes, but it has not been put into the form in which our constitution could be presented to the people.
>
> *Yoshida*: We will have a cabinet meeting on Tuesday [February 26]. After that meeting we will be able to tell you how many days the work of translation and form will take. We trust that you will preserve perfect secrecy on these discussions.
>
> *Whitney*: Complete secrecy will be maintained, of course. I will report to General MacArthur that you, Dr. Matsumoto, will have this *work of translation* [emphasis added] completed well before the end of the next week.

These remarks make clear that Whitney expected Matsumoto and his team simply to translate the SCAP draft into proper Japanese[11]—and to do it as quickly as possible. Matsumoto's worry about "form and translation" did not concern Whitney and Kades. How the document sounded in Japanese was not important to them, as long as it contained a clear statement of everything the Americans had written. Given their emphasis on secrecy and their strategy of convincing the FEC that this was a Japanese government draft, it seems odd that they would risk exposure by using careless language. The answer was, as Whitney had told Matsumoto earlier in the conversation: "General MacArthur feels that since he is in complete charge of the situation, he can put a document such as this through [the Diet]." To MacArthur and Whitney, time was of the essence. Having the document finished before the FEC could issue orders was more important to the Americans than getting the language right so the Japanese people would regard it as a Japanese draft. But having it properly written would be more convincing to all concerned—the Japanese people as well as the FEC—that it was a genuine Japanese draft. Matsumoto had not yet fully grasped the problem of timing for MacArthur, and MacArthur did not understand the problem of style for Matsumoto. To the Japanese, there were two imperatives: to produce a document that offered some protection to the emperor and his prerogatives *and* to hide its American origins.

Foreign Minister Yoshida asked the Americans, once again, to "preserve perfect secrecy on these discussions." Whitney agreed but seemed willing (or was he bluffing?), if necessary to get his way, to reveal the American authorship to the Japanese public. Whitney's insistence on translation was self-defeating. Translation was relatively easy, as the Foreign Ministry had shown when rendering the American draft into colloquial Japanese. But neither the style nor the substance could pass muster as the work of the cabinet's legal scholars. No translation was

likely to convince the Japanese people, the press, and the FEC that the document had been drafted in Japanese and translated into English, rather than the
reverse. That is what Matsumoto knew and was telling Whitney. This divergence
of positions would produce an explosive clash between the two sides in early
March.

The Cabinet Meets Again

The Japanese cabinet, meeting on February 26 to hear Matsumoto's report on
his talk with Whitney, made two important decisions about constitutional reform. First, with little debate and less time to study Japanese translations of the
American document, the cabinet agreed to accept SCAP's February 13 draft as
the model on which to base a new constitution for Japan. Having been assured
by MacArthur and Whitney that the Americans required only that the basic
principles and forms of that draft, not the precise wording, need be incorporated
into a Japanese version, most of the ministers expressed support for the decision.
However, Minister Matsumoto, the man in charge of the reform issue since the
Shidehara cabinet was formed in October of the previous year, did not.[12]

The cabinet's second decision put Matsumoto in charge, again, of preparing
the Japanese cabinet's draft to be presented to General Whitney and his staff.
Matsumoto himself tried to decline the dubious honor, pleading a lack of ability
and time.[13] But, as Whitney and his staff had done a few days earlier, the cabinet
expressed confidence in his ability to carry out the task. In retrospect, it might
have been wise to give the assignment to someone else, perhaps Foreign Minister
Yoshida or Minister of Welfare Ashida. Neither of them, however, was a legal
expert, and giving the task to another minister would have required a reshuffling
of the cabinet. Besides, Matsumoto, despite his volatile personality, enjoyed the
trust and respect of both Shidehara and Yoshida. He was a leading legal mind,
even if in the field of commercial law; by March 1946, with two draft constitutions bearing his name, it was easy to regard him as a specialist in constitutional
law as well. Shidehara and Yoshida largely ignored evidence of growing tension
between Matsumoto and the Americans in GS, a fact that did not augur well for
future relations.

Time was of the essence. Following the cabinet's February 26 decision, Matsumoto and his assistants set to work immediately. Their goal was to have a
draft ready by March 11, only thirteen days later. To preserve absolute secrecy,
only Matsumoto, Irie Toshio, and Satō Tatsuo could be involved in the drafting.
Other members of the Legislation Bureau remained unaware of the SCAP draft;
the ministers who knew were unwilling to risk a leak by involving others. The
task of preparing a draft in less than two weeks was next to impossible for three
men: getting the Japanese language right, making copies, rendering their draft
into English for the Americans. Their failure was virtually guaranteed when
Whitney repeatedly pressed them to hurry and finally ordered that the draft be
submitted to GS by 10 A.M. on Monday, March 4, "even without the English
translation."[14]

Why the Rush?

Here we encounter a crucial question. Why the rush to complete a draft constitution that would be identified publicly as the work of the Japanese cabinet? Some critics have assumed that SCAP was simply angry with Japanese delay, or that SCAP's staff, as conquerors, was acting arbitrarily. The explanation is more complicated. The Japanese government, for its part, thought MacArthur was motivated by a desire to protect the emperor from anti-Hirohito forces in the world. This was true, as we have seen. And the SCAP draft, retaining the reigning emperor on the throne was evidence of that. The cabinet and the emperor himself blamed a news story by Associated Press correspondent Russell Brines, quoting "a high personage of the Court," that many members of the imperial family favored the emperor's abdication.[15] This palace cabal could undo MacArthur's strenuous efforts to save the emperor from trial. The news story, they reasoned, had triggered MacArthur's sudden order to "announce a democratic Constitution . . . to be submitted to him without delay."[16] It was in the Japanese government's interest to comply.

MacArthur's concern, however, was not only to save the emperor but to defend his own authority as supreme commander against the Moscow Agreement. His goal was to have a draft constitution ready before the commission began its meetings in Washington, one he could pass off as the work of the Japanese government. The commission scheduled its first meeting on February 26. As the date approached, SCAP increased the pressure on the Japanese quickly to convert the American draft into a Japanese document. MacArthur was playing a complicated game. Having a draft constitution "initiated by the Japanese" through a revision process that predated the Moscow Agreement might block the FEC from assuming direction of constitutional reform.

MacArthur could have told the FEAC delegates on January 30 in Tokyo that a Japanese draft, in the works since the fall of 1945, would soon be forthcoming. This might have preempted the FEC from asserting control over the revision process. But he did not do that. On the contrary, he said that constitutional reform had been "taken out of my hands by the Moscow Agreement."[17] A few days later, advised by Whitney[18] that indeed he did have authority over constitutional reform until the FEC convened, MacArthur ordered GS to write a model constitution in a week and present it to the Japanese cabinet. The die was cast. He had either openly to defy the new international commission or to order the Japanese cabinet to join SCAP's conspiracy and conceal the true authorship of the new draft constitution. He chose the latter course.

The March 2 Japanese Draft

The Japanese draft was the product of the same officials—Matsumoto, Irie, and Satō—who had prepared the Matsumoto committee's draft which SCAP rejected in early February. This time, however, they worked under very different conditions: They faced a SCAP-imposed deadline only days away; they had the SCAP draft, accepted by the Shidehara cabinet on February 26, as their guide to contents; and they had the Foreign Ministry's translation of the SCAP draft to help them understand the contents. Cabinet discussions on February 22 and 26 had provided little guidance beyond the need to protect the emperor and preserve the imperial institution.

When work on the draft began on February 27, Matsumoto and his aides expected to finish it by March 11, but Whitney's newly imposed March 4 deadline allowed only four days for writing the draft. The task was formidable: to incorporate the "fundamental principles and basic forms" of the SCAP draft into a document written in formal literary Japanese (*bungotai*) customarily used in laws. They never considered it their task simply to adopt the words, phrases, and articles of the Foreign Ministry's translation and rewrite them in the vocabulary, grammar, and style of suitable constitutional language.

Working in complete secrecy in a radio recording studio of the prime minister's official residence, Irie and Satō assisted Matsumoto in preparing the Japanese draft. Satō later described the assignment: "Because we were required to maintain the strictest secrecy, we could neither discuss the matter with our colleagues in the Legislation Bureau nor borrow the reference works we needed. Working under a strict deadline . . . we did our best to write out our own draft quickly."[19] Matsumoto, using the Foreign Ministry's translation of the SCAP draft, wrote preliminary chapters on the emperor, renunciation of war, the Diet, and the cabinet. In the chapter on the Diet, Matsumoto ignored SCAP's preference for a unicameral legislature and provided for a national legislature with lower and upper houses. Satō drafted chapter III on the people's rights and obligations. Irie and Satō together then produced a second draft, including chapters on the Diet and the cabinet. The three met twice during this time to discuss their work.[20]

Matsumoto provided a long "note explaining the first Japanese draft," an explanation and justification of the Japanese draft for Whitney and his staff in GS.[21] But because he provided no English translation, it is unlikely that Whitney, Kades or others in GS saw the document before the marathon conference of March 4–5 that produced a new Japanese draft much closer to SCAP's original. Yet Matsumoto's explanatory note is important as a reflection of his understanding of the task with which he had been charged. Specifically, the note explains why the Japanese draft had departed in significant ways from SCAP's draft. He wrote: "This provisional draft has been prepared with the utmost concern in carefully observing the fundamental principles of SCAP's draft and, to the maximum extent possible, in following faithfully the basic forms."[22] It is clear that Matsumoto had not attempted either to make a literal translation of SCAP's draft or to rewrite in formal constitutional language the Foreign Ministry's translation of that draft.

The Americans' expectations were quite different, as we have seen. Kades reiterated this point in a 1973 interview:

> *Interviewer*: Were you expecting that the Japanese would present a literal translation of your GS draft, or did you think they were doing a draft of their own?

Kades: No, I expected a translation of our draft—that would translate back into our draft, which theirs didn't. I didn't think that at that time they would just be adhering to basic principles.[23]

On March 2 (Saturday), without time to make an English translation due to Whitney's strict deadline, the Japanese hastily put their draft in order and produced thirty mimeograph copies for submission to GS.

Summary of Japanese March 2 Draft

A comparison of the American and Japanese drafts reveals significant differences in the position of the emperor in articles 1 and 2:

SCAP DRAFT

Article 1: The Emperor shall be the symbol of the State and of the Unity of the People, deriving his position from the sovereign will of the People, and from no other source.

Article 2: Succession to the Imperial Throne shall be dynastic and in accordance with such Imperial House Law as the Diet may enact.

JAPANESE DRAFT

Article 1: The Emperor derives his position from the supreme will of the Japanese People, maintaining his position as a symbol of the State and as an emblem of the Unity of the People.

Article 2: The Imperial Throne shall be dynastic and succeeded to in accordance with the Imperial House Law.

In article 1, while the Americans clearly spoke of "the sovereign will of the People," the Japanese avoided the word "sovereign" and described the will of the people as "supreme." When Prime Minister Shidehara examined the draft, he substituted the word "supreme" (*shikō*), as in the "supreme will of the people," for SCAP's "sovereign will of the Japanese People."[24] This was his way of avoiding the unpalatable truth of MacArthur's decree: Sovereignty in Japan must shift from the emperor to the Japanese people. This discrepancy in language would remain until the Americans finally noticed it four months later, in July 1946, and ordered it changed.

In article 2, SCAP made succession to the throne, and other important matters concerning the composition and continuity of the imperial family, subject to a law enacted by the people's representatives in the Diet. The Japanese draft, on the other hand, provided for succession according to the Imperial House Law,[25] without giving the popularly elected Diet a role in the matter.

Chapter III of the two drafts revealed sharp differences between American and Japanese concepts of how to establish constitutional protection for all forms of expression. The American draft said, in article 20, "Freedom of assembly, speech and press and all other forms of expression are guaranteed." This broad, un-qualified language accorded well with American constitutional practice. But article XXIX of the Meiji Constitution allowed freedom of expression only "within limits not prejudicial to peace and order" or "within the limits of the law." The Japanese draft of March 2 rewrote SCAP's unqualified guarantee as "All of the people shall have the freedom of speech, writing, press, assembly and association to the extent that they do not conflict with the public peace and order." Moreover, the Japanese draft omitted some of the human rights articles in SCAP's draft, including those on the rights of women, state ownership of land, public health, and social security.

We have already noted Matsumoto's strong objection to a unicameral legislature in the American draft. Article 45 of the Japanese draft provided for two houses, a House of Representatives and a House of Councillors. An upper house was needed, Matsumoto explained, to restrain "an unjust and oppressive majority and . . . to check temporary excesses" of a majority party in the House of Representative.[26] Matsumoto believed that "a flaw of the Japanese national character" made the people easily swayed and inclined to extremes. If unrestrained, this would lead to political instability. He proposed that the upper house "reflect the people's will in the healthiest way" by gathering educated representatives of all the people in regional professional bodies. It would be very different from the existing House of Peers in which members of the imperial family and hereditary nobles constituted the principal elements. Earlier Matsumoto drafts A and B had also provided for a House of Councillors to replace the House of Peers. He envisaged a system that would altogether exclude the imperial family and peers from hereditary seats in the upper house of the national Diet. Some members of the upper house would be elected from "the various districts or professions" and others would be appointed by the cabinet.

The March 2 draft gave the emperor the authority to initiate amendments to the imperial house law on the advice of the cabinet.[27] The SCAP draft deprived the emperor of autonomy in matters concerning the imperial family, making no distinction between the imperial house law and other laws.

Matsumoto omitted SCAP's statement of popular sovereignty and the plan to have constitutional amendments initiated by the Diet rather than, as in the Meiji Constitution, "submitted to the Imperial Diet by Imperial Order." For the same reason, he omitted SCAP's preamble entirely. As a declaration of the Japanese people, he said, it was in conflict with article LXXIII of the Meiji Constitution, which gave the emperor the sole right to initiate constitutional amendments.[28] While embracing the commendable intention of SCAP's preamble, Matsumoto suggested that the same objective could be achieved through an imperial rescript or a Diet resolution to be issued when the new constitution was adopted.

In making his draft, Matsumoto had also changed the order of some articles in the SCAP model, eliminating what he called "relatively unimportant" articles, while adding and rewriting others. For example, he told Satō to "omit the provision about [nationalizing] land and other natural resources, and to reduce as much as possible the numerous provisions on criminal litigation."[29] Satō shared Matsumoto's concern with what he deemed SCAP's poor drafting and the "unnatural, confused and disorderly" way the articles in chapter III were written.[30]

Matsumoto concluded in his accompanying note that "these insignificant changes have no connection with the fundamental forms of the SCAP draft."[31] In other words, he clung to the view that SCAP's directive to incorporate certain "fundamental principles and basic forms" afforded him wide latitude in writing a Japanese draft constitution.

8 . . . .

"Do Your Best"

• THE MARATHON MEETING

•

• The divergence between Japanese goals and American expectations created sharp conflict between the two sides during the marathon meeting of March 4–5. Matsumoto's leading role in reforming the constitution, which had continued since October 1945, ended abruptly. His assistant, Satō Tatsuo, won some concessions as he and the Americans struggled through a 30-hour meeting to produce a draft that MacArthur and Shidehara would announce to the world on March 6 as the Japanese government's draft constitution. In the process, Whitney and his GS staff placed their indelible mark on Japan's basic law.

At 10 A.M. on Monday March 4, Matsumoto and Satō entered the GS offices on the sixth floor of the Daiichi Building. One of the few buildings in central Tokyo that escaped the American fire bombings, the Daiichi was MacArthur's headquarters, and the sixth floor was the heart of SCAP's operations. MacArthur, his chief of staff, his adjutant, and GS all had offices here. Awaiting Matsumoto's and Satō's arrival were Shirasu Jirō of the CLO and two Foreign Ministry officials, Obata Kaoru and Hasegawa Motokichi, who were to help with interpreting and translating.[1]

Responding to Whitney's demands, Matsumoto had rushed his draft to GS before there was time to submit it to the cabinet or to translate it into English. Satō, it turned out, would bear much of the burden of negotiating during the long conference that was now commencing, and his presence was fortuitous. He had not known in advance that he would have to go with Matsumoto that day. Satō met Matsumoto by chance in the Legislation Bureau that morning as the minister was preparing to depart for his meeting with Whitney. "Suddenly," Satō recalled, "he said he wanted me to go along with him. . . . There was no way I could refuse."[2] Satō was filled with apprehension about meeting the American military occupiers. Although a ranking bureaucrat in the cabinet's Legislation Bureau who had worked on constitutional reform since October 1945, he had never set foot in MacArthur's headquarters. He recalled years later: "Rain was threatening that day. I was wearing rubber boots covered with mud and a badly worn Western-style suit, dressed exactly like a citizen of a defeated country."³ Despite his appearance, he was enormously capable and had a turn of mind and character that suited him well for this historic task.

Matsumoto presented copies of the Japanese draft and an explanatory note to Whitney, cautioning that it "was not a final draft since it had not been approved by the Cabinet." Whitney handed the Japanese draft to Kades, his second in command, who summoned two GS translators to another room to join Obata and Hasegawa in rendering it into English. Satō cautioned Obata and Hasegawa when possible to employ the words of the SCAP draft in doing their translating. Kades then took Satō to a room marked "Translators Pool" to help two young Japanese–American soldiers who were struggling to translate the long Matsumoto explanatory note written in difficult literary Japanese (*bungotai*). Consulting dictionaries, and with Satō's help, they translated Matsumoto's comments on the draft.⁴

Kades Confronts Matsumoto

As work on the draft proceeded, Kades noticed differences between the Japanese draft and SCAP's own draft. The Japanese had omitted SCAP's preamble. Kades said sharply to Satō: "You can't omit the preamble. Add a preamble that is precisely the same as the one in the MacArthur draft."⁵ Satō attached the foreign ministry's translation of the SCAP preamble. Reading further, Kades noticed in chapter I differences between the SCAP and Japanese drafts. SCAP's version said the emperor derived his position "from the sovereign will of the people and *from no other source*," and that succession to the throne would be determined by "such Imperial House Law *as the Diet may enact*." The Japanese had omitted the italicized words from their draft. Kades demanded to know why.⁶ They involved the principle of popular sovereignty and the imperial family's subordination to the national assembly. Angered by the omissions, Kades ordered the translators to stop their work until he could get an explanation from Matsumoto.

Matsumoto defended his wording as more succinct, coherent, and suitable for the articles of the Japanese constitution than those in the SCAP draft. The Japanese draft did clearly state that the emperor "derived his position from the *sovereign* will of the people." Adding "and from no other source" was redundant, Matsumoto said. But the provision exempting the Imperial House Law from Diet control weakened his argument and aroused Kades's suspicions. It did no good to urge Kades, as Matsumoto did, to read his note explaining changes made in the Japanese draft.

To pursue the matter further, Kades took Matsumoto into another room with Shirasu as interpreter. Kades pointed to other discrepancies. Why, he asked, had Matsumoto in article 3 used the word *hohitsu* (advice) of the cabinet instead of saying, as the American draft had, that an act by the emperor required "advice and consent" of the cabinet? Following the recommendation of his American translators, Kades wanted the word *kyōsan* (consent) used in this context. Matsumoto objected. He said the word *kyōsan* was used "only in relation to the Diet," as in "consent of the Diet." It sounded strange to Japanese ears when used about the cabinet. But Kades refused to accept that explanation, noting that *hohitsu* (advice) alone was significantly different from "advice and consent." The disagreement continued about other words and phrases and soon escalated into an ugly confrontation. Matsumoto recalled: "[Kades] was extremely upset. His hands were trembling so hard that they shook the table. I was upset too. I couldn't wait for Shirasu to translate what Kades was saying. I began to reply directly in my broken English. I asked him, 'Have you come to Japan to correct our Japanese?' I was so mad that I said something like that. He too was very angry . . . and we couldn't get anything done."[7]

Underlying the clash between the two were differing assumptions about Matsumoto's task. Kades assumed the Japanese draft would be a translation of the SCAP draft.[8] Matsumoto, on the other hand, had prepared a draft that, in his view, followed instructions from MacArthur and Whitney that allowed the Japanese side freedom in drafting as long as they incorporated the "fundamental principles and basic forms" of the SCAP draft. More broadly, age, status, and cultural differences between Kades and Matsumoto sharpened their disagreement over constitutional and legal traditions. The 68-year-old Matsumoto was especially incensed that this young, mid-level American officer, who knew no Japanese and little about Japan's legal tradition, would presume to "come to Japan to correct our Japanese."[9]

A lunch break separated the two combatants and allowed tempers to cool. Matsumoto, fearing that his clash with Kades might escalate to the point of exchanging blows, decided it would be best for him to leave.[10] After telling the Americans and Satō that he must attend an important cabinet meeting, he departed at 2:30 P.M. Incensed and determined to finish the job without further interruption, Kades ordered the door of the conference room locked.

The Drafting Session

Translation of the Japanese draft was completed at 6 P.M. The GS staff left the conference room and gathered in General Whitney's office to examine it.[11] Two hours later Kades returned and announced that "a final draft would have to be completed during the night, and the Japanese officials present were required to participate."[12] An article-by-article comparison of the Matsumoto and SCAP drafts began about 9:00 P.M.

Satō, faced with the prospect of confronting the GS staff aided only by interpreters, scrambled to round up support from his colleagues. He telephoned Matsumoto at the Legislation Bureau, then at the minister's home, but failed to reach him. No other senior member of the Legislation Bureau volunteered to join Satō at GS. The cabinet secretariat, responding to his plea for help, dispatched Kiuchi Shirō to break the bad news to Satō: Minister Matsumoto had arrived home feeling ill, suffering from high blood pressure, and would not be returning to MacArthur's headquarters. He sent word to "do your best." Kiuchi then parted with "warm words of support," while Iwakura remained to serve as a courier between Satō and the cabinet during the drafting session that followed.[13]

Satō was thus abandoned and alone, a virtual prisoner. Kades said that an acceptable draft must be completed before he could leave. The sad truth was that no cabinet minister, not even his immediate superior in the Legislation Bureau, Irie Toshio, would come to MacArthur's occupation headquarters, sit beside him facing the Americans, and defend the Japanese draft constitution.[14]

Kades and Hussey returned to the conference room from their meeting with Whitney and directed the proceedings during the next 19 hours. Other Americans—Hays, Roest, Rizzo, Swope, Nelson—joined the group as the focus moved from one chapter to another.[15] Kades passed out a few typed copies of the English translation of the Matsumoto draft, but Satō never received one and had to share the copy that Hasegawa and Obata were using. Nor were reference works available to him.[16]

None of the American military officers spoke Japanese. Rizzo, who could read some Japanese, sat at the table with his Japanese-English dictionaries checking words and Japanese characters to determine their dictionary meaning. Satō was the only Japanese constitutional expert in the room. His English was limited. A young civilian woman on the GS staff, Beate Sirota, helped as his interpreter. Hasegawa and Obata, the Foreign Ministry translators, wrote out and put the various articles in proper order as agreement on wording was reached. G.I. coffee arrived in five-gallon gasoline cans. For Satō, the only pleasure of the grueling session was the ample supply of sugar and cream for the coffee—rare items among the Japanese at the time. Kades ordered a guard stationed at the door to prevent anyone from leaving without his permission. He described the scene: "[I]t was a little bit like a school-room, because I told the people there that anyone who wanted to use the facilities should not hesitate to raise their [sic] hand. Then we'd unlock the door and have somebody accompany them. . . . We didn't want any communication with anybody else. We wanted to get it finished."[17]

The long, difficult negotiations began with a single step that Kades had demanded when he first saw the Matsumoto draft: SCAP's preamble, written by Hussey and omitted from Matsumoto's draft, was restored verbatim.

The chapter on the emperor next came under close American scrutiny. Kades was already alert to Matsumoto's wording in the chapter on the emperor, which violated SCAP's draft. In the morning, after seeing a translation of the first chapter, on the emperor, he had ordered the Japanese to restore SCAP's precise words on the location of sovereignty and the constitutional functions of the emperor. A literal translation of the first article read: "The Emperor shall hold the position of symbol of the state and symbol of the unity of the Japanese people, based on the supreme will of the people." Kades rejected the words "shall hold the position," and Satō's substitute "shall have that position," and insisted that the emperor "shall be" that symbol.[18]

In article 2, the Americans gave the Diet authority to enact the imperial house law and a bill on succession to the throne. Matsumoto's draft said nothing about the Diet role in this. The Americans demanded that Satō restore their wording, as it was a law and the Diet enacted all laws. Satō argued that it was a special law, one relating only to the emperor and his family, and it should be enacted only on the emperor's own initiative. Kades insisted that the SCAP draft was "absolute" with respect to the emperor, and the imperial house law must be "passed by the Diet." The original wording was restored.[19]

The Americans now reminded Satō of their earlier objections—voiced initially to Matsumoto—to article 3, which changed SCAP's "advice and consent" of the cabinet for the emperor to act in state matters to "advice" only. The Japanese wished to avoid subjecting the emperor to cabinet control and requiring his ministers' authorization for his acts. Kades said another word meaning "consent" must be added to ensure that the cabinet authorized such acts and that the emperor could not act independently in matters of state. Like Matsumoto, Satō argued that the one word *hohitsu* was sufficient, because it had the meaning of consent as well as advice. But GS was skeptical and insisted on restoring SCAP's original wording.[20]

Through these changes of words and phrases, the Americans showed their determination to deprive the emperor of any independent constitutional authority, power, or function and to make him a "symbol" and nothing more. The Japanese resisted, trying to preserve some semblance of the emperor's dignity and authority found in the Meiji Constitution since 1889. The unequal struggle played out in the discussion of all articles of chapter I, concerning his appointing the prime minister (as designated by the Diet), performing such "functions of state" as convoking the Diet, promulgating laws and treaties passed by that body, or other ceremonial duties—always "as provided by law."

Chapter II (article 9), "Renunciation of War," was the most radical and controversial change in Japan's 1946 constitution. The Matsumoto draft, however, made no attempt to challenge or change it. On the contrary, Matsumoto tried to improve the writing of the article by (1) merging the two sentences of the first paragraph of SCAP's draft, and (2) refining the language of the second paragraph in which Japan gave up "war potential" and the nation's right of "belligerency." Whitney noted the changes in his discussion with GS staff and commented that this was "not quite our version." He called it "incomplete" because it "does not contain definite prohibition of maintenance of forces." It needed "some more clarification."[21]

In the joint session, the Americans made minor changes of wording and punctuation in the first paragraph. Following Whitney's instructions, they changed the second paragraph of Matsumoto's draft, which read: "The maintenance of land, sea, and air forces, as well as other war potential, and the right of belligerency of the state will *not be recognized*." GS judged the phrase "will not be recognized" too weak and ordered the paragraph changed to: "The maintenance of land, sea and air forces, as well as other war potential, *will never be authorized* and the right of belligerency of the state will not be recognized."[22]

The Vexing Issues of Rights

Chapter III (articles 10–38) set forth the "Rights and Duties of the People." This sprawling chapter (six pages and thirty articles, more than a third of the total) represented the most radical ideas on individual liberty found in twentieth-century constitutions outside Scandinavia. In writing it, the Americans had borrowed freely from the constitutions of the Soviet Union and Weimar Germany. Satō was largely responsible for this chapter in the Japanese draft, and he followed Matsumoto's order to cut back the "disorderly, confused and unnatural" articles of the SCAP version.[23] Especially rankling to the Japanese was Whitney's rhapsodic rhetoric regarding the "age-old struggle of man to be free," MacArthur's and Roest's provocative statements that the "feudal system of Japan shall cease" (article 12),[24] and that "enslavement, serfdom and bondage shall be prohibited" (article 17).

In any case, to Japanese legal specialists, protecting human rights was not the principal purpose for drafting a constitution. Democracy could best be achieved through laws passed by a popularly elected House of Representatives. SCAP's draft recognized certain basic freedoms as inalienable constitutional rights. Matsumoto's draft, by contrast, regarded basic freedoms as existing "within the limits of the law" and "not prejudicial to peace and order," as the Meiji Constitution had said. Matsumoto and Satō viewed chapter III of SCAP's draft as the work of misguided foreign amateurs trying to fashion a new legal tradition in Japan. Matsumoto had warned against efforts to plant a foreign legal system in the soil of a nation with different customs, traditions and history.[25] Consequently, his draft omitted Roest's statements and rewrote most of the articles of this chapter.

For example, article 10 of the Japanese draft reduced Whitney's words about "the age-old struggle" to a simple statement that "fundamental human rights . . . shall be conferred upon the people of this and future generations as eternal and inviolate rights." At the meeting in Whitney's office, the Americans enclosed these words in parentheses and wrote in the margin: "USE ORIGINAL ARTICLE X [from the SCAP draft]." The Japanese draft had also omitted Roest's declaration at the beginning of article 12, on respect for individual rights, that "the feudal system of Japan shall cease." At Whitney's meeting, Roest and John Maki favored restoring Roest's words "to mark dramatically the end of the old."[26] Hussey however was opposed, and Kades sided with Hussey, saying that the words "feudal system" were meaningless in a context in which the constitution provides a modern legal system to protect people as individuals.[27] In the joint session, when Satō was asked why he had omitted Roest's controversial declaration, he replied that nothing corresponding to a feudal system existed in Japan. The Japanese people would think such a statement, in the constitution, very strange indeed. What, he asked, did the GS drafters have in mind? The only example of "feudalism" they could identify was the tenantry system of the Japanese countryside.[28]

SCAP's article 13 said that "all natural persons are equal before the law";

banned discrimination based on race, creed, sex, social status, or *national* origin; and abolished Japan's system of European-style nobility dating from the 1880s. In the Japanese draft, Satō omitted paragraphs abolishing the nobility but sought to achieve the same effect by banning discrimination because of *family* origin. Hussey and Kades demanded the restoration of wording that would deprive the nobility of any "national or civic power of government" and abolish the peerage at the end of the current generation.[29]

For Satō, peerage and feudalism were not the main concerns. He was troubled that SCAP, in providing for individual equality, was insisting that foreigners be given the same protection under the law as Japanese citizens. This could mean that foreigners would enjoy, for example, the right to vote in Japanese elections. He had therefore changed SCAP's statement that "all natural persons are equal before the law" to "all of the people [*kokumin*] are equal under the law," where *kokumin* meant, specifically, the Japanese people or Japanese nationals. The Americans ordered him to replace *kokumin* with "all natural persons," which included foreigners as well as Japanese. In article 16, SCAP had added another layer of protection for foreigners by saying, "aliens shall be entitled to the equal protection of the law." Why, asked Satō, was this needed if article 13 contained the inclusive phrase "all natural persons?" The Americans finally agreed that it was redundant and allowed it to be dropped.[30]

At this point, the Americans, frustrated by having to consider each article of Matsumoto's chapter III, announced that negotiations would henceforth follow the SCAP draft.[31] Satō accepted SCAP's article 14 (right of the people to choose and dismiss public officials through inviolate secret elections) and article 15 (right of peaceful petition) much as written, with little debate.[32]

SCAP's article 17 again revealed American ignorance of Japanese society. It prohibited "enslavement, serfdom and bondage of any kind" and "involuntary servitude, except as a punishment." Matsumoto and Satō had omitted this article entirely. When the Americans reviewed the Japanese draft with Whitney, Roest insisted that "some form of bondage" must exist in Japan. He agreed to drop the reference to enslavement and serfdom, but stuck to his guns on bondage, demanding that "our text be restored."[33] In the joint session, Satō strongly denied that slavery, serfdom, or bondage existed in Japan, or had existed for a long time. Compromise was reached on an article retaining Roest's favorite words: "No person shall be held in bondage. Involuntary servitude, except as punishment for crime, is prohibited."

Both sides agreed on freedom of thought and conscience (article 18) and freedom of assembly, speech, and press and other forms of expression (article 20). But SCAP also prohibited censorship in Article 20.[34] Although Satō included this in the Matsumoto draft, he added "except in cases specifically provided for by law." In the joint session, he referred to the Weimar Constitution, which allowed censorship of movies, photographs, and books harmful to public morals, to make the case for allowing censorship of such things as "obscene pictures." Kades rejected the argument and ordered him to "restore our Article XX as written."[35] There were no basic differences in articles on freedom of association and choice of abode, emigration and change of nationality, choice of occupation, academic freedom, and the right to a free elementary education.

Article 24, on the family, marriage, property rights, and inheritance, proved to be the most contentious of the long negotiating session. In February, the SCAP drafters mounted a broad attack on Japanese marriage and family customs and decreed "the indisputable legal and social equality of both sexes." All matters relating to marriage and the family were to be based on the principles of individual dignity and equality of the sexes. Sirota's draft denouncing the evils of the Japanese family, marriage, parental coercion, and male domination and demanding equality of the sexes revealed a feminist's attempt to impose her ideas on Japanese society.

In their draft, Matsumoto and Satō omitted such SCAP wording as "marriage shall rest upon the . . . social equality of both sexes," "cooperation instead of male domination," and "the essential equality of the sexes." Rather, they endorsed in less sweeping language the notion of marriage based on mutual consent of both sexes, mutual cooperation, and "with equal rights of husband and wife as a basis." Even this was a major concession, for they believed that marriage and other family matters, such as the legal status of women, should be treated in the family chapter of the civil code, not in the constitution.

As the Americans and Japanese debated this issue on March 5, Satō persuaded the Americans to drop the first sentence of SCAP's article 24 ("The family is the basis of human society and its traditions for good or evil permeate the nation") as an assertion unsuitable for a nation's constitution, to tighten the language and eliminate repetition,[36] and to accept all his language in the second sentence as an improvement on Sirota's.[37] Satō also proposed simplifying the broad statement that laws "shall be designed" to promote and extend social welfare through free public education, protection of children, public health, social security, and working conditions. This proposal produced agreement on four separate articles: guaranteeing rights of equal education, free elementary education for children, the right to work and working standards, wages and hours fixed by law, and the right of workers to organize and act collectively.[38] The two sides quickly reached agreement on the status and rights of private property (article 27) and the right of the state to take that property with compensation (article 29).[39] Satō's legal drafting skills again brought clarification to both articles.

They now confronted the "red article" (article 38 in the SCAP draft), which said, "The ultimate fee to the land and to all natural resources reposes in the state as the collective representative of the people." Matsumoto, appalled at what he considered evidence of communist influence in GS, had with trepidation dropped the article from his March 2 draft.[40] But it remained in the SCAP draft on March 5, and Satō had to confront its author, Kades. His argument was that the average Japanese citizen would not understand the concept of the state being the ultimate owner of all land and natural resources. In terms of the constitution's appeal to the average citizen, it would be better to eliminate the whole article. "When I said this," Satō recalled, "the Americans simply agreed."[41] Kades made no attempt to defend the notion that the state is the ultimate owner of the nation's land and natural resources. Nor did any other member of the GS staff support their leader's article.[42]

Agreement was not so easily reached on basic rights of citizens and judicial powers of the state. A long section of the SCAP draft (the latter half of chapter III) offered protection against arbitrary arrest, detention, torture, seizure of property, trial without counsel, double jeopardy, and so forth. Comparable articles in the Japanese draft of March 4 qualified all such rights and protections with the phrase "except as provided for by law." This was anathema to the Americans. As it was debated in the presence of Whitney, Ellerman recorded a dramatic reaction: "Restore our 32 to cover [their] 25 and 26, restore our 34, restore our 35," and so forth, through eleven articles of the Japanese draft. In an angry outburst, Hussey complained: "[B]etter to merely give [the Japanese] our Bill of Rights again and say use this. [The] Japanese have casually violated our draft, chopped up articles, spoiled our logic."[43] Later in the joint session, Hussey quickly squelched Satō's efforts to salvage some of his work by refining the language in several of these articles. In the end, no other section of this chapter adhered so faithfully to the language of the original SCAP draft.

Determining the Diet

Chapter IV of the draft contained provisions for Japan's national assembly, the Diet. SCAP's draft provided for only one chamber, a House of Representatives elected directly by the voters. Matsumoto had included a House of Representatives and a second chamber, a House of Councillors, some of whose members would be elected for six years, representatives of professions, and cabinet appointees recommended by a joint Diet committee. This provision had already provoked a heated debate when Whitney and his staff met in his office to go over the Japanese draft.[44] Andrew Grajdanzev and Roest expressed opposition to allowing a second house. They seemed to think that a second chamber must, like the U.S. Senate, represent states, or former feudal classes of society, as the House of Lords did in Britain. Whitney argued that a bicameral legislature was "not opposed to democracy" and if the Japanese "wanted to have two houses," he had no objection.[45] Swope, a former legislator himself, agreed that an upper house, which he called "the senate," would be acceptable. He pointed out, however, that either they accepted the principle of two houses "or the whole chapter [of the Japanese draft, which provided for two houses] is out." If their decision was to allow a bicameral system, he continued, the "upper house as provided by the J[apanese] is unacceptable." To satisfy SCAP's understanding of democracy, its members—all members—would have to be elected directly by the voters. Roest, citing SWNCC 228, agreed that an upper house must be fully representative of the electorate and could find no justification for members representing trades or professions.[46]

Whitney's troops proceeded to examine the Japanese draft, tightening the language on the number of members in each house, qualifications of candidates, terms of office, annual salary, and so forth. They decided that the House of

Representatives would "act as the Diet until the House of Councillors shall be constituted." They also decreed that the legislative powers of the House of Representatives would be superior to those of the House of Councillors, ensuring that the latter could not "stifle bills by just not acting on them."[47]

In the session with the Japanese, the Americans added their articles on the upper house, setting forth the organization of the two houses, the number of members in each, term limits, elections, and qualifications and defined the Diet (article 40) as the "highest organ of state" and "the sole law-making authority of the State." The atmosphere of the meeting was captured in an exchange over this wording. The Japanese draft said the Diet "shall alone exercise the legislative power." Kades asked why SCAP's phrase was not used, and Hussey told Satō to "leave it in the form we originally had it—the "sole law-making authority of the State." But Satō persisted, trying to find words that could be used. Hussey snapped: "What about the exact translation? Doesn't that give absolutely what we say in our draft? What is the objection to that—the sole law-making authority?" "No objection," replied Satō. "Then use it," Kades ordered. "Use it as written in our draft."[48]

The Americans next added language to ensure that members of both houses were "representative of all the people." This language clearly rejected the Japanese desire that the upper house repesent districts and professions rather than national constituencies. They were strict on this point when Satō timidly raised it. "Is there no chance," he asked, "of including Article 45 of the Japanese draft concerning organization of the House of Councillors?" The Americans, however, were adamant. As Satō wrote later, he suspected what their answer would be judging from Matsumoto's talk with Whitney on February 22.[49]

Considering the Cabinet

Chapter V, the cabinet, provoked little discussion among the GS staff, in the meeting either with Whitney or with the Japanese. They made small editorial changes in several articles, none involving substantive matters. Only article 76 of the Japanese draft got much attention. This provision gave the cabinet the authority to issue an emergency order, with the force of law, should a national crisis occur when the Diet could not be convoked due to the dissolution of the House of Representatives. Such an order could temporarily substitute for law or provide funding. The Americans had strongly objected to this provision in their session with Whitney and agreed to discard it. They told Satō, when they met him, that such a provision was "unprecedented in foreign constitutions." Satō knew more constitutional history than they did, but he had no reference books with him to prove that the constitutions of Denmark, Spain, Portugal, Czechoslovakia, and Greece, among other European nations, did indeed have such provisions.[50] Kades and Satō would return to the issue in later meetings.[51]

The Judicial Thicket

Negotiations on the judiciary (chapter VI) entangled the two sides in a thicket
of conflicting legal traditions and constitutional issues. The Americans, speaking
from their own history in Hamiltonian cadence, had sought to create a system
of independent courts and judges, capped by a supreme court, to protect the
people's rights. They used inspiring rhetoric and sweeping generalizations to underline the importance of an independent judiciary. "A strong and independent
judiciary being the bulwark of the people's rights" began the first article. Judges
would be independent, not subject to removal or disciplinary action by the executive branch, and bound only by their conscience, the constitution, and laws
supporting it. Public prosecutors would be officers of the courts, not officials of
the ministry of justice. No "extraordinary tribunal" or agency of the executive
branch could have final judicial power on any matter. Only the courts would
enjoy that privilege.

Matsumoto's draft omitted the rhetoric, saying only that "the courts of law
shall exercise the judicial power independently." Prosecutors were not mentioned,
leaving them part of the executive branch. Judges could be dismissed in a variety
of ways and were subject to reduction of salary as a disciplinary measure. The
Japanese draft diluted the powers and privileges of the courts and judges in the
SCAP draft.

In the meeting with Whitney, Hussey complained that the "first article of our
draft [is] omitted." He wanted it restored. He and others complained that the
Japanese draft had weakened or left out provisions of the SCAP draft that guaranteed the independence of the judiciary and supreme court.[52] The Americans
restored verbatim the first two articles of the chapter (establishing a strong and
independent judiciary system) and replaced, discarded, or rewrote more than half
the chapter of the Japanese draft.[53]

In the joint session with the Japanese,[54] Kades began by playing down differences between the two sides, "but we feel we expressed it better." He demanded
to know why the first article had been changed. "Why have you moved sentences
and clauses around"? Satō responded quite frankly that some of the SCAP language did not fit the Japanese legal tradition. "Much of what we have here in
Judiciary belongs in the Civil Rights [chapter] and is repetitious of clauses in the
Family [articles], and is flowery." Hussey denied it was flowery, "but straightforward simple law."

He and Kades then made a concession, agreeing to remove the first clause of
the chapter ("A strong and independent judiciary being the bulwark of the people's rights"). Shirasu, in a rare comment, requested that the Americans also
"leave out 'no extraordinary tribunal shall be established.'" Hussey initially
agreed, but after talking it over with his colleagues reversed himself: "No, this
[removal] would permit . . . extraordinary courts of the Legislature." And, presumably, it would allow other bodies with judicial powers in the executive branch.
That is the point, Satō said. Prohibiting this provision in the Japanese constitution

would make it impossible to establish such family and juvenile courts as existed in the United States. Hussey agreed, but still required the phrase be restored.[55]

The Americans did concede on three provisions the Japanese challenged. Responding to Satō's argument, they agreed that the procurators could be part of the executive branch rather than officers of the court but must be "subject to the rule-making power of the supreme court." Second, SCAP's draft had muddled the separation of powers rule by defining the Supreme Court as the court of last resort, except in some cases in which "the judgment of the Court is subject to review by the Diet" and "may be set aside by the concurring vote of two-thirds of the whole number of representatives of the Diet" (article 73). Satō pointed to the contradiction of calling the supreme court the "court of last resort" while allowing the Diet to trump the court and be the final judge of some of its own laws. After a few moments hesitation, the Americans conceded Satō's point and ordered the article rewritten as follows: "The Supreme Court is the court of last resort with power to determine the constitutionality of any law, order, regulation or official act."[56] The third provision was an article (74) which gave the Supreme Court "exclusive original jurisdiction" in all cases involving foreign diplomatic officials. When Shirasu, a member of the Foreign Ministry, remarked sarcastically that this was a fine article, the Americans quickly discarded it.[57]

But the Americans refused to compromise on provisions they considered essential for the independence of judges. The Japanese wanted to provide a way of taking disciplinary action (reduction of salary) against judges short of impeachment. They proposed dropping the clause which prohibited reduction of compensation during tenure, allowing reduction of salary "for minor infractions not serious enough for impeachment."[58] Hussey rejected this, saying that only the supreme court should have the power to take disciplinary action against judges. Anything else would reduce the independence of the courts.

Taking up Finances

During the morning of March 5, as the negotiations moved into their second day and focused on chapter VII (finance), Satō received assistance from two councillors of the Legislation Bureau, while GS now relied more on Rizzo, who had drafted this chapter. The principal issues were the Diet's power to raise and appropriate funds for the state, control the budget process, create a reserve fund for unforeseen shortfalls in the budget, imperial household property and income from it, prohibit use of public funds for organizations not controlled by the state, and prepare annual audits of government expenditures and revenues.

The Japanese considered the first half of this SCAP chapter "a confused jumble."[59] SCAP had given the Diet exclusive power to levy taxes, borrow money, and appropriate funds. The cabinet was required to submit an annual budget to the Diet and was prohibited from imposing new taxes or modifying existing ones without Diet approval. Nor could the cabinet enter into contracts in the absence of Diet appropriations. The cabinet could create a reserve fund for "unforeseen budget deficiencies" but was accountable to the Diet for payments from the fund. In eight out of ten articles of the chapter, the Diet was described as approving, authorizing, or controlling government finances. The American basic distrust of the Japanese executive branch was clear.

Matsumoto and Satō offered a much trimmer version, with few references to the power of the Diet. The multiple financial functions of government were to be done "as provided by law." The Diet passed and modified such laws, of course. And the cabinet had no special powers outside these laws, including the creation of a reserve fund for emergency expenditures. But the wording of Matsumoto's draft gave the distinct impression that the cabinet would be in a dominant position vis-à-vis the Diet. The Americans reacted by marking up the Matsumoto draft.[60] Rizzo, especially, was looking not only for an accurate "translation" of the SCAP draft but for any evidence that the Japanese were attempting to avoid Diet control of government expenditures.[61]

A good example was the debate over the provision for a reserve fund to meet government emergencies. Rizzo scrutinized the language regarding expenditures outside the budget and creation of a reserve fund for a supplementary budget not authorized by the Diet. During the GS meeting with Whitney, Swope had seen little difference between the SCAP and Matsumoto versions of a reserve fund, and in the joint session Satō agreed with Swope's evaluation.[62] But Rizzo, fearing that the language of the Matsumoto draft created a "loophole" for unauthorized government expenditures, insisted on restoring the original SCAP wording.[63]

Imperial Household Property

The provision on imperial household property touched on perhaps the most sensitive issue of chapter VII—and perhaps of the whole constitution. SCAP said, bluntly, that all property of the imperial household, except the "hereditary estates," belonged to the nation, and all income from these properties must be paid into the national treasury.[64] This provision rendered the imperial family directly subject to the people's representatives in the Diet for their allowances and expenditures. It was popular sovereignty with a vengeance. The Japanese imagined a British-style monarchy with its hugh wealth in lands, stock and bonds, art works, and jewelry. The Americans wanted a symbolic monarchy stripped of private wealth, beholden to "the people."

Matsumoto's March 2 draft had avoided the sweeping first sentence of SCAP's draft which, in effect, nationalized all imperial property, except hereditary estates. His article said: "The budget for the Imperial Household expenses shall be part of the national budget; and so shall the income and expenditures arising from Imperial House property, except for inherited property." He spoke first of the imperial family's expenses; it would be part of the national budget and thus have to be voted every year by the Diet, a fact Matsumoto chose not to state. The rest of the article essentially agreed with SCAP's article. Matsumoto's indirect language

softened the harshness of SCAP's draft nationalizing imperial property and making the whole family financially dependent on the Diet.

But GS quickly rejected Matsumoto's attempt at obfuscation. "Replace [Mat-
sumoto's article] with our 82," Ellerman's note read, "this is a C[ommander] in
C[hief] mandate."[65] Rizzo thought it was unnecessary to have an article on imperial property in this chapter of the constitution. Hussey disagreed. He thought
it useful to emphasize in the chapter on national finances that "upon adoption
of the Constitution, title to I[mperial] P[roperty] becomes vested in the nation.
The Japanese version is an attempt to slide out." Whitney agreed, and so SCAP's
article replaced Matsumoto's.[66]

In the meeting with the Japanese, Kades assumed direction of negotiations and
told Satō: "Obviously this [article 82] is a matter of principle. We will discuss
the language but its purpose is to nationalize the Imperial property."[67] Kades
meant that nationalizing imperial property was one of those "fundamental principles" of the SCAP draft mentioned to Matsumoto back in February. He was
unwilling to compromise on this. Satō resisted, knowing that this would be a
bitter pill for his government to accept, but in the end he had no choice but to
surrender to the American dictate. It would remain a major bone of contention
until the debates in the Diet ended in August.

Local Government

The local government chapter of the SCAP draft created something new for Japan.
Under the Meiji Constitution, Japan had no local government organization; the
central government appointed local officials. None of the previous Japanese draft
constitutions proposed anything like SCAP's draft. In preparing the Japanese government draft, Matsumoto and staff, determined to continue central government
control, rewrote the local government chapter of the American draft.[68] They
changed the title of the chapter to "Local Self Government," called local government bodies "local public entities," instead of "prefectures, cities and towns," and
added a new article at the beginning of the chapter which said: "[All] regulations
concerning organization and operation of local public entities shall be fixed by
law." In short, nothing concerning local government was to be determined by
constitutional mandate. Rather, it was to be "fixed by law in accordance with the
principle of local autonomy."

In the GS meeting, Whitney and his staff had rejected the Matsumoto version
as violating their writ from Washington, SWNCC 228.[69] They concluded that "to
comply with 228, we must put in our article 86." This required "all officials of
government bodies having taxing power to be elected by direct popular vote." In
fact, this went well beyond SWNCC 228's short statement that one general objective of political reform should include "The popular election or local appointment of as many of the prefectural officials as practicable." Roest, a scholar of
European background, agreed with Matsumoto and Satō. He seemed wary of the
decentralized system of U.S. local government. If the Japanese object to having

it in the constitution, he said, then let the Diet decide how local government will be organized. Hussey, on the other hand, was adamantly opposed and argued that "[SWNCC] 228 requires that we provide for a greater amount of democracy in local affairs." In this meeting, Whitney had the last word and supported Hussey's position. "Put in our whole Article on Local Gov[ernment]," he said, "[we] should insist on ours, which is very clear."[70]

In the joint session with the Japanese,[71] Satō won several important concessions, revealing a lack of American agreement on local government and on the meaning of SWNCC's charge to them. Initially, the Americans wanted all local officials to be elected but later accepted the Japanese provision that only the chief executive and members of local assemblies "be elected by direct popular vote," while lesser officials would be "permanent" administrators. The American terminology ("prefectures, cities and towns") was dropped in favor of Satō's "local public entities." Kades agreed that, concerning the organization and operation of local government, the Diet should have "unrestricted power to do as it deems advisable." But local communities did receive protection from such "unrestricted power." The final article of the chapter prohibited the Diet in Tokyo from enacting a special law for any one locale without "the consent of a majority of the [local] inhabitants." Local autonomy meant, as Satō had written in the Japanese draft, that the residents of the local public entity would have the right of self-government and could enact rules and regulations "within the scope of such laws as the Diet may enact." This was a solid compromise between the very different American and Japanese views on local government.

The Amendment Process

What later became one of the most controversial features of the Shōwa Constitution—the amendment process—caused remarkably little friction during the negotiations of March 4–5. In article 89, SCAP gave a clear signal that it wanted this American-drafted constitution to last. It said: "Amendments to this Constitution shall be initiated by the Diet, through a concurring vote of two-thirds of all its members" and ratified by a majority of the voters in a national referendum. Two-thirds of all members was a high bar for anyone proposing an amendment. By comparison, SCAP required, for *ratification* of the 1946 revision, only two-thirds of "the [Diet] members present" (article 92). The tougher amendment provision was SCAP's way of protecting what it had wrought, of ensuring that popular sovereignty and renunciation of war, for example, would not be easily overturned after the occupying forces went home.

The Japanese government draft, following SCAP's model, adopted a similar requirement for amendment—a "concurring vote of two-thirds or more of all members of each House." Whitney and his staff nevertheless decided to "substitute our Article [89, which is] much clearer than the Japanese version."[72] In the combined session on March 5, Satō questioned whether amendments should be "proclaimed by the Emperor, in the name of the People" or "on behalf of the

People."[73] Yet neither he nor any one else raised the slightest objection to the two-thirds provision.

The Cabinet and Emperor Consider the Draft

The 30-hour drafting session ended in the afternoon of March 5 with a brief dispute over whether separate chapters should enshrine provisions on amendments, define the constitution as the "supreme law" to which the emperor and all government officials and Diet members would be bound to observe and protect, and include a statement regarding ratification. The Japanese draft put all these in one chapter, "Supplementary Provisions." Matsumoto had also inserted an article (106) limiting to the emperor the power to initiate revisions to the imperial house law. Again, the Americans ordered Satō to follow their model,[74] using three separate chapters for these provisions. In the chapter on the "Supreme Law," to which Satō objected as unprecedented, they inserted as one article Whitney's rhapsodic statement: "The fundamental human rights by this Constitution guaranteed to the people of Japan result from the age-old struggle of man to be free." They also discarded the article on the imperial house law, because it was provided for in article 1, and made their chapter on ratification part of the amendment chapter.

When the marathon session concluded around 4 P.M.,[75] the Foreign Ministry translators rushed to insert last-minute changes, while Satō gathered up his copies of the Japanese and American drafts and prepared to return to the prime minister's office. At that moment, he recorded, "Whitney, who had not shown his face even once, came into the conference room with a look of relief, shook our hands, and effusively thanked us for the work we had done. To us Japanese, this seemed so unnatural."[76] Whitney acted as though the Japanese had voluntarily collaborated in making the draft. In fact, as we have seen, Whitney had ordered them to come to GS, and his staff kept them there until the work was done.

Satō recalled returning to his office after thirty hours without a wink of sleep feeling "deeply dejected . . . with my head hanging."[77] He had been unable to contact his wife and daughters, who were worried by his long absence. His older daughter remembered her mother searching desperately for a telephone in working order to call his office and watching the road leading from their house to the train station. When he finally appeared on that road the morning of March 6, "he was utterly exhausted and appeared to be creeping up a steep hill."[78]

In the early afternoon of March 5, as the work of drafting and collating entered its final stage, Shirasu left the conference room with ten copies of the draft constitution in English and delivered them to the cabinet. He reported that MacArthur intended to publish the English draft that evening and asked whether the cabinet would accept it "before the day was out."[79] Satō's final version of the Japanese draft did not reach the cabinet until shortly after 7 P.M., when the ministers reconvened after a dinner break.[80] They were in a quandary. To them, the Japanese version "sounded like a direct translation of the American draft, especially the preamble." It was "too poorly written to be published right away." They believed further work was needed before it could be published. Even Ashida, a proponent of constitutional revision, considered the Japanese draft to be nothing more than "a translation of the American draft."[81] The cabinet meeting continued that evening and into the next day, March 6.

The cabinet decided to rework the preamble, which began "We, the Japanese People," and was intended by its American author, Hussey, to be a ringing endorsement of democracy by the Japanese people. It sounded foreign to Japanese ears, exactly like the translation that it was—pretentious, full of inflated rhetoric, nothing that the "Japanese people" would write. Education Minister Abe, himself a skilled writer, made a new translation of Hussey's composition and presented it to the cabinet the next morning. But Irie informed the ministers of SCAP's sensitivity over the preamble and the matter was dropped.

The ministers were especially concerned about chapter III, Rights and Duties of the People, and asked Irie to review it. The style and wording made the cabinet uneasy. But faced with MacArthur's determination to publish the draft as it was on March 6, they adopted a novel, inspired proposal by Irie: Leave some wording, especially verb endings, unfinished, call the draft a yōkō (gist or summary), and finalize it after publication.[82] Irie and his staff made no changes in the English text that emerged from the marathon conference. Rather, using it as their guide, they spent the night of March 5 putting the "expressions and words in the Japanese text in proper order."[83] The cabinet polished the "wording of the preamble and so forth" early on March 6. The upshot was that the document presented on March 6 to the Japanese people and the world as "the Japanese draft Constitution" was not in final form.

More important than stylistic features was an issue of constitutional form. How could the ministers approve this massive revision when, according to article LXXIII of the 1889 constitution, only the emperor could initiate amendments? Under the circumstances, they saw no alternative but to join MacArthur's conspiracy by releasing it to the press that evening "as the Japanese Government's draft."[84] The cabinet used an imperial rescript to provide cover for proposing such fundamental changes in the existing constitution. Usually, the prime minister would have gone to the palace and sought the emperor's agreement on the proposal and then drafted the rescript for the imperial signature. Faced with the pressure of SCAP's inflexible timetable, however, the cabinet drafted the formal statement for the emperor to sign and issue along with the draft constitution. The task of writing it fell to Ashida. Shidehara and Matsumoto rushed the statement and draft constitution to the emperor for his approval.[85]

Prime Minister Shidehara had earlier presented to the emperor the March 4 provisional draft constitution as "Matsumoto's personal draft," which they could still revise at that moment. Twenty-four hours later, in the early evening of March 5, Shidehara and Matsumoto returned with the new draft constitution, which they could not further revise before publication. The emperor was unhappy. He wished to reserve for himself the right to initiate changes in the imperial house law and to preserve the privileged nobility. Under the circumstances, however, the ministers had to reject his proposals. SCAP was demanding the cabinet's immediate approval of the document, and the cabinet needed an imperial rescript that would give the emperor's seal of approval. Hirohito signed off on the text of the proposed rescript with the understanding that it would then go to MacArthur for final approval before publication.[86] Meanwhile GS, without telling the Japanese, made additional minor changes in the English-language draft. Satō learned of these when he returned to the Legislation Bureau on March 6 and incorporated them into the Japanese version.[87]

The Final Deception

The final act of this historical drama within a drama starred Commander Hussey. Following the SCAP script, Hussey prepared thirteen copies of the English version of the new draft Constitution, along with a brief statement from the Japanese cabinet, and carried them to Cabinet Secretary Narahashi for his signature. Narahashi recalled that Hussey said eleven of the copies were to be sent by special plane to Washington "for members of the Far Eastern Commission." He remembered signing thirteen copies, eleven for the FEC countries, one to be kept by the American side, and one for the Japanese cabinet.[88] Why did SCAP want these copies certified by an official representative of the Japanese cabinet? Hussey's answer: "The final draft was approved by the Cabinet on the morning of [March] 6 and immediately thereafter the Chief Secretary, in the presence of Commander Hussey, certified the English version as *the exact and official translation of the original Japanese.*"[89] The conspiracy had reached its climax: The SCAP draft of February 13 had been transformed by this deceptive procedure into the "Japanese Government draft" of March 6 and was now certified by the cabinet secretary as having been originally written in Japanese. Hussey himself then boarded a plane and flew off to Washington to present certified copies of the document to the Far Eastern Commission.

Despite the best collaborative efforts of GS and the Legislation Bureau, the deception produced a document that read like a translation from English to Japanese. As we shall see, it provoked strong reactions in Japan and in Washington. It also required further negotiations between the Americans and Japanese to try to remove ambiguities and the strong "odor of translation." The complete and final text of the "March 6" draft was not issued until April 17, a week after the general election that SCAP interpreted as a popular ratification of the document.

9 . . . .

"Grave Danger"

• THE ALLIES CHALLENGE MacARTHUR

•

The publication of a draft constitution on March 6 set off shock
• waves in Tokyo and Washington. In the media, the appearance of
the draft rivaled *Mainichi*'s scoop of Matsumoto's draft on February
• 1, just over a month earlier. Newspapers, magazines, and radio reported on it for days, speculating on the contents and style and
• whether it was indeed a Japanese government draft. The press solicited the views of various legal associations and individual scholars
• and devoted much space to the "symbol" emperor and the antiwar
clause.

•

• International Reaction

• An angry FEC sent a series of messages to MacArthur in March and
April, virtually accusing him of usurping the international commis-
• sion's authority. The Allies objected to MacArthur's public "approval" of the March 6 draft as well as his plan to submit the doc-
• ument for ratification to a new Diet, to be elected in April. In the
FEC's view, the Moscow Agreement had given the commission sole
• authority to approve a new constitution for Japan. The FEC's strong
reaction challenged MacArthur to explain and justify his actions.
• This challenge posed a threat to MacArthur's bold conspiracy to
make Japan's imperial institution a basic part of Japan's new con-
• stitutional order. If the FEC succeeded in delaying the general election or derailing debate of the draft constitution by the Diet, the
whole intricate plot hatched in Tokyo might fall apart. To fend off
the FEC, MacArthur would have to make a strong legal case to
persuade his government, if not the FEC, and to convince the Japanese to accept several FEC demands at the end of the process.
During the next three months MacArthur repeatedly rejected the
commission's attempts to assert its authority over the political reform of Japan. The State Department, the War Department and
SWNCC, although embarrassed by MacArthur, closed ranks behind
him.

On March 10, when the FEC complained to the State Department about MacArthur's action, the department itself was still ignorant of what he had done. Hugh Borton, then acting director of the Japan Office in the State Department, later confirmed that Washington "had not been informed of the activities of MacArthur's Government Section in February and March."[1] There were no copies of the new draft constitution available in Washington when the document appeared in Tokyo. From the office of SCAP's Political Adviser (a State Department representative), Max Bishop wrote Secretary Byrnes on March 8 that the announcement of the new draft "came as a surprise."[2]

Byrnes attempted to soothe the bruised feelings of the FEC countries. He told newsmen on March 12 that "before the Constitution becomes effective, it will in some way or other come before the Far Eastern Commission."[3] And he assured the press that the draft constitution had been drawn up by the Japanese government "under its right to do so."

The War Department, meanwhile, reacting to MacArthur's apparent diplomatic faux pas, quickly proposed a strategy to him for aligning his actions with the Moscow Agreement's provision giving the member nations of the FEC authority over Japan's constitutional revision. Army Chief of Staff Dwight Eisenhower, in a telegraphic "inquiry" to MacArthur on March 10, suggested how SCAP's public endorsement of the new draft constitution could be made consistent with the Moscow Agreement. Eisenhower cautioned that the FEC might question his right to approve a new constitution without directives from the commission. The State Department, Eisenhower continued, wanted to know the basis of his approval. He then offered a suggestion:

> View of War Department has been that if Japanese Government were to proceed with constitutional reforms prior to action in December [signing of the Moscow Agreement], you would intervene only if such reforms were inconsistent with directives already issued by you. It appears therefore that your action in personally approving this new Constitution is consistent with War Department view since (a) the Constitution was issued not by your Headquarters but by Japanese Emperor and Government in compliance with directive issued by you prior to Moscow Conference, and (b) constitutional reforms appear to be consistent with directives received by you. Request your early confirmation of views expressed . . . above or comments thereon.[4]

The telegram offered a strategy that had been thought out *before* the announcement on March 6, suggesting that the Pentagon had advance knowledge of the event.[5] Moreover, it implied that the Moscow Agreement had indeed become binding on MacArthur the day it was signed, December 26, 1945. A SCAP directive issued *after* that date would violate the international agreement. Therefore, the March 6 draft must be a product of a revision process that began before December 26. Eisenhower invited MacArthur to confirm this point.

Before responding to the JCS's telegram, MacArthur ordered a new review of his authority regarding constitutional revision. The memorandum[6] by Kades repeated arguments contained in Whitney's memorandum of February 1, which Kades had also drafted:

> It is abundantly clear that SCAP's powers over Japan within the scope of the basic directive [JCS 1380] are absolute and that SCAP has the authority to undertake whatever measures it deems appropriate to effectuate the surrender terms, and that such authority necessarily includes the right to approve such measures as the Japanese themselves initiate to establish a responsible government in conformity with the surrender terms.

Kades never mentioned the Moscow Agreement. He said that SWNCC 228 was only for MacArthur's "information," not a directive and not the controlling policy document. In fact he asserted: "Nowhere is there any requirement, stated or implied, that SCAP consult the Joint Chiefs of Staff in connection with constitutional changes excepting only insofar as they may involve removal of the Emperor."

After reading Kades's memorandum, MacArthur responded to Eisenhower on March 12 that "the reasoning advanced by you is correct." He endorsed the premises that (1) the process of constitutional revision, based on his suggestions, was continuous since the fall of 1945; and (2) that process was undertaken by the Japanese government. He revealed nothing about SCAP's role in all of this. He went on to say that he had told the FEC "that for several months revision of the constitution had been in progress in accordance with the directives covering this matter which I had already received and I expected an acceptable draft revision shortly. No expression of dissent was offered. The proposed new constitution is still subject to acceptance or rejection by the Japanese people in the coming election."[7]

Thus MacArthur embraced the War Department's interpretation that confirmed his earlier strategy and offered him a cover of legitimacy. He omitted any reference to his own unilateral action in conspiring to draft a model constitution for Japan and having it published as a "Japanese Government Draft." Eisenhower and MacArthur did disagree on one central point, however. Eisenhower believed the signing of the agreement on December 26 had immediately imposed restraints on SCAP's actions, whereas MacArthur maintained that no such restrictions would exist until the FEC issued a policy directive on constitutional reform.[8]

MacArthur ended his telegram with a grossly misleading statement regarding the process ahead, particularly the significance of the coming general election: "The proposed new constitution is still subject to acceptance or rejection by the Japanese people in the coming election."[9] In fact, the general election scheduled for April 10 would make no provision for Japanese voters to accept or reject the draft. They were to elect new members of the Diet, not pass judgment on the draft constitution. MacArthur's statement served a different purpose; it was clearly intended to reassure his government, and the FEC, that constitutional revision under his guidance was proceeding in accordance with the principles agreed on by the Allies at Potsdam.

The FEC Challenges the Election

By March 20 the FEC had decided by unanimous vote to challenge MacArthur over his announcement of an election in early April. The FEC's message to MacArthur reveals apprehension, even confusion, about the body's authority and its relations with SCAP. The first approach was circumspect. The FEC expressed concern that Japanese voters were unprepared for an election, especially one intended to serve, as MacArthur indicated, as a referendum on the draft constitution. The FEC feared that "the Japanese people have little time to consider it." In addition, holding the election on April 10, just twenty days away, "may well give a decisive advantage to the reactionary parties and thus create the embarrassment of [electing] a Japanese Government which might not, in fact, truly represent the people's wishes."[10] The FEC posed three questions to MacArthur: Did SCAP share its apprehensions about the general election? Would he consider postponing the election? Or would he "prescribe" the election as a test "of the ability of the Japan to produce a responsible and democratic government."[11] The FEC clearly wanted MacArthur to delay the election but was reluctant to confront him by bluntly saying so.

The American representative and FEC chairman, retired Major General Frank R. McCoy, encouraged a deferential attitude toward MacArthur. Though older than MacArthur, McCoy was subordinate in rank and had served under him before the war. On the day he became FEC chairman, McCoy had sent a personal message to MacArthur, saying: "You may rest assured of my determination to safeguard your interests at all times."[12] He now had to explain why he had not vetoed the FEC's decision to question MacArthur about his hasty actions. Despite his personal loyalty, McCoy also questioned MacArthur's decision to approve the March 6 draft and rush the general election.[13]

MacArthur's response to the FEC and McCoy was to point to the reforms he had already undertaken: election law revised, voting age lowered, suffrage extended to women, and the purge of 90 percent of the existing Diet members and thousands of "undesirable personnel," including party members, from office. These measures, he insisted, would ensure a fair and representative election, with the reactionary elements having no advantage. The only political group in Japan that wished to delay the election, MacArthur pointedly noted, was the Japan Communist Party. Should the new Diet turn out to be less democratic than expected, he could always dissolve it and hold another election.[14]

The second issue was how the March 6 draft constitution would be considered and adopted. MacArthur and his co-conspirators in the Japanese cabinet preferred having the emperor submit a revision bill as prescribed in article LXXIII of the Meiji Constitution. A new Diet, to be selected in the April general election, would meet in June and debate and pass the bill. MacArthur insisted on this procedure in part because it appeared to conform to the Potsdam Declaration, requiring that the Japanese people freely express their will in the matter. Doing so through their elected representatives involved less risk—than a referendum or a national assembly—that the draft constitution would be rejected. In addition, an early election gave SCAP greater control over who would be elected and forestalled interference by the FEC.

But there was another consideration. As the Japanese public became more vocal about constitutional revision, many expressed a preference for a special national assembly, members of which would be elected solely for the purpose of adopting a new constitution. More than half of those who responded to the question wanted the public election of a special commission or assembly to debate a revision bill.[15] Other Japanese citizens, including some government officials, thought it only natural "to radically reform the deliberative procedure" when revising the constitution. One plan put forth in the Legislation Bureau proposed a "constitution Diet" to prepare a draft constitution which would then be submitted to a national referendum.[16] This plan sounded highly democratic, placing the process squarely in the hands of the people. But it had little appeal to MacArthur and his staff, who were determined that the March 6 draft, or something close to it, be adopted by the Diet.

The FEC also preferred a special constitutional assembly or special Diet to consider the draft but insisted that the FEC itself, rather than the Japanese people, be the ultimate authority for judging whether the document was in accord with the Potsdam Declaration. MacArthur steadfastly resisted the commission's entreaties and demands. He refused to postpone the general election or to consider an enactment procedure, such as a referendum, that would directly reflect the will of the Japanese people. For the commission, McCoy cautioned MacArthur on April 9, while the general election was under way [Japan time]: "[The] Constitution . . . should receive due consideration of [the] Japanese people, possibly over considerable time. Unless this is done, and unless [the] Commission has full opportunity to express itself before final adoption of the document, there is grave danger that it will not be approved by the Commission."[17]

On April 10, the FEC unanimously adopted a resolution requesting MacArthur to dispatch a member of his staff to Washington to confer on Japanese constitutional reform and the principles that should determine the commission's approval of any specific constitutional draft. The FEC's resolution said: "The Commission, in its concern that any constitution adopted by the Japanese should embody the 'freely expressed will of the Japanese people,' is particularly interested in the procedures by which it is contemplated a new constitution will be adopted—whether, for example, by the Diet, by a constitutional convention, or by a plebiscite."[18]

Clearly, the FEC did not accept MacArthur's contention that the general election would constitute a referendum on the March 6 draft constitution. And MacArthur did not accept the FEC's claim to controlling authority over the process of Japan's constitutional reform. Japan's April election was already in process when the FEC adopted its resolution. The impasse would continue for another two months while MacArthur and the Japanese cabinet proceeded to push the March 6 draft through the Privy Council and to the floor of a newly elected Diet.

The April 1946 General Election

The April 10, 1946, general election may have been the most consequential election in Japan's history. Certainly it became the most misrepresented. It took place under the control of American forces and in the midst of widespread purges, mass political protests, and desperate cries for food. SCAP justified it as a test of the new election law revised in December 1945 and as a gauge of popular support for the general principles of the draft constitution.[19]

We need to address two questions about the election. First, to what extent was it a fair election, allowing the Japanese people freely to express their views on constitutional reform? Second, did the election serve as a referendum on the draft constitution? That is, did the candidates themselves discuss constitutional reform, indicate their approval or disapproval of the March 6 draft, and make their views clear to the voters?

MacArthur's contention was that, since publication on March 6, the draft had received extraordinary publicity in the media. The Japanese people had had time to read and debate it and to acquaint themselves with its major provisions.[20] They could, he told the War Department, accept or reject it "at the coming election."[21] Because no formal referendum was planned, presumably MacArthur meant that the general election would be an opportunity for candidates and voters to engage in a discussion of the draft.

There were several factors that weaken the claim of free elections serving as a referendum on the constitution. First was SCAP's sweeping purge—instituted in January 1946—of all persons who had held positions of responsibility since 1937 in politics, industry, finance, commerce, and agriculture.[22] SCAP ordered the Japanese government to submit information on the actions and views of all prewar politicians. A SCAP press release said this order would "strike the shackles from the efforts of the Japanese people to rise toward freedom and democracy." Whitney, with his usual bombast, said it removed those who "enslaved and beat the Japanese people into abject submission and hoped to do the same with all the world."[23] By the time of the general election in April, this order had removed from office and disqualified hundreds of politicians of all the major parties. Several ministers of Shidehara's cabinet, facing purge, resigned immediately, and by March all but three (Yoshida, Ashida, and Shidehara himself) had been forced to resign.

The purge order devastated the House of Peers and the major political parties. Between January and April 1946, 37 members of the House of Peers resigned rather than be removed, and more than 100 were expected to be removed. In the House of Representatives, the largest party, the Progressives, lost all but 27 of its 274 Diet members, including most of its leaders. The Liberal Party learned that half of its 50 members were purged, including its president Hatoyama Ichirō. By the time of the general election in April, the Social Democrats had lost 10 of their 17 Diet members. The result was that hundreds of Japan's Diet members and party politicians were barred from participating in the April 10 general election.

SCAP then extended its investigation from the prewar politicians and political parties to all who wished to stand for election on April 10. He ordered the Japanese government to examine the qualifications of all 3,384 candidates according to the regulations of the purge order. Some 252 were disqualified, and another 268 were not allowed to file.[24] In short, the purge greatly narrowed the approved political spectrum and denied the electorate the chance to vote for many experienced candidates.

The general atmosphere in which voters approached the polls in April is suggested by the wave of left-wing enthusiasm that surged over Tokyo in the spring of 1946. The Communist leader Nosaka Sanzō's promise to create a "lovable Communist Party" accompanied the powerful swell of union members and workers mobilized by the political left. Workers in the "production control" movement, beginning in late 1945, had seized offices, factories, and mines until management gave in to their demands.[25] Numerous such incidents continued in the first three months of 1946. Yoshida's "sea of red flags" began filling the streets of Tokyo three days before the election and posed a threat to the Shidehara cabinet.[26] Led by the Communist leader Tokuda Kyūichi, 50,000 workers and farmers advanced on Shidehara's official residence. Dozens of demonstrators broke through the gate and occupied his offices, denounced and verbally abused him, and shoved him against a wall as he tried to leave. Threats to the elderly prime minister continued until the U.S. military police restored order.[27]

The Election Is Held

SCAP's official account of the April 10 election emphasized vigorous campaign activities, fair allocation of radio time to candidates, press coverage encouraging citizens to vote, and the government's efforts to stimulate interest in the election and voting and to explain the plural voting system.[28] All major parties appealed to voters by making vague promises of providing basic necessities such as food, clothing, housing, and jobs. They criticized the government's system of compulsory rice deliveries and called for the rationalization and "democratization" of the system that provided people with basic foods. In short, the food shortage, not constitutional revision, was the major issue for most voters, who spent much of their time searching for food.[29]

In an attempt to assure "fairness," SCAP employed heavy-handed tactics that cast a pall of apprehension over the whole election process during the campaign and on election day. GS's account said: "The campaign and the election itself were brought under the close personal observation of the Occupation forces by a directive which provided surveillance by troops in the field."[30] Whitney arranged for counterintelligence teams and combat units to reinforce military government teams already assigned to prefectural capitals.[31] These field forces, distributed throughout each prefecture, contacted local governors, prefectural and local police, and all mayors and village headmen. American soldiers checked Japanese campaign expenditures, received complaints, and wrote news articles on procedures of the election and penalties for violating such procedures.[32]

On election day, SCAP ordered careful observation of the voting.[33] American military forces visited more than half of the 21,000 polling places in Japan, some two or three times, checking the posting of election regulations, consulting officials in charge, and observing how voters entered polling places and cast their ballots. They even oversaw the counting and recording of ballots.[34] One cannot read the GS description of these actions without feeling the chilling effect of such oversight. Americans believed, of course, that their presence would guarantee the "untrammelled and free expression" of the Japanese voters. It seems likely, however, that the mass of American faces and uniforms at the polls aroused suspicion in the minds of Japanese voters that the election was taking place under the shadow of Yankee bayonets.

Japanese and American officials worried that the Japanese public would be apathetic toward voting in this first postwar political contest. Prime Minister Shidehara, in a printed statement and a radio address, urged all citizens to exercise their franchise. The daily *Asahi Shinbun* called April 10 the "point of departure of the democratic revolution" and urged voters to support the "democratic parties." Registered voters surprised most observers by voting in large numbers (according to official figures, 72 percent of them cast their ballots). They strongly supported conservative party candidates over socialists and communists (234 to 97). The Social Democrats did make some gains, and female candidates won thirty-nine seats while the Communist Party, fielding candidates for the first time, captured only five seats in the new Diet. Still, adding the members of small parties and independents gave conservatives 70 percent of the vote and leftists 30 percent.[35]

More important perhaps than the shift in the political parties in the Diet was the change in backgrounds of the new members. SCAP's purge had eliminated many members of the prewar Diets and political parties, among them professional politicians, lawyers, and representatives of big business and large taxpayers. As MacArthur proudly proclaimed on April 25, prewar professional politicians were replaced in large part by a group of "intellectuals," including thirty-two educators, twenty-two authors, and thirteen physicians. Forty-nine farmers added further to the nonprofessional cast of the new Diet.[36] But SCAP's claims and numbers are misleading, for slightly over half of the new representatives had experience as prefectural (33 percent) and municipal (20.4 percent) assemblymen.[37]

The Election as "Referendum"

Did the April general election provide a clear measure of the Japanese people's support for the draft constitution? Because the issue itself was not on the ballot, perhaps the only way to judge is to examine, whenever possible, candidates' comments about constitutional reform in their campaign speeches and literature, and whether they embraced or endorsed the basic principles of the draft constitution. The only solid evidence is from a survey that Japan's Commission on the Constitution, created by the House of Representatives in 1956 to investigate the origins of the constitution, published in 1961.[38]

The commission studied the statements contained in the official "election bulletins" of 535 candidates from eight electoral districts around the country.[39] The major conclusion from this survey is that the draft constitution was hardly an issue at all in the election. Of the 2,697 candidates, only 17.4 percent even mentioned the constitution in their campaigns. Of this small minority, nearly three-quarters indicated their support for it, a handful (6 percent) were opposed, and the rest (about a quarter) made remarks about the draft revisions that were ambiguous. The important point is that more than 80 percent never mentioned the draft constitution in their campaigns at all, despite the fact that its existence had been widely publicized since early March. This fact casts a long shadow over MacArthur's assertion that the April elections were a "referendum" on the draft, tantamount to popular ratification of its fundamental principles.

The commission also attempted to determine whether the candidates in this election discussed another issue of constitutional reform—the emperor system. Did the voters favor retention of the emperor system, either as it had existed in the Meiji Constitution or as it was redefined in the March 6 draft constitution? Of the candidates of these eight districts, nearly 80 percent mentioned the emperor during the campaign, and of those, nearly three-quarters indicated support for the imperial institution. However, according to the survey, two-thirds of these supporters of the emperor failed to make clear whether they supported a Meiji-type imperial institution or a "symbol" emperor system of the kind presented in the draft revisions. Of those who did make this important distinction (a little over a quarter of the total number of candidates surveyed), an overwhelming majority gave their support to a revised status for the emperor. Only a small minority of the total (less than 5 percent) favored abolishing the imperial system outright.

Another fundamental issue presented in the draft constitution was the antiwar clause, article 9. Only about one-third of the candidates surveyed (36.6 percent) even talked to the voters about this issue. In fact, most of these (over three-quarters) merely spoke of opposing militarism or supporting pacifism. Only a small minority (a little over one in five) said they supported the type of provisions contained in article 9. Based on this limited sample, it seems clear that, among the candidates for the House of Representatives in the April election, there was much stronger support for the imperial institution than for the pacifism of article 9. *Kokutai* was very much alive in the hearts of the candidates in April 1946.

The evidence here indicates that the FEC was only partly right in its criticism of the election. Japan's prewar conservative party politicians clearly were not able to preserve their hold on power through the election. This was largely due to the fact that MacArthur's purge and strict censorship barred them from either holding office or expressing their views on the draft constitution. On the other hand, the FEC and the State Department may have been right in their suspicion that Japanese votes would find it hard to express their political will freely during the early days of a foreign military occupation. Whitney's concern about staging a "fair" election and protecting the polling places may actually have intimidated some voters. Yet when all is said and done, the fact remains that a large majority of eligible voters did turn out on election day, and they elected a new Diet that was mainly conservative.

MacArthur Replies to McCoy

With the election behind him, MacArthur replied to McCoy's warning that the FEC might not approve the revised constitution. In his telegram to McCoy on April 15,[40] MacArthur quoted extensively from SWNCC 228 ("Reform of the Japanese Governmental System"), reviewed the long "course of revision" leading to the March 6 draft, and defended his responsibilities and authority as Supreme Commander. He said his approval of the draft constitution was "personal" but at the same time contended that he was acting in accordance with a directive implementing the Potsdam Declaration. He described the draft as evolving "from joint studies between the Japanese Government and SCAP Headquarters" and characterized his approval as merely encouraging liberal forces in Japan, without committing the FEC or himself except on general principles. He attempted to turn the wording of the Potsdam Declaration against the FEC, warning that any interference from the Allies would deprive the Japanese people of their right to "freely express" their will in adopting a new constitution.

As for the FEC's insistence that it be given "an opportunity to pass upon the final draft of the constitution," MacArthur rejected it with scorn. The FEC had no business as a policymaking body trying to execute policy or exercise administrative powers in Japan. These functions "are reserved exclusively to the Supreme Commander."[41] This was a Japanese project which he, as Supreme Commander, had the exclusive authority either to allow or to prohibit. As for the FEC's request that he send a member of his staff to Washington to confer on constitutional reform, MacArthur stated bluntly: "I do not believe . . . that the dispatch of an officer from my staff to confer with the Commission would provide a solution to the problem."[42]

Washington Defends MacArthur

The State Department, caught between SCAP and the FEC, resorted to cajoling and delaying. General John Hilldring, who now represented the State Department on SWNCC, urged MacArthur to be more forthcoming with the FEC. He wrote on April 15: "This government believes that such personal contacts between GHQ and the Far Eastern Commission will be of great assistance to all concerned and are of special importance at the present time."[43]

John Carter Vincent, head of the Office of Far Eastern Affairs, sought to involve Secretary Byrnes in the matter. On April 19, he wrote Byrnes[44] that the "general agreement among concerned American officials" was that MacArthur "should not have approved the draft" and that his telegram to McCoy "is not to the point." While disapproving MacArthur's actions, Vincent sought to construct a defense for him against the FEC. MacArthur had told the Allied Council in Tokyo on April 5 that changes in the March 6 draft might result from public debate and "ultimate consideration of the National Diet and the Allied Powers." He had therefore acknowledged the FEC's legitimate role in constitutional reform. Further discussion of the matter "would serve no useful purpose." Vincent reminded Byrnes of the secretary's own public statement on March 12 ("before the Constitution becomes . . . effective, it will in some way or other come before the Far Eastern Commission") and added: "We must . . . bear in mind that the control of Japan is, by agreement, an Allied responsibility."[45] At the same time, the department wished "to extend the fullest protection to General MacArthur's position as the executing authority" of the Occupation.[46]

The State Department faced a serious dilemma. How could the United States honor the Allied agreement and protect MacArthur's position at the same time? Vincent's tactic was to block communications between MacArthur and the FEC, to delay sending MacArthur's April 15 telegram (which rejected the FEC's proposals and request for direct communication with SCAP) to the FEC until June 4.[47] McCoy, while cooperating with Vincent in concealing MacArthur's message from the FEC, attempted to placate MacArthur. On April 20 he wired the general to assure him that the FEC was not challenging his authority as Supreme Commander.[48]

Meanwhile, the FEC was growing impatient with what it considered MacArthur's stalling tactics. On May 13, FEC members voted unanimously to adopt a mandatory policy that contained three "Criteria for the Adoption of a New Japanese Constitution":

1. Adequate time and opportunity should be allowed for full discussion and consideration of the terms of the new Constitution.
2. Complete legal continuity from the Constitution of 1889 should be assured.
3. The new Constitution should be adopted in such a manner as to demonstrate that it affirmatively expresses the free will of the Japanese people.[49]

The second point was considered necessary to forestall a later claim that the constitution was illegal and should be considered null and void. The main purpose of the commission's policy, however, was to guarantee that the Japanese people had an opportunity freely to express their will on the basic law of their land. Many FEC members seriously doubted that the draft constitution expressed the Japanese people's will. Indeed, a majority of the commission wished to reject the March 6 draft entirely and to require the Japanese instead to elect a constituent assembly or a new Diet to draft a constitution and then to give the voters a chance to express their will on the draft through a referendum. However, McCoy opposed this proposal—effectively vetoing it—as "an intrusion into an area of discretionary jurisdiction which should be left to the Japanese."[50]

The FEC's frustration was compounded by its inability to consult fully with MacArthur. The State Department was still sitting on MacArthur's telegram of April 15, which rejected the commission's earlier proposals. On May 24 the FEC sought to have another message sent to MacArthur to request his opinion on the FEC's own recently adopted "criteria for a new Constitution." The commission also wished to dispatch a representative to Tokyo to inform MacArthur of the FEC's views on constitutional reform and to study directly the "constitutional situation" and report back to the full FEC.

This forced the State Department's hand. On May 29 the department had to admit that "a reply has now been received from General MacArthur" expressing his desire for a closer working relationship with the FEC but saying "that it is impossible to send an officer to act as his deputy in broad matters involving constitutional reform." Faced with the Allies' dismay, the State Department finally relented and on June 4 forwarded MacArthur's April 15 telegram to the FEC. McCoy rather lamely defended the six-week delay as "due to a misunderstanding," not intentional.[51] The FEC, angry at the State Department's delaying tactics, interpreted MacArthur's refusal to send an officer for consultation as a "disposition not to cooperate fully with the commission."[52]

MacArthur never responded directly to the FEC's proposed criteria for constitutional reform, which he understood as an attempt to control constitutional revision in Japan. But pressure from the commission and the American government began to have their effect. On May 23, SWNCC had the Joint Chiefs of Staff transmit the FEC's three "criteria for the adoption of a new Japanese Constitution" as a directive to MacArthur.[53] These criteria would allow sufficient time for full discussion of the terms of the new constitution, ensure legal continuity with the 1889 constitution, and guarantee that its method of adoption expressed the free will of the Japanese people. MacArthur relayed the intent of the FEC's criteria to the Japanese government, where it had an immediate effect. Within days the new prime minister, Yoshida Shigeru, would tell the Privy Council, which was then discussing the draft, that it would be possible for the Imperial Diet to offer amendments.[54] This was less than a full acceptance of the FEC's three criteria, but it did ensure that the newly elected Diet would have an opportunity not only to debate the bill for a new constitution but to offer its own amendments to it.

SWNCC also concluded by early June that a directive from President Truman was the only way to persuade MacArthur to cooperate with the FEC. A presidential letter, drafted in the State Department as "information and guidance" for MacArthur, endorsed the FEC's demands that he allow more time for "consideration of the Constitution" and permit ratification by a specially elected "Constituent Assembly or another Diet elected with the Constitution as a campaign issue, or a popular referendum."[55] This endorsement would have gone a long way toward satisfying the FEC as well as many Japanese. However, Vincent, considering "the complexities of this problem," decided against sending the letter to the president for his signature or to MacArthur.[56]

MacArthur addressed the FEC demands indirectly on June 21, following the opening of the newly elected Diet to debate the draft constitution. In a statement issued "to the Japanese people," he stated (without attribution to the FEC) the three criteria the FEC had adopted on May 13 and said:

These criteria governing the mechanics involved in constitutional revision thus far have been scrupulously followed, and they must continue to guide now that the issue is before the National Diet. . . . The Government Draft now before the Diet is a Japanese document, and it is for the people of Japan, acting through their duly elected representatives, to determine its form and content—whether it be adopted, modified, or rejected.[57]

After three months of turning aside any and all inquiries, requests, and demands, this was MacArthur's response to the FEC, and to his own government. His statement reasserted his earlier stance: The draft constitution "is a Japanese document" and the process of considering it has been and will be open and democratic. In other words, an international commission sitting in a distant city would not be allowed to intervene.

The FEC continued to discuss the draft constitution section by section, and to spar with MacArthur as the debates in the Diet proceeded during the summer of 1946. Some of the discussion reflected FEC objections regarding the composition of the cabinet, qualifications for suffrage, the precise location of sovereignty (to state clearly that "sovereignty resides with the people"), the composition and method of election of the two houses of the Diet, and how the prime minister should be chosen.[58] The FEC insisted, for example, that the prime minister and members of the cabinet should be members of the Diet. MacArthur initially objected but then acquiesced and pressured the Yoshida government to persuade the Diet's committee on revision to amend the draft accordingly.

Even as late as September, when the draft bill had passed the House of Representatives and was being debated in the House of Peers, the FEC again insisted on making inconsequential amendments to the draft. The Chinese member of the FEC wanted this antiwar constitution, which banned all military forces, explicitly to say that all cabinet ministers must be civilians. MacArthur ordered the amendment. The FEC also demanded that it be given enough time "to pass upon the final draft of the Constitution . . . before it is finally approved by the Diet and becomes legally valid."[59] Further conflict over this issue was avoided when normal delays in Diet proceedings enabled the FEC to complete its examination of the draft constitution before the Diet had formally approved it. In the end, all members of the FEC, except the Soviet Union, "expressed at least qualified approval" of the document.[60]

10 . . . .

"Seize This Opportunity"

• REWORKING THE MARCH 6 DRAFT

Following our review of the reaction of the FEC and developments in Washington triggered by MacArthur's "approval" of the draft on March 6, we must return to Tokyo, to the halls of the cabinet's Legislation Bureau and SCAP's Government Section, to see how the draft evolved in spring 1946. In the period March 7–24, Japanese cabinet officials gathered reactions, comments and suggestions from the many government ministries and offices as it prepared for further negotiations with SCAP. Irie and Satō of the Legislation Bureau met on April 2, 9, and 15 with Kades and Hussey at SCAP headquarters to seek further revisions in the draft. Meanwhile, in a major development, bureau officials rewrote the March 6 draft in colloquial Japanese. Although the English version of the draft remained the same, except for the revisions made in the April negotiations, the Japanese version, to the public's astonishment, appeared in a colloquial rebirth on April 17. We consider these developments next, starting with the rewriting in Japanese.

The draft made public on March 6 was not only written in legal terminology, with numerous technical words and difficult Chinese characters (*kanji*), but in a literary grammar seldom used in daily life. The decision to rewrite it in the colloquial language of daily speech and script was a revolution in Japanese political culture. How did it happen?

Converting to the Colloquial

The first proposal for rewriting the draft came from the youngest member of the Legislation Bureau, Watanabe Yoshihide.[1] Two or three days after the March 6 draft was published, Watanabe heard a senior colleague, appearing on Japan National Radio, say that such a permanent legal code as the constitution must be written in literary form. Foreign constitutions, he said, were always written in refined legal language, not colloquial speech. Moreover, he said, colloquial Japanese was unstable, changing too easily. Watanabe, a proponent of using common language in writing laws, not only disagreed with this analysis but thought that writing in spoken language would at least give the Japanese "control over the *style* if not the content of their constitution." He therefore broached the matter with Irie, the new director general of the bureau, who supported the idea and encouraged Watanabe to discuss it with a leader of the People's National Language Movement, Yamamoto Yūzō.[2] When a law student at Tokyo Imperial University, Irie had heard lectures by his professors on a movement advocating use of the colloquial language in writing laws.[3]

In 1946, Yamamoto, Andō Masaji, and other members of several language and literary associations became advocates of using colloquial language in the constitution.[4] Following Watanabe's contact with them on March 21, Yamamato, Andō, and others prepared a written petition requesting that laws and public documents henceforth be written in colloquial language and avoid archaic grammar and obscure, difficult words and expressions. They also urged the reduction of the number of pictographic symbols (*kanji*) then in use from 5,000 to 2,000 and the standardization of both the *kanji* and the phonetic script (*kana*) used in writing laws and government regulations. Other groups were also agitating for reform of the writing system used in common publications and taught in the schools. The draft constitution thus became a focus for reform of a writing system that many regarded as not only unnecessarily difficult but undemocratic.

On March 26, Andō, Yamamoto, law professor Yokoto Kisaburō, and judge Miyake Shōtarō delivered their petition to the prime minister's office. Support from officials of several ministries,[5] who were studying the March 6 draft, reinforced Irie's inclination to "seize this opportunity." Matsumoto, though initially cool to the idea,[6] soon changed his mind and threw his weight behind the proposal, arguing in favor of it in a cabinet meeting. His principal reason was that writing in the vernacular "might at least make it [the draft] seem a little more Japanese."[7] As he explained some years later: "I considered the draft a translation; no matter what was done, it was clearly a translation. Therefore, to hide this fact the only thing we could do, as I told the cabinet, was to rewrite the draft in colloquial Japanese."[8]

Irie canvassed the views of his senior colleague in the Legislation Bureau, Kanamori Tokujirō. Kanamori would soon emerge in the new Yoshida cabinet as the chief spokesman and defender of the draft constitution in the Diet debates. His opinion was important, and it was very positive. Irie then consulted a key senior cabinet member, Home Minister Mitsuchi Chūzō. A specialist in Japanese language, Mitsuchi had the rank of deputy prime minister in the cabinet. Irie approached him with considerable trepidation, for he knew opposition from Mitsuchi would kill the proposal. He pointed out that language specialists often disagreed on what was proper grammar of spoken Japanese. Mitsuchi agreed but countered that the same could be said of the literary language, which had changed a great deal over the years. "If our criterion is ease of understanding," he said, "it would be better to write [laws] in the colloquial language."[9] Mitsuchi knew that many citizens found the constitution difficult to read and comprehend. In this brief statement, he was embracing the goal of removing linguistic barriers and making the principles of the nation's basic law and democracy more available to the Japanese people. This was a sea change in the government's attitude toward the constitution.

At a meeting with Kades and Hussey on April 2, Irie and Satō told them of the plan to convert the draft into colloquial language. The Americans did not seem to understand what difference it would make to do this. Kades's major concern was whether this would change the meaning of any of the provisions of the document. He cautioned Irie and Satō that, when the work was completed, they should quickly translate it into English again, annotate it, and inform SCAP of any changes. SCAP, he said, would have to send the new version to the FEC.[10] They assured him that the English version would remain the same, that, in effect, using standard spoken Japanese would make it easier for the average citizen to read and comprehend the democratic principles of the new constitution.

On April 3, Watanabe, Irie, and Satō spent the day in the prime minister's office working on a colloquial version of the draft. Irie then persuaded Yamamoto, noted for his style, to write "the preamble and articles one through nine in the spoken language, to compare it with our version."[11] Unaware that the preamble had been crafted by a vain senior member of GS, Yamamoto, working at home, rewrote Hussey's long, convoluted first sentence as follows:

> We, the Japanese people, love truth, freedom and peace. We will exert all of our strength for the search and realization of these for the benefit not only of ourselves and our descendants but for the people of the whole world, and do not wish ever again to be drawn into war by a few leaders. We hereby proclaim through our duly elected representatives in the National Diet that sovereignty resides in the wishes of the people and do establish this Constitution.

Yamamoto sought Yokota's assistance. Yokota rewrote in modern Japanese MacArthur's "fundamental principles" in chapters I and II. Although the English version remained unchanged, the stiff, formal verb endings and phonetic script of the literary Japanese gave way to the more familiar words, grammar, and script of the language seen in the press every day. They completed the rewriting of these chapters in one evening and reviewed and recast their work for several hours the next day.

When they presented their work to Watanabe the next day, he seemed surprised at what they had done and quickly returned the text to the safer environs of the Legislation Bureau.[12] Officials of the bureau would have the final say in how the draft was rewritten. Fearing that Yamamoto had gone too far, they rejected his preamble, recalling perhaps Kades's order on March 4 that the SCAP preamble be "restored verbatim." They may also have known of Hussey's pride in his own prose. They knew, too, that the colloquial version would have to pass muster in the cabinet, which it did in a formal meeting on April 5 (even while Satō and Kades were still making changes). Fearing strong conservative reaction, the Legislation Bureau "concealed from the world the fact that we were working on a colloquial version of the constitution until the cabinet announced it on April 17." Irie explained that "we were concerned that some clever scheming might block this advance of culture while public opinion on the matter was still fluid."[13]

The Impact of the March 6 Draft

While work on the colloquial text was going on, Satō focused on further editing and revision of the March 6 draft. He had incorporated some of his marginal notes after leaving the Daiichi building the afternoon of March 5. That evening, he had Shirasu negotiate by telephone with Kades, excising two phrases from article 13 that specifically guaranteed the rights of foreigners and their legal equality with Japanese citizens.[14] On March 6, back at his office, Satō compared his March 5 draft with the "certified" copy of the English language version that Hussey had left with the cabinet secretary. He discovered "discrepancies of wording in several places" and made corrections. As both sides reviewed what they had wrought at the marathon drafting session of March 4–5, they agreed to make further changes in four meetings in early April.

The March 6 draft sent shock waves through the bureaucracy, especially the imperial household ministry. The whole government would have to operate under a new basic law, requiring interpretation of numerous articles, and the rewriting of legal codes and thousands of government regulations. As questions began pouring in, the Legislation Bureau prepared a detailed timetable for consulting with all the ministries and agencies. For advice on foreign constitutions and legislation, the bureau sought the assistance of three professors of the law faculty of Tokyo Imperial University.[15] Formal consultations, which began March 18 and continued through the end of the month, involved the ministries of imperial household, foreign affairs, home affairs, finance, justice, education, and health and welfare and the secretariats of both houses of the national Diet.

Officials of the imperial household ministry wasted no time expressing serious concern about the treatment of the emperor in the March 6 draft. Articles 8 and 84 would prohibit gifts to the imperial family, place all their finances under Diet control, and nationalize all imperial property, except "hereditary estates." During the next two weeks the ministry raised many questions about the status of the emperor when the imperial house law became subject to the Diet (article 2) and all persons were declared equal under the law (article 14). The press also expressed concern about the emperor's property as defined in the draft.[16]

Irie's attempts to quiet such concerns were not entirely successful. Palace officials sent a note to the cabinet objecting to the provisions of article 84 which exempted imperial hereditary estates from government control but confiscated the remaining property and put all finances of the imperial family at the mercy of the Diet.[17] The issue of subordinating the imperial institution to the Diet continued to roil negotiations and Diet debates till the very end.

Questions Posed and Answered

By March 24, consultations with other ministries, especially the finance and foreign ministries, produced a lengthy list of comments, suggestions, and protests on every provision of the draft.[18] Irie discussed their questions with Matsumoto, who was still minister in charge of constitutional matters. Most were satisfactorily answered by Irie and his colleagues. However, some were important enough to refer to Kades and Hussey. On April 2, Irie and Satō submitted to GS the issues raised by the ministries, in the form of three sets of questions.[19] The Japanese proposed to modify fifteen articles of the March 6 draft—five articles in chapter III (Rights and Duties of the People), five in chapter IV (the Diet), and five in chapter V (the Cabinet).[20] Most involved nothing more than attempts to achieve greater clarity by reversing sentences, changing a word or two, eliminating repetition, tightening up the language. As Kades and Hussey examined the proposed changes, they readily granted permission to make most of them. But they disallowed several which, in their opinion, involved "matters of substance."

On this day, the principal Japanese concern was that "unqualified freedom of expression" by speech and publication might encourage obscene publications or disobedience to law. Satō had raised this issue before, during the marathon meeting on March 5, citing the Weimar Constitution's provisions allowing censorship to protect public morality. He and Irie now proposed to insert a clause that would permit the censorship of any expression which might allow publications injurious to public morals or encourage citizens to violate laws. Kades responded much as he had earlier. He rejected as undemocratic any such provision in the Japanese constitution.[21]

A week later, on April 9, Japanese representatives raised the issue of the emperor's role in foreign affairs.[22] They wanted a ruling by the chief of GS regarding the procedure for signing and ratifying treaties, and to whom foreign ambassadors would present their credentials. These were weighty matters, indeed, for officials of the Foreign Ministry. Shirasu Jirō, the deputy director of the CLO, and Hagiwara Tōru, the head of the Foreign Ministry's treaty bureau, took their questions directly to General Whitney. They did not wish to have decisions on this issue rendered by Kades or Hussey. Hagiwara, who in October 1945 had made preliminary recommendations on constitutional reform, now wanted to know what the emperor's role would be in conducting diplomatic relations. Would the emperor be treated as a "contracting party" of a treaty for the Japanese nation? Could the emperor meet and sign the credentials of ambassadors and instruments of ratification? Whitney agreed that, yes, he could act in both cases.

With this out of the way, Irie and Satō returned that same day to GS for a second conference with Kades and Hussey.[23] They posed questions about several articles, some involving no more than minor adjustments in wording. Kades and Hussey made a ruling on each and every one of them, either approving or disapproving. They quickly approved most, as they involved no basic constitutional principles. The most controversial had to do with gifts to the imperial family (article 8) and disposition of imperial properties (article 84). The latter was to be a bone of contention over the next five months, coming to a head finally in late August during a rancorous debate between the House of Representatives and GS.[24]

The Issue of Imperial Property

In the meeting of April 9, however, the Japanese side sought clarification of the wording of article 8, which seemed to place all financial matters of the imperial house under direct control of the Diet.[25] This provision reflected deep distrust of the imperial family as an institution. American propaganda during the war had painted the emperor as super-rich, the largest of the *zaibatsu*, accountable to no one. He was said to possess hundreds of thousands of acres of land, countless shrines and palaces, and enormous wealth in stocks and bonds. A paper written in 1944–1945 in the Foreign Economic Administration contributed to the American occupation's concern with "excess" imperial wealth.[26]

American official policy, as stated in SWNCC 150/4, was to promote "wide distribution of income and of the ownership of means of production and trade" and "the dissolution of the large industrial and banking combinations." U.S. policy regarded concentrations of wealth in Japan as undemocratic. Moreover, Washington's directive to MacArthur on political reform (SWNCC 228) targeted the imperial wealth: "The entire income of the Imperial Household shall be turned into the public treasury and the expenses of the Imperial Household shall be appropriated by the legislature in the annual budget." Articles 8 and 88 in the draft constitution accurately reflected this policy.

At the meeting with Kades and Hussey on April 9, Irie and Satō sought clarification of the GS interpretation of article 8. Did the provision prohibit the customary small gifts given to the imperial family by any Japanese citizen? Did "Imperial House" mean the emperor and his immediate family, or all his relatives? Did this mean gifts to the imperial family as a corporate body, or to each and every member of the family? What about New Year's gifts from one member of the family to another? Could the emperor give his wife and children gifts without seeking Diet permission? Kades and Hussey reiterated SCAP's tough line: All the imperial family's property, income, and other assets, were to be placed under Diet control. They resisted Irie's and Satō's attempts to change the wording or establish an interpretation of the provision favorable to the imperial family. But what was the American rationale for prohibiting individual gifts to the royal family? Gifts could not be allowed because of the danger that one of the Japan's large corporations (*zaibatsu*) might convey its property to the emperor as a gift from an individual. "All gifts," Kades told them, "must therefore be authorized by the Diet." Moreover, he interpreted the article's prohibition of giving valuables to "the Imperial House" to mean that no gift could be given to *any member of the imperial family* without Diet authorization.

Kades and Hussey also rejected the Japanese effort to exclude the emperor's "personal property" from state control under article 88. Such property might include, for example, his stocks and bonds, cash and gold, and even revenue from them. The intention of this article was to have revenue from imperial property, except "hereditary estates," paid fully into the national treasury. Kades halted further probing by saying negotiations on article 88 were under way between Major General William F. Marquat, head of the economic and scientific section of SCAP, and representatives of the imperial household ministry. Marquat was investigating the extent of imperial "hereditary property." Kades cautioned that article 88 might have to be revised once that investigation was completed.

"The Supreme Law"

Another source of conflict was article 94, which identified the constitution as "the Supreme Law." As Satō had done during the March 4–5 marathon negotiations,[27] he again objected to this as essentially a rhetorical statement unsuited for the constitution. The Japanese negotiators, uncomfortable with the article, proposed omitting the first paragraph, or placing it in the preamble. They had no objection to the second paragraph but wished to make it an independent article. In rejecting the proposal, Kades claimed that such revisions would cause this provision to lose its meaning. It was, he asserted, the "masterpiece of this draft Constitution, is highly regarded in the United States and cannot be eliminated."

What the Japanese did not know was that the author was none other than the director of GS, General Whitney himself. Just as no change would be allowed in the preamble, of which Hussey was the proud father, article 94 represented Whitney's effort to enshrine his rhetoric on freedom and human rights in the constitution of a foreign country. Whitney's prose had first appeared as article 13 of the SCAP draft, related directly to human rights of chapter III. It was moved to chapter X, "Supreme Law," during the March 4–5 marathon meeting. There it would remain, a provocative reminder of the constitution's roots, through the long debates in the Privy Council, in both houses of the Diet and to the promulgation.

Local Government Again

Irie and Satō next turned to the chapter on local government. In March, Satō had lost his battle for a system of indirect elections of prefectural governors and other local officials.[28] He was determined to try again, under less pressure this time. Kades replied that SCAP considered this issue—democratizing local government—an important commitment. The FEC agreed with SCAP on this, he said. Kades was right: Both FEC and SCAP were committed to direct popular elections of local officials. Irie and Satō pointed out the problems of excessive spending for direct elections, multiple candidates, a fragmented vote that would produce no absolute majority and resulting political instability. They preferred a system of indirect elections, with members of local assemblies acting as nominators who could select candidates for whom the voters would cast their ballots. But Kades insisted on direct popular elections, including run-off elections if necessary. In accordance with U.S. and FEC policy, he vetoed the method of selecting local officials preferred by the Japanese bureaucrats.

Emergency Powers

The third set of questions prepared by the Japanese involved the issue of government during an emergency. The Japanese feared a paralysis of government might occur unless the cabinet had power to act when the lower house of the Diet was dissolved. Several contingencies were mentioned to justify such a provision: sudden death of a prime minister, a large-scale natural disaster, an urgent need to conclude an international treaty or agreement or to ratify one already concluded.[29] The same arguments had been used at the April 2 meeting to justify a special Diet committee for this purpose. Kades had rejected them then. This was deeply troubling to the Japanese government, and on this day Satō was determined to press the issue. He presented in English drafts the provision his government wished to have inserted. The provision said that the cabinet, when faced with an "urgent necessity," would be authorized to take emergency measures when the Diet had been dissolved or could not be convoked. The measures would be provisional and would become null and void unless the cabinet could get the approval of the Diet within a period of ten days after the opening of the next session.[30] The emergency power granted to the cabinet would thus be limited and would expire quickly unless the Diet approved it.

Kades still balked. He would not approve granting emergency power to the cabinet in this way. He considered it dangerous to democracy. He thought the death of a prime minister could be dealt with under article 67 (when the cabinet resigns it shall continue to function until a new prime minister is appointed). And he could think of no case when ratification of treaties might have to be done quickly. In short, Kades again rejected Satō's proposal to give the cabinet limited emergency power.

If not in the cabinet, Satō countered, how about providing such power in the House of Councillors, which continues when the lower house is dissolved? Satō was proposing creation of a standing committee in the upper house to act on behalf of the Diet while the lower house was dissolved. Kades also rejected this proposal as "the worst method because it runs the risk of ignoring the Diet." (The House of Councillors was, of course, also part of the Diet, consisting according to article 38 of "elected members, representative of all the people.")

Kades advanced another solution to the problem, namely, to revise article 50 to permit the Councillors to be convoked in emergency session to meet a crisis. A second paragraph could be added to the article, he suggested, as follows: "Measures enacted at such session shall be provisional and shall become null and void unless agreed to by the House of Representatives within a period of ten (10) days after the opening of the next session of the Diet." Although Kades's formulation borrowed some of Satō's own language, it did not satisfy Satō or Katō. Katō, who interpreted and took notes during the conference, observed laconically: "He [Kades] persisted in his opinion on this point, and we decided it would not be good policy to press too hard. The result was that we adopted Kades' proposal in that form."[31]

Following this careful scrutiny and control of what went in the draft constitution, Kades said something that surprised the Japanese negotiators: "It was unnecessary for the Japanese Government always to have SCAP's approval for each and every alteration in the wording of this draft." The changes they had been discussing, he said, were problems for the Japanese themselves to resolve. The Japanese were astonished by the statement. SCAP's approval had been required for every significant (and often even insignificant) change in the draft since negotiations began in February. The pattern was continuing in these talks in April. Satō responded that "in view of the circumstances of the preparation of this draft, we thought it appropriate to obtain your [Kades'] 'advice' when making changes in the wording and could not arbitrarily alter even the word 'estates'."[32] Katō recorded that "without responding, Kades allowed a slight smile to appear on his face." The incident reveals, again, SCAP's continuing tight control over the draft. The truth was that GS would not permit the Japanese cabinet to alter any wording without careful scrutiny and approval.

Talks between the two sides resumed at a fourth conference on April 15. Satō submitted the government's full draft constitution with changes agreed on in the previous three meetings. It was now in the form of a legislative bill, ready to be presented to the Diet, written in colloquial language and popular cursive script (hiragana). The Legislation Bureau had also prepared a new English-language draft incorporating the agreed-on revisions. In seeking GS's permission for immediate publication of both documents, Satō agreed, as directed, not to use the Supreme Commander's name when making the new draft public. To the Japanese, this seemed odd in light of MacArthur's prominent endorsement of the March 6 draft when it was released to the press. Clearly SCAP, through Kades, was responding to FEC complaints.[33] MacArthur had become sensitive to criticism and was attempting to hide his staff's involvement in every step of the drafting process. After consulting Whitney, Kades offered one small concession: The Japanese government might mention "informal consultations" with MacArthur's headquarters.

On April 19, two days after the "final draft of the Japanese Constitution" (SCAP's term for the April 17 English version) had been published, Shirasu reported to Satō that Kades was upset over the Japanese words used to render "advice and consent" in the draft. When SCAP's translators, using the English and Japanese drafts of March 6, spotted what they thought were changes in the colloquial draft, SCAP officials were quick to charge the Japanese with manipulation and bad faith. Shirasu told Satō that GS believed the Japanese side had acted in bad faith by inserting words not agreed on.[34] Alarmed, Satō grabbed his Japanese-English dictionary and rushed to Kades's office. With his interpreter at his side, he told Kades that the words (hosa to dōi) in articles 3 and 7 did accurately translate into colloquial Japanese the English phrase "advice and consent." Some changes in wording were unavoidable when the document was rewritten in colloquial language. Kades accepted this explanation.

Even though the new draft had been published two days earlier (April 17),

Kades raised questions about wording in several other articles. He was especially careful about any changes concerning the emperor or imperial household. When these were examined, usually they were accounted for by the use of colloquial language in the April 17 draft.[35] On the question of imperial property, however, the two sides continued to disagree over the meaning of "hereditary estates." Though they discussed their differences at this meeting, no decisions were reached, and negotiations continued between specialists on both sides.

"No Choice But to Abide"

● THE PRIVY COUNCIL AND BUREAUCRATS PREPARE

Although the draft of March 6 had been approved by the cabinet and abruptly taken by Hussey to Washington, negotiations, revisions, and translations had continued for several weeks before producing a text for submission to the Diet. Meanwhile, before the draft could go to the Diet, the 1889 constitution required the Privy Council, a consultative body for the emperor, to sign off on it. Following this procedure helped reinforce the impression that Japan and SCAP were observing all the rules in revising the constitution. The emperor had "initiated" the changes to the Meiji Constitution drawn up in draft form by his government. The Privy Council would debate the draft before it went to the Diet for debate and adoption. Then it would be returned to the Council for a final stamp of approval in the presence of the emperor. All very neat, done in accordance with existing constitutional provisions. This was the line MacArthur reiterated to the FEC in his message of April 13: SCAP is advising on constitutional reform but not dictating its course or content.

The Privy Council

The Privy Council's responsibility under the Meiji Constitution was "to deliberate upon important matters of state, when they have been consulted by the Emperor" (article LVI). In the spring of 1946, this body of twenty-five advisers included many senior statesmen and leading scholars, such as Suzuki Kantarō, former admiral and prime minister in 1944–1945; Shidehara Hiroshi, younger brother of the prime minister, who won his spurs in the ministry of education and in colonial service in Korea and Taiwan; Nomura Kiichirō, former admiral, foreign minister, and ambassador to the United States in 1940–1941; Minobe Tatsukichi, prominent constitutional scholar; Hayashi Hiroku, diplomatic historian and former president of Keiō University; and Sekiya Teizaburō, who had served as a senior palace adviser in the fall of 1945.

Historians have tended to ignore the debates in the Privy Council, believing that it could only rubber stamp whatever the government submitted. In general this was true, but the council did anticipate many of the questions raised later in the Diet. In this sense, it served a useful purpose in identifying some major concerns of conservative Japanese as they read the bill containing the draft: the status of the emperor, whether sovereign, whether one of the people, and the meaning of "symbol"; the future of *kokutai*; the no-war provision and defense; the possibility of revising the draft; and much more. The councillors found many faults in the bill. The major principles of the draft disturbed and agitated them, as did the awkward language in which they were expressed. They were frustrated that, as the government spokesmen told them, they could neither amend the principles of the bill nor improve its language. In the course of their meetings, they came to understand the international circumstances that tied their hands.

Shidehara Addresses the Council

At the opening of the Privy Council on March 20, Prime Minister Shidehara offered informal comments on chapters I (emperor) and II (renunciation of war) and touched on the circumstances leading to the draft constitution.[1] His cautious remarks conveyed the impression that the cabinet, under pressure from SCAP and fearing an Allied threat to the emperor, had taken the initiative in making the draft. He said MacArthur had acted to prevent the FEC from interfering in MacArthur's policy of attempting to protect the imperial household. General MacArthur, to create a fait accompli, rushed the announcement of the draft constitution. The prime minister explained the cabinet's reason for joining in MacArthur's conspiracy: "Considering these circumstances, I believe the completion of this draft before us today is something for which, for Japan's sake, we should be pleased. [Without this draft] I believe the Imperial Household would have been in grave danger."[2]

Shidehara linked the chapter on the emperor to the chapter renouncing war. Japan must give up this right, normally enjoyed by all nations, to preserve even a truncated imperial institution. Chapters I and II were the most important provisions of the draft constitution. He said not a word about democracy, the rights and welfare of the people, the expanded powers of the people's representatives, or an independent judiciary.[3]

Almost a month passed following Shidehara's presentation on March 20 before the cabinet again consulted the Privy Council. Shortly after the colloquial draft appeared in the press on April 17, Irie briefed the president of the council, Shimizu Tōru,[4] on recent negotiations with GS.[5] He also reviewed the draft's origins and responded to questions about its major provisions. He requested that the council quickly give its approval so the draft could be sent forward to the Diet.[6]

Shimuzu appointed a "deliberation" committee of thirteen councillors, under the chairmanship of Ushio Shigenosuke, to examine the draft constitution and report to the full council. The committee met in eight sessions from April 22 to May 15 before adjourning while the Shidehara cabinet was replaced by the new

Yoshida cabinet (May 22). The committee then held three additional meetings on May 29, June 1 and June 3. On June 8, the committee reported to a plenary session of the council in the presence of the emperor.[7] Cabinet members were present at most of the meetings: Prime Minister Shidehara at the plenary meeting of the council and occasionally thereafter; Minister Matsumoto Jōji, responding to many questions of the deliberation committee, until relieved of his duties on May 22, when the Shidehara cabinet's resignation became effective; and other ministers. Also attending these meetings were key members of the Legislation Bureau, who served as experts to assist in answering the councillors' questions.

Committee Deliberations

Formal deliberations on the draft began on April 22. By this time a final version of the draft had been approved by SCAP and rewritten in the colloquial language. Also, the FEC's dissatisfaction with MacArthur's approval of it had been reported in Japanese newspapers.

At the first session of the deliberation committee, Prime Minister Shidehara again explained the basic principles of the draft. Minister Matsumoto assisted, responding to most of the questions about the drafting process and special features of the document.[8] Other ministers and members of the Legislation Bureau stood by to field questions of a more specialized nature.

In this opening meeting of the Privy Council, the cabinet faced several sensitive questions. What was the relationship of SCAP and the FEC to this draft? Could the draft be amended by the Privy Council or the Diet? Matsumoto replied that the government could not make or accept substantive changes in the bill while it was before the Privy Council, but later the Diet probably could. However, he quickly added, the bill could not be amended by adding new provisions to it. He ended with a weak comment which revealed just how hobbled he thought the government was: "In actuality it is uncertain to what extent it can be amended."[9]

Minobe Tatsukichi, professor emeritus of Tokyo Imperial University and the nation's most respected constitutional authority, rose to speak. He questioned the legitimacy of the bill and the government's action in presenting it to the council. He argued that article LXXIII of the 1889 constitution, which gave the emperor sole authority to initiate amendments, had become null and void in August 1945, at the moment the Japanese government accepted the Potsdam Declaration. Why? Because the government had accepted the declaration's premise of popular sovereignty, where government was determined by "the freely expressed will of the Japanese people." This was the August Revolution, so-called in an article published while the Privy Council was meeting.[10]

Minobe denounced as false the statement in the draft's preamble that "the Japanese people . . . establish this Constitution." The people had nothing to do with it, he said. The proposal for revision came from the emperor, the draft was drawn up by the government (he did not mention SCAP's role), and the Diet had only a limited right of revision. He deplored the plan of pushing this draft through a severely constrained Diet and urged the government to withdraw it immediately. How then should revision be done? Minobe's answer was that "a democratic constitution should freely be discussed and drafted by representatives of the people." By what procedure? "Procedures for the revision of the Constitution should be discussed at the coming Diet and . . . determined by the Diet [itself]." This was an argument for care and deliberation in considering the draft. Matsumoto's lame response was that submitting the bill to the Diet for approval at the next session "does not necessarily mean that we [have] ignored the will of the people."[11]

Councillors Takegoshi and Izaka wanted to know which of the drafts, the English or Japanese, should be considered the original. Further, what relation would the English-language draft have to the Japanese constitution in the future? Matsumoto, following the conspiracy's line, asserted that the Japanese draft was the original, despite what he had already revealed about its origins. With greater candor, Irie told the meeting that "in the negotiations with the Americans, agreement was reached on the English-language version. Therefore, in the future it will be an authoritative reference work in interpreting the Japanese Constitution."

As the hearings continued, the councillors scrutinized the preamble and every chapter of the proposed constitution, agonizing especially over chapters on the emperor, renunciation of war, and the legislature. They called the concept of popular sovereignty foreign to Japan. One councillor characterized the proclamation of sovereignty by the people and their "establishing this Constitution" as a "bloodless revolution." Irie denied this, telling them that the emperor himself, as initiator of the preamble, was declaring these principles. Besides, the emperor was the "nucleus" of the people. It was no revolution if one accepted this interpretation of "the people." But this was a transparent maneuver by the government to preserve some semblance of imperial sovereignty and prestige. The government, forced to defend SCAP's dictate on popular sovereignty, attempted to legitimize it by advancing the myth of the emperor's authorship.

One member wondered whether the traditional national character (kokutai) had been protected by the provisions of article 1. Matsumoto equated kokutai with the emperor system but denied that the emperor had ever personally conducted state affairs. When pressed further, Matsumoto responded that the most important feature of the national character was the existence of the emperor system at the head of state, not his personal conduct of state affairs.[12]

The distinction was important. Even a powerless symbolic emperor at the head of state preserved kokutai, according to Matsumoto, because the emperor had never functioned as head of state. The words "at the head of the state" had been used in MacArthur's note of February 3. Ironically, Matsumoto was now using these words to persuade the Privy Council that kokutai would continue. The draft constitution preserved the emperor system and kokutai by limiting the emperor's involvement in state affairs. This was neither good history nor convincing argument; Matsumoto and his subordinates had to offer other arguments to bolster their case.

Government spokesmen said in many ways that the people and emperor are one, implying that sovereignty was shared. The people were to be raised to the elevated level of sovereignty, but the emperor would not be brought down from the plain of high heaven. "One can't imagine the 'people' [*kokumin*] apart from the existence of the Emperor." "The Emperor is the nucleus of the people." "Sovereignty is possessed by all the people with the Emperor at the center." "The Emperor is the symbol and center of the people." "The ruler and the people are one." The councillors were left shaking their heads. Former admiral Nomura, who had been ambassador to Washington in 1941, attempted to cut through the rhetoric by urging the government to acknowledge and accept popular sovereignty. "In the English text it is clear that sovereignty resides with the people. The Japanese text has taken great pains to obscure this, but since Japan has accepted the Potsdam Declaration, we have no choice but to abide by it. How about making it clearer that sovereignty resides in the people? Otherwise, one can't understand this constitution. We must make up our minds to state clearly that this is a bloodless revolution."[13]

The Right of Self-Defense

Members of the Privy Council expressed apprehension and concern over a provision that seemed to renounce Japan's right of self-defense. From the first day of hearings on April 22, they attempted to learn from the government the meaning of the two paragraphs of this article. Initially, at least, they were confused rather than angry over the provision or apprehensive for Japan's future. Hayashi began by probing the connection between the concept of renouncing war and the right of self-defense. He noted the apparent contradiction between the first and second paragraphs. The first, although it renounced war and the use of force as a means of settling international disputes, did not explicitly renounce war for the purpose of self-defense. But the second paragraph in a practical sense seemed to make war, for whatever purpose, impossible by denying Japan any military forces, war potential, or the right of belligerency. Even if Japan had the right of self-defense, how could it be exercised without military forces?

Matsumoto agreed with Hayashi's interpretation of the first paragraph. As for the second, he said there was no explicit provision for self-defense, even if Japan were attacked, to prevent "its being used as a pretext." Thus although "it is impossible to wage war" without military forces, it is also unreasonable to prohibit a recourse to arms in self-defense. The "right of belligerency" in paragraph two implies a declared war but "does not purport to prohibit even acts of self-defense."[14]

The committee returned to Article 9 at its fourth hearing on May 6. The issue this day was how the renunciation of war would affect Japan's future membership in the United Nations. Could Japan join without having armed forces? Irie, speaking for the government, speculated that Japan might be exempted from the United Nations where all members were expected to contribute to the common defense. Hayashi suggested two theories about how Japan might join as a member without arms: (1) it might seek an exemption from the obligation of member's contribution to the common defense or (2) it might join the United Nations after revising article 9. He then asked, "Which of the two does the Government intend to adopt?"

Hayashi's question offered government spokesmen a chance to say Japan might repudiate the no-war clause once the occupation ended. Such a statement would certainly have angered SCAP and the FEC. Here was a chance for Matsumoto to lash out at this restriction on Japan's sovereignty and independence. But he resisted the temptation. Instead, he deflected the question with the laconic remark that the future of the United Nations was uncertain. Irie reminded the councillors that this bill expressed "the desperate attitude of . . . 'burning one's boat'." Neither he nor Matsumoto would explicitly endorse Nomura's suggestion that the nation was being denied the right to maintain war potential "because of pressure from without."[15] Whatever the Privy Council thought of the provision—Japan was being unjustly punished, Japan was being left without protection against civil conflict—government spokesmen did not attack it in front of a sympathetic audience.

Clearly disappointed with the government's position, Hayashi, an outspoken critic of the draft, finally summarized his own views on article 9 during the last meeting of the council on June 8. It is less important, he said, that other countries follow Japan's example in renouncing war than that Japan go forward "on the royal road of justice." The progress of science and development of arms with dreadful power of destruction would awaken the nations of the world and make them think seriously about renouncing war as a way of settling international disputes. This argument, embraced by others in the coming months, implied that Japan's constitutional act of renouncing war might become a guide to other countries in the future.[16]

The Concern With Rights and Duties

The discussion moved from the antiwar provisions to the rights and duties of the people. Councillors' concerns were heightened by the mass "Food May Day" rallies in front of the imperial palace and surrounding the prime minister's official residence a few days earlier. Hayashi spoke directly to this when he questioned whether a constitutional guarantee of freedom of expression might threaten the public order or violate public morals. He worried that the principle of individual equality would require the abolition of the family system in the civil code. And he wondered whether guaranteeing the right of workers to organize and to bargain and act collectively was not going too far. Why, he asked, was there no provision establishing the duty of citizens to pay taxes?

Others questioned the wisdom of granting such broad rights to the people. As Isaka put it, "the rights of the people are too broad; and, on the other hand, duties . . . have not been provided for." He urged the government to put more emphasis on duties of the people. In responding for the government, Matsumoto—in his last official comments on the draft constitution—seemed sympathetic to the views of Isaka and others. Yet he argued that the exercise of individual rights should not conflict with personal good behavior or threaten the public order. In the end, he agreed that it would be necessary "to control the abuse of rights."[17]

A New Prime Minister Faces Some Old Questions

No meetings were held between May 15 and May 29 while Yoshida Shigeru maneuvered to form a new cabinet and replace Shidehara as prime minister. As the new prime minister, Yoshida met with the Privy Council for the first time on May 29. The official record reproduced Yoshida's answers to questions in one terse sentence, offering nothing of substance. But, off the record, Yoshida provided a fuller account of the SCAP-imposed constraints under which the government was operating. At last, the councillors heard directly from a key member of Shidehara's cabinet how the conspiracy between MacArthur and Japan's top leaders had come about. Yoshida spoke candidly, revealing what MacArthur and Whitney had told him in February about the circumstances surrounding MacArthur's decision to have his own staff draft a model constitution in English. And he shared with the councillors his understanding of the reasons for rushing the draft to completion.[18]

According to Yoshida, MacArthur had said that renunciation of war and continuing the imperial house were closely linked, important objectives for the Occupation. MacArthur praised the emperor for ensuring a peaceful surrender in 1945. He told Yoshida that time was of the essence. Getting the revision done quickly was more important than worrying unduly about the content. Writing an excellent constitution would mean nothing if time was lost. Yoshida confirmed what others had suspected, that MacArthur had "wanted the draft published around the time the FEC began its meetings on February 26."[19] It was important to assuage the FEC's suspicions that Japan was planning to rearm or that its democratization effort was a sham.

MacArthur had wished to have the draft done quickly for several reasons. He wanted to forestall any interference by the Allied Council, which was scheduled to arrive in Tokyo in late February. He considered, too, possible shifts in Japanese domestic opinion and the addition of troops of other countries to the occupation forces. Finally, he had wanted the draft published before the general election in April and to make it an issue in the election campaign.[20] Yoshida also told the council that in subsequent negotiations with SCAP he had complained about the article on imperial property. Yoshida said: "I myself discussed this with them several times. They said 'wouldn't it be alright to revise this provision in the Diet? At this time we want to finish the draft and publish it quickly.' "[21]

Even if that were so, Hayashi pressed, why continue to rush the deliberation process after the draft had been published? The first of the FEC's three criteria for constitutional revision reported in the press on May 15[22] had been to ensure the necessary time and opportunity for the Japanese people to study the draft. What procedure did the FEC expect Japan to follow? Yoshida did not respond directly to this question. Instead, he stressed that it was most important for Japan to end the occupation and recover sovereignty as soon as possible. Many Americans in the Occupation were saying the same thing. Among some, he joked, the abbreviation GHQ meant "go home quickly." It was important to assure the world immediately that Japan was serious about carrying out thorough democratization and avoiding rearmament. The best way to do that was to enact without delay a constitution embodying these principles. As for the FEC's recent resolution on constitutional reform, Yoshida considered it an attempt to soften the earlier Soviet demand for a direct hand in the Occupation's policies and administration.[23]

What was the government's position on revising the draft, Hayashi wanted to know? Yoshida said: "I think General MacArthur would have no objections to revisions so long as the fundamental principles and basic forms were not changed."[24] As for specific revisions the councillors wished to make, Yoshida replied that he would have to study the matter before replying. By "study the matter," Yoshida apparently meant he and his subordinates would have to ask GS whether the change could be made. Actually, Satō had already discussed with Kades the FEC's May 13 resolution calling for sufficient time for a careful study of the draft. He explained that some Japanese interpreted this to mean that the FEC wanted Japan to take more time before submitting the draft to the Diet. Kades strongly denied this interpretation. He said: "The Japanese government should not be swayed by the FEC's statement. I myself have already forgotten the contents of the statement." Just proceed with the revision as planned, Kades emphasized.[25]

On the location of sovereignty, Hayashi quoted MacArthur's March 6 public endorsement of the draft constitution which, he said, "places sovereignty squarely in the hands of the people." By contrast, Matsumoto had told the councillors that "as a matter of law sovereignty resides in the State." Consequently, he explained, "the Emperor is an organ of the State." Hayashi questioned Yoshida on the new government's view on this important issue and whether this interpretation could be defended in the coming Diet debates. Although Yoshida was not prepared to reply to the question, he said SCAP had made it clear in their negotiations that, by making the emperor a symbol in article 1, the "person" of the reigning emperor was protected and would be saved from any warmaking responsibility. The emperor was, in short, divorced from any political responsibility. This, he was convinced, is what the Allied powers wanted, and they were satisfied with the wording in article 1. He declined to get involved in a theoretical debate over the "organ theory" of the emperor's position and asked the council for advice on how to respond to such questions when they came up in the Diet.[26]

Councillors Nomura and Shidehara reiterated to Yoshida their worry about foreign invasion and internal disorder when the occupation forces left Japan. Without armed forces or war potential, how could Japan defend itself? Shouldn't the second paragraph of article 9 be eliminated? Didn't it go too far? The Potsdam Declaration demanded only the elimination of existing military forces. Even a permanently neutral country such as Switzerland maintained military forces.

Accepted—With Reservations

In the end the Privy Council voted to refer the bill to the Diet without modifications. The examination committee reported to the full council and members had an opportunity to offer any final comments. The committee report outlined the objectives of constitutional reform as contained in this bill and concluded that, despite some shortcomings, "this measure [draft bill] must be said to be the proper step [in achieving the objectives] and the contents of the bill may on the whole be regarded as conforming to these objectives." The revision was unprecedented, but due to "the critical situation both at home and abroad, there seems to be no alternative but to approve of the general import of this bill."

Hayashi announced his support of the bill despite his reservations about its many imperfections. He refrained from trying to modify any provisions of the bill, in view of the circumstances, but felt compelled to share with the council his concerns. The bill is historic and revolutionary, he said. It deserves utmost prudence and care in examining every provision and every word and phrase, many of which he thought were ambiguous and obscure. In the "ten days of deliberations" allowed the committee, this kind of thorough inquiry had not been possible. Much about it is "unsatisfactory" and "regrettable." Hayashi ended his statement complaining about the ambiguity of location of sovereignty, the emperor's powers, the provision concerning imperial household property, the uncertainty of the right of self-defense, lack of protection against "publications detrimental to public morals," and lack of clarity about the organization and character of the House of Councillors.[27]

Nomura also indicated his support for the bill, nevertheless complaining that "there is hardly any room for negotiation before submitting the bill to the discussion of the Diet." He hinted that Japan faced a threat from radical domestic forces supported from the outside. And he expressed concern that article 9 "will make it difficult for Japan to maintain public peace in our territorial land and water." The public police force is "utterly insufficient for this purpose and I feel most uneasy about . . . depend[ing] upon the Allied forces."[28]

And what would happen, he continued, when the occupying forces of the Allies were withdrawn from Japan, as the Potsdam Declaration provides? Here we see the real dilemma of conservatives like Nomura: An unarmed Japan, unless protected by Allied forces, would face a serious risk of revolution led by domestic Communists aided by the Soviet Union.[29] Nomura alluded to mass demonstrations demanding food in the streets of Tokyo since March and warned that "nobody can tell what unexpected occurrence might issue." He concluded that "we must, after the withdrawal of the Allied forces, be ready with all satisfactory preparations for maintaining the public peace without depending upon others."[30]

Similar concern and dissatisfaction with the bill were expressed by Prince Takahito, the emperor's brother, just before the close of the hearings. In the presence of Emperor Hirohito, the prince offered rambling comments on the bill's treatment of the imperial family and complained about "a translated constitution" which the Japanese people would find difficult to accept as their own. He proposed settling the question of amendment authority (article LXXIII) at the coming Diet session and leaving "the work of making the Constitution to the next session." The prince ended as he had begun, in a state of confusion, saying he did not oppose the bill or approve of it, announcing in the end his abstention and withdrawing from the meeting.[31] The subcommittee's report confessed its acceptance of the inevitable: "The Government authorities . . . declared that the bill would be left to the deliberation of the Imperial Diet to ensure its perfection. Thereupon the Examination Committee . . . decided to pass the bill by majority without any modification."[32] Chairman Suzuki, the prime minister who in August 1945 had announced to the Allies Japan's decision to surrender, brought the debates to a close on June 8. With no one else wishing to speak, he omitted the second reading of the bill and asked members who supported it to stand. Only Minobe Tatsukichi, the nation's premier constitutional authority, remained seated, adamantly opposed to the bill. The meeting ended and "His Majesty retired." Thus after eleven meetings stretching over six weeks, the council voted to approve the bill containing the draft constitution and to send it to the Diet for debate.[33]

The Legislation Bureau Prepares for Diet Debates

The Legislation Bureau was an important part of the prime minister's staff. There legal experts were responsible for drafting most of the legislation and laws under the Meiji Constitution. In April and May officials of the bureau had prepared a list of questions and answers for every article of the draft. In June, following the Privy Council hearings, they revised and expanded the list, taking into account the councillors' inquiries and comments. In June and July the ministries pitched in with their own expert advice on many provisions of the draft. Such efforts had one major objective: to mobilize the government in support of the cabinet as it prepared to face the House of Representatives.[34]

Two issues were expected to be especially troublesome: (1) the locus of sovereignty and (2) the revision procedure. The bureau developed arguments to persuade conservatives in the House of Representatives that the draft would preserve *kokutai* unchanged. The bureau knew that as a result of the election of April 10, conservatives, who were in a majority, would be "waving the flag of protecting the *kokutai*." To answer them, the bureau had to come up with a convincing explanation. Kanamori, Irie, Satō, and others spent days studying the issue and formulating arguments to persuade the representatives that Japan's *kokutai* was not changed by this revision. To do this, as Satō wrote, "we had to abandon such fixed notions as *kokutai* being determined by the location of sovereignty and rethink the issue from the beginning."[35] Two weeks fielding questions in the Privy Council was an excellent chance for the bureau to hone its skills for a more public audience ahead. Bureau officials approached the challenge systematically. What emerged in the end was a long list of possible questions and answers that served as a guide for the cabinet ministers, especially the new minister, Kanamori Tokujirō, on the floor of the House of Representatives.[36]

Anticipating Questions

First, an article-by-article explanation was prepared. Bureau officials attempted to place their task in a wider political setting, drawing on the history and experience of other countries. They included, for example, information on the property holdings of the British monarchy, Anglo-American appeal practices, quotations from academic studies of freedom of expression, search and seizure and detainment, a paper on "Soviet democracy," and excerpts from American state constitutions.[37]

Second, the bureau identified "fundamental problems" and tried to anticipate questions that might arise about each. The list included the proper procedure for revising the constitution, *kokutai*, and sovereignty. Special attention was given to these three before considering individual chapters of the draft. The bureau prepared to field a variety of questions about whether the draft had been prepared according to proper legal procedure, as defined in the Meiji constitution, in revising the basic national charter. The press had already raised many questions about the draft constitution's origins: Who had prepared it? Was it done originally in English or Japanese? Was it a translation of the original English version? Did it violate article LXXIII of the existing constitution?

The authorship of the first draft was obviously a sensitive matter for the Japanese government. No government spokesman could admit openly in the Diet that SCAP had done the work. Yet the bureau made no special effort to prepare a set of questions and answers on this issue. There were several reasons. First, the answers to such questions were already quite clear to intelligent readers of the press, including Diet members. Also, such questions, although embarrassing, were not substantive in the sense of involving basic constitutional principles. No legal research was required to prepare a truthful answer for the Diet. More important, the Legislative Bureau's decision to ignore such questions was an indication that Yoshida had firmly associated himself with MacArthur in supporting the SCAP line—that he was prepared, in short, to assume the role of co-conspirator. By early June, the fundamental issue was less about who wrote the first draft or whether the Japanese draft was a translation of the SCAP draft. It had become, at this stage, whether the document's basic principles, which the cabinet had come to affirm, could be made acceptable to the Diet and to the Japanese people. It was whether a new political system, embodying the demands of the Potsdam Declaration, could be adopted quickly. Irie and Satō entertained the vain hope that House members, suspecting the truth about the drafting, would be more discrete than the press had been in speculating on the matter.

The proper procedure for adopting the new constitution concerned the bureau more than did its authorship. It was a basic constitutional matter as well as a sensitive political issue. Legal scholars and the press had already raised it. However framed, it was a basic issue that was sure to be raised when the bill reached the House of Representatives.[38] The typical question bureau officials anticipated would be posed like this: Why is the revised constitution presented to this session of the Diet? Isn't it necessary to convoke a special session to consider amending the constitution?

The answer preferred by the bureau, and the one Yoshida had offered the Privy Council in May, was the logical one. It began with a reference to "the circumstances that our country is in today." This was a powerful reminder, if one was needed, that Japan was under foreign military occupation. Even the most contumacious representative could not ignore it. It appealed to Diet members as Japanese to consider the plight of the nation before splitting hairs over legal procedures. Calling a special session of the Diet or holding a national referendum at this stage risked entangling Japan in the SCAP–FEC dispute over their relative authority. It could only prolong the agony of a foreign occupation.

Next came the argument that reconstruction of the nation must be based on a new political system. Constitutional revision must therefore be completed as soon as possible. This argument echoed the appeal that Yoshida had directed at the Privy Council: Put aside the question of who initiated the draft; adopting a new constitution quickly is more important than quibbling over who initiated it. Only with this new political system, Yoshida reasoned, could Japan preserve important elements of its heritage and regain its status as an independent and sovereign nation.

Having repeated Yoshida's position, the bureau then concluded, in indirect language, with a restatement of MacArthur's argument to Yoshida: "It doesn't seem improper for this session of the Diet to debate the draft because it was publicly announced before the [April 10] general election that constitutional revision would be done at this session of the Diet."[39] The claim is more accurate and less sweeping than SCAP's assertion that the election was, in essence, a popular referendum on the new draft constitution. The Japanese cabinet merely claimed that the voters knew when they elected their representatives on April 10 that they were choosing men and women who would debate the bill to revise the constitution.

Several follow-up questions focused attention on article LXXIII, which provided for an Imperial Order "to amend the provisions of the present constitution." First, critics might contend that complete revision or rewriting of the constitution was never anticipated under article LXXIII. The wording does seem to refer to amending one or several provisions, though it does not prohibit a complete rewriting of the document. However, the bureau quickly disposed of this contention, suggesting it was not a serious issue.

But a second related issue did require at least a brief defense. Miyazawa Toshiyoshi argued that article LXXIII had become null and void in August 1945 when Japan accepted the Potsdam Declaration.[40] The bureau's paper rejected Miyazawa's thesis. Accepting the Potsdam Declaration did not destroy the basis of Japan's existence as an independent state, nor did it produce a revolution. To bolster the argument, the bureau added a populist and democratic touch by attempting to mobilize on its side the opinion of the Japanese people. The average Japanese citizen, it asserted, agrees with the government's interpretation of the August surrender. Therefore, the current (1889) constitution is still in force and valid.

Next, the bureau anticipated questions about the role of the House of Peers. The central issue here was the legal propriety of the House of Peers, which was not elected by the people, participating in revision of the constitution. The government again invoked the will of the Japanese people to justify its position. Considering the circumstances Japan faced, it was essential for the nation to frame a new political system as soon as possible. Consequently, the desire and decision of the Japanese people was to proceed under the present system. "We do not think that the Peers' participation will produce a result that will violate the will of the people."[41]

The bureau's Q&A guide also anticipated questions about the preamble of the draft constitution. For example, wasn't the statement that the people "establish this Constitution . . . through [their] duly elected representatives in the Diet" a fiction? Again, here was the embarrassing question of the authority for "establishing this Constitution." Nobody on the Japanese side liked the wording of the preamble, and the government's draft of March 2 had omitted it. But at the March 4–5 negotiations, Kades had ordered it restored, unaltered. It fell to the Legislation Bureau therefore to fashion arguments to defend it. Would the government again remind the critics that Japan was under a military occupation? This argument would have conceded that the critics were right, that the statement was a fiction, and that Japan had little choice in the matter. Another argument was needed.

The Critical Issues: Sovereignty and *Kokutai*

The bureau took seriously SCAP's assurance that the people's representatives would have the final say in voting on the revision bill. The House of Representatives would meet for this very purpose. The government therefore could say, "because the decision of the House of Representatives [is required], it is not a fiction." In other words, revision of the constitution would be determined by the will of the people. The decision of the House of Representatives itself, representing that will, would be the decisive factor. The bureau added that hereafter important matters of state would be based on the general will of the people.[42]

Satō recalled later that several cabinet members met at least twice to discuss the principles and issues contained in the draft constitution.[43] On May 28 and June 13, Justice Minister Kimura Tokutarō and Ministers of State Saitō Takao and Uehara Etsujirō met with Kanamori and Irie. A list of questions about the draft constitution was prepared for discussion. Sovereignty and *kokutai* were the two issues receiving major attention: To whom did sovereignty belong? Did it reside in the people? Did the draft change *kokutai*? Was the authority of the emperor reduced unduly in this draft? Was the right of self-defense recognized? Considering the way the revision had been undertaken, wasn't the preamble a fiction?

Minister Saitō ventured that the draft did indeed change the location of sovereignty from the ruler to the people. The authority for enacting amendments to the constitution had also changed in this draft. If *kokutai* were defined in terms of the ruler being sovereign, Saitō reasoned, then one must conclude that *kokutai* has also changed. This was a bold admission by a cabinet minister, but perfectly logical.

Justice Minister Kimura disagreed with Saitō on *kokutai;* he believed that it remained unchanged, if understood as something—a force or power—which bound the people and the emperor harmoniously into one body. Here, from the outset, a major cabinet member advanced the useful proposition that the whole emotional issue of *kokutai*, in its essence, revolved around definition. The trick was to find the right definition. This approach was certain to provoke long debates in the Diet unless the bureau could come up with a persuasive definition of this elusive concept.

Minister Uehara tried his hand at defining what it meant. He began with the emperor, who he believed both represented and symbolized the consolidated will of all inhabitants of the country. In the past it had been considered a mistake to think of the people and the emperor existing apart one from the other. He noted in the draft that the power to enact the constitution had changed from the emperor to the Diet, representing the people. He attempted to reconcile this important point in the 1889 constitution and the new draft by asserting that, in actuality, the Meiji Constitution itself, though drafted by a few bureaucrats and promulgated by the emperor, was indeed based on the desires and demands of the people.

This was revisionist history, with an element of truth, to be sure; the Meiji government did act under pressure from political opponents. More important in the 1946 context, however, Uehara reflected in his comments an emerging tendency in the cabinet to recognize "the people" as the dominant political force of the nation.

The issues of sovereignty and *kokutai* were potentially the most explosive for the government's team in the Diet debates on the constitution bill. Both received careful consideration as the bureau fashioned the cabinet's defenses in early June 1946. Less than a year before, on August 10, 1945, officials in both the cabinet and the Foreign Ministry had raised questions about *kokutai* when accepting the Potsdam Declaration as the basis of surrender. Determined to protect imperial sovereignty, the government accepted the Allied declaration, "with the understanding that the said declaration does not comprise any demand that prejudices the prerogatives of his Majesty as a Sovereign Ruler." Protecting the sovereignty of the emperor was, at least in a narrow constitutional sense, the same as protecting *kokutai*. The two were inextricably linked in the minds of Japanese officials. Also, for the many conservatives elected to the Diet in the April general election, "preserving *kokutai*" was a central pledge. The bureau felt compelled to find ways of describing and defending the bill on revising the constitution that would persuade the conservatives that *kokutai* had not changed.

Most Japanese, the bureau believed, wished to preserve imperial sovereignty and *kokutai*. The April election results seemed to confirm this reading of public opinion on the issue. The challenge was to hit on a definition of this elusive word broad enough to encompass the understanding of a wide range of Japanese political interests and the draft constitution. As for the issue of sovereignty, the wording of SCAP's draft, the "sovereign will of the people" had forced the question to the fore. The government's initial translation of the phrase as "*supreme will of the people*" showed a reluctance to acknowledge a shift in the locus of sovereignty. Conservative senior statesmen in the Privy Council noted the discrepancy and urged the government to correct it and acknowledge popular sovereignty. The Legislation Bureau itself anticipated that Diet members would ask why the cabinet, a coalition of the conservative parties, was submitting a revision that substituted popular sovereignty for rule by the emperor. Was this not a repudiation of *kokutai*? Bureau officials would have to come up with a more persuasive argument to support the government's contention that *kokutai* was preserved, unchanged, in the draft, or else abandon it.

The strategy developed by the Legislation Bureau and cabinet ministers drew on constitutional scholar Hozumi Yatsuka's argument that *kokutai* as embodied in the concept of *imperial sovereignty* was the fundamental characteristic of the country.[44] If lost, the cohesion and identity of the nation, achieved with the restoration of imperial power in the nineteenth century, would be destroyed. According to Hozumi, the Japanese people believed the nation's identity had been unchanged throughout history. In the popular mind that identity had always been linked to the existence of the emperor, even though he had not personally wielded political power very often. Thus *kokutai* required the existence of the imperial institution, whether or not the reigning emperor actually ruled. In this sense— based on scholarly opinion as well as the beliefs of the people—*kokutai* as the fundamental character of the nation was not changed in the draft constitution.[45]

In the materials prepared for the ministers' meeting of June 13, however, this argument took a significant populist turn.[46] The bureau staff, while noting the complexities of the issue, paid less and less attention to scholarly writings and debates. They separated *kokutai* from imperial sovereignty and reduced it to a concept of popular feeling toward the emperor. They reasoned that what counted most was not what scholars, even Hozumi, said but what the people believed and how they felt. To a majority of Japanese it was not enough to equate *kokutai* with the mere existence of the emperor or imperial institution. *Kokutai* meant that feeling for the *tennō* (emperor) was rooted in the hearts of the Japanese people; he was the power or principle that united the whole people, "forming the basis of the state's existence."[47]

In preparing for the meeting with the ministers, Satō struggled to find proper words to express what he thought was the people's feelings toward the emperor. In a paper submitted to the bureau on June 12, "*Kokutai* and Sovereignty and the Bill to Revise the Constitution," he wrote of "the emperor as the center of the people's devotion [*akogare no chūshin*]."[48] Usually conveying a feeling of yearning or nostalgia, the word *akogare* seemed out of place in this political context. Satō struggled to make it fit. The tie between the emperor and the people was not a contract, not a sacred feeling, not even a feeling of authority. Neither did the expression "the emperor as the center of devotion" convey the people's true feelings for the emperor. He defined the emperor as the people's *akogare no chūshin*, which he described in a handwritten memorandum as "center of devotion, not as a god, nor as a lord, but as the feeling one has towards parents.

Legally, this has no direct connection with the Constitution but is the groundwork and the raison d'etre of Article 1 [Emperor as symbol of the state and unity of the people]."[49]

Kanamori, the minister who defended the draft in the Diet debates over the next three months, was strongly attracted to Satō's description of the emperor as the "center of devotion of the Japanese people." He would borrow the words to explain not only what the *tennō* meant to the people but to insist that *kokutai* had not changed, because the Japanese people's feelings had not changed.[50]

The Legislation Bureau distributed copies of Satō's paper and other materials to ministers who attended the June 13 meeting. This was the last preparatory session they would have before the plenary session of the House of Representatives on June 20. While the focus was still on *kokutai* and sovereignty at this meeting, the bureau had completed its Q&A guide to the whole draft constitution.[51]

Three months had passed since the government had published the March 6 draft. During that time, officials of the Legislation Bureau had solicited comments from all concerned ministries, continued negotiations with SCAP's GS, and made minor revisions in the draft, rewritten it in colloquial Japanese, and carefully observed the Privy Council's deliberations on the draft. By mid-June bureau officials had prepared a series of questions and answers for Yoshida and Kanamori, who would guide the bill to revise the constitution through the debates of the ninetieth Imperial Diet. They were ready for the final stage of this long struggle.

TRANSFORMING A DRAFT
INTO A CONSTITUTION

Preview

THE DIET GOES TO WORK

In accordance with the terms of article LXXIII of the Meiji Constitution of 1889, Prime Minister Yoshida Shigeru on June 25 presented his cabinet's draft of a revised Japanese constitution to the Imperial Diet (still so-called). There was no precedent for the process on which Japan was about to embark; the Meiji constitution had never been amended. Nevertheless, it was commonly expected that the proposed revision would be presented first to the House of Representatives, then to the House of Peers. After each house adopted amendments and any differences were reconciled, the revised constitution would be taken to the Privy Council for formal approval, then promulgated by the emperor.

How long this process would take was anybody's guess. Initially the cabinet and SCAP hoped that it could be expedited, to be finished perhaps by mid-summer. But nothing like this had ever happened before in Japan. In fact—inevitably perhaps, given the nature of deliberative assemblies—it took a good deal longer than either SCAP or the Japanese cabinet expected. It was not until October 7 that the House of Representatives took its final vote on the amended text, concluding the Diet's consideration.

In outline, this is how the Diet conducted its deliberations.

The government, as we have seen, published its draft on April 17 and forwarded it to the Privy Council. Beginning April 22, the Privy Council devoted eleven sessions to it, granting preliminary approval on June 3. The Privy Council made no changes in the text.

Yoshida presented the government's draft to the House of Representatives on June 25. For three days thereafter, the House in plenary session held preliminary "interpellations" (questioning the government). The bill was then referred to a specially created panel, the Committee on Revision of the Constitution, consisting of seventy-two members and chaired by Ashida Hitoshi. It met in twenty sessions, July 1–23.

The work of the committee coincided with intensive negotiations between the cabinet officer in charge of the revision project, Kanamori Tokujirō, and SCAP's designated liaison on constitutional is-

183

sues, Colonel Charles Kades. Colonel Kades's assignment was to decide whether amendments proposed by the Japanese were consistent with SCAP's "fundamental principles" for constitutional revision. The negotiations between Kades and Kanamori produced several significant changes in the text.

On July 23, the Committee on Revision created a subcommittee of fourteen members, also chaired by Ashida, to refine the draft's language and prepare amendments that reflected the committee's consensus. The subcommittee met thirteen times, through August 20. Again, there were concurrent negotiations with Colonel Kades.

On August 21, the Committee on Revision met to receive the subcommittee's report and decide on the amendments it had drafted. After a brief debate, the revised draft was put to a vote. The committee approved it by a standing vote.

With that, the project was returned to the House of Representatives, which met on August 24. Ashida presented the committee's report and explained the proposed amendments. After speeches by party leaders, the vote was taken. By a margin of 421–8, the House passed the bill as amended by the Committee on Revision.

The next step required by article LXXIII was consideration by the House of Peers. The upper house began its deliberations in plenary session on August 24. For three days, the full house listened to speeches by its leading members. The bill was then referred to a special Committee on Revision consisting of forty-five members, chaired by Abe Yasunari. The committee met twenty-four times, from August 31 through September 26. A subcommittee then scrutinized the bill's language and prepared amendments. This panel, like its counterpart in the House of Representatives, met in secret. It held four meetings and reported to the Committee on Revision on October 3.

On October 5, the committee reported back to the full House of Peers, recommending amendments. These were adopted on October 6. The House of Peers passed the amended bill that same day. On October 7, 1946, the House of Representatives accepted the Peers amendments, and the bill was enacted, with just five members remaining seated for the standing vote. On October 29, the Privy Council added its approval, and on November 3, Emperor Hirohito proclaimed the new constitution. It came into effect on May 3, 1947.

12 . . . .

"Along Democratic and Peace-Loving Lines"

• YOSHIDA PRESENTS HIS DRAFT

•

• When the House of Representatives convened on June 25 to begin deliberations on a revised constitution for Japan, the occasion was marked by a minimum of ceremony. The new prime minister, Yoshida Shigeru, was a man of few words. A distinguished diplomat, the crown of his career had been his posting as ambassador to Great Britain in 1936. Taciturn, canny, tough as leather, he had spent the war years under a kind of self-imposed house arrest because of his refusal to participate in a war he deemed ill-advised He was only now emerging into the bright light of the political arena. At age 68, he was serving his first term as a cabinet officer. His conservative temperament made him a natural leader of the right. His refusal to participate in the war protected him from the Occupation's purges. But he paid a price for the independence he had shown during the war: His fellow conservatives respected him and trusted his judgment, but his personal reserve kept them from loving him. By those on the left, Yoshida was regarded with deep suspicion. They did not trust what he said. They were suspicious that he was cutting deals with MacArthur to protect the emperor. They did not believe him when he declared an intention to lead Japan toward democracy and social justice.

In truth, Yoshida was ideally suited for the task at hand: to hold together the elements participating in Japan's constitutional reconstruction. He had MacArthur's confidence. He had consistently opposed those who took Japan into war. Culturally he was deeply Japanese, but he accepted the Potsdam Declaration without reservation. During his diplomatic service, he had witnessed the operation of the parliamentary system on which the new draft was modeled. He knew how it worked, he knew the role of monarchy in it, and he trusted its compatibility with conservative social institutions. He knew that it lent itself to conservative political leadership. He was, in short, quite comfortable with the prevailing current of reform.

From Yoshida's perspective, however, there were dangers ahead. He would have to fend off the challenge of the left, who saw an opportunity, in the present chaos, to commit Japan to collectivism. He would have to be watchful against rationalists who failed to understand the value of myths in fostering cohesion. He would have to resist rightists, who wanted desperately to deflect insults to the emperor's dignity. Essentially, he had to be prepared to fight from various angles against those who failed to appreciate the complicated arrangements surrounding the first three chapters of the draft: those dealing with the preservation of the emperor, the renunciation of war and armed forces, and the commitment to human rights.

The prime minister had one staunch ally in this struggle: Kanamori Tokujirō. A scholar by temperament, author of several books on the interpretation of the Meiji constitution and on constitutionalism generally, Kanamori had served before the war as director of the cabinet's legislative office. From that vantage point, he had had ample opportunity to observe the way bureaucracies worked in Tokyo. He had never been comfortable with then-prevailing interpretations of Meiji constitutionalism, but he had reluctantly made his peace, in his published writings, with the advocates of imperial mysticism. Despite these efforts to accommodate the royalists, Kanamori's career as a legislative bureaucrat had been cut short by suspicions that he was not strong enough in his support of imperial prerogatives. Nevertheless, he did not have Yoshida's record of quiet defiance, and he would pay a price during these summer debates for passages in his books that accommodated the prewar regime's newly invented doctrines about the emperor's "sovereignty."

Despite these difficulties, Kanamori turned out to be the perfect man to handle the government's brief for this revision project. His knowledge of constitutionalism was masterly, his commitment to it entirely genuine. Day in and day out, many hundreds of times from late June until mid-October, he would rise to his feet to defend a particular clause or phrase in the draft, to demonstrate its compatibility with Japanese history, to explain its source in British or French history, or to show the light shed on it by an American Supreme Court case. His facility and his patience in these exchanges were truly astonishing. One of his main themes was to insist that the emperor must be protected from any involvement in politics, in order to ensure his absolute impartiality. Kanamori himself, by his performance that summer, came about as close as any human being can come to attaining such a superhuman standard, and he did it while playing the lead role in a high-stakes political drama.

Reading the transcripts of these debates, an American student of the Federal Convention of 1787 is often reminded of James Madison. Success in making a constitution for a great nation requires political leadership that can rise above the usual routines of "who gets what," the give and take of deal making among elected representatives. Both Kanamori and Madison may have been deficient in some of the small arts of legislative politics, but both were quite at home at the level of constitutional argumentation, and they had rare gifts of being able to draw other men (and women, in Kanamori's case) to the high level of constitutional principle. It was a great blessing for Japan that he was there in 1946.

Revision "Absolutely Necessary"

On June 25, the prime minister opened the debate. Without mincing words, he sketched the government's case for revision. The Potsdam Declaration, he declared, made it "absolutely necessary" to revise Japan's constitution. The existing constitution enshrouded the emperor in "mysticism and unreality," giving him "wide imperial prerogatives." Until it was revised, there would be danger that persons in power, "having erroneous notions of their own, might, in the name of the emperor, mislead the people, abuse the powers of government and in pursuance of their reckless policies, lead the country and the people to destruction and other unpredictable plight." The revision eliminated that danger. Henceforth it would be clear that the "position of the emperor originates in the will of the people." His participation in affairs of state would be done at the direction of the cabinet. Such were the arrangements, he noted coolly, in most European democracies.

Then came an even bigger bombshell. In words that would have been laughable from any anyone else, this most realistic of Japanese statesmen declared that Japan would henceforth entrust its "future security and her existence itself to the fair play and good will of the nations of the world." By now, of course, everyone in Japan knew that the proposed revised constitution contained these two chapters (on the emperor and the renunciation of war). Still, it must have been quite astonishing to hear Yoshida affirm them without equivocation.

Yoshida hurried on to conclude his introductory summary. Rights, he said, would be unambiguously guaranteed, and the powers of government "divided." The Diet would be "highest," the sole lawmaking authority; the executive would be vested in a cabinet responsible to the Diet; and there would be a supreme court, with power of judicial review. The constitution would be written in the vernacular, so as to be "easily understood by the general public."[1]

First to respond was a senior member of the Yoshida's own (Liberal) party, Kita Reikichi. Sixty-one years old, he had graduated from Waseda University and done graduate work at Harvard and in Europe. Before the war, he had written several books analyzing Asian contributions to the history of philosophy. He had been a member of the House of Representatives since 1936. Apart from a brief absence when the Occupation purged him from politics (for his work as editor of a magazine called Shōkoku [Fatherland]), he would remain in the Diet until 1958. Kita began by noting how closely Yoshida's opening remarks had tracked MacArthur's announcement on the publication of the draft revision, even to the point of using the same strange terms to describe past sins—the "mysticism and unreality" of the emperor's position, and the like. Not everyone agreed, said Kita, that revision was necessary. The distinguished scholar Minobe Tatsukichi had written a magazine article in February arguing that the fault lay not in the constitution but in faulty execution. The circumstances leading up to the current crisis were particularly troubling. Last fall, he recalled, the government appointed the Matsumoto Commission to prepare revisions. When published reports of its preliminary proposals produced an outcry, various political party committees prepared drafts of their own, all of which were more progressive than the government's. Then "all of a sudden when we least expected it," the present draft revision was published. No one disputed that it was far more radical than any of the party drafts, including the one produced by the Socialists. What, asked Kita, could explain such a drastic development? General MacArthur had urged the Diet to discuss the proposed revision candidly and not hesitate to amend it in accordance with the will of the Japanese people, whom they represented. Yet Yoshida now admonished them to conduct their deliberations "with the foreign relations and the actual position of Japan in mind." How were Diet members to understand these conflicting signals?[2]

Yoshida's reply to this sharply worded question set the tone for the government's defense of its revision project. Acknowledging Minobe's opposition, Yoshida said it was naïve to expect the world to believe that Japan's constitution made no contribution to its misbegotten aggression. As for the government's performance in the matter of constitutional revision, Yoshida insisted that when the so-called Matsumoto draft was published, it was only one of several that the government was working on. Some, he said, were a good deal more progressive than the one published. In the midst of pondering its options, however, the government discovered "something very grave in the international relations of this country," a shift in "the sentiments and attitudes of the European and American nations toward Japan." The Allies had come to suspect that something in Japan's national character (*kokutai*) represented a menace to the peace of the world. "Of course," said the prime minister, "this is born of . . . a misunderstanding that Japan is a militaristic and ultra-nationalistic state, that we are by nature a warlike people." Nevertheless, in light of the catastrophic results of the war, it had to be admitted that such apprehensions were quite justified.

Now, he said, "in the face of a disastrous defeat, if we are to preserve our national character, our statehood, and the happiness of our people," we must consider "how we can dispel such a misunderstanding and such apprehensions." In the world's view, "the fact that there is an imperial family on the top, and our loyal and brave people are solidly united with the imperial family as the center," constitutes a serious threat to world peace. In the face of such dangerous suspicions, the government concluded that a thorough revision of the constitution was necessary. Between Matsumoto's draft and the present one, international factors of the gravest import intervened. "I earnestly hope," he concluded, "that you will make a careful study of the international situation" as you deliberate on this project.[3]

What were the ominous "international factors" that developed so suddenly in February to persuade Yoshida and the rest of the Shidehara cabinet to proceed with the "radical" GHQ draft as its own? As Yoshida came to terms with the revision project, he had doubtless learned about mounting Allied (not just Soviet) pressures to try the emperor as a war criminal and to inflict a draconian peace. His speech to the Diet on June 25 reflected his own understanding of the fierce diplomatic pressures on both MacArthur and himself. MacArthur had concluded they could be held at bay only by stripping the emperor of all "state functions" and promising the permanent disarmament of Japan. As Yoshida saw it, Japan had no choice on these matters. MacArthur's package now seemed to be the only viable strategy for salvaging the essence of *kokutai*, stripped of its "mystical" features.

So intent was the prime minister on carrying a deeply skeptical House with him that he allowed himself to exaggerate his government's achievement in defense of *kokutai*, a self-indulgence that would cost him acute embarrassment in the days ahead. In recounting what had happened in the exchanges leading to Japan's surrender in August, Yoshida recalled the "deep yearning" of the Japanese people to preserve its national character. "For this reason," he said, Japan accepted the Potsdam Declaration, "being assured herself that her national character [*kokutai*] would thereby be preserved." Yoshida acknowledged that President Truman, while reiterating the Allied promise to base government on the collective will of the Japanese people, specifically rejected the notion that peace was grounded on an American promise or contract with Japan:

> In the midst of what I might call misunderstandings concerning Japan, . . . [including] the mistreatment of war prisoners and various instances of the violation of laws of war that have since come to light, and in the lurid atmosphere . . . pervading the world in the wake of the war, in the midst of these things—it is not difficult to imagine that . . . the Allied Powers may not have been in a position to give immediate clear-cut assent to Japan's desire for the preservation of her national character.

Nevertheless, the Allied Powers repeatedly promised to base governance on the collective will of the Japanese people. Yoshida concluded with these fateful words of assurance to his Japanese audience: "The collective will of the Japanese people concerning the preservation of their national character has been fully brought home to the Allied Powers."[4]

With these words, the recipe for Allied irritation had been fully cooked. Yoshida would spend much of the next three days eating these words about Allied assurances to Japan concerning the terms of surrender.[5]

The hasty publication of the government's draft drew anguished criticism from the left as well. Morito Tatsuo was a leading Social Democrat, from Hiroshima. In 1920, he had been dismissed from the faculty of Tokyo Imperial University and spent three months in jail for publishing an article on the Russian anarchist P. A. Kropotkin that was deemed insufficiently critical by the authorities. His trial had been a cause célébre. During the interwar period, Morito had studied Marxism in Germany. He was serving his first term in the House of Representatives. He was struck, he said, by the government's contention that the new constitution would be an expression of the "freely expressed will of the Japanese people," as required by the Potsdam Declaration. He contrasted the government's efforts with those of the private Society for the Study of the Constitution (*Kenpō Kenkyūkai*), of which he was a member. "This was not a large society," he said, "but when last winter it produced a draft revision, "it was circulated for criticism among a goodly number of experts in different circles." Then a second draft was made up and the same process repeated. Only then was a final draft produced and made public. Surely the government had made a similar effort, though no one he knew seemed to be aware of it. Did the government consult important political organizations, academic societies? Did it hold public hearings and inquiries to ascertain the popular aspirations?[6] The government lamely replied that the time had been too short.

Democracy was the great shibboleth of these deliberations. No one could allow an opponent to take this high ground. Yoshida showed his keen appreciation of this imperative. Commenting on the Potsdam Declaration demand that Japan commit itself to democracy, the prime minister coolly remarked that most Japanese found this demand thoroughly congenial. After all, he said, Japan had been democratic in spirit from the beginning. Imperial poetry from time immemorial had celebrated the unity of feeling between the emperor and the people, and at the beginning of the modern era, the Emperor Meiji had put this commitment into immortal language in the Charter Oath of 1868.[7]

Not everyone in the chamber shared this assessment of the Charter Oath and its significance in Japanese history. First to rise in explicit contradiction to Yoshida was Hososako Kanemitsu. A lawyer for labor unions and other left-wing causes during the interwar period, Hososako's perception of the harshness of Meiji-era politics was based on personal experience, having been arrested in 1932 under the Peace Preservation Law. He insisted that the government's approach to constitutional reform had been grudging from the start. The people of the United States, Britain, and France, he said, had secured their liberty by fighting. Japan was committing itself to democracy only because the Allies insisted on it in the terms of surrender. Replying tersely, Yoshida said, "I agree to your opinion regarding the necessity of revising the constitution along democratic and peace-loving lines. As for the reasons for my agreement, I hope you will be satisfied with what I have stated here."[8]

More blunt in criticizing the prime minister for invoking the Charter Oath was the leader of the Communist Party in Japan, Nosaka Sanzō. Nosaka had traveled to Britain in 1919, joined the newly formed Communist Party and been promptly deported. After visiting the Soviet Union, he returned to Japan in 1922 and became a charter member of the Japanese Communist Party. He engaged in underground work in the United States during the 1930s and was with Maoist forces in Yenan from 1940, indoctrinating Japanese prisoners of war. In 1946, encouraged by the Allied amnesty, he had returned to Japan and was elected to the central committee of the resurrected Japanese Communist Party. He was now serving his first term in the Diet.[9] As far as he was concerned, said Nosaka, the Charter Oath was simply the Meiji government's declaration of intent to substitute bureaucrats for the feudal barons of the Tokugawa Shogunate. Far from encouraging democracy, the Meiji leaders constantly oppressed those who participated in popular movements for the establishment of a parliamentary system through popular elections. An American prosecutor at the war crimes trials, Brigadier General H. G. Nolan, had been closer to the truth, said Nosaka, when he characterized Meiji Japan as an oppressive regime, utterly devoid of democratic spirit.[10]

With these preliminary skirmishes, the plenary session of the lower house concluded its initial review. The next step would be for the ad hoc Committee on Revision to examine the draft.

13 . . . .

"Free and Untrammeled Debate"

• THE EMPEROR'S PREROGATIVES

•

After its initial survey, the House of Representatives forwarded the revision project to an ad hoc committee for detailed examination. It consisted of seventy members, chosen by the speaker and distributed proportionally among the parties (including the Communists). At its organizational meeting on June 29, Inukai Ken nominated a fellow Progressive Democrat, Ashida Hitoshi, to serve as chair. It was an excellent choice. Ashida was a conservative in politics, but broad-minded, even-tempered, courageous, and fair-minded. For the occasion, he bought himself a new briefcase, inscribed on the inside flap with the words, "Commemorating Revision of the Constitution." For their part, officials of the Occupation must have welcomed the choice. They had developed a high opinion of Ashida, partly because of his contacts with Socialists during the war.[1]

The members would work with great intensity for almost two months. The appalling conditions of Tokyo that summer were frequently reflected in the debates. One member, recalling the fires of the summer of 1945, said that he had lost everything: "no cup, no razor, no chopstick, indeed nothing whatever was left intact after the fire." Kanamori replied that he too was "one of those victims who have lost their houses and am present here today in a borrowed suit from coat to shirt."[2] The seriousness of the work was reflected in the fact that the prime minister and leading members of his cabinet frequently attended the committee's meetings, even though a blasted nation clamored for attention to matters of life, death, and dislocation.

One notable feature of these discussions was the members' awareness that they were taking part in a historic event and that their words might later be studied by people seeking to understand the "framers' intent." Kanamori's careful responses seemed to indicate his sense of this responsibility.[3]

For the Sake of Continuity: Using Article LXXIII

Opening the committee's inquiry, Kitaura Keitarō, a leading conservative from Nara, questioned the legitimacy of the revision project. The draft proposed to restrict the emperor's powers. The emperor himself had presented it. Was he voluntarily limiting his own powers? If so, on what authority?

This question, apparently so simple, presented Kanamori with a trap set by the decision to use article LXXIII of the Meiji constitution as the basis for constitutional revision. The Occupation and the Japanese government tacitly agreed that they could not take the time, or run the political risks, to revise the constitution by a thoroughly democratic process. Amendment by article LXXIII required only the initiative of the emperor and the acceptance of two-thirds of the Diet. But how could the emperor, on whose will the authority of the Meiji Constitution rested, now restrict the exercise of that very will? Did the sovereignty of the people's will, proclaimed in the preamble and in chapter I, depend on the emperor's recognition of it? Or did the emperor's position as "symbol" of the nation depend on the people's will, as article 1 seemed to state? If the latter, how could the revision stem from article LXXIII of the Meiji Constitution, which in turn rested on the emperor's will?[4]

There was no good answer to these questions.[5] The amendment process established in article LXXIII was chosen for the sake of convenience, because it lay at hand, because generations of Japanese knew it was there (though none had ever used it), and because the process it ordained skirted the troublesome demands of democracy. That it left a riddle of illegitimacy seemed a small price to pay.[6]

Another basic question haunted these proceedings. How free was the Diet to amend the government's draft? At first Kanamori answered this question with studied vagueness, saying that the government would accept any amendment "in harmony with the world situation."[7] One key element of the "world situation," which apparently went without saying, was that GHQ would not accept any amendments to chapter I designed to restore the emperor's position or to erode the safeguards against its reassertion.

A week later, Kitaura sharpened the question, and this time he got a more candid answer. He recalled that General MacArthur had called for "free and untrammeled debate." Did this mean that the Diet could alter the articles defining the emperor's position? Kanamori replied that he could not answer such a question in the abstract. What if a large majority of the Diet favored an amendment? Even if the Diet favors an amendment and the government finds its contents reasonable, said Kanamori, the government would have to consider whether the proposed change was "compatible with the international obligations imposed on our country. . . . We cannot afford to lose sight of [this consideration] even for a moment." "I understand," said Kitaura. "The words 'international obligations' have made everything clear to me."[8] The exchange with Kitaura indicated the pressures Kanamori and the cabinet faced, from both directions, in seeking to adapt the position of the emperor to the requirements of constitutional democracy.

Hozumi Shichirō was a graduate in economics of the University of Tokyo. During the 1930s, he had joined a left-wing agricultural training institute and taken the lead in many labor disputes. He had also served as an editorial adviser to the distinguished general-interest magazine, *Chūō Kōron*. He was a newcomer to elective office, serving his first (of seven) terms in the House.

He began his interrogation of Kanamori harshly. The very style of the draft's language made him "dizzy." Of which country was this supposed to be the constitution, he asked? It was so un-Japanese. The government insisted that the "revision" arose from a commitment to democracy. Democracy was not so easily achieved. It grew from an intense and continuous social process, and it required deep self-respect. No culture that despised itself and its own creations could ever be democratic, or truly international. The first priority was the emancipation of the workers, who had been treated like rodents. If we try to bypass the hard work of cultural reconstruction, we will be little different from the authoritarian masters of wartime Japan. No less than they, we will be trying to force-feed an idea into the heads of our countrymen.[9] The draft sounded like a tinny replay of the French Revolution. Montesquieu, the source of much of the thinking behind this constitution, was "outdated." We need a charter of our own, not one "lettered in the blood of foreign people." We should not be embarrassed about myths, what the government was calling mysticism. Christianity, upheld by Western, democratic nations, preaches "many miracles and legends such as deeming the son of a carpenter the Son of God." It is mindless, said Hozumi, to denounce such beliefs as illogical or unreal. Nor should Japan be drawn into quarrels about whether its history is 600 years shorter than hitherto supposed. The point is that "it is the expression of unbroken endeavors put forth by the Japanese people." Viewed in this light, it is "reasonable to say that the emperor has constantly existed with the people and for the people." Japan's national history must be grasped in an "organic manner." "Oriental" people, like the Japanese (Hozumi did not hesitate to admit that his ideas were based on racial theories), have been guided throughout history by ideals of "unity and harmony, not opposition and subjugation or division and struggle." In demanding recognition of the emperor as the focal point of national unity, he did not mean to deny that "militarists and landed interests" had used him cynically in the past. Indeed, a concern for the suffering of the Japanese people under its current "feudalistic and capitalistic order" is the very thing that drove him to seek a foundation for Japan's renewal with deep cultural roots. The emperor, "the cornerstone of the spiritual and educational life of the nation," was thus the key to the "democratization of the political structure of this country."[10] Hozumi acknowledged that there were dangers in using the imperial person in this way, but in his view, there was no alternative. You could not create democracy in Japan out of thin air. The draft revision was like an iceberg.[11] The problem was that the vast bulk underneath would be unaffected by the government's cosmetics at the surface.

The Draft's Language

Ōshima Tazō, a school teacher from Kyushu, indicated a preference for the British example. Could we not say that the emperor reigns, though he did not rule? He suggested that the word "head" (*genshu*) was better than "symbol" to describe the emperor's position. Kanamori acknowledged that the word *genshu* was widely and customarily used for the head of state. But it was, after all, a direct translation of the German word *Oberhaupt*. When we use this expression, the state is likened to a human body, and the emperor is figuratively called its head. Therefore, the word *genshu* was not appropriate to represent the emperor as a spiritual center of our country, uniting the people. The word "symbol," said Kanamori, had been chosen after careful consideration. He hoped that in time it would help people to develop a "true image of our country . . . thereby rejecting mysticism and preventing international suspicion."[12]

There would be many more words spoken about this matter as the summer wore on, but Kanamori's remarks on July 3—particularly those about "rejecting mysticism and preventing international suspicion"—expressed how and why the Japanese government had come to affirm Kades's term, "symbol."

As often happened where delicate matters were concerned, it was Nosaka, the incorrigible Communist, who roiled the waters. Calling attention to an English translation of the draft revision that had been published "yesterday," he asked whose it was. The cabinet had issued it, replied Kanamori. Well, said Nosaka, it was full of "mistakes." Readers abroad would get the impression that Japan had under consideration a truly democratic constitution, whereas the "original" (the Japanese version) was "ambiguous."[13] Kanamori replied that there would, of course, be differences, attributable to variations in the two "language systems," but he disagreed with Nosaka that the differences would mislead foreign readers.[14]

Nosaka then pointed to a discrepancy that was, he thought, material. In the preamble, the English version referred to the people's will as "sovereign," but the Japanese version used the word "supreme." Questions had repeatedly been asked on this point, Nosaka noted, "which is extremely clear in the English version and extremely ambiguous in the Japanese." Kanamori claimed not to understand the question. "To express the idea of supremacy," he said, it is the "common practice of English translators to use the word 'sovereign,' the meaning of which dates as far back as to the days of Bodin." He did not think there was "any difference in meaning between the will that is supreme and the 'sovereign will'." As Nosaka sat down, he said rather ominously that he would not pursue the matter at this time.[15] The thunder rumbling around this point was continuing to build.

The Paradox of Potsdam

At its meeting on Friday, July 5, one of the youngest members of the Diet, Akazawa Masamichi, took the floor. He raised a question that went right to the heart of the paradox of Potsdam. Why were the Japanese people forced to accept chapter I when the Potsdam Declaration promised them a government based on their own political will, freely expressed? Veneration of the emperor, he insisted, was not a creation of ideologues in the 1930s. It had roots in traditions that were both ancient and still lively in Japan. To ignore this fact would not promote democracy; it would guarantee chaos. (He was applauded when he said this.) The Potsdam Declaration wisely promised the Japanese people a government based on their own will, freely expressed. The democratization of Japan, "not only political, but economic, industrial, and cultural," was not inconsistent with the "permanent maintenance of the venerability of the emperor." The one depends on the other. He hoped, he said, that article 1 did not contradict this essential dimension of the Japanese mentality. It made "no difference," did it, in Japan's age-old devotion to the emperor? Kanamori answered that although the "country itself is incarnated in the person of the emperor," the actual legal system was stipulated by the constitution itself. Thus, courts would perform the judicial function; general administration centered on the cabinet. "But at the root of all these, the people look up to the emperor as symbolizing the nation as a whole."[16]

Akazawa said it all looked pretty disjointed to him. He wondered where sovereignty would finally be located. Could we say that sovereignty lay with the issuer of the constitution? If so, the preamble seemed to indicate that the Diet would be sovereign. Kanamori thought not. If such were the case, the Diet could determine future amendments for itself. The human source of sovereignty in the new Japan would be the whole people, including the emperor himself. Less metaphorically, he concluded, somewhat warily, that it might make some sense to say "that this constitution itself is more or less a unified form of sovereignty."[17] (Kanamori here echoed Tom Paine's remark, in *Common Sense*, that "in America the Constitution is king.")

Well, then, asked Akazawa, what form of government will we have? Would it be a monarchy, a presidential system, a cabinet system, a Soviet system, a republican system, or what? A complete answer, said Kanamori, would require an explication of all 100 articles of the text. In a phrase, we might say that it is "essentially founded on the emperor system derived from the aggregate will of the people."[18]

This inconclusive exchange satisfied no one. No wonder these politicians were having a hard time grasping the new system. This new form of government was in no meaningful sense an "emperor system." In due course, Kanamori would have to come clean.

Will *Kokutai* Survive?

Would Japan's traditional structure survive the revision of the Meiji Constitution? Many of Japan's leading politicians were on record as determined that it should. With that in mind, Hayashi Heima called attention on July 4 to discrepancies between the official positions on constitutional revision taken by the ruling parties (in January and February, before their leaders became aware of the SCAP draft)[19] and the stand now taken by the cabinet formed by those parties. According to a report compiled by researchers for the House of Representatives, Hayashi noted:

> [I]t is the consensus of the Liberal Party that the subject of sovereignty is the state and that the emperor is the person who exercises it. . . . The consensus of the Progressive Party on the revised constitution is stated in the following terms: "The emperor shall exercise sovereign rights with the assistance of the people, according to the provisions of the [Meiji] Constitution." This is rather vague, but we may interpret it to mean . . . that sovereignty is vested in the emperor.[20]

How did Kanamori interpret these statements? Kanamori's answer was unresponsive to Hayashi's challenge. Opinions about the seat of sovereignty were "a matter of theory," he said. The issue before the Diet was the text of the proposed revision. It was not necessary to decide about "explanations, methods and ways of thinking underlying the draft."[21]

Two days later the interrogator was Kanda Hiroshi, serving his first of eight terms in the House. He began by expressing "profound respect to the government for its labors and efforts . . . at this unprecedented crisis," and especially his "gratitude and sympathy . . . to Mr. Kanamori for his untiring efforts in making explanations continuously day after day."[22] Nevertheless he pleaded with his friend to offer explanations that the Japanese people could readily understand. General MacArthur, in basing revision on article LXXIII, had stressed the importance of continuity. The cabinet, for its part, had insisted that the revision required no change in the nation's foundations. Yet the people noticed that the preamble of the existing (Meiji) Constitution declared the sovereignty of the emperor's will, whereas the preamble of the revision said that the people's will was sovereign. How did these charters fit together?

Again, Kanamori was in a tight place. His audience was complex. The Occupation was taking careful note to these debates (as events would soon show), and General MacArthur answered to a government, and to Allied nations, that were deeply suspicious of Japan's intentions. He repeated that article LXXIII ensured that "the fundamental law of the country is not interrupted in its continuity." But the continuity went far deeper than that: "The make-up of Japan has not in the slightest changed in its essentials through the process of the termination of the war. I do not think, and I believe none of the people think, that our country has discontinued its life and is to be born afresh under a new fundamental setup." He admitted that the "the wording of the draft revision" might be misleading in this respect. It seemed to suggest that "Japan's fundamental system has almost completely changed, root and branch." But we must train our eye on "what is most fundamental to the makeup of Japan. It lies," he said, "in the position of the emperor. The people are mentally linked together with the emperor as the center, and on this foundation the state of Japan exists. . . . So long as we continue to form a state with this national character as the foundation, I do not think there is any room for entertaining the slightest suspicion that discontinuance has ever come to the life of the state."

Why was there so much confusion on this point? It could be traced, Kanamori thought, to "some Japanese scholars," who have been "obsessed with an illusion" that the Potsdam Declaration somehow "altered the fundamental character of the nation." He insisted that there was "no ground, either theoretically or practically, for that illusion." He begged to repeat: "the fundamentals of the Japanese state lie in the unity of the will of the people." He admitted that, in the Meiji Constitution, "it is expressly stated that in actual practice the emperor forms the center in the exercise of the right of rule." The "fundamental shape" of the government was not visible to the eye. But Kanamori urged the committee to "penetrate to the roots." We need to "wake up," he said, "and consider what really constitutes the fundamental national character of Japan." With that, he repeated his familiar incantation: "In the final analysis, the foundation of the Japanese state lies in the general will of the people, which is formed with the emperor as the center of the link. . . . Sovereignty resides in the whole of the people, among whom is included the emperor."[23] Kanamori would soon discover that these remarks sowed a field of trouble. He might have gratified Kanda's concern for imperial dignity and scored points in his quarrel with the scholars, but he was also feeding suspicions at GHQ. There his insistence on the continuity of Japan's governing arrangements would not prove a winner.

Close Examination

Toward the end of the second week in July, the committee on revision began to examine the draft "article by article." To some (mostly on the left), it seemed anomalous that the first chapter of a democratic constitution should deal with a ceremonial vestige of feudalism. Most, however, were perfectly comfortable with this ordering, recognizing that coming to terms with the myth of *kokutai* was the first priority in reconstructing Japan along democratic lines.

In reviewing this debate, we need to bear in mind that article 1, reducing the emperor to symbolic status, was one of SCAP's "fundamental principles" for the revision project. The Diet was not free to change any of the language of chapter I contrary to the wishes of SCAP. In this respect, Potsdam's promise of government in accordance with the "freely expressed will of the Japanese people" and MacArthur's call for "free and untrammeled debate" were misleading. No matter what the Japanese people or their elected leaders wanted, chapter I would have to strip the emperor of his prerogatives.

Inevitably, thinking about the emperor's place meant reviewing Hirohito's role in starting and ending the war against China and the United States.[24] The session on July 12 produced a notable exchange between Kitaura and Kanamori on that vexed and vital subject. It also provided an uncommonly clear exposition of the mythology about the imperial institution that prevailed in the mind of politicians on Japan's right wing.

MacArthur (in Kitaura's paraphrase of the Supreme Commander's March 6 announcement) had said that "the new constitution would deprive the emperor of his powers relative to government and of all his property owned in the name of the country, and make the emperor, as the symbol of the state, follow the will of the people." This may be "the spirit of democracy," said Kitaura, and "I am all in favor of democracy." But democracy takes various forms: republican in the United States, monarchical in Britain, communistic in the Soviet Union. Japan needed to develop a form for herself.[25]

Prejudice against the emperor was rooted in the idea that it was because of him that the militarists and bureaucrats wielded their evil power. But that idea, said Kitaura, was "quite wrong." Only those who knew nothing about Japanese history could believe that "doing away with the power of the emperor" would bring permanent peace. Japan, he said, had never been at peace when the emperor was persecuted. He cited the fifteenth-century Great War of Ōnin as one example among many of what happened when Japan failed to respect the emperor. At that time, a shogun who had no son adopted his brother, then had a son of his own. Civil war ensued over the issue of succession. For eleven years the struggle raged, laying waste to Kyoto and its environs and ending only in the exhaustion of the parties. He found similar abuses in other periods, including modern times. He described Tōjō Hideki, prime minister during World War II, as a modern shogun, leading Japan to disaster by abusing imperial authority. (Kitaura cast Emperor Hirohito as the hapless victim of Tōjō's evil machinations.) That, he said, was what happened when people failed to respect the emperor. Subjecting the emperor to the will of the people was no better than subjecting him to shoguns. Furthermore, it was unprecedented in Japanese history and incompatible with hopes for peace and cultural reconstruction: "If the Japanese nation is to live in real peace and contribute to the peace of the world, the emperor must be made the central object of profound respect of all Japanese people. This is an unshakable truth verified by history, and this will remain true forever."

As a concrete example of the mistaken spirit of the revision, Kitaura cited the provision (in article 7) that the emperor must perform state functions with the advice and approval of the cabinet. In Kitaura's view, this made clear the intention to "subjugate the throne to the people's authority." Might it not be possible, he asked, instead of saying in article 1 that the emperor is "the symbol of the state," to say instead that he is "among the people as an object of adoration and respect, and [that] he administers the affairs of the state together with the people." Kitaura concluded by putting his argument in an international context.

> I believe that our earnest wish for peace is in perfect conformity with the policy of the Allied Powers.... The emperor is the symbol of peace, and I believe that the greatness and sagacity of General MacArthur as a statesman lies in having left the emperor system unmolested.... I am sure that the peace-loving peoples of the world will not object to [my suggestion], nor is there any reason why General MacArthur will be against it.[26]

Kanamori was of course obliged to reject this suggestion out of hand, for reasons both internal and diplomatic. Kitaura's history was highly suspect—not so much his ancient history (though that too was disputable) but his implied account of the emperor's role in World War II. How could you absolve the emperor of everything that happened before August 1945 but, at the same time, credit him with ending the war on August 15? Why had he not acted sooner, before Japan had been laid waste?

As for General MacArthur, the cabinet knew perfectly well that he could protect the emperor from arrest and trial as a war criminal only by assuring the Allies that Japan would accept a thoroughly democratic form of government, with the emperor strictly and explicitly confined to ceremonial functions. Kitaura said it was "quite wrong" to hold that militarists and bureaucrats wielded power only because they were able to manipulate the imperial authority. But that is exactly what the Americans believed, and they were determined that in the future political authority in Japan would be less ambiguous, more transparent, more responsible.

A more effective argument for the emperor was made by Ōhashi Kimi, a secondary schoolteacher from Kyushu and a Progressive Democrat. Ōhashi said that the difficulty in framing a constitutional government for Japan was that the emperor system was unique; thus there was no precise model. Government in Japan, she said, was "patriarchal." The emperor had not attained his position by military exertions.

> The Japanese people compose one family. Its parents are the imperial family, from which the Japanese race has developed into this large family of seventy million people in 3,000 years. . . . [Admittedly] the kinship between us and the imperial family has become thin and remote, due to the infiltration of different races and blood, but we are still bound to it by blood and heart.[27]

Japan, she concluded, was bound into a nation by the power of love.

This was of course a familiar notion in Japan, often used for right-wing purposes. But Ōhashi turned it to a different end. She commended Kitaura for calling attention to the fact that the emperor is a "symbol of love and peace, and Japan is made by the power of love." The challenge for the scholars and political leaders of Japan, she said, was to fashion a constitutional system that incorporated both this unique cultural bond and proper safeguards against abusing it. Being fully committed to democracy, we "must not be ignorant, but be steady and see to it that the emperor should not be led to commit an error."[28]

Kanamori heartily welcomed this comment. The draft stood on the "people's true sentiment," but it sought at the same time to leave no room for the abuse of imperial authority. He warned against the traditional doctrine that the emperor could not be held liable for his actions. The experience of Germany following World War I showed that this doctrine did not protect the kaiser from condemnation or prevent the ruin of the imperial system.[29] To make the emperor system "eternally unalterable and unwavering," the system must be so designed that the emperor is protected from criticism not only legally but also in fact.[30]

This was a deeply significant exchange. Ōhashi's invocation of the Japanese sense of family identity would be cited several times by subsequent speakers. Her remarks were not only moving to her audience; they incorporated a viable notion of the emperor's place in a constitutional democracy.

Much of the rest of the two days devoted to chapter I dealt with the implications of this doctrine. Kanamori said that although he had been accused of sloppy draftsmanship, the various provisions of chapter I had been carefully crafted, like a jewel.[31] For example, article 7 ensured that the cabinet, not the emperor, would decide on amnesty. Several members had argued that the emperor should decide whether to suspend the operation of the laws. If the cabinet granted amnesty, it would inevitably have a partisan tinge. The emperor's amnesty told the convict that he owed his liberation to an awesome grace; he would not dare to soil such a gift. Kanamori steadfastly rejected such arguments. The emperor, he said, being human, can make mistakes. If he had substantial powers to exercise, he could also be pressured by political "wirepullers." Of course the cabinet too could make mistakes, but the cabinet could be held responsible, and replaced, if it lost the people's confidence.[32]

The ensuing discussion shed light on one small feature of article 7, part of its "gem-like quality," perhaps. Whereas the emperor would merely "attest" to the appointment of cabinet officers, the granting of amnesty and ratification, he would award honors himself, after obtaining the advice and consent of the cabinet. One member wondered why the emperor could not make such awards on his own authority. The awarding of honors, said Kanamori, was different. The emperor awarded honors "to make people share in his glory." Though the cabinet's advice and approval would now be required, it was suitable that the awarding of honors should be "the emperor's creative act." Therefore, the term "attestation" was not used regarding honors. "I do not think that any political evil will ensue," concluded Kanamori, "if the awarding of honors is done formally on the emperor's initiative."[33] Perhaps not, but the exception—and this candid exposition of it—did mark a significant remnant of the old tennō system. The spell, the mystique of the emperor was not completely broken.

It was paradoxical for Kanamori to defend the emperor as the source of honors in the most sentimental terms but at the same time to oppose any attempt to restore the emperor's prerogatives. His best formulation of this paradox came in answer to a question by Inoue Tokumei, a 60-year-old member from rural Kagoshima. Inoue remarked that he had been born in a Buddhist temple and had been a religious educator throughout his life. When he left his province to attend the Diet, "all the believers of my temple entreated me to see to it that the emperor is safeguarded." Article 1 spoke of the emperor as a "symbol" of the nation. How could he explain such a concept to his constituents, many of whom were illiterate?[34] Kanamori began his answer by explaining that it was not strange—indeed it was universal—to find millions of people functioning as an organic whole, a community. But functioning communities have their own source of cohesion. For the Japanese people, the emperor was the "center of the unity of the people, around which we all gather and to which the will of the people as an organic whole is focused." But suppose this focal center came under the sway of a particular will. Suppose, for example, there were two contending forces in the country, two opposing parties, one representing capital and the other labor. "If the emperor, who is the symbol of the state and of the unity of the people, should favor one of the two, how could we expect to have a rational structure of the state?"

In speaking to this Buddhist priest, in a national culture strongly under the influence of Buddhist ideas, Kanamori continued his explanation in religious terms. "It is only natural," he said, "that a person who is to be the symbol of the united will of the nation ought to have embodied in himself an impartial mind, comparable to a state of 'nothingness.' . . ." For the emperor to descend from this position and enter the scrum of politics was a mistake, for the emperor and for the nation.

> In the past . . . we have committed error in bringing down the emperor from this ideal, transparent and colorless position and letting him take sides in actual politics, approve or reject legislation and seek the people's opinion in state affairs, and thereby caused his dignity to be marred. . . . It is due to these circumstances that the war responsibility of the emperor is some-times made a topic of discussion internationally, if not internally.

The "dignity" of the emperor's position lies in his power to "crystallize the will of the nation," to carry its destiny forever and embrace everyone without discrimination. "Our country has existed on the basis of this principle."[35]

This was as clear a statement of Kanamori's position as he made all summer. The difficulty for him was that it satisfied neither the right nor the left or the authorities at GHQ.

Article 4 became a flash point for conflicts over these dueling conceptions of the emperor's role in Japan's new constitutional order. It provided that "the emperor shall perform only such state functions as are provided for in this Constitution. Never shall he have powers related to government." For conservatives, the diminishment in the first sentence and the implied insult in the second were a jarring contrast to the reverence of the preceding fifteen years. Repeatedly they urged Kanamori to seek a softer way to express the changes in the emperor's responsibilities. Hara Fujirō, a sharp critic of the language of the Japanese version,[36] urged that the first clause be struck altogether, or at least that the order of the clauses be switched, so that the general point would be stated first.[37] But Kanamori insisted that the clause about "state functions" was necessary, to make clear that the emperor would not need the "advice and consent" of the cabinet to perform religious rites, cultural work, or his beloved scientific research. The two clauses together, in the order proposed, defined the emperor's role quite precisely.

There was a deeper issue here, though, relating to the Japanese terms used to translate the terms "state functions" and "powers" in articles 4 and 7. The first to broach it before the committee was Kojima Tetsuzō, a lawyer whose practice served mostly foreign clients. It was imperative, he said, to lay down clearly in the constitution that the emperor could not be involved in any political or judicial affairs.[38] Article 7 listed various "functions" to be performed by the emperor, with the cabinet's advice and consent. None, however (with the rather odd exception of dissolution, the procedures for which were *not* adequately spelled out elsewhere in the constitution[39]), could be regarded as involving imperial prerogatives or "any substantial power." Why then, Kojima asked, had the government chosen the terms used in article 4? In the first paragraph of the Japanese version, the text said that the emperor will perform certain state functions (*kokumu*) but shall have no powers (*kennō*) related to government. The second paragraph said that the emperor may delegate his functions (*kennō*, in the Japanese version) as provided by law. "I cannot help thinking that the word *kennō* was deliberately used here [in the second paragraph] to demonstrate that what the emperor performs are not mere business affairs, but that he had *kennō* (powers) related to government."[40]

Kanamori's answer, referring vaguely to awkwardness in translation,[41] was not adequate. Whether or not these linguistic issues masked a deep plot to lay the foundation for some future recovery of the emperor's position as head of state, they certainly did point to a matter that needed attention, if only because they were arousing deep suspicions, both here in the committee and, as would soon become apparent, at GHQ.

The committee's discussion (July 12 and 13) reinforces the impression that SCAP's initiative on constitutional revision had been essential. There is simply no way that Japanese politicians, representing a nation after 15 years of intensive indoctrination about *kokutai*, could have written provisions that stripped the emperor's powers and reduced him to a list of "functions," to be undertaken with the advice and consent of a parliamentary cabinet. Japan could not have done that by itself. With their own tenacity, Japan's conservative politicians helped to preserve the emperor, but it took SCAP's insistence to ensure that his role in governance was constitutionally restricted.

Problems in Translation

During the second week in July, voices outside the revision committee began to indicate that something was amiss in the Japanese version of the draft, particularly those sections relating to the nation's commitment to democracy. It may have been Matsumoto Shigeharu[42] who first noticed the problem. In a front-page editorial in the Sunday (July 7) edition of his newspaper, *Minpō*, Matsumoto drew attention to discrepancies between the Japanese and English versions of the preamble and chapter I in passages referring to the sovereignty of the people's will. First he cited language in the preamble, where, in the English version, it read: "We, the Japanese people . . . do proclaim the sovereignty of the people's will." The Japanese version, however, "only said: ' . . . do proclaim the supremacy [*shikō*] of the people's will.' " That, wrote Matsumoto, was "not so clear an expression as the English version." In article 1, the same terms were used. The English read, "deriving his [the emperor's] position from the sovereign will of the people," but the Japanese text read, "This position is based on the supreme [*shikō*] will of the people." Articles 4 through 7 contained a related difficulty. In the English version, the phrase "acts in matters of state" was used consistently, and it was made clear that the emperor would performs such acts only cere-monially, "on behalf of the people," following the determination of the Diet (in the case of naming a prime minister) or with the advice and approval of the cabinet (in the case of acts listed in article 7). In the Japanese version, different terms were used for these various acts, leaving some confusion about the status of the emperor's prerogative under the revision.[43]

Matsumoto's observations reflected concerns being raised at the same time by the FEC. On July 2, SWNCC had forwarded to SCAP, "as a directive for your guidance," a set of requirements for constitutional revision, including the demand that the text explicitly affirm popular sovereignty.[44] In replying on July 10, SCAP pointedly noted that its comments referred only to the *English* version, "without reference to the Japanese language version."[45] In the English text, SCAP asserted that popular sovereignty was affirmed "even more emphatically" than in the U.S. Constitution.[46] The qualifier suggested that SCAP too had become concerned about the implications of the Japanese version.

On July 10, Kades met with Japanese officials to review progress on the Diet's consideration of revision. In the course of the meeting, he mentioned his concern that the phrase "sovereignty of the people's will" in the English version "certainly does not have the same meaning as the translation '. . . declare that the will of the people is supreme.' "[47]

Kades's comment was apparently not a casual observation. It drew on staff work at GHQ. On July 11, a group that had been assigned to monitor transcripts of debates in the Diet[48] presented a memo outlining its own analysis of the Japanese version of the revision. In this case (unlike Matsumoto's editorial), there was no hesitation about speculating as to Japanese motives. The American memo began by calling attention to the use of "supremacy" in place of "sovereignty" in the preamble and in chapter I. Why had the Japanese translators done this? It was, in the Americans' opinion, to "pave the way" for crafting article 4 as the foundation for reserving certain prerogatives for the emperor. In the English version, article 4 directed the emperor to perform "only such state functions as are provided for in this Constitution."[49] It explicitly barred him from exercising any "powers related to government" but said that he could delegate his "func-tions," as provided by law. The Japanese version changed the meaning of these clauses by using "state affairs" (a "much more positive, dynamic term") in place of "functions" in the first clause. It barred the emperor from exercising "powers related to government" (using a term that implied politics). But then, in speaking of delegating, it used the term for "powers," rather than "functions" (as in the English text). Thus, in the Japanese version, the second and third sentences ap-peared contradictory (the emperor had no powers relating to government, yet he had powers to delegate). The contradiction might be resolved if one understood that the emperor should abstain from "government" in the sense of politics or routine administration, as sophisticated Japanese had always believed he should. But the text as rendered in Japanese implied that the emperor retained sovereign prerogatives. These he might delegate, even while he was refraining from poli-tics.[50]

Thus, according to the SCAP analysts, by the clever use of terms in translation, the "bureaucrats," those sly manipulators, had sought to establish a basis in the constitution for their pet ideas. Kanamori himself, having in the 1930s promoted Minobe's theory that the emperor was an "organ" of government, was a prime suspect in this plot to reserve powers for the emperor, according to the SCAP group's analysis. Nor would these traditional bureaucrats be content just to "warp" the text of the constitution. SCAP should anticipate a drive during the transition period (between November 1946 and May 1947) to pass organic laws that would reestablish the authority of something akin to the Meiji-era privy council.[51] The SCAP analysts noted that the laws to create such a body would be passed, not through the government established in the new constitution but, rather, during the transition period, through the lame-duck regime, including the old Privy Council and House of Peers.[52] The only way to prevent this catastrophe would be for SCAP to intervene forcefully, at great political cost. Much better, they concluded, to intervene now and demand that the Japanese version of the constitution be corrected.

Tensions in the Diet

The revision committee, continuing on July 11 with its article-by-article examination, heard next from Oikawa Tadashi, a middle-school principal from Kanagawa. He recalled Kanamori saying that the revised constitution rested government, including the emperor's authority, on the will of the people and that this was a traditional concept in Japan, despite some recent scholarly misconceptions. Oikawa found this logic tortured. Surely the people had not misunderstood when they read the imperial edicts of the Meiji period as emanating from the emperor's will. As for democracy, when members campaigned for election to the Diet in April, they—and the voters who elected them—had, in mind and heart, a concept very different from Kanamori's when they promised to defend the emperor's traditional position. Most people in Japan understood that the preservation of the imperial system was a "condition" for Japan's acceptance of the Potsdam Declaration as the basis of surrender. Yoshida seemed to encourage such an understanding, and the emperor himself had said recently that the Allies recognized his sovereign rights. For 15 years, the government had hammered away that the emperor alone was sovereign. As an educator himself, he had been an integral part of this campaign. In the face of all this, Kanamori's doctrine seemed like an academic invention, pure theory. If the government believed it was necessary to stand on a new doctrine, the people could understand that. But it should come clean, admit its mistakes. Kanamori replied that Japan was in a whirlwind. It was hard to think clearly. A dispassionate view of history, however, would show that his conception was closer to traditional practices than were the doctrines that prevailed during the 1930s. He agreed with Oikawa that a drive to reeducate the public would be necessary once the new constitution was adopted.[53]

Nosaka spoke last that day. Belaboring what had become a sore point, the Communist leader asked why the cabinet insisted on using the word *shikō* (supreme) to describe the people's will, rather than *shuken* (sovereign)? Partly, said Kanamori, for the sake of simplicity. The word *shuken* produced quarrels about its meaning even among academics. *Shikō* was not a household word either, but at least people would understand the syllable "shi-," often used in combinations to signify "the highest."[54]

What are we to make of these suspicions? They seem to have been shared by Japanese journalists, SCAP staff members, and many Diet members. Were conservative politicians and bureaucrats deliberately trying to leave the door open for a resurgence of imperial authority? Were the Japanese words chosen for article 4 part of a dark conspiracy? Where did MacArthur stand? And how far apart were Kanamori and Kades? Dramatic clashes over the next ten days would help to answer these questions.

The Kades-Kanamori Confrontation

In light of mounting concerns at GHQ and FEC, and in the Diet, it was imperative that Kades obtain a clarification of the Japanese cabinet's ideas about the preservation of *kokutai*, as well as a commitment to make changes in the Japanese text. To this end, there ensued a series of meetings between Kades and officials at the Legislative Bureau and CLO.

The first had been on Wednesday, July 10, attended by Irie and Satō. Kades indicated (perhaps reflecting the first reaction to Matsumoto Shigeharu's editorial) that the Japanese term used to translate "sovereignty of the people's will" should be rethought.[55] On Monday, July 15, they met again. This time, Kades drew attention specifically to problems in article 4, involving the use of the term *kennō* (powers) to describe the emperor's actions, the same term used elsewhere in the text to describe the powers of the Diet, cabinet, and judiciary. Kades asked that his concerns be treated as "informal and technical amendment problems between legal scholars."[56]

The following day (Tuesday, July 16), however, Kades—"suddenly," according to the Japanese account—demanded a meeting with Kanamori himself. Kades reported that Kanamori's recent replies to questions in the Diet had raised serious concerns at GHQ. These comments suggested that Kanamori had "his own firm constitutional theories." It seemed, said Kades, that the constitution MacArthur had endorsed and the one now propounded by Kanamori had "drifted very far apart," so far, in fact, that it might be necessary for MacArthur to "reconsider his approval." At the very least, he said, SCAP could expect embarrassing questions from the FEC.[57] It was time for Kades to express his concerns directly to Kanamori and to hear the minister's explanations.

And so, on Thursday morning, July 17, at the prime minister's official residence, the first of two fateful meetings took place between the American colonel and the cabinet minister responsible for the revision project.[58] Kades was there alone for the American side; two officials from the Legislation Bureau (Director General Irie Toshio and his deputy, Satō Tatsuo), and a translator, Katō Tadao, accompanied Kanamori. Kades opened the meeting by saying that because Matsumoto Jōji's draft had been replaced by the SCAP draft as the basis for revision, he had felt that GHQ and the Japanese cabinet were "on the same team." He came today, he said, "entirely in that spirit." He reviewed why SCAP had rejected the Matsumoto draft: It had been an attempt at reform along the lines of Minobe's "organ theory" of the emperor, and as such it could not protect Hirohito from the Allied demand that he be tried as a war criminal, or from the demand of many Japanese that he abdicate. The only way to do that was to redefine the emperor's constitutional position entirely. This SCAP had done, in its draft revision. The trouble now was that the Japanese text, coupled with Kanamori's explanations in the Diet, made it appear that some leading Japanese intended to resurrect the old ideas about the emperor. At first he had hoped that the problems of translation could be resolved as technical matters. In light of Kanamori's answers in the Diet, however, he now needed to know whether political issues lurked here.

Kanamori responded by outlining his ideas about *kokutai*. There was no doubt, he began, that *kokutai*, in the sense of Japan's traditional political structure, was completely revised by the proposed constitution. Under the Meiji constitution, the emperor could do anything he wished, but under the new constitution, he could do nothing except act in strict accordance with its articles. In the Meiji constitution the emperor's position was based on his own will and on the hereditary will of the imperial household, but in the new constitution the emperor's position derived entirely from the people's sovereign power. The emperor continued to be the center of the people's devotion, but his *constitutional* position had completely changed.[59]

Kades replied that these ideas were "exactly the same as SCAP's own."[60] His concerns had arisen from newspaper accounts, mainly; perhaps they were in error. Newspapers, he said, had reported Kanamori as saying that, "under the new constitution, there would be no change in Japan's *kokutai*." Abroad, this meant that Japan's traditional conception of itself as unique, a family under the emperor as father figure, would not change. Add to this the rumor, published in some provincial newspapers, that the revised constitution would take effect on Kigensetsu (February 11, 1947), Japan's most nationalistic holiday,[61] and it was not hard to understand why many foreign observers were growing apprehensive.

Kanamori replied that he had been deeply frustrated by newspaper reports of his comments in the Diet. He had tried his utmost to explain the difference between *kokutai* and the nation's political structure, and he thought most Diet members understood the difference. He said that there was absolutely no basis for the rumor that the Japanese intended to promulgate the revision on Kigensetsu. Regarding SCAP's insistence on substituting *shuken* (meaning "sovereign") for *shikō* (meaning "supreme") to describe the people's will in the new Japanese system, Kanamori said that only the Communists in the Diet were calling for such a change.

Kades insisted that he was certainly no Communist, but he noted that the terms in English had different meanings. Someone could be supreme without being sovereign. To assert that the people were sovereign, in places where monarchs had been called sovereigns, had a distinctive meaning. Thus using a Japanese word for "supreme" where the English text used "sovereign" inevitably raised questions, especially for those who did not speak Japanese. He hoped Kanamori would look for another place, if not in the preamble, to use the stronger term *shuken* to describe the people's will. And he asked Kanamori to set down in writing his ideas on the meaning of *kokutai*.

The meeting ended amicably. In the car returning him to his office, Kades remarked to Katō, the interpreter, that he thought Kanamori understood his concerns. He asked Katō for a copy of the memorandum of the meeting. Kades also mentioned that his meeting with Kanamori was unauthorized. If MacArthur reprimanded him for it, he said, he would have to resign.

What Kades meant by this last comment became clearer from Whitney's report to MacArthur later that day (July 17).[62] Whitney told his chief about the study by GHQ staffers that pointed to a problem in the Japanese version of chapter I. Recalling MacArthur's public promise that there would be no interference with Japanese deliberation on the revision project, Whitney said that he and his staff intended, if possible, to "treat these matters as technical discrepancies that had crept in despite the best of faith on the part of the Japanese." He hoped the problem could be ironed out on a staff level. He warned, though, that "Matsumoto" (i.e., the traditionalist faction) might still be "contriving" behind the scenes, and that Kanamori might be part of a conspiracy.

> If [Kanamori] is successful in establishing the idea that the new Constitution is based on this unchanged concept of "national polity," it will be possible to defeat the democratic letter of the new Constitution by interpreting it in terms of this spirit, which will have been established as being the philosophical basis of the Constitution. The will of the people will be constantly subjugated to the mystic concept of the "national polity" which is considered to be something inclusive of, but at the same time above and beyond the will of the people.

Despite these disturbing signs, Whitney reported there was reason to hope that the matter could be resolved quietly, at the staff level. Kanamori and Kades had met and discussed it "with encouraging frankness and in an atmosphere of friendliness and mutual understanding," he wrote, and Kanamori had "tentatively agreed, subject to confirmation by the cabinet," that appropriate changes in the Japanese text would be made.[63]

A week later, on July 23, Kades and Kanamori held a second meeting, and here it became apparent that the matter was so fraught with significance for all concerned that it could not be finessed. Earlier that day, the House's revision committee had ended its deliberations; the draft would now be referred to the subcommittee for the preparation of amendments. Kanamori requested a meeting at 5 P.M. with Kades to explain the changes that would be sought, pursuant to the discussion in the special committee. Again, Kades came, alone, to a Japanese venue (this time, the Chief Cabinet Secretary's residence) to meet with Kanamori, Irie, and Katō. Opening the meeting, Kanamori presented, for Kades's approval, several points that the Diet wished to change: the deletion from article 4 of the sentence that the emperor would "never" have any powers related to government, which Kades refused; several changes in the bill of rights, all of which Kades approved; the elimination of Diet consent for cabinet appointments (Kades said he would have to consult General Whitney on that; SCAP's approval was later given); changes in the article on the imperial properties, which Kades refused; and changes in chapter X, establishing the constitution as the supreme law. On the latter, Kades suggested that some of that material could be repositioned "when the preamble is rewritten." Kanamori replied that about one-fifth of the Diet wanted to make verbal changes in the preamble, but most seemed satisfied with its general content.[64]

At this point, Kades delivered what Irie recalled as "an unusually passionate speech."[65] He began by indicating that the matter of popular sovereignty was still bothering him. He noted that this meeting, unlike the one last week, was "official": Whitney knew that he intended to speak as he now intended to. Members of the FEC (he mentioned the Soviet Union and Australia specifically) believed that the principle of popular sovereignty was insufficiently affirmed in the text as it stood. It was no longer possible to ignore this sentiment. The text would have to be amended. Kanamori replied that if SCAP insisted on amending the draft's language, he would have to resign. It would be impossible for him to explain why he had changed his mind.

According to Irie, Kades seemed "very perplexed" by this response. He said people at the FEC were beginning to suspect that the Japanese translation was a "double-cross." Nor was the FEC alone in believing an amendment was necessary. People in America suspected that Japan was swallowing this constitution without chewing it. Indeed, MacArthur himself was growing apprehensive. In March, he had made a statement affirming the draft revision as a commitment to popular sovereignty. People would now think either that the Supreme Commander was trying to pull the wool over people's eyes or that he himself had been duped by the Japanese. Besides, Kanamori would not have to repudiate his earlier explanations. He need only say that his government was asking for an amendment, adding an affirmation of popular sovereignty to article 1, just to "make doubly sure."[66]

The atmosphere was very tense. Irie, sensing there was a "very strong force" behind Kades's statements, insisted there had been no intentional deception. "We compared the Japanese text with the English version, and we tried to write a Japanese text that was faithful to the English." The first paragraph of the preamble, he said, made Japan's commitment to popular sovereignty perfectly clear. He explained the passages in the preamble and in article 4, to which exception had been taken, as a problem of context; minor amendments could correct the mistaken impressions here.[67] Kades replied: "I do not doubt for a moment that all of you are honest. But the issue is not how you interpret this preamble, but that the intention of the English text is not made clear [in the Japanese version]."[68] He pleaded with Kanamori to consider the international context. If Japan refused to bend on this issue, he warned, people around the world would suspect that Japan harbored secret reservations about constitutional democracy.

The Japanese minutes of the meeting (there is no American record of it) note that the Japanese, sensing that Kades was being "stubborn," said they would try to "accommodate" him. Kanamori said he was sorry to hear Kades utter suspicions that the Japanese were attempting a "double-cross." Kades said it was not he, but world opinion, that might come to that conclusion. The meeting ended, according to Katō's minute, on friendly terms.

The next day, Kades called Kato to say he was "tickled to death" to hear reports that Kanamori was seeking an amendment that would use the word *shuken* in the preamble. But now he had to make the "formal request" that the word be used in article 1 as well. The Allies were demanding it; Kanamori was free to say that if he liked. Perhaps, Kades added to Katō, if the change had been made in the preamble two or three days sooner, it would not now be necessary to make it in article 1. But it was too late. The Allies were now insisting on it.[69]

14 . . . .

"Fervent Hopes"

- ## PACIFISM AND HUMAN RIGHTS

-
-   When the revision committee turned to chapter II (consisting of
-   just one article, article 9, on the constitutional renunciation of war
    and armed forces), discussions revealed broad support for its radical
-   affirmation of pacifism, mingled with anxious concern about inter-
    nal security and Japan's future role in world affairs. Yoshida, the old
-   diplomat, seemed resigned to accept it as the price for an early
    restoration of independence; the future would take care of itself.
-   Some members of the Diet committee were considerably less pas-
    sive.
-

-   ### General Principles

-   Early discussions revealed considerable distress about the tone of
    the article. Why, asked Hayashi Heima, was it couched in such neg-
-   ative terms? Japan had a 3,000-year-long commitment to interna-
    tional peace. General MacArthur said recently[1] that Japan's daring
-   renunciation of arms was not just a "culprit's song of submission."
    It put Japan in the vanguard of a movement for world peace. Hay-
-   ashi admitted that Japan had behaved deplorably in the recent war,
    but that was an aberration. Japan had the densest population in the
-   world, because the Japanese people had a "peculiar attachment to
    their homeland, desiring to live in it at any cost and not to leave it
-   to settle in a foreign country." "If you look out through a train
    window," he said, "you see land cultivated everywhere, even as far
    as the top of a hill." It was a "symbol of the Japanese people, who
    . . . sustain a poor livelihood by diligent and hard labor." Such peo-
    ple "do not belong to a race inclined to conquest and invasion."
    Hayashi called on the prime minister to respond to MacArthur's
    address by proclaiming Japan's commitment to peace and bidding
    the world to follow suit. "We must have it understood that we are
    the most peace-loving people on earth."[2] With an almost deflating
    economy of words, Yoshida replied, "I am quite in sympathy with
    the opinion expressed. The government is going to take proper steps

fully in line with the purport of the question." The committee, perhaps appreciating that the prime minister was in no position to proclaim such sentiments on the world stage, quietly applauded his reply.[3]

Miura Toranosuke, a liberal from Yokohama, took a different tack. In the course of a question about internal security, he contributed a little folk history. In the days of yore, he said, from the shogunate of Yoritomo (late twelfth century) through three centuries of the Tokugawa regime (ending in the mid-nineteenth century), Japan's politics was dominated by the military, "a specially privileged class entirely apart from the masses." The Meiji Restoration (1868) promised respect for human rights, but "the parliamentary government of Japan for fifty-odd years following the enactment of the Constitution in 1889 . . . in name and in substance was nothing other than a military government." Now, "as a consequence of our surrender and acceptance of the Potsdam Declaration, the military has disappeared, *zaibatsu*[4] will be dissolved and bureaucracy will lose its power." All this was quite wonderful, he said, but how would we deal with disturbances or riots? "We remember well what commotion was caused by wild rumors concerning the Koreans, at the time of the big earthquake in the Tokyo and Yokohama area in 1923." Martial law had been proclaimed then, but such a proclamation would be out of the question under the revised constitution. "What measures, if any, do the authorities have under contemplation to cope with emergencies?" Kanamori explained that Japan would of course have police forces, properly regulated, capable of handling such situations.[5]

Fujita Sakae, a young Social Democrat from Hiroshima, asked Kanamori whether article 9 would prevent Japan from defending itself against attack or joining with an ally to defend itself against unlawful aggression. National self-defense, he said, was not a war to advance national interests, nor was it a means to settle disputes. It was not prohibited in international law, nor by the Kellogg-Briand Pact. How could Japan provide for its security if it renounced even wars of self-defense? Kanamori replied that article 9 "does not clearly say that war of self-defense is renounced," though he admitted that the second clause, barring armed forces, made self-defense practically impossible. In fact, said Kanamori, Japan was "not yet" in a position to provide for its own security.[6]

When the prime minister arrived, Mori Mikiji renewed the question about Japan's response to aggression. War, he said, could not be avoided by the will of any single country. He recognized that Japan could not secure a guarantee against aggression before establishing this revised constitution. But did the government have a long-range plan for saving the country from the horrors of war? Yoshida replied that the purpose of article 9 was to remove the suspicion that Japan was plotting rearmament or acts of aggression. It would be a powerful indication that Japan was a "peace-loving nation." If any other nation threatened world peace by attacking us, he said, the United Nations would apply sanctions in accordance with article 43 of its charter. Thus, "if any country should invade Japan, all the United Nations would protect the peace of our country."[7] No one said so out loud, but taking Yoshida's words at face value, it must have seemed that the old codger had taken leave of his senses. Any man of his experience who would say these words could say anything.

A clue to the reason behind his almost cynical response came with his answer to the next inquiry. Mori, noting that the conclusion of a peace treaty must precede Japan's joining the United Nations, asked when the prime minister expected the peace treaty to be concluded. It depended entirely on Japan's attitude, he said, as perceived by the Allied powers. "The earlier it is recognized that Japan is democratized, peaceful, and a worthy member of the peace-loving nations of the world, the sooner the peace treaty will be concluded."[8] This terse response was Yoshida's policy for the postwar period in a nutshell. He was as tactical in his commitment to pacifism as he was about "democracy." With a conservatism like Winston Churchill's, he moved forward with an enigmatic smile.

The highlight of the committee's discussion of article 9 was a brilliant oratorical performance by the chairman, Ashida Hitoshi. His remarks and questions indicated that he had been doing some hard thinking about the implications of article 9. Why, he began, is Japan hastening to revise its constitution? The demand of the Allies, stated in the Potsdam Declaration, was a part of the reason. But Japan had deep purposes of its own. "When we look out of the windows of this Diet building, we see nothing but a great and desolate stretch of debris. Tens of thousands of corpses lying there, and tears shed morning and night by orphans and widows who live in temporary huts built on the ashes! Out of these is the Japanese constitution destined to be born." Indeed, the crisis in Japan was part of a worldwide calamity.

> Not only in Japan, but also in England, in the fields of the Ukraine, and under the shade of willows along the Yangtze River, similar cries of misery are to be heard. When we contemplate this lamentation of mankind and ravage of society, we come to realize that herein lies the fundamental problem common to mankind. There is no doubt that fervent hopes common to mankind for renunciation of war, aspirations for higher culture, and wishes for a better life, combined with the defeat, forced a way to a great change.

To recover the world's respect, Japan would have to remove all feudalistic tinges and establish a government of separated and balanced powers, truly accountable to public opinion. It would have to demonstrate respect for fundamental rights. In addition, before it could regain independence and rebuild herself, it would have to renounce war and armed forces. Only then could it begin to think about joining the United Nations.[9]

At that point, however, said Ashida, Japan would confront a problem. How could it meet its obligations under the U.N. Charter, to join in collective measures for international security, without armed forces? Article 9 had been discussed "enthusiastically" at these committee meetings, he said. The renunciation of war was "undoubtedly a demand originating in the bottom of the hearts of the people pining amid the ruins." But it needed to be analyzed "more concretely."[10] He saw three specific questions that the government had not yet answered candidly. First, the right of self-defense was clearly recognized in the U.N. Charter. Was Japan expected to give it up? Second, if Japan could not defend itself, was its territory not likely to become a battlefield in the event of war between other countries? Third, because Japan would not be able to provide armed forces as a member state of the United Nations, would it not be denied admission to the organization? The government's answers to these points had not been clear. It was time for the government to clarify its position.[11]

Kanamori's response to this challenge was formulaic and evasive. He admitted there was "something missing" in the link between the proposed article 9 and what the U.N. charter required of its member nations. This discrepancy would be "made good . . . when necessity arises . . . as the occasion demands."[12] In truth, the Japanese government could not answer Ashida's perfectly reasonable questions. The U.S. government—having imposed article 9 (banning armed forces in Japan) and also having led the way in drafting the U.N. charter (ensuring the right of self-defense to all nations and requiring all member nations to contribute peace-keeping forces)—would have to deal with these contradictions when Japan sought admission to the United Nations, as it was surely U.S. policy that it should ultimately do.

On July 12, just as the dispute between Kades and Kanamori over *kokutai* was coming to a head, Kitaura, the voice of Japan's right, asked again about national self-defense. General MacArthur's statement of June 21 said that Japan would "never" be permitted to accumulate "war potential." Did that mean that even self-defense would never be possible? Kanamori's response revealed some exasperation.

> It goes without saying that this constitution is to be decided by our country, not by the will of any foreign country. But in deciding on various matters to be prescribed in the constitution, we have to abide by the various international restrictions placed on our country. . . . I have no exact knowledge as to what terms a foreign general used regarding the renunciation of war which you have just referred to, but I hope you understand the rough idea from my reply.[13]

Later in the morning, Kasai Jūji reprimanded Kanamori for this "slip of the tongue" in referring to the Supreme Commander.[14] It did seem to betray irritation. Kanamori might be a willing "sacrifice," as he once remarked,[15] but he was also a proud man.

Prime Minister Yoshida Responds

On July 15, after several postponements, Yoshida finally showed up for a second meeting of the committee. It is not known whether his delays reflected contempt for the work of constitutional revision or irritation with Ashida, chair of this committee, for whom Yoshida sometimes exhibited thinly veiled contempt, or simply preoccupation with other affairs of government. In any event this was a long-awaited opportunity for committee members to try again to pin down the prime minister on his policies regarding the renunciation of war and armed forces.

The questioning began with a set of discourses by Katō Kanjū, a fiery labor leader. What did Yoshida think about the population problem as the leading cause of modern warfare? Yoshida replied that it was indeed a difficult problem. "It is impossible to support an unlimited number of [people] on these narrow islands." The solution depended on economic policies. "If we rely on agriculture, the population we can support will necessarily be limited." A larger population cannot be supported without the "mechanization and rationalization of agriculture." That, and the conversion of Japan to a "trading nation," were the challenges confronting the leaders of the new Japan.[16] This could not have been the answer sought by the husband of Japan's leading advocate of birth control.[17] It did, however, afford an insight into the priorities of Japan's most important postwar leader, and his answer was a key to the reasons for his acceptance of article 9.

Members who followed Katō in questioning the prime minister were less theoretical. Sasamori Junzō had lived in the United States for 20 years and earned a doctorate from the University of Denver. He was a Christian, and, as president of Aoyama Gakuin University before the war, he had strongly opposed militarism. His question dealt with domestic insurrection. "If a revolt occurs somewhere in Japan after the conclusion of the peace treaty, and the rebels occupy and declare that area to be independent, will Japan be precluded from the use of armed forces against them because she has renounced war by this constitution?[18] Kanamori replied that article 9 as drafted would not prevent the use of force to preserve "peace and order" in Japan's internal affairs. A line could be drawn, he said, between police power and the "land, sea and air forces, as well as other war potential," prohibited by the constitution. He did, however, add this significant statement of the "intent of the framers" of 1946: "If we undertake to maintain land, sea, or air forces of considerable size under the pretext of police power necessary for the maintenance of domestic peace and order, it will constitute a violation of article 9 of this Constitution."[19]

Not all the concerns about article 9 focused on its future impact. Takahashi Eikichi noted the failure of the victor nations to repatriate Japanese soldiers, in violation of the Potsdam Declaration and international law. This was a serious matter. At the end of the war, approximately 6.5 million Japanese were stranded in Asia, Siberia, and the Pacific Ocean area, of whom roughly 3.5 million were soldiers and sailors. The civilians, including many women and children, were regarded as agents of Japan's imperial establishment. Of these 6.5 million, 2.6 million Japanese were in China, 1.1 million in Manchuria, 500,000 in Taiwan, 900,000 in Korea, nearly 1 million more in Southeast Asia and the Philippines, and hundreds of thousands more on scattered islands in the Pacific.

Getting the people back to Japan was one of the great tasks facing Occupation authorities. It was slow work, and it encountered considerable resistance from the Allies. By September 1946, over 2 million Japanese remained unrepatriated. By mid-1946, over 100,000 were still being held by the British in south and southeast Asia to work on rebuilding projects. As late as April 1949, 60,000 Japanese were still being held in Communist-controlled areas in China. By far the greatest offender, however, and the one most deeply resented by the Japanese, was the Soviet Union. That nation had entered the war on August 8, one week before it ended, just in time to accept the Japanese surrender in Manchuria and northern Korea. Japanese authorities estimated that more than 1.6 million Japanese nationals became Soviet prisoners in August 1945. None were released until December 1946. By the end of 1947, fewer than 1 million had made it back to Japan.[20]

It was in the gradually dawning awareness of this situation that Takahashi asked how these people would be rescued. "When I asked the prime minister the other day whether the detention of our disarmed men abroad long after the end of war did not constitute a violation of the Potsdam Declaration," said Takahashi, "he replied in the affirmative." Would Japan be able to present this case to the United Nations?[21] Kanamori replied that foreign affairs was not his portfolio, so any answer from him would not be authoritative.

In the end, the revision committee was left in the position Yoshida had outlined at the outset. If Japan wanted to end the Occupation quickly, it would have to swallow this chapter. SCAP viewed it as integral to constitutional revision. On the other hand, the depth and persistence of Japanese concerns were evident. Toward the end of July, Ashida and his colleagues on the revision subcommittee would find language, acceptable to SCAP, that opened a narrow path for creative interpretation.

Human Rights

Everyone realized that Japan was emerging into a new era, as far as the rights of the people were concerned. During the Meiji era, constitutional rights had been hedged about with qualifications. The stressful years of war in Asia and in the Pacific saw the government seize on these constitutional qualifications to impose disciplines in the interest of full national mobilization.[22] At the end of the war, the Potsdam Declaration called for the removal of "all obstacles to the revival and strengthening of democratic tendencies among the Japanese people" and "respect for the fundamental human rights," including freedom of speech, religion and thought.[23]

What personal experience and attitudes did the Japanese framers, particularly those in the Diet, bring to the consideration of human rights? Many members of this committee were quite familiar with the West's evolving notion of human rights, having studied or toured extensively abroad.

- Tahara Haruji, for example, who spoke up for the outcast *burakumin* during the discussion of article 14 (the equal protection and antidiscrimination clause)—and who later left the Diet to lead an alliance of supporters of the *burakumin* cause—had a degree from the University of Missouri.
- Kojima Tetsuzō, who sought to add explicit safeguards against libel and defamation, had studied law in the United States.

- Kasai Jūji, who suggested adding a provision, like the one in Oregon,[24] for initiative and recall to the guarantee of suffrage in article 15, had degrees in political science from the University of Chicago and Harvard.
- Tanahashi Kotora, a labor lawyer who insisted that a guarantee of the right to work implied that the state was the employer of last resort, had traveled to Weimar Berlin and the Soviet Union during the late 1920s.

So there were certainly cosmopolitan influences at work in this chamber. In fact, however, the most strenuous and sustained pushes for human rights came from legislators newly entering the political arena, people whose experience as schoolteachers and principals, labor lawyers and social activists, journalists, and assemblymen informed their evaluation of these guarantees.

- When Koshihara Haruko sought protection for pregnant women and infants and pressed for equal pay for equal work, she was drawing on her experience as a selftaught school administrator in Nagoya.
- Satō Gizen, who would lead the minister of education through a long interrogation about the place of religion in elementary and secondary schools, had spent the war years teaching at a commercial high school in Kobe.
- Ono Takashi, a schoolteacher from Aomori, in the far north of Honshu, "took [Kanamori] to task" for refusing to interpret the rights to education and work as imposing obligations on the government.

One topic that drew close attention was the conflict of rights. Takeya Gentarō asked whether the guarantees of "freedom of assembly, association, speech and press, and freedom from censorship" would be "absolutely guaranteed in time of emergency." Pointing to article 12, Kanamori said that people would be bound not to abuse their rights but to use them for the public welfare. Accordingly, he said, "in time of emergency these rights are guaranteed within necessary limits."[25] Fujita noted that articles 11 and 97 both said rights were eternal and inviolate. What would happen if rights written in different articles imposed contradictory commands? Kanamori replied in classic liberal terms. The Meiji Constitution, he noted, relied on statutes to set the framework for making such adjustments, but the revision rejected that approach as "basically wrong." How would articles 12 (responsible use of rights) and 21 (freedom of assembly and expression) be reconciled? The courts would eventually adjust them. This approach would tend to favor human rights.[26] Fujita reduced his inquiry to examples. Suppose, he said, there arose a political movement aimed at repudiating the emperor system as outlined in the constitution, or an association banded together to advocate rearmament, against the constitutional commitment of article 9. Kanamori said the courts would probably protect such movements. But what about the government? asked Fujita. Would agitators be arrested for acting against the public welfare? Kanamori replied that it was difficult to speak of hypothetical cases. But it did seem likely that administrative action would be taken as the government deemed necessary. "If the concrete [government actions] prohibit what should not be prohibited or punish what should not be punished, and if it becomes a constitutional question, it will be placed before the Supreme Court, where it will be dealt with properly." Fujita was not contradicted when he summed up the exchange by saying, "I understand by your explanation that the government will regard such a movement as against the public welfare."[27]

Fujita's question may have been hypothetical, but it was not framed in a vacuum. On May 1, and on a second day of popular uprisings, May 19—called "Food May Day"—central Tokyo had been the scene of boisterous demonstrations. A government crackdown ensued. A demonstrator who displayed a placard was charged with the serious crime of lese majesty,[28] which at that time still carried stiff penalties. Even if rights of association and protest were ultimately vindicated in court, repression by the police could have a chilling effect, and there was no guarantee that the courts would prevail in a system without a strong tradition of personal liberty.

The Question of Positive Social Rights

Another concern of many members was whether chapter III was modern enough for the new Japan. Mori Mikiji called attention to article 97, where the rights guaranteed in this constitution were described as products of an "age-old struggle." The reference, he assumed, was to the Magna Carta (1215), the French Bill of Rights (1789), and the American Declaration of Independence (1776). These were indeed "milestones," he said, but what they marked were advances for "individualistic" liberty. Germany's Weimar Constitution, responding partly to twentieth-century conditions of urban congestion and industrialization, also deserved emulation. Article 29 (guaranteeing private property) particularly needed updating. It promised just compensation for public takings but omitted the duty to use property for the general good. Kanamori's reply was not defensive. He pointed to article 12. It was better than Weimar, he said. It recognized that all rights must be exercised in light of the public welfare. As for property rights, the language of article 29 was carefully guarded and gave every encouragement to conceptions of the public good in the regulation of property rights.[29]

There were other questions about social rights in chapter III, and initially the government's responses were encouraging to members on the left. Sakai Toshio asked whether article 27, guaranteeing the right to work, might be construed as promising that workers were being guaranteed the *opportunity* to work. In the absence of the welfare minister, a vice minister replied that article 27 meant that people who had the ability and the will to work would be given the opportunity to work. Sakai pressed for clarification. Did that mean that people who were able to work but unemployed would have the right to demand that the state provide them with a job? The minister replied that if people are willing to work but unable to find employment, "the government, in my opinion, should undertake some works for their relief."[30]

It soon became apparent that this answer was, to put it mildly, misleading. Ono Takashi was apparently the first to realize that Kanamori's reading of chapter III differed from the junior minister's. On July 18, addressing a question about article

26 (on the right to an education), Kanamori said it meant not that the state would provide a free education for everyone, but that the state could not interfere with a citizen's right to an education. Ono was incredulous. Did Kanamori read article 27 (guaranteeing a right to work) the same way? Earlier, Ono said, a spokesman for the government had given a different answer. Kanamori replied that Ono must have misunderstood him. At any rate, the articles in question did not oblige the government to provide either a free elementary education or jobs for everyone. Ono, stupefied, declared that this was a "very important answer." It would alter the understanding of the whole text for many Japanese people.[31]

That afternoon, Sakai Toshio, a member of a center-right party, rose to express astonishment at Kanamori's words. When he heard Kanamori's explanation, he said, he felt astounded, "as if the earth had crumbled at my feet." The working class, said Sakai, "had felt greatly reassured" by the government's earlier answers. It made them "rejoice over the enactment of such a splendid democratic constitution." He never dreamed that Kanamori would give an opposite interpretation. "Which interpretation shall we accept?"[32] Ashida intervened at this point to observe that "the government's replies lack unity." He hoped, he said, that the government would sort out its differences and state its authoritative interpretation "at a suitable opportunity, say at tomorrow's meeting of the committee."[33]

The following morning (July 19), Kanamori gave the cabinet's reply. He admitted there were grounds for misunderstanding, but he insisted that he and Kawai Yoshinari, the welfare minister, were now in agreement as to the meaning of article 27. The article, he declared, expressed a "fundamental right of individual liberty." It meant only "that the people will not be deprived of the fundamental right to work, not that the people are guaranteed the opportunity for various kinds of actual work." Legislation providing a guaranteed income could be built on article 25 (guaranteeing "social welfare and security"), but a right to these benefits could not be inferred from article 27. He acknowledged that his reading was a "cool, juridical interpretation of the letter of the constitution." He added that it was "natural to conclude," as the welfare minister had, "in view of the right to work so clearly stipulated in the constitution, that the state is obligated politically as well as morally to make every effort to uphold this principle and make it sufficiently effective." That would be a perfectly valid *political* interpretation. But juridically, he insisted, the interpretation he now offered was the correct one.[34]

This fight may have left a mistaken impression of Kanamori's politics. Kanamori was certainly opposed to entrenching certain economic benefits in a constitution. In this sense, he was a classic liberal. At the same time, however, he indicated his support for an active state, responsive to modern social realities. For example, he made clear that the government under this constitution would have broad powers to regulate the conditions of labor. He defended labor's right to organize under article 28, even to the point of replying affirmatively when Sakai asked him if it included the "right to sabotage." And when Kasai, the American-educated political scientist, expressed alarm that the government, egged on by SCAP, seemed to be encouraging social movements that amounted to "class strife,"[35] Kanamori replied, so be it. A true libertarian, he said there must be no repression of workers' rights. Class strife could certainly be troubling. He hoped owners and workers would show a sense of responsibility and concern for the public interest. But Japan's commitment to political freedom must be unswerving. The revised constitution was criticized by some as "extremely retrogressive and conservative, protecting only rights recognized since the 18th century." It was not so. Its "quiet phraseology" aimed at a modern objective. He agreed that, if labor disputes took an unrestrained form, it would doubtless have a dampening effect on Japan's industry. "But is it better to kill an ox in an attempt to straighten its horns, or let the ox play to the full of its ability with its horns as they are?" The times called for courage, "but we have drafted this project in the ardent hope that [a constitution] having such progressive meanings will be operated successfully, by appealing to the sense of responsibility of the Japanese people."[36]

Religion in the New Japan

Religious freedom, its extent and limits, was another vexed topic during these discussions. Answers given by Tanaka Kōtarō, then minister of education and future chief justice of the supreme court, indicated how his ideas and experience would inform his judgment. Mori began by pointing out that superstition and bigotry often masked themselves as religion. Shouldn't the revised constitution contain language like that in article XXVIII of the Meiji Constitution, promising the enjoyment of religious freedom "within limits not prejudicial to peace and order"?[37] Tanaka thought not. Mori's apprehensions were understandable, but discriminating between good and bad religion was a delicate business, particularly for public officials. It exposed religion to great pressure, as it had during the war and the "critical period that preceded it." Presumably now the standard of screening would be different, but it would be pernicious nonetheless. "Religion in its essence," he said (rather naively), "has nothing to do with politics or state administration; it is something unworldly in nature and not political; it has not worldly aims, but is only concerned with the problems of souls." In its "degenerated forms," he admitted, fraudulent religions sometimes violate penal codes, harm public sanitation, or outrage public decency. But the criminal code existed to deal with such matters. The question of right and wrong among the various types of religion ought to be left to "free competition and natural selection among them."[38]

Sakai posed a related question. Wasn't there danger that freedom of thought (guaranteed by article 19) would strip Japanese defenses against fascist organizations? Again, Tanaka appealed to a distinction between thought and criminal behavior. The latter would be punished; the former should be given the widest possible protection. To illustrate his point, Tanaka recalled that, during the Tokugawa Shogunate, "Christians were forced to abandon their faith, and, to test their faith, they were made to tread upon a copper tablet of the crucifix."[39] Tanaka, himself a Christian, concluded that measures like this "should not be resorted to." Articles 19 and 21 would make them unconstitutional.[40]

The need to adjust the claims of religious faith to the premises of a secular polity is a delicate issue for all liberal democracies. The discussion in the revision committee occurred in the shadow of the 1930s and early 1940s, when religion became an engine of Japan's imperial program. There was agreement among many Japanese leaders in 1946 that this kind of thing must not be repeated. But how could the abuse of religion be prevented without interfering with religious liberty? The bill of rights in chapter III, drafted by the Americans, sought to achieve that end by providing that "no religious organization shall receive special privileges from the state, nor exercise any political authority . . . ; no person shall be compelled to take part in any religious act, celebration, rite or practice . . . ; [and] the state and its organs shall refrain from religious education or any other religious activity." In addition, the SCAP draft provided that "no public money or property shall be appropriated for the use, benefit or support of any . . . religious institution or association, or for any charitable, educational or benevolent purposes not under the control of public authority."[41] By such language, Americans sought to draw a firm line between religion and the state. Some of these Diet members, however, were personally religious. Others represented communities of devout people. Many of them saw Japan's postwar crisis as partly spiritual. These circumstances guaranteed that the clauses in question would be closely examined to see whether they would permit religious people to practice their faith and allow "the state and its organs" to reflect and foster the religious sentiments of the people.

Satō Gizen began the inquiry by noting that the United States was itself a spiritual country, whose public life began with a religious compact aboard the *Mayflower* and continued to reflect the conviction that religious belief is the "source of democracy" and a key to world peace and justice. Was it not hazardous to insist that Japan's public institutions be barred from religious expression in any form?[42] Tanaka, minister of education, replied that he understood the importance of spirituality but that church and state must be kept separate. The state must not take sides in the struggle over religious convictions. In our schools, he said, we must promote morality by using the classic texts of all the great religions.

Satō jumped on Tanaka for this answer. Earlier, he recalled, someone had asked Tanaka how the government intended to deal with the Imperial Rescript on Education, the widely revered credo of the Meiji era.[43] He had replied that "not only the Imperial Edict on Education, but the Holy Bible, the Analects of Confucius, the Book of Mencius, and the Buddhist Sutras may be utilized for education." Satō apologized for "tripping you upon your words," but when Tanaka had urged that these great teachings be employed in a utilitarian fashion, "it makes me feel as though I am peeping at the armor of feudalistic bureaucracy under the cover of the clothes of democracy." Teachers and government officials must kneel before religion, not attempt to manipulate it.[44] He recalled that, under the Meiji constitution, Japanese "subjects" were entitled to enjoy freedom of religion "within limits not prejudicial to peace and order, and not antagonistic to their duties as subjects." In this draft, no such conditions were attached. This was unrealistic, Satō thought, given the "present degree of Japanese intelligence." He cited a recent publication that ranked Japan next to Germany in matters of superstition. In these circumstances, wasn't it "the duty of the state to take positive measures for imparting the right faith to the people" and to foster religious sentiment in children?[45] Tanaka held his ground. He was confident that "good religion" would prevail in a free marketplace of ideas. Teachers, he said, must be particularly careful about propounding their own doctrines in school. They must treat all sects and religious teachings evenhandedly.[46]

Inoue Tokumei, the Buddhist educator from Kagoshima, shared Satō's concerns about the capability of the Japanese people to handle religious freedom.[47] Did the government intend to be "absolute" on this issue? Kanamori replied that article 12, with its warning that the people must "refrain from any abuse of these freedoms and rights and shall always be responsible for utilizing them for the public welfare," gave the government some leverage. He added, however, that it was "unthinkable from its very nature that religion . . . will conflict with other public welfare." Thus, the draft's language "substantially approaches absolute freedom." Inoue thought this approach unwise. "Our people in the level of present religious knowledge and sentiment lack power of judgment." How did the government plan to cope, if religions cropped up that interfered with "social peace, happiness and welfare"? Kimura, the justice minister, replied that criminal behavior would be dealt with as such, via the penal code, but that otherwise there would be no interference with religion.[48]

Women and the Family System

One issue stirred particularly deep passions. With its apparent promise of a revolution in the traditional Japanese family system, article 24 proved to be nearly as explosive as the demand for change in *kokutai*, and perhaps even more so than the renunciation of war and armed forces. A speech by Hara Fujirō indicated the stakes, as far as the conservatives were concerned. "I need not enlarge upon the fact that the family system and the emperor system are time-honored institutions, closely related to each other." The family system was "God-ordained, an established institution since the very foundation of our country." The unity of the emperor and the people, a prime objective of government, is essentially related to the family system. Hara indicated he was not opposed to the concept behind article 24, but he did wonder what impact it might have on "a few matters of the family system," such as the traditional succession to the headship of a family and the rights of the head of a family.[49] Yoshida was ready for such a sympathetic question. Remarking that the principal object was "to sweep away . . . so-called feudalistic relics," he declared that article 24 posed no threat to the rights of the family head, family membership, inheritance, and such traditional institutions. "The family system and the family succession of Japan is a good custom peculiar to Japan," he declared. The government would make "proper amendments [to the civil code], taking into full consideration the discussions in this House and the views of the committee."[50]

These smooth words did not satisfy everyone on the right. Kitaura Keitarō saw family relations as Hara did. "By the present draft constitution," he said, "Japanese subjects are relieved of their duty to be loyal to the emperor." The extension of equal rights to women was quite right, but he was afraid that unless great care were taken, the family system would be destroyed, replaced by mindless individualism and social disintegration.[51] In his reply, Kanamori indicated that a fair measure of change in the family system and the inheritance system could be foreseen as a result of article 24. However, as Yoshida had already explained, it would not necessarily lead to the loss of the rights of the family head or parents. Reform would be designed to establish a "legal order most suited to Japan, after getting detailed views from various quarters."[52]

The hornet's nest that lay underneath these glib reassurances was pretty thoroughly disturbed by the Socialist leader, Suzuki Yoshio, who followed Kitaura to the podium. Noting that article 24 "provides for equality of the sexes in marriage, etc.," Suzuki said he expected that "in dissolving the time-honored family system," it would be necessary to bring about a "rationalization of relations, etc., between parent and child, between each brother and sister." If so, he said, he hoped that "provisions for the protection of home life would also be supplemented." As Suzuki started to address the changes he foresaw in education, the transcript records that shouting broke out and the "whole House [was] thrown into commotion." The Speaker shouted, "Be quiet!" Suzuki tried to continue, but again, the transcript reports, "many members" began to shout.[53] Such an outburst was unusual. Suzuki's call for a "rationalization of relations" between the sexes and within families outraged many members. The perception that family relations were fundamental to Japanese society, and fundamental, therefore, to the prospects for democracy, was entirely correct.

Katō Shizue's Speech

On July 6, the first woman to speak, Katō Shizue, took the floor. She had attended the exclusive Gakushūin School, where children of the imperial family and of noble families were prepared, with exquisite care, for lives of refinement. As expected, she married a baron. In 1919, her husband's work took him to New York City. When his young wife followed, he left her to fend for herself, believing that she needed to be more independent. She took an apartment in The Bronx and attended the Ballard School, to learn shorthand and typing so that she could earn a living. One evening in New York she attended a lecture by Margaret Sanger. Soon she was involved in the birth control movement. Returning to Japan, she campaigned for birth control, provoking a minor scandal, and was instrumental in arranging for Sanger to visit Japan. Having grown apart from her husband, she obtained a divorce (itself a scandal in those days, especially for a woman of her class), then went to work to support herself and two sons. In 1937 she was arrested for involvement in a campaign for family planning. That year she published (in English only) an autobiography, *Facing Two Ways*. During the war, she came in contact with a labor leader, Katō Kanjū, whom she married in 1944. In April 1946—the first election in which women had the right to vote and to stand as candidates—she won a seat in the Diet as a Social Democrat, one of thirty-eight women elected to the House of Representatives that year.

When Katō rose on July 6, she must have presented a disconcerting image to her fellow politicians. She came from an aristocratic background, as refined as anyone in the room. Yet she was a famous radical and newly married to a rough-and-tumble labor leader.[54] She was also a favorite at GHQ. Just two weeks before, on June 21, she had led a delegation of women to meet with General MacArthur, who had basked in her praise for enfranchising women.[55]

She began powerfully, capturing her theme in a complex opening sentence. "When this constitution is enacted and promulgated," she declared, "it will have an important bearing upon the liberation of women, which is closely related to the democratization of Japan that arises from the acceptance of the Potsdam Declaration."[56] She made clear from the outset that she would be talking of women's rights but that her concern was for the well-being of the nation as a whole. Many members, she said, worried that article 24 might "have the effect of destroying the good manners of the traditional family system in this country." She recalled Prime Minister Yoshida's reassurance that "the good manners of Japan's traditional family system should by all means be respected and maintained." Perhaps he meant that "members of a family should have the spirit of proper harmonization and mutual concession; . . . abide by the rules of etiquette; . . . have industrious habits." If so, no one could disagree. But if he was thinking of preserving the family system as a legal institution, as it existed in the present civil code, there would indeed be a problem.[57]

With that, she subjected Japan's domestic mores to candid examination. Despite all the sentimental rhetoric, Japan's family system, like those in every country on earth, reflected the "political and economic structure of the age" and would have to evolve. No matter how "high-sounding" a nation's laws may be, even if its constitution appears to vindicate fundamental human rights, it could not "develop any racial power, or hope for any cultural progress, if its people were an incoherent riffraff," unsupported by healthy, progressive social relations.[58]

Margaret Sanger's disciple then laid out a vision of domestic life for Japan that must have seemed a "brave new world" indeed to many of her listeners. Family life, she said, should include a "lawful and well-ordered sexual life" for both sexes. Its function was "maintaining and adjusting the population of the race." The home should be a "place where all the members of a family can live freely and pleasantly, develop their individuality, and perfect their personality." Because it promised to encourage these goals, article 24 was to be "most heartily welcomed as forming the groundwork of an epochal democratization of our family life." But such a reordering would not come without fundamental change. Many provisions of the existing civil code were incompatible with article 24. They did not treat husband and wife as legally equal. The wife was legally incompetent, and other members of the house were also placed under the restraint of the head of the house. "This seems to me an oppression of the personality of family members and an infringement of their rights of pursuing happiness." She asked Kanamori what he thought.[59] Kanamori said he agreed. "The existing order of things should be subjected to stern criticism, and . . . matters requiring reform should be set right."[60]

Katō turned next to Kimura Tokutarō, minister of justice. Did he agree that many provisions in the existing civil code were inconsistent with the proposed article 24? Under current law, any act done by the wife in court without the permission of her husband could later be repudiated and rescinded, by her husband or even by herself. Also, unless specific contractual arrangements were made before marriage, which was rarely the case, the administration of a wife's property belonged to her husband. Katō noted that a government committee[61] had recently recommended revision of this system, along more democratic lines. That was encouraging, but subsequent reports indicated that the so-called time-honored manners and customs of this country would be the "yardstick" in assessing these reform proposals. Was that true? she asked.[62] Kimura agreed that the current civil code was in many respects "feudalistic." "The power held by the head of a house and by the husband is too great." He pointed specifically to article 14 of the current code, giving the husband an extensive right of permission over acts of his wife. This provision, he said, was "quite rich in the complexion of feudalism." Also no longer defensible, he thought, was the right of the head of a house to disapprove the marriage of a member of the house or to appoint a place of residence for him. What then would become of the "time-honored manners and customs of this country" when the revised constitution came into effect? He agreed with Katō that manners and customs were "moral" in nature. Family members "should assist each other, should uphold the good name of their family, and should revere their ancestors." But these were moral considerations. When the family was considered as a legal institution, things "feudalistic" should by all means be eliminated. There was no doubt, he concluded, that the civil code would have to be thoroughly revised, in light of the requirements of article 24 of the proposed constitutional revision.[63]

Katō pressed on. What about chastity and the grounds for divorce? Under the present civil code, she noted, "while the husband can sue for divorce on the ground of a wife's adultery, the wife cannot do so unless the husband is convicted for adultery." Even under the government committee's proposed revisions, the causes for divorce are listed as "1. Unfaithful act of the wife. 2. Gross misconduct of the husband." Here again, a distinct difference is shown in the obligation of chastity. How did Kimura think these things would be dealt with hereafter?[64]

Kimura replied cautiously. No doubt, he said, from a moral point of view, chastity should be observed by husbands as well as wives. But whether a breach of chastity should be regarded as grounds for divorce was a different and more difficult question. In revising the code, the Diet would need to think carefully.

Katō was not happy with that answer, but she forged ahead. Article 24 as drafted guaranteed equality of the sexes, but that was too simple. "Women have a special and important mission in regard to pregnancy, childbirth, and up-bringing of children." Protection of motherhood needed to be "expressly stipulated in the constitution." If a husband dies or deserts a woman with children, she must undertake both earning a livelihood and educating her children. Thus, it is not enough to lay down equality of the sexes. The constitution needed to recognize a woman's special circumstances. Kanamori said that such matters could be handled under provisions for the general welfare. But Katō feared that unless the interests of mothers and children are specifically recognized, the promise of equality would not be honored.[65]

Kawai, the welfare minister, agreed that mothers bore special burdens in aspects of daily living. Men too had special roles in the natural order of things. "Take the example of birds. What duty is the cock to fulfill? What duty is the hen to fulfill? Their duties are naturally different. In the same way, the duties of human beings are different, according to their respective spheres of natural duty." Kawai agreed that legislation governing the conditions of work should be different for men, pregnant women, other women and girls, and children.[66]

Katō responded that draft legislation coming out of the welfare ministry was not reassuring on this point. That is why she was asking for specific constitutional guarantees. For example, to qualify for aid under the draft bill for so-called livelihood protection, war widows had to demonstrate that they were "destitute." Considering that the state was the cause of their plight, was this not unduly harsh? It was like giving medicine to a sick person only after all hope was lost.[67]

Katō's other great concern was for education. Schooling for girls in Japan, she said, had hitherto been based on the ideal of "good wives and wise mothers," a slogan that smacked of feudalism. Japan needed a completely revamped approach to the education of girls. She called on the education minister to make clear by what means the future education of children and women would be guided. Tanaka said he welcomed the opportunity to speak of the education of the new Japanese woman. At all levels, he said, beginning with the primary education of young children, the aim of democratic education should be to "cultivate personality and promote a healthy development of individuality, and in the long run, to have them take constant interest in the pursuit of truths." Traditional slogans were not bad things in themselves, but they had been "much distorted," to fit the demands of "extreme nationalism or racialism." The principle of "good wives and wise mothers," as hitherto practiced in Japan, had encouraged an atmosphere in which "the personality of women is not respected, their freedom is not respected, women are made a tool in the hands of men, or women are sacrificed on the altar of the family." Tanaka concluded by summarizing how his ministry would approach renovating the education of girls: "The ministry of education calls for equality of opportunity in education, equalization of standards of education for boys and girls, and mutual respect between boys and girls."[68]

Katō pronounced herself "perfectly satisfied with the reply just given by the minister of education." She wished, she said, to add only a few words.

> The quality of Japanese women has in the past been valued very highly by European and American philosophers. . . . However, [women in Japan] have been unable for a time to give proper play to their intrinsic traits, owing to the too feudalistic principle of "good wives and wise mothers." Now we are able to entertain the hope that, thanks to educational methods based on a broad point of view, the excellent quality of Japanese women will again come to be recognized in the world, and with this hope I am greatly satisfied.[69]

With this, she sat down, amid cheers. It had been a maiden speech to be remembered. In a way, the speech, and the responses it elicited, may have created false hopes. Article 24 would not produce an immediate revolution in Japanese mores.

Cultural resistance to sexual equality would not collapse. But Katō Shizue had drawn the issues clearly. Male dominance would no longer go unchallenged.

Other Women Join the Debate

Ōhashi Kimi taught at a high school for girls in Kyushu. She was thrilled, she said, that for the "first time in world history," women were involved in writing a national constitution.[70] For her colleague, Koshihara Haruko, a school administrator from Nagoya, this was not enough. She made a strong case for protections for infants and pregnant women, as in Germany's Weimar Constitution. Kanamori dismissed Weimar as "idealistic" and rather patronizingly advised that such protections be given in legislation.[71] Koshihara countered by asking whether any female members of the Diet were serving on either of the committees that were preparing revisions of the civil code. Kimura, the justice minister, answered that he thought a "female member" was sitting on one of them.[72]

The following day, Koshihara renewed her question about the drafting committees. "The essential traits of women can be known only by women," she insisted. She had learned that no woman representative was participating on the panel drafting of the revised civil code. Did the justice ministry have any intention of naming one? Kimura replied that "formalities have already been gone through for a woman representative's participation. You may rest assured."[73] The transcript does not indicate how Koshihara and her colleagues reacted to this promise, but it seems unlikely, after Kimura's dismissive and misleading report the day before, that they would "rest assured."

The discussions provided ample evidence that women knew the stakes in these new constitutional arrangements, though they were not always sure what to make of them. Ōhashi, for example, expressed concern about the individualistic assumptions of the bill of rights generally, and specifically as it related to widows and orphans. At the beginning of the Meiji era, she noted, Western individualism was introduced into Japan, with sometimes tragic results. She hoped that this time, reformers would aim at a more cooperative and compassionate social system.[74] Takeda Kiyo wanted to know exactly what equality would mean for women. What if a father and a mother disagreed about their children's education? Whose preferences would prevail? Kimura replied that legislation to regulate such details had not yet been worked out. Women needed special protections, she continued. As women age, sexual desire diminishes, and women are often cast out by men who crave fresh delights. Japan aspired to become a "cultured nation," she said. Mothers carried the weight of that expectation, and it limited their freedom. No doubt legislation would be needed to ensure the necessary protections, but it ought to have a secure constitutional foundation. Kawai, the welfare minister, sought to parry this attack by noting that a so-called Livelihood Protection Law (the Japanese equivalent of a social security law) would include protections for needy women. He took the occasion, while he was "on his feet," to apologize for his earlier use of the analogy of cocks and hens. He meant no disrespect.[75] Takeda was not satisfied. The Livelihood Protection Law would provide protection for the poor. Mothers need help and protection, not because they were poor but because of their condition and responsibilities. As for animal analogies, she noted that poultry farmers wanted ten or more hens for every cock. Why? "Hens lay eggs and rear chickens." What women were demanding was respect for their essential role in building civilization.[76]

These arguments by women did not go unanswered. Resistance by traditionalists was manifest in speeches by Amano Hisashi and Ii Seiichi, both experienced legislators. Amano was a sake brewer. He argued that Japan could never achieve true democracy by simple imitation of Western democracies. Japan's family system was essential to its makeup. He admitted that it contained many features that were relics of feudalism. It needed reform, but he insisted that revisers of the civil code must be careful not to destroy it altogether. Farmers toiled in obscurity for decades, just to have something to leave their families. If the rights of inheritance were disturbed, the fabric of rural life would unravel, with dire consequences for Japan.[77]

Ii, an attorney, was active in the Federation of Farmers' Unions. His concerns were similar. "The very marrow of our family system," he said, "is our traditional and deep-rooted belief that there is an unbroken lineage in our family continued from generation to generation, from ancestors down to posterity, which is the backbone of our social structure." How did the cabinet regard these traditions? How did it understand the bearing of article 24 on the family system? That was the question, and the committee on constitutional revision needed to know how the government was treating the matter.[78]

Kimura[79] stood pretty strong under this assault. The Japanese family system, he said, was based on respect for the "family pedigree and the worship of ancestors." He repeated that various drafting groups were studying to see how the Japanese family system might be maintained without violating the promise of individual dignity and essential equality.

There was nothing intrinsically wrong with this response. However, when Ii replied, "I understand that the idea . . . is to keep alive the import of the family system as of yore," and Kimura allowed his comment to go unrevised, it seemed apparent that any agreement on this issue was superficial. And when Ii followed up by asking whether article 2, dealing with succession to the throne, would be affected by the promise of equality in article 24, and Kanamori replied, not necessarily,[80] it was evident that any social revolution produced by article 24 would likely be slow in materializing.[81]

Reforming the Criminal Justice System

The other focus of this examination of chapter III, the bill of rights, was the protections for persons in the criminal justice system. From the standpoint of many Diet members who had had experience as defense attorneys, the existing system was brutal, routinely subjecting suspects to cruel mistreatment. Ibaragi Kazuhisa, a lawyer from Niigata, said that, despite prohibitions in existing codes, the torture of suspects was common in Japan. Holding pens for detaining sus-pects, commonly called pig sties, were like the Tower of London, imposing brutal punishment before conviction. Kimura said he agreed with much of Ibaragi's criticism, but remedies would be hard to find because the problem spanned several ministries. Police work was the province of the home ministry. The justice ministry handled prosecution at trials. Improvement of facilities, costing money, would involve the budget makers at the finance ministry.

Tanaka Isaji put the problem of administrative detention in the context of meeting the terms for ending the Occupation. The Potsdam Declaration required that the Occupation continue until Japan corrected its human rights abuses. None was more flagrant, he said, than the abuses committed while holding suspects for interrogation. Japan would not have a peace treaty until these abuses were ended. Kimura, reacting to what he called Tanaka's "vehement opinion," said that his ministry intended to protect liberties, "with or without the provisions in the Potsdam Declaration." He would not deny that there had been abuses, but he offered the performance of his ministry during the recent general elections as evidence of a new spirit and commitment to human rights.[82]

Bland assurances did little to calm the anxieties of representatives on this committee. Commenting on article 36 (banning torture and cruel punishments), Tanaka told of an actual case he had handled just a short while ago.

> There was a woman who was badly tortured at the police station, her cloth-ing taken off, hanged upside down, her legs separated, and [abused] in other manners which I hesitate to mention. No confession was obtained from her, but she was committed for trial on a false charge. She sent me a postcard asking me to defend her. I tried to get the evidence of torture, but could not get any on her person, because there was no wound or scar. Then I learned from the woman that while being hanged, she moved one of her legs so violently that one of the porcelain hat racks on which her legs were fastened was broken to pieces, and those pieces were thrown away by the policemen into the wheat field outside the window. After three days' search of the field with the help of my assistants, I could finally find some of the broken pieces of the hat rack. As a result, the policemen concerned were tried and sentenced to imprisonment with hard labor.[83]

To counter such practices of wringing confessions out of terrified suspects, police agencies should be trained to gather evidence themselves, scientifically, as they do in the United States, said Tanaka. Kimura readily endorsed this idea, even though it would be costly to implement, he warned.[84]

Several times Kimura was asked about the death penalty. Did he not think it inherently cruel? Should Japan not join other progressive nations in outlawing it? Kimura thought this was not the time to do that. The draft constitution carried no implication that the death penalty was cruel (if it were, article 36 would prohibit it); indeed, article 31 seemed specifically to anticipate its retention ("No person shall be deprived of life . . . except according to procedure established by law"). It might eventually be outlawed by legislation, but he was not prepared to agree, in the tumultuous circumstances of the postwar period, that it was wrong or unjustified.

Kimura was similarly firm in interpreting the exclusionary rule in article 38. Kimura Kōhei put a series of questions about this. Would a prosecutor be permitted to use "leading questions"? Would confessions obtained at midnight be admitted? How about confessions obtained after long detention? To each of these questions, the justice minister replied that it would depend on the circumstances. None of these instances would be unconstitutional on its face.[85]

There was really no quarrel about these articles on criminal justice. Everyone seemed to agree that there had been widespread abuses in the past, and Japan as a constitutional democracy would need reform in this area. The provisions in chapter III seemed like a start in the right direction.

These discussions provided a training ground for politicians in the tradition of constitutional democracy. Many people, in and out of Japan, criticized the formulation of rights in the Meiji Constitution as too heavily qualified by exceptions, and rights grounded in the emperor's "gracious gift" as seeming fragile. The American bill, with its absolute language for First Amendment freedoms ("Congress shall make *no law* . . ." restricting speech and press, association, religion, etc.) is seen from this viewpoint as vastly superior. This dichotomy, however, is too simplistic. Westerners need to acknowledge that rights in the American tradition, however they are phrased in the bill of rights, are not absolute. Legislatures in the United States qualify constitutional rights in all sorts of ways. So do courts in interpreting them.[86] American citizens do not understand these qualifications very well; they continue to celebrate the Bill of Rights as if its guarantees were absolute. But political leaders gradually come to grasp the realities of adjustment, as they work through the challenges of governance in actual situations.

For Japanese political leaders in the postwar period, discussions of chapter III provided an intensive introduction to governance in the context of a liberal bill of rights. It was not a seminar. Kanamori himself remarked that when he presented juridical interpretations of particular clauses, he was not speaking as in a law school class, where distinctions between legal provisions and their political implications could be treated separately.[87] Nevertheless, in the dialogue between cabinet officers and the newly elected representatives, Japan was taking important steps in appropriating and shaping its new polity.

15 . . . .

"Complex and Labyrinthine"

THE STRUCTURE OF GOVERNMENT

On July 19, the revision committee finally turned full attention to chapters IV, V, and VI, where the principal institutions of government were outlined. Having spent nearly three weeks on the role of the emperor, the renunciation of war and the bill of rights, members would now devote two businesslike days to the balance of the draft, including the legislative, executive, and judicial branches of government. It is perhaps a measure of the ascendancy of Anglo-American ideas about constitutional governance that these chapters generated relatively little controversy.

Yet there was an irony in this brevity. The American framers had indicated their sense of the importance of chapter IV, on the Diet, by declaring in its opening article that the Diet would be the "highest organ of state power." Diet members engaging in this framing process could not have felt very powerful. Not only had the draft under consideration been prepared by American occupiers. Elected under the Meiji constitution, they were themselves operating in a constitutional framework that made them distinctly subordinate to other authorities. They were still surrounded, institutionally, by all the old bodies. The procedure for amendment was the one outlined in article LXXIII of the old constitution. The government's draft had come to them from the emperor, via the Privy Council. It still faced consideration by the House of Peers, whose powers and discretion were uncertain. It would be promulgated by the emperor.

So here was the House of Representatives (through its committee on revision), considering a draft that would dramatically increase the powers of the lower house, both within the Diet itself and within the larger governmental framework. Indeed, by the terms of the preamble, the new constitution would be sent forth in the name of "the Japanese people, acting through our duly elected representatives in the National Diet." (That could only mean the House of Representatives, as the other branch of the Diet, the House of Peers, consisted of appointed members.)

How would this new House, soon to be the "highest organ" of the state, behave?

How the System Would Work

Earlier, at the plenary session, Kanamori had provided a useful overview of how the system would work. Kanda Hiroshi had asked whether the separation of powers might not leave the nation paralyzed in a crisis. Would it not be important to have an authority capable of taking charge in a crisis? The emperor was the symbol of the nation and of the unity of the Japanese people. Would it not be wise to empower him to act as the ultimate arbiter in times of extreme emergency? Or, if that were not feasible, how about having the people at large exercise that function, by making provision for a popular initiative, allowing the people to introduce and enact bills or demand the dissolution of the Diet?

Kanamori's reply provided a comprehensive account of how he expected the system to work. Kanda had granted that the separation of powers gave the popular will "full expression," but every culture, every nation had to develop its own way of dealing with the paralysis that occasionally threatened to overwhelm constitutional governments. The Meiji Constitution had to some extent adopted the model of the separation of powers, but ultimately it rested on the prerogative of the emperor. That might have worked. Indeed it had worked, down through the 1920s. But gradually constitutional government was destroyed, as "unscrupulous politicians, militarists and bureaucrats made use of imperial prerogatives to carry out their ill-conceived policies."[1] Now it was necessary to replace that system decisively, to make the operations of government more transparent. How would it work? How would its disparate parts be brought together, to function harmoniously? Here Kanamori invoked what he called a "common example": "When we go to see a 'No' performance, we see a variety of musical instruments. We see flutes, drums, tabors, and others; there are also human voices to play their parts. What . . . makes it possible that all these things should be controlled perfectly? The control is rendered possible by a number of principles."[2] The drama of constitutional democracy would work similarly. The system seemed to lack a central power of control. Yet everything was based on the "general will of the people."

Major responsibility for realizing the public good lies with the Diet, the principal representative of the popular will. But what if the Diet oversteps, or falls short? What if it commits a "temporary error" in implementing the popular will? Part of the remedy is the bicameral system. The lower house has the major power, but the upper chamber has some limited powers of amending the expressions of the other body. Similarly, the Diet and the courts are separated, so that the courts may protect the freedom of the people. The supreme court is vested with special authority to void legislation it finds contrary to the constitution. Of course, the supreme court may abuse that power. That is why "cool and intelligent criticism by the people is to be applied in regard to the judges of the Supreme Court after their appointment, and then at an interval of about ten years thereafter." In the fullness of time, adjustments can be achieved.

If a clash develops between the Diet and the executive branch, the adjustment must be quicker, "because this is a field in which living politics works." Thus the constitution provides for dissolution, including the resignation of the cabinet and the election of a new House of Representatives. In this way, clashes can be settled by bringing the "general will of the people to bear on the matter."

The system, Kanamori admitted, is "complex and labyrinthine." The Meiji system probably allowed speedier adjustments, by depending on its "principle of leadership." But leadership can lead a nation astray, as Japan knew to its sorrow. Criticisms of constitutional democracy often came from academics who tried to grasp its operation "all at once, as a scholastic theory." In actual practice, he said, "disharmonies occur singly, calling for separate adjustments."[3] It was a mistake, he thought, to try to provide for every eventuality. In a culture as advanced as Japan's, "when the fundamental principles of democratic government are firmly laid down, any inconveniences that may stem from them . . . can be left to the intelligent efforts of the persons who participate in government."[4]

Leading off the discussion in the revision committee, Katō Sōhei asked Kanamori what it meant to call the Diet the state's "highest organ," in light of the provision in article 81 enabling the supreme court to declare acts of the Diet unconstitutional. Wouldn't it be more accurate to say, as the next clause did, that the Diet was the "sole law-making organ," and leave it at that? Kanamori did not, at this stage, offer an elaborate account of judicial review. Instead, he stressed that the Diet, as the only directly elected representative of the people, would have enormous prestige in Japan's new democratic regime. It would be not only the "sole law-making organ." It would create the government, by choosing the prime minister and (at this stage, still) confirming his choices for cabinet ministers, and it would have final authority over the budget and all other public financial obligations.[5]

All this was reassuring to advocates of democratic constitutionalism for Japan. But what would it mean in practice? Would it mean that the Diet would take control of the government, or at least of the legislative process? That was surely what the American framers intended, drawing on their experience with the U.S. Congress as the 900-pound gorilla of American politics. These Americans had experienced the New Deal and World War II, so they knew something about executive leadership. But they also knew that Congress was a proud, well-staffed branch, keenly aware of its prerogatives in matters of taxing and appropriations and its ability to shape public programs through the legislative process. The American governing process involved a complex, ever-changing dialectic between president and Congress, but Congress had both the constitutional means and political incentives to fight back, particularly when presidential leadership got too far ahead of popular sentiment.[6]

For the Diet to assume an analogous role in the Japanese system would mean a tremendous change in the behavior of its members. In the eyes of some members, the prospects were not promising. Sakai Toshio noted that the old, prewar

Diet also had substantial powers, on paper. Yet it always caved in to the bureaucrats. The transcript showed some grumbling among members of the committee when he said this. Members of the current House were showing a similar lack of gumption. Most had been elected because of their support for the emperor's sovereignty. They had deserted that cause as soon as they saw the government's draft. Sakai said he was "glad they have done so, because it is progress."

> However, their abrupt change of attitude . . . without making a single statement of explanation towards the people, is taken by some people . . . as proof of a want of conviction on their parts. [*Voices*: "No, no."] If a promise given two or three months ago is to be ignored so soon [*Voices*: "Make it snappy, make it snappy!"], I think there will arise a serious question as to the future operation of the Diet and the trustworthiness of its members.

Japan had adopted constitutional government "quite a long time ago," he concluded, but the attitude of deference, with roots in the feudalistic period, persisted. He was afraid that despite the brave words of the draft, the Diet would remain "a tool of the bureaucrats."[7]

There was searing truth in Sakai's words, and the hecklers' efforts to intimidate him only underscored it. At first Kanamori replied defensively, and somewhat irrelevantly, saying that the draft "left no loophole" for bureaucrats to abuse the democratic intention for their own benefit. He then turned to the deeper issue, addressing the charge that members had cravenly abandoned their defense of the emperor: "I want to add further that though you have said there has been evidence of change within the hearts of representatives during the past several months, it was a special phenomenon necessitated by the international situation, which they had to accept willy-nilly. [*"Hear, hear!"*]."[8]

This brief, emotional exchange revealed the irony of SCAP's attempt to impose constitutional democracy. Democracy requires people willing and determined to govern themselves. The legislators were quite determined to adopt constitutional government. Their take on it, however, was closer to the British model than to the American. In that sense, the attempt to reproduce the American model by verbal exhortations—by insisting that the Diet was the "highest organ," for example—was ill advised and doomed to failure. Wisely, SCAP's framers, despite their high regard for the congressional model, had adopted the British model of parliamentary government as the basic framework.[9] The British model was more suitable to traditional Japanese ways, certainly as long as men such as Yoshida, a fervent Anglophile, were in charge.

One clear mark of the parliamentary, rather than congressional, demeanor of Japanese legislators was that they seemed so dependent on the government's initiative, even on matters centrally affecting the Diet's role and procedures. How do you draw the line between laws and regulations, "legislative matters" and "cabinet orders," they humbly asked. It is a worldwide problem, answered Kanamori, best left to political developments and the conscience of leaders.[10] Did the government have any intention of allowing for legislation by popular referendum? No, said Kanamori somewhat patronizingly, the "steady" Japanese people disliked such destabilizing procedures.[11] The draft said that either house could "conduct investigations in relation to national affairs." How far did that extend? It was virtually unconfined, answered Kanamori.[12] Wasn't it risky, someone asked, to allow the Diet itself, likely to be dominated by one or a few political parties, to settle disputes over the qualifications of its members, including election results? That was the way it was done in Britain, Kanamori pointed out. To ask the courts to decide such disputes would violate the separation of powers.[13] Shouldn't the Diet be equipped with a first-class library and staff to support its work? Here Kanamori was more diffident, perhaps because he already anticipated the possibility of being named to lead the Diet Library into existence as its first director. That is for the Diet to decide, he remarked. He agreed that when Japan escaped from its current straitened conditions, it ought to build a world-class national library.[14]

Partly, of course, the tone of these dialogues came from the fact that Kanamori was explaining the meaning of the government's draft, while at this stage Diet members were still trying to understand its logic. Some of them would have their own chance to do some drafting and revising when the subcommittee began its work on July 26. Nevertheless, there was an unmistakable spirit of deference at work here. The position of the House of Representatives was theoretically strong. This constitution would never come into force without its acquiescence. But even that ultimate legitimizing role was attenuated by the fact that Japan desperately wanted to end the Occupation, and everyone knew that acceptance of the revised constitution was a precondition. Thus this crucial birthing drama of constitutional democracy placed Japan's "highest organ" in a deeply compromised position.

There were exceptions, instances of strong insistence on a point of view different from the cabinet's. A good example was the plea for unicameralism (i.e., a single legislative chamber). Hara Kenzaburō asked why a second chamber was necessary. Kanamori replied that the Diet, and particularly the House of Representatives, would have great power. It might move too quickly, too passionately. The system needed a safety valve. Hara was not convinced. Other nations had second chambers to accommodate special conditions: The British needed one to represent the nobility; the United States, to represent the states. With the peerage ending in Japan, there was no more need for such an institution here. Besides, a second chamber gave no guarantee of prudence. One chamber might pass something ill advised, relying on the other to block it, but the other chamber might be equally irresponsible. The great disadvantage of bicameralism was that it complicated the relationship between the Diet and the executive. What if the upper chamber were controlled by a different party or coalition from the one that controlled the lower chamber and cabinet? That could produce stalemate and endless, unproductive haggling. The future belonged to cabinet governments, formed by responsible parties. Japan should commit itself without backward glances. Kanamori replied that democracy was indeed a complicated form of government. Fascism cleverly played on these complications. After more than a decade of ghastly warfare, however, a chastened world had learned that efficiency in government came with a high price. Kanamori noted that France had recently rejected a unicameral constitution.[15] Hara was still unconvinced. We follow the American and British examples blindly, he said, without any good reason.[16]

Hara then asked how the House of Councillors would be composed, to ensure that its members would bring prudence to the legislative process. Here indeed was a basket of crabs. Members of this committee would try all summer to wring a proposal out of the cabinet regarding the composition of the House of Councillors.[17] The cabinet's unresponsiveness was not entirely its own fault. GHQ and several of the Allied powers had firm ideas of their own on these matters, sometimes contradictory ones. There seemed to be two main problems: the inherent complexity of electoral law and the reluctance of Kanamori and the cabinet to accept SCAP's insistence that the second house, no less than the first, would have to consist, in the words of article 43, of "elected members, representatives of all the people." Kanamori reported that the cabinet committee responsible for generating a proposal had labored long and hard, but so far inconclusively. They seemed to favor a house smaller than the lower house but were still uncertain about the size of electoral districts. They were also looking for a way to screen candidates and examining the idea of indirect versus direct election. Combining various options, the cabinet group had generated seven plans and was trying to decide which to put forward. Hara pressed him to state his own preferences. Kanamori said it was a "very annoying" question, but he indicated a preference for indirect election for at least some members. What about the requirement in article 43, asked Hara. Kanamori said he thought that objection was not insuperable.[18]

Hara concluded by arguing that time spent perfecting electoral schemes for the second chamber would better be spent thinking about electoral schemes for the House of Representatives.[19] Hara's point was well taken. In the April elections, voters confronted 2,770 candidates representing 363 political parties,[20] far beyond the conditions that drew Hitler's ridicule of "vier-und-dreissig Partien" (thirty-four parties). Those concerned about the shades of Weimar should have spent less effort objecting to social and economic guarantees in the bill of rights and more on framing electoral laws that could give voters an effective choice.

Here again, the remarkable thing was the passivity of the members, waiting for the government to come up with a scheme that bore directly on their own place in the constitutional system. Hara showed more gumption than most, pressing awkward inquiries, offering strong arguments, and criticizing the government's neglect of important issues. Yet even Hara did not put forth a proposal of his own, or demand that the Diet be equipped with necessary staff to generate its own legislation.

Dissolution and the Role of the Cabinet

Hara raised another important issue during these discussions: the mechanics of dissolution. Who, he asked, would decide on dissolution? Article 7 indicated it would be the emperor, with the advice and approval of the cabinet. Article 45 used the passive voice, saying that the term of House members would end "in case the House of Representatives is dissolved." None of this clearly allocated the power to dissolve the lower house. (The House of Councillors was not subject to dissolution.) Kanamori replied that the power to dissolve would belong to the cabinet. Under what circumstances could the cabinet dissolve the House? It was impossible to anticipate them. Political leaders would be guided by common sense. Basically, when the cabinet and the Diet clashed, the people would have to arbitrate, through an election. Or the government might wish to have a fresh expression of the popular will when a grave issue was at stake. It would have to be decided in concrete circumstances.[21]

This was a sensible answer. It gave great power to the cabinet, or rather to the prime minister, because he would control the composition of the cabinet. But, as Kanamori pointed out, dissolution entailed the resignation of the cabinet and the hazards of an election, so no prime minister would embark on it lightly. Later, Kojima Tetsuzō asked whether dissolution would necessarily depend on an explicit resolution of no confidence, or could a loss of confidence be implied if a cabinet-sponsored bill failed to pass? Kanamori's answer was not clear,[22] but again, the best answer was that it would depend on circumstances and on the willingness of Japan's leaders to "breathe the soul" of parliamentary democracy into their political system.[23]

There was another important issue addressed in these discussions: the collective responsibility of the cabinet, set forth in article 66 of the draft. Under the Meiji Constitution, each minister was directly accountable to the emperor rather than to the prime minister. That system deliberately invited differences to emerge within the cabinet, allowing the emperor, or his agents in the Privy Council or the Imperial Household, to decide. The question was how this collective responsibility would be affected by the requirement, in article 68, that the prime minister's cabinet appointments be confirmed by the Diet. Again, it was Hara who raised this question. Calling attention to the prime minister's power, in article 68, to remove any cabinet minister "as he chooses," Hara asked what sense it made to tie the prime minister's hand in appointments. Was it not enough that the Diet chose the prime minister and could dissolve his government whenever it lost confidence in him?

Kanamori defended giving the prime minister the power of dismissal by saying that it ensured both the unity of the cabinet and its acceptability to the Diet. Hayashi thought the scheme was "too conservative." It would tie the government's hands unduly. Kanamori said he used to feel that way, too, but he had changed his mind. Democracy was a complicated process. In confirming ministerial appointments, Diet members would grasp the details of government. Your way, he told Hayashi, was like an army. The prime minister gave an order, and all heads turned the same way. Under the Meiji Constitution, the government tended to be a "serpent with eight heads." We need to find a way between these extremes, he said, one that encouraged unity without imposing the excessive discipline of fascism.[24]

The Judiciary

On the afternoon of July 20, the committee turned to chapter VI, on the judiciary. Earlier, during the plenary session, Hara had objected to the electoral review of judges. Montesquieu, he noted, taught that judges needed to be insulated from political pressures, yet here we find judges subject to decennial review—by the voters, of all people. It was a weird provision, "probably found only in the Constitution of the United States."[25] Would it not be advisable at least to postpone implementation of this idea for ten or twenty years?[26] Kanamori responded that Hara's apprehensions were not warranted. The supreme court, having powers of judicial review, might indeed be "pitted against the Diet and the cabinet." Therefore it would be improper to vest the Diet or the cabinet with the power of dismissal. But what if the judges' actions "diametrically oppose state policy"? There would have to be some way to decide whether to retain them in office or dismiss them. We clothe them in "armor" to protect their independence, but we must also provide for possible misconduct, for judges are human. In the final analysis, "the key to this problem should be left with the people who, when considered in a broad sense, are most clever and act with the highest degree of intelligence." It is true, he said, that the system was "not only novel to the Japanese people, but also not common in the world." Hara was also justified in saying that individual voters were sometimes ill informed or inattentive. "However, when taken as a whole, [the voters] in most cases represent justice and give expression to the will of heaven."[27]

Honda Eisaku, vice chairman of the Liberal Party, opened the discussion on the judiciary in the committee by regretting the absence of any language like that in article LVII of the Meiji Constitution, that justice was administered "in the name of the emperor." Whatever one might conclude about the Meiji system in general, he said, there could be no doubt that the administration of justice had been "almost flawless, except for some criticisms leveled against the prosecution system." The success of Japanese courts stemmed from the people's faith that the "judicature was exercised . . . in the name of the emperor," even though he never exercised his power in this sphere directly. Why were we abolishing such a useful fiction?

Kanamori's answer was one of the most important he made on the provisions relating to the emperor. The attribution of justice to the courts, rather than to the emperor, reflected one of the basic principles of this constitution. "A right judgment is right because it is right," he said. The idea that the name of the emperor makes it right had better be avoided. In the past, even though the emperor never concerned himself in administrating justice, a wrong judgment was sometimes given in the name of the emperor. Because of that, people sometimes bore a sense of grievance toward him. This constitution must reflect the "actual state of things." That is why it stated, quite plainly, that judicial power belongs to the courts, in the same way that legislative power belongs to the Diet.[28]

Honda also found it irritating that judges, by article 76, would be "independent in the exercise of their conscience," bound only by the constitution and laws.

Such language was an "insult" toward judges, and it made him "indignant." The point, replied Kanamori, was that other officials were bound to obey superiors, whereas judges were "independent," bound only by their consciences. He noted a related provision, in article 78, that made judges subject to "no disciplinary action" by executive organs or agencies. Kimura Tokutarō, the highly respected minister of justice, added that his reaction to the draft's language on the judiciary was "entirely different" from Honda's. Rather sheepishly, Honda later admitted that he too found most of chapter VI "splendid."[29]

In truth, despite some calls for fine-tuning, most members found these chapters (IV through VI, outlining the structure and processes of government) quite satisfactory.

16 . . . .

"Fresh Trouble"

- ## THE HOUSE SUBCOMMITTEE FRAMES AMENDMENTS

-
- On Tuesday, July 23, the House Committee on Revision moved to create a subcommittee to prepare amendments to the draft. Ash-
- ida asked that members and political parties submit proposals to this group. When the subcommittee had distilled these suggestions
- into a tentative revised draft, he would invite the parties to offer their reactions. The subcommittee would then prepare a final
- draft and submit it to the revision committee for debate and action.
- Suzuki moved that Ashida appoint "about ten members" to serve on the subcommittee, balanced to reflect the partisan com-
- position of the House. There being no objection, Ashida appointed ten members, all male: two Liberals, Hatsukade Takashi and Etō
- Natsuo; five Progressive Democrats, Inukai Takeru, Yoshida An, Kasai Jūji, Hayashi Heima, and himself; two Social Democrats, Su-
- zuki Yoshio and Morito Tatsuo; and one from the People's Co-operative Party, Ōshima Tazō.[1] When the subcommittee convened
- for its first meeting that afternoon, Ashida announced four additional members, also males: two Liberals, Kita Reikichi and Taka-
- hashi Yasuo; one Progressive Democrat, Hara Fujirō; and one Social Democrat, Nishio Suehiro. His aim, he said, was to name one
- man to the subcommittee for each of the thirty-five party members in the full House.[2]
- Ashida then suggested that, "as it is desirable to proceed . . . in an informal manner," the meetings be held "behind closed doors." Shorthand notes would be taken and a communiqué issued daily, summarizing the proceedings. Members of the subcommittee voiced no objection.[3] The agreement on secrecy immediately became controversial. At the subcommittee's very next meeting, on July 26, Suzuki bitterly complained that conservatives had pulled a fast one on the Social Democrats. At the organizational meeting on Thursday, Kita had remarked, in the context of generally positive remarks about the preamble, that he especially liked the proposals of the Social Democrats and Communists for new language on popular sovereignty. Others had murmured agreement, and it appeared that

240

the amendment had general support. The agreement was apparently reported to the Progressive caucus, and reporters soon got wind of it. Morning newspapers on July 26 reported the consensus on popular sovereignty, attributing it to a decision by the Liberals and Progressives (parties led by Yoshida and Ashida). Suzuki and the Socialists were furious, noting that the Social Democrats had been pressing for this change for months. Responding to Suzuki's angry charge, Ashida admitted that he had called reporters' attention to language in the amendments proposed by the Liberals and Progressives. Kita and Yoshida An both admitted contacts with reporters that could have contributed to the misunderstanding. Everyone expressed sympathy for the Socialists and agreed to take extra care not to reveal anything done in the subcommittee, beyond the brief communique Ashida would release after each session.

This episode underscored the tenderness of feelings surrounding the whole revision effort. Another indication came when Hatsukade said that he and the other members would be "risking our lives in this effort." This was not intended as hyperbole.[4] Ten years from now, said Hatsukade, people might look back on the revision as a great calamity for Japan. If that happened, those involved would be viewed in a light similar to that now cast on persons involved in the Imperial Rule Assistance Association.[5] There was real danger here, he asserted, but members would have to forget their personal fates, abandon all concern for safety, and resolve to do their best.[6]

In several important respects, the proceedings of the subcommittee differed from those of the full committee on revision. No longer was discussion based on a series of questions directed at the cabinet. Now Diet members put their heads together to consider specific proposals for changing the language of the text. It was a dialogue in which men such as Kita and Inukai assumed leadership because others respected their political acumen and linguistic skills.

The government was present in the discrete person of Satō Tatsuo, but Ashida emphasized that he would attend "not to represent the government's opinion, but to offer his own opinions on technical points."[7] Occasionally members would ask Satō why certain Japanese words had been chosen, or why ideas had been expressed as they were. Satō was not, however, in a position to negotiate with the Diet on behalf of the cabinet. Kanamori, who closely monitored transcripts of the subcommittee's meetings, was the only one who could do that. Backdoor channels between the subcommittee and the cabinet, and between the subcommittee and GHQ, were operating as well. For example, when Suzuki offered to redraft the preamble "in a more sublime and succinct style," less "negative and prolix," he asked whether any such wholesale revision would be permitted. We must find out, he said, implying that the limits of GHQ's tolerance could be ascertained by informal inquiries.[8]

Dealing with Language

The subcommittee's task was to comb through the Japanese text, improve its expression, and make changes in accordance with ideas expressed during the revision committee's interpellations. This was a delicate and difficult assignment. It demanded knowledge of a domestic political situation that was close to chaos, where political parties formed and reformed almost daily. It required an ability to use vernacular language for constitutional purposes. It meant staying within bounds set by the Occupation, when the Americans themselves were under extreme pressure from their own government, led by a new president and a Congress controlled by the opposition, and from the leaders of a wartime alliance that was exploding into bitter feuds.

In this maelstrom, the safest course was to revert to the English text, to seek better ways to express its meaning in Japanese, and to test whether it might be possible to amend it in places that offended Japanese sensibilities. By examining the transcripts of these meetings, we can see where the constitutional garments fashioned by GS and the cabinet chafed most uncomfortably.[9] These records are the best indication of how leading Diet members viewed the revision project. Despite the agreement on secrecy, members of the subcommittee were aware that they were speaking for the historical record. Kita, for example, remarked at one point that the cabinet's Legislation Bureau had "misread" the English text in translating it, and he specifically asked that his opinion be recorded.[10] They knew that ears were attuned, both at SCAP and in the cabinet. But they also knew (despite Suzuki's sad experience) that they would not have to answer immediately for press reports of what they were saying. Thus they were relatively free to speak their minds.[11] Moreover, they were meeting with colleagues who were experienced and trusted political leaders and had a deep understanding of constitutional government, so they did not have to spend a lot of time setting the stage for the expression of their opinions.

Another important difference between these subcommittee transcripts and those reporting discussions in the full committee is the candor here concerning which text was the "original." Kanamori never permitted members of the House to treat the Japanese text as a translation. Here that pretense is dropped almost entirely. Working on the preamble, members regularly referred to the English version as the "original" and the Japanese version as a "translation."[12] Indeed, many expressed a preference for the English version, urging that it be treated as a model.[13]

However much they may have admired the principles of the preamble, they believed to a man that the style of the Japanese version was awful, embarrassingly so, that it read like a translation and would make Japan "contemptible," a "laughingstock" among nations, "ridiculed by posterity."[14] For two days they considered whether to rewrite it entirely or try to polish its expression. Several members offered to write fresh drafts.[15] Would GHQ allow it? Kasai, in portions of the transcript deleted by Kanamori from the version supplied to SCAP, mentioned having heard that GHQ had spent a great deal of time on the preamble. He had been given to understand, he said, that they were not free to ignore the English version.[16]

Problems with the Preamble

Suzuki suggested that they form a small task force to work on a new draft of the preamble. At first Ashida seemed sympathetic to the idea. Then, on Friday morning, Suzuki offered that the Social Democrats would produce an alternative for the subcommittee to consider. Ashida observed that it would be an enormous task to prepare something in Japanese that would both satisfy the subcommittee and be able to gain the approval of "the quarters interested" (GHQ). Suzuki apparently agreed.

> Arguments on this point have been repeated many times, so I shall hasten to reach a conclusion. The reason we had not made a draft ourselves [before now] was that if we had done this and sent an English translation of it for [GHQ's] consent, it would be quite possible that such a draft . . . would occasion fresh trouble. It was thus decided that the drafting be put off till the time when it would have become possible. Now the time allowed us is short. . . . I think there is no alternative but to adopt [the government draft], subject to an improvement in Japanese phraseology.[17]

By Friday afternoon, Ashida had concluded that the subcommittee ought to work together to polish the existing draft, rather than preparing a new one.[18]

Having decided on this course, members of the subcommittee confronted several serious controversies. One that was fundamental to the constitutional project related to the opening phrase: "We, the Japanese people, *acting through* our duly elected representatives in the National Diet." Kita strenuously opposed this language, and Ōshima and Hatsukade agreed that the text seemed confused. Kita asked Satō what the drafters were thinking of. Satō replied that the phrasing reflected the general notion that the Diet should be at the center of the new regime. Kita was not persuaded. The resolve of the Japanese people, he said, was to "secure the fruits of peaceful cooperation with all nations and the blessings of liberty." They were acting through the Diet, because theirs was a representative government.[19] The crucial point was to establish limits on the powers of government. Only the people could properly do this.

The subcommittee also paid careful attention to the terms used to translate the preamble's paraphrase of Lincoln's "government of the people, by the people, for the people." Kita noted that two of the cabinet's leading constitutional scholars, Uehara and Saitō, had urged the Progressive caucus to use the term *seifu* here, meaning administration, rather than *kokusei*, referring to the whole government, including executive, legislative, and judicial branches. Kita thought the suggestion had merit. In Japan, "unlike Britain or America," the recent war had been waged "through the action of government alone, without a vote of the Diet." The Tōjō and Koiso governments had operated by imperial prerogative. The Japanese people were determined never to permit a recurrence. It was not necessary to dwell on the judicial and legislative branches of government. Sovereign power in Japan would now reside with the people: The authority of government would derive from the people, and the prime minister would be designated from among the members of the Diet, representatives of the people. The powers of government would be exercised by the representatives of the people, and the benefits of government, such as social security and stability of life, would be enjoyed by the people. By using the proper terms, the preamble could present a coherent statement of these principles.[20]

A controversy developed over the effort by Socialists to insert the phrase "poverty and exploitation" into the litany of abuses that international society was seeking to banish. As Morito explained, the text's "tyranny and slavery" referred to political matters, "oppression and intolerance" to spiritual. The phrase the Socialists wanted to add spoke of a third major category, economic abuses. Morito insisted that the catalogue would be incomplete without it.[21] Ashida diplomatically pointed out that all the other parties had been satisfied with this section. He urged Morito to yield to this consensus. It would require a great many changes to achieve utopia. Why insist that this particular one be in the preamble? Would it not be better to push for economic guarantees in the bill of rights than to make an issue about it in the preamble? Morito replied that insisting on this phrase was "not my personal opinion, but that of the [Socialist] Party, which places special emphasis on this third item." It was, he said, a "matter to which we attach greater importance than any other."[22]

Etō thought he heard echoes of ideological warfare in Morito's proposal. Not true, Morito replied. The British Conservatives claim that a capitalist country can overcome poverty. The principal object of Socialists is to eliminate poverty, but it is not they alone that declare this object. Anyway, he said, the new international society cannot be unconcerned about eliminating poverty.[23] Kita complained that this loaded term was inconsistent with the rest of the constitution. The idea underlying the constitution was that if the people thoroughly act on liberal principles at home and peaceful principles abroad, the peoples of the world would be set free from fear and want. "The word *sakushu* (exploitation) is a socialistic expression, without your explanation." A flavor emanated from the word, a peculiar color. Kita offered a political carrot. "When the Socialists gain in influence and take the reins of government with support of the people," he said, "exploitation will naturally disappear." He opposed adding the term to the preamble.[24]

Seeking to bridge the conflict, Inukai asked if another term might be substituted, to attain the Socialists' goal without using a loaded term. "Christianity also calls for the elimination of poverty. May I suggest the word *kokushi* (overtask)?"[25] Morito suggested "cruel dealing" or "hardship," but Inukai objected: "Then the field before us will be broad indeed."[26] Kita tried a different tack. Many things, he said, not just economic exploitation, were omitted from the draft's catalogue of ills. If Japan were truly independent, instead of a defeated nation, "we might hope to insert here such terms as 'banishment of racial prejudice,' 'equitable distribution of resources,' 'equitable division of territories,' and some other loftier ideas." Instead, he said, we must be "content with the liberalism and pacifism entertained by the 'have' countries, which are . . . based on the ideas of Roosevelt. This," he added, "is the case with the whole of this constitution."[27] Ashida and Inukai pleaded with Morito to accept the offer of amendments to chapter III to incorporate the Socialists' commitments, but Morito agreed to move on only when Ashida promised that they could return to the issue later.[28]

The Right Word for "People"

Leftist terminology entered the picture again in a dispute about which term to use for "people." In expressing the idea of popular sovereignty, conservatives objected to the term *zaimin* (residing or vested in the people), on grounds that *min* usually meant the people as distinguished from the monarch. They preferred a more precise term, such as *zaikokumin*, as in the phrase, *shuken zaikokumin*, literally meaning "sovereignty vested in Japanese nationals." Hatsukade and Yoshida An were particularly adamant on this point. Ashida explained why they were so sensitive. Under the influence of European political thought, he said, *min* had come to indicate the people as distinguished from the sovereign ruler. But Kanamori had been advancing, as the "official interpretation of the present government," the idea that *min* included the emperor. However, this usage had not yet taken hold with the general public. That was why Hatsukade suggested the use of *kokumin*, instead of *min*, "so as not to give the wrong impression to the people."[29]

Kita added that the idea of popular sovereignty derived from Rousseau's *Social Contract*, where it signified, he said, that "sovereignty is vested in the people of a nation." On the other hand, Kanamori's theory was explicit in vesting sovereignty in a "corporate body of the emperor and the people." In this context, the term *shuken zaimin* (people's sovereignty) gave the impression that sovereignty is vested in the people, as over against the emperor. The situation was not helped by the fact that the Communists were using *min* in such a term as "Popular Front." In common usage, *min* denoted the "ruled class as against the ruler, the government, and the ruling class." This was the background that made conservatives prefer terms that did not use *min*.[30]

Suzuki said he understood these sensibilities but hoped that members would not be rigid about the matter. Socialists had grown accustomed to the term *shuken zaimin*. It was not their intention to juxtapose popular sovereignty and the role of the emperor as symbol of the state.

There was also a brief flurry of questioning about the last phrase in the first paragraph, promising to "reject and revoke all constitutions, laws, ordinances, and rescripts in conflict herewith." The Japanese text did not include the word "constitutions." Suzuki said he thought the word was superfluous; "we need not stick too strictly to the original text." It went without saying, he thought, that "constitutions" were included; besides, it was "unlikely that we shall enact in the future constitutions in conflict with it." Satō was asked whether "laws and ordinances" ordinarily included constitutions. He was unsure, he said, but he thought the term could be interpreted in a broad sense. Ashida remarked that he had intended to ask Justin Williams, a staff member at GHQ, about this point, but had forgotten to do so.

But what did "herewith" mean? Were they rejecting all enactments in conflict with "this constitution," or those in conflict with the "universal principle of man-kind" embodied in the previous sentence (paraphrasing Lincoln's phrase: "government of the people, by the people, for the people")? Or, asked Inukai, could "herewith" refer to natural law, as Tanaka, the minister of education and future chief justice of the supreme court, thought? Suzuki said the text did not support Tanaka's reading. For the moment at least, most seemed to accept Suzuki's interpretation that " 'herewith' represented the preceding term 'this Constitution,' written in capital letter C."[31]

One way to get a feel for the work of the subcommittee is to read the following exchanges about the verb in the phrase: to *reject* all constitutions . . . in conflict herewith.

> *Ōshima*: Mr. Chairman, I have a question to ask. In the phrase, *shōchoku wo haijo suru* (reject and revoke rescripts), what character will you use for that *hai* [(revoke)]?
> *Takahashi*: Isn't it the character *hai* (reject) (to reject or pump out) in the word *haisui* (drainage)?
> *The Chairman [Ashida]*: Do you use that character?
> *Yoshida An*: It is the character *hai* (revoke) in *sōzokunin haijo* (the abolition of a successor).
> *Suzuki*: Isn't it the character *hai* (reject) of *haikyū* (volley-ball)?
> *The Chairman [Ashida]*: It is the translation of "disinherit." *Hai* (revoke) is better. . . .
> *Takahashi*: It may not be idiomatic, but I think *hai* (to abolish or dis-inherit) is more appropriate for expressing the significance of this case.
> *Hara*: The *hai* (to abolish or disinherit) of a successor means the removal of a person having a right of inheritance from the order of succession.

Then, after a digression to discuss another issue, they return to *hai*.

> *Suzuki*: How would you decide the *hai* (to abolish or disinherit) we were discussing a short time ago?
> *The Chairman [Ashida]*: Let us decide on *hai* (abolish or repeal).[32]

It was no easy task to divine precisely what the English text meant, then find the appropriate Japanese characters to express it, accurately and gracefully.

Waiting for GHQ

In due course the subcommittee came to chapter I, on the emperor. Ashida opened the session by confiding, "I do not know whether this may be said openly or not, but the fact is this: the authorities concerned [GHQ] have suggested the insertion of a word in Article 1 to indicate that sovereignty rests with the people."[33] The Legislation Bureau would have to study the form, he said, in consultation with GHQ. Ashida suggested moving on, reserving article 1 for later consideration.

During this initial look at chapter I, there was surprisingly little controversy. Just three matters drew attention, none of them arousing serious disagreements. Suzuki argued that matters of succession should be settled in article 2 of the constitution, not left to legislation, as the draft anticipated. He noted that the government was drafting a revised Imperial House Law, drawing on research that described the practices of other countries. He hoped that the government's draft of the Imperial House Law would be available soon. In the meantime, he gave some examples of matters that ought, in his opinion, to have a constitutional foundation: that succession to the throne not be limited to males; that provision be made for abdication; and that disputes about accession be referred to a council of elders, including the prime minister, the presidents of both chambers of the Diet, and judges of the supreme court.[34] Ashida said the matters raised by Suzuki were "very important," but the question of amending the constitutional text should be postponed until the government's draft was generally available.

Several members representing the smaller parties wanted to remove from article 4 the statement that the emperor would "never have powers related to government." It sounded, said Hayashi, as if the emperor were an "incompetent person." Suzuki, however, insisted on retaining the prohibition, to prevent mischief, and Inukai, flattering Hayashi as a "true Japanese" for raising the point, asked him to yield his feelings and accept the majority's position. Hayashi reserved his position for later discussion.[35]

Another debate arose over the emperor's power (in article 7), with the advice and approval of the cabinet, to convoke and dissolve the House of Representatives and proclaim general elections. It was inconsistent with the emperor's revised status, said Suzuki. The cabinet would make the necessary determinations; let the formalities conform to the political facts. Morito added a theme Kanamori often used in explaining the emperor's altered role: We should keep the emperor far removed from politics, to preserve his dignity. Inukai responded that life abounds in fictions. They give us courage and inspire our dreams. Suzuki acknowledged that such sentiments had a place in public life; that is why we retain the emperor's role in granting honors and receiving ambassadors. But dissolution and calling elections were political acts. The emperor's involvement might give moral authority to a shabby political trick.

Amending Article 9

On Monday, July 29, Ashida presented an amendment to article 9 that has been a source of intense controversy ever since.[36] An examination of the transcripts surrounding the decision to attempt this amendment sheds light on the "framers' intent."

The background was that Suzuki, on the preceding Saturday, had lamented the defensive, "whining" tone of the article as drafted. Japan was a "peace-loving nation." Its decision to renounce war "forever" and "never" to maintain military forces ought to be made in ringing terms. Inukai agreed. The article sounded like "whimpering"; it lacked "vigor." Ashida replied that the Foreign Ministry also wanted to add some words of affirmation to the declaration.[37] Inukai asked whether they were free to amend it. "Of course," replied Ashida.[38] The day's deliberation ended with a remark by Ashida that there was no need to settle the matter immediately. He urged people to think about it over the weekend.[39] Note that there was no hint here of any desire to open the way to rearmament, not even a mention of the right of self-defense.

When Ashida called the subcommittee to order on Monday morning, he mentioned that he and others who had arrived early had put together some language that he hoped would be responsive to the concerns mentioned on Saturday.[40] He read the proposal: It began with a participle affirming pacifism and then, in the main clause, converted a passive construction ("war is renounced") into an active one, using "the Japanese people" as the subject of the declaration. It also switched the order of the two main clauses (renunciation of arms and belligerency first, and of war second). The purpose of these changes, said Ashida, was to put a more positive cast on the article.

Conservative members—Yoshida An for the Progressives, Hayashi for the Co-operatives, Takahashi for the Liberals—immediately announced their support.[41] Suzuki, however, the Social Democrat, hung back. He said there was "no precedent the world over" for using the word "declare" in a context such as this. He thought the whole article looked more like a treaty. Moreover, its phrasing sounded odd. He also repeated his earlier opinion that because of its importance, the commitment to pacifism belonged in the preamble. Ashida agreed with the latter point but recalled that GHQ insisted that it come in the body of the document, immediately after chapter I.[42]

Ashida then asked Satō, the technician from the Legislation Bureau, what he thought about it. Satō, saying that he would speak frankly, indicated that he agreed with Suzuki.

> The original draft makes it clear . . . that if we maintained land, sea, and air forces, or other war potential, apart from any question concerning the right of belligerency of the state, our conduct . . . would be denounced as an infringement of the provisions of the constitution. But in accordance with the provisions in the amended draft, our conduct might be denounced as contrary [merely] to such a declaration or announcement.[43]

This brought from Ashida a statement of the stylistic "motive" that shaped the amendment.

> We thought that the wording in the original draft, reading, "The maintenance of land, sea, and air forces, as well as other war potential, will never be authorized," was rather awkward as a Japanese sentence. It was as if we were telling something to ourselves. . . . As a Japanese sentence, it sounds much better and natural to say *Ore wa uso wo iwanai no da* (I will not tell

a lie) than to say *Ore wa uso wo ittewa naranai noda* (I shall not be allowed to tell a lie). . . . But to insert these words at the beginning of the chapter would give an abrupt appearance to the entire chapter. Therefore, after a careful study of all things concerned, we thought of an introductory remark to be inserted at the beginning of the Article, "Aspiring sincerely to an international peace," and then introduced the principal provision, reading, "For the above purpose, land, sea, and air forces, as well as other war potential, will never be maintained." Introduced by an order like this, the entire article sounds quite natural. Such was one of the motives for which the amendment was proposed.[44]

Nishio, another Social Democrat, then asked whether GHQ was likely to accept what Ashida and his colleagues had drafted. Satō admitted that a concern on that score had been behind his suggestion that the substitution of a declaration for a prohibition had "deprived the sentence of its vigor." On the other hand, he said, "if you gentlemen say that the new wording is more vigorous, I feel very much assured." Ashida added that if "some quarters" objected to it, "we can reconsider it." But we had better "express frankly the will of the people," in any case. What if GHQ insists on something worse, Nishio asked. They won't, replied Ashida. But you do plan to submit it to GHQ first, before announcing it, don't you, asked Yoshida An. Yes, replied Ashida; otherwise there might be embarrassment. What if it leaks, asked Suzuki. "We cannot help that," replied Ashida, with re-markable sangfroid.[45]

Still Suzuki was worried. It sounds "clumsy," he said. Besides, he said, Satō is right. It weakens the commitment to state it as a moral declaration rather than a legal prohibition. Ashida disagreed. He thought the new language was emphatic and stately.[46] And there they left it, reading at this stage as follows:

Aspiring sincerely to an international peace based on justice and order, the Japanese people hereby declare that land, sea, and air forces as well as other war potential, will never be maintained and that the right of bellig-erency of the state will not be recognized.

In order to accomplish the aim of the preceding paragraph, they forever renounce war as a sovereign right of the nation, and the threat or use of force as means of settling international disputes.[47]

A further discussion took place the next day, Tuesday, July 30, though the record of it was suppressed, eliminated entirely from the transcript delivered to SCAP. In a brief reprise, Ashida asked Kanamori, attending specially that day, whether he had an opinion about using the word "declare" in article 9. Kanamori said that in preparing the government draft, he had carefully avoided using the verb "declare" in the body of the constitution (though it did appear in the pre-amble), precisely because, though it looked emphatic, it was substantively weaker than a simple prohibition.[48] (The word "declare" was later removed from the amended article 9.)

Suzuki then asked him about the order of the clauses. "From the perspective of legislative technique," did Kanamori think it was a good idea to keep the clause renouncing arms and belligerency first and put the renunciation of war in the second clause? Kanamori's reply is worth quoting in full:

> This is indeed a very delicate issue, and it should be mentioned very carefully. The first clause [as the government had drafted it, with the renunciation of war in the first paragraph] uses words such as "renounces forever" and says it very strongly. However, the second clause does not use the word "forever". This may be merely my intuition, but I think that there remains an area to be considered in Japan's relations with the United Nations, in the future, in [connection with] the second clause, with regard to the right to maintain war potential. Therefore, we redrafted Article 9 into two clauses, moving that part which very clearly mentioned "permanence" or "forever" to the first clause. This is what we were thinking.[49]

In other words, though quite indirectly, Kanamori was suggesting that to leave open the possibility of self-defense, the two clauses of article 9 should be presented in their original order (renunciation of war "forever," first; then disarmament). Ashida may not immediately have caught Kanamori's drift, for, on August 1, he told Suzuki that the order of the clauses was "a question of personal preference." Nevertheless, when Inukai asked that the original order be restored (renunciation of war "forever" coming first), Ashida agreed. Satō remembers whispering into Ashida's ear that whichever way it was done, the changes would have to be taken to SCAP for approval, where Kades might detect a "scheme to rearm for the purposes of self-defense." According to Satō, Ashida laughed at this remark but did not reply.[50] However, sometime before Ashida published his *Interpretation of the Constitution* (written in September, 1946; published on November 3, 1946), he developed an interpretation of the revised article 9 that limited its application to "aggressive war," renouncing it as a means of resolving international disputes. "Consequently," he wrote of article 9, "this provision does not renounce war and the use of force for the purposes of self-defense."[51]

As the records of July 29 clearly show, however, none of this was spoken of when the amendments were fashioned and discussed by the subcommittee. The subcommittee's records show that the framers of the article 9 amendments, including Ashida, had no intention of opening the door to rearmament—unless Ashida was concealing his personal intentions from his fellow committee members.[52]

17 . . . .

"Fundamental Principles of Democracy"

• HUMAN RIGHTS AND IMPERIAL PROPERTY

From July 29 until July 31, the subcommittee on revision worked on the bill of rights. The hottest issue was article 24, on marriage and the family, but there were other flash points as well: article 20, banning "religious education" in the public schools and articles 25–28, to which the Social Democrats wished to add a guarantee of "minimum standards" of living.

Marriage, Family, and Women's Rights

Part of the problem regarding the language on marriage and the family was that the subcommittee had no women. This led to such fruitless efforts as Suzuki Yoshio's half hearted suggestion that a provision be added to article 24 that people "receive due protection with respect to their family life." There was something like this, he said, in the Weimar Constitution. When Yoshida An challenged him, saying it made no sense, Suzuki quickly retreated, saying that, to tell the truth, the idea had come from a "lady member." He apologized, but he thought article 24's concern for "individual dignity" ought to be balanced with a concern for the family.[1] There may indeed have been "something missing" from article 24, as Morito put it the following day,[2] but Suzuki was obviously not the person to supply it.

The discussion over article 24 occasioned much drivel about human nature and the obstacles it erected to the "essential equality" of the sexes. A disquisition by Kita provides a good example. While unusual in citing academic sources, it represented widely held concerns that article 24 was at odds with nature. There had been a number of views "since olden times," said Kita, on whether human beings were equal in nature. For example, Lipps, "famed ethicist of the Kantian school," was of the opinion that man and woman are different in essential nature: "The reason . . . is that, as a woman makes sexual life the center of her life, the whole personality degrades when she sexually degenerates. On the other hand, the sexual life of a man is secondary in importance, and though he may get somewhat stained sexually, he does not degenerate in personality." To illustrate the point in a Japanese context, Kita cited the Meiji-era political leader, Itō Hirobumi. Chastity was "no strong point" for him, Kita recalled, "yet his personality was great." As this was an important question, Kita begged leave to cite another example.

> In his *Man and Woman and Genius,* translated by Katayama Koson, Weininger (a young Austrian philosopher who killed himself) says sex life is the center of a woman's life. In her maiden age, she hopes for marriage; in her old age, she looks back on her bridal days. . . . Sex is the center of a woman's life. Famous philosophers, including Schopenhauer, say so. On this point, even American authorities cannot deny the theory.[3]

Kita reported that article 24 had become a "great problem" for the Liberal and Progressive parties. It had assumed the "same importance as . . . the principle that sovereignty lies in the people."[4] It threatened to undermine the land reform program. The government planned to purchase vast areas of land held by landowners and virtually give plots to tenants and poor farmers. Ownership of land would henceforth be restricted to three *chōbu.*[5] If a farmer had five children, and all children had an equal right to inheritance, soon there would not be enough for anyone to live on.

Kanamori was not normally in attendance at the subcommittee's meetings, but on July 30 he responded to a call by Ashida to answer questions on this point. "Most of the committee members," the chair reported, feared that if the provisions of article 24 were retained in their present form, Japan's whole system of domestic relationships would be "blown off," victim of a "frontal collision" with the constitution. They supported changes in favor of women's rights, but they regarded the draft's insistence on the "essential equality of the sexes" as an "overdose."[6] Hara Fujirō added that if farmers and factory owners were required to distribute their property equally among their children, it might lead to dire consequences, as it had in France, where experts traced a decline in population to similar provisions in the civil code.[7] Kanamori sought to quiet these fears. The second sentence of article 24 was intended to correct two defects: insufficient respect for individual dignity and "unreasonable discrimination between the sexes." Accordingly, the constitution would not deny the right of succession; it required only that "unreasonable discrimination" be avoided. In purging these defects, however, it would be important to bear in mind the purpose of the house and of its head, which included maintaining fêtes in commemoration of ancestors and preserving a family lineage and purity of blood. He acknowledged a "feeling" in favor of such traditions, as long as the idea of the "house" continues to exist in Japan. As for succession to a property, he urged members "not to take it so seriously." Although he hesitated to commit himself before the revisers had finished their work, he said there were circumstances when succession by a male is preferable. If a female were to succeed to the headship, she would have to adopt a son, and things might not work out smoothly. As for inheritance of land, he did not think the draft's language required an equal division of farmland each time there is an inheritance.[8]

Members gave considerable thought to amendments. Several objected to the phrase "laws shall be enacted from the standpoint of individual dignity and the essential equality of the sexes." Hayashi thought the first sentence, providing equal rights for husband and wife, was sufficient. In light of Kita's point about differences between the sexes, the second sentence need only assert that females deserved respect in all matters relating to family life. Hara agreed. He especially regretted the term "individual dignity." Would it not be better to say that laws must be based on "mutual respect and love and the nature of both sexes"?[9]

Ashida replied that the terms "individual dignity" and "the essential equality of the sexes" were given great importance (he did not say by whom: GHQ or female legislators and their allies). If "individual dignity" were replaced by "mutual respect and love," he said, "I am afraid that more than half of the spirit of this article will be lost."[10] For a different reason, Morito thought it best to leave *songen* (dignity) as it stood. The spirit of the article was to bring democratic principles to the Japanese family, just as we must democratize the state. "In the feudalistic family system," he observed, "individual personality is not valued." Women were placed in a "slavish position." The Japanese family system would have to be transformed to a certain extent.[11]

Earlier Ashida had suggested that the word "essential" be deleted from the phrase "essential equality of the sexes." Now the chairman was unsure. If we struck it, he said, "it would need a long explanation." How about changing just the Japanese word, from *honshitsuteki* to *kihonteki* (roughly, from "essential" to "fundamental"), on the ground that the former is not a good Japanese expression. He doubted that a more radical amendment (of both English and Japanese versions) would pass. "It may appear ridiculous to take into consideration such things. But circumstances being as they are, we rather hesitate to strike the word out." Satō, the cabinet's technician, liked Ashida's suggestion.[12] In due course, the change was made, without comment. No one at SCAP seemed to notice.

The Role of Religion

The subcommittee also addressed the place of religion in a liberal democracy. It began when Hayashi moved to add the word "sectarian" to the prohibition in article 20 against religious education. Kita responded with a strong statement of the argument that it was dangerous to encourage religion in public schools. There were, he acknowledged, strong pressures from his (Liberal) party behind Hayashi's amendment. Andō Masazumi, former chair of the political affairs investigations committee of his party, had supported it, and Kita himself had had a representation from the Buddhist community at his home yesterday. Also, Tanaka, minister of education, had expressed hope that religious sentiment might be fostered in schools, if it could be done without partiality to one religion or another. Despite these indications, Kita had concluded—and Andō now agreed—

254 TRANSFORMING A DRAFT INTO A CONSTITUTION

that it was better to leave the article unamended. Why? Because it would not work in practice. The name of Buddha would be invoked when Buddhists led classes in religious sentiment, and the name of Christ would be mentioned, or words in the Bible quoted, if Christians were teaching it. Some contended that it would be all right as long as teachers referred to religion broadly, but not good when they showed prejudice in favor of particular sects. But even if education in religious sentiment were confined in such a nonsectarian fashion, it might involve difficulties. Education that precluded partiality to one sect or another would "wipe off the individual color" of faith. It would be like "drinking whiskey that had been watered so much that there would be no smell to it."

To illustrate the mischief of intermixing religion and politics, Kita cited the French experience, where a strong secularist impulse among teachers stood vigilant against "too deep a penetration by religion into school education." The long delay in the realization of women's suffrage in France was due in part, he said, to opposition by progressive statesmen, on the ground that if women were enfranchised, many Catholic priests would be returned to the National Assembly and make it more reactionary and conservative. For all these reasons, although he felt sympathetic toward school education in religious sentiment, he favored retention of the provisions as they stood. Opening the door to religious education would simply invite confusion.[13]

This barrage from their leader did not immediately convince other conservatives. Yoshida An supported Hayashi's suggestion of inserting the word "sectarian." Surely, he said, there was no harm in teaching the doctrines of Shinran, Nichiren, or Shaka for cultural purposes. What must be condemned is education based on some particular sectarian consciousness. Hayashi argued that it was impossible to ignore religion. It was part of life and culture. Certainly teachers should avoid bias, but people in their earlier years needed to acquire an appreciation of religious sentiment and a critical ability regarding religion, so that they might make an informed choice for their own lives. Ōshima recalled Tanaka saying that schools, though "organs of the state," might offer instruction in religion, as long as it was not partial to a sect or denomination. Article 20 gave the impression that any and all religious education was prohibited, and it made many religious people anxious. To eliminate such misgivings, he hoped Hayashi's amendment could be inserted.[14]

The Socialists preferred to leave the article as it was. Unlike their European counterparts, they did not insist that education entirely ignore religious sentiment. After all, said Morito, religion plays a big part in the life of the Japanese people. But it was best to leave religious education to private organizations. Parents who wanted their children instructed in particular doctrines should send them to sectarian schools.[15]

As the discussion proceeded, it became apparent that conservatives and social democrats were not far apart on this issue. Hatsukade said he did not really mind leaving the article as was. He himself had been principal of a school, and while he was always careful not to promote particular doctrines, he made sure that children in his school were "immersed" in his own faith. "I call it religious education to impart only such an earnest, all-devoting or pious feeling," he said.

He agreed that "denominational education...should be prohibited," but he thought that the article, as explained by his philosophical friends (Kita and Morito), would do that without discouraging the inculcation of religious sentiments.[16]

As the debate wound down, Kita offered summary reflections. He cited the argument of Andō Masazumi[17] to the effect that Japan's educational system in the prewar years had become a tool of nationalism and militarism; that it needed now to be grounded in universal morality; that such "world religions" as Christianity and Buddhism offered sound approaches in this direction; and that, without embracing "the fundamental spirit of world religion, the finishing touch in education is missing." He acknowledged that education devoid of religious underpinning would not serve Japan in its present spiritual crisis. "Nevertheless," he said, "I am firmly resolved to support the existing provisions." If religious education were explicitly tolerated, Shintō, with its ambiguous status as a quasi-religion, might again be allowed to foster undesirable thoughts in close association with the concept of the national polity of Japan.[18]

In light of Japan's internal and international circumstances, most Diet members seemed ready to accept the position outlined in article 20, as interpreted by Kita and Tanaka. They opposed any provision that explicitly countenanced or encouraged religious teaching in publicly supported education. They agreed that the state and its organs must not give financial assistance to religious institutions. On the other hand, they were profoundly concerned about Japan's spiritual crisis. To leave religious training entirely to private institutions, without assistance from the government, seemed unwisely passive. Summing up, Hayashi said that, "with the understanding that general religious education at school is tolerated," he would agree to drop his amendment.[19] And so it was done. The discussion left many important issues unresolved. Japan's decision—to retain language that gave the state some leverage to deal with the abuses of Shintoism and extremist faiths without banning religious sentiment from schools and other public institutions—was not unlike the balance struck by many Western nations. There was still plenty of room for sharp controversies over these provisions, in Japan as elsewhere.

Should Social Rights Be Entrenched in the Constitution?

Another major struggle erupted over the constitutional foundations of social policy. The cabinet draft of June 20 vaguely promised that "in all spheres of life, laws shall be designed for the promotion and extension of social welfare and security, and of public health." Kanamori insisted that the bill of rights protected individual liberty but contained no positive obligations enforceable against the state. Many Diet members thought this view reflected an outmoded understanding of constitutional government, more in tune with eighteenth- and nineteenth-century theories than with twentieth-century realities. Social Democrats now moved to insert language in article 25 that would establish the commitment to advance social welfare through positive public programs. At the beginning of the article, they proposed to add, "All people shall have the right to maintain minimum standards of wholesome and cultured living." Their intent, they said, was to oblige the state to provide each citizen with the wherewithal to lead wholesome, cultured lives.

Why was this necessary? asked Hatsukade. The Diet had recently enacted a dole (approximately $4 per day) to assist needy people.[20] Everyone accepted the necessity of it. Morito replied that his party was calling not for charity but for a social contract. People would be obliged (by article 27) to work. In return, the nation should guarantee the material requisites for a decent life.[21] Liberals thought article 13 already covered the matter. It established the right to "life, liberty and the pursuit of happiness," making them the "supreme consideration in legislation and in other governmental affairs." That, together with article 25 as drafted, provided a secure constitutional footing for the programs desired by the Social Democrats. Nishio replied that article 13 did not suffice. It protected the right to pursue happiness, through industrial strikes and social movements. Article 25, if amended, would go far beyond that. It would guarantee minimum standards of living. That is what the Socialists were demanding.[22] Suzuki added that social and economic rights needed specification, just as political and legal rights did. Ashida's argument, that the general principles of article 13 were enough,[23] was like arguing that the rest of the bill of rights was superfluous after article 11 ("the people shall not be prevented from enjoying any of the fundamental human rights"). No one believed that.[24]

The debate over amending article 25 produced some of the summer's sharpest exchanges over Germany's Weimar Constitution (1919) as a model. For Social Democrats (in Japan as elsewhere), the Weimar Constitution was a prime example of twentieth-century constitution making. It showed a spirit of democracy adjusting constitutional doctrine to modern conditions. In modifying the commitment to private property, it recognized the state's obligation to buffer workers and their families from the agonies of the market system.

Conservatives saw Weimar as a symbol, too, but of a different sort: of idealism gone haywire. For the right, the collapse of Weimar Germany was no accident. It came because Germans failed to tailor their idealism to the realities of Germany's postwar condition. The results—hyperinflation and social chaos, leading to Hitler's totalitarian repression—were utterly predictable.

These polar perspectives led to sharp clashes between Suzuki, the Socialist leader, and Ashida, the Progressive Democrat. Typical was a brief but acerbic exchange over a proposal to insert an obligation to work. Our amendment is "modeled after the Weimar Constitution of Germany," said Suzuki. "It is there stated that all healthy German people shall contribute labor for the benefit of the public welfare, and that the state shall always give employment to those who wish to work, in order to encourage them to do so." "The Weimar Constitution miscarried," replied Ashida. "I am shocked to hear its name." "I protest against such a remark," rejoined Suzuki. "It is not the fault of the Weimar Constitution that the German government failed." Ashida retorted that he hoped Japan's new constitution would not follow suit.[25]

Later Ashida made another attempt to explain why he reacted so negatively at the invocation of Weimar. Suzuki moved to insert a right of tillage and tenancy, to protect farmers. "I may be taken to task again if I quote the Weimar Constitution, but there is a similar provision in it," he said. Ashida said he did not mean to be rude, but the Weimar Constitution had proven abortive, without realizing any effective results. Why? "Because it did not accord with the real conditions of Germany at the time." He hoped "day and night" that Japan's new constitution would not follow suit. I hold a different view, said Suzuki. If the Weimar Constitution had been truly in force, Germany might have been saved. The Nazis seized Germany without any chance for a popular front. "In short, her constitution had utterly been distorted." Exactly, said Ashida. That is why "we must establish a constitution that can actually be put into practice by the Japanese people."[26]

On July 30, the committee considered a list of amendments[27] proposed by the Social Democratic Party. The proposal to insert an obligation to work as part of the social contract, alongside the right to work, met resistance from liberals who feared that the government might use it to requisition labor, as it had during the late war. Hayashi countered that with no more military service, few ties remained between citizens and the nation.[28] This argument helped to enlist centrist support and carried the day for an amendment to article 27. Other initiatives, however, were less successful. Social Democrats proposed a right to leisure, to vacations, to sanitariums, and to equal pay for equal work but got little support beyond the left. The prevailing argument was that these worthy goals ought to be considered when Japan's economy emerged from exigent circumstances, but it was wrong to entrench them in the constitution. The constitution needed a clear basis for legislative enactments along these lines, but that was already present in existing provisions.

The gulf between the left and the right on social and economic rights was finally unbridgeable. By July 30, this was obvious. Ashida summarized the subcommittee's dilemma. "None of us is against the policies proposed by the Social Democrats," he said. "The dissent has arisen over whether we should insert detailed provisions in the constitution, or content ourselves with a summarizing provision. We seem unable to settle the question by debate here. How shall we deal with it?"[29] Nishio pleaded with the subcommittee not to turn down the Social Democrats' proposals summarily but to deal with them one by one, so that he and his colleagues might offer explanations. Ashida replied that they had already adopted the proposal to insert an obligation to work, but a majority of committee members were opposed to their other proposals, and so, he said, "I must ask the [Social Democratic] party to reconsider."[30] Ōshima noted that the Social Democratic representatives were reserving their position on these amendments. If that continued, he feared the deliberations could never be concluded. Was it not time to have a vote?[31] Ashida replied that the subcommittee could, of course, do that at any time, but he hesitated to impose such a solution.

In a spirit of resignation, he proceeded to article 29 (property rights), where the Socialists made one last stand. As it had stood since February, when the SCAP committee drafted it, the article pronounced the right to own property "inviolable" but added that "property rights shall be defined by law, in conformity with the public welfare." The Socialists now proposed to begin the article with a declaration that "the object of the order of economic life shall be the advancement of the public welfare" and only then proceed to establish a qualified "right to own property and economic freedom . . . insofar as they do not contravene the above object." The notion of an "inviolable" right to own private property "derived from the French Constitution," said Morito. The world has changed greatly since the eighteenth century. He recognized that "we do not live in a society where socialism prevails, so we must recognize economic freedom or the right to own property." But the public welfare should be placed above them. Only so could the constitution meet the "changing conditions of society."[32] Conservatives responded by calling attention to article 12, where people were warned against the abuse of rights and made responsible to use them "always . . . for the public welfare." It was agreed to postpone consideration of the Social Democratic amendments, but clearly this committee was not likely to change article 29.

Despite these discouraging defeats, however, the Social Democrats of 1946 left their mark on the Japanese bill of rights, most notably in article 25, guaranteeing the "right to maintain the minimum standards of wholesome and cultured living," and in article 27, with its "obligation" to work. Thus, by the end of July, the subcommittee, though dominated by Liberals and Progressive Democrats, was ready to go further than Kanamori's insistence on a strict liberal interpretation of economic rights. Indeed, Ashida stated that the need to accept the Socialists' amendment to article 25 stemmed from the government's failure to offer a clear and persuasive explanation of the constitutional foundations of social policy. Kita agreed.[33]

Criminal Rights

As for the second half of the bill of rights (articles 31–40, dealing with criminal rights), the subcommittee made few changes. The most significant resulted from a proposal by the Socialists to include protections for those falsely accused of crimes or who had suffered damage as a result of official malfeasance. Suzuki acknowledged that article 32 (guaranteeing the right of access to the courts) provided constitutional foundation for suits against the government, but he insisted on language making it explicit that Japanese citizens had the right to sue the government. "The Japanese generally think it is impossible to bring a lawsuit against government authorities and preposterous to take such a step." It was therefore "very important" to make clear that people could "bring a suit against the administration even without a special court for the purpose."[34] There was little resistance to Suzuki's proposal. In fact, two articles (17 and 40) were added for this purpose. They were extremely important undertakings in the constitution of a nation emerging from an era when the state, conducted in the name of imperial authority, had been beyond challenge by ordinary citizens. They were adopted by this subcommittee after only a minimum of complaint that they were technically unnecessary, in a spirit of unanimity—a strong mark of commitment to constitutional principles.

The Crisis over Imperial Property

For the subcommittee on revision, as for the Diet as a whole, perhaps the most sensitive issue in the constitution concerned the disposition of the imperial family's property. Article 88[35] was sensitive, not only because of the size and complexity of the emperor's holdings but because the status of these properties was intimately bound up with *kokutai*, the doctrine concerning the place of the imperial family in the nation and the esteem and devotion that Japanese people felt for them.

A Preliminary Discussion

On July 22, just as the revision committee was about to hand the draft to the subcommittee for fine-tuning, attention had turned briefly to article 88. As written at this stage, it provided that all property of the imperial household, "other than the hereditary estates," would henceforth belong to the state.[36] What were the "hereditary estates"? And why was not all the emperor's property covered by the guarantees in article 29, where property rights were made "inviolable" and "just compensation" promised for any taking? Kanamori sought to answer the first question by distinguishing three types of imperial property: that belonging personally to members of the imperial family; that held by the imperial family in its corporate character, to secure the continuous existence of the institution (these were the so-called hereditary estates); and all other properties. The latter would be transferred to the state. The hereditary estates would remain with the family, but any income derived from them would go into the national treasury. How much property, and of what types, was included in this second category? Kanamori indicated that its value was considerable (he mentioned the figure of $27 million, a large sum at that time),[37] but he said that an accurate accounting had not been completed. The idea behind the admittedly strange terms of article 88 was that the so-called hereditary properties needed to remain in imperial hands for the sake of continuity, but that, "in view of various circumstances at present" (probably code words indicating pressure from Occupation authorities and the Allied powers), it was imperative to protect the emperor from the "political entanglements" necessarily attendant upon managing such huge assets.

Members who commented on these provisions were unanimous in asserting that the people of Japan bitterly opposed them. Hara Fujirō said that article 88, coupled with the provision (article 8) that barred the emperor from accepting or making any gift, was severely restrictive. He conceded that the provisions had been written "with a view to respecting the Imperial House" and were "quite consistent with the purport of the constitution." But viewing the emperor as the symbol of the state, with a "status respected by the people," article 88 seemed unreasonably tight. Why not allow the imperial family to retain these properties and defray the expenses of their position with the proceeds?[38] Kanamori replied that the article requiring Diet authorization for any gifts to the emperor must stand, but that Hara's position on the hereditary properties was certainly worth considering. A great deal of wealth was at stake here, he said. The important thing was to separate the emperor from controversial entanglements.

At this point, the other Hara, a firebrand named Kenzaburō, entered the fray. In England, he said, the royal court was authorized to have its own property and to take income from it. Kanamori defended article 88 as necessary to remove suspicions, but "we the people," said Hara, "entertain no such fears." This attempt to strip the emperor of his property, contrary to the guarantees of article 29, arose from a mistaken ideology. "I am deeply convinced that such provisions are quite contrary to the genuine feelings of the Japanese people."[39] The difficulty, of course, was that the issue of imperial property stood at the juncture of fierce pressures.

The Subcommittee Tackles the Issue

From the beginning of the revision project, the Allies had demanded that the emperor no longer play any part in the governance of the nation. Grudgingly, most members of the Diet had come round to accepting that position. Accord on that point, however, did not settle the question of the properties. If anything, it exacerbated it. In Kanamori's formula, the emperor must be kept free from political entanglements, the better to serve as the center of devotion for all Japanese. But was it consistent with this devotion—indeed, was it fair to him as a person in a constitutional system that guaranteed the rights of property—to strip most of his property and deny him the fruits of whatever was not expropriated? The problem was aggravated by the aura of uncertainty and mystery surrounding it. It was hard to get reliable information about the extent of imperial holdings, in part because they were so vast and complicated, but also because it seemed vulgar and impertinent to ask.

After many hours of agonized debate in the House revision committee, the text of article 88 stood essentially where SCAP had left it. SCAP had shown willingness to consider amendments on most other points, but on matters affecting the emperor, the Americans were adamant. It would fall to the Legislation Bureau to negotiate an understanding with MacArthur's headquarters.

The parties interested in this explosive issue were legion, emotional, and very determined. On one side were conservatives in the Diet. On August 3, Ashida told the Legislation Bureau that prevailing sentiment in the Diet wanted to delete the provision that all income from imperial properties must be paid into the national treasury.[40] It would accept the language in the SCAP draft only on direct orders from GHQ. In fact, this demand came solely from the conservative parties (Liberals and Progressives). Ashida himself acknowledged at a subcommittee meeting on August 2 that it might not be possible to gain the two-thirds majority in the Diet needed to amend the government draft.[41] Even so, Ashida was correct that conservatives in the Diet were dead set against stripping the emperor of his properties. The Social Democrats were less emotional on the subject of imperial property. They supported the imperial institution, but they wanted a clear accounting, both of overall holdings and of annual expenditures. The Japanese Communists were small in number but noisy and bold in their search for a constituency. The backing of the Soviet Union in the FEC strengthened their position. On issues affecting the emperor, they were sometimes inconsistent, but they strongly supported the demand for a full accounting, and they insisted on eliminating the financial power of the imperial institution.

The dominant player in all this was, of course, GHQ. Kades made it clear to the Japanese that SCAP regarded article 88 as one of the "fundamental principles" of the constitution. In putting the point this way, the American was using heavily loaded language, and the Japanese knew it. GHQ viewed a certain few things as "fundamental principles of democracy." Most of chapter I, on the emperor, was "fundamental." So was article 9, the antiwar clause. On these items, there would be no compromise. Much of the rest of the draft was negotiable—but not article 88. GHQ was convinced that the imperial household was a prime example of *zaibatsu*, the concentration of economic power in politically unaccountable hands. In the eyes of the Americans, constitutional democracy could not be secure in Japan until the financial power of the imperial institution was liquidated.[42]

The international context here was particularly important. MacArthur was convinced that the preservation of the imperial institution, and the protection of Hirohito personally, was essential to the speedy and successful conclusion of the Occupation. He realized the potential for abuse of the institution, but he believed that setting clear limits on the emperor's authority in the constitution could solve these potential problems. But MacArthur was not a free agent on this issue. Not everyone on the FEC agreed that the emperor was essential to the achievement of Allied purposes. The Soviets were bent on abolishing the imperial institution entirely. The Australians, Filipinos, and Chinese were also hostile, at least to the current emperor. By the summer of 1946, GHQ could not afford to ignore these opinions.

Officials at the Legislation Bureau were the other major players here. Politically, they took orders from the conservative coalition that dominated the cabinet. However, they also felt pressure from the Foreign Ministry and from GHQ, with which they were in frequent contact. Ashida indicated the attitude of many politicians toward the Legislation Bureau when, in the midst of the negotiations with GHQ, he wrote in his diary that he must try to get former Prime Minister Shidehara involved. The Legislation Bureau, as he put it, was too "weak-kneed."[43]

On July 31, the subcommittee turned its full attention to article 88. Even from the dry bones of the transcript, one senses that the discussion touched tender feelings. Everyone recognized that the emperor—a human being after all, as Ashida noted[44]—needed a "private purse." On the other hand, the imperial household harbored many "parasites," as Morito observed. The Social Democrats advised that the subcommittee would not be able to avoid an examination of the finances of the imperial establishment.

The discussion focused on a Progressive Party motion to strike from article 88 the clause directing that all income from imperial properties be paid into the national treasury. If this deletion had been accepted, the imperial establishment could have relied on the income from the hereditary estates, which, by the first sentence of article 88 as it then stood, had been left to the imperial household.

The Progressives' amendment raised two questions. What was the extent of the hereditary estates? And how much money did it cost to maintain the imperial establishment? No one on the subcommittee seemed able to answer either question.

Discussion focused on the second question. Under the Meiji Constitution, the Diet had appropriated 4.5 million yen annually (about $75,000 at 1946 exchange rates) for the expenses of the imperial household. That figure had been set in 1887 and had been kept there over the ensuing years, even though actual expenditures had risen greatly and were thought now to be anywhere from six to ten times greater annually. The difference was made up with income from imperial forests and other holdings of the imperial family. Clearly, as Kasai pointed out, if the annual national budget were forced to absorb that cost, it would cause great strain on national finances and provoke public controversy. True enough, Ashida acknowledged, but if the state were to take over the imperial properties, the burden would presumably be at least partially absorbed.[45] For the Social Democrats, the main point was transparency. They readily granted that the emperor, as symbol of the state, needed adequate support, but they insisted on a full accounting of imperial holdings, including the hereditary estates. They cited sensational rumors of imperial wealth (including huge investments in industrial properties) flying through the press and in the corridors of the Diet. It was imperative to get accurate information as a basis for framing a fair and sound provision. The Social Democrats knew they were outvoted but asked how far the conservatives planned to push their demand. Did they intend to confront GHQ on this issue? Ashida replied that he did not know yet. On August 3, Ashida called the Legislation Bureau's negotiators to his office. He reported that the subcommittee intended to seek an amendment to Article 88. Only a direct order from SCAP would deter them.[46]

When the Legislation Bureau relayed this message to Kades, the American colonel was firm. "We view the issue of imperial property, along with the issue of the location of sovereignty," he said, "as the most important points in the new constitution." If article 88 had been in the form of the proposed amendment, he said, General MacArthur would probably not have approved the draft published by the Japanese cabinet on March 6. The American was dismayed that the Japanese were proposing such an amendment at this late hour. He expected at least that SCAP would have been warned in advance that the Diet was contemplating an amendment on such a fundamental point. The Diet, said Kades, must have the same control over the expenses of the monarchy as the Parliament in England. He cited a SCAP directive of November 24, 1945, to the effect that imperial property would henceforth be taxed like any other property, but Kanamori had "gone so far" as to contradict this policy in a speech to the Diet.[47] Kades said he had heard there was a move afoot to include imperial stocks and bonds among the hereditary properties exempted from expropriation. But the Japanese side well knew this was never the intent of those who undertook the drafting of this article. The exemptions from this article were only palaces—detached palaces, and gardens used by the imperial family in their daily lives—and the emperor's personal items. No intangible wealth should be included.[48]

Kades concluded by reporting that people close to the emperor supported SCAP's policy on imperial properties. Continued resistance, stemming (he said) from "a small group of persons who depend on the imperial household," would only damage the emperor's own interests. SCAP did not wish to impoverish Hirohito. "Is it not better that the imperial family receive all necessary expenses from the national treasury, with the approval of the National Diet?"[49] To resolve the issue, Kades proposed adding "as defined by the Diet," to the clause exempting hereditary properties from the expropriation. After the meeting, however, he consulted General Whitney, who disapproved of this suggestion. Instead, Kades told his Legislation Bureau counterparts, if the subcommittee insisted on removing the phrase about income going to the national treasury, SCAP would insist on striking the exemption for hereditary properties.

On August 5, Kades delivered GHQ's decision on the wording of article 88 to Irie, Kanamori, and Satō. It eliminated both the exception for hereditary estates and the provision that all income from imperial property would be deposited in the national treasury. The latter was rendered moot by the fact that there would no longer be any imperial property per se.[50] It would all belong to the state. Irie warned that the Diet might react badly to such a blunt demand. He reminded Kades that the proposed amendment had come from a Diet subcommittee. Kades replied that it was up to the Legislation Bureau to explain to the Diet that this way was better for the emperor. General Whitney understood Japanese sensitivities, but the situation internationally was "extremely delicate." If it looked as if the constitution's language left any loophole for the restoration of the imperial estates, the Soviets, in particular, would exploit the situation for all it was worth. It was therefore critical to handle the matter discreetly, providing the necessary explanations confidentially. As for the exemption of so-called hereditary properties, it was better not to try to settle such matters in the constitution. There would be time later to make distinctions between public property and the emperor's personal property. Let the Diet provide the necessary definitions by law and let the supreme court be the final arbiter of the meaning of the constitutional text. The wording in the constitution was "fundamental," from the American standpoint.[51]

What Kades was proposing was to leave it to the Japanese government (cabinet and Diet) to draw the line between the "property of the imperial household," which would henceforth "belong to the state," and the holdings of the emperor's family, which would remain his. The conservatives, while suffering an apparent defeat on the explicit terms of the language of article 88, had succeeded in gaining the point that the emperor, "the symbol of the State," had to have resources to live in dignity. All that remained after August 3 was to persuade the conservatives in the Diet to accept the article without stirring up a public storm. It would not be easy.

Ashida's diary traced the steps. He began his entry for August 10 by basking in the glow of praise in the press for his adroit handling of his work as chair of the subcommittee. The committee was finished by then, he reported, except for article 88. He mentioned a visit from Justin Williams, a mid-level aide at GHQ, with whom he discussed the emperor's property. Williams reported that the issue touched "fundamental principles." "Surely," Ashida replied, "you do not mean to take away the man's hat and pencils." Would it not be possible for the cabinet, GHQ, and the imperial household to work out a fair and practical division of property? It was at this point that Ashida mentioned the possibility of getting Shidehara involved, to strengthen the spine of the cabinet's bureaucrats.

By August 13, Ashida had learned from Shidehara that the cabinet had acceded to SCAP's demand to amend article 88, not by preserving an income for the emperor from the "hereditary estates," as the conservatives in the Diet were demanding, but by deleting the exemption for the hereditary properties altogether. According to Ashida's diary, Shidehara admitted that he had let his friend down by agreeing to this deal.[52]

The Legislation Bureau made one more effort to accommodate the Diet conservatives. Would GHQ accept the phrase "now accredited" to the first sentence, leaving open the possibility of future accumulations. Article 8 in chapter I, they explained, would enable the Diet to control any future accretions to imperial wealth. According to the minutes of the Japanese negotiators, Kades put on a "sour face" upon hearing this suggestion. Article 8 was totally inadequate for this purpose, he said. The imperial family controlled vast wealth, over one billion yen, according to some estimates. The imperial household was indeed a powerful *zaibatsu*. It must be liquidated and no door left open for it to be restored.[53] Then how about moving article 88 to a separate chapter in the constitution, one devoted to "transitional matters"? At first Kades reacted positively to this suggestion, but after consulting with Whitney, he withdrew his acquiescence.[54]

On August 16, the new, stripped version of article 88 came before the subcommittee. Ashida asked Kanamori to explain what had happened. Negotiations with GHQ over this article had been long and extremely difficult, Kanamori said. GHQ had insisted that the subcommittee's amendment, leaving income from the hereditary properties to the emperor, would threaten the purity of the imperial institution. It would also violate a principle that SCAP considered "fundamental" to Japan's new constitutional order. Kanamori explained that henceforth all imperial property would belong to the state, but all the emperor's personal property would be private. He urged that any public discussion of these arrangements be extremely discreet, as the negotiations with the Americans were highly sensitive.

Hatsukade was the first to respond. He wondered whether this deal could be sold to the Diet without explaining all the circumstances. Those who were privy to the negotiations would have to reassure the people about the emperor's private holdings. Would they be believed, if they could not tell what had happened? Ashida responded by claiming (in remarks not included in the version sent to GHQ) that he had tried to get this article put into a special section on transitional matters, but MacArthur had personally told Prime Minister Yoshida that it was not possible. Hatsukade was still not satisfied. The emperor is a "sacred being," he said, a "living god." It was wrong to reduce him to poverty and to publicize his affairs as if he were a common thing. "Stubborn conservatives" would certainly bitterly resist such an approach.[55] (In this, Hatsukade proved to be a keen prophet!)

Kanamori made one more attempt to state the terms of the deal. The emperor's villas and palaces would remain private. So would his laboratories and personal effects. This was only "reasonable," and SCAP knew it. The forests were different. They had been acquired during the Meiji era, and they represented considerable productive wealth. They must be turned over to the state. As for the ancient imperial treasures and the artworks at the imperial museum in Ueno Park, their status had not yet been determined, but members could trust that SCAP was not being unreasonable. GHQ's main concern was the vast wealth accrued by the imperial household during the Meiji era and the potential for abuse that it carried. Suzuki, a leading Social Democrat, and Inukai, a maverick conservative, expressed satisfaction that there would finally be an accurate accounting of all this wealth and its uses. Inukai added that he hoped the imperial household would divest itself of industrial holdings, as well.

The Issue Comes to a Head

At the surface, maneuvering over article 88 concluded at this August 16 meeting of the subcommittee. Ashida's diary, however, reveals that the crisis continued for another week. In fact, the third week in August saw one of two genuine crises during this summer of constitutional revision (the other being the Kades–Kanamori meetings of mid-July over *kokutai*).

Ashida began his entry of August 17, "The enemy's attack has become stronger and stronger."[56] The context makes clear that the "enemy" in this case were members of his own coalition, the "stubborn conservatives" to whom Hatsukade had referred at the subcommittee meeting that afternoon. Ashida wrote that deliberations on the constitution began to "falter" on August 15, after a meeting between Yoshida and MacArthur that confirmed the settlement between GHQ and the Legislation Bureau on imperial property. The caucus of the Liberal and Progressive parties immediately accepted the amendments, but just as he was preparing to leave for the subcommittee meeting, Ashida was approached by two fellow Progressives, who pleaded with him not to take these amendments to the subcommittee. "Red in the face," one of them exclaimed that the people of Japan would passionately oppose the proposed language. Ashida replied that on the subcommittee, he must act as chair rather than representative of his party. He went off to his subcommittee meeting, where the changes were formally adopted. After the meeting, Ashida met Katō Kazuo (a prominent Social Democrat) in the corridor, who confirmed that there was a "hubbub" among Liberals in the Diet over this issue. Katō suggested that Ashida attend the Liberal Party meeting then in session, but Ashida, anticipating an effort to embarrass him, declined to go.

On the morning of August 17, Ashida changed his mind. He decided to attend a meeting of the executive council of the Liberal party, to explain the reasons for amending article 88. As soon as he entered the room, he sensed tension. Seven leading members of the party—including the speaker of the Diet, Higai Seizō, "looking like a warlord"—were arrayed against him.[57] Uehara, a distinguished senior cabinet member without portfolio, joined him at the meeting. Ashida does not report what he and Uehara told the Liberal dissidents, but somehow they seemed to succeed in changing the atmosphere. Later in the day, however, three of the dissidents, including Speaker Higai, reported that Prime Minister Yoshida had told them he would try to renegotiate the settlement with the Americans, though he could not do so until "next week." This report infuriated Ashida

After completing his rounds, explaining the agreement to caucuses of the other parties (Progressive, Social Democrats, Kyōdō, and two others), Ashida, still hot under the collar, decided to ask the prime minister directly about his reported willingness to reopen negotiations with GHQ. Yoshida was not in his office when Ashida got there, but he ran into Hara Fujirō, a Progressive member of the subcommittee, who told him that the Progressives and Social Democrats were also furious with Prime Minister Yoshida for encouraging the dissidents.[58] Reinforced by growing irritation among subcommittee members, Ashida demanded an appointment with the prime minister.

At 5 P.M. on August 17, twelve members of the subcommittee met Yoshida, who was clad, with studied informality, in a kimono. He began by explaining in detail how the revision had come about (most, if not all present, knew the story as well as Yoshida did, having heard it from Kanamori, who had been at the center of the negotiations). Yoshida concluded by asking the subcommittee to proceed with the draft as revised.

Ashida and the others in the delegation were "flabbergasted" by this performance, "so different from what we had heard earlier." Ashida admitted out loud that he was "taken aback" and said that the prime minister's statement was at odds with what he had been told by three men who had seen him earlier in the day. Suzuki was more blunt. He asked Yoshida why he had promised the conservatives that he would seek to renegotiate the matter with GHQ. "I thought they were members of the constitution committee," he replied coolly. "You know, the Speaker of the House was with them." Ashida then asked if the text distributed by the Legislation Bureau was to be considered the "final draft" of article 88. "Yes, it is," Yoshida replied.[59]

Suzuki, still sore at the prime minister's apparent betrayal of the subcommittee's efforts, lamented the poor communications between the prime minister and the subcommittee. There were rumors in the newspapers, he said, that Ashida was in cahoots with GHQ, acting against the interests of the emperor. He implied that Yoshida was seeding these reports. Several members of the subcommittee, representing a wide spectrum of parties, defended the chairman against these rumors, saying his actions had been completely justified. Ashida quickly drafted a summary of the meeting and gave it to the chief cabinet secretary. He then turned directly to the prime minister and said, "Unless you, as head of the Liberal Party, admit the rightness of the action I took and support me, I cannot continue my job. I will have to resign from the chairmanship." Yoshida nodded, apparently to indicate his support for Ashida, "although in a vague manner." Elated by this small triumph, Ashida went home, "filled with courage." "The war has already started," he confided to his diary. "The time has come for me to fight."[60]

Next day, however, there was an eerie silence in the press. Newspapers did not carry the statement Ashida had drafted. Nor was there any evidence that Yoshida was delivering on his promise of support for the subcommittee and its chairman. Ashida feared that a "frontal clash" was in the making between the Liberal Party and the Diet's committee on constitutional revision.[61]

Soon the Japanese press was full of reports of intense infighting among conservatives. According to these reports, Yoshida was using his ties to SCAP in the battle for control over the political right. Liberals were beginning to admire and respect him for delivering some relief on food shortages and for keeping the political left off balance and at bay. His ties with Hatoyama Ichirō, the purged but by no means disgraced lion of the right, were said to be "very intimate."[62]

Another Crisis Intervenes

By awkward coincidence, just as the subcommittee was meeting to decide how to respond to the prime minister's intrigues, Ashida was summoned to a meeting with Shirasu Jirō (Yoshida's close aide), Irie, and Kanamori. GHQ "had issued another order," he was told. SCAP was now demanding changes in the text to require that all cabinet members be "civilians" and that the prime minister and at least a majority of the cabinet be members of the Diet.[63] They handed Ashida a typed English text of the revisions to articles 66, 67, and 68, asking that the matter be presented to the subcommittee. This was not a good moment for such a demand, Ashida replied. He insisted that Kanamori be the messenger.

When Ashida returned to the subcommittee, he found members deep in conversation about how to react to Yoshida's snub (his failure to publicize his support for the settlement concerning imperial property). Four members, headed by Suzuki, had drafted a statement. It criticized "Prime Minister Yoshida's carelessness and Chief Secretary Hayashi's neglect of duty" but focused its condemnation on the Speaker of the House for seeking to undermine the work of the subcommittee.[64] Learning the tenor of the statement his colleagues had prepared, Ashida withdrew and went home. He knew the statement would be a political bombshell, but he was reluctant to intervene. He agreed that the subcommittee could not allow the conservatives' maneuver to pass without some rejoinder.

As Ashida had anticipated, newspapers on August 20 gave great prominence to the statement from the subcommittee. It caused a furor, particularly in the Liberal Party.[65] Attention now focused on the effort to remove Higai, the Speaker of the House. When Inukai indicated his support for the uprising, Shidehara made an appeal to Ashida to call off his supporters. If a motion of no confidence against Speaker Higai succeeded, said Shidehara, the cabinet would fall. Meanwhile, Kitaura and other conservatives in the Diet took the subcommittee to task for its campaign against Higai. The Socialists, however, held firm, refusing to sit with the revision committee (convening now to receive the subcommittee's report) while Higai remained in the speaker's chair.

By August 21, it appeared that the Liberals had enough votes to defeat the motion of no confidence, but the Socialists skillfully filibustered. On August 22, Higai made a speech attempting to justify his actions, but it was ineffective. On the afternoon of August 23, he resigned. Ashida himself was apparently considered as a replacement for the speaker, but the choice fell on Yamazaki Takeshi.[66]

The Crisis Resolved

In retrospect, the crisis of mid-August 1946 involved two great issues: the disposition of imperial properties and the new, FEC-inspired provisions affecting the construction of cabinets.[67] These issues were difficult and emotional in any case, but their severity was inflamed by political rivalries. On imperial properties, SCAP's interference probably could not have been avoided. The Yoshida cabinet and its allies in the Diet were determined to alter article 88 in favor of allowing the emperor to retain substantial property. SCAP could not be seen as yielding to this demand. The FEC would not have tolerated it. A clash over this point was inevitable. The coincidence of the FEC intervention over articles 66 through 68, however, was unfortunate. The Japanese were deeply irritated by SCAP's insistence on language that all ministers be "civilians," whatever that meant. In light of article 9, which promised that armed forces would "never" be maintained, it seemed gratuitous. Moreover, it flew in the face of MacArthur's promise that the Diet would have substantial leeway in shaping the final draft. It brought them up short, just as they were beginning to feel confidence in their proprietorship over this constitution.

No doubt these last-minute negotiations strained Yoshida's enthusiasm for his chosen role as joint conspirator in constitutional revision. It was his pride that suffered the most. Not only did his government have to swallow the apparent delivery of imperial properties into public hands, but his vaunted relationship with MacArthur had not produced any softening of the terms, at least not publicly. And his "intimacy" with Hatoyama was doubtless strained by this episode. Despite his embarrassment, the prime minister asked his fellow conservatives to accept, on faith, that the deal he had made with GHQ would benefit the emperor. By late August, he seemed to have succeeded. The constitutional crisis over the imperial properties was over.

18 . . . .

"Sincere and Steady Efforts"

• DENOUEMENT

•

The three-week span from the end of July until August 20 was a critical period in the making of Japan's postwar constitution. Sensing that events were moving rapidly to a conclusion, the cabinet of Prime Minister Yoshida, built on a coalition of the two major conservative parties (Liberals and Progressive Democrats) suddenly came to life, becoming an active participant in negotiations with GHQ, especially on the vexing issue of the imperial properties. For its part GHQ also took a more active role, bringing forward several amendments it had received from the FEC in early July but had sat on until the end of the month. These modifications were negotiated at a series of meetings in GHQ. Kades was again the dominant player. As the man responsible for approving any amendments proposed by the Japanese, he was also, somewhat reluctantly,[1] the channel for FEC demands.

Renunciation of War Revisited

First there was a brief but highly significant reprise on article 9, the antiwar clause. As it stood after the Diet's amendment to the GS draft, it provided, in the first clause, that Japan would not maintain armed forces; in the second clause it renounced war and the threat or use of force. Ashida had remarked that the sequence of the clauses was "a matter of taste," but to him it made sense to clear the deck of armaments first, then build to the climax of renouncing war. Kanamori quietly, but with considerable intensity, disagreed, urging that the order be left as the GS draft had it. Members of the subcommittee now returned to this point. Suzuki preferred the original sequence. He recalled Kanamori's suggestion, that renouncing "forever" the right to wage war first, and only then promising not to maintain armed forces, had the effect of reserving the right to self-defense. Inukai shared Suzuki's (and Kanamori's) concern. He asked Satō whether Kanamori had meant to imply that the second clause, banning armaments, was more flexible than the first.[2] Satō did not know.

The ostensible purpose of Ashida's participial phrases modifying article 9 had been to make the renunciation of war more positive. Everyone agreed that was desirable. On the question of sequence, however, many seemed to feel the weight of Kanamori's preference, without ever saying exactly why. At this point Ashida, a skilled and experienced diplomat, offered an acute observation. Whether Japan eventually armed itself for self-defense or for participation in United Nations (UN) peacekeeping would be decided, he said, "not by the way the constitution is written, but by the extent of Japan's democratization and the international situation. Therefore, having the word 'forever' in the clause might be very important as a formal issue, but as a practical issue I don't think it makes very much difference."[3] Ashida's comment was deleted from the minutes made available to GHQ, not so much, perhaps, because it would have surprised or offended Kades or Whitney but because it seemed to drain some of the idealism out of Japan's renunciation of war.

In the end, the subcommittee voted to restore the cabinet's original sequence: renunciation of war first ("forever"), then the ban on armaments ("never"). Yoshida An spoke for several members when he said he was not sure exactly what was at stake, but if Kanamori thought his version might allow greater flexibility in the future, it should prevail.[4] Ashida persisted in the opinion that it was a "matter of taste,"[5] but he finally acquiesced in restoring the original.

On another matter, though, Ashida was less compliant. It concerned the negative term in the clause barring rearmament. We ought not to agree blindly "never" to maintain armed forces, said Ashida. Others on the subcommittee agreed; it was a "bitter pill." But how to amend it? Ashida thought it would be dangerous to try to amend the English version. Instead, the subcommittee adopted a phrasing in the Japanese version that said simply that armed forces would "not" be maintained. Ashida said the difference in meaning was not material, but it would help to ease Japanese sensibilities.[6]

Article 9 had two aspects: It renounced war and it banned armed forces. The Japanese people were quite ready for the former. About the latter, many were deeply ambivalent.[7] A poll taken in May 1946 by the *Mainichi Shinbun* showed 72 percent in favor of the renunciation of war in article 9. The poll also showed strong sentiment in favor of retaining Japan's right, and capacity, for self-defense. Diet members doubtless shared these views, but they also knew that MacArthur had his heart set on this article.[8] Many of them understood that it was an essential part of the bargain that was protecting Emperor Hirohito from the vengeance of his enemies, foreign and domestic. In any case, they had no choice. They accepted it, both clauses. At the same time, there is no doubt that Ashida served a broad constituency in finding language to put a more positive face on the article, stating it in the active voice, with Japan as the subject, and adding phrases that based the declaration on Japan's "sincere aspiration" for peace. Many of them also welcomed Kanamori's hint that the modifiers in the Japanese version might leave some wiggle room for self-defense and for Japan's eventual participation in UN peacekeeping.

How Much to Guarantee in the Bill of Rights

It was also during this period that arguments over the Social Democrats' proposal to add social guarantees to the bill of rights came to a head. Earlier the Social Democrats had wanted to add a whole set of specific guarantees. They now fell back to demanding that a single clause be added to article 25, asserting that "all people shall have the right to maintain the minimum standards of wholesome and cultured living." Ashida countered by suggesting that article 13 be amended instead, adding a right to a living to the familiar coupling of life, liberty, and the pursuit of happiness. To the Social Democrats, however, it seemed important to place the guarantee of social benefits alongside the right to social security, rather than among the general provisions at the beginning of chapter III.

The discussion of this issue was sometimes heated. Hara asked why social rights needed to be specified at all. It boils down, said Suzuki, to "whether our constitution should remain in the old form of the 19th century, or be framed after the new pattern, as adopted by various countries since the advent of the 20th century." He thought it was "very regrettable that . . . we will accept without objection anything written in the American Constitution, but nothing from the French, the Soviet, or the German [Weimar] Constitutions."[9] Hara proclaimed himself tired of Suzuki's lectures, provoking Suzuki to declare that "cooperation is impossible" with people who harbored such attitudes. The irenic Inukai stepped between the battlers to wonder if compromise might not be possible. Hatsukade suggested it was time for a vote[10] (which the conservative opposition would surely win), but the subcommittee adjourned for lunch before one could be taken. No more was heard during the subcommittee's deliberations about the Social Democratic amendment to article 25. Yet it was made part of the text sent forward to the revision committee, to the full house, and on to the emperor for promulgation. Thus, the subcommittee seems ultimately to have concurred that it belonged in their new, twentieth-century constitution.

Commitment to International Law

There were two remaining issues over article 98. As drafted, it made this constitution "and the laws and treaties made in pursuance thereto" the supreme law of the nation. First, the conservatives moved to strike out the quoted phrase. Agreeing, Ashida said that if all laws and treaties made prior to this constitution were rendered suspect and inferior, as they would be with the original language, some treaties (ones entered into in the future) would be "supreme law" but older ones would not. The language seemed awkward.[11]

The next day, Ashida returned to article 98. In removing the offending phrase, the subcommittee had deleted the only reference (apart from the preamble) to Japan's intention to abide by treaties and international law. Ashida reported that the Foreign Ministry wanted article 98 to include a commitment to observe international law.[12] Satō said it was unnecessary, but he had no objection to it.

Ashida thought it might help when Japan sought admission to the United Nations.

Kita took a stronger position. To him it was important—"at any cost"—that the constitution declare Japan's intention to respect treaties. The brief speech of this respected conservative thinker is worth quoting.

> Japan in the past violated anti-war agreements. . . . It was also obliged to withdraw from the League of Nations. . . . Japan as a sovereign power could withdraw from the League, but she called names at the League of Nations at that time, in spite of the fact that it had joined it willingly. These events paint the Japanese as if they lack the spirit of respecting international treaties. So if the existence of this spirit is represented . . . in this article, I think it will stand us in good stead when we shall join the United Nations in the future. Our people should enter into the comity of nations as a peaceful, moral and cosmopolitan people. . . . The renunciation of war alone is not enough to show Japan's positive decision to cooperate with other nations; and therefore, to enable Japan to escape from isolation, I hope that the proposed amendment can be realized.[13]

Suzuki followed with a similar call to signal a new spirit of international cooperation. "It has been a great fault of the Japanese people as well as the government in past generations not to have been strict about respecting treaties," he said. "I think it is very good to insert this provision.[14]

The Formation of Cabinets

The final meetings of the subcommittee also saw significant changes in the articles dealing with the makeup and recruitment of the cabinet. In the text submitted to the Diet on June 20, the executive had one distinctly American feature: The prime minister's choices for his cabinet would require the approval of the Diet. This was, of course, modeled on the requirement of senate approval of the president's choices of cabinet officers. It strengthened the legislature at the expense of the executive, though the president's unencumbered power of removal kept him in control and responsible, once the appointments cleared the senate.

The large parties on both right (Liberals, Progressives) and left (Social Democrats) liked the idea of requiring Diet approval, but the smaller conservative parties were wary. Hayashi pointed out that the Diet could remove the Prime Minister at any point, by withholding its confidence. This by itself would ensure ultimate Diet control over the government. Requiring Diet approval every time a vacancy developed would be cumbersome and costly.[15]

When Hayashi and Ōshima first raised this argument, on July 31, it was strongly rejected. Suzuki, noting that future ministers could be recruited from outside the Diet, argued that Diet confirmation would be especially important for these people. Ashida thought that eliminating Diet approval would give too much power to the prime minister. Sensing the prevailing opinion, Oshima withdrew his amendment (to eliminate Diet approval), but he warned that people would later regret this feature.[16]

There the matter rested until the meetings between GHQ and representatives of the Japanese cabinet in mid-August. On August 19, Ashida was abruptly summoned from a meeting of the subcommittee to confer with Shirasu, Irie, and Kanamori. They told him that GHQ had presented them with revisions of articles 66–68, which they hoped the subcommittee would quickly adopt.[17] The changes were as follows:

1. To stipulate (in article 66) that the prime minister and all other cabinet ministers must be "civilians";
2. To eliminate (from article 68) the provision for Diet approval of ministerial appointments; and
3. To insert (in articles 67 and 68) provisions that the prime minister and a majority of cabinet ministers must be chosen from among the members of the Diet.[18]

These demands had come from the FEC,[19] where preferences for the British model were prevalent and suspicions of resurgent Japanese militarism died hard. MacArthur hesitated to impose these new demands at this late date. It spoiled the image he was trying to cultivate, of permitting maximum freedom to the Japanese to fashion their own revision. The imposition in this case was particularly galling, inasmuch as spokesmen for the leading parties—Liberals and Progressives, and even Social Democrats—had defended the existing provisions just two weeks earlier.

Of the changes SCAP was now demanding, the most controversial was the first. Hayashi had already proposed the second. Though the leaders of the three large parties thought it would trammel the executive, they recognized that there was strong precedent—in the United Kingdom, "Mother of Parliaments"—for entrusting the makeup of the government to the prime minister and then holding him accountable for it. Article 66 made the cabinet "collectively responsible to the Diet" for the executive. That, plus the provisions for dissolution, was enough to ensure accountability.

As for the proviso that the prime minister and cabinet be chosen from the Diet, Ashida pointed out that the American example, where service in the government was incompatible with membership of Congress, was not apposite. He also dryly observed that the current prime minister would have to get himself elected (Yoshida was not a Diet member). Inukai called attention to the important contribution currently made by Wada, the welfare minister, who was not a member of the Diet. He called Wada a useful "refrigerant" in a cabinet of hot-blooded conservatives.

In the end, the changes demanded by the FEC were accepted without much dissent. The item that stuck in their throats was the first, the demand that all ministers be "civilian." Kanamori admitted it made little sense, in light of article 9, prohibiting the maintenance of armed forces. But he had been given to understand that there was no choice on this issue. (Some members of the FEC had insisted on it.) He pleaded with subcommittee members to treat this matter with discretion, especially in commenting to journalists, because GHQ was sensitive and could be volatile in reacting to press reports.[20] Inukai asked whether the ban would apply to ex-infantrymen, men who had not graduated from military academies. Satō admitted that it would be hard to define legally. He added that GHQ, soldiers themselves after all, agreed that the proposed insertion was unreasonable; they would surely allow the Japanese to set the regulations and definitions. A further difficulty was that there was no good term in Japanese for "civilian." Did it mean someone who had never served in the military, or one who no longer served? Ashida and Suzuki pointed out that many distinguished statesmen in the United States and Great Britain came from military backgrounds.

In the end, despite Kanamori's report that the FEC demanded language requiring that ministers be "civilians," the subcommittee omitted it from the draft submitted to the full committee and to the House.[21] It was not added until later, in the House of Peers.

With these amendments, the contours of the executive were set. It would follow the British model of cabinet government very closely. The anomaly of requiring confirmation of ministerial appointments by the Diet was eliminated, strengthening the hand of the chief executive. The constitution still referred to the Diet as the "highest organ of state power," but these eleventh-hour changes ensured that the prime minister, with a strong hand in the makeup of the cabinet, would have the constitutional tools needed to give Japan firm executive leadership, as required by modern government.

Final Maneuvers in the Revision Committee

The subcommittee completed its work on August 20. For nearly a month, in close consultation with party leaders, members had hammered out the language of several significant amendments. They were presented to the revision committee on Wednesday morning, August 21. The committee's concluding session began with a carefully choreographed pas de deux between Ashida and Kanamori explaining the settlement on imperial property. The principal declarations were that "the property owned by the emperor as a purely private person is deemed entirely outside the purview of Article 88," and that, "even after the imperial property is transferred to the state, it is deemed natural that the emperor shall use as his right, so to speak, the property closely and inseparably related to his official position."[22]

Ashida then introduced the subcommittee's work. Commenting first on the preamble, he acknowledged that, as it was "drafted in haste," its rhetoric was "spoiled by many unpolished phrases and difficult passages." The subcommittee had tried hard to agree on a thorough revision of it. However, "in view of the situation at home and abroad, which necessitates enactment of the bill as soon as possible," he said, "we gave up . . . and contented ourselves with a minimum of modifications in respect to the phraseology." He hoped members of the full committee would understand the awkward position they were placed in.[23]

As for article 9, he explained that the subcommittee's insertion of phrases at the beginning of both clauses was "to clarify that our determination to renounce war and discard armaments is actuated solely by our sincere desire for the amicable cooperation of mankind and for world peace." As amended, the article would "proclaim to the world" that the Japanese people, "fervently endeavoring to create a peaceful world based on justice and order," had decided to take this risky initiative.[24]

After completing his survey of the other principal amendments, Ashida introduced a "rider" that the subcommittee hoped the committee would adopt. It renewed its call on the government to present bills as soon as possible on the imperial household, the cabinet, and the makeup of the House of Councillors (the subcommittee hoped that a way could be found to recruit "men of learning and experience" to the upper house). It also called on the government to establish, as soon as possible, "facilities and institutions" capable of redeeming the constitution's promise of a decent living for all the people. Finally, it called on the government to "forge ahead with vigor and enthusiasm for the reconstruction of the fatherland and for the completion of its independence."

Before the final vote, this concluding session of the revision committee was the occasion for two loud complaints and a minority report. Kitaura demanded to know why the subcommittee's meetings had been closed. Why were members of the full committee excluded? The reason, said Ashida, was to expedite the process. Subcommittee members were in constant contact with their parties' caucuses. There were no secrets about what was going on. Kitaura said he was satisfied with the explanation.[25] Nosaka protested the exclusion of the Communist Party from the process. Ashida responded that their numbers in the full House did not warrant representation on the subcommittee. He added dryly that the subcommittee was well aware of the recommendations of the Communists from newspaper accounts.[26]

At this point, the Social Democrats were permitted to present to the full committee a set of amendments already disapproved by the subcommittee. They fared no better here. After brief statements in opposition by representatives of the other parties (including the Communists, who favored some of the Social Democrats, but not others), the proposals were rejected by a standing vote. The way was cleared for a vote on the text as amended by the subcommittee, plus the rider. They both passed, by an (uncounted) standing vote.[27]

On August 24, the amended bill for a new constitution finally came before the House of Representatives for debate and a recorded vote. The political dynamic surrounding the revision had changed dramatically since June. No longer were conservative politicians grudging and smoldering with resentment. Now they were champions of the government's project, and their advocacy was virtually unqualified. Now it was the left's turn to express serious reservations. The Communists opposed it, root and branch.[28] As for the Social Democrats, one leading member (Kikuchi Yōnosuke) went so far as to warn that unless the Socialists' amendments were accepted (they were not), the imperial institution might again become a "hotbed" of militarists, bureaucrats, plutocrats, and assorted sappers and parasites.[29]

A Time for Eloquence

The day of the final vote in the House of Representatives (Saturday, August 24) was an opportunity for eloquence, and it was not lost. Inukai called the revision a "masterpiece." He particularly saluted chapter III, the bill of "rights and duties."

> Especially, we members of the House, quite unlike the executive officials, have inherited the will of many of our predecessors who bequeathed to us a precious heritage of the vindication of the idea of the people's right, and as a result, some of us were subjected to intimidations and cross-examinations by the military as well as judicial authorities concerning the trend of our thoughts. [*Cheers!*] Some of us here present, and that not a few in number, suffered the indignity of imprisonment and actually experienced ourselves the inquiry of the court. Especially the declaration vindicating the human rights in Chapter III comes to us all, to everybody, as a revelation of a long-cherished hope finally fulfilled. [*Cheers!*][30]

He added that their predecessors in the Diet (including his father, the martyred prewar prime minister) would have been particularly pleased with the provision requiring that prime ministers be chosen from the Diet.[31]

On the left, Katayama, the Socialist who would soon be prime minister, called the revision idealistic and forward-looking, though not utopian, and remarked that, just as the Germans sought inspiration from the spirit of Kant and Goethe, the Japanese would be carried forward by this practical charter of liberty.[32] Ozaki Yukio, the great populist patriarch, now 87 years old, bestowed his blessing. Saying that the "democratic regeneration" embodied in this charter would prove more important for Japan in the long run than the Meiji Restoration, he pronounced the charter, despite infelicities in phraseology, "a far better instrument" than the one it would replace.[33]

Ashida, concluding his service as leader of the revision effort in the Diet, also invoked the Meiji Restoration at the final meeting of the committee on revision. Recalling the proclamation of the Charter Oath in 1868 at the dawn of the Meiji era, he said it had inaugurated "the era of modern democracy" in Japan. The Imperial Constitution of 1889, "simple and bold in phraseology, vast and concise in content," had launched Japan on the road to modernization and integration into the world culture. Had it been faithfully implemented, Japan might have developed into a full-fledged constitutional democracy on its terms. Instead, he said, "misguided fellows, blind to the trends of the world," perverted the use of it, "driving our beloved fatherland and brethren into its present predicament." In the grip of "profound emotions," he said that members now found themselves "on the brink of taking eternal leave of the Meiji Constitution."

> Owing to a defeat in war unprecedented in history, by far the greater part of the capital has been laid in ashes, and today the tearful eyes of widows and orphans, running into tens of thousands in number, are scarcely dry.

At this juncture, how can we give them a ray of hope? How can we attain the establishment of a peaceful, democratic and responsible government in Japan, as mentioned by the United States in its statement of postwar policy toward Japan? Nobody doubts that all this can be attained only through the enactment of a democratic constitution and through the advancement of the people's culture and civilization as the background for the new constitution. [*Cheers.*]

Calling the new constitution a "great canon of epochal importance," he said it had two aspects.

One is the realistic or organizational phase, as represented by an attempt to eliminate all feudalistic hangovers from the national structure of this country in order to establish parliamentary, cabinet and judicial systems of a really democratic character. The other is the phase covering idealistic elements in regard to our future international life, as revealed in the expression of a will to respect fundamental human rights within the land and to bring about peaceful cooperation with foreign countries, so as to obtain an honored position in the international society.[34]

The "greatest characteristic of the new constitution," he concluded, was that it proclaims, boldly and straightforwardly, the renunciation of war. "This is the very thing hankered after by all who have experienced this bloody war, victimizing tens of millions of human lives. It also constitutes the road to world peace. Under the banner of this ideal, we are going forth to make a call to the whole world. . . . God be praised for this opportunity given to the Japanese people. [*Cheers.*]"[35]

No one—certainly not Ashida—thought the revision was perfect. Twice he called attention to infelicities, particularly in the preamble.[36] Yet even here, the governing parties found mitigating circumstances. Inukai, greatly admired by his fellow framers for his literary style, noted that the awkwardness of the preamble was traceable in part to the immaturity of the colloquial style, particularly for use in formal, legal writing.[37]

Social Democrats Make a Final Push for Amendments

The misgivings of the Social Democrats gained expression as they presented their amendments one last time at this final session of the committee on revision.[38] Most of these ideas had been presented seriatim in the course of the committee and subcommittee deliberations. For this final push for amendment, they were assembled into a package. In presenting them to the plenary session on August 24, Hara Hyōnosuke claimed that the draft prepared by the subcommittee on revision already included "80 percent" of the Social Democrats' proposed changes in the government draft—including such fundamental improvements as more direct wording in the preamble and in article 1, of the commitment to popular sovereignty, and new language in article 25 securing the right to "minimum standards of wholesome and cultured living."[39] Now, citing strong support from editorialists and radio commentators, he urged the House to heed popular sentiment and perfect its work by adopting certain remaining fundamental items.

The two most important of the Socialist proposals aimed at underlining popular sovereignty and reducing the governmental role of the emperor. The Socialists fervently wanted a new chapter at the beginning of the constitution, asserting that all governmental authority arises from and rests on the sovereign will of the people. To them, it was anomalous that popular sovereignty gained expression in a chapter devoted to the emperor, in an article declaring that he was the "symbol of the state and of the unity of the people." Popular sovereignty deserved a separate chapter and article, at the threshold of the constitution. A twin proposal would have amended article 7 (vesting in the emperor certain "acts in matters of state," to be performed "with the advice and approval of the cabinet") by deleting the first four items from the list: those relating to the promulgation of constitutional amendments, laws, cabinet orders, and treaties; convocation of the Diet; dissolution of the House of Representatives; and calling general elections. These items would have been removed to article 73, where the powers of the cabinet was listed. Article 7 as currently drafted, the Socialists insisted, was full of mischief. Japan's recent calamities had come about through the exercise of power by shadowy elites, hiding in the folds of the emperor's garments. Japan's new constitution should eliminate any possibility of a repetition.[40] Other items in this final Socialist proposal called for a right to public financing of higher education for qualified poor people, an assertion (in article 29, on property rights) of the primacy of the public welfare, and the inclusion of "exploitation and poverty" in the preamble's list of evils to be eliminated by the new constitutional order.[41]

Kitaura Keitarō—60-year-old lawyer and publisher, vice minister of justice in Yoshida's cabinet, the man who had, the day before, expressed the Liberals' outrage at the sacking of Speaker Higai—was the man chosen to respond to the Socialist demand for these amendments. He began by acknowledging their contributions to the drafting process. He noted with appreciation the differences between their approach and that of the Communists. But there was too much "democratic rationalism" in these proposals, too much mimicry of the Weimar and French constitutions. They were too academic, too verbose and fussy. He recalled that the Socialists had backed the idea of involving the emperor in the appointment of the chief judge of the supreme court. It was inconsistent for them now to object to the emperor, with the advice and consent of the cabinet, performing certain other high acts of state. He was sure, he said, that when Katayama's time came to serve as prime minister (a remarkable prophecy, as it turned out), the Socialist leader would be pleased to receive his call from the emperor.[42]

The Socialist effort to set bounds on the emperor reminded Kitaura of the proposal to put huge lightning rods on the five-storied pagoda in his native city of Nara. The remedy was disproportionate, ugly, and unnecessary. The pagoda had already survived centuries of lightning. His friends were acting like "nervous college professors." All across the world, along the Danube River, in China, people were choosing. Would they side with communism or freedom? For Japan, the *tennō* system was part of that choice. He urged the Diet to reject the Socialists' proposed amendments. With that done, he hoped the Socialists would join in affirming Japan's new constitutional order.[43]

Despite Kikuchi's anguished cry, that allowing the emperor to perform state functions sowed seeds of trouble for the future, it was clear that support was lacking to carry the Socialists' proposals. A vote was taken, and the amendments soundly defeated.

At last the house turned to the decision on the final draft. There were lingering signs of irritation. Ashida remarked that it seemed odd to many Japanese that the emperor, alone among property owners, would be expropriated and forbidden to keep any income from his hereditary estates. Despite the precise explanation of terms thoroughly favorable to the emperor and imperial family, on August 21 during the concluding session of the revision committee, Ashida now indulged himself in yet another tortured summary of the revised article 88.[44]

Inukai, however, put a more positive face on the settlement. He said he was "profoundly moved" to hear that the emperor has set his mind on an "exceedingly simple life." Our fear had been that the emperor's personal properties would revert to the national treasury. This, he said, "would have been indisputably irrational." However, we now had assurances that the emperor's private properties would be "distinctly and rationally separated" from those going to the state. The emperor's private properties would not fall within the scope of this law. Further, it was now clear that the emperor would retain use even of the properties of the imperial household being turned over to the state if they were deemed inseparable from his position as symbol of the state. The emperor's expenses as symbol of the state would be included in the national budget, submitted to the Diet for decision. Inukai concluded by expressing the hope that the Diet, in making decisions about the imperial family's budget, would take an attitude, "both calm and immaculate," to show to the world our nation's broad and profound sentiment. Inukai's speech was repeatedly interrupted by cheers.[45] His calm words articulated an understanding that enabled the House of Representatives to accept this agitated part of the draft.

Kita uttered another cautionary note. Article 97, he thought, sounded a bit sour in Japanese ears in asserting that the fundamental human rights guaranteed by this constitution "result from the age-old struggle of man to be free." It made this affirmation sound, he said, like the experience of "some other country." During the late war, he said, Japan almost died from suffocation under the stern control of bureaucratic and militaristic cliques. Thus, "the present freedom is not obtained as a result of the long years of our toiling, but is given as a result of the defeat."[46] "We may better maintain it as a common heritage of human beings, though not without feeling a bit ashamed. Our contribution has been almost nothing, but with a view to giving lessons to ourselves, we have decided to accept the provision."

He had similar feelings about article 98. In earlier times, he said, "the Japanese people were known as scrupulous observers of international treaties." However, since the Manchurian incident, "it has become a habit of Japan to break treaties."

Japan violated, one after another, the Nine Power Treaty respecting Chinese territory and sovereignty, the antiwar pact renouncing war as a means of settling international disputes, and others. Therefore, it was quite natural to introduce into the constitution a promise to observe international treaties, to underline Japan's desire to live in a peaceful world society, and its determination to regain the world's confidence. Though he regretted the circumstances that made it necessary, it had his full support.[47]

But these indications of regret over the revision were the exception on this day of affirmation. More characteristic was Ashida's proud comment that Japan would henceforth have "a parliamentary cabinet system on the British pattern." The Potsdam Declaration, he said, had promised that "the ultimate form of the government of Japan would be determined by the freely expressed will of the people." This was the essence of democratic government. Pursuant to this ideal, article 41 made the Diet "the highest organ of state power." This was a "striking advance compared with the provisions of the current constitution."[48] He noted that the power of the supreme court to prohibit the implementation of unconstitutional legislation qualified the Diet's power, but "common sense" revealed that the power of the Diet, as the most direct representative of the people's will, would be controlling in the new regime.

They were proudest, however, of article 9, the renunciation of war and armed forces. As originally drafted, Kita said that it sounded like a convict's confession. Inukai had found it negative and spiritless. As revised by the subcommittee, however, it expressed a heartfelt commitment and uttered a brilliant call to other nations to follow Japan's lead toward world peace. It had not been dictated to a reluctant nation, said Katayama; it welled up from the deepest reaches of the Japanese soul. It was "adventurous" and unprecedented. Other nations (Ashida mentioned Brazil and France) had outlawed war, but none had taken the additional step of banning armed forces. This was fateful; it marked Japan as unique in its commitment to world peace. Hayashi said that the peace and survival of the world in the age of atomic weapons depended on the success of this historic initiative. (Incidentally, there was no hint, in comments on article 9 during these concluding debates, that the subcommittee's amendments were intended to open a door toward rearmament, or even national self-defense. On the contrary, their purpose as represented here was to underline the commitment to pacifism and put a positive face on it. That was emphatically the intent of these framers.)

Finally it was time for the vote. On a preliminary standing count, there were seven nays. Then came the final vote, a ballot where casting a white one meant "aye," blue for "nay." The record listed 421 members casting white ballots; 8, including all 5 of the Communists, cast blue ones.[49]

At this point, Yoshida rose to speak for the first time on this historic day. Taciturn to the end, the prime minister's comments were stunningly flat. They can be quoted in full:

The draft of the revised constitution has been approved just now in this House of Representatives. Representing the government, I should like to make a few words of address. The sincere and steady efforts rendered by the gentlemen of the House of Representatives in the deliberation on the draft constitution in the plenary sessions and the committee meetings, since it was introduced into this House on June 25th, command my heartfelt respect. Needless to say, the present draft was drawn up with a view to laying a foundation for the construction of new Japan and to taking the lead in establishing world peace. I am confident, and it gives me great pleasure to see, that the speeches made today by the members of this House in support of the present draft will echo in and out of the country as representing the general will of the people and will make still clearer the significance and character of the draft of the New Constitution. Although there still remain some procedures before the present draft comes into being, I beg to express herewith our deep gratitude towards you gentlemen's untiring efforts.[50]

That was it. Was he elated or merely stoical? Was his endorsement deliberately tepid? Did he think the occasion unworthy of rhetorical razzle-dazzle? Or did he prefer to let others spin the verbal garlands? It was impossible to tell.

With that, the House of Representatives sent the draft off to the House of Peers. Yoshida's reference to "some procedures" necessary before the draft could come into being indicated his impatience—widely shared—to get on with it. Meanwhile, the press was full of warnings that the lame-duck Peers must not attempt to modify the text or delay its promulgation unduly.[51] Clearly, the government, with strong support from the House of Representatives, was ready to set Japan on this foundation.

19 . . . .

"Last Service to the Fatherland"

- ## THE HOUSE OF PEERS ADDRESSES

- ## CONSTITUTIONAL REVISION

- For the sake of legal continuity and to keep control in the hands of the Yoshida cabinet, SCAP and the Japanese government had agreed
- to treat constitutional revision as a matter of "revising" the Meiji constitution. The procedure for amending the Meiji constitution
- was outlined in article LXXIII. It provided that the emperor must initiate any proposed "amendments." Amendments would be
- adopted on approval by two-thirds of the Diet.

-

The Peers Must Act

-

The emperor's initiative, under the conditions of 1946, was fairly easy to arrange. The Diet's assent was another matter. The Diet consisted of two houses, the democratically elected House of Representatives and the aristocratic House of Peers, a body modeled on the British House of Lords. The lower house had accepted a new constitution that would, among other things, end the peerage and abolish the House of Peers. The revision, now put before the House of Peers, called on that body to commit institutional suicide.

The problem was compounded by the Potsdam Declaration, requiring that Japan's governance be established in accordance with the will of the people. The Occupation and the Japanese cabinet had agreed to accept the House of Representatives as surrogates for the Japanese people, acting on their behalf.[1] The House of Peers, however, was in no meaningful sense a democratic body.

Thus, the role of the House of Peers in the revision process was problematic. By the terms of article LXXIII, the Diet's upper chamber under the old regime must be given an opportunity to deliberate on this legislation and, if it chose, to pass amendments to it.[2] On the other hand, as an aristocratic body, the House of Peers did not dare attempt to thwart or frustrate the government's decision (not to mention SCAP's demand) to adopt this democratic constitution. The prime minister[3] and the Supreme Commander[4] both indicated that they expected consideration by the House of Peers to be perfunctory and inconsequential. Meanwhile, Japanese editorial writers reminded the Peers that the nation would not tolerate any attempt by them to tinker with the text adopted by the House of Representatives.[5] Leading members of the House of Peers indicated they had gotten the impression that they were not to alter the text passed by the House of Representatives in any material way.[6]

In light of these reinforcing expectations, what is the significance of the House of Peers' deliberations, protracted through the entire month of September 1946? First, they had the potential for disaster—and they came close, two or three times, to realizing it. What if the Peers flatly refused to affirm the new constitution? Admittedly, to withhold assent would have been a reckless act for any responsible Japanese organ of government. But what if they gave the appearance of only begrudging acceptance, or of being coerced? These were proud men (no women), most of them elderly, with reputations for integrity and deeply ingrained habits of independence. They were highly respected members of Japan's civilian elite[7]: scholars and educational administrators of the first rank, distinguished former public servants, men of considerable wealth. If they openly refused their consent, the project—perhaps not the revision of the constitution per se but the establishment of a firm foundation for Japan's transformation into a constitutional democracy—might have been strangled in its crib.

Preview of the Process

The revision project remained in the House of Peers for over a month. Consideration began on Monday, August 26. For a week, through five plenary sessions, peers presented speeches, many of them impressively learned. The text was then referred to an ad hoc committee for detailed examination. On Saturday, August 31, a so-called special committee convened for the first time. It met twenty-three times, through Saturday, September 28, then created a subcommittee that met behind closed doors[8] four times, through Tuesday, October 2. The revisions prepared by the subcommittee were sent back to the special committee, which debated them on Thursday, October 3. At the end of the day, it accepted them by a standing majority vote.[9]

The full House of Peers received the report of the special committee and debated the matter for two more days (Saturday and Sunday, October 5 and 6). On Sunday afternoon, October 6, the House of Peers passed the revised constitution by a standing vote, recognized by Speaker Tokugawa Iemasa as greater than the necessary two-thirds in the affirmative.[10]

Peers Consider Their Role

Traditionally the House of Peers had served as a typical second chamber, tempering, slowing, forcing politicians in the cabinet and lower House to take second thoughts. On August 30, Akita San'ichi, addressing his fellow peers, offered a sketch of occasions when the House of Peers had played a decisive role in Japan's governance over the previous 50 years. He counted four times when the House of Peers had "exercised powerful restraint" on the system. In 1900, it blocked a tax bill to defray expenses incurred in Japan's intervention in the Boxer uprising. In 1913, it "severely rebuked the cabinet for the Siemens Affair," demanding a "clean-up of navy circles," and blocked expenditures for new naval construction, causing the collapse of the Yamamoto cabinet. In 1920, "on a question of official discipline and public morals," it impeached an education minister for duplicity, against the majority vote of the lower House exonerating him. And in 1929, it passed an impeaching resolution on steps taken by Prime Minister Tanaka "in connection with the invocation of a gracious imperial message."[11]

Akita further contended that throughout the recent great war, the House of Peers had been a voice of prudence. "Having many men of scholastic achievement and authority in various scientific fields among its members, . . . alive to the trends of international affairs and the limits of the real strength of this country," many members of the House of Peers had been "opposed to commencing hostilities" and strongly favorable toward a "speedy settlement of the Sino-Japanese Incident." They entertained "extremely unpleasant feelings against the militarists meddling in politics and warned them on occasions." Had it not been for "undue pressure" from the militarists and the suppression of freedom of speech, the "pacifist view" of the House of Peers might have "carried the day and nipped the war in the bud." The House of Representatives, composed "entirely" of "members recommended by the government-sponsored party," in full cooperation with the military authorities, "stirred up the national fighting spirit to the highest pitch, by adopting a resolution for a death-defying struggle by one hundred million people."

After the emperor's declaration of war, the upper house cooperated "wholeheartedly" in voting the necessary appropriations, but on "noticing" the lack of military strength, individual members of the House of Peers "discussed in private how to seize the earliest opportunity to lay down arms." Though 180 members of the House of Peers had now been purged for the positions they held during the war effort, it was Akita's "unbiased opinion" that they were "most pacific and farsighted" men. In light of this history, he concluded, it was a "pity" that this House now had to be abolished.[12]

Akita doubtless spoke the mind of many of his fellow peers in this assessment. The general public mood, however, was probably better reflected in the House of Representatives' decision to amend the draft by ending not only the House of Peers but peerage itself, immediately on the institution of the new constitutional system in May 1947.

Despite these awkward facts, everyone agreed to pause in the rush toward ratification while the House of Peers conducted its solemn review. The peers for their part took this responsibility seriously. This would be their "last service to the fatherland," said Nanbara Shigeru; it was a "mission of grave importance."[13] It would help to determine whether Japan could "liquidate" its immediate past and rise again, perfected, from the ashes of war and defeat.

Two Speeches, Two Themes

Two speeches—one pro and one con—laid out the principal themes of the debate in the House of Peers. Takayanagi Kenzō was the first to speak on Monday morning, August 26, 1946. Fifty-nine years old, professor of English law at Tokyo Imperial University since 1921 and frequently a lecturer on law at leading universities in the United States and Europe, he spoke with quiet authority on the whole range of constitutional studies.[14]

He began by setting the historical context, and he did not mince words. The revision project arose, he said, "in fulfillment of our international obligations to execute the terms of the Potsdam Declaration." But that was not all. Behind the revision bill stood the "blood and tears shed by Japanese and foreign nationals, not alone in the Far East, but in different parts of the world from the outbreak of the China Affair up to the end of the Pacific War." Further, there lay "deep-felt demands for freedom, even if not loudly proclaimed, on the part of the Japanese people, who had to submit for some years to the political and economic oppression of militarists and bureaucrats." Thus the new constitution, which would "determine the direction of our national life in all its main spheres," was "at once a product of the past and a charter for the future."[15]

Takayanagi acknowledged that the revision looked and sounded strange to many Japanese minds. That was partly because it was based not on continental European traditions of civil law, as the Meiji system had been, but on "Anglo-American legislative techniques."[16] But he reminded his fellow peers that the Meiji constitution had also seemed strange when first introduced. It too represented a marked shift, from Chinese traditions to Prussian, and it had taken some getting used to.[17]

At the same time, he pointed out, many of the distinguishing features of the draft—even article 9—had roots in Japanese tradition. "The late Uchimura Kanzō once said that if he were Prime Minister, he would set an example to the world by carrying out the total disarmament of Japan."[18] As for chapter III (the bill of rights), it was misleading to say, as some commentators had, that it was a mere replica of America's eighteenth-century bill. Much of its phrasing was indeed "individualistic in a high degree." When one took into account such features as the invocation of the "public welfare" in article 13, it was clear that chapter III represented a halfway house between capitalism and socialism. Articles 25 to 28 contained additional clear concessions to socialistic ideas. As presently drafted, chapter III reflected the American Bill of Rights as modified by twentieth-century judicial interpretation.[19]

Takayanagi did have some concern for the future. Democracy, he said, was a relativistic faith. Unlike communism and fascism, unlike the teachings of Plato, Confucius, and St. Augustine, democracy was rooted in skepticism and tolerance. It flourished best in cultures that were empirical and inductive and allowed law to accumulate and evolve. Japan had only recently emerged from feudalism and had until recently been heavily dependent on imperial rescripts as a source of law. Its people were law-abiding and its culture authoritarian. Dissent was suppressed, not encouraged and supported. These traits were not conducive to democracy, Takayanagi said. If constitutional democracy were to flourish in Japan, "the traditional morality of the Japanese people needs fundamental reconstruction."[20] He therefore believed that it would take a strenuous campaign of education to build a culture of democracy in Japan. Despite these qualms, Takayanagi believed that the draft laid out a "sound policy" for reconstructing Japan on peaceful and democratic foundations. He thought it deserved to be supported.

If Takayanagi's magisterial words heartened the supporters of the cabinet's project, the mood did not last long. The next speaker, on Monday afternoon, was Sawada Ushimaro, a 72-year-old former instructor in the police academy and bureaucrat in the army and home ministries. He had served before the war as an appointed governor in several prefectures. A member of the House of Peers since 1939, he would soon be purged from political life, presumably for his activities before and during the war. He was a blunt-spoken, tough old man who expressed, with passion and candor, the views of those who abhorred the entire revision project.

He had felt the cabinet's pressure to rubber-stamp the revision, but he refused, he said, to be rushed. He spoke harshly of Prime Minister Yoshida, who had declared with satisfaction, as the House of Representatives concluded its deliberations, that only "some procedures" remained.[21] He agreed with the distinguished constitutional scholar Minobe, that it would have been far better first to amend article LXXIII before altering the nation's foundations. The whole project, he thought, was wrong-headed.[22] The mistakes that led to the disastrous war lay not with the Meiji Constitution but with the emperor's advisers. He was "dazed" when he first read the proposed revision. The preachy tone—he cited articles 12, 13, and 99, especially—made the Japanese people sound like "South Sea Islanders," incapable of determining for themselves what the situation required. He noted rumors that it had been drafted in two nights of work. The "inexpertness" of the draft's language, its "ambiguous," "careless," "queer" provisions, lent credence to such charges and heightened Japan's humiliation. Virtually every article of the proposed revision contained errors. He called on the government to withdraw this doomed project and start over, drawing this time on the skills and spirit of experienced people in Japan to consider whether constitutional amendments were truly in order.[23]

Kanamori, responding for the cabinet, treated Sawada's blast with elaborate respect, lauding him for "sincere patriotism." Commenting on Sawada's sense that the project had been put together "hastily," Kanamori admitted that it looked that way. In the wake of Japan's surrender, most Japanese had not regarded constitutional revision as a priority. Soon, however, the attitude of what he called the "intelligentsia" began to change. Although the Meiji system had been worthy of "our sincere adoration," it had produced "deplorable" results. The emperor's prerogatives had many merits, facilitating the adjustment and integration of the branches of government and providing a means to correct a mistaken course, there had been far too much secrecy, giving opportunity for cabals to betray the national interest. As knowledgeable people reflected on this experience, they saw a need for "fundamental reconstruction of our national Constitution." Thus the impulse for revision came not only from the Potsdam Declaration but for "internal reasons," as well.[24]

Measured Support

Following these two bold opening shots, several other Peers made statements, most of them offering carefully measured support of the project. Itakura Takuzō was newly appointed to the upper house. A former journalist and professor of international law, he had during the 1920s called for the reduction of military forces and incurred the wrath of the police by exposing the murder of a prominent anarchist by military police after the Tokyo earthquake of 1923. Itakura congratulated the cabinet and the House of Representatives for adapting monarchy to democracy. The revision would bring a "glorious revolution" to Japan (he was cheered when he said this). Indeed, if it were true, as some alleged, that the monarchy was still potentially a factor in British politics, the new constitution would move Japan further in a democratic direction.

Miyazawa Toshiyoshi spoke next. For several months he had been arguing that Japan's acceptance of the Potsdam Declaration had in itself constituted a revolution, inasmuch as it had committed Japan to a government based on the freely expressed will of the people. He repeated that argument here, adding that basing the revision on article LXXIII obscured the real situation.[25] Kanamori replied that Potsdam by itself did not establish popular sovereignty in Japan. (Presumably the people could choose to be governed by the emperor alone.) Only acceptance of a new constitution could bring democracy to Japan. Potsdam did not require that constitutional revision be submitted to the Diet; article LXXIII did. Because Japan's deepest principles (including national unity based on adoration of the emperor) had not changed, the use of article LXXIII was justified. By blending Potsdam and article LXXIII, Japan was laying a firm foundation for democratic governance.[26]

The second day opened with an address by Nanbara Shigeru, another newly appointed member of the House of Peers. As a young man, Nanbara had resigned from the home ministry when his superiors rejected his draft of a progressive labor union law. He had joined the law faculty of his alma mater, Tokyo Imperial University, studied in Europe and America between 1922 and 1925, and become a Christian. In March 1945, he had joined with Takagi Yasaka, Tanaka Kōtarō, now the education minister, and other colleagues in devising a plan to end the war. He had recently assumed the presidency of his university. Generally, Nanbara's speech reflected strong support for the revision draft. However, he took the government severely to task for its approach to the project. He called the work of constitutional revision a "touchstone to determine whether our fatherland can liquidate its errors ... after its defeat in war and rise once again on its own feet as a perfect independent State."[27] The grave importance of the task made it all the more deplorable that the government had moved so sluggishly in December and January to correct the errors of the past. Every signal during this period—the leaked report of the Matsumoto committee, the position papers of the major government parties—underlined the government's intention to preserve articles I–IV of the Meiji Constitution, the bedrock of the old order. Thus the nation reacted with shock to the publication in March of a "government bill" that amended the provisions on the emperor in fundamental ways. Yoshida, then foreign minister, attributed the surprising development to a "sudden change in international conditions," but were these circumstances not predictable, asked Nanbara. Why hadn't the cabinet at least started, during the fall of 1945, to raise inquiries in the Diet about constitutional revision?

As for GHQ, its honor too had suffered from the cabinet's clumsiness. Officers there had had to bear the onus of seeming to impose a draft on Japan; if the government had met its responsibilities in a timely fashion, this could have been avoided. This regrettable situation reached a climax at the end of June, said Nanbara, when General MacArthur called for "untrammeled debate," but Yoshida urged Diet members to keep foreign relations and the "actual position of Japan" in mind as they deliberated on whether or not to amend the government's draft. It appeared that SCAP approached constitutional revision in a more liberal spirit, more trustful of democracy. The work of constitutional revision offered Japan a "training in democracy"; invoking the so-called international situation as a "hiding place" had tended to stifle it.[28]

Peers on the Role of the Emperor

Despite its reputation as an elite body, out of touch with the masses, the House of Peers debate mirrored Japanese culture quite faithfully. This was especially true in the obsession with *kokutai*, the belief that Japan uniquely owed its national existence and culture to a shared adoration for the emperor. Attachment to the emperor was indeed an ancient sentiment in Japan, but it had reached a fevered pitch in the struggle against China and the Western powers. Now Japan had lost the war, and the Occupation was attempting to reverse this tide, to build a wall of separation between sentiment for the emperor and the business of government. It was a daunting task. *Kokutai* had a powerful sentimental appeal. Many Japanese people felt they had to do all in their power to defend *kokutai*; some went so far as to say that Japan should not agree to any revision that undermined *kokutai*, whatever the consequences, even if it meant a confrontation with the Occupation. Such an opinion was strongly held in Japan in 1946, and it had vigorous champions in the House of Peers.

Emotional voices insisted that chapter I of the Meiji Constitution, setting forth the emperor's sovereignty and resting his authority on ancient lineage and blood rather than popular consent, must be left undisturbed. *Kokutai*, said Sawada, along with the authority of the male heads of families, was a *sine qua non* of cohesion for Japanese society. The proposed revision, he thought, would eviscerate both.[29]

A calmer voice for tradition, though no less committed to derailing the revision if possible, was that of Sasaki Sōichi. Sasaki's position was poignant. A distinguished academic, he had served on the ill-fated Konoe Commission.[30] He was still not convinced that revision was necessary. Above all, it irritated him that this project had fallen into profane hands. Specifically concerning the importance of the emperor to the Japanese system, Sasaki noted that Hirohito had rescued him from persecution during the tumults of the early 1930s. He also recalled the emperor's role in ending the war. It was militarists who had led Japan into that disastrous conflict. Reducing the emperor to impotence would make Japan even more vulnerable to tumult and error. The revised constitution would create three separate branches, without anyone or anything capable of unifying them for constructive action. Political parties might perform that function, but parties carried terrible dangers of their own. In due course, Japan would have its own Hitler or Mussolini.[31]

Sawada's and Sasaki's arguments were not new. What was striking about the debate in the House of Peers was that answers came not just from Kanamori but from other peers. In fact, several leading peers strongly criticized the government for not being bold and radical in repudiating the errors of the past.

Asai Kiyoshi, one of the newly appointed peers, hoped the government would stop pretending that kokutai was left unchanged by this revision. He recalled Kanamori's attempt, in the House of Representatives, to insist that the term meant nothing more than "the people's yearning adoration for the Emperor," and that as such, it had not been disturbed by the revision. On the contrary, Asai noted, for the past two decades, kokutai had had a far more sinister meaning, one clearly stated in harshly enforced laws. The Peace Preservation Law of 1925 made it a crime to agitate against kokutai. In 1929, the Supreme Court of Japan offered an authoritative definition of the term: "The meaning of kokutai lies on the point that Japan shall be reigned over by a line of Emperors, unbroken for ages eternal, and the Emperor combines in himself and exercises the rights of sovereignty." Asai acknowledged that the Peace Preservation Law had been abolished since the war, but the conventional meaning of the word kokutai had surely not vanished with it. Japan had fought a war to the bitter end to uphold kokutai. Through this terrible ordeal, the people of Japan had not doubted its meaning. Now they were being told that its meaning had "altered in an instant," yet the government was insisting that somehow, deep down there had been no change. How, he asked, could the government, defending a text that designated the Diet as the "highest organ of state power" and vested in the supreme court the power to determine constitutionality of any act of government, claim that these provisions left kokutai unaffected?[32]

Nanbara, dean of the law faculty and president of Japan's leading university,[33] added some hard-hitting points to this indictment of the government's stance. Citing outlines for constitutional revision published by the "ruling parties" (Liberals and Progressive Democrats) in January and February,[34] Nanbara noted that they had clung to the notion that the emperor was "sovereign." No wonder the nation was shocked when the government blithely published a draft revision in March that rested on popular sovereignty, made the emperor a "symbol" of the state, and barred him from exercising "powers related to government." To pretend that such a draft faithfully preserved kokutai as commonly understood was ridiculous. It was pure "self-deception." Worse, it obscured the "revolution" currently transforming Japan. The government's connivance in the mystical notion that Japan's cohesion was somehow unique was untenable. No informed person believed it. Unless the government was more candid, it was courting a political explosion when future events revealed the truth.[35]

On the other hand, if it were admitted that *kokutai* had to be rejected, how was Japan to understand its new order? Would it evolve into a constitutional monarchy, or become a republic, or would it develop its own hybrid form? Here the peers offered divergent interpretations, reflecting divisions that sometimes surfaced even within the cabinet itself.

Itakura Takuzō, a crusading journalist and professor of international law, said it was time for Japan to admit that the new constitution would inaugurate a "sudden change." He called it a "glorious revolution." (This remark was cheered.) Japan would become a "republic in disguise," like Great Britain, according to Walter Bagehot. Some contended that in Britain the monarch had residual powers. If so, said Itakura, Japan's constitution would be superior because it would permit no such departure from true democracy.[36]

Nanbara returned to the question of the emperor's place in Japan's governance. It was a mistake, he argued, to see either the old emperor system or popular sovereignty as the only choices for Japan. If the government would give up its insistence that *kokutai* never changes and admit that it evolves "with the progress of the times," a form of democracy fit for Japan, its mentality, and traditions would develop naturally. Such a notion would have deep roots in Japan's experience and traditions, but it would not expose the emperor to the abuses of the recent past. He thought the ruling parties' manifestos on constitutional reform contained the kernel of a good idea, positing sovereignty in the state, with the people, not as individuals but as a collectivity, being the ultimate authority.

The draft's provision for three separated powers was "all to the good," but it left out an "organ to guarantee the unity of the state." It was imperative to "restrict" the emperor from the sole exercise of power. "All functions of the emperor concerning cares of state [should] require the advice and approval of the Diet, and the Cabinet [be] made responsible to the Diet, all along the lines of the present draft, thus establishing a form of parliamentary government." In such a system, there would be "no longer any room for despotism by a few men to intervene between the emperor and the people . . . absolutely no menace of war towards foreign countries and no danger at home of the freedom of man being trespassed upon in the name of the emperor." The emperor need not be reduced to a "mere symbol." He is "the manifestation of the will of the Japanese nation to unify itself . . . an organ of the state, an organ which guarantees the unity of the state." Nanbara concluded that "when such an emperor system and democracy are naturally combined without any contradiction to each other, it will be possible for democracy of a Japanese pattern to materialize." There was no reason that a new constitution amended in this way should not be "understood by the Allied Powers and the rest of the world."[37]

In calling for candid national repentance and reform, critics such as Nanbara, Sasaki, and Asai were quite blunt in reminding cabinet officers, particularly Kanamori, of their past efforts to explain and defend *kokutai*. Replying to a particularly nasty taunt along these lines from Asai, Kanamori said he was thoroughly weary of academic disputation about *kokutai*.[38] He repeated his insistence that *kokutai* had not changed, only our understanding of it. The people, he said, were now accepting the change. They knew that their adoration of the emperor was as strong as ever, and they accepted that he (the emperor) needed to be relieved of the twisted expectation that he must bear the burden of day-to-day, routine governance.[39]

The next day, answering further taunts by Sasaki, who may have envied Kanamori's prominent place in the revision project, Kanamori graciously and with evident sincerity admitted that in his prewar writings, he had been among the worst offenders in building support for a mistaken notion of *kokutai*. Sasaki asked whether Kanamori had "relinquished his old idea ... that the question of who exercises sovereign power decides the essential quality of the national character of the country." He admitted his error and said he deserved censure for changing his idea about *kokutai*. But he begged to clarify his error. He had not erred, he insisted, in saying that the Japanese people had always embraced the emperor in their midst as an object of loyalty. His error came in stating that on this account, the emperor should be recognized politically and juristically as the sovereign power, and that this recognition constituted the "national character of the country." He recalled a poem by Tsu Fu: "the river flows but pebbles remain." He had confused the pebbles with the river, he said. Many others made the same mistake. Since the war, the nation was wakening from these awful errors as from a bad dream.[40]

One other exchange during these opening debates in the House of Peers added nuance to the changing sense of the role of the emperor. Nanbara took Tanaka (minister of education, later chief justice of the supreme court) to task for an article he had written during the autumn of 1945, titled "In Defense of the Emperor." Did the minister, who now vigorously defended a text that barred the emperor from a meaningful role in government, repent of those earlier views? He did not, replied Tanaka. As a republic, Japan would quickly fall into anarchy, revolution, and despotism, like a Latin American country. The emperor was "essential" to Japan as a "symbol of the public order."[41]

This remark, from an unusually thoughtful, if distinctly conservative, politician, is worth bearing in mind when one considers the suggestion that the Occupation should have taken the opportunity presented in 1945–1946 to eliminate the emperor system entirely.[42] It is difficult, if not finally impossible, to gauge the resistance that would have met such an attempt. MacArthur estimated that it would require "a minimum of a million troops ... for an indefinite number of years" to stabilize and pacify Japan without the emperor.[43] He too was strongly biased in a conservative direction. What is remarkable, though, is how far Japan was willing to go toward constitutional democracy, as long as their emperor was not violated or subjected to unbearable indignities.

The Renunciation of War

Article 9 also drew fire during these opening debates in the House of Peers. Nanbara thought that the American press might be right in dismissing it as "merely utopian." Self-defense was the first and most basic human right, universally recognized, even in the U.N. charter. To renounce it smacked of the "quiet resignation peculiar to the Orient." The hope for the future lay in the establishment of a supranational force, under U.N. auspices, to keep the peace, but article 9 would make it impossible for Japan to contribute to peace-keeping operations.[44]

Shidehara replied by reciting a lengthy paraphrase of MacArthur's defense of article 9 in his grandiloquent speech to the Allied Council on April 5. Some people, MacArthur had contended, insisted that Japan "in a childish manner" was trusting its fate to a "dreamlike ideal." It was these people, however, who were indulging in fantasies, pretending that the world can live safely with weapons designed by modern science for the "annihilation of mankind." It was this kind of "irresponsible optimism," not Japan's courageous stand for peace, that constituted the gravest danger to civilization. Shidehara said that he was proud to have participated in drafting the renunciation of war.[45]

A few days later (August 31), Hayashi Raisaburō, a prewar chief justice of the supreme court and minister of justice, gave a long speech on what he called the "fighting instinct," which he called natural and the source of much good, as well as undoubted evil. Article 9 seemed to deny its existence. Was it not unrealistic and foolish for Japan to pretend that it could be effaced from human nature by a clause in one nation's constitution? Shidehara replied with some eloquence of his own, garnished with homely wisdom. "At the present day," he acknowledged, "we are marching alone in the wilderness of international relations with the large banner of war renunciation." But soon others would follow:

> When the first announcement was made of the draft Constitution, I expressed this conviction to a group of foreign correspondents assembled to see me on that day. I told them that these unstable conditions cannot last forever and that the discovery of the atomic bomb alone gave food for reflection to the war proponents, reminding them that such a state of things should not be allowed to continue. I told them that Japan was now leading a drastic peace movement with a huge banner held high in her hands, and that others will follow her example.

He added that there was also a practical reason for Japan to take this step.

> If war were renounced, there will be no need for armaments of any kind. If no armaments are needed, there will naturally be no need for expenses for armament that hitherto we have been spending. Considering in this light, we can say that our country in her peaceful activities has a great advantage over those nations who are consuming a major portion of their annual expenditures on unproductive armaments. In order to elevate the

national status of our country among nations, nothing is more keenly needed than the much-desired development of peace industries and the promotion of science and culture. I believe it is solely on these peaceful activities that Japan's future depends.[46]

Here, quite candidly expressed, was a decisive answer to the suspicion that Shidehara and Yoshida had taken leave of their senses in agreeing to article 9.

The Bill of Rights

The House of Peers also touched on chapter III, the bill of rights, during this preliminary survey. At times the conversation seemed like a seminar or workshop in the law faculty at Tokyo Imperial University. Takayanagi remarked that to implement this modern constitution, "the traditional morality of the Japanese people needs fundamental reconstruction." Two days later, Tanaka, the education minister, replied that some people "misinterpret" democracy and liberalism, contending that Japan's "good morals and good customs" are reactionary and feudalistic and incompatible with modern requirements. The government, said Tanaka, rejects this view, believing that certain fundamental principles of morality are universal and that many traditional Japanese customs are fully in accord with these values.[47]

Speakers generally agreed that the bill in the Japanese revision represented a creative bridging of nineteenth-century capitalist and twentieth-century socialist ideals. Nanbara noted that the Japanese bill reflected not so much the original American Bill of Rights as recent judicial adaptations thereof. Nevertheless, he thought it was still excessively individualistic. Japan's future lay with a planned economy and cooperative democracy, and that would require greater emphasis on communitarian values.[48] Kawai Yoshinari, the welfare minister, agreed. Democracy tended to awaken the individual; in the twentieth century, there was need to emphasize the common good.

This concern for the compatibility of a liberal bill of rights with Japanese mores found a flashpoint in article 24, with its stress on individual dignity and the essential equality of the sexes in matters pertaining to marriage and the family. Makino Eiichi, repeatedly invoking the "community of family members," asked why article 24 required the consent only of the couple and not other interested parties, like the family, in making a marriage. He also warned of the impact of article 24 on viable agriculture, if the laws based on article 24 required all children, regardless of their gender or the number of them, to be treated equally in distributing real property.[49] Kimura Tokutarō, the justice minister, said that such undesirable results could be avoided if families would work together, by mutual consent, to divide property equitably. Kimura defended article 24 for leading Japan beyond feudalism, but he insisted that it did not necessarily undermine ancestor worship, a mainstay of Japanese society.[50]

On August 30, the plenary session of the House of Peers completed its preliminary survey of the revision project and turned it over to an ad hoc committee for intensive examination.

20 . . . .

"A Borrowed Suit"

• PEERS ACCEPT THE INEVITABLE

On August 31, the "special committee," consisting of forty-five members, met for the first time, under the chairmanship of Abe Yoshishige. Its task was to examine the draft revision reported by the House of Representatives and to prepare amendments, if it thought any were needed. The committee would meet twenty-four times altogether, until October 3.[1]

Spirited Discussion

Discussions in the special committee were painstaking and marked by candor that was occasionally stunning. Members criticized one another, sometimes almost brutally, for the roles they had played before, during, and after the war. Kanamori was scolded, again, for prewar writings that skirted around the issue of the emperor's sovereignty. Sasaki was taken to task for his work with the Konoe Commission.[2] Shidehara and Yoshida were severely chided for their failure to take the initiative on constitutional revision, creating a situation that required SCAP to move in and take charge. Why, asked Sasaki bitterly, had the government failed to publish its proposed revisions in January? Yoshida replied that "the grandeur of the enterprise made it necessary to listen to the views from all quarters." That could not be finished until early March.[3]

In one particularly tense exchange on September 4, Nanbara called attention to the government's inconsistent answers when asked why it took so long to produce a draft. Shidehara had said that "internal investigations" convinced them that articles I through IV, on the emperor, would have to be rewritten, and doing that had proven enormously difficult. Prime Minister Yoshida stressed the "international situation." Which was it? asked Nanbara.

Shidehara responded that, out of consideration for the nation's harmony, he would not comment further on the process that led to the government's draft. Nanbara was not quieted. The foreign press had carried stories about the origins of this constitution, he pointed out. Young intellectuals, increasingly fluent in English, were reading these accounts. The government's lies were making them cynical, and that would have a "great bearing on the stability of the new Constitution."

Recognizing the dangers lurking in Nanbara's statement, Shidehara replied with the summer's strongest affirmation of the government's responsibility for constitutional revision. He too was aware, he said, that a foreign magazine was reporting that the revision "had been forced on us by some foreign country." Now Nanbara was contending that it was "undesirable" that people should be given such an impression. Indeed it was, said Shidehara. "But we have never stated such a thing." The revision project reflected the profound convictions of the government. "We have never been prevailed upon by any foreign country. ... We are not acting against our will by the compulsion of others." He pointed out that the House of Representatives had amended the text in a number of significant respects. These efforts, along with those of the House of Peers, would make the constitution thoroughly Japan's own.

Nanbara accepted Shidehara's statement at face value. He took the occasion to urge the government to embrace the new constitution with enthusiasm.

> When this draft constitution has been legislated, with firm determination on the part of the government, as well as the members of the House of Peers who have seconded it, to enforce it as our own constitution, they shall have to hold themselves responsible for it—especially the government, as it was drawn up by the government.

Some had hinted that the constitution, having been made under the occupation, might be revised as soon as the Allies left. Nanbara urged the government to repudiate such "indiscreet remarks" explicitly and forcefully.

> Whatever the circumstances may have been, when the constitution has been drawn up by the Japanese government and approved by the Diet, the responsibility rests upon Japan. Therefore, we must enforce the constitution as the constitution of Japan. In this respect, the government's responsibility is especially heavy. ... What I want to request from the government is enthusiasm for the foregoing matters.[4]

In truth, the work of September 1946 would go a long way toward determining whether Japan would take this constitution as its own. The House of Peers was an institution mounted on principles at odds with those underlying the new constitution, but it represented values that had deep roots in Japanese culture, and Japanese public opinion could not ignore the assessment of its distinguished membership. If this constitution failed to pass muster with these men, its legitimacy would be gravely compromised.

Kokutai and Sovereignty Revisited

To understand these deliberations, we must again try to appreciate what kokutai meant and why it mattered so much. Why did they devote so much precious time to debating whether the foundations of Japan's governance—everyone agreed that these foundations rested on feelings for the emperor—would change with the adoption of this constitution?

The issue came into the open early in the special committee's deliberations when Shimoyama Seiichi, a distinguished jurist, cited what he called the consensus among scholars that the traditional notion of *kokutai* was encapsulated in articles I through IV of the Meiji Constitution. Did not the revision of these articles change the concept? He asked three members of the cabinet present— Uehara, Saitō and Tanaka, all of them scholars as well as cabinet ministers—to comment on whether they thought *kokutai* would be altered by the adoption of the revised constitution. Uehara, an elderly state minister in the Yoshida cabinet, said that the revision would amount to a "revolution" in forms of government but not in Japan's commitment to monarchy. Even during the Tokugawa period (1600–1868), he said, the emperor's symbolic status as Japan's ruler had persisted. As a democracy, Japan would be more like Britain than the United States or the Soviet Union. Saitō noted that he had not spoken publicly on this point before, believing that the government should speak with one voice.

But now that he was asked point blank, he would have to admit that he demurred from the cabinet consensus: From a legal standpoint, there was no doubt that this revised constitution would transform *kokutai*. From ancient times until now, sovereign power rested with the emperor. Now it would shift to the people. Ethically, Kanamori was "not wrong" in insisting on continuity, but revision would bring a change in *kokutai*. Tanaka focused his remarks on the contention that such differences of opinion as this discussion revealed were to be expected, no disgrace and not a problem. Let scholars debate the issue. The government would not issue authoritative pronouncements.[5] Beliefs, even about fundamental matters, should be subject to discussion, debate, and decision by the nation.

The following morning, Matsumoto Gaku noted that newspapers overnight had highlighted disarray in the cabinet over whether or not *kokutai* would change. It was one thing for scholars to debate such an issue, he said, but quite another for the cabinet to have no coherent position on an issue so fundamental to the interpretation of the revised constitution. Prime Minister Yoshida responded with another recital of the government's formula, to the effect that the revision would bring about a change in the form of government but not in the underlying feelings of the people toward the emperor. He insisted that there was no inconsistency between cabinet ministers on this point. Kanamori, for his part, repeated that the government would make no attempt to propound an orthodoxy on *kokutai*.[6]

The government's attempt to satisfy the members' concerns around *kokutai* was not entirely successful. It was widely believed that social cohesion in Japan depended on attachment to the imperial institution. Tanaka reflected general sentiment when he said that if an elected president replaced the emperor, the nation's social structure would collapse into chaos. Some members feared that the articles defining the emperor's place in the new order would dangerously erode his position. Sasaki, noting that the emperor would lose his "sovereign rights," worried that "in tens of years to come, the devotion rooted deep in the hearts of our people towards the emperor . . . might disappear." He appreciated the devotion of the people towards the emperor. He doubted it would last, however, if the emperor were totally separated from government.[7]

Sawada, as usual, put the challenge more bluntly. This constitution, he said, was nothing less than an attempt at revolution. Beyond that, it was illegitimate, or, as he put it, "*ultra vires*, since the Imperial Throne existed before the Constitution and it exists superior to the Constitution." It was not for the constitution to say whether or not the Throne was "dynastic." The constitution erred in presuming to acknowledge and define a place in Japan for the emperor. Only the emperor could establish and legitimate the institutions of government.[8]

Yamada took particular exception to the word "symbol" to describe the emperor's relationship to the state and nation. "Plainly speaking," he said, "it does not meet the feelings of the Japanese people." When the draft revision was published prior to the elections in April, "the word '*genshu*' was translated into English as 'sovereign of the state' in the *Nippon Times*." Most of the parties assumed that the word used here would be *genshu*, meaning "head" in Japanese. That expressed the "true voice of the nation." It was on the basis of that understanding that members had been elected to the Diet in April. Why had the government changed the term? To most ears, the word "symbol" sounded strange.[9] "The whole Japanese nation is confiding and desiring that the emperor be recognized as the 'head' of the state."[10]

Kanamori responded to Yamada, noting that there had been strong sentiment for *genshu* in the House of Representatives, too, to describe the emperor's relation to the state. But if the word "head" meant anything in this context, it meant sovereign, or chief executive. No matter how carefully the word was qualified elsewhere in the text, it would tempt the people, "falling in with the magic of words," to regard the emperor as "more powerful" than this bill intends. *Genshu* had a "bewitching power, which was experienced even at the meetings of the House of Representatives." For this reason, the novelty of the term "symbol" was perhaps appropriate. It would cause the people to "study and contrive for themselves anew" the place of the emperor.[11]

In the course of this important debate, Shidehara contributed a comment on how the word "symbol" came to be used. Shidehara had been prime minister when the revision was drafted and published. He recalled that, as the drafters of the Japanese revision were searching for a term to describe the emperor's new relationship to government, someone[12] recalled the meeting in London between the prime ministers of Great Britain and all its overseas dominions, called to redefine their relationship to one another, being independent nations, under one crown. The Statute of Westminster (1931) adopted the term "symbol" to describe the role of the Crown. Though this term had no precise Japanese equivalent, the drafters thought the concept would be apt here, too. As the monarch of Great Britain symbolized the unity of the Commonwealth, the emperor symbolized the state and the unity of the Japanese people.[13]

The most eloquent and persuasive answer to these various challenges over the emperor's role in the new order came from Takayanagi Kenzō. Several times during these debates, often at points at which the outcome seemed to hang in the balance, Takayanagi offered interpretations of the revision that laid ground on which these men could confidently stand. This was such an occasion. A republican system, he said, may seem in some ways more fitting to the principle of democracy, making it logical to abolish the emperor system. In the history of governments, the emergence of the sovereign people had been "the dynamite that played a powerful role in abolishing the monarchical system," launching such cataclysms as the French Revolution. In this light, "the Japanese people are indeed blessed" to be able to maintain the emperor system in the wake of the recent worldwide convulsion, "because it is so evident that disorder would prevail here without the emperor system." He credited Shidehara with a major role in saving Japan's emperor system "through his strenuous efforts." The central point of the revised constitution, he said, was "the democratization of the Japanese governmental structure around the emperor." He drew a parallel with the English system.

> If you ask an Englishman where sovereignty lies, he will answer that it lies in the Parliament. Then what is the Parliament? It is king and Parliament. The combination of king, the House of Lords, and the House of Commons can do anything legally without restriction; sovereignty resides in the cooperation of the three bodies.

Like the English, the Japanese people "favors things concrete and dislikes the metaphysical," making them "more like the English people than any other people." Despite this, he said, ever since the Meiji era, Japanese culture had been "strongly influenced by the civilization of the European continent [more than by Britain's]." The effects of the continental civilization had been particularly strong in the fields of legislation and philosophy. Since the Meiji restoration, Japanese legal culture had been strongly rooted in civil law. The transition now to Anglo-American common law was very difficult and was making the postwar reconstruction of Japan all the more traumatic.

Where then did the revision lodge sovereignty? That was a complicated question, Takayanagi admitted. An Englishman might observe that amending this constitution would require "the cooperation of the Diet, the people, and the emperor. In that sense," he said, "the emperor is not excluded from the legal sovereignty," though from a political standpoint, the final decision lies with the people, exclusive of the emperor, "as in England." It can therefore be said that "the influences of militarists or senior statesmen who concealed themselves under the protection of the emperor's prerogatives have been eliminated . . . ; and the Prime Minister, representing the people, has assumed the entire responsibility for . . . advising the prerogatives."[14]

The Emperor's Prerogatives

Takayanagi's subtle argument did not quiet all concerns about chapter I. In fact, he had at least one major concern of his own. He teamed with Yamada Saburō, Tokyo Imperial University's distinguished authority on international law, in offering an amendment to article 7 ("The emperor, with the advice and approval of the cabinet, shall perform the following acts in matters of state on behalf of the people"). Item 8 in article 7 called for "attestation of instruments of ratification and other diplomatic documents as provided by law." Yamada and Takayanagi pointed out that it was a diplomatic convention without exception that treaties were formally ratified not by prime ministers but by heads of state. Already article 7 generally provided for cabinet "advice and approval" and declared that the emperor performed these acts "on behalf of the people" and "as provided by law." It also provided that the emperor promulgate constitutional amendments, convoke the Diet and dissolve the House of Representatives, and award honors, again with the same careful safeguards. It was only logical that the emperor formally ratify treaties, rather than merely attesting to their ratification.

Responding to this challenge, Kanamori (backed by Ōkōchi, Asai, and others) did not question the logic of the would-be amenders' arguments but said that amending article 7 in the manner proposed could not avoid being perceived, in Japan and abroad, as a backward step in the effort to curb the emperor's prerogatives. To move in this direction would stir up a hornet's nest that could only embarrass the emperor. Ironically, General Whitney would give GHQ's blessing to the Yamada–Takayanagi amendment, allowing it to come to a vote.[15] Nevertheless the Peers rejected it, decisively, by a vote of 72 in favor to 228 opposed.[16]

Speaking of the emperor's prerogatives, Makino noted that the revision's revolutionary purpose was best expressed not in chapter I but in article 15, asserting that "the people have the inalienable right to choose their public officials and to dismiss them." Some might dismiss this article as rhetorical, but the keen-eyed Makino, perhaps the chamber's most astute draftsman of statutory language, noted with evident approval that it took away the emperor's most important prerogative. "The whole structure of the constitution has been completely turned around by this single article," he declared.[17]

The fundamental requirement of the Potsdam Declaration was that Japan adopt a *democratic* form of government. Everyone understood this, but Japan's leaders responded in various ways to the Allies' demand. Yoshida was sometimes petulant on the subject.[18] "From time immemorial," he said, "the fundamental political principle of Japan has included a democratic way of thinking or principle, though the term employed may not have been democracy. The successive emperors have taken the people's mind and heart as their own and have had great concerns for the welfare of the people, which fact is clearly shown in their Imperial poems. . . . [D]emocracy has not been adopted for the first time here only in these days." He admitted that the emperor's position would not be "what it used to be." The emperor's powers had been "greatly modified." "But our political principle has always embodied the democratic way of thinking, both before and after the new Constitution."[19]

Such a bombastic assertion convinced no one. A more thoughtful, nuanced answer came from Kanamori. Someone asked if the emperor were reduced to a "mere symbol," how could the government, based on a separation of powers, avoid being "torn in pieces," having no unity. The constitution relied on democracy, the rule of the majority, but that was "far from perfect." Kanamori replied that democracy should not be equated with rule of the majority. "Government by persuasion" was a more appropriate description. A constitutional democracy rules by "general conviction, understanding and accord," not merely by majority rule. He also acknowledged that the executive side of government needed to be strengthened by adopting the "better side of the oligarchic principle." (His questioner had argued that "a fascist government has some really strong points.") Japan, like its allies in the recent war, had learned the hard lesson that oligarchy was subject to abuse. He thought the revised constitution represented a sound balance of democratic and oligarchic features. "Someone in an old book said that really good government would be possible if and when such factors as democracy, aristocracy, etc., were interwoven in the administration of a country. ... My conclusion is that government in this country must adopt the norm of democracy and, led by the opinions of superior persons, be conducted in accordance with the principle of persuasion."[20]

It is clear that the commitment to democracy of the leading framers of this revision, Japanese and American, was tempered. One enlightening exchange took place when Sawada, the House of Peers' leading opponent of constitutional revision, took issue with article 96, making constitutional amendments subject to referendum. Such a provision was "not appropriate to our national condition," he said. It might be all right in a city-state, as in Switzerland or ancient Greece, but not in Japan, with a population of 80 million. Kanamori answered that the constitution reflected the will of the people in a special way. Representatives could make legislation, but the constitution was more fundamental. The people could be trusted to "give a right judgment," he said. Recently in France, he said, the people had rejected a misguided draft-constitution, refusing to support a "rash and unconsidered action." The Japanese people would prove to be similarly "self-possessed."[21]

Sawada replied to this lofty pronouncement by asking, if a referendum were as "good and effective" as Kanamori said, why would the government not trust one now, to ratify this wholesale revision? Clearly Kanamori was "hoist." He answered that the government had decided, "very calmly," to use the amendment procedure in article LXXIII of the Meiji Constitution in the interest of continuity. The people's will had been consulted in the April elections. The "substance of the draft" had been published at the beginning of March, and there had been a full discussion in the ensuing month. Thus the April elections had "practically about the same effect" as a referendum.[22]

Clearly Kanamori was in an awkward position. The April elections were in no way a referendum on the text currently before the Diet. In fact, negotiations between GHQ and the Japanese government over the text of chapter I had taken little, if any, account of the "freely expressed will of the Japanese people." The conspirators (SCAP and the Japanese cabinet) had hit upon the tactic of using article LXXIII of the Meiji Constitution in part as a way to *avoid* having a popular referendum on revision. To cite the April elections in this context was little more than a rhetorical trick.

Electoral Review of Judges

The cabinet's commitment to democracy faced another severe test in the debate over article 79, providing for an electoral review of appointments to the supreme court at the first general election after appointment and at ten-year intervals thereafter. For the most part, the new arrangements for the judiciary met enthusiastic approval. It seemed right to most of the peers that the emperor appoint the chief justice, giving him the same status as the prime minister and symbolically underlining the independence of the judiciary from political control. They also liked the idea of judicial review, which Kanamori explained as the power of the court to refuse to enforce statutes in particular cases where it found the law in conflict with the constitution.[23]

However, the idea of electoral review of judicial appointments seemed "ridiculous"[24] to many peers. It had been tried in "a certain Western state,"[25] but the American Bar Association strongly opposed it, Takayanagi reported.[26] As Iida put it, didn't the system need a "trump card" to play against the tyranny of the majority in the Diet? Kanamori did not flinch from this challenge. "This constitution is built on the view that the position of those without popular support is not strong," he said. If a faction seeks to impose tyranny, the hope of democratic government lies ultimately with the wisdom of the people. For that, we must have universal education, freedom of speech, and "stability, within appropriate limits, of the administrative machinery."[27]

Kanamori's strong defense seemed to work. No doubt it pained him to part company with Takayanagi on this issue, but his reply was Lincolnian. Japan was placing its bet on the democratic faith. Having a periodic electoral review of judges would create an incentive for popular education about the work of the judiciary. The press would have to pay more attention to the role judges play in constitutional governance. Kanamori's explanation seemed to satisfy most of the doubters. Miyazawa contributed the sensible point that nothing would insulate judges completely from political pressure. He thought there was "more to be feared from cabinet influence [over the judiciary] than from popular review."[28] When the proposal to eliminate electoral review from article 79 came up for a vote in the special committee, not a single peer rose to support it.[29]

Several peers renewed the struggle to get the government to commit itself on a procedure for electing the House of Councillors,[30] but to no avail. One useful by-product of this debate was a clarification of the reasons for adopting a bicameral system for the Diet. Kanamori recalled that SCAP originally proposed a unicameral legislature but had yielded to the cabinet's earnest desire for a second chamber with two conditions: that it consist entirely of elected members and that the general electorate have the final say in choosing all of its members.[31] This meant that the usual reasons for having a second chamber (to represent the nobility, or states in a federal union) would not pertain in Japan's case and, further, that designating some seats for representatives of special constituencies (scholars or farmers or trade unionists or whatever) was unacceptable to GHQ.[32] It took a long time for SCAP's insistence on these points to sink in.[33] Kanamori warned that there had been strong support in the House of Representatives for a unicameral legislature, on grounds that a parliamentary system worked better that way.[34]

More Quarrels over Language

Some of the most passionate quarrels of September came over the language of the revision. There were several flashpoints in the bickering over linguistics: the preamble, with its paraphrases of American rhetorical favorites, out of context, strange-sounding, and awkwardly translated; the articles on the emperor's powers; some expressions in the bill of rights and in chapter X (The Supreme Law), which struck many ears as unduly preachy; and the last-minute demand to add the word "civilian" to article 66 defining the cabinet's role and qualifications.

The language of the preamble irritated almost everyone who read it. It had, of course, been a rich object of resentful comment in the House of Representatives, too. In the House of Peers, it came under examination by experts such as Yamamoto Yūzō, novelist, editor, and eminent leader of the effort to simplify the writing of Japanese language.[35] Yamamoto tried several times to introduce amendments, designed to make the preamble more felicitous to the Japanese ear, but they always seemed untimely or were otherwise deflected.[36] Toward the end of the proceedings, Yamamoto tried once more to suggest a few changes in the wording of the preamble. In the course of his remarks, he strongly affirmed the use of vernacular expression for the constitution. Formal Japanese sounded "feudalistic" to most people. It was entirely appropriate that the new constitution be written in the style of oral Japanese, so that its democratic content and expression might fit together admirably. There was a cost, however, and it should be minimized, if possible. He recalled that Stendahl used to read the Code Napoleon, not from an interest in law but because its style was "simple and good." It was unlikely, he said, that this constitution would attract Japanese stylists, unless it could be made "free of verbosity."[37] He hoped he would be given a chance to make it so.[38] But it was not to be.

Nor was Yamamoto alone in attempting to produce a better preamble. Sasaki,[39] Makino,[40] and Takayanagi[41] all turned their hand to this task. The drafting subcommittee did not confront the matter until September 30, and by that time, the pressure to conclude deliberations in the House of Peers had become positively fierce. Everyone seemed to agree that the content of the preamble as approved by the House of Representatives was acceptable. Most were reconciled to the fact that they should try only to make the Japanese text into a felicitous expression of the ideas in the English text. As Takayanagi reported, "GHQ said that in regard to the preamble, they did not want changes in the English text, but that it did not matter if the Japanese text was changed in order to make the meaning of the English text crystal-clear." Takayanagi's draft came closest to doing that, so they accepted it.[42]

The Debate over Chapter X

Chapter X was a repository of pet American ideas, some at least of dubious relevance to Japanese circumstances. It had three articles. Article 97 was pure rhetoric (rights resulting from the "age-old struggle of man to be free," etc.). It was deeply offensive to Japanese sensibilities, as it must have been intended to be. Article 98 was the supremacy clause. In the American constitution, it asserted the supremacy of the national constitution over those of the states. Here, where there were no states, it was anomalous at best. Article 99 said that the emperor and all public officials must "respect and uphold" this constitution. The debate over these three articles was one of the most bitter for these peers.

Takagi Yasaka, an authority on Anglo-American law, led the charge. He reminded Kanamori of his own doctrine, that a constitution should be spare, not prolix, like a treatise. It should contain only essential provisions, expressed with economy. Article 97 had no place in a constitution drafted under this rubric. A supremacy clause might be vital in a federated republic, like the United States, but not in Japan, with a different history.[43]

To this opening foray, by a friendly critic, Kanamori offered only a weak response. He admitted that article 97 was similar to article 11, in the bill of rights, but the concept bore repetition, "for the enlightenment of the people." Consideration had been given to including it in the preamble, but it was decided that it might "weaken the tone" of the declarations made there. "So we excluded it from the preamble, but it being necessary to include it somewhere, we have given it as Article 97." Concerning article 99, obliging the emperor and other public officials to obey the constitution, Kanamori contended that it was "not superfluous." In the existing Meiji Constitution, this thought was contained in the emperor's promulgation. For the revision, the preamble, rather than a statement from the emperor, would set forth the source of the constitution's authority. Again, it seemed better to include these thoughts within the text, rather than in the preamble. In general, chapter X contained important provisions, "and I do not think their existence is of no value."[44]

Takagi let the matter drop here, but when it came Sawada's turn, he tore into Kanamori. "Chapter X," he began, flatly, "must be discarded." The fact that this constitution reads like a "translation" of America's was nowhere more apparent than in this chapter. These provisions were an insult to the Japanese people ["*Voice*: You are right!"[45]]:

> If we were such people as the aborigines of the South Sea Islands or the Hottentots of Africa, we might not be able to understand what a constitution is or whether a constitution is a supreme or a lowest law. . . . It might then be necessary to write that it is the obligation of the people to respect the Constitution, and many other matters. . . . But for the people of Japan, where legislation has been much developed [and] the system of law has been well set . . . such writings as may be given to primitive aborigines are insulting.

Sawada drew attention also to article 99, warning the emperor and public officials (but not the people) to respect the constitution. In answer to an earlier challenge by Makino on this point, Kanamori had noted that, inasmuch as the people were the authors of this constitution, they did not need to be reminded to obey it. Sawada found this fiction deeply offensive. Indeed, he said, "If this splendid constitution had been made by the initiative of the people with their real consciousness, Chapter X would be absolutely unnecessary." Laying aside the promise in article 98 to observe treaties "faithfully" (that provision could be inserted elsewhere), the whole of chapter X was indefensible and should be deleted in its entirety.[46]

Kanamori responded with a somewhat more spirited defense of article 97. Under the Meiji Constitution, he said, rights were simply not respected. It was not superfluous to remind Japanese people that human rights were the fruit of struggle. These struggles had taken place in Europe, not Japan.

The mood was getting ugly. Note taking had to be suspended. When the stenographer resumed, Sasaki and Matsumura[47] added their voices to Sawada's side of the argument. Sasaki attempted a softer approach. These provisions were not a great disgrace for Japan, he said, but they were unnecessary and ought to be removed.[48]

The Basis of Constitutionalism

At this point, mercifully, the proceedings broke for lunch. Perhaps Kanamori mentioned that Whitney had been the author of the offending language. At any rate, when the peers returned, they sat down for a brilliant little lecture by one of their most distinguished members. Takayanagi began by saying that, in his opinion, chapter X "was very important and should be retained by all means." It is true, as Takagi had said, that the phrase "supreme law of the land" was used in the U.S. Constitution, but it originated from the Magna Carta. It symbolized the basic tenet of constitutionalism: the supremacy of law. The dignity of law was particularly important to assert in a democratic state. Without respect for the law, democratic government would be ruined. Government by majority rule was a kind of government by power. In many circumstances, autocracy by one person and autocracy by the majority come to the same thing. Far from being superfluous, the provisions of chapter X were a fitting "crescendo of the whole constitution, concluding it with the idea of the rule of law." Earlier, he recalled, this draft constitution had been compared (by Yamamoto) to a literary work. In that sense, it was "of no little significance" to place the commitment to law at the climax of the document.

It had often been claimed that the revision had copied too much from the U.S. Constitution. Takayanagi thought it more accurate to say that Japan's new constitution adopted the principle of the Magna Carta. Even in the much lamented article 98, the borrowings were well advised. The notion that the acts of legislatures and the executive should be subject to examination in court, under the principle of constitutionality, had been "much discussed in England during the 17th century," he said, but only in the United States had the principle of judicial review been perfected. The adoption of this "technique of the American style in our draft constitution is a proper step, I believe," he said. As for the provisions of article 99 (binding the emperor and public officials to obey the constitution), they were "of profound significance." They helped to clarify the "fundamental idea of constitutional government," that even persons of supreme authority should obey the "eternally unchangeable and universal principle: that a ruler must govern under God and the law."[49]

This brief comment by Takayanagi, coming at a critical moment in the deliberations of the House of Peers, was one of the most important speeches of the summer of 1946. Tactically, it ended the debate over chapter X. Yamada later suggested that chapters IX and X be reversed in order, putting the provisions about the rule of law ahead of the article on amendments, but that idea failed for lack of a second. No more was heard of the idea of eliminating chapter X.

More important, Takayanagi laid to rest the idea that the constitution of Japan came exclusively, or even primarily, from American sources. He set it in the context of the entire tradition of constitutional development. To that tradition, America had made important contributions, as he acknowledged in his comments on judicial review. The United States, however, did not invent constitutionalism.

Even more fundamentally, Takayanagi underlined the relationship between constitutionalism and democracy. Japan's new constitution would begin with a commitment to democracy, but it would end in an invocation of the rule of law. Japan was to become a *constitutional* democracy. Law would temper even the people's power.

The Issue of "Civilians" and the Article 9 Revisions

There was one more major struggle over the language of the revision. It arose from the demand that article 66 pledge that the prime minister and members of his cabinet "must be civilians." This demand was awkward for a number of reasons. First, it seemed to raise a question about the true effect of Japan's promise in article 9 that armed forces would "never be maintained." If there were no armed forces, wouldn't all Japanese be civilians? The second problem was that there was no word in Japanese for "civilian." One would have to be invented. And third, the demand came at the eleventh hour, in the face of MacArthur's major effort to build the fiction that Japan was making its own constitution.

It was in fact a demand not from MacArthur's headquarters but from the FEC.[50] Not that SCAP was treating it lightly for that reason.[51] MacArthur was under pressure from both Washington and the Allies to guarantee that Japan would not return to its bad old ways under the revised constitution. As Kanamori reminded the Peers, "General MacArthur, feeling that this constitution supports the emperor system, approves it, but he is not almighty. The allied nations can still summon the emperor to testify as a war criminal in a trial." If this change would reassure some skeptics, it needed to be done.

It was the amendments to article 9 made in the House of Representatives that had aroused new suspicions. Diplomats at the FEC had grown alarmed that the door to future rearmament had been opened.[52] To lessen the likelihood of repeating the pattern that led to war in the Pacific, they were insisting that the constitution guarantee civilian control of the military.[53] Kanamori seemed to share the apprehension. "After the withdrawal of the army of occupation," he said, "we do not want our various institutions to go back to what they were."[54] Was article 66 intended to disqualify from government service forever every man who had served as a corporal of infantry? Kanamori assured them that was not the intent. Rather, it was meant to "erect barriers to a resurgence of the military."[55]

No one seemed to worry that this amendment introduced into the text of the constitution the possibility that Japan might one day again have noncivilian politicians. Yoshida, as usual, was cryptic and opaque in his explanations. Summoned before the special committee on October 1, he reported that Whitney and Kades had approached him "rather apologetically" with a request that Japan add the requirement that ministers be "civilians." General MacArthur regretted having to make this request, "but he has had to swallow it." Asked about the relation between this clause and article 9, Yoshida said Whitney and Kades could not explain it.[56]

This still left the problem of finding a Japanese equivalent for the English word "civilian."[57] Several Peers wondered exactly what it meant. The transcript of the subcommittee reveals that Kawamura Takeji was the first to suggest the term, *bunmin*, meaning citizen.[58] "In one dictionary," Asano pointed out, "it was defined as someone who is not a soldier or a Buddhist priest."[59] At any rate, it seemed to fill the bill. Unlike many words meaning "official," it carried no connotation of "retainer," and again, as with "symbol," its very novelty in this connection underlined the freshness of the arrangement.

However, even after the problem of translation had been cleared up, serious trouble loomed. Some of those most sympathetic to the revision project were deeply offended to be asked to accept these changes at the eleventh hour. It made a mockery of the notion that this constitution was a Japanese project, said Takagi. Oda wondered which would involve worse consequences: to reject this demand outright or to "choke it down." He suggested a tactical approach. Why not trade this amendment (requiring that cabinet ministers be "civilians") for some others we greatly desire for our own reasons?[60] The demand to accept this amendment irritated Miyazawa. It was simply contradictory for SCAP to encourage a "free discussion" of this draft and then force the acceptance of this amendment. "To say that we have even a little autonomy is nothing more than self-deception," he added. Tadokoro was also despairing. "It was our real intention from the beginning to reject this constitution completely," he said, "but that turned out to be completely impossible." Shimojō disagreed with these assessments, though he too was strenuously opposed to knuckling under. "In the House of Representatives," he recalled, "the government initially said that there could only be a few revisions, but it turned out to be an unexpectedly large number." He thought the House of Peers should fight on this one.[61]

Eventually cooler heads prevailed. Takayanagi and Takagi were dispatched to

see Kades and others at GHQ, to ascertain the depth of SCAP's commitment to
these FEC-induced amendments. The minutes are cryptic at this point, but they
seem to indicate that SCAP's own predicament was the controlling argument.
When Miyazawa asked Takayanagi if he had relayed the committee's view that,
if possible, the demand for "civilian" be withdrawn, Takayanagi replied that "since
MacArthur as an international statesman must defend Japan . . . it would be better
[for us] to swallow this matter."[62] In the end, it boiled down to a demand from
the FEC that MacArthur dared not resist at this stage. The Japanese decided to
"choke it down" for his sake, as much as anything else.

One effect of Japan's acceptance of the "civilian" amendment was that it led
the FEC to table any further consideration of article 9. At the instigation of the
Chinese and Australian representatives, the FEC resolved that the demilitarization
and demobilization of Japan should depend on Allied policy rather than the
Japanese constitution, which might later be amended by the Japanese themselves.
Regardless of the wording of article 9, the future of Japan's military establishment
would depend on the peace treaty and related international agreements.[63] The
constitutional guarantee of civilian control of the military was more important
than unenforceable, utopian promises not to maintain armed forces.

It is interesting that article 9 itself was not a major focal point of the revision
debates in the House of Peers.[64] Yoshida was asked again whether the commitment not to maintain armed forces would preclude entry into the United Nations.
He usually answered such questions by saying that he did not know: the future
would take care of itself. But in the secrecy of the subcommittee, he said, "Since
we are renouncing war, we cannot contribute men" to the projected U.N. peacekeeping forces.[65] There would have to be a reservation when Japan joined the
United Nations.

Another time, Nanbara asked Kanamori about the meaning of the amendments to article 9 added in the House of Representatives. Their purpose had been
simply to emphasize Japan's peaceful intentions, he said, to give them a positive
expression.[66]

Also noteworthy was Takayanagi's strong speech on September 13, explaining
the significance of article 9. The renunciation of war was "nothing very new,"
he said; it would be found in the prewar constitutions of Spain and Brazil, and
as far back as the first revolutionary constitution (1791) of France. What made
article 9 special was the renunciation of "war potential, a step hitherto taken by
no country." When added to the second paragraph, renouncing the right of belligerency, article 9 became "epoch-making" in importance. A revolution in the
methods of making war had made not just war but "the armed sovereign states
of the old days worse than anachronisms." In light of these new realities, the
world was moving toward a federation. International police belonging to no particular country would soon serve as guarantors of order in the world community.

When a world federation comes into being, all countries will have to
adopt such provisions (as article 9) in their constitutions. In that event,
just as the member states of the American union have no independent

military force, so there will be no need for the member states of the world community to maintain independent military forces.[67]

Takayanagi's vision was utopian, but he was in good company.[68] His speech was the summer's most cogent articulation of the oft-spoken idea that Japan, in affirming article 9, was in the vanguard of nations that had taken to heart the grim lessons of World War II.

The Committees Conclude Their Work

There was a somber atmosphere as the House of Peers moved in early October to conclude its work on the revision project. Everyone knew this would be the last significant act of this august body. With an acute sense of gravity, the House of Peers was about to do much more than sign a warrant signaling the end of its own existence and that of the Japanese nobility. It would be taking a decisive step in committing Japan to constitutional democracy, laying a new foundation for the nation.

The subcommittee of fifteen ended its work on October 2. In reporting the document back to the Peers' special committee on revision, it made several suggestions for amendments.

Of these, the special committee made short work. It rejected a series of changes in the Japanese language of the preamble and of several articles proposed by Yamamoto Yūzō. Mainly the subcommittee would have substituted Japanese syllabary for Chinese characters, but the committee apparently felt that such changes were more trouble than they were worth at this stage.[69] The committee also rejected the amendments proposed by Yamada and Takayanagi that would have given the emperor power, with the advice and approval of the cabinet, to ratify treaties and make diplomatic appointments. It was generally agreed that the changes made perfect sense logically, but Kanamori insisted ("not a shadow of doubt," he said) that the "possibility of attributing responsibility to the emperor would be increased." Ōkōchi added that many people blamed Japan's current distress—including the cruel necessity of adopting this revised constitution—on the treaty of 1940 that created Japan's so-called Triple Alliance with Germany and Italy. In the new Japan, criticism of the emperor would no longer be a crime. If the Yamada–Takayanagi amendment were adopted, the emperor would surely be blamed for controversies surrounding future treaties, including the coming treaty of peace.[70] These arguments prevailed; the proposal to amend article 7 was rejected.

So were Tadokoro's notion to add "respect for family life" to article 24[71] and the effort to delete the periodic electoral review of judges.[72] These latter proposals especially enjoyed wide support, but in the circumstances, they were deemed untimely.

As for the demand of GHQ to add a requirement that cabinet members must be "civilians," it occasioned a brief debate. Matsumura worried that it would encourage challenges in court to a minister's acts (had he always been a "civilian"?). On the other hand, Oda raised the intriguing suggestion that it might be "to the advantage of the state in some future date, in relation to the constitutional article pertaining to the renunciation of war."[73] Did he mean that the language restricting cabinet membership to "civilians" implied the existence of some Japanese who were *not*, thus opening the door to armed forces? If so, that would be an ironic consequence of the FEC's attempt to fortify the barrier against the remilitarization of Japan. At any rate, the amendment quickly passed.

Having disposed of the amendments, the special committee moved directly to vote on draft revision as a whole, as amended. After brief speeches by Sawada (opposed) and Iwakura (tepidly in favor), the committee voted to forward the text to the full House of Peers with its approval.[74]

Presenting the Text for a Vote

On October 5, Abe Yoshishige, chair of the Special Committee on Revision, presented a summary of the committee's work to a plenary session of the House of Peers. Concerning the status of *kokutai* under the revision—the point "most discussed" by the committee, he said[75]—he reported that its meaning remained ambiguous and that the government flatly, and probably wisely, refused to issue an authoritative statement on it. He said some members wished to augment the emperor's powers, but the government consistently rejected such ideas, contending that no more strain should be put on him. Some had asked whether the emperor ought to retain powers to bale the nation out of emergencies, as he had in ending the late war. The government's answer, Abe reported, was that Japan must henceforth act as a mature democracy and learn to be self-reliant in operating a "cold and hard system."[76] Abe admitted that the language of the bill, particularly the preamble, seemed "crude," but again, the government resisted changes at this late hour. An exception had been made for adding "civilian" to Article 66, he said, as a contribution to the "lasting peace of the world."[77] As for the bill of rights, he noted that its guarantees were not explicitly made available to aliens "for the present." However, the Japanese term for "the people" (*nanbitomo*, rather than *subete kokuminwa*) had been chosen carefully, "so as not to prevent its application to aliens" later, by statute.[78]

Abe's peroration struck a delicate balance. He noted that the revision had been criticized for its wording and for its defensive tone. People needed to bear in mind that constitutional revision had become "a necessity" when the existing constitution had been turned to "evil account." He absolved the general public, but "those in power, Diet members, scholars, government officials and the like, cannot evade their responsibilities." Those people must now take the lead in "materializing a new constitution." He admitted that he did not feel "overjoyed," but it was time for a new beginning.[79]

As Abe concluded, a member rose to ask a pertinent question. Would the House of Peers be permitted to make "an important amendment," or would it be limited to discussing the bill before voting it up or down? Prime Minister Yoshida replied, "[you may] discuss it to your heart's content and make amendments or proposals on it as freely as you want." But he warned against frivolous obstruction. "This country has been placed in an extremely difficult position since its defeat." There would be no relief until Japan met the terms of the Potsdam Declaration, to the satisfaction of the occupiers. In these circumstances, he said, "useless political controversies or rivalries are quite undesirable."[80] This was, in a nutshell, the understanding that prompted the cabinet's decision to participate actively in the process that produced this constitution.

Final Debate in the House of Peers

A two-day debate ensued that summarized the arguments for and against accepting this constitutional revision. Sasaki led off for the negative. In a speech of carefully chosen words, the eminent professor of lofty reputation said he spoke from "unspeakable pain." Such a radical revision was not justified by the Potsdam Declaration, he said, which had, after all, promised a democratic government "in accordance with the freely expressed will of the Japanese people."[81] Efforts to demonstrate that this revision required no modification of *kokutai* had utterly failed, he said. *Kokutai* was clearly defined in countless imperial rescripts, statutes, and court decisions. The first chapter of the revision contradicted those definitions. The people knew that from common sense, and it trifled with them to pretend otherwise. He drew a contrast between the nobility of the Meiji founding and the shameful process that had produced this revision:

> One day when deliberation was going on, a man from the ministry of the Imperial Household came to Prince Itō Hirobumi, who was then presiding over the meeting, and whispered something to him. Prince Itō stepped forward to the Emperor and reported something to him. But the Emperor continued with his work as if nothing had happened. Later it was revealed that one of his sons had passed away that day. . . . But the Emperor would not listen, and it was only after they had finished with a certain article on which they were deliberating that he left the room. How deeply moved we are to hear of the noble action of the Emperor![82]

Sasaki concluded by paying "homage" to the government for its efforts in preparing and presenting the draft and for explaining and vindicating it for many months. "I understand their most difficult position," he said. With apologies for his "obstinacy," he would withhold his support. "I am awfully sorry," he concluded. His fellow peers warmly applauded his speech.[83]

Matsumura led off for the supporters. It was a miracle, he argued, that Japan had emerged from the calamity of defeat with its imperial institution intact. He noted that the Potsdam Declaration contained no requirement that Japan give up the emperor, and he insisted that with the revision, it would not happen. Unlike Europe, where kings and subjects fought for many centuries over forms of government, "Japan was a country in which the emperor and the people were fused together into the sovereign right of maintaining national order." Japan had committed awful blunders on the road to war. He cited particularly the government's attempt to project Shintō as not a religion, so it could require worship at Shintō shrines, despite the guarantee of religious freedom in the Meiji constitution,[84] as well as the edict of 1936 that freed the ministries of war and navy from political control.[85] The revision erected strong barriers against a repetition of those mistakes.

Then it was Sawada's turn, and he immediately turned up the rhetorical heat. (As Yoshida had said, "You can say anything you want.") Only an independent state should attempt to frame a constitution, he began. The constitution should not be revised until "Japan has recovered perfect independence as a state." It had been said that we should cast off old clothes and put on new ones. But these new garments were "borrowed ones and full of patches, with tails and sleeves too short to fit." We were about to throw off "the finest silk clothes of first order Nishijin'ori and put on a borrowed suit of poor fiber cloth."[86]

Unlike this new text, so full of insulting preachment, the Meiji Constitution was refined and dignified, with no superfluous expressions. This new text mangled important legal distinctions. It confused public and private law, as in the article on marriage, where matters of civil law were jumbled together with constitutional provisions. Its separations of power were muddled. It provided for judicial review of the "highest organ." It put the prime minister in charge of foreign relations. The style and phraseology were in a state of extreme confusion; correcting them was a hopeless task.

An account in an American newspaper had put the point better perhaps than he could. The reporter had written, "This is not a Japanese constitution; it is an American constitution for Japan." He was quite right: This is "not a thing Japanese."[87] Why had the government offered such a thing? Japan had many able constitutional authorities; the cabinet itself had "creditable experts in this line." Part of the problem, he thought, was that this revision was based on Anglo-American law. Japan's codes were of continental origin. If we adopt this revision, we will have to adopt revised codes "one a day for a long time to catch up." Was this what Potsdam meant by democracy? There was nothing to do but to return this revision to those who introduced it, he concluded.[88]

The final speaker on Saturday afternoon, October 5, was Ōkōchi. He acknowledged some concern that the revision expected too much from the Japanese people, who were not well trained in the culture of democracy and who tended to look to various guardians for protection. On balance, however, he favored this attempt to "make the flower [of democracy] open in full bloom in this corner of the Orient . . . affording an example to other nations."[89]

There were two notable addresses on Sunday, October 6, before the final vote. Mitsuchi Chūzō, former journalist and cabinet minister both before and after the war, lamented that bad men had led Japan into "unwarranted war and devastating defeat." He attributed the calamity partly to "disgusting, sycophantic scholars," whose false counsel had corrupted the Meiji system. In the future, he said, we must trust our own instincts as democratic citizens. He regretted, he said, Kanamori's attempt to define *kokutai* in mystical or sentimental terms, describing the emperor as the "center of devotion." It was better simply to recognize, as a fact, that "the emperor, who comes of the imperial line unbroken for ages eternal, forms the center of the unity of the people." This explanation was not only "exactly in accord with the truth, but also easily intelligible to the general public." One need only consider what had happened at the end of the war. Millions of servicemen, who stubbornly kept fighting despite a series of crushing defeats, and the majority of the people, who desired the continuation of the war, blindly accepted the propaganda of military authorities. Yet as soon as the emperor spoke, they laid down arms. He was immediately obeyed, not because he was a generalissimo or because constitutional authorities regarded him as the "supervisor of the rights of sovereignty" but because, simply struck with his dignity, "they could not bring themselves to act against the imperial wishes." He concluded that his differences with Sasaki were slight, but for him, the balance tipped the other way.[90]

The other notable address came from Matsumoto Gaku, a former police official who had made many friends in Europe and America while representing Japan at international conferences. He had been a peer since 1934. He began his speech with a paean to the Meiji Constitution, but he said revision had become "inevitable" with Japan's defeat. He paid respect to the cabinet for preparing this revision and to SCAP for its "thoughtful" supervision of the project. The result, he said, was not perfect in style, but it was thoroughly creditable. He drew attention to four respects in which the revision seemed to him deeply imbued with Japanese ideals. The preamble identified the people as the locus of sovereignty. The government had consistently held that the people here included the emperor. This idea of a fused identity of the people and the emperor was full of meaning to the Japanese sensibility. He quoted an ancient poem:

Letting alone the people who look upon herself in joy or grief,
The moon is shining e'er serene
Above the hills in cloudless sky!

The poet, he said, was expressing "in exquisite symbolism . . . the permanence of our national character." (He was applauded at this point.) In this sense, he added, article 1 and the preamble gave voice to "the most essential and most characteristic phases of Japanese national character."[91] Similarly, he interpreted article 9 in terms of classical poetry, citing a work by Ōe no Masafusa (1041–1111) depicting the military spirit as like that of a newborn chick. "Think of the small chicken just about to come out from the shell," he said. "That power, that feeling, that power of will: this is what we call military spirit in our country." If this could be well appreciated by European peoples, it would wipe away the various suspicions they have about our nation. In this sense, article 9 "fully represents Japan's inherent characteristics and Japanese-like character."

The bill of rights too had a distinctly Japanese flavor. It borrowed many phrases from the great international tradition of rights, but as shaped by the summer's consideration, it was now more Japanese than either British or American. Indeed, several of its provisions were characteristically Japanese. Article 12, for example, declared the freedoms and rights guaranteed by this constitution would be "maintained by the constant endeavor of the people, who shall refrain from any abuse of these freedoms and rights and shall always be responsible for utilizing them for the public welfare." That was lovely, and it expressed a distinctly Japanese approach to human rights. Finally, articles 8 and 88, dealing with the property of the imperial family, were quite unlike the provisions relating to royalty in European lands, and they perfectly reflected the Japanese imperial spirit. Just as Japanese emperors, unlike their European counterparts, had no family name, so it was right that their purity should not be compromised by the cares of property.[92]

It was a dramatic speech. Matsumoto had drawn attention to some of the deeply resented parts of the revision and cited them for being particularly valuable expressions of the Japanese sensibility. Now he drew his assessment to a close: "On these four points, the revised constitution brings out a typical Japanese complexion in strong relief and shows off Japan's intrinsic character. . . . Inwardly toward the people, it indicates the guiding principles to be followed; outwardly toward foreign countries, it clarifies the true shape of our country and also proclaims our ardent desire for international peace based on justice and order."[93]

For these reasons, he concluded, "the bill has my hearty approval."

One more speech, by Kinoshita Kenjirō, interpreted the text as an expression of ancient Confucian wisdom. With that, the morning session ended.

That afternoon, the peers assembled to vote. One more time, Yamada and Takayanagi presented their amendment to article 7, to enable the emperor, with cabinet advice and approval, to ratify treaties. It failed, by a vote of 72 in favor to 228 opposed. Makino was given leave to move that the words, "Family life shall be respected," be added to article 24 (on marriage and family). After Makino's brief explanation, the speaker called on the prime minister to respond. With apologies, Kanamori took the podium[94] and offered familiar reasons for opposing the amendment. The government had no intention of moving radically to reform the family system. There was, however, he said, no need to include an explicit reference to it in the constitution. Social mores were shifting, and it was not yet clear what form they would take in the future. A phrase such as that proposed "contains no feature substantial enough to serve as a standard for shaping the ideas of the coming generation." He recalled that a similar proposal had been made in the House of Representatives, but it was concluded there that "the question should be settled by means of law." It was "exceedingly desirable" that the question of the family system be dealt with similarly here. Indeed, it would be "expedient" for the government if the revision could be approved "as it stands." "Excuse me," he added, "for using such a word as expedient."[95]

With that, the vote was taken. It showed 165 in favor, 135 opposed.[96] The amendment was rejected, lacking the two-thirds margin necessary for passage.

The House of Peers passed immediately to the final votes. By standing votes, the speaker (Tokugawa Iemasa) found the necessary two-thirds majorities[97] in favor of each of the amendments proposed by the committee (minor alterations in the wording of the preamble, plus the FEC amendments to articles 15 and 66 and a minor addition to article 59[98]). He then asked those in favor of the whole bill, as amended, to stand, and again he found two-thirds in the affirmative.[99]

The meeting concluded with brief remarks from Prime Minister Yoshida, who offered "heartfelt respect" to his colleagues in the House of Peers. The bill, he said, "aims at establishing the cornerstone of a new Japan and at bringing peace to the world." The opinions expressed during their deliberations had evoked "resounding echoes" throughout Japan, "as representing the general will of the intelligent classes of our country." They had also played an important role in making the revision better understood by the people. "This is indeed a matter for great joy."[100]

With this, as the sun set on a Sunday afternoon, the House of Peers concluded its deliberations. There was little exaltation among the peers. They had done their part. There was no escaping it. As they had joined in the drift toward war and the descent into defeat and disaster, they had now to cooperate in the work of reconstruction. With few dissenters, they agreed that accepting this revision was a necessary step in that direction.

SEQUEL

21 • • • • • • • •

"Broaden and Deepen the Debate"
• ## FIFTY YEARS WITHOUT REVISION

•

•

The work of laying a new constitutional foundation for Japan did
not end on November 3, 1946, when the emperor promulgated the
ratified draft, or on May 3, 1947, when it took effect. For the remaining five years of the Occupation, the Japanese government,
guided by MacArthur's staff, revised all legal codes to implement
the text of the new constitution and took political and judicial action
to interpret its provisions.[1] After the Occupation ended in 1952 and
Japan regained its independence, debate on the constitution focused
on whether and to what extent it should be amended. This chapter
sketches out a few of the leading developments that shaped debate
on the constitution after 1946 and reviews the arguments in favor
of revising it. Of particular concern are the formal committees and
commissions investigating its origins and offering proposals to revise
its major provisions.

The FEC Keeps the Issue Alive

Criticism of the 1946 constitution had been common from the beginning. SCAP's strict control of the press and other media outlets
could, and did, silence many critics, and SCAP's widespread purges
removed powerful conservative leaders from the political arena between 1946 and 1950. But one critic MacArthur could not control
was the FEC in Washington. The FEC's continuing concern with
constitutional reform in Japan helped keep the issue alive until it
could be fully resuscitated after 1950 by Japan's own angry conservatives.[2]

The FEC's tussle with MacArthur culminated in a series of meetings in Washington in late September 1946, where members expressed their final opinions on the draft constitution. The conspiracy
by a small coterie of Americans and Japanese in Tokyo had not
convinced the FEC of Japanese authorship. A review was necessary,
according to the Australian representative, "because the present
Constitution was not an expression of the free will of the Japanese

people." The FEC must have an opportunity to ascertain the opinion of the Japanese people. Agreeing with this assessment, New Zealand threatened to oppose FEC approval unless a review was provided for in the near future. Many of the FEC nations supported these two American allies. Accordingly, on October 17, 1946, the FEC voted to require a review of the new constitution "not later than two years" after it had been in operation. It warned that "the Far Eastern Commission . . . may require a referendum or some other appropriate procedure for ascertaining Japanese opinion."[3]

Reaction in Tokyo

Angered by the FEC's action, MacArthur refused to tell the Japanese government about it. He told Washington that it would "be viewed in the [Japanese] public mind as a display of force by the Allied Powers" and would "invite the collapse of the Constitution."[4] The dispute dragged on until December, when Washington agreed with MacArthur that only the Japanese government—not the Japanese public—should be informed of the FEC's review requirement. In early January 1947, MacArthur informed Prime Minister Yoshida. Yoshida himself showed little interest in the matter, barely acknowledging MacArthur's letter regarding it.[5] Not until March 1948, almost two years after the FEC's decision, did MacArthur inform the Japanese public of that decision.

It was August 1948 before the Diet took up the issue, setting up a committee in its Legal Affairs Office and identifying certain provisions of the constitution for review. One member of the office suggested looking at the procedure for designating the prime minister and conditions under which the Diet would be dissolved.[6] But the Diet had little stomach for another go at revising the document it had debated and approved just two years before. There was also brief press speculation about a national referendum on the document or on specific provisions of it. On the whole, however, neither the Diet nor the Japanese public showed much interest in the FEC's "review requirement."

Meanwhile, the Ashida cabinet, racked by scandal and the arrest of several high officials, collapsed in June 1948, after only eight months in power, without taking a stand on reviewing the constitution. Yoshida returned to power and ignored the issue until April 1949. Only when questioned in a Diet committee meeting did he deign to mention it. In his usual abrupt manner, he denied knowing anything about the FEC decision requiring a review, but he did tell the committee his government had no intention of amending the constitution.[7]

The SCAP–FEC squabble did, however, spark an interest in amendments by some private organizations. For example, the Constitution Research Association, a group of young law scholars of Tokyo University, accepted the fundamental principles of the constitution but proposed rearranging them. SCAP, they pointed out, had written its draft along the lines of the Meiji Constitution, placing the chapter on the emperor first. They thought it more appropriate to place provisions on popular sovereignty and "permanent pacifism" in the first chapter, basic human rights in the second, and the emperor in the third. Another group, the

Public Law Forum, a group of scholars on the left, proposed, in March 1949, a new provision stating clearly that "sovereignty resides in the Japanese people," and changing the emperor as "symbol" to "emblem." They also wished to rewrite article 9 to replace "ambiguous" wording and restore the spirit of the original provision to make it a "declaration of complete pacifism renouncing all war."[8]

More important than these scholarly groups, powerful revisionist groups would soon emerge to lead a strong backlash against the new constitution. Prewar conservative politicians had been purged before the draft reached the floor of the Diet in June 1946. But some Diet members of the (conservative) Liberal and Progressive parties did denounce the preamble and various provisions relating to the emperor, his family, and property; war renunciation; rights and duties of citizens; the judiciary; and the organization and powers of the Diet itself. Thus arguments that many revisionists would later make were already being aired in the press and in the Diet by the fall of 1946. While this early agitation died down after the constitution was promulgated, it resumed in the early 1950s when the prewar conservative leaders were depurged. Their return to the political stage after the Korean War started in June 1950 signaled the beginning of the first sustained assault on the new constitution.

The Cold War and Change in U.S. Policy

As the Cold War developed, American policymakers began to view Japan as a potential ally against the Soviet Union in East Asia.[9] One of the problems for Japan was the mixed signals coming from American occupiers in Tokyo and Washington, especially regarding the promise of permanent disarmament imposed by article 9. Sometimes MacArthur would boast about Japan staking out a position of moral leadership against war and armed forces, at great risk to itself. As late as March 1949, MacArthur described Japan as the "Switzerland of the Pacific," giving encouragement to those who championed a policy of neutrality for post-Occupation Japan.

Meanwhile, however, officials in Washington were having serious second thoughts about forcing total disarmament on Japan.[10] As American policy developed to encourage European economic recovery and to contain Soviet expansion, the State Department began worrying that SCAP's reforms might make Japan vulnerable to Communist pressures and takeover.[11] Between February and October 1948, therefore, the Policy Planning Staff under George Kennan abandoned preliminary plans for an early peace treaty with Japan and moved U.S. Occupation policy toward the goals of economic recovery and political stability. On October 9, 1948, President Truman approved a new statement of U.S. policy, known as National Security Council 13/2, which signaled relaxation of the purge and censorship of the Japanese media, hastened the end of war crimes trials, and encouraged measures for economic recovery.[12] By April 1950, Washington was talking about keeping U.S. military bases in Japan after a peace treaty, a possibility first discussed by MacArthur and Emperor Hirohito in 1947.[13]

The change in U.S. policy was soon reflected in SCAP policy toward the Japanese left. MacArthur responded in 1949 to the threat of internal violence by clamping down on the labor movement and questioning whether the Communist Party "should be permitted to function as a legal party."[14] A year later, on June 6, 1950, SCAP ordered the purge of Communist Party members and leftists in government and industry.[15] Thus the reassessment of the need for security in Japan, both internal and external, had already begun before the outbreak of the Korean War on June 25, 1950.[16]

This shift in Occupation policy led to the depurging of many of Japan's prewar bureaucrats and politicians, who quickly filled the ranks of the conservative parties. By the end of the Occupation in April 1952, these prewar politicians and bureaucrats made up more than a third of members in the Liberal and Progressive parties and controlled a large block of seats in the House of Representatives.[17] Their angry voices would be heard for the first time after Japan regained its independence. Ishibashi Tanzan, an editor and future prime minister, referred to "the dictatorial men . . . of the Occupation" who would not "admit a single criticism of their own actions."[18] Revisionist publications and conservative leaders demanded an outright scrapping of the Constitution. They would question not only article 9 and other specific provisions but the very legitimacy of the constitution.

Commission on the Constitution

Hatoyama Ichirō, the purged leader of the Liberal Party, accused the Americans of blatant hypocrisy and expressed his contempt for them. In the fall of 1953, Hatoyama, having regained influence in the Liberal Party, pressured Yoshida to create a committee to consider constitutional revision. The Progressive Party followed suit in early 1954. Diet members and youth groups formed committees demanding an "independent constitution." Conservative Diet members began calling for the creation in the Diet of a special commission to study the constitution. As the agitation reached a feverish pitch in 1955, the president of the House of Representatives, Kiyose Ichirō, declared that in writing the constitution, SCAP had violated the Hague Conventions and the Atlantic Charter.[19]

When the two leading conservative parties merged in November 1955, creating the Liberal Democratic Party (LDP), one of the principal aims of the new party was to revise the 1946 constitution. In 1956, the third Hatoyama cabinet, after a furious struggle with the Socialists, won passage of a bill establishing a Cabinet Commission on the Constitution (Kenpō Chōsakai).[20] The LDP's party platform said the purpose was to "prepare a draft of a new constitution." Under the law that created it, however, the commission was charged only with investigating and deliberating on the constitution and reporting the results to the cabinet and the Diet.[21] Meanwhile, the LDP organized its own investigative committee whose principal task was to generate support for revision by educating the public about the origins of the constitution. The Socialists, who controlled more than one-third of the Diet seats, boycotted the commission. They saw it as a conservative government's attempt to confer respectability on revisionism.

The commission held its first public meeting on August 13, 1957. By the time the commission began its work, the origins of the constitution of 1946 were already well-known. GS had published its version of events in 1949. The Liberal Party's investigation had heard testimony from Japanese insiders—Matsumoto Jōji, Irie Toshio, Satō Tatsuo, and others. Satō had published his famous series of articles in the legal journal, *Juristo*, on how the Shōwa Constitution came to be. Memoirs by MacArthur, Whitney, Shidehara, and Yoshida revealed much about how the constitution saved the emperor and turned Japan into a pacifist nation.

Proposals for Revision

A majority of the commissioners favored revision of one kind or another, and some wanted a new and independent constitution while preserving the principles of popular sovereignty, democracy, pacifism, and respect for fundamental human rights. The most persistent demand in the commission, was for a constitution written in good style by the Japanese themselves. Other demands did, however, involve more than mere style. For example, a majority of the commissioners favored rewriting the preamble. They wished to discard the American wording and style and what they viewed as a weak appeal of a dependent pacifism. A majority also wished to preserve the emperor-as-symbol system and keep it subordinate to the people's sovereignty. But they favored a clear statement that the emperor was "the head of state," especially in representing the government in foreign affairs. A minority of commissioners viewed the emperor as the spiritual foundation of the nation—the familiar *kokutai* argument. They thought the term "symbol" demeaned him and undermined the nation's historical unity. In a word, they advocated democracy under a *sovereign* emperor.

A majority of the commissioners also wished to amend the controversial antiwar clause, article 9. The politics surrounding article 9 were a maelstrom. In a "Memo on Security in Post-War Japan," dated June 23, 1950, MacArthur wrote: "It must be understood that despite Japan's constitutional renunciation of war its right to self-defense in case of predatory attack is implicit and inalienable."[22] Following the outbreak of the Korean War two days later, MacArthur authorized Japan to organize a Police Reserve of 75,000 men and to enlarge the existing Maritime Safety Agency. Then, in his New Year's address on January 1, 1951, he went further, raising the question whether Japan ought to consider rearming for defensive purposes.[23]

By 1954, the Police Reserve had evolved into Japan's Self-Defense Forces (SDF), and the nation became part of the U.S.–Japan Mutual Security Treaty.[24] These developments sparked an intense debate over article 9. Emotions ran high; the issue soon split the nation between critics and defenders of that provision.

Over the years there have been several protracted legal battles over the compatibility of military forces with article 9. A prominent leftist, Suzuki Mosaburō, asked the supreme court in 1952 to rule that legislation authorizing military forces, for whatever purpose, was unconstitutional per se. The court refused jurisdiction on the ground that courts in Japan were limited to hearing cases in which "there exists a concrete legal dispute between specific parties." Japan had no constitutional court in the European tradition. Suzuki's personal stake was deemed insufficient to give him standing in a Japanese court. In due course, cases were brought that met the criteria for standing, but still the courts found ways to duck the issue.

This was the political background that the commission knew so well as it considered what to do about article 9. Japan's SDF existed. Japan's Security Treaty with the United States since 1952 was a fact that the commission could hardly ignore. Japan, in short, was arrayed on the American side in the Cold War.

The commissioners agreed that every nation has the right of self-defense, and thus the right to maintain war potential. But article 9 seemed to say otherwise. Some contended, logically, that article 9 needed to be revised to clarify the issues arising from Japan's maintenance of its own SDF and its cooperation with other nations in collective security. Others believed that article 9 should be modified, not by changing existing wording but by expanding it, by adding to it a phrase that would serve to legalize Japan's SDF. Still others felt that Japan could stand on the moral high ground of renouncing war but still maintain its self-defense forces.

The Bill of Rights

As the commissioners moved from renunciation of war and national defense, they confronted another set of principles in chapter III (rights and duties of the people) which affected every community and individual in Japan. This chapter entailed the most emphatic statement of Western individualism. It embodied values that often were an affront to Japanese culture, with its commitment to collective, communitarian values.

It is hard to imagine elected officials expressing a desire to reduce the "rights of the people." None of the commissioners did so candidly, but many did wish to revise chapter III of the 1946 constitution. They believed that Japan's basic law needed to strike a better balance between the people's rights and duties, giving more weight to duties and a better balance between individual freedom and social responsibility. The modern welfare state, they argued, requires more emphasis on the rights of the community and society and less on the rights of the individual. Some even suggested that "welfare and obligations of the people" should replace the concept of "rights and duties." While acknowledging the importance of society's welfare to the ultimate freedom of the individual, defenders of chapter III rejected revision in favor of adjustments through legislation and court decisions. In the end, this argument carried the day on the commission.

The Diet

Chapters I and II of the constitution had been the main focus of heated debate during the drafting and adoption process in 1946. To many participants, articles on the location of sovereignty and the renunciation of war were the major principles for both sides. Yet, a truly representative Diet, a parliamentary cabinet system, and an independent judiciary were basic to the Americans' understanding of democracy. The commission on the constitution also took them seriously.

The nature and powers of the Diet had been the objects of debate since SCAP wrote its draft in February 1946. Major disagreement existed over whether there should even be an upper house and, if so, what kind. The compromise was a bicameral legislature in which the upper house, House of Councillors, represented national and prefectural constituencies, served longer terms, was weaker than the House of Representatives, and, initially, was less involved in party politics.

It took until the summer of 1948 to solve the riddle of how to elect members of the upper house. The election law of March 1947 established 117 multimember districts for House of Representative elections. The House of Councillors Election Law of August 1948 provided that 100 members elected for fixed terms would represent the whole nation as a single electoral district in hopes of securing the election of well-known leaders from all walks of life. The remaining 150 councillors were to be elected, also for fixed terms, from 46 prefectures, each constituting one district electing 2 to 8 members depending on its population.[25]

To some commissioners, the constitution gave the legislature too much power, violating the doctrine of the separation of powers and weakening the role of the cabinet and the prime minister. Some supported proposals that would abolish the House of Councillors, creating a unicameral legislature, or give it special responsibilities, and that would strengthen the executive branch against the Diet and local government through direct election of the prime minister. Others thought party politics should be confined to the lower house and the councillors should be nonpartisan.[26]

Concern about a weak cabinet in relation to the Diet continues to exercise Japanese politicians. Frequent changes in cabinets, weak prime ministers, and divisive party politics are often mentioned as faults deriving from the constitution. But others, on the commission and since, hold it would be dangerous to Japan's democracy to have an elected prime minister or a powerful executive branch that would dominate the Diet.[27]

Dissolution of the Diet was another issue that exercised the commissioners. Dissolution is the power, in a parliamentary system, to end the terms of representatives in the legislative assembly[28] and cause elections to select new representatives. Under Japan's postwar constitution, this was to be done with the "advice and approval of the cabinet," and dissolution must be followed by general elections within 40 days (article 54). But when should, or must, the cabinet advise the emperor to dissolve the Diet? Article 69 directs that if the House of Representatives passes a nonconfidence resolution, or rejects a resolution of confidence, the cabinet must resign unless dissolution is proclaimed within ten days.

All this is clear enough: The House controls the fate of the cabinet. It can hold the cabinet accountable and cause it to collapse. But what if the House does not pass a resolution of nonconfidence? Must the House and cabinet soldier on together, no matter how paralyzed or crippled they are? Or does the cabinet have discretion to ask the emperor to dissolve and call new elections, even without a resolution of nonconfidence? In other words, can the cabinet use dissolution as a means of discipline over the Diet members who would prefer not to face a general election?

As it turned out, these latter questions describe not the exception but the usual situation in postwar Japanese politics. Never has a majority of the Japanese House of Representatives passed a resolution of nonconfidence against the wishes of the cabinet.[29] The parties in the Diet have always reached a *modus operandi* without dissolving the house.

The commission on the constitution issued its final report on July 3, 1964. Its seven years of operation produced 40,000 pages of hearings, testimonies, and documents, which added much detail and nuance to the story of the Shōwa Constitution's framing. The hearings produced a host of arguments in favor of revising the constitution. But the Diet, hamstrung by the provision that required two-thirds of all of its members to pass an amendment (article 96), never took action on any of the proposals that flowed from the commission.

Commission's Conclusions Regarding the Constitution

On the whole, the commission's proposals for revising the constitution were conservative. The revisionists favored amendments that would strengthen public rights against individual private rights and claims, strengthen the cabinet and executive branch, and reduce the powers of the Diet, local governments, and political parties. Although none was achieved through the amendment process, some have been implemented through constitutional interpretation. Others remained alive 30 years later, when revisionists again explored some of the weaknesses of the 1946 constitution.

Revisionism in the 1980s

The revision issue faded from the political scene as the national passion for economic growth gripped Japan from the early 1960s. The conservative champions of Japan's political tradition failed to break through the solid bloc of Socialists and Communists in the Diet, which controlled over one-third of the seats, making amendments to the constitution impossible without their support. The leftists deftly turned the antiwar feelings of the Japanese people against all efforts to revise the constitution, interpreting them as an attack on article 9. The Yoshida bureaucrats who controlled the government lacked the stomach for engaging the left on this issue. Besides, most of the leaders of the LDP, like their mentor, Yoshida, supported the national security arrangements with the United States arising from the antiwar clause.

Perennial critics of the 1946 constitution, such as Nakasone Yasuhiro, who had been a member of the commission on the constitution, lacked the clout in the LDP to press the issue. This situation began to change, slowly, when the LDP's victory at the polls in June 1980 encouraged the revisionists. In early 1981, the party's committee on the constitution dusted off old revision proposals. When Nakasone became prime minister in November 1982, the press speculated that he would mount an attack on the constitution. His visit to the shrine of the war dead, Yasukuni Jinja, and his defense of Japan's traditional values alarmed the leftist press and sparked rumors that he was preparing to rearm Japan. He did talk informally about what he considered the contradictory policy of supporting a large "self-defense force" while article 9 remained in the Constitution. Nakasone's more immediate target, however, was the arbitrary limit on defense spending (1 percentage of gross natural product) adopted by previous conservative administrations. His advisers, fearing a political backlash if he tried to amend the constitution, persuaded him he could exceed the artificial limit on defense spending without tackling the larger revision issue. Consequently, Nakasone never seriously proposed revision, preferring instead to build on Japan's powerful economic status in the world.

The Gulf War Stirs Debate on Article 9

The collapse of the Soviet Union, the end of the Cold War, and the Persian Gulf War—all occurring between 1989 and 1991—provoked the most serious debate on Japan's constitution since the 1950s. The end of the Cold War created an opportunity to discuss revision in terms other than the antiwar clause. Economic prosperity, and the subsequent collapse of "the bubble economy," highlighted urgent social problems: a weakening family system, an aging population, changing concepts of human rights in matters of privacy, and the environment. But above all, the Gulf War raised questions about Japan's ability to meet its international responsibilities under the UN charter. Japan's initial response, a financial contribution (about $1 billion) seemed weak to the U.S. government. Eventually this was raised to a total cash contribution of $13 billion to the coalition effort against Iraq.

The question of contributing military forces per se, however, proved to be a good deal more difficult. Japan was unable because of article 9 to contribute forces to the American-led coalition against Iraq or to participate in UN peacekeeping operations. Criticized harshly by its foreign friends, Japan had to question the wisdom of continuing the "one-country pacifism" required by article 9. The Diet was eventually able to pass a measure that sent civilian medical personnel and transportation equipment to the Persian Gulf, but no soldiers or weapons.[30] The response still seemed inadequate to many Japanese leaders. Accordingly, they introduced a bill into the Diet to enable Japan to contribute to UN peacekeeping efforts, albeit under strict limitations. In June 1992, it passed. The measure limited Japan's contributions to logistical and humanitarian support, monitoring elections, aiding civil administration and the like, while maintaining the prohibition on monitoring cease fires, disarming combatants, and patrolling buffer zones. Even with the limitations, this legislation marked a milestone: It breached the ban on deploying SDF abroad.

In September 1992, when a contingent of several hundred personnel (most of them engineers) joined a UN peacekeeping effort in Cambodia, Japan had taken an important step out from the shadow of article 9, toward a more active role in international affairs.[31] But nationwide polls in 1991 and 1994 still showed little public support for revision of article 9 that would legitimate Japan's armed forces.[32]

A Newspaper Provokes a National Debate

A turning point came in 1992 when the *Yomiuri Shinbun*, Japan's largest daily newspaper, touched off a national debate on the constitution. Concerned about the Diet's confused debates over Japan's international obligations and constraints of its constitution, the newspaper established its own "Constitution Study Council," composed of twelve experts. To "broaden and deepen the nationwide debate on the Constitution," *Yomiuri* asked its outside experts to prepare a revised text of the constitution, which was printed and distributed widely the next year.[33] The Yomiuri council recommended revision of the constitution by the end of the century. Its major proposals suggested a range of possible amendments that have been widely discussed in recent years.

First, the council would rewrite the preamble, abandoning much of its righteous rhetoric and saying in plain language that the people are sovereign, desire peace for all time, respect human rights, and wish to promote the people's welfare. The principles of popular sovereignty and "symbol emperor" would be preserved but rewritten in clear and unambiguous language. The council proposed one change in the emperor's functions: that he be accorded "the ceremonial status of a head of state" in such matters as foreign relations.

The most controversial and interesting proposal concerned article 9. Here the council would change the title of chapter II from "Renunciation of War" to "National Security." The council proposed to retain the wording of the first paragraph unchanged, renouncing war and embracing world peace. In a new paragraph, Japan would pledge not to manufacture, possess, or use weapons of mass destruction. But the council would delete the current prohibition on the maintenance of armed forces in the second paragraph and would expressly recognize Japan's right to possess self-defense forces under the command of the civilian prime minister, without national conscription. These changes would be reinforced by a new chapter acknowledging Japan's obligation to support with its SDF "peace-keeping and humanitarian efforts of international organizations." The proposed wording would clarify the constitutional status of Japan's SDF. By curbing efforts to turn Japan into a major military power, this would reassure Japan's neighbors and the world of Japan's peaceful intentions.

The *Yomiuri* council also proposed rewriting parts of chapter III (rights and duties of the people) to provide greater clarification of existing rights and to add some new ones: rights of privacy, freedom of occupation and conduct of business, and the "right to enjoy a favorable environment." In the chapter on the Diet, the council proposed creating greater equality between the two houses of the national legislature. To do this, it would give the House of Councillors precedence over the House of Representatives when considering treaties and certain personnel matters. And it would give the upper house the exclusive right to designate justices of a new constitutional court and exercise oversight of the judicial branch. The council also proposed changes that would strengthen, or at least clarify, the prime minister's powers in appointing and dismissing cabinet members, dissolving the House of Representatives, supervising the bureaucracy, and designating a prime minister pro tempore in case of emergency.

The Japanese judiciary has been under attack for years. Of particular concern is how notoriously slow the courts are in conducting trials and hearing appeals. The supreme court has come in for its share of criticism for allowing constitutional conflicts over treaties and laws to go unresolved for years. The *Yomiuri* draft proposed, first, to create a new constitutional court to exercise sole power to determine the constitutionality of treaties, laws, executive orders, and official acts. This would, in theory, accelerate the resolution of debates on constitutional matters that have often tied the judiciary in knots. Second, a reorganized supreme court, freed of appeals on constitutional grounds, could hear other appeals more quickly and resolve complicated legal cases.

Finally, the *Yomiuri*'s experts confronted the article on amendments (article 96), which required for approval a concurring vote of two-thirds of all members of both houses. Since 1955, when the Socialists gained one-third of the seats in the House of Representatives, no proposal for amending the constitution has had a chance of passing. The *Yomiuri* draft would require the concurrence of only a majority of those present and voting, provided that two-thirds of all registered in each house were present. This change, if adopted, would dramatically ease the current requirement for amendments to be passed.

The national debate touched off by the *Yomiuri* draft has blossomed, often in unexpected directions. The mass media have taken a leading role, with newspapers and television networks running special programs. Theatrical groups have reenacted the SCAP drafting session of February 1946, with Japanese actors dressed as the American army and naval officers present at the event.[34] Some participants have engaged in extended lecture tours talking about their role in the drafting sessions. Japanese proponents and opponents of revision are often paired in debates. For example, two former conservative prime ministers, Miyazawa and Nakasone, have published a book together to air their opposing views on revision.[35] Every year on Constitution Day (May 3) the media offer "specials" on some aspect of postwar constitutional history. On special anniversaries, major newspapers, and the Diet itself, invite Americans to Japan who helped write the SCAP model constitution in February 1946, often pairing them with Japanese politicians and scholars of similar ideological persuasion.[36]

New Commissions on the Constitution

In July 1999, both houses of the Diet voted to establish "Research Commissions on the Constitution" (*Kenpō Chōsakai*), which began operating in January 2000.[37] This was a historic development, made possible by a broad ruling coalition of three parties (LDP, Liberal Party, and the New Kōmeitō), with support of one opposition party, the Minshutō. The aim appears to be to develop proposals for revision which could lead eventually to a complete rewriting of the Shōwa Constitution. However, proponents of revision have been cautious in their public comments. Former Prime Minister Nakasone, for example, noted that the purpose of the two Diet commissions is only "discussion of the Constitution [*ronken*] . . . because discussion will not be conducted on an a priori assumption of revision." He called for a broad national debate over ten years, with five years for "general discussion" and another five years "to consider revisions to the Constitution."[38]

Doi Takako, leader of the SDP, complained that "what revision advocates really contrive to do is change article 9. Supporters of the 'constitutional debate' are playing right into their hands." She pledged to spearhead the effort to "protect the Constitution." Others have noted that the LDP's own commission on the constitution is calling for a complete rewriting so that the "style and content will make Japanese who read it proud of their Constitution."[39]

Like the *Yomiuri's* study council, the LDP speaks of principles that might be added, such as protection of privacy, the family, rights of children, the "right to know," and environmental rights. An LDP spokesman also points to constitutions of other countries that refer to pacifism without foregoing the right to maintain armed forces for defense. Article 9 is thus likely, again, to stir the greatest controversy. Other issues the LDP seems certain to study are independence of the judiciary, public assistance for private schools, autonomy of local governments, and organization and powers of the Diet itself. This debate, along with recent legal recognition of the "Rising Sun" flag as a national emblem and the nineteenth-century *Kimigayo* as the national anthem, promises to become part of the conservatives' continuing effort to raise national awareness among the Japanese people.

What amendments may eventually be proposed, and whether any can be enacted, is difficult to predict. The press has, of course, given full attention to the creation of the Diet commissions. Daily reports provide a wide range of information. On Constitution Day (May 3), 2001, the Diet announced a "working" schedule for the commissions over the next five years.[40] Both groups plan to hold public hearings and seek expert testimony and advice from many sources. Both also plan to travel abroad for consultation. So far, however, the commissions have offered little in the way of substantive deliberations.

The revisionist effort was given new life with the election of a new prime minister in April 2001. Koizumi Jun'ichirō immediately rekindled debate over the "Peace Constitution." At his first news conference as prime minister, he pointed out that article 9 concealed a "lie" about Japan not having a standing army. But his interest went beyond article 9 to popular election of the prime minister, making the emperor the head (*genshu*) of state, reform of the judiciary, and a host of other constitutional issues. With his refreshing straight talk, he appeared willing, even eager, to enter the fray over Japan's constitution and complex issues of the nation's postwar history. His candid comments may spur the kind of wide-ranging national debate that could lead to a rewriting of the 1946 constitution.

Conclusion

·

·

·

We conclude our study of the origins of the Japanese constitution at a time of growing concern about Japan and its political system. Can Japan find a way out of a decade of economic and political stagnation? Is the Japanese state up to meeting the political and diplomatic challenges of the new century? Can Japan ever be made whole politically, without a constitution expressed in its own idiom?

In 2001, the fifty-fifth year under the Shōwa constitution, a new prime minister, Koizumi Jun'ichirō, injected a bracing tone of adventure into Japanese politics. In his inaugural press conference of April 2001, he called for reconsideration of the constitution's renunciation of war and armed forces. Many Americans, including top government officials, were quick to agree. The new American ambassador, Howard Baker, told reporters on July 17, 2001, two weeks after he arrived in Tokyo: "I think the reality of circumstances in the world is going to suggest to the Japanese that they reinterpret or redefine Article 9 of their constitution." He noted that "things like missile defense and international operations with peacekeeping forces" will ultimately require a decision by Japan.

Once again, Americans were explaining "reality" to the Japanese. Yet Prime Minister Koizumi acknowledged that it would be difficult to put revision of the article on the political agenda any time soon. His caution seemed to reflect two factors of Koizumi's situation: the strongly pacifist stance of his party's main coalition partner and opinion polls that show 74 percent of the Japanese public opposed to revising article 9.

This concern with article 9, although not unimportant, tends to obscure some deeper trends. Japan since 1946 has become a stable constitutional democracy. The events of 1945 and 1946, recounted in this book, laid the foundation for that development.

Quite aside from the many decisions and reforms imposed on the Japanese by General MacArthur and the Occupation, constitutional reform was the decisive step in America's remodeling of Japan and in Japan's eventual recovery of control over its own political destiny. After several months of inconclusive debate in Washington over treatment of the emperor, MacArthur seized the initiative and shaped U.S. policy to suit himself. In particular, MacArthur insisted publicly that Japan's salvation from its militaristic past required not only democratic reform but spiritual renovation according to Christian principles.

The emperor's entourage, including several Christians, was quick to take advantage of this opportunity to save their emperor. They told MacArthur that Hirohito would collaborate with him in achieving U.S. policy goals. They also hinted that the emperor and the royal family were eager to support his goal of Christianizing the Japanese nation. This was misleading, of course. Hirohito had no intention of embracing Christianity or of encouraging his people to do so. Nor did he need to. His advisers (even the Christian ones) believed that democratic values and institutions could flourish without Christian moral foundations. Japan's experience in the 1920s seemed to support this premise. Besides, any attempt to link democracy with Christianity ran the risk of causing the Japanese to reject democracy as a front for a foreign religion (less than 1 percent of the Japanese were Christian) and a modern form of Western colonialism. Ironically, had MacArthur also acknowledged this important distinction, he would have been less inclined to "civilize and Christianize" Japan. He might also have felt less need to protect Hirohito. This, in turn, might have opened for MacArthur new paths for democratization and constitutional revision.

Japan's own early efforts at democratic reform looked quite promising at first. Ranking bureaucrats in the cabinet and the foreign ministry, having analyzed the Potsdam Declaration, recognized that occupation policy required Japan to revise its constitution. They were ahead of leading politicians on this central issue. By moving quickly, they hoped to gain control of the process and determine the extent of such revision. They turned to scholars and studied foreign constitutions as they considered how to revise the Meiji Constitution. Although preliminary, some of their proposals moved in the direction the Americans wanted. Yet, few of the proposals from these officials had much influence with the reform committees led by Konoe Fumimaro, the emperor's man on constitutional issues, and Matsumoto Joji, the head of the cabinet's task force on revision. As technical experts, these bureaucratic officials lacked the weight of the top politicians and their scholarly assistants. The one positive benefit of these early reviews in fall 1945 may have been that officials in the Legislation Bureau, for example, were better prepared for the cascade of demands for constitutional reform that flowed from SCAP in early 1946.

Fierce infighting between the Konoe group and Matsumoto's cabinet committee was a major obstacle to progress. The tension arose from the disorderly power arrangements of the Meiji Constitution and from Konoe's attempt to resume his special position in the power structure. We must also acknowledge, however, that the problem came in part from MacArthur's own careless words to Konoe, leading the hapless courtier to believe that MacArthur wanted him to take charge of constitutional reform. The conflict might have given way to cooperation and progress had MacArthur continued his initial role as overseer of the effort and provider of ideas. Instead, when he was sharply criticized in the American press for seeming to embrace Konoe, he made Konoe the scapegoat and told his political advisers to have no further contact with the Japanese. This tack prevented Washington's thinking on constitutional revision from informing the Japanese and Japanese ideas from reaching MacArthur's political advisers.

In early October 1945, the State Department had sent George Atcheson an outline of the constitutional revision the United States wished Japan to adopt. Atcheson shared these ideas with Konoe but could not continue the meetings of their two staffs to ensure that the American ideas would be included in the drafts on which Konoe and Sasaki were working. To be sure, Matsumoto's stubborn personality and his mistaken assumption that Japan was free to make its own revisions would have made coordination with the Americans difficult. Atcheson twice appealed to MacArthur to allow him to resume contact and share Washington's latest thinking on constitutional reform with Matsumoto's committee. But MacArthur short-sightedly rebuffed him. The next bilateral discussion about reforming the constitution would not come until February 13, 1946.

Meanwhile, the Allied powers asserted their right to exercise a veto over any basic changes in Japan's political structure by setting up a policy control group, the FEC. Henry Luce, the powerful publisher of *Time* and *Life* magazines, advanced the thesis that the United States alone was the "powerhouse" from which democratic ideals and a new moral order would spread throughout the world. His call found resonance at the highest levels in Washington. But America's allies, including Britain, questioned this view and insisted that Washington modify its policy of excluding other powers from control of Japan. They demanded that MacArthur, in theory their surrogate in occupied Japan, be accountable to them when making decisions about Japan's political future. The Moscow Agreement of December 1945 changed the rules of the occupation. It gave the Allies control over Japan's future political structure. They were concerned about preventing Japan's revival as a military power, and they insisted on trying Hirohito as a war criminal. MacArthur then developed a strategy to create a new political order in Japan before the FEC could assert its authority. He defiantly ordered his staff to draft a model constitution that would permanently disarm Japan and preserve the emperor in a symbolic role. He persuaded Shidehara and Yoshida that he was their ally in trying to protect the emperor and committing Japan to pacifism, and that the rest was negotiable.

Using threats and promises, SCAP's GS compelled the cabinet to adopt MacArthur's line that the draft was a Japanese government product, approved by the emperor in accordance with the existing constitution. He then tried to convince the FEC (and the world) that it was a Japanese draft, months in the making, supported by the "freely expressed will of the Japanese people." Whitney and his staff intimidated Japanese officials in secret negotiations, forcing them to accept most of the SCAP draft as a Japanese product, and then offered the FEC fictitious "evidence" of Japanese authorship. When the suspicious allies demanded more information, MacArthur stonewalled.

We have argued in this volume that MacArthur did not act alone; he had Japanese collaborators. We have even suggested that constitutional revision resulted from a joint conspiracy. Shidehara and Yoshida, not to mention Hirohito and his aides, cooperated with MacArthur to ensure protection of Japan's imperial institution. They also hoped that such reform would satisfy the Potsdam demands for democratization and thus hasten the end of the Occupation. The roles of these co-conspirators are amply documented in this volume. As the conspiracy blossomed, it enveloped first the Privy Council, then Kanamori, and ultimately Ashida and political leaders in both houses of the Diet. All recognized the same imperatives that had driven MacArthur and Shidehara at the beginning.

On the American side, key figures in the Pentagon and State Department also joined the effort to support MacArthur and hold the FEC at bay. They gradually came to understand the dilemma that MacArthur faced. FEC demands for a controlling role in constitutional reform ran the risk of endangering the emperor, whom MacArthur was committed to protect. By May 1946, MacArthur's warning of the previous January, about the troop levels that would be necessary if the Allies moved against the emperor, no longer seemed hyperbole to many in Washington. Neither the Americans nor the Japanese wished to run the risk. Support of MacArthur's strategy became the real wisdom for both sides.

Through the spring of 1946, cabinet bureaucrats and SCAP officials refined the text and persuaded the Privy Council to approve it without change. During the summer they guided it through a long, careful examination in the newly elected Diet. But the question that arouses controversy to this day is: Was the draft that the Diet approved in August virtually a translation of SCAP's original model constitution, as some have charged, or had it been substantially modified to reflect Japanese wishes? We have examined this issue carefully in the context of the marathon meeting of March 4–5, 1946, subsequent meetings in April, and the Diet debates in the summer. To be sure, the SCAP draft of February 13 was translated by the Foreign Ministry, and that translation was used by the Japanese to aid in understanding what the SCAP draft said. But the Matsumoto/Satō draft of March 2 was substantially different from the Foreign Ministry translation. So was the March 6 draft, which grew from the marathon negotiating session of March 4–5. This version, often called the first Japanese government draft, underwent further changes in early April through negotiations. Then came a dramatic style change in Japanese when it appeared on April 17 rewritten in colloquial language.

Some key provisions and the preamble were preserved as literal translations throughout this process. It is also true, as critics have charged, that the whole document has "a translation odor" about it. But the constitution ultimately approved by the Diet was far from being a literal translation of SCAP's model draft. Indeed, Satō has been accused of hoodwinking the Americans with some of his legal terminology and translations of English words. We find little merit in this accusation. Our sense is that much of the confusion over words and phrases derived from the difficulty of translating, from Satō's imperfect knowledge of English, and from the enormous pressure of time under which he was working. As we have shown, he did use words that served Japan's interests without telling the Americans. Generally, however, he openly confronted differences between the Japanese and American drafts and candidly debated them with the Americans.

Our examination of American and Japanese records leads us to conclusions that differ in some ways from previous accounts. First, we note that different legal backgrounds of the two sides influenced their arguments. As heirs to a European legal tradition, the Japanese trusted more to the flexibility of statutes, rather than absolute constitutional language, for guaranteeing certain rights and regulating branches of government. The Americans preferred to spell out such matters in the constitution. Similarly, Japan, following European practices, had no history of a strong, independent judiciary. Second, we conclude that the meeting on March 4 of Whitney and his staff to review an English translation of Matsumoto's March 2 draft deserves special attention. It is seldom mentioned in accounts of the March 4–5 marathon negotiations. This meeting revealed differences of temperament and ideas among the American drafters themselves. The senior officers (Whitney, Kades, Hussey) tended to be more conciliatory toward the Japanese draft than some of the junior officers. This may have been in part because the former came to know their Japanese counterparts personally through face-to-face encounters, whereas some of the latter never experienced joint sessions.

No doubt American constitutionalism, as it came to bear in Tokyo in 1946, was a muddle of contradictions. Bicameralism was all but incompatible with the classic Westminster model. So was Diet confirmation of cabinet appointments. Judicial review was anomalous in a system explicitly committed to parliamentary supremacy. Local self-government had no roots in modern Japanese history, yet the Americans insisted on it. And the preamble on which they insisted was not only awkwardly expressed; it was almost risible in its claim to be an expression of the Japanese people. However, the viability of constitutionalism does not depend on its being internally consistent, or expressed in elegant prose. The American framers did get a few basic things right. They insisted, in the face of Japanese resistance that was both fierce and sometimes very subtle, that the emperor's position must fundamentally change, that he be stripped of his governmental power, and that all but his personal property be subject to public control. And they demanded that all those who directed the affairs of state (oddly, for Americans, including even judges of the supreme court) be electorally accountable.

The essential ingredient was to persuade the grassroots politicians in the lower house of the Diet to affirm the new arrangements. How free were they to express their reservations and objections? When the Diet convened in June, MacArthur called for "untrammeled debate" of the draft. He and his subordinates said the Japanese Diet was free to debate and amend it without interference from them. This public stance was not candid. SCAP had in the fall of 1945 established tight control over the Japanese news media and publishing industry. It had carried out a massive purge of politicians before the April 10 election and had set the rules under which the House of Representatives was elected. Would MacArthur now back off and allow the debates to proceed freely or would he simply push the draft constitution through a compliant Diet?

Kades was assigned to monitor the debates. A team of translators at the Foreign Ministry worked round the clock to provide him with an English version of the transcripts. His notations on these transcripts show that he read them with care. The question is whether he, and others in MacArthur's headquarters, interfered in the debates. On several major issues, recounted previously, the answer is yes. The most dramatic instance involved his confrontation with Kanamori over the latter's defense of *kokutai* and his assertion that it had not changed. Other instances involved the debate over popular sovereignty and imperial property. In both cases, SCAP pressured the Japanese representatives to accept things in the draft that most disliked. In addition to these instances of overt pressure, a fear of displeasing GHQ pervaded the Diet debates, imposing a form of self-censorship on the proceedings. Kanamori and his staff often signaled that an issue was off limits or that a proposed amendment would be out of bounds. They used circumlocutions to signal a sensitive issue. From time to time, the shorthand recording of proceedings was stopped to allow more candid conversation between the Diet representatives and Kanamori. These discussions allowed criticism, without mentioning the Occupation or MacArthur in the official record. Kanamori himself read through the daily transcript of the debates and occasionally removed language he feared the Americans might find offensive before sending it for translation and delivery to Kades.

Diet members were well aware of the implications of the draft constitution for Japan's future and its bearing on the end of the Occupation, a consummation for which they and their constituents devoutly wished. Yoshida and Kanamori frequently reminded them of the relationship between these goals. But from their various perspectives, Diet members were intensely concerned about the content of the deal, too. They knew it would determine their country's future. They knew they would have to answer for their votes on it and to live with it themselves as well. Thus they took it seriously, as a constitution.

Two things especially made these politicians uncomfortable: the rough treatment of the emperor and the extreme pacifism of article 9. The cabinet's translators and negotiators had softened some of the language about the emperor, removing its most offensive phrases (compare chapter I of the SCAP draft with the final version). Even so, many Diet members thought the emperor could perform a more useful role than the text allowed. Surely he could be trusted to stand as head of state in formal dealings with foreign powers, as the monarch of England did. Might he not also intervene helpfully when the political system was paralyzed by indecision or by commitment to a failing course, as he had at the end of the war? And why could he not keep his property, as the bill of rights guaranteed to everyone else? Kanamori's argument, that the emperor must be separated from any and all governmental responsibility and set safely beyond involvement in political quarrels, persuaded some but certainly not everyone in the Diet.

The other major sticking point was article 9. In the ghastly light of Japan's charred cities, not only Hiroshima and Nagasaki but the fire-bombed environs of Tokyo and other metropolitan centers as well, virtually every Japanese could affirm the renunciation of war. But was it wise to disarm, unilaterally and permanently? Could they ever participate responsibly in a peaceful world order if they did that? Wouldn't membership in the United Nations require Japan to contribute armed forces to international peacekeeping efforts? Yoshida and Kanamori tried to explain that such questions could not be answered now. The simple fact, by the summer of 1946, was that an end to the Occupation required Japanese acceptance of article 9, not as a basic principle of constitutional democracy but as the price of having lost the war. This constitution was not simply about democratization of Japan; it was also about saving the emperor. To do so, it had to deprive the new Japanese state of sovereign rights that other nation states enjoyed. Diet members ultimately swallowed this painful reality, though many of them not happily.

For the project as a whole, the decisive vote in the House of Representatives in late August reflected a knowledgeable and heartfelt affirmation of constitutionalism. Japan was ready to commit itself to liberal democracy, and this variant seemed a solid enough foundation.

As for the House of Peers, it was in a bind. The peers knew by September, when they got the project, that their house—indeed the peerage itself as an institution—was finished. Did they have any useful role to play in this drama? They did only if they could reconcile this new framework to Japanese traditions and interests. For several weeks, they worked hard on that. Many members made important contributions, some by their blunt criticism, which drew powerful responses from other members. The fact that there were learned answers to these criticisms must have been reassuring to thoughtful opinion throughout Japan. After a thorough vetting by this body of honored scholars and distinguished citizens, the House of Peers added its assent. Everyone knew that the members were not free agents, but neither were they easily intimidated. They acted for the good of the country. They performed their duty by adding their authority to this fresh start.

What are Americans to conclude about MacArthur's victory in leading Japan to affirm a Western-style constitution as the basis for its new regime? One option might be triumphalism: that it was a great moment in the inexorable American-led advance of liberal democracy. According to this view, Americans, following the providential victory of its armed forces, brought democracy to Asia. At first many Japanese sullenly resisted the imposition of Western constitutionalism, but gradually they came around. Eventually with conviction, they affirmed the wisdom of what was offered to them. The end—that Japan has been, for over a half century now, a prosperous, stable democracy, firmly allied with the United States—more than justified the Occupation's sometimes heavy-handed methods.

This picture, while gratifying to the notion of American power benevolently serving the cause of universal democratization, glosses over some awkwardness. One that is most notably ignored by American triumphalism is that the 1946 constitution imposed on the new Japanese state a unique feature: national pacifism in a world of nations armed to the teeth. No other major nation has so radical a constitutional commitment to pacifism. Whatever may be said about the imperative of radical Japanese disarmament as part of the strategy to save the emperor, was it truly a good idea constitutionally?

A second awkwardness reflects the warning of social scientists that institutional arrangements cannot be transported from one culture or country to another with predictable effects. Just as the United States cannot fix what is wrong with the separation of powers by a wholesale importing of features of the parliamentary system, Japan cannot become a stable liberal democracy simply by dressing itself in Western institutions. Matsumoto Jōji reflected this concern early in his troubled negotiations with SCAP when he pointed out that roses, transplanted from England to Japan, lose their fragrance. His contention would have found a sympathetic audience among many American professors, then and now.

On the other hand, parliamentary institutions have developed a unique flavor in Japanese culture. The Japanese royal family is not the House of Windsor. The machinations between factions within the Liberal Democratic Party are unlike the struggles between Tories and Labour in Britain. No Japanese prime minister since World War II has had the power or impact of Margaret Thatcher or Tony Blair.

Even so, the commitment to parliamentary government has generally had the effect in Japan desired by the American framers. The framers believed that the exercise of governmental power was not transparent enough in prewar Japan. There were too many opportunities in the Meiji regime for shadowy bodies to use the emperor's authority in unaccountable ways. They hoped that the elimination of these bodies would empower the cabinet and Diet, and that a reformed parliamentary system would ensure government rooted in the will of the Japanese people.

There is an irony in imposing democracy, and Diet members in Tokyo keenly felt it in 1946. Japan's constitution proclaims that human rights "result from the age-old struggle of man to be free," but knowledgeable Diet members, familiar with the history of constitutional liberty in the West and knowing the provenance of the draft they were mulling, could not help feeling like guests at someone else's party. Americans insistence on keeping this language in the text revealed a tutelary impulse that marked the entire American Occupation. It was deeply galling to many Japanese and reminded them of their experience with Western colonialism in the nineteenth century. That they could swallow their pride was quite remarkable.

But democracies are often instituted by undemocratic means. The case of the United States is no exception. The American founding was seriously flawed from the democratic standpoint, not only by excluding women, blacks, Native Americans, and many who owned no property but by manipulated votes for ratification, after hasty debate, in many states. Moreover, institutions to realize democracy—in the election of a president, for example—did not begin to take shape in American until well into the nineteenth century and are manifestly imperfect still.

It is not unusual for founders of democratic regimes to resort to unlawful and undemocratic processes. What made the Japanese "refounding" in 1946 especially problematic was that it depended on outside intervention by a foreign military force. Even West Germans had greater autonomy in framing their postwar political system than did the Japanese. From the beginning, American planners had warned that "the knowledge that [a revised constitution] had been imposed by the Allies would materially reduce the possibility of its acceptance and support by the Japanese people for the future." Yet virtually everyone in Tokyo suspected that American military officers had drafted the constitution Japan was adopting.

It has also been generally known ever since. The Japanese people have had to live with this embarrassing reality. It has made their constitution vulnerable to right-wing fulminations, and it has left a sour taste.

These are serious considerations. They lie behind the longing in many Japanese hearts to become a "normal" country, to throw off the American yoke. The truly remarkable thing is that defenders of the constitution have so far been able to fend off these nationalistic passions. No amendment has ever been made. The reasons are many, some having to do with partisan factionalism and the alignment between left and right. Also, the Cold War persuaded many that any revision might lead to Japan's direct involvement. Despite these reasons external to the text, however, we must also conclude that the constitutional model crafted in 1946 was, despite its sometimes irritating phrasing, fundamentally well adapted to Japan's needs.

At the outset, in our introductory chapter, we urged readers to join us in viewing Japan as a "case study," that is, as one among the many countries undergoing transitions to democracy during the twentieth century. We noted there that Japan's prospects were propitious in many respects. Though devastated by war and not yet truly a developed country economically, Japan had a literate, well-trained, and confident labor force. It was unified ethnically, protected from the hostility of its neighbors, and eager to learn from the examples offered by the successful democracies.

The principal problem, we noted, was the ideology that had shaped Japan's politics over the preceding decades. Japan's leaders had converted Shintoism from a folk religion into a powerful engine for inducing mass obedience and sacrifice. On its face, the Meiji Constitution formally placed the emperor at the head of the state. In the immediate prewar years, this framework came to be interpreted literally. Obedience to the emperor became the hallmark and primary obligation of good citizenship. The politico/religious ideology, encapsulated in the term *kokutai*, was incompatible in its prewar form with constitutional democracy.

We have followed the debate over *kokutai* closely because it was in fact central to Japan's political revolution embodied in its new constitution. Japan's public philosophy had to change (this the Allies insisted on), but it could not be done carelessly (this the Japanese understood). It had to be transformed, incorporating the people's emotional attachment to the emperor, but explicitly and decisively rejecting the notion that he was the sovereign ruler. That this transformation of ideas was ultimately accomplished was a major achievement, and it was profoundly a joint achievement. Neither side could have produced this constitutional revolution alone.

It might be interesting to speculate what would have happened if SCAP had built a system with a separately elected chief executive. Over the years, and now, some Japanese apparently want to try that: direct popular election of the prime minister. It might give the prime minister greater autonomy over administrative actions, in the application of police and military power, and in foreign policy. But it might also lead to conflicts with the Diet and to paralysis, if different parties took control of the two political branches. Would the system need some other authority, such as the French or German presidency, to guide the regime through such crises and to take power in emergencies? Might the emperor have to be rehabilitated for such a role?

Politically, the parliamentary system, framed in 1946, has worked reasonably well. One problem seems to be the inability of the system to register shifts in public opinion. Japan has lacked a competitive two-party system for most of the last half century. Factional competition within the LDP has been a weak substitute, as far as democratic accountability is concerned. The fault seems to lie with the electoral process. It encourages a parceling out of political territories among factions and punishes unsuccessful forays into enemy territory very severely. Efforts to reform the system have been halfhearted. Japanese politicians seem to prefer stability and consensus to decisiveness. Who can say that the economic distress of recent years proves that they are wrong?

There is a malaise in Japanese politics at the present time, but it does not seem to threaten the consensus that supports liberal democracy. Whether the virtues of constitutional democracy and pacifism will prove permanently satisfying or will represent the ultimate achievement in political happiness in Japan or anywhere else is unclear. But it is hard to deny that the system has delivered for Japanese what the framers of 1946, both American and Japanese, wanted for them.

Notes

The most comprehensive collection of documents in English on the making of the Japanese Constitution is Ray A. Moore and Donald L. Robinson, eds., *The Constitution of Japan: A Documentary History of Its Framing and Adoption, 1945–1947* (Princeton University Press, 1998; a CD-ROM). It contains the electronic equivalent of more than 8,000 pages of material. The numerous references to this collection in our endnotes appear as RM plus document number, followed in many cases by numbers identifying paragraphs or other markers within the document. Included in the collection are the initial SCAP draft of February 1946 (RM189), the final version approved by the National Diet (RM481), and five intermediate drafts (RM208, RM225, RM280, RM312, and RM417).

Introduction

1. An article in the *New York Times* (January 6, 1999, p. A9), to quote a typical instance, says, "Most historians agree . . . that the Constitution was imposed on Japan by the United States in the aftermath of World War II."

2. For an analysis of the distinction in the African context, see H. W. O. Okoth-Ogendo, "Constitutions Without Constitutionalism," in Douglas Greenberg et al., eds., *Constitutionalism and Democracy: Transitions in the Contemporary World* (Oxford University Press, 1993), 65–82.

3. There is a considerable and growing literature on the relationship between democracy and constitutionalism. Specifically to the point here, see Adam Przeworski et al., *Sustainable Democracy* (Cambridge University Press, 1995), especially part I; Juan J. Linz and Alfred Stepan, *Problems of Democratic Transition and Consolidation: Southern Europe, South America and Post-Communist Europe* (Johns Hopkins University Press, 1996), especially part III, on South American cases; and Samuel P. Huntington, *The Third Wave: Democratization in the Late Twentieth Century* (University of Oklahoma Press, 1991).

4. Kyoko Inoue, *MacArthur's Japanese Constitution* (University of Chicago Press, 1991).

5. SCAP called its history of the early years of the Occupation *Political Reorientation of Japan*. Perhaps the play on the word "orient" seemed clever.

6. *Political Reorientation of Japan* (U.S. Government Printing Office,

1949), Vol. II, 737, 747; Douglas MacArthur to Douglas Horton, October 19, 1946, in CinC's Personal File, MacArthur Memorial Library, Norfolk, VA.

7. Tanaka Hideo, "The Conflict between Two Legal Traditions in Making the Constitution of Japan," in Robert A. Ward and Sakamoto Yoshikazu, eds., *Democratizing Japan* (University of Hawaii Press, 1987), 107–132.

8. Potsdam Declaration, RM024.

9. For important statements of American policy, see SWNCC 150 (Initial Postsurrender Policy), RM030; Secretary of State James F. Byrnes's statement, released September 1, 1945, RM031; Five Fundamental Reforms, statement by SCAP, October 11, 1945, RM041; and Initial Postsurrender Directive, issued by the Joint Chiefs of Staff for the guidance of the Supreme Commander (JCS 1380, dated November 3, 1945), RM044.

10. Quoted from a brief statement by Secretary of State Byrnes, September 1, 1945, RM031.

11. "Five Fundamental Reforms," RM041. The phrase, "for centuries," was curious. It revealed SCAP's thin understanding of Japanese history; the Americans were apparently unaware of Japan's nineteenth- and early twentieth-century social and political reforms.

12. In explaining this reform, SCAP said that women, "being members of the body politic, [would] bring to Japan a new concept of government directly subservient to the well-being of the home." RM041.P3.11.

13. RM041.P1.

14. RM041.P1.

15. RM030.1.P1.B(b). This document (SWNCC 150) was approved by President Truman and sent to MacArthur on September 6, 1945. The same language was repeated in JCS 1380, dated November 3, 1945, which the military regarded as its basic orders for the Occupation.

16. Peter Duus, *Party Rivalry and Political Change in Taishō Japan* (Harvard University Press, 1968).

17. These questions are beyond the scope of the present book. They are the subject of two important recent books. One, by a Japanese historian, Daikichi Irokawa, is titled *The Age of Hirohito: In Search of Modern Japan,* transl. by Mikiso Hane and John K. Urda (foreword by Carol Gluck) (Free Press, 1995); see especially 27–39 and chap. 3, 71–107. The other, a biographical study by Herbert Bix, is titled *Hirohito and the Making of Modern Japan* (HarperCollins, 2000), chap. 10–13 et passim.

18. RM043.TEXT2.P7.

19. An all-too-typical example of this neglect was the project on comparative constitutionalism organized by the American Council of Learned Societies, beginning in 1987. A volume of papers produced for the project's worldwide series of conferences contains no treatment of the Japanese case and only one passing reference to it. See Greenberg et al., pp. 12–13.

20. *Time* magazine was an early proponent of this image. An article titled "We, the mimics" (March 18, 1946) caused acute pain in Japan.

21. For an affirmation of these values, see Bilahari Kausikan, "Asia's Different Standard," in *Foreign Policy* 92 (1993): 34–37.

22. For a brilliant evocation of these feelings, see Murray Sayle, "Letter from Japan: A Dynasty Falters," in The *New Yorker,* June 12, 2000, 84–91.

23. We have in mind works like that of Adam Przeworski and his associates, titled *Sustainable Democracy.* See also Huntington, *Third Wave,* especially chap. 2 (especially the list on pages 37–38) and 3, and sources cited there.

24. By the mid-1960s, Japan ranked third in the world in total gross national prod-

uct, behind the United States and the Soviet Union, but ahead of West Germany, France, Italy, and the United Kingdom. As late as 1952, however, per capita GNP in Japan was "only $188, below that of Brazil, Malaysia and Chile, among other less developed countries." Hugh Patrick and Henry Rosovsky, eds., *Asia's New Giant: How the Japanese Economy Works* (Brookings, 1976), 3, 11.

25. Ronald P. Dore, *Education in Tokugawa Japan* (Oxford University Press, 1965).

26. Patrick and Rosovsky, 15.

27. Robert Dahl offers empirical evidence, in *Polyarchy* (Yale University Press, 1971), 110–111. Przeworski and his associates present a detailed critique of Dahl's argument, particularly as it relates to central and eastern Europe in the post-Communist era, in *Sustainable Democracy*, 19–33.

28. On Hume's contributions to the thought of American framers, see Donald L. Robinson, *"To the Best of My Ability": The Presidency and the Constitution* (W. W. Norton, 1987), 31–34.

29. For an exception, see Ernest Barker's admirable *Reflections on Government* (Oxford University Press, 1942). For a poetic expression of anxiety, see "September 1, 1939," in W. H. Auden, *Another Time* (Random House, 1940).

30. For a discerning analysis, see Clinton L. Rossiter, *Constitutional Dictatorship* (Princeton University Press, 1948).

31. On the tensions between democracy and liberal constitutionalism, see Walter F. Murphy, "Constitutions, Constitutionalism, and Democracy," in Greenberg et al., 3–7; and Bhikhu Parekh, "The Cultural Particularity of Liberal Democracy," *Political Studies* [Special Issue] 60 (1992): 160–175.

32. Huntington, *Third Wave*, 3–13.

33. Adam Przeworski, Michael Alvarez, Jose Antonio Cheibub, and Fernando Limongi, "What Makes Democracies Endure?" *Journal of Democracy* 7.1 (1996): 50.

34. Huntington, *Third Wave*, 301.

35. Toshio Nishi, *Unconditional Democracy: Education and Politics in Occupied Japan, 1945–1952* (Hoover Institution Press, 1982), ix.

36. Ibid., 123.

Chapter 1

1. "General Principles Applicable to the Postwar Settlement of Japan," September 29, 1943, Notter File, Box 64. U.S. National Archives, Washington, D.C.

2. "Status of the Japanese Emperor," State Department Decimal File 894.001.3-443, U.S. National Archives.

3. State Department Decimal File 894.001/11–2244, National Archives. Also Notter File, Box 116. *Kokutai* refers to Japan's political structure built around the imperial institution. It was, as will be evident, a major concern throughout this period.

4. For these papers, see RM009–RM015.

5. Theodore Cohen, *Remaking Japan: The American Occupation as New Deal* (Free Press, 1987), 28.

6. Notter File, Box 116, U.S. National Archives.

7. See Feis's memo to Marchu, January 10, 1945, in Record Group 165, Civil Affairs Division 321, Section 7, U.S. National Archives.

8. Between March and August 1945 General Curtis LeMay's B-29 bombers "dropped 147,000 tons of incendiary bombs and laid over 12,000 mines in Japanese waters." In 2,148 sorties, LeMay lost only two B-29s to enemy fire. According to the Office of Air Force History, *Strategic Air Warfare* (Office of Air Force History, 1988), 40, n. 28, the

attacks devastated sixty-six cities, causing 900,000 deaths and 1.3 million injuries, and forcing a quarter of Japan's urban population to evacuate the cities.

9. Hugh Borton, *Japan's Modern Century* (Ronald Press, 1955), 389. Borton served on the SFE for the State Department.

10. Grew's account is in his *Turbulent Era* (Houghton Mifflin, 1952), vol. 2, 1428–1431.

11. Ibid.

12. For the controversy over the development of U.S. policy leading to the Potsdam Declaration, see *Foreign Relations of the United States, Conference of Berlin* (U.S. Government Printing Office, 1945), vol. 1, 889–892 and 894 (hereafter FRUS).

13. Acheson later admitted that "Grew's view fortunately prevailed. I very shortly came to see that I was quite wrong." See James Chace, *Acheson: The Secretary of State who Created the American World* (Harvard University Press, 1998), 106–107.

14. See RM018–RM024.

15. FRUS, vol. 1, 893.

16. Ibid., 893, n. 4, and 899.

17. MacLeish's memo to Byrnes, dated July 6, 1945. See RM019.

18. RM020.

19. RM021.

20. Officially known as the "Potsdam Proclamation," it came to be more commonly known as the "Potsdam Declaration." We have followed this conventional usage here. For the text, see RM024.

21. Robert J. C. Butow, *Japan's Decision to Surrender* (Stanford University Press, 1954), 143; and Tōgō Shigenori, *The Cause of Japan* (Simon and Schuster, 1956).

22. For the Japanese Foreign Ministry's record of the last days of the war, see *Shūsen shiroku* (Tokyo, 1952). Chapters 43–44 contain published accounts of many participants in the August 9 imperial conference.

23. Butow, 162

24. Quoted in Butow, 175

25. Quoted *ibid.*, 175–176. Butow reconstructed the speech from testimony of those present. For a summary of the conference and the emperor's comments by Cabinet Secretary Sakomizu Hisatsune, see *Shūsen shiroku*, 588–589. Herbert P. Bix, *Hirohito and the Making of Modern Japan* (HarperCollins, 2000), 506, argues that the emperor delayed Japan's surrender in the summer of 1945 while trying to win a guarantee of the "authoritarian imperial system with himself and the empowered throne at the center."

26. The devastating American air raid on May 25 had completely destroyed the Foreign Ministry's main building. *Shūsen shiroku*, 601.

27. Kase Toshikazu translated the Japanese text into English. See his *Journey to the Missouri* (Yale University Press, 1950), 238, 243. Matsumoto's account is in *Shūsen shiroku*, 602.

28. The transmission was intercepted by U.S. intelligence and passed to the White House immediately. The question remains whether this constituted an "official" notification that Japan had surrendered.

29. Butow, 181. The raids continued until August 15, well after Washington knew of Japan's decision to surrender. Leon Sigal, *Fighting to a Finish* (Cornell University Press, 1988), 254–255; and Curtis LeMay, *Mission with LeMay* (Doubleday, 1965), 388.

30. Early in the morning of August 10, Byrnes, Forrestal, Leahy, and Stimson met with Truman in the Oval Office to consider the Japanese shortwave radio transmission. Walter Millis, *The Forrestal Diaries* (Viking, 1951), 83; and Leahy, *I Was There* (Whittlesey House, 1950), 434. Cited in Sigal, 250, nn. 68 and 69.

31. President Truman noted the appeal of "unconditional surrender" to Congress and the public. See his *Memoirs* (Doubleday, 1955), vol. 1, 42. According to public opinion polls in June 1945, 33 percent of a national sample wanted Hirohito executed, 17 percent wanted him put on trial, and another 18 percent preferred imprisonment or exile for him. A mere 3 percent favored using him to run Japan after the war. Cited in Sigal, 95.

32. For an account of the meeting in the Oval Office, see Sigal, 249–250. Byrnes's statement is in his *Speaking Frankly* (Harper, 1947), 209.

33. Sigal, 249–250.

34. For Kido's account of his meeting with Anami, see *Shūsen shiroku*, 678.

35. *Shūsen shiroku*, 681.

36. Butow, 208.

37. Truman said: "I deem this reply a full acceptance of the Potsdam Declaration which specifies the unconditional surrender of Japan. In the reply there is no qualification." Quoted in Sigal, 272.

38. The full story is told in Pacific War Research Society, *Japan's Longest Day* (Kodansha, 1968).

39. See RM030.

40. See Acheson's letter of September 5 to Truman, in FRUS, 1945, vol. 6, p. 591.

41. See chapter 2 in this volume for SFE's heated debate on this issue.

42. RM056. The document was sent to MacArthur in its final form on January 9, 1946.

43. See RM040, JCS directive 1380/15, dated November 3, 1945.

44. See RM030.

45. In October 1945, these powers formed the Far Eastern Advisory Council (FEAC) and in December the United States, China, Great Britain, and Soviet Union signed the "Moscow Agreement" creating the Far Eastern Commission. See RM049.

46. The most important were the "Initial Post-Surrender Policy for Japan" (SWNCC 150) and the "Basic Directive for Post-Surrender Military Government in Japan" (JCS 1380). See RM030 and RM044.

47. MacArthur saw earlier drafts of this document. The September 3 version referred to here was the final one which President Truman signed on September 6, 1945.

48. For the cable exchange between MacArthur and Marshall, see Radio Message File, CM-IN-2193, War Department, U.S. National Archives, Washington, D.C.

49. For an excellent guide to the main sections and personnel of MacArthur's General Headquarters, see Takemae Eiji, *GHQ* (Iwanami Shinsho, 1983).

50. It was called *shūsen renraku jimukyoku* in Japanese.

51. *Nihon senryō kenkyū jiten* (Tokuma Shoten, 1978), vol. 3 of *Nihon senryōgun*, 60.

52. Acheson, *Present at the Creation: My Years in the State Department* (Norton, 1969), 126.

53. *Political Reorientation of Japan* (hereafter PRJ) (U.S. Government Printing Office, 1949), 737, 785; and Douglas MacArthur, *Reminiscences* (McGraw-Hill, 1964), 20.

54. MacArthur to Douglas Horton, October 19, 1946, in Commander-in-Chief's personal file, MacArthur Memorial Library, Norfolk, Virginia.

55. Ibid. and PRJ, 737, 747.

Chapter 2

1. RM030.

2. RM040.

3. Later called SWNCC 55/3. See RM040. The discussion that follows is based on the SWNCC 55 Series, Scholarly Resources microfilm, reel 7; and Minutes of the Subcommittee of the Far East, National Archives microfilm T1198.

4. RMO36.

5. The reference here is to a draft policy paper, SWNCC 228. See RM056.

6. Chairman Vincent defended the statement as policy because "Mr. Acheson had approved such a policy." RM040.

7. RM042.

8. Robert Fearey took a draft copy of SWNCC 55/6 to MacArthur's political adviser in Tokyo in early October, but the official directive reached MacArthur in November. RM interview with Fearey, October 16, 1978.

9. War Department Messages, 1001-1094, April 29 to August 2, 1945, in MacArthur Memorial Library, Norfolk, Virginia.

10. Etō Jun, ed., Senryō shiroku (Kōdansha, 1981), vol. 1, 270-275; and MacArthur to Marshall, War Department General Staff, DPD Messages, CM-In-2193, September 3, 1945, Record Group 165, U.S. National Archives.

11. For Kagawa's activities, see his autobiography, Kagawa-den (Kirisuto Shinbunshi, 1956); Cyril J. Davey, Kagawa of Japan (Epworth, 1960), and Thomas Mackin, "Kagawa Sees Japan's Future," Christian Century (October 10, 1945).

12. "Sekiya Nikki" is Sekiya's handwritten diary preserved in the National Diet Library in Tokyo.

13. Published in the English-language Nippon Times, September 2, 1945.

14. Mackin, "Kagawa Sees Japan's Future."

15. An American independent missionary born in Colorado and raised in Flagstaff, Arizona, Vories had served in Japan since 1905 and taken Japanese citizenship in 1940. Vories's wife, Hitotsuyanagi Makiko, also a Christian educated in the United States, was the daughter of a nineteenth-century feudal baron, with ties to the emperor's mother and other members of the royal family. Her father had once served in the palace of Hirohito's father, the Taishō Emperor.

16. Vories Diary, September 6-12, 1945. We thank the Ōmi Kyōdaisha in Ōmi Hachiman for permission to copy several pages of the diary.

17. Bartlett's record of his meeting with Vories is from MacArthur Memorial Archives, RG-5, B.2, F.1, "Japanese File" correspondence, 1945-1946.

18. The emperor developed this argument in his memoirs on the coming of the war, which were dictated to several aides in the spring of 1946. The document was published in 1991 as Shōwa tennō dokuhakuroku (Bungei Shunjū, 1991).

19. This was the imperial rescript rejecting "false views and myths" regarding his "divinity." See RM096.

20. Koseki Shōichi, The Birth of Japan's Postwar Constitution, ed., and trans. Ray A. Moore (Westview Press, 1997), 7.

21. Koseki, 8.

22. For the only record of the meeting, see RM057. Konoe's report to Higashikuni is discussed in Satō Tatsuo, Nihonkoku kenpō seiritsushi (Yūhikaku, 1962), vol. 1, 160.

23. Nippon Times, September 22, 1945. The quote is from Darley Downs, "Effects of Wartime Pressures on Churches and Missions in Japan," 83, M.A. Thesis, Union Theological Seminary, 1946; also Davey, Kagawa of Japan, 131.

24. In January 1946, Hirohito invited Kagawa to give a lecture on Christianity at the palace. Uemura Tamaki, the daughter of a famous Meiji period Protestant leader, taught Bible classes and Christian hymns to the empress. See R. A. Moore, Tenno ga baiburu o yonda hi (Kōdansha, 1983), 39-41.

25. *Kawai Michiko Bunshū* (comp., pub. Keisen Jogakuen Shiryōshitsu Iinkai, 1985), 592–594.

26. For more on Fellers's military background and service on MacArthur's staff, see John W. Dower, *Embracing Defeat: Japan in the Wake of World War II* (New Press, 1999), 280–286.

27. Kawai Michi, *Sliding Doors* (Keisen Jogakuen, 1950), 84–86, and an interview with Isshiki's daughter in May 1983.

28. 1880–1950. See entry in *Seijika Jimmei Jiten*, 287–288.

29. Our thanks to the National Diet Library staff in Tokyo for help with Sekiya's diary and an introduction to his son, who kindly shared his father's unpublished diary entries for the fall of 1945.

30. MacArthur claimed Hirohito had assumed personal responsibility for the war. See MacArthur, *Reminiscences* (McGraw-Hill, 1964), 288. After MacArthur's death in 1964, the Reverend Billy Graham revealed that MacArthur had told him in 1955 that the emperor had privately declared his willingness to make Christianity the state religion of Japan. According to Graham, MacArthur, after considering the proposal, replied to the emperor: "No nation must be made to conform to any religion. It must be done on a voluntary basis." *New York Times*, April 7, 1964, p. 16. Also *Church and State*, vol. 17(6) (June 1964): 10. The notes of their first meeting on September 25, 1945, by the Foreign Ministry interpreter, Okumura Katsuzō, offer no support for either of these claims. See Kojima Noboru, "Tennō to Amerika to Taiheiyō Sensō," *Bungei Shunjū*, (November 1975): 115–119.

31. Tanaka, professor of law at Tokyo Imperial University, served as minister of education in the first Yoshida Cabinet, 1946–1947, and later became chief justice of the Supreme Court. He was married to the daughter of Matsumoto Jōji, who, as a minister in Shidehara's cabinet, chaired the committee on constitutional reform.

32. Higashikuni and his cabinet resigned on October 5 to protest MacArthur's directive on civil liberties. Shidehara became prime minister the following day.

33. Etō Jun, ed., *Senryō shiroku*, vol. 4, 87.

34. See RM038. We thank Professor Theodore McNelly for a copy of this memorandum.

35. *Kagawa-den*, 427

36. See RM056.

37. Joe J. Mickle letter to Joseph C. Grew, 1/26/45, "Cooperation with Japan." Archives of Foreign Missions Conference of North America, New York City.

38. Two of the four, James C. Baker and Luman J. Schafer, were former missionaries in Japan. The other two, Douglas Horton and Walter Van Kirk, were prominent leaders in the Federal Council of Churches. Their report is contained in *Return to Japan* (Friendship Press, 1946). See also Charles Inglehart, *International Christian University* (International Christian University, 1964), 12.

39. MacArthur's full speech is in PRJ (U.S. Government Printing Office, 1949), vol. 2, 736.

40. *Return to Japan*, 26.

41. *Return to Japan*, 27; and Inglehart, *International Christian University*, 12.

42. His monologue on causes of the war referred to deep anger Japan felt in the 1920s when the United States discriminated against Japanese immigrants in California. See *Shōwa Tennō Dokuhakuroku*, 20.

43. *Nippon Times*, October 31, 1945.

44. George Atcheson to Secretary of State, October 31, 1945; National Records Center, SCAP, POLAD, Box 2275.

45. *Return to Japan*, 28.

46. See MacArthur's statement to Paul Rusch—Japan cannot be a democracy without Christianity—in William P. Woodward, *The Allied Occupation of Japan and Japanese Religions* (E. J. Brill, 1972), 359.

47. See Bonner Fellers, "Our Friends the Japanese," *Nation's Business*, (February 1948).

48. Inglehart, *International Christian University*, 12; Woodward, *The Allied Occupation*, 243.

49. Bruno Bitter to SCAP, November 7, 1946; National Records Center, SCAP, Adjutant General's File, Box 478.

50. MacArthur to JCS, December 29, 1945, and November 22, 1946, National Records Center, SCAP, Adjutant General's File, Box 408 and Box 478. In 1949, Royall wrote to Truman of the "religious opportunities now open to us in Japan," and said he had ordered the Department of Army to "give active encouragement to Christian missionary work . . ." and help disseminate "Christian ethical, cultural and political ideals through all levels of Japanese society." Assistant Secretary Tracy Voorhees incorporated "work of this nature" into the U.S. program for rehabilitation of occupied areas. He reported to Royall: "Conversations have been held with leaders of both Catholic and Protestant communions seeking their help and advice as to the most appropriate means that might be utilized." Royall to Truman, April 27, 1949; Truman Correspondence, Subject File, Truman Library, Independence, MO.

51. See "General MacArthur's Statements Concerning Christianity in Japan," in Woodward, 357–359.

52. PRJ, vol. 2, 770.

53. From Paul Rusch's unpublished manuscript, cited in Woodward, 359.

54. Douglas MacArthur, *A Soldier Speaks* (Praeger, 1965), 309–310. MacArthur is referring here to a campaign to distribute New Testaments in all Japanese schools.

55. For SCAP policies supporting Christianity, see Moore, ed., *Tennō ga baiburu o yonda hi*, 42–50.

56. Atcheson to MacArthur, January 7, 1946, State Department Decimal File 894.001/1–746, National Archives.

57. "Ningen Sengen" in Japanese, which affirmed the human qualities of the emperor. The Americans preferred to call it the emperor's "Denial of Divinity."

58. The fullest account of CIE's role is Woodward, 250–269, 317–321; and Wilhelmus H. M. Creemers, *Shrine Shinto after World War II* (E. J. Brill, 1968), 124–132.

59. Woodward, 267. For MacArthur's press release, see PRJ, vol. 2, 471. For a detailed account, see Dower, *Embracing Defeat*, 308–317.

60. RM002

61. Fearey's memo to Atcheson, 10/13/45, Record Group 84, Box 2275, WNRC.

62. Atcheson to MacArthur, January 7, 1946, State Department Decimal File 894.001/1–746, National Archives.

63. Ibid.

64. On trying the emperor for war crimes (January 25, 1946), General MacArthur to General Dwight D. Eisenhower, RM054.

65. For the Japanese government's argument, see Etō Jun, ed., *Shūsen o toinaosu* (Hokuyōsha, 1980), 112–130.

66. War Department Operations Division, ABC 014 Japan, Section 5, Record Group 113, National Archives; and FRUS, 1946, vol. 8, 395–401.

67. MacArthur's note to Whitney, RM141.

Chapter 3

1. For example, Koseki Shōichi, *The Birth of Japan's Postwar Constitution* (Westview, 1997), 64–65; and Dower, *Embracing Defeat: Japan in the Wake of World War II* (New Press, 1999), 359–360.

2. See Satō Tatsuo, *Nihonkoku kenpō seiritsushi* (Yūhikaku, 1962) (hereafter NKSRS), vol. 1, 154–155. The four published volumes of this work are indispensable. Volume 2 was published in 1964; volumes 3 and 4, published in 1994, were supplemented and edited by Satō Isao.

3. The American press published SWNCC 150/4 in the United States on September 22, and the Japanese press published it two days later. See NKSRS, vol. 1, 87.

4. Yoshida replaced Shigemitsu as Foreign Minister on September 17.

5. NKSRS, vol. 1, 152.

6. SWNCC 150 and JCS 1380. The final version of SWNCC 228, "Reform of the Japanese Government," was sent to MacArthur in January 1946. There is no evidence it was shown to the Japanese government at any time during 1946.

7. NKSRS, vol. 1, 153.

8. Higashikuni, *Ichigunjin no sensō nikki*, cited in NKSRS, vol. 1, 160.

9. NKSRS, vol. 1, 154–155.

10. Ibid., 155.

11. Ibid., 152–153,

12. *Hōseikyoku* in Japanese.

13. Irie Toshio, *Kenpō seiritsu no keii to kenpōjō no shomondai* (Daiichi Hōki Shuppan, 1976), 4–5.

14. Both have left detailed accounts of the constitutional revision process. Satō's papers in the National Diet Library contain a wealth of information for students of this period.

15. RM058, drafted by Irie Toshio. See Irie, *Kenpō seiritsu*, 5.

16. NKSRS, vol. 1, 164.

17. For more on Miyazawa's activities in 1945–1946 and his "August Revolution," see Koseki, 124–129. David Titus analyzed Miyazawa's role in popularizing the new constitution, in "The Making of the 'Symbol Emperor System' in Postwar Japan," *Modern Asian Studies*, 14(4) (1980): 529–578.

18. For a summary of the lecture, see RM059.

19. Article LXXIII. Miyazawa believed this article "served as an obstacle to hasty amendment," but acknowledged it would have to be revised as a prelude to constitutional reform and democratization.

20. For earlier references to the Japanese emperor as a "symbol," see Nakamura Masanori, *The Japanese Monarchy: Ambassador Joseph Grew and the Making of the "Symbol Emperor System," 1931–1991* (M.E. Sharpe, 1992), chap. 9.

21. Yabe's given name is also read "Sadaji." For his report, see RM062.

22. Yabe edited a two-volume biography of his mentor, *Konoe Fumimaro* (Kōbundō, 1952) and served as vice chairman of the Committee on the Constitution (*Kenpō chōsakai*) from 1957.

23. RM062.

24. *Tennō* was first translated as "emperor" in the nineteenth century. T. Fujitani, *Splendid Monarchy: Power and Pageantry in Modern Japan* (University of California Press, 1996), shows brilliantly the Meiji government's transformation of a "mysterious figure" into a Western style imperial ruler called emperor (*tennō*).

25. Yabe Teiji, *Konoe Fumimaro* (Kōbundō, 1952), vol. 2, 581–583.

26. See RM064.

27. The Moscow Agreement of December 26, 1945, established the FEC and gave the Allied organization veto power over certain political reforms in Japan.

28. For both documents, see "Outline of Constitutional Amendments," in RM068.

29. George M. Wilson, *Radical Nationalist in Japan: Kita Ikki, 1883–1937* (Harvard University Press, 1969).

30. The Privy Council was a constitutional body whose members had the responsibility to "deliberate upon important matters of State, when they have been consulted by the Emperor [Article LVI]."

31. RM068. The memorandum was discovered in 1975. See Ray A. Moore, "Japanese Government Materials on the American Occupation," in *The Occupation of Japan and Its Legacy to the Postwar World*, ed. L. H. Redman (MacArthur Memorial, 1976).

32. Tatsuki seems to have in mind military force such as guns and tanks; he never mentions ultimatums or SCAP directives, which indeed were used frequently.

33. See the previous chapter.

34. Max Bishop's report on meeting with Hiranuma. POLAD No. 101, enclosure, December 14, 1945, in Record Group 84, Box 2275, WNRC.

35. Ibid.

36. See Meirion and Susie Harries, *Sheathing the Sword: The Demilitarization of Postwar Japan* (Macmillan, 1987), chap. 4.

37. RM072.

38. See RM007.

39. The Socialists took credit for this in Diet debates in July 1946.

Chapter 4

1. See chapter 2 (in this volume) and RM057.

2. The interpreter was Okumura Katsuzō, head of the CLO, who had served in the same capacity at the first meeting of MacArthur and Emperor Hirohito a week earlier.

3. Okumura's memo for record, RM061.

4. Ibid.

5. Ibid.

6. See RM039 for the SCAP order.

7. Technically, Konoe remained a cabinet member until the new Shidehara cabinet was appointed on October 9.

8. RM213.SP2.P4.

9. RM065.

10. RM066.TEXT2.P5.

11. RM071.

12. Based on SWNCC 228.

13. RM071. Emmerson writes in his memoirs: "I handed a copy of these principles to Professor Takagi for the Konoe group." *The Japanese Thread* (Holt, Rinehart and Winston, 1978), 266. See also Takagi's account of this meeting in Kenpō Chōsakai Jimukyoku, comp., *Kenpō seitei* Jimukyoku, *no Keika ni kansuru shōiinkai hōkokusho* (Ōkurashō, 1961), 37. (Hereafter *Kenpō setei*)

14. *Kenpō seitei*, 19.

15. See Sasaki's outline of revisions, RM083; and Konoe's recommendations to the emperor, RM088.

16. RM049.

17. *Kido Kōichi nikki* [diary] (Tokyo Daigaku Shuppankai, 1966), vol. 2, 1241.

18. Ibid, 1241–1242.

19. *Kido Kōichi nikki*, 1242.

20. For Matsumoto's 1954 recollection of the events, see RM213.SP2.P4.

21. See Takagi's testimony in Koseki, 11.

22. This agrees with Koseki's interpretation. *The Birth of Japan's Postwar Constitution*, trans. R.A. Moore (Westview Press, 1997), 12.

23. Even Matsumoto was uncertain what might develop. See RM213.SP2.P6.

24. *Mainichi Shinbun*, October 23.

25. *Kenpō Seitei*, 148–149.

26. Ibid.

27. RM074.

28. *New York Times*, October 26, 28, 1945.

29. RM078.Text1.P2.

30. RM075.

31. *Kenpō Seitei*, 155.

32. RM079.

33. *Kenpō seitei*, 39

34. Norman, a secret member of the Communist Party since 1935, was later accused of being a Soviet agent and committed suicide. See Roger Bowen, *Innocence Is Not Enough: The Life and Death of Herbert Norman* (M.E. Sharpe, 1986). Theodore McNelly disagrees with Bowen in an unpublished paper, "Herbert Norman: Security Risk or Victim of McCarthyism?" (Presented at Southeast Regional Seminar on Japan, George Mason University, October 7, 2000). Cited with permission of the author.

35. *Herbert Norman zenshū* [collected works] (Iwanami Shoten, 1977), 2:345. Quoted in Koseki, 17.

36. RM077. Koseki, 19, denounces Atcheson for this "dishonorable and shockingly false charge against the interpreter, Okumura Katsuzō."

37. RM078.

38. See RM056.

39. RM073.

40. Konoe's proposed revisions are in RM088.

41. Sasaki's proposals submitted to Hirohito are in RM083.

42. Koseki, 21.

43. *Shidehara Kijūrō* (Shidehara heiwa zaidan, 1955), 255–256.

44. PRJ, vol. 1, 91; RM213SP2.P3. *Kenpō seitei*, 195–197.

45. RM213.

46. Abe Shinnosuke, quoted in Koseki, 52

47. Suzuki Tadao, quoted in Koseki, 52.

48. RM213.SP2.P6.

49. Satō Tatsuo's account in RM076 and *Kenpō Seitei*, 199.

50. No specialists on the American system of law served on the committee. See RM076 for a complete list of the committee's members and advisers; and cf. Koseki, 50–51.

51. Irie, *Kenpō seiritsu*, 25.

52. See RM082 and RM078.

53. NKSRS, vol. 1, 296.

54. Quoted in Koseki, 54.

55. Summary based on Satō's memo in RM076, and Koseki, 56.

56. RM080, RM081, and RM085.

57. RM087.

58. NKSRS, vol. 2, 617–618.

59. NKSRS, vol. 2, 618–619.
60. Koseki, 60.
61. RM113.P2
62. RM111.P2.

Chapter 5

1. See chapter 2 (in this volume) for details of these meetings. On October 11, 1945, MacArthur told the new prime minister, Shidehara, that satisfying the Potsdam requirements would "unquestionably involve a liberalization of the Constitution." RM041.

2. Quoting SWNCC 228. See RM056.

3. See chapter 4 (in this volume).

4. Kades regarded Hays as one of the most valuable members of his staff. When Kades returned to the United States in 1948, Hays would replace him as Whitney's deputy at GS. Donald Robinson's (DR) interview with Charles Kades (CK), September 24, 1994, in Greenfield, Massachusetts; see also Justin Williams, *Japan's Political Reform Under MacArthur* (University of Georgia Press, 1979), 69.

5. For Whitney's role in GS, see Williams, chap. 5.

6. CK, Northampton, March 1, 1994.

7. RM132.P5.

8. These notes and impressions are based on Koseki, *The Birth of Japan's Postwar Constitution*, 82; Williams, 53; and on DR's interview with CK, Greenfield, MA, February 12, 1994.

9. RM132.P2. Reading this memo, one cannot help wondering what effect it might have had if SCAP had *encouraged* contact between Rowell and Matsumoto rather than prohibited it.

10. Rowell identified several: the Imperial Conference ("not authorized by any written law but decides policy on the most important matters of state . . . normally meets prior to commencement of war"), Lord Keeper of the Privy Seal (already "voluntarily abolished"), the cabinet, the Privy Council, and the House of Peers. The latter three were constitutional, in the sense that the Meiji Constitution mentioned their existence. Rowell's point was that the constitution did not make them "responsive to the people or their representatives." RM132.ANNEXB.1.PA.

11. RM132.ANNEXB.4.PC.

12. RM132.ANNEXB.4.PD.4–16.

13. Rowell's warning against any interference with these rights apparently applied only to the Japanese. Under the Americans, protection extended only to freedom of religious worship, opinion, speech, press and assembly "not incompatible with the security of the occupational forces." RM132.ANNEXA.2.P1.

14. RM132.ANNEXC.1.

15. RM102.14.

16. RM474.

17. RM056.P4.A.

18. A section later in the document does mention that courts in Japan were subservient to social pressures and notes that MacArthur had issued an order (RM039), dated October 4, 1945, guaranteeing basic civil liberties.

19. At the end, SWNCC 228 says that electoral laws can be "safely left, and would be better left," to the Japanese, in statutes. Takayanagi Kenzō, Ohtomo Ichirō and Tan-

aka Hideo, eds., *Nihonkoku kenpō seitei no katei* [*The Making of the Constitution of Japan*], vol. I (documents), (Yūhikaku, 1972), 434–436 (hereafter MCJ).

20. RM056.P4.D.

21. RM056.P4.C.1. It is not clear what other bodies are intended here—presumably the Privy Council and the Imperial Household. But if the imperial institution were abolished, would these others not be abolished, too?

22. RM056.P4.D3 and D1.

23. MCJ, 420–422.

24. It was to correct this flaw that Matsumoto's draft made individual ministers susceptible to removal by votes of no confidence. RM101.ART55.

25. RM005.ART71. This was the clause borrowed by Meiji leaders from the Prussian constitution.

26. The irony here is that this ordinance was designed by Yamagata to control the military. See George Akita, *Foundations of Constitutional Government in Japan in Modern Japan, 1868–1900* (Harvard University Press, 1967), chap. 10. The ordinance was repealed in 1913 but restored in 1936. It was a major factor allowing military leaders to control Japanese policy on the road to the Pacific War.

27. MCJ, 428.

28. RM056.P5.

29. Perhaps earlier. Kades remembered that, when he left Washington bound for duty in Japan, he asked Ward Cameron, Civil Affairs Division liaison to the JCS Secretariat, to assemble "important policy papers" for him. Included, he said, were early drafts of SWNCC 228 and JCS 1380. DR interview with CK, March 1, 1994.

30. RM056. The authors directed that SWNCC 228 not be published, so that the Supreme Commander could retain control of the process. RM056.P7.

31. Kades noted that it deserved respect and received respect in GS, both for its merits and because SCAP would have had to answer to authorities in Washington for deviating from its recommendations. He also noted that, coming from an interagency committee, rather than directly from JCS, SWNCC 228 was not a "directive" for SCAP. DR interview with CK, March 1, 1994.

32. RM147.6.P1. Note also that SWNCC 228 was used to measure the adequacy of the revisions proposed by Matsumoto. RM118.

33. See, for example, RM146.3, RM147.6, and RM161.1.P2 and RM161.2.P2.

34. Ward notes three exceptions to this generalization: "SCAP's initiative in building the imperial institution into the framework of the new constitution"; Article 9 ("SWNCC 228 nowhere contemplates" incorporating demilitarization into the constitution, rather than in the peace treaty or statutory law); and an upper house of the legislature (*not* part of the GS model originally). Ibid., 34–35.

35. Eventually India and Burma also joined the FEC.

36. RM030.

37. George H. Blakeslee, *The Far Eastern Commission* (U.S. Government Printing Office, 1953), 8–9.

38. Blakeslee, 18. For the Moscow Agreement, see RM049.

39. Blakeslee, 15.

40. Blakeslee, "Negotiating to Establish the Far Eastern Commission," in *Negotiating with the Russians*, ed. Raymond Dennett and Joseph E. Johnson (World Peace Foundation, 1951), chap. 5.

41. RM049.A.3.p3.

42. See RM049.

43. Quoted in Blakeslee, *The Far Eastern Commission*, 16.

44. Blakeslee, *The Far Eastern Commission*, 16–17.

45. Ibid., 19.

46. Ibid., 19.

47. SCAP records referred to the occasion as "A meeting between Government Section and the FEC." Hussey Papers, reel #5, quoted in Koseki, *The Birth of Japan's Postwar Constitution*, 73, n.19.

48. RM053.33.SP1–RM053.33.SP10. The document purports to be a verbatim record of the conversation.

49. RM053.33; see especially RM053.33.SP 1–4, 7–8, 13–14, 19–21.

50. The memo was apparently the work of several people at GS. In forwarding it to MacArthur, Whitney said that it "represents the composite view of all officers of the Government Section who have examined this question." RM140.7.P1.

51. RM140.2.P1 and P2.

52. RM140.1.P2; RM140.2.P1; and RM140.3.P1.

53. Cf. RM139.P4.

54. In relevant part, the Moscow Agreement stated: "The United States Government may issue interim directives to the Supreme Commander pending action by the Commission whenever urgent matters arise not covered by policies already formulated by the Commission; provided that any directives dealing with fundamental changes in the Japanese constitutional structure . . . will be issued only following consultation and following the attainment of agreement in the Far Eastern Commission." (RM049.A.3.P3)

55. This ignored Washington's statement, cited earlier, that the terms of the agreement took effect on the day it was signed.

56. The memo reads: "It is my opinion that the [prohibition against an 'order' regarding constitutional revision] . . . would not embrace a mere approval by you of constitutional reform measures submitted to you by the Japanese government." RM140.5.

57. RM148.P4. There is indirect evidence, however, that SCAP divulged its secret to an American member of the FEC delegation, Colonel James McCormack, who had represented the Pentagon on the SFE of SWNCC. McCormack did not depart with the FEC on January 30 but stayed in Tokyo for a few days before flying home two weeks later. Sasakawa Ryūtarō argues that Pentagon officials were thus prepared to support MacArthur's claim when the March 6 draft constitution was published, and that it was a Japanese government product the origins of which predated the Moscow Agreement and the FEC. See Sasakawa, "Makkasa no kenpō seitei sakusen to Pentagon no kokuitachi," in *Kōhō no shisō to seido*, ed. Arata Masahiko (Shinsansha, 1999), 202–203.

58. RM139.P4. This document is a summary of MacArthur's comments to the FEC based on notes by the commission's secretary general, Nelson T. Johnson.

59. SWNCC 150 (RM030).

60. RM139.P4.

61. RM139.P12.

62. The countries represented were the United States, the United Kingdom, China, Australia, France, Canada, the Philippines, the Netherlands, and New Zealand.

Chapter 6

1. RM096.P6.

2. RM140.

3. RM112, 118.

4. So much so, that many have wondered whether it was a plant. But no evidence has ever been found. Koseki, 78.

5. Whitney memo to MacArthur, quoted by Koseki, *The Birth of Japan's Postwar Constitution*, 79.

6. RM141.

7. RM143.1.1.P0. Kades altered the quoted phrase to read: "a model constitution for submission to the Japanese people." RM144.0.P1. We have used the blunter language in the Ellerman version because it sounds more like Whitney. The Kades version conforms to the line taken by the Americans that engineered this event.

8. RM143.1.1.P4. Kades's amended version of the minutes omits this threat entirely. RM144.3.P4. Note also that Milo Rowell, who was present at the meeting with Whitney, swore out an affidavit, eighteen years later, denying that the words ascribed to Whitney had ever been spoken, or that he had spoken to that effect "in substance." RM143.2.P3. It is impossible to tell whether Whitney uttered words to this effect at that meeting. He was certainly capable of it. On the other hand, Rowell's integrity was well-known. Suffice it to say that the threat of forcing a revised constitution on Japan, one way or another, was always there.

9. RM143.1.1.P5.

10. RM143.1.3.P1.

11. Much of the biographical information that follows is gleaned from DR's interview with Kades, July 28, 1994; also, from Williams, *Japan's Political Revolution under MacArthur* (University of Georgia Press, 1979), chap. 5.

12. Geoffrey Perret, *Old Soldiers Never Die: The Life of Douglas MacArthur* (Random House, 1996), 368–370; a photo of the Leyte landing can be found between pages 344 and 345 of Perret's book.

13. As the original drafter of the preamble, Hussey's pride of authorship may have been a factor in discouraging the Japanese from rephrasing its alien echoes and rhetoric.

14. Quoted in Koseki, 82.

15. In Tanizaki's great novel, *The Makioka Sisters*, the heroines display their sophistication by attending a concert in Osaka where Leo Sirota was the soloist.

16. Beate Sirota Gordon and Hiraoka Makiko, *1945 nen no kurisumasu* (Kashiwa Shobō, 1995), 124–125. Gordon's memoirs were translated as *The Only Woman in the Room* (Kodansha International, 1997).

17. Koseki, 89–90.

18. Later Wildes would write *Typhoon Over Tokyo: The Occupation and Its Aftermath* (Macmillan, 1954), a harsh critique of the occupation from a leftist perspective.

19. Not Kades, though. He had prepared to do civil affairs work in Europe.

20. DR interview with Kades, February 12, 1994. The historian Hajo Holborn, a distinguished scholar—but not a specialist on Japan—helped to prepare a "handbook" of information that was used in some of these courses. Excerpts can be found in RM016.

21. See also MacArthur's "Five Fundamental Reforms," directive of October 11, 1945, which called for a "liberalization" of the constitution. RM041.P1.

22. Kades asked SCAP's drafting group on the Diet why there was no executive veto. Commander Swope replied with the quoted phrase. RM152.P4.

23. Alexander Hamilton set forth the case for a "unified executive" in *The Federalist*, no. 70.

24. Williams, 57.

25. RM166.P3 (memo cosigned by Esman and Jacob I. Miller).

26. RM161.2.P1.

27. RM187.2.P1.

28. Ellerman's notes indicate that the GS team may have viewed unicameralism as a bargaining chip, to be given up in return for Japanese compromise on a more important matter. RM146.2.P1.

29. Hussey viewed the collective responsibility of the cabinet as crucially important to the strength of the Diet in the proposed system. RM187.2.P1.

30. Kades wanted to call the SCAP draft, "An Agreement Among the People," like Cromwell's constitution of the 1640s. But Hussey and Rowell thought it sounded odd; so did Hays. So he gave it up. DR interview with Kades, June 25, 1994.

31. "The powers not delegated to the United States by the Constitution, nor prohibited by it to the States, are reserved to the States respectively, or to the people."

32. RM189.

33. RM149.1.P0.

34. RM149.1.P5.

35. RM149.1.P4.

36. RM149.1.P3. The idea here was to elevate the judiciary, but other ways would have to be found.

37. RM161.1.P1.

38. RM189.ART40.

39. RM147.5.P1 and P2.

40. Born in Sicily, Rizzo had studied with Kades at Cornell. After graduate work, he joined a Wall Street investment firm. When General Hilldring asked Kades to recommend someone to work on financial policy for the Occupation, Kades reached outside of government to recommend Rizzo. When Kades resigned in 1949, Rizzo replaced him as deputy chief of GS. In 1973, he received the First Class Order of the Sacred Treasure from Emperor Hirohito (Williams, 61). Kades never received a comparable honor from Japan.

41. RM155.

42. Kades later recalled that the phrase, "highest organ of state power," was "derived from my recollection of some such clause referring to some government body in the U.S.S.R. constitution." He thought it "dovetailed nicely" with the provision for a two-thirds Diet override of supreme court decisions on the unconstitutionality of statutes. Letter to DR, February 6, 1994. The override provision was dropped during the translating session in early March.

43. RM146.7.P1. Compare RM147.5.P2, where Kades again emphasized that "the Diet has all powers not explicitly prohibited to it by the Constitution."

44. RM172.1.P1. Hussey added that it was stated elsewhere in the constitution that "the will of the people, exercised through the Diet, is supreme." It is not clear what he meant. The Preamble, which he himself drafted, says, "We, the Japanese People, acting through our duly elected representatives in the National Diet . . . do ordain and establish this Constitution, founded upon the universal principle that government is a sacred trust the authority for which is derived from the people. . . ." RM181.Pre.P1.

45. RM149.2.3.P1.

46. Kades denied that the Americans pressured Japan into accepting a stronger judiciary. In his memoir about constitutional revision, he pointed out that two of the leading private (nongovernmental) Japanese drafts—one prepared by *Kenpō Kondankai*, a group headed by "the venerable Yukio Ozaki," and another by the Progressive Party—proposed that the constitution give powers of judicial review to a court. They also stressed the importance of keeping the judiciary independent of the executive, outside

the control of the ministry of justice. "The American Role in Revising Japan's Constitution," *Political Science Quarterly*, vol. 104 (September 1989): 227.

47. Kades and Roest discussed the meaning of the clause on February 9, 1946. RM174.P3; cf. RM189.ART28 for the text. While practicing law in New York City from 1930 to 1933, Kades made a close study of a five-volume *Constitutional History of New York State*, by Charles Z. Lincoln (Lawyers Cooperative Publishing Company, 1906). Though he did not have a copy in Tokyo, at least two of his ideas came from this treatise: the "red clause" (article XXVIII of the SCAP draft) and the election of judges. Rowell and others on the GS team killed the idea of electing judges, and the "red clause" failed to make it through the translating marathon in early March. DR interview with Kades, February 5, 1994.

48. Williams, 57–58; Koseki, 86; and DR interview with Kades, February 12, 1994.

49. RM172.11.P1–3.

50. RM172.11.P4.

51. RM175.3.ART2.11.

52. RM176. The other two drafters were Lt. Commander Roy Malcolm and Philip Keeney. Reviewing it 50 years later, Kades found Tilton's text quite good, certainly workable as a point of departure.

53. We know of no copy of this Hussey draft.

54. RM177.

55. A person's academic training sometimes has far-reaching effects. Kades's draft of the due-process clause bears the influence of Felix Frankfurter, his instructor at Harvard Law School. In the early 1950s, Justice Frankfurter suggested to a visiting Indian jurist that India model its due-process clause, not on America's flawed example but on Japan's better version. He probably never knew that he was pointing to his own indirect influence. DR interview with Kades, December 10, 1994.

56. RM189.ART 87.P1.

57. RM172.6-8; RM173.ART34.P1; RM174.P5; cf. RM175.2.

58. RM172.2.P1–3. At the eleventh hour, just before preparing the final version to hand to the Japanese government, MacArthur and Whitney struck out the provision limiting the power to amend chapter III, the bill of rights, for ten years. Kades, Rowell, and Hussey welcomed the change. They were firmly convinced that any such inhibition on Japanese democracy would be a mistake. RM188.

59. RM172.2.P2.

60. RM147.3.P1 and P2.

61. RM185.

62. In a set of "explanatory notes" that accompanied the transmission to MacArthur, Whitney remarked, with characteristic bombast, that Japan's renunciation of war and armed forces would have "such far-reaching implications that uncounted future generations may well come to look upon it with the same reverence as the Magna Charter [*sic*]." RM190.4.C.P1.

63. There were eighteen signatures (Kades, Hussey, Rowell, Ellerman, Hays, Swope, Hauge, Norman, Peake, Miller, Stone, Roest, Wildes, Tilton, Malcolm, Rizzo, Poole, and Nelson) on the covering memo to Whitney dated February 13. RM186. Comparing this list with the undated roster listing members of the committees assigned to draft various parts of the draft (RM145), we find three additional names: Sirota, Esman, and Keeney (not counting secretaries and interpreters).

64. Yoshida Shigeru, *The Yoshida Memoirs* (Heinemann, 1961), 133.

65. Ibid. "Framing" was not quite right. The opening sentence stated that the people

"do *ordain and establish* this Constitution." As for the framing, the people were "acting through our duly elected representatives in the National Diet." Nevertheless, Yoshida put his finger on the essence of it.

66. As a brash, young New Dealer, Kades had been a strenuous defender of Roosevelt's so-called court-packing plan.

67. It was originally scheduled for Tuesday (RM148; cf. RM143.1.1.P4), but had been postponed for a day, ostensibly to give the Japanese cabinet a little more time to prepare its proposed constitutional revisions. Obviously the additional time also suited SCAP's needs at this stage.

68. RM191. It was signed by Kades, Rowell, and Hussey.

69. The "gist" of Matsumoto's proposals had been "informally" delivered to GHQ on Friday, February 8. RM114, RM118.

70. RM191.P3.

71. During this half hour, an American plane roared overhead, and Whitney commented to Shirasu, who had joined them in the garden, "We are out here enjoying the warmth of atomic energy." RM191.P5. Thus were the Japanese rather brutally reminded of the circumstances that had brought them to this pass.

72. RM191.P10.

73. The exact terms of Whitney's reference to the emperor's safety later became a matter of controversy. Hasegawa's official record of the February 13 meeting reflects Whitney's expression of concern about the emperor, but mentions no threat. Following the meeting on February 13, Matsumoto seemed quite sanguine about being able to persuade the Americans that he could frame revisions that would satisfy their "principles." On February 18, however, Whitney told Shirasu bluntly that Matsumoto's revisions did not merit any further examination. The next day Matsumoto reported to the Japanese cabinet that Whitney had said that acceptance of the SCAP draft was "the only way of protecting the person of the emperor from those who are opposed to him." Koseki reviews the evidence concerning Whitney's supposed threat about the "person of the emperor" (100–106), noting that "those present at the February 13 meeting—Yoshida, Shirasu, Hasegawa, Rowell, and Hussey—have denied 'hearing such words.'" Koseki concludes (106) that "there is no evidence anywhere [concerning Whitney's words on February 13] that supports Matsumoto's testimony."

74. RM191.P11.

75. Hasegawa, the Japanese interpreter, also prepared an account, shorter but not significantly different, save in one respect. Hasegawa says it was Whitney who asked that the existence of a SCAP draft be kept secret; the American account attributes the call for secrecy to Yoshida. Koseki, 101.

Chapter 7

1. The reference is clearly to the imperial institution. Whitney to Shirasu (RM193).

2. RM195.

3. RM196.

4. This account of the cabinet meeting is based on *Ashida Hitoshi nikki* (Iwanami Shoten, 1976), 77–78 (hereafter *Ashida nikki*).

5. This is not quite accurate. The Matsumoto committee's drafts had been discussed by the cabinet for two days at the end of January, before the *Mainichi* scoop interrupted the proceedings.

6. *Ashida nikki*, 78–80, for Shidehara's report to the cabinet on his meeting with MacArthur.

7. *Ashida nikki*, 80.

8. The Foreign Ministry did the translation.

9. See Irie, *Kenpō seiritsu*, 204. Koseki, *The Birth of Japan's Postwar Consitution*, 108–109, finds no evidence that the cabinet ever saw the fifteen copies in English that Whitney had given to Matsumoto and Yoshida on February 13.

10. RM201 for Matsumoto's record of the February 22 meeting. For a more detailed GS stenographic record, see RM203.

11. Kades confirmed this in an interview with Dale Hellegers in 1973. See RM221.

12. *Ashida nikki*, RM216

13. Ibid.

14. NKSRS, vol. 3, 72; and RM214. According to NKSRS, 72, n.2, Matsumoto showed the draft to the prime minister but perhaps not to the emperor.

15. RM216.

16. RM217

17. RM049.

18. RM140 for the memorandum discussed earlier.

19. NKSRS, vol. 3, 72.

20. Ibid. Also Nishi Osamu, *Nihonkoku kenpō wa kōshite umareta* (Chūō Kōron Shinsho, 2000), 263.

21. See RM211, "Note Explaining the First Japanese Draft (3/2/46) by Matsumoto Jōji."

22. Ibid.

23. RM221.

24. Satō, Jurist 83 (3) (June 1, 1955): 9

25. Under the Meiji Constitution, the so-called Imperial House Law was not enacted by the Diet. It prescribed the order of succession to the imperial throne, membership in the imperial family, as well as marriage and adoption; establishing a regency; honorific titles, imperial funerals and mausoleums; and the composition and operation of an imperial house council. For the text, see PRJ, vol. 2, 846–849.

26. Matsumoto's "Explanatory Note on the Japanese Draft." See RM211.1.P2.

27. RM211.2.P1.

28. RM211.3–4.

29. From Matsumoto's 1954 testimony. RM213.SP1.P3.

30. Testimony at the Commission on the Constitution. See *Kenpō chōsakai daiyonkai sōkai gijiroku*, 34–35.

31. Ibid.

Chapter 8

1. NKSRS, vol. 3, 105; Irie, RM214

2. Satō, RM214

3. RM215

4. NKSRS, vol. 3, 105–106.

5. Koseki, *Birth of Japan's Postwar Constitution*, 117, quoting from Satō's testimony at the Commission on the Constitution. Also, NKSRS, 106.

6. Matsumoto, RM214; cf. Matsumoto's report to the Cabinet on March 5, *Ashida nikki*, RM215.

7. Matsumoto, RM214.

8. See Hellegers's 1973 interview with Kades. RM221.

9. Matsumoto, RM214.

10. RM214. For Kades's account, see Hellegers's 1973 interview, RM221.

11. The record of their discussion is available only from brief notes. Rather than summarize them here, we will refer to major points below as we present an account of the American-Japanese joint negotiating session that immediately followed this meeting. Handwritten notes are in "Ellerman Notebook E" in Hussey Papers (HP), microfilm reel 4, 19-C-5, 1–38.

12. RM215.

13. Satō's account in RM214 and RM215.

14. Ibid. Also, NKSRS, vol. 3, 107.

15. NKSRS, vol. 3, 152–153, lists fifteen Americans present.

16. NKSRS, vol. 3, 110.

17. 1973 interview, RM221

18. NKSRS, vol. 3, 111.

19. Ibid.

20. For this dispute, see NKSRS, vol. 3, 112, n. 1, and Hussey Papers 26-C-2-1.

21. Ellerman's notes in HP 19-C-5, 15.

22. Satō believed the confusion over wording in article 9, which led to another rewriting in the Diet debates in July, was in part due to his own inattention to the matter in the joint drafting session. NKSRS, vol. 3, 115–116.

23. *Kenpō chōsakai daiyonkai sokai gijiroku*, 34–35.

24. HP 26-C-2-3. While Roest drafted the sentence, MacArthur's note contained these precise words.

25. RM 211. On the Japanese tradition concerning rights, see Tanaka Hideo, "The Conflict Between Two Legal Traditions in Making the Constitution of Japan," *Democratizing Japan*, ed. Robert E. Ward and Sakamoto Yoshikazu (University of Hawaii Press, 1987), 114.

26. HP 26-C-2-3.

27. For Ellerman's brief note on this debate, see HP 19-C-5, 1–2.

28. NKSRS, vol. 3, 117–118.

29. HP 19-C-5, 3.

30. NKSRS, vol. 3, 118.

31. NKSRS, 119.

32. The rhetorical and redundant first sentence of article XIV ("The people are the ultimate arbiters of their government and of the Imperial Throne") was dropped. NKSRS, vol. 3, 119.

33. NKSRS, vol. 3, 120; and HP 19-C-5, 6.

34. SCAP enforced its own strict censorship of all Japanese media and publishing during the occupation period, 1945–1952. See Toshio Nishi, *Unconditional Democracy: Education and Politics in Occupied Japan* (Hoover Institution Press, 1982), 86–93, 100–105; and Etō Jun, "Genron tōsei: senryōka Nihon ni okeru ken'etsu," in Ray A. Moore, ed., *Tennō ga baiburu o yonda hi* (Kōdansha, 1983), 115–154.

35. NKSRS, vol. 3, 121 and 122 n.1; and HP 19-C-5, 6.

36. The SCAP draft included such statements as "Marriage . . . founded on mutual consent *instead of parental coercion*, and maintained through cooperation *instead of male domination*." It also repeated the language of Article 90 that "Laws contrary to these principles shall be abolished." NKSRS, vol. 3, 123.

37. Ellerman's jottings in HP 19-C-5, 7, are too brief to convey the flavor of the discussion.

38. NKSRS, 122–123.

39. Articles 35 and 36 in the Matsumoto–Satō draft.

40. Matsumoto's 1954 testimony. RM213.SP1.P4.
41. NKSRS, vol. 3, 124.
42. NKSRS, vol. 3, 124–125.
43. Ellerman Notebook E, in HP 19-C-5, 9.
44. Ibid.
45. Ellerman's notes on the discussion of the Diet is in HP 19-C-5, 10–25.
46. Ibid., 13.
47. Ibid., 23–24.
48. Ibid., 38–39.
49. NKSRS, vol. 3, 133.
50. NKSRS, vol. 3, 131.
51. See chapter 10 (in this volume).
52. Ellerman notes in HP 19-C-5, 27–29.
53. See the marked-up English translation used in the meeting with Whitney, HP 26-C-2, pp. 3–16.
54. Ellerman notes in HP 19-C-5, 47–53. And NKSRS, vol. 3, 138–142.
55. NKSRS vol. 3, 139.
56. Ibid., 141–142.
57. Ibid., 142.
58. HP 19-C-5, 52–53.
59. NKSRS, vol. 3, 143.
60. HP 26-C-2–15, and HP 19-C-5–30.
61. Ibid.
62. NKSRS, vol. 3, 145.
63. See his comments in HP 19-C-5–31.
64. This wording followed closely SWNCC 228's provision *d*.(6): "The entire income of the Imperial Household shall be turned into the public treasury and the expenses of the Imperial Household shall be appropriated by the legislature in the annual budget."
65. HP 19-C-5–33.
66. Ibid.
67. HP 19-C-5–57.
68. See HP 26-C-2–16 for this chapter of the Matsumoto draft.
69. HP 19-C-5–35.
70. Ibid.
71. For details, see NKSRS, vol. 3, 146–148; and Ellerman notes in HP 19-C-5, 58–60.
72. Ellerman notes in HP 19-C-5, 37.
73. NKSRS, vol. 3, 148.
74. Ellerman notes, HP 19-C-5, 37, 61–63.
75. Satō describes what happened next in NKSRS, vol. 3, 151–152.
76. Ibid., 151.
77. Quoted in Koseki, 121
78. Quoted in Nishi Osamu, *Nihonkoku kenpō wa kōshite umareta* (Chūō Kōron Shinsho, 2000), 273.
79. *Ashida nikki*, RM216
80. Accounts of the cabinet meetings of March 5–6 are from Ashida, Matsumoto, Iriye, and Satō. RM216, RM218, RM219, RM220.
81. RM216.
82. See Irie's account, RM224. The word *yōkō* is usually translated as "gist," "summary," or "outline," none of which captures the real meaning. Kenkyūsha's Japanese-

English dictionary defines it as "itemized." The peculiar pattern of ending statements, which may be numbered or itemized, with a certain verb ending followed by *koto*, is found in rules and regulations issued by schools to students, and governments to citizens. Professor Kyoko Inoue, a linguist and author of *MacArthur's Japanese Constitution*, says "the March 6 version [of the draft Constitution] was 'a draft with itemized articles.'" Personal correspondence, January 27, 2001.

83. RM223.

84. Ibid.

85. *Ashida nikki*, RM216.

86. RM217.

87. NKSRS, vol. 3, 175–176. The principal one was a sentence regarding double jeopardy which was added to article 33.

88. RM230.

89. PRJ, 107 (emphasis added).

Chapter 9

1. Hugh Borton, *Japan's Modern Century* (Ronald Press, 1955), 424.

2. FRUS (1946), vol. 8, 173.

3. RM250

4. RM246

5. Sasakawa Ryūtarō, "Makkasa no kenpō seitei sakusen to Pentagon no kokuitachi," *Kōhō no shisō to seido* (Shinsansha, 1999), 202–203.

6. For Kades's memorandum, see RM248.

7. SCAP to War Department, RM249.

8. In his memorandum of February 1, Whitney had written to MacArthur: "Your authority to make policy decisions on constitutional reform continues substantially unimpaired until the Far Eastern Commission promulgates its own policy decisions on this subject." RM140.

9. Ibid.

10. FEC to SCAP, RM253.

11. RM253; Koseki, *The Birth of Japan's Postwar Constitution*, 146–147.

12. Quoted in Koseki, 147.

13. Personal cable from McCoy to MacArthur, March 22, RM253.

14. RM254.

15. Koseki, 147–148.

16. The plan was designed by Irie Toshio, deputy director of the Legislation Bureau, but opposed by conservative members of the Cabinet since it "could not possibly be done in the time we have in the present circumstances." Quoted in Koseki, 149.

17. McCoy to SCAP, RM273.

18. For the FEC resolution, see RM274.

19. PRJ, vol. 1, 320; and Justin Williams, *Japan's Political Revolution under MacArthur* (University of Georgia Press, 1979), 10.

20. MacArthur's response to McCoy, RM254

21. SCAP to War Department, RM249.

22. See SCAPIN 548 and 550 in RM051 and RM052. For SCAP's account of the purge, see PRJ, vol. 1, 12–13.

23. Ibid., 14.

24. Ibid., 27.

25. The basic study in English of the "production control" movement is Joe Moore, *Japanese Workers and the Struggle for Power* (University of Wisconsin Press, 1983). For the economic effects of "demonstration strikes" and other labor problems, see Miriam Farley, *Aspects of Japan's Labor Problems* (John Day, 1950), 82–84.

26. Dower, *Embracing Defeat* (New Press, 1999), 258–259.

27. Ibid., 261. For an eyewitness account of the assault on Shidehara, see Mark Gayn, *Japan Diary* (Charles E. Tuttle, 1981), 166–171.

28. PRJ, vol. 1, 319.

29. Shinobu Seizaburō, *Sengo nihon seiji shi*, vol. 1 (Kōdansha, 1965), 294–295. Also Koseki, 148; and Dower, 263.

30. PRJ, vol. 1, 316.

31. These included units of the U.S. First Cavalry Division, the Eleventh Airborne Division, the Second Marine Division and British Commonwealth Forces. PRJ, vol. 1, 316.

32. PRJ, vol. 1, 316–317.

33. PRJ, vol. 1, 317–318.

34. Ibid., 317–318. For an American monitor's memory of the experience, see Williams, *Japan's Political Revolution under MacArthur*, 10–11. General Whitney himself visited polling places in Tokyo, accompanied by several American journalists. Gayn, *Japan Diary*, 176.

35. Shinobu, *Sengo nihon* (Kōdansha, 1965), 297. SCAP's official figures for the leading parties were: Progressives 93, Liberals 139, Social Democrats 92, Independents 83, Communists 5, and minor parties 38. PRJ, vol. 1, 321.

36. Figures from a Kyōdō News survey, cited in PRJ, vol. 1, 322. For MacArthur's statement, which was prepared by Whitney, see PRJ, vol. 2, 719–720.

37. Masumi Junnosuke, *Postwar Politics in Japan, 1945–1955* (Center for Japanese Studies, University of California, 1985), 97.

38. Kenpō Chōsakai Jimukyoku, comp., *Kenpō seitei no keika ni kansuru shōiinkai dai yonjūnana kai gijiroku* (Ōkurashō, 1961), 449–451.

39. "Election bulletins" were official publications containing "program statements" and biographies of candidates. SCAP required prefectural governors to distribute these, unedited, to all registered voters. PRJ, vol. 1, 316.

40. MacArthur to the FEC, RM275.

41. MacArthur to McCoy, April 15, 1946, RM281.

42. Ibid.

43. RM281.

44. See Vincent to Byrnes, RM282. MacArthur's statement of April 5 to the Allied Council of Japan is in PRJ, vol. 2, 746–748.

45. RM282.3.P1.

46. RM282.2.P2.

47. Blakeslee, *The Far Eastern Commission* (U.S. Government Printing Office, 1953), 50–51.

48. See McCoy to MacArthur, RM283.

49. For this FEC "mandatory policy decision," see RM249.

50. See Blakeslee, *The FEC*, 53.

51. Ibid., 50–51.

52. Ibid., 52

53. See PRJ, vol. 2, 659.

54. Yoshida made his statement on May 29, shortly after he took office. See Koseki, 158.

55. Quoted in Koseki, 156–157.
56. FRUS (1946), 8:247 n.14.
57. PRJ, vol. 2, 660.
58. Blakeslee, 56.
59. Quoted in ibid., 57.
60. Ibid., 58.

Chapter 10

1. Watanabe's role is described in Nishi Osamu, *Nihonkoku kenpō wa kōshite umareta* (Chūō Kōron Shinsho, 2000), 285–286.
2. Yamamoto (1887–1974), a popular dramatist of progressive political persuasion, was elected to the House of Councillors in 1947.
3. Nishi, 286.
4. Koseki, *The Birth of Japan's Postwar Constitution*, 134–135; NKSRS, vol. 3, 274ff.
5. NKSRS, vol. 3, 278, n.3.
6. Nishi, 287.
7. Quoted in Koseki, 135.
8. NKSRS, vol. 3, 274.
9. RM234.P3.
10. NKSRS, vol. 3, 299.
11. RM234.P4.
12. Koseki, 136.
13. RM234.P4.
14. RM223, and Koseki, 129.
15. Miyazawa Toshiyoshi, Osakabe Tsuyosi, and Satō Isao, all of whom had served on Matsumoto's committee to revise the constitution in late 1945. See NKSRS, vol. 3, 269–270.
16. See *Asahi shinbun*, March 9, in RM243.
17. Irie, *Kenpō seiritsu*, 461ff.
18. For this long document, see NKSRS, vol. 3, 236–269.
19. See RM260, "Observations and queries on the March 6 draft," and RM262, "Conference on March 6 draft."
20. See RM260, RM261, and RM262.
21. RM260.
22. See RM266, "Issues in the Draft Constitution Relating to Foreign Affairs."
23. Accompanied by their interpreter and note taker, Katō. See RM269 for Katō's notes on the meeting.
24. See the Diet debates in chapter 17 of this volume.
25. Article 8 in the March 6 draft said: "No property can be given to, or received by, the Imperial House, and no receipts and disbursements can be made thereby, without the authorization of the Diet." This was the exact wording in the SCAP draft, the Matsumoto draft, as well as the March 6 draft. During the April negotiations, the word "gifts" replaced "receipts and disbursements."
26. "Administration of the Property of Imperial Houseld of Japan," in file 7, box 2047, RG 331 of the WNRC.
27. See chapter 8 in this volume.
28. See ibid.
29. RM276.
30. NKSRS, vol. 3, 324 n.3.

31. RM236, last paragraph.

32. RM278.P1.

33. See chapter 9 in this volume.

34. NKSRS, vol. 3, 365–367.

35. NKSRS, vol. 3, 368–371.

Chapter 11

1. Irie, *Kenpō seiritsu*, 316–319; NKSRS, vol. 3, 374–376. Satō was present at most of the Council's meetings. The official record of the deliberations are in Kawakami Ichirō, ed., *Teikoku kenpō kaiseian gijiroku* (Kokusho Kankōkai, 1986). English translations of the deliberations are in R. A. Moore and D. Robinson, eds., *The Constitution of Japan: A Documentary History of its Framing and Adoption, 1945–1947* (Princeton University Press, 1998).

2. Irie, 318–319.

3. This emperor-centered argument, delivered by Shidehara in soothing tones, was put more bluntly by his successor, Yoshida Shigeru, in a speech to the House of Peers on June 23: "At this moment of defeat in war, we have presented [this] bill having . . . in mind the questions of how the nation can be saved and how the safety of the Imperial House can be assured." Quoted in Koseki, *The Birth of Japan's Postwar Constitution*, 166.

4. Irie, 321.

5. Ibid.

6. Irie, 321.

7. Ibid., 323.

8. According to Satō's notes. NKSRS, vol. 3, 389–390. Satō's notes do not reveal whether Matsumoto described the crucial marathon meeting on March 4–5. Matsumoto's comments were not included in the official record of the April 22 PC meeting. See RM287, "First Meeting of the Privy Council" (April 22, 1946). This refers to the council's first formal deliberation on the draft constitution.

9. NKSRS, vol. 3, 390.

10. On Miyazawa Toshiyoshi's "thesis," see Koseki, 124–129.

11. RM287.PM.SP32–33.

12. RM287.PM.SP27–29.

13. Ibid.

14. RM288.PM.SP7–10.

15. RM295.AM.SP3–7

16. RM307.AM.SP2.P3.

17. RM287.PM.SP25–26.

18. NKSRS, vol. 3, 423ff.

19. Ibid., 423.

20. Ibid.

21. Ibid., 423–424.

22. Adopted on May 13. See RM285

23. NKSRS, vol. 3, 424.

24. Ibid.

25. NKSRS, vol. 3, 418.

26. Ibid., 426.

27. RM307.AM.SP3.

28. Ibid.

29. The same concern would persuade Yoshida a few years later to seek a security arrangement with the United States.

30. RM307.AM.SP4.

31. RM307.AM.SP7.

32. RM307.AM.SP2.P4.

33. RM307.

34. NKSRS, vol. 3, 447–448.

35. Ibid., 395, 447–448.

36. Kanamori replaced Matsumoto as minister in charge of constitutional revision in the Yoshida cabinet. Before assuming this portfolio, he had been attached to the Legislation Bureau helping with revision preparations. See NKSRS, vol. 3, 448.

37. Ibid., 395, 447–448.

38. The FEC had already complained about the procedure, as had domestic critics. See RM273 and Koseki, 148.

39. Koseki, 149.

40. The "August Revolution" thesis was popularized by Miyazawa Toshiyoshi, who apparently heard it from Maruyama Masao at an academic seminar. See Koseki, 124–127.

41. NKSRS, vol. 3, 450–451.

42. Ibid., 451.

43. Ibid, 456.

44. Hozumi (1860–1912) was professor of constitutional law at Tokyo Imperial University and an opponent of parliamentary rule. For his views on *kokutai*, see his *Kenpō teiyō* (Yūhikaku, 1935), 74–75.

45. NKSRS, vol. 3, 457–458.

46. Satō prepared the materials for the meeting of June 13. See NKSRS, 456–457.

47. Quoted in NKSRS, vol. 3, 456.

48. See Irie, 361.

49. NKSRS, vol. 3, 459 n.4.

50. RM361.P6. For an extensive treatment of the *kokutai* debate in the Diet, see the following chapters of this book, especially chapter 13.

51. See NKSRS, vol. 3, 447–491.

Chapter 12

1. RM317.PM.SP7.P6.

2. RM317.PM.SP9.P3.

3. RM317.PM.SP10. P1.

4. RM319.PM.SP3.P1.

5. See, for example, his reply the following day to Yoshida An. RM320.PM.SP5.

6. RM320.PM.SP12.

7. The first clause of the Charter Oath (RM002) stated: "Deliberative assemblies shall be established and all measures of government decided in accordance with public opinion."

8. RM322.PM.SP11.

9. In 1950, he was purged from political life in Japan. He remained underground until 1955. During this period he was bitterly criticized by Cominform (an agency, controlled by the Soviets, that published propaganda touting international Communist solidarity) for advocating that the Japanese Communist Party use peaceful methods and participate in political life. Upon reinstatement, he was elected to the House of Council-

lors and served there from 1964 to 1977. After the collapse of the Soviet Union, documents in the Kremlin implicated him as a Soviet agent in the betrayal and execution of fellow Japanese Communists. He died in 1993, at the age of 101.

10. RM322.AMPM.SP32, SP36.

Chapter 13

1. Uchida Kenzō, "Japan's Postwar Conservative Parties," in *Democratizing Japan*, ed. Robert E. Ward and Yoshikazu Sakamoto (University of Hawaii Press, 1987), 212.

2. RM331.PM.SP8–11.

3. RM336.AM.SP18.P1 and SP19.P1.

4. RM326.PM.SP36–41.

5. For SCAP's attempt to address the problem of legitimacy, see RM316.TEXT2.

6. The American founding posed similar problems, and they too were finessed, rather than solved. The Articles of Confederation contained a process for amendment, but it was found impractical in the circumstances of 1787. The Federal Convention was convened under its authority, but once the Constitution was framed, its requirement of unanimous ratification was not given another thought.

7. RM330.AM.SP6–7.

8. RM346.AM.SP5–7.

9. RM329.AM.SP19.P6–7.

10. RM329.PM.SP2.P5–6.

11. RM329.AM.SP19.P11.

12. RM329.PM.SP28.

13. RM331.AM.SP75–77.

14. Kanamori came close to lying about the origin of the draft. "It is needless to say that the Constitution proper is drafted in Japanese and is submitted to the Diet for deliberation in the Japanese original form itself, while it has been caused by officials concerned to be rendered into English just for secretarial convenience." RM331.AM.SP78.P1.

15. RM331.AM.SP81–83.

16. RM331.AM.S2–3

17. RM331.AM.SP3 and S15.

18. RM331.AM.SP17.

19. For examples, see RM103, "The Liberal Party Outline for Constitutional Revision" (January 21, 1946); and RM120, "The Progressive Party Outline for a Constitution Revision Bill" (February 13, 1946).

20. RM330.AM.SP18.P2.

21. RM330.AM.SP19.

22. RM333.AM.SP2.

23. RM333.AM.SP3.P1.

24. For a harsh appraisal of Hirohito's role, see Herbert P. Bix, *Hirohito and the Making of Modern Japan* (HarperCollins, 2000), part III. For a more balanced assessment of the policies that led to Japan's conflict with China and the West, see James Crowley, *Japan's Quest for Autonomy: National Security and Foreign Policy, 1930–1938* (Princeton University Press, 1966).

25. RM346.AM.SP2.P6.

26. RM346.AM.SP2–8.

27. RM346.AM.SP34.P2–3

28. RM346.AM.SP34.P3.

29. Kanamori had made this point earlier that morning, in responding to Katō Kanjū. RM346.AM.SP19.P2.

30. RM346.AM.SP35.P2.

31. RM346.AM.SP19.P3.

32. RM347.AM.SP64–66 (Yoshida An and Kanamori); also RM347.PM.SP6.P2 and SP7 (Kanamori and Kitaura).

33. RM347.PM.SP79.P3.

34. RM346.AM.SP28.P1.

35. RM346.AM.SP29.P1.

36. See especially a spirited exchange with Kanamori at RM347.PM.SP26–27.

37. RM347.PM.SP30. For another expression of concern about article 4, see RM346.PM.SP88–90.

38. RM346.PM.SP62.P2.

39. Dissolution of the House of Representatives, said Kojima, "may be regarded as the only supreme power retained in the hand of the emperor, because there is no provision in the constitution authorizing the cabinet to decide the dissolution of House of Representatives." RM346.PM.SP70.P2.

40. RM346.PM.SP70.P3. On July 20, Nosaka added his voice to those who smelled a rat in articles 4 and 7. Article 7 speaks of the *kokumu* of the cabinet. Why was the same term used for the emperor's "state functions"? The English "translation," he said, makes a distinction. Why doesn't the Japanese version? RM364.PM.SP71 et seq.

41. RM346.PM.SP71.

42. This Matsumoto is not to be confused with Matsumoto Jōji. Matsumoto Shigeharu (1899–1988) was a journalist and informal political adviser.

43. RM335.

44. RM327. The quoted phrase was strong language; it indicated that the FEC meant business.

45. "This statement is based upon an examination of the official English translation of the Draft Constitution, without reference to the Japanese language version." RM341.P0.

46. RM341.P1.Q2.P1.

47. RM340.P1.1(1).

48. Later Kades noted that the group that prepared this memo had been carefully balanced. It consisted of left-leaning T. A. Bisson, right-leaning Kenneth Colegrove, and centrist Cyrus Peake. DR interview with Kades, June 25, 1994.

49. RM312.ART4.P1.

50. RM343.P4–6.

51. RM343.P7.

52. The memo did *not* point out that such organic laws would also have to be passed by the House of Representatives elected in April 1946, where anything of the kind apprehended by the SCAP staffers would probably have been dismissed with ridicule.

53. RM342.PM.SP40–48.

54. RM342.PM.SP78–79. Nosaka may have picked up some leads in informal conversations at GHQ. His query aligned closely with the concerns expressed in Whitney's memo of July 17 (RM359).

55. RM340.P1.

56. RM340.P2.

57. RM340.P3.

58. RM358.

59. RM340.P7. Cf. RM 361, Kanamori's July 17 memo outlining his "Six Principles on Constitutional Reform."

60. RM358.SP3.P1.

61. According to Shintō mythology, February 11 was the day, in 660 B.C.E., that the first emperor, Jimmu, ascended the throne. During the Occupation, SCAP prohibited celebrating this holiday.

62. RM359.

63. RM359.P4. and P5.

64. RM368.1.

65. RM369.P1.

66. RM368.2.P7 and P9.

67. RM369.P3 and P4.

68. RM369.P4.

69. RM369.P6.

Chapter 14

1. MacArthur's April 5 speech to the Allied Council in Tokyo is at RM264.

2. RM330.AM.SP2.P3.

3. RM330.AM.SP5.

4. *Zaibatsu* were family-owned business corporations, operating in many industries.

5. RM331.PM.SP4–5.

6. RM337.PM.SP16 and 17.

7. RM337.PM.SP38 and 39.

8. RM337.PM.SP41.

9. RM337.PM.SP51–55.

10. RM337.PM.SP53.

11. RM337.PM.SP59.

12. RM337.PM.SP60.

13. RM346.AM.SP6–7.

14. RM346.AM.SP40.P2.

15. RM337.PM.SP62.P2.

16. RM349.AM.SP24.

17. On Katō Shizue, see the section titled "Katō Shizue's Speech" in this chapter.

18. RM349.PM.SP26.

19. RM349.PM.SP27.

20. Dower, *Embracing Defeat* (New Press, 1999), 50–52.

21. RM349.PM.SP8.

22. Thomas R. H. Havens, *Valley of Darkness: The Japanese People and World War II* (Norton, 1978).

23. RM024.P10.

24. RM352.AM.SP74.

25. RM337.AM.SP40–41. Cf. RM363.PM.SP23–27.

26. RM337.AM.SP50–51.

27. RM337.PM.SP3–6.

28. For an account of these street actions, see Dower, *Embracing Defeat*, 259–267.

29. RM336.PM.SP18–19.

30. RM336.PM.SP66–69.

31. RM360.AM.SP53–65.

32. RM360.PM.SP2.

33. RM360.PM.SP3.

34. RM363.AM.SP2.

35. For an account of serious labor troubles in early 1946, see Richard Finn, *Winners in Peace: MacArthur, Yoshida and Postwar Japan* (University of California Press, 1992), 49–54.

36. RM360.PM.SP67.

37. RM336.PM.SP26.

38. RM336.PM.SP27

39. The story is told by Endō Shūsaku, *Silence* (Pivot Books, 1980).

40. RM336.PM.SP62–63.

41. Articles 19 and 83, respectively. RM189.

42. RM352.AM.SP92.

43. Issued in 1890, it called on the Japanese to be "good and faithful subjects," ready, in any emergency, to offer themselves "courageously to the State, and thus guard and maintain the prosperity of Our Imperial Throne, coeval with heaven and earth." RM006. Under pressure from the Occupation, the Diet repealed it on June 19, 1948.

44. RM352.AM.SP94.

45. RM352.PM.SP2.

46. RM352.PM.SP2, 3.

47. MacArthur apparently shared them. He gave great offense by referring to the Japanese people as "like a boy of twelve compared with our development of 45 years," during testimony before two committees of the U.S. Senate on May 5, 1951. Dower, *Embracing Defeat*, 550 ff. It is worth noting that, in these exchanges, Kanamori, Tanaka, and Kimura rejected Inoue's paternalistic view.

48. RM352.PM.SP41–44.

49. RM319.PM.SP2.P3.

50. RM319.PM.SP3.P2.

51. RM319.PM.SP5.P15–16.

52. RM319.PM.SP6.P5.

53. RM319.PM.SP18.P5 and SP20.P2.

54. Mark Gayn, *Japan Diary* (Charles E. Tuttle, 1981), 172–174, tells of her dramatic speech on April 9, 1946, to a huge Socialist election rally in Tokyo.

55. RM314.

56. RM333.PM.SP2.P1. Compare this formulation to Akazawa's mealy-mouthed relay of a question from female members he presumed to represent. RM331.AM.SP8.P2.

57. RM333.PM.SP2.P2.

58. RM333.PM.SP2.P5.

59. RM333.PM.SP2.

60. RM333.PM.SP3.P2.

61. The Temporary Legislation Investigative Committee (TLIC).

62. RM333.PM.SP4.

63. RM333.PM.SP5.P3.

64. RM333.PM.SP6.

65. RM333.PM.SP12.

66. RM333.PM.SP13.

67. RM333.PM. SP14.P1

68. RM333.PM.SP26.P2.

69. RM333.PM.SP28.

70. RM349.PM.SP89. Ōhashi's claim was exaggerated. Women had been active participants in the drafting of Germany's Weimar Constitution in 1919.

71. Kanamori suggested that articles 13 (asserting a right to the pursuit of happiness) and 25 (committing the state to "use its endeavors" to promote social welfare and public health) provided ample grounds for the kind of legislation Koshihara had in mind. RM357.PM.SP2–3.

72. RM357.PM.SP4–5.

73. RM360.AM.SP82–85.

74. RM349.PM.SP87.

75. RM357.AM.SP49.P2.

76. RM357.AM.SP50.

77. RM357.AM.SP16.

78. RM357.AM.SP52.

79. Kimura was answering in Kanamori's absence. This being July 17, Kanamori was engaged in critical negotiations with Kades over *kokutai*.

80. RM357.AM.SP53–55.

81. Compare Kanamori's response to Miura's question about whether ancestor worship would be protected under article 11. The constitution, he said, was not designed to produce a revolution in national morality. RM349.PM.SP66–69.

82. RM363.AM.SP4–9.

83. RM363.AM.SP51.P2.

84. RM363.PM.SP51–56.

85. RM363.AM.SP71–84.

86. For a demonstration that these complexities are grounded in the framing of these rights, see Akhil Reed Amar, *The Bill of Rights* (Yale, 1998), especially chapter one.

87. RM360.PM.SP25.P2.

Chapter 15

1. RM333.AM.SP7.P1.

2. RM333.AM.SP7.P2.

3. RM333.AM.SP7.P2–3.

4. RM333.AM.SP17. This last comment looks a little facile, but improvisation beyond the bounds of strict constitutionality is essentially what Great Britain relied on to cope with Hitler's aggression, as did the United States in meeting the challenge of secession. See Clinton Rossiter, *Constitutional Dictatorship* (Princeton University Press, 1948).

5. RM363.PM.SP17–22.

6. For a thoughtful analysis of this dialectic, see James L. Sundquist, *The Decline and Resurgence of Congress* (Brookings, 1981).

7. RM363.PM.SP29.P3.

8. RM363.PM.SP30.

9. Some might insist that it was not incidental to its genius that the Westminster model was never written down in England. Israel follows England in this regard, though many Commonwealth nations do not.

10. RM363.PM.SP6–14.

11. RM363.PM.SP35–36.

12. RM364.AM.SP71–74. In the final version, it was changed to read, "Each House may conduct investigations in relation to government."

13. RM364.AM.SP32–33.

14. RM363.PM.SP47–48. Tanaka and Kanamori both mentioned the American Library of Congress as a model. RM364.AM.SP58–64.

15. The vote, on May 5, 1946, was 53 percent opposed to 47 percent in favor. A

second vote, on October 13, 1946, was 53.3 percent in favor of a draft that included a bicameral legislature, 46.7 percent opposed.

16. RM363.PM.SP51–57. He might have added that Britain sharply curtailed the House of Lords in 1911.

17. See, for example, Katō Kazuo at RM349.AM.SP2.P4, and Ashida at RM346.PM.SP43.P2 and RM366.AM.SP1.P2.I1.

18. On this, as we shall see, he was mistaken. For SCAP's insistence on the direct election of the House of Councillors, see RM447, a Whitney memo dated September 10, 1946.

19. RM363.PM.SP63. On July 20, Miura called for measures to reduce the influence of money in politics and for consideration of proportional representation. RM364.AM.SP22–25. Both suggestions were ignored.

20. Dower, *Embracing Defeat* (New Press, 1999), 259.

21. RM364.AM.SP2–11.

22. RM364.PM.SP43–48.

23. The quoted phrase is Kanamori's. RM364.PM.SP29.

24. RM364.PM.SP37, 38. Later, when the subcommittee revisited this issue, it would come down on the side of Hayashi and Hara, against Kanamori, strengthening the prime minister's control of the cabinet.

25. In fact, this provision was borrowed from the twentieth-century constitution of California. It appealed to some of SCAP's drafters as a way to discourage courts in Japan from thwarting a strong popular will, as many New Dealers thought the U.S. Supreme Court had done in the 1930s.

26. RM326.PM.SP20.

27. RM326.PM.SP21.

28. RM364.PM.SP84–85.

29. RM364.PM.SP88–91, 96.

Chapter 16

1. RM366.AM.SP1–4.

2. RM367.AM.SP7. In the fluid political circumstances of the immediate postwar period, it is difficult to tell how close Ashida came to proportionality. The membership of the subcommittee does seem heavy on Progressive Democrats and quite light on Social Democrats. But no one seemed to complain. In one respect, though, the membership was defective. There were thirty-eight women in the House of Representatives (RM290.2.3.8.P3) but none on the subcommittee.

3. RM367.AM.SP1.P1.

4. Kazuo Ishiguro's novel, *An Artist of the Floating World* (Faber & Faber, 1986), presents a vivid portrayal of cultural currents in postwar Japan.

5. Prime Minister Konoe launched the Imperial Rule Assistance Association (IRAA) in October 1940. Every Japanese automatically became a member. The organization was designed to replace traditional political parties with a nationwide network of local cells to mobilize Japan for an all-out war effort. It was resisted at first, not only by political party elites but by those who believed that such an organization might interfere with natural ties of affection between the emperor and his subjects. Gradually it became an instrument of the home ministry, organizing the populace into local, even neighborhood, groups to encourage greater industrial and agricultural productivity, increased savings, and civil defense. After the war, Occupation authorities saw the IRAA as analo-

gous to the Nazi and Communist parties and purged former officials for their IRAA work. The analogy, also drawn by some postwar Japanese commentators, seems strained. Despite its totalitarian ambitions, the IRAA did not serve as an instrument of terror or lawlessness on anything like the Nazi model, nor was it a major source of influence on public policy.

6. RM367.AM.SP16.

7. RM367.AM.SP1.P2.

8. RM375.AM.SP36. Kasai (SP34, 38) and Morito (SP39) had the same concerns and suggested the same inquiries.

9. These transcripts were prepared for the CLO and translated into English for the benefit of Kades and other officers at SCAP.

10. RM380.AM.SP63.

11. Koseki Shōichi, *The Birth of Japan's Postwar Constitution* (Westview Press, 1997) writes (chapter 9; see especially 199) that Kanamori deleted many passages from the transcripts of the subcommittee's deliberations submitted to GHQ. Most of Kanamori's deletions dealt with comments on SCAP's likely attitude toward proposed revisions. To that extent, Kades saw the deliberations through a flawed glass. The passages Kanamori deleted are restored, marked, and translated in the version published in Moore and Robinson, *The Constitution of Japan: A Documentary History of Its Framing and Adoption, 1945–1947* (Princeton University Press, 1998). See, for example, RM367.AM.SP16 and RM384.PM.SP87.

12. See, for example, Kita (RM367.AM.SP17), Kasai (RM367.AM.SP18), even Takahashi, the acting chair in Ashida's temporary absence (RM375.PM.SP67); also Hara (RM380.AM.SP159) and Morito (RM380.PM.SP58).

13. On July 26, Morito, while complaining that the Japanese version sounded wooden and flat, called the English version of the same ideas "excellent." Kasai and Kita agreed. RM375.AM.SP39; cf. SP37 and 38. All three wondered how much latitude they had to depart from a verbatim translation of the English text.

14. Kita, at RM367.AM.SP17; Hatsukade, at RM367.AM.SP16; Suzuki, at RM375.AM.SP36; Morito, at RM375.AM.SP39; Kasai, at RM367.AM.SP18.

15. Kasai, at RM367.AM.SP18–21. Hatsukade said that he had spent two brain-wracking days writing a new version of the first paragraph (RM380.AM.SP2), but the effort was apparently fruitless.

16. RM375.AM.SP34 and 38.

17. RM375.AM.SP47–48.

18. RM375.PM.SP1. Morito summarized the goal of their work. Speaking of a particularly complex phrase in the first sentence of the preamble, he remarked that "the first consideration must be for the sentence to be understandable to the Japanese people, on the condition that it is not too different from the English version." RM380.AM.SP10.

19. RM380.AM.SP63–72.

20. RM380.AM.SP79.

21. RM380.PM.SP8.

22. RM380.PM.SP8.

23. RM380.PM.SP16–17.

24. RM380.PM.SP18.

25. RM380.PM.SP53.

26. RM380.PM.SP20–25.

27. RM380.PM.SP51.

28. RM380.PM.SP39, 47–50.

29. RM375.AM.SP16.

30. RM375.AM.SP18.

31. RM375.PM.SP487–503.

32. RM375.PM.SP504–511, 526–527.

33. RM380.PM.SP81.P1. Ashida was referring to the discussions between Kades and Kanamori.

34. RM380.PM.SP86.

35. RM380.PM.SP121–142.

36. For an account of the shenanigans surrounding the forgery (by the newspaper *Tokyo Shinbun*) of Ashida's diary for July 27 and 29 and the sealing, though not until 1956, of the stenographic record of the subcommittee, see Koseki, *Birth*, 192–198. Koseki shows, and the transcripts examined here confirm, that the idea of using the amendments to Article 9 to legitimate wars of self-defense was not broached in July 1946, by Ashida or anyone else.

37. RM380.PM.SP194, 203, 242.

38. RM380.PM.SP229–230.

39. RM380.PM.SP264, 272.

40. The text of Ashida's wording is printed in Koseki, 198.

41. RM381.AM.SP1–14.

42. RM381.AM.SP26, 29, 38–39.

43. RM381.AM.SP44.

44. RM381.AM.SP56.P1.

45. RM381.AM.SP62–83.

46. RM381.AM.SP84–85.

47. RM384.PM.SP8.P2, 3.

48. RM384.PM.SP82.

49. RM384.PM.SP86–87. This material was deleted from the transcript sent to Kades. Given his editing of MacArthur's second (of four) basic points for the drafting in February (RM142.2.P1), however, it is doubtful that Kades would have been upset if he had seen these remarks by Kanamori. Of course, others at SCAP might have reacted more strongly.

50. Koseki, 200.

51. Quoted by Koseki, 194, who notes that Ashida repeated this argument during a roundtable discussion of the new constitution broadcast the day it was promulgated, November 3, 1946. Ashida said, "In this article, the question of self-defense is definitely not included in the renunciation of war." Suzuki Yoshio and Inukai Takeru, who knew as much as anyone about the provenance of the article 9 amendments, were there when he said this.

52. Koseki is severe in accusing Ashida and *Tokyo Shinbun* of deliberate deception. His evidence is convincing. He adds that Kanamori must have regarded Ashida's cold-blooded falsifications of the record as "unbearable" (197–198).

Chapter 17

1. RM381.PM.SP50–54.

2. RM384.PM.SP90.

3. RM381.PM.SP88.

4. RM381.PM.SP64.

5. One *chōbu* equals about 2.5 acres.

6. RM384.PM.SP77.

7. RM384.PM.SP67–68.
8. RM384.PM.SP78.
9. RM381.PM.SP78, 79.
10. RM381.PM.SP80.
11. RM381.PM.SP81.
12. RM381.PM.SP87, 96, 97.
13. RM381.PM.SP105.P5.
14. RM381.PM.SP106, 107, 108.
15. RM381.PM.SP110.
16. RM381.PM.SP111.

17. Andō Masazumi, journalist and politician, was former editor-in-chief of *Tokyo Asahi Shinbun* (newspaper) and was elected to the House of Representatives ten times. He was purged in 1946, reinstated in 1950, and named minister of education in the Hatoyama cabinet (1954).

18. RM381.PM.SP116.
19. RM381.PM.SP128.
20. RM381.PM.SP179.
21. RM381.PM.SP184.
22. RM381.PM.SP195.
23. RM381.PM.SP185.
24. RM384.PM.SP96.
25. RM384.AM.SP146–149.
26. RM387.PM.SP221–224.
27. RM371 and 372.
28. RM384.AM.SP154.P2.
29. RM384.PM.SP127.
30. RM384.PM.SP128–130.
31. RM384.PM.SP133.
32. RM384.PM.SP141.
33. RM381.PM.SP165, 166.
34. RM386.AM.SP3, 5.

35. The text of article 88 evolved through several stages. In the Matsumoto Commission draft (January), it read: "The budget concerning allowances and expenses of the imperial household shall constitute a part of the national budget. The same shall apply to the income and expenditure arising from imperial properties other than the hereditary estates."

The SCAP draft (February) had it: "All property of the imperial household, other than the hereditary estates, shall belong to the nation. The income from all imperial properties shall be paid into the national treasury, and allowances and expenses of the imperial household, as defined by law, shall be appropriated by the Diet in the annual budget."

In the Japanese Cabinet draft (June), it read [underlined portions later deleted by the Diet subcommittee on revision, at the behest of GHQ]: "All property of the imperial household, other than the hereditary estates, shall belong to the state. The income from all imperial properties shall be paid into the national treasury, and allowances and expenses of the imperial household, as defined by law, shall be appropriated by the Diet in the annual budget."

36. RM312.ART88.
37. RM365.PM.SP18.P2.
38. RM365.AM.SP89.

39. RM365.PM.SP4. For a different impression of the events of May 12, see Dower, *Embracing Defeat*, 262–266.

40. RM390.1.P1.5

41. RM389.PM.SP30.

42. RM404.1.P1.

43. RM394.P11. Shidehara soon joined in accepting the position that the Legislation Bureau, under intense pressure from SCAP, had taken.

44. RM386.PM.SP84.

45. RM386.PM.SP81–82.

46. RM390.1.P1.5.

47. RM390.3.P1.3

48. RM390.3.P1.4.

49. RM390.3.P1.5.

50. RM392.1.5.P1.

51. RM392 and RM 393. Compare Kanamori before the revision committee. RM412.AM.SP1–7.

52. RM394.

53. RM404.

54. RM404.

55. RM405.AM.SP109–111.

56. RM406.P1.

57. RM406.P3.

58. RM406.P4.

59. RM406.P7.

60. RM406.P8–9.

61. RM407.P4.

62. RM408.

63. SCAP had received these requirements from FEC in early July. RM327.TEXT2.P3.Bb. See chapter 18 (in this volume) for a discussion of these amendments.

64. RM409.

65. RM419.1.P2 (Ashida's diary entry for August 25).

66. RM419.

67. For a discussion, see chapter 18 (in this volume).

Chapter 18

1. RM382.1.

2. RM387.AM.SP92.

3. RM387.AM.SP114.

4. RM387.AM.SP113.

5. RM387.AM.SP128.

6. RM387.AM.SP108.

7. RM292.2.2.B.P1.

8. RM387.AM.SP161–163.

9. RM387.AM.SP199–201. Suzuki's crack about the American Constitution was excised from the version of these minutes forwarded to GHQ.

10. RM387.AM.SP259.

11. RM386.PM.SP149.

12. See RM388 (memo by Hagiwara, of the Foreign Office) for background.

13. RM389.PM.SP44.

14. RM389.PM.SP46. Ashida pointed out that the inserted provision ought not to be restricted to treaties adopted pursuant to this constitution, lest people question Japan's intention to abide by such agreements as the Hague and Geneva conventions. RM389.PM.SP59.

15. RM386.AM.SP216–220.

16. RM386.AM.SP221–228.

17. The FEC had demanded these changes as early as July 2. The American JCS communicated them to MacArthur shortly thereafter. RM327. Apparently MacArthur had been sitting on them, perhaps hoping that they would go away so that he would not have to interfere further with Japanese deliberations on their government's draft.

18. RM409.

19. RM411.AM.SP2. This point was stricken from the record forwarded to GHQ.

20. Loc. cit. This point too was stricken from the transcript for GHQ.

21. RM411.AM.SP19–20.

22. RM412.AM.SP2 and SP4.

23. RM412.AM.SP7.P3.

24. RM412.AM.SP7.P6.

25. RM412.AM.SP9–11.

26. RM412.AM.SP12 and 13.

27. RM412.AM.SP46, 47.

28. RM420.PM.SP33–36.

29. RM420.PM.SP10.P2.

30. RM420.PM.SP19.P5, P8.

31. RM420.PM.SP19.P12.

32. RM420.PM.SP21.P3.

33. RM420.AM.SP2. Ozaki was a major figure in Japanese politics, a reputation signaled by the fact that he was chosen to give the second major address (after Ashida) at this "solemn session." He had been elected a member of the Diet twenty-four times, beginning with the first Diet in 1890.

34. RM420.AM.SP1.P30–31, P3–4.

35. RM420.AM.SP1.P30–33. Ashida was very proud of this speech and of the warm, vigorous reception it got. For expressions of his vanity, see his diary entry for August 24, at RM419.3.P3–7. Earlier, at the concluding session of the revision committee, he had tossed congratulatory oratorical bouquets to the committee and subcommittee on revision, the government, and the press (but not to SCAP or GHQ). RM412.AM.SP49.P2 (August 21, 1946).

36. On August 21, he had remarked that the text was "spoiled by unpolished phrases and difficult passages," especially in the preamble. RM412.AM.SP7. Cf. RM420.AM.SP1.P20, where he admits crude rhetoric, especially in the preamble, explaining that the need for haste (to restore Japanese independence) precluded attention to niceties of style. Ōshima also called attention to marks of haste in the preamble. RM420.PM.SP25.

37. RM420.PM.SP19.

38. The Social Democratic amendments were presented to the committee on revision by Suzuki (RM412.AM.SP16), and to the plenary meeting of the House of Representatives by Hara Hyōnosuke (RM420.PM.SP6).

39. RM420.PM.SP6. The government draft published in March must have been "quite a surprise" to the Liberals and Progressives, Hara said. Citing documents that outlined the conservatives' initial position (in January 1946) on *kokutai* and the consti-

tutional foundations of imperial authority, he noted that the draft had already traveled a considerable distance in a leftward direction. Indeed, at the concluding meeting of the subcommittee on revision, Suzuki, a Social Democrat, had declared that the text was "now almost perfect." RM412.AM.SP16.P1.

40. RM420.PM.SP6.

41. Loc. cit.

42. This was an unfair taunt. The Social Democrats had not proposed to alter this ceremonial power of the emperor.

43. RM420.PM.SP8.

44. RM420.PM.SP1.P18, 25. Ashida's exposition of article 88 in the latter passage is particularly convoluted. Why was he so grudging? He seemed particularly eager to distance himself from the government's position on this unpopular article. Perhaps he was paying Yoshida back for leaving him exposed during the quarrel that led to the removal of Speaker Higai. See chapter 17, "The Issue Comes to a Head," 265–266.

45. RM420.PM.SP19.P11

46. RM420.PM.SP17.P18.

47. RM420.PM.SP17.P19.

48. RM420.AM.SP1.P15.

49. RM420.PM.SP28–36.

50. RM420.PM.SP38.

51. RM422.

Chapter 19

1. The opening words of the preamble read: "We, the Japanese people, acting through our *duly elected representatives* in the National Diet. . . ." RM417.PRE.P1.

2. There was a question in some minds as to whether, under article LXXIII, the Diet could amend an imperial project for constitutional revision. Presumably, however, if the House of Representatives could, the House of Peers could, too.

3. RM420.PM.SP38.P2.

4. RM438.P2.

5. RM422.

6. RM473.4.AM.SP2.P4.

7. Military members had already been purged. Also, the ranks of the Peers had been swelled by the emperor's postwar appointment of men of peaceful and humanitarian reputation. To that extent, the deck was stacked.

8. Note that the revision subcommittee of the House of Representatives had also done its work of drafting amendments behind closed doors.

9. RM475.PM.SP159.

10. RM478.PM.SP51.

11. RM430.AM.SP5.P9.

12. RM430.AM.SP5.P9–11.

13. RM423.AM.SP2.P1, 38. Cf. Sawada, RM421.PM.SP2.P1.

14. Takayanagi's reputation is indicated by the fact that, when the Japanese government decided in the mid-1950s to conduct an inquiry into the origins of the postwar constitution, it named him to head the inquiry. The so-called Takayanagi Report was submitted to Prime Minister Ikeda Hayato in 1964. (See chapter 21, this volume.)

15. RM421.AM.SP4.P1 and P2.

16. This is one of the themes found in an illuminating study by Tanaka Hideo, "The Conflict Between Two Legal Traditions in Making the Constitution of Japan," in Robert

E. Ward and Sakamoto Yoshikazu, eds., *Democratizing Japan: The Allied Occupation* (University of Hawaii Press, 1987), 107–132.

17. RM421.AM.SP4.P4.

18. RM421.AM.SP4.P18.

19. RM421.AM.SP4.P5–8.

20. RM421.AM.SP4.P22.

21. RM421.PM.SP2.P4. Yoshida's speech is at RM420.PM.SP38.P2.

22. Sawada expressed regret that the new system would abolish the peerage. Japan would still be a monarchy, he noted, and peerage went with monarchy. RM430.PM.SP2.P1.

23. RM421.PM.SP2.P15–21.

24. RM421.PM.SP3.P1–7.

25. RM421.PM.SP4.P1 and SP7.P4.

26. RM421.PM.SP8.P7 and P8.

27. RM423.AM.SP2.P1.

28. RM423.AM.SP2.P1–11. MacArthur's call is at RM313.

29. RM421.PM.SP2.P17.

30. See chapter 4 (in this volume).

31. RM428.AM.SP2.P45–P46.

32. RM426.AM.SP7.P6–P8.

33. In 1946, still called Tokyo Imperial University (the name was changed to the University of Tokyo in March 1947).

34. Texts of these outlines can be found at RM103 and RM120.

35. RM423.AM.SP2.P13–17; RM423.PM.SP3.P4–5. The word "revolution" was not used by Nanbara, but it was attributed to him by Kanamori (at RM423.AM.SP6.P3), and it fairly summarizes Nanbara's views, as expressed here.

36. RM421.PM.SP4.P2–3, 10–14.

37. RM423.AM.SP2.P20–22.

38. RM428.PM.SP2.P22.

39. RM426.AM.SP8.P8–13.

40. RM430.AM.SP11.

41. RM423.AM.SP9.P4.

42. James Fallows, a prominent journalist with a special interest in Japan, has taken this position, in a commentary on National Public Radio.

43. RM054.

44. RM423.AM.SP2.P23–P26.

45. RM423.AM.SP3. Shidehara's boast here was a bit of a stretch. Theodore Mc-Nelly's research has established that article 9 was drafted at GHQ. ("General MacArthur and the Constitutional Disarmament of Japan," in T. H. McNelly, *The Origins of Japan's Democratic Constitution* [University Press of America, 2000].) At a meeting with MacArthur on February 21, Shidehara was persuaded that the constitutional renunciation of war and armaments was an essential part of the revision package. RM200. In that sense, he "participated in drafting" article 9.

46. RM430.AM.SP10.P2–3.

47. RM421.AM.SP4.P22; RM426.AM.SP5.P1–2.

48. RM423.AM.SP2.P27.

49. RM423.PM.SP8.P33; SP10.P1–8.

50. RM426.AM.SP3.P1–7.

Chapter 20

1. Originally, the House of Peers was supposed to have taken just three weeks to conduct its review of the revision. As the meetings stretched out, Yoshida's cabinet became increasingly impatient. For its own reasons, GHQ was also determined to avoid unnecessary delay; it could only provide opportunity for further FEC meddling.

2. RM439.AM.SP2.P4. For Sasaki's defense of the Konoe Commission's effort, see RM437.AM.SP15.

3. RM437.AM.SP12.P1.

4. RM436.PM.SP31.P2.

5. Abe, in his report to the plenary session, took note of this assertion, adding that the government had no intention of issuing an official interpretation of the Constitution similar to Itō Hirobumi's *Commentary* on the Meiji Constitution. RM477.AM.SP3.P11.

6. RM435.AM.SP2.P4 (Matsumoto Gaku), SP5.P3 (Yoshida), and SP9.P9 (Kanamori).

7. RM446.PM.SP12.P2.

8. RM448.PM.SP63.P3.

9. Abe later reported that the word "symbol" had been chosen partly *because* of its unfamiliarity. It carried the least baggage. RM477.AM.SP3.P24.

10. RM448.PM.SP43.P2. Recall that "head" was the word MacArthur used, in his brief guidelines for the GS drafting committee. RM141.

11. RM448.PM.SP44.P1 and SP44.P2.

12. Shidehara did not indicate whether it was the American or Japanese drafters who had come up with this term. It was in fact Kades. As an avid student of British constitutional history, he was well acquainted with the Statute of Westminster. Shidehara, like Yoshida an Anglophile, was probably pleased to learn where the term had come from.

13. RM448.AM.SP6.

14. RM437.PM.SP9.P12 and SP9.P13.

15. RM473.4.PM.SP29.

16. RM478.PM.SP16; cf. SP22 for the names of those in favor and opposed.

17. RM457.PM.SP40.P3.

18. Finn reports a remark Yoshida made when he first met Kades: "So you're the man who is going to make us democratic. Ha, ha." Richard B. Finn, *Winners in Peace*, (University of California Press, 1992), 124.

19. RM437.AM.SP9.

20. RM439.PM.SP6.P6 (Matsudaira's question); RM439.PM.SP7.P2–P4 (Kanamori's answer).

21. RM468.PM.SP94 and SP95.

22. RM468.PM.SP96 and SP97.

23. RM467.AM.SP76.P4. Sawada thought judicial review conflicted with the supremacy of the Diet. Kanamori's reply was Madisonian: The separation of powers should not be absolute; constitutional balance required checks. RM467.AM.SP73 and SP76. Sasaki would have preferred a special court for assessing constitutionality, the kind they had in Germany and Austria. RM467.PM.SP35.P2.

24. Takayanagi used this word. RM467.PM.SP56.P2.

25. Takayanagi was probably referring to California.

26. RM473.2.PM.SP14; cf. RM467.PM.SP56.P1.

27. RM473.2.PM.SP17–19.

28. RM473.2.AM.SP25.

29. RM475.PM.SP154.

30. See, for example, RM445.AM.SP2–25; also RM464.AM.SP5 and SP7, where Kanamori presents a thorough discussion of the history and theory of bicameralism. In the latter remarks, he observed trenchantly that "responsible cabinet government cannot be realized in the United States," owing to the existence of two chambers of practically equal power.

31. RM473.1.AM.SP6.

32. SCAP's policy was outlined in a memo of September 10, written by Frank Hays. It said "there must be no discrimination between electors for the House of Councilors and electors to the House of Representatives." RM447.P4.

33. Kanamori finally got it right on October 1. RM473.3.PM.SP98.

34. RM473.4.AM.SP21. Even the Progressive Party found it difficult to swallow a second chamber, he said.

35. In the spring of 1946, Yamamoto had drafted a version of the preamble in spoken Japanese, but cabinet officials declined to submit it to the Americans. See chapter 10 (in this volume).

36. On this occasion, Abe, the chairman of the subcommittee, asked Yamamoto to submit suggestions about changes in expression in writing, for consideration later. RM455.PM.SP6.P1.

37. The quoted terms are used in a colloquy on September 13 between Yamamoto and Abe. RM475.PM.SP13.P1.

38. RM475.PM.SP12. Cf. RM475.PM.SP136, where Mishima Michiharu notes that alternates versions of the preamble had been prepared not only by Yamamoto, but by Takayanagi and Makino as well.

39. RM445.PM.SP72.P1.

40. RM473.2.PM.SP23.

41. RM473.2.PM.SP30.

42. RM473.2.PM.SP21–SP31.

43. RM469.AM.SP2.

44. RM469.AM.SP3.

45. RM469.AM.SP31.P2.

46. RM469.AM.SP31.

47. RM469.AM.SP36 and SP72.

48. RM469.AM.SP36.

49. RM469.PM.SP2.

50. The concern seems to have come from many members of the FEC, including the Chinese, Canadians, Soviets, Australians, and British. Smelling a rat in the changes to article 9, they decided to demand this additional assurance against a military resurgence. See Koseki, 202–204; and cf. RM470.P1.

51. RM473.1.PM.SP7, SP8.

52. RM471.2.P1.

53. These concerns also led Kades to insist on a re-phrasing of the second clause of article 9, renouncing armed forces. "For the above purpose" seemed too vague. It would become "In order to accomplish the aim of the preceding paragraph." RM471.3.P13.

54. RM473.1.AM.SP6.

55. RM473.1.AM.SP3. Or, as Takagi put it, GHQ wanted to be sure that "a civil official [will] be the minister of military affairs when we can create an army in the future." RM473.3.PM.SP90.

56. RM473.3.PM.SP71. Earlier Kanamori had reported that GHQ did not want this

request to be "written up in the newspapers." If it had to be talked about, it should be presented as a "wish of GHQ that had actually originated outside GHQ." RM473.1.AM.SP3.

57. In his report to the plenary session, Abe listed several of the options considered. RM477.AM.SP3.P44. At the same session, Ōkōchi provided an illuminating review of the reasons for choosing *bunmin*, at RM477.PM.SP11.

58. RM473.2.AM.SP7.

59. RM473.2.AM.SP14.

60. Perhaps he was referring to deleting the electoral review of judges, or adding respect for family life to article 24, one of Tadokoro's favorite ideas. See RM473.4.PM.SP32.

61. RM473.3.AM.SP75, SP76, SP80, SP86.

62. RM473.4.AM.SP3, SP4.

63. RM474.

64. Abe's report to the plenary session slid past article 9 almost without comment. RM477.AM.SP3.P29

65. RM473.3.PM.SP80.

66. RM437.AM.SP7.P1. Kanamori's comments to the subcommittee in the House of Representatives were a good deal more candid and illuminating.

67. RM455.PM.SP38.P4.

68. Besides MacArthur and Shidehara, one might cite the postwar efforts of U.S. Supreme Court Justice Owen Roberts.

69. RM475.PM.SP93–97. The committee did decide to keep copies, in its records, of the revised drafts of the preamble made by Yamamoto, Takayanagi, and Makino. RM475.PM.SP136–137.

70. RM475.PM.SP65.

71. RM475.PM.SP92–93.

72. RM475.PM.SP154. Ōkōchi had been the principal proponent of eliminating the electoral review of judges (article 79). Here he withdrew his proposal without comment. Presumably he found Kanamori's argument before the subcommittee persuasive, to the effect that officials lacking the sanction of popular support would be weak in the new Japan. RM475.PM.SP153.P1; cf. RM467.AM.SP76. It might actually have been politically possible to eliminate this provision. Kades opposed it, as did many at GHQ, according to Takayanagi. Also, an editorial in *Jiji Shinpō* called it "reckless," "the greatest defect in the new constitution." Citing criticism of the idea in America, the editorial concluded: "There is no need for hastily adopting new systems which are still in the testing stage." RM479.3.P2

73. RM475.PM.SP145.P1.

74. RM475.PM.SP156, 157, 159.

75. RM477.AM.SP3.P3. Cf. P24, where Abe noted that "a hot controversy raged in a tense atmosphere" over the whole of chapter I.

76. RM477.AM.SP3.P13.

77. RM477.AM.SP3.P23, P44. Paragraph 44 contains a review of various terms that had been considered as translations of the English word, "civilian," and tells why the committee chose the neologism, *bunmin*, antonym to *bushin* (military person).

78. RM477.AM.SP3.P31.

79. RM477.AM.SP3.P45.

80. RM477.AM.SP5 and SP6.

81. RM024.P12.

82. RM477.PM.SP2.P41.

83. RM477.PM.SP2.P43.

84. RM477.PM.SP4.P14, P41, and P37. Matsumura said that articles 20 and 89 of the revision would prevent a repetition of that mistake. Article XXVIII of the Meiji Constitution reads: "Japanese subjects shall, within limits not prejudicial to peace and order, and not antagonistic to their duties as subjects, enjoy freedom of religious belief."

85. Matsumura presented a detailed analysis of these edicts, the most comprehensive of the summer. RM477.PM.SP4.P30-35.

86. RM477.PM.SP9.P2-P4.

87. RM477.PM.SP9.P12.

88. RM477.PM.SP9.P16, P14.

89. RM477.PM.SP11.P27.

90. RM478.AM.SP5.P2, P6, P8, P10, P12.

91. RM478.AM.SP7.P8-9.

92. RM478.AM.SP7.P12, P13, P17, and P18.

93. RM478.AM.SP7.P22.

94. Pressed for his own comment, Yoshida simply endorsed what Kanamori had said.

95. RM478.PM.SP26.

96. RM478.PM.SP34. This was a record vote; the names of those voting for and against were listed.

97. The actual vote was not recorded.

98. It added a third paragraph to article 59, empowering the House of Representatives to call for a conference committee between the two houses of the Diet, in the event they passed different versions of a bill. The purpose of the amendment, said Abe, was "to make assurance doubly sure." RM477.AM.SP3.P43.

99. RM478.PM.SP51.

100. RM478.PM.SP53.

Chapter 21

1. The best general account is Alfred C. Oppler, *Legal Reform in Occupied Japan: A Participant Looks Back* (Princeton University Press, 1976).

2. For a summary of the tedious exchange between SCAP, Washington, and the FEC in 1947–1949, see Blakeslee, *The Far Eastern Commission* (U.S. Government Printing Office, 1953), 63–65.

3. Ibid., 58–59.

4. Ibid., 59, 60.

5. RM509. See also Koseki, *The Birth of Japan's Postwar Constitution* 244–245

6. Koseki, 246. See also Satō Isao's comments in Koseki, 247.

7. Ibid., 250.

8. See *Hōritsu jihō* 31(4) (April 1949), and Koseki, 248–249.

9. For background and details of this policy change, see Richard B. Finn, *Winners in Peace* (University of California Press, 1982), 195–210.

10. Ibid., 171.

11. George F. Kennan, *Memoirs* (Little, Brown, 1967), 368–369, 375–377.

12. For NSC 13/2, "Recommendations with Respect to U.S. Policy Toward Japan," and related documents, see Ōkurashō zaiseishishitsu, comp. *Shōwa zaiseishi* (Tōyō Keizai Shinpōsha, 1982), vol. 20, 183–195.

13. Finn, 250–251.

14. Ibid., 232.

15. Ibid., 234. Finn calculates that 1,200 were purged from government jobs, many of them teaching jobs, and 11,000 from private-sector jobs.

16. This point is developed by John W. Dower, *Empire and Aftermath* (Council on East Asian Studies, 1979), chap. 10.

17. H. Fukui, "Twenty Years of Revisionism," in Dan Fenno Henderson, ed., *The Constitution of Japan* (University of Washington Press, 1969), 46.

18. Ibid., 47 n.20.

19. Ibid., 49 n.27.

20. We have two excellent reports on the committee: Robert E. Ward, "The Commission on the Constitution and Prospects for Constitutional Change in Japan," *Journal of Asian Studies*, 24(4) (1965): 401–429; and John M. Maki, "The Documents of Japan's Commission on the Constitution," *Journal of Asian Studies*, 24(3) (1965): 475–489. Maki published an expanded version by the same title in Dan Fenno Henderson, ed., *The Constitution of Japan: The First Twenty Years, 1947–1967* (University of Washington Press, 1969), 279–299. Also, John M. Maki, *Japan's Commission on the Constitution: The Final Report* (University of Washington Press, 1980), a translation of the Committee's final report and introduction.

21. Maki, 20–21.

22. *Shōwa zaiseishi*, vol. 20, 253–254.

23. Finn, 263–266.

24. For a thorough account of these events, see Dower, *Empire and Aftermath*, chap. 10.

25. RM523.

26. Maki, 296–300.

27. Ibid., 304–308.

28. Only the House of Representatives can be dissolved. The House of Councillors has a fixed term. But the lower house dominates the Diet, including the process that produces prime ministers and cabinets.

29. For a review of the first eight dissolutions (1948–1966) when this pattern was set, see D. C. S. Sissons, "Dissolution of the Japanese Lower House," in *Papers on Modern Japan* (Australian National University), (January 1968), 106–137.

30. J.A.A. Stockwin, *Governing Japan* (Blackwell, 1999), 72–77.

31. Kenneth Pyle, *The Making of Modern Japan*, (D.C. Heath, 1996), 277.

32. Stockwin, 168–169.

33. An English text, "A Proposal for the Revision of the Text of the Constitution of Japan" (Yomiuri Shinbunsha, 1994), appeared on November 3, 1994. See our analysis in Moore and Robinson, "Yomiuri shian o kaibō suru," *This is Yomiuri* (January 1995): 108–121.

34. NHK television aired in 1981 a one-hour docudrama on the SCAP drafting session of February 4–10, 1946, culminating in the February 13 meeting of MacArthur's GS members with Ministers Matsumoto and Yoshida.

35. Miyazawa Kiichi and Nakasone Yasuhiro, *Kaiken Goken* (Asahi Shinbunsha, 1997).

36. See Theodore McNelly, *The Origins of Japan's Democratic Constitution* (University Press of America, 2000), 171–174.

37. For a brief description, see Odawara Atsushi, "The Dawn of Constitutional Debate," in *Japan Quarterly* (January–April 2000).

38. Ibid.

39. Hanshi Nobuyuki, chairman of the LDP's commission on the constitution, quoted in Odawara Atsushi, "The Dawn of Constitutional Debate," *Japan Quarterly* (January–April 2000): 20.

40. *Yomiuri Shinbun*, May 3, 2001.

Bibliography

-
-
-

- *Primary Sources*

Alfred Hussey Papers. Microfilm reels 4–6. University of Michigan Library.

Archives of Foreign Missions Conference of North America. National Council of Churches (New York City).

Charles L. Kades Papers. Amherst College, Frost Library Archives.

Congressional Information Service. *Framing the Constitution of Japan: Primary Sources in English, 1944–1949*. Bethesda, MD: University Microfilms, 1989.

Congressional Record. 19th Cong., 1st Sess. (Sept. 18, 1945). pp. 8671–8680.

Donald Robinson's Correspondence and Notes on Interviews with Charles Kades, 1993–1994. Kades Papers. Amherst College, Frost Library.

"Ellerman Notebook E." In *Hussey Papers (HP)*, microfilm reel 4.

Gaimushō gaikō bunsho [Japanese Foreign Ministry Records]. Microfilm reel A'0092.

Kenneth Wallace Colgrove Papers. Northwestern University Archives, Evanston, IL.

Papers of Major General Courtney Whitney. MacArthur Memorial Archives and Library, Record Group 16.

Prange Collection, Kades Papers. University of Maryland at College Park, McKeldin Library, pt. B.

General Douglas MacArthur's Private Correspondence, 1848–1964. MacArthur Memorial Archives and Library, Record Group 10.

Sangiin jimukyoku, comp. *Teikoku kenpō kaiseian tokubetsu iin shōiinkai hikki yōshi* [Summary of the Subcommittee Proceedings of the House of Peers Special Committee on Revision of the Imperial Constitution]. trans. John M. Maki. Tokyo: Zaidan Hōjin Sanyōkai, 1997.

Satō Tatsuo Papers, nos. 601–603. Tokyo: National Diet Library.

Sekiya Teizaburō Diary. Tokyo: National Diet Library.

Shūgiin teikoku kenpō kaiseian iin shōiinkai sokkiroku [Shorthand Record of the Debates on the Bill to Revise the Imperial Constitution in the Subcommittee of the House of Representatives]. Tokyo: Shūeikai, 1995.

Takagi Yasaka. "Memorandum on Prince Konoe's Contribution in 1945 to Constitutional Revision in Japan." An informal talk to faculty members of International Christian University, May 30, 1952 (copy on file in Kades Papers, Frost Library, Amherst College).

U.S. National Archives, Record Group 226 (OSS File).

U.S. National Archives 2 (College Park, MD), Record Group 331. Box 2208.

U.S. Department of State. *Bulletin*, Sept. 23, 1945.

U.S. Department of State. *Foreign Relations of the United States, Conference of Berlin (1945)*, 2 vols. Washington, DC: U.S. Government Printing Office, 1956.

U.S. Department of State. *Foreign Relations of the United States, 1944–1946*. Washington, DC: U.S. Government Printing Office, 1965, 1969, and 1971.

William Merrill Vories Diary. Ōmi Brotherhood, Ōmi Hachiman, Japan.

Books and Articles

"A Proposal for the Revision of the Text of the Constitution of Japan." *Yomiuri shinbun* (November 3, 1994).

Acheson, Dean. *Present at the Creation: My Years in the State Department.* New York: Norton, 1969.

Akita, George. *Foundations of Constitutional Government in Modern Japan, 1868–1900.* Cambridge: Harvard University Press, 1967.

Amar, Akhil R. *The Bill of Rights.* New Haven: Yale University Press, 1998.

Auden, W. H. "September 1, 1939." In *Another Time.* New York: Random House, 1940.

Barker, Ernest. *Reflections on Government.* London: Oxford University Press, 1942.

Bix, Herbert P. *Hirohito and the Making of Modern Japan.* New York: HarperCollins, 2000.

Blakeslee, George H. "Negotiating to Establish the Far Eastern Commission." In *Negotiating with the Russians*, ed. Raymond Dennett and Joseph E. Johnson. Boston: World Peace Foundation, 1951.

Blakeslee, George H. *The Far Eastern Commission: A Study in International Cooperation, 1945–1952.* Washington, DC: U.S. Government Printing Office, 1953.

Borton, Hugh. *Japan's Modern Century.* New York: Ronald Press, 1955.

Bowen, Roger. *Innocence Is Not Enough: The Life and Death of Herbert Norman.* New York: M.E. Sharpe, 1986.

Butow, Robert J. C. *Japan's Decision to Surrender.* Stanford: Stanford University Press, 1954.

Byrnes, James F. *Speaking Frankly.* New York: Harper and Brothers, 1947.

Chace, James. *Acheson: The Secretary of State Who Created the American World.* Cambridge, MA: Harvard University Press, 1998.

Cohen, Theodore. *Remaking Japan: The American Occupation as New Deal.* New York: Free Press, 1987.

Creemers, Wilhelmus H. M. *Shrine Shinto after World War II.* Leiden: E.J. Brill, 1968.

Crowley, James B. *Japan's Quest for Autonomy: National Security and Foreign Policy, 1930–1938.* Princeton, NJ: Princeton University Press, 1966.

Dahl, Robert. *Polyarchy.* New Haven: Yale University Press, 1971.

Davey, Cyril J. *Kagawa of Japan.* London: Epworth Press, 1960.

Dore, Ronald P. *Education in Tokugawa Japan.* London: Oxford University Press, 1965.

Dower, John W. *Embracing Defeat: Japan in the Wake of World War II.* New York: New Press, 1999.

Dower, John W. *Empire and Aftermath: Yoshida Shigeru and the Japanese Experience, 1878–1954.* Cambridge: Council on East Asian Studies, Harvard University, 1979.

Downs, Darley. "Effects of Wartime Pressures on Churches and Missions in Japan." M.A. thesis, Union Theological Seminary (New York City), 1946.

Duus, Peter. *Party Rivalry and Political Change in Taishō Japan.* Cambridge, MA: Harvard University Press, 1968.

Emmerson, John K. *The Japanese Thread: A Life in the U.S. Foreign Service.* New York: Holt, Rinehart and Winston, 1978.

Endō Shūsaku. *Silence.* New York: Pivot Books, 1980.

Farley, Miriam. *Aspects of Japan's Labor Problems.* New York: John Day, 1950.

Fellers, Bonner Frank. "Our New Friends the Japanese." *Nation's Business* 36 (February 1948): 41–43.

Finn, Richard B. *Winners in Peace: MacArthur, Yoshida and Postwar Japan.* Berkeley: University of California Press, 1992.

Fujitani, Tadashi. *Splendid Monarchy: Power and Pageantry in Modern Japan.* Berkeley: University of California Press, 1996.

Fukui, H. "Twenty Years of Revisionism." In *The Constitution of Japan,* ed. Dan Fenno Henderson. Seattle: University of Washington Press, 1969.

Gayn, Mark. *Japan Diary.* Tokyo: Charles E. Tuttle, 1981.

Gordon, Beate S. *The Only Woman in the Room.* Tokyo: Kōdansha International, 1997.

Greenberg, Douglas et al., eds. *Constitutionalism and Democracy: Transitions in the Contemporary World.* New York: Oxford University Press, 1993.

Grew, Joseph. *Turbulent Era.* 2 vols. Boston: Houghton Mifflin, 1952.

Hamilton, Alexander, James Madison, and John Jay. *The Federalist Papers,* ed. Clinton Rossiter. New York: New American Library, 1961.

Harries, Meirion and Susie Harries. *Sheathing the Sword: The Demilitarization of Postwar Japan.* New York: Macmillan, 1987.

Havens, Thomas R. H. *Valley of Darkness: The Japanese People and World War II.* New York: W.W. Norton, 1978.

Hellegers, Dale M. *We the Japanese People: World War II and the Origins of the Japanese Constitution.* 2 vols. Stanford, CA: Stanford University Press, 2001.

Henderson, Dan Fenno, ed. *The Constitution of Japan: Its First Twenty Years, 1947–1967.* Seattle: University of Washington Press, 1968.

Horton, Douglas. *The Return to Japan.* New York: Friendship Press, 1946.

Huntington, Samuel P. *The Third Wave: Democratization in the Late Twentieth Century.* Norman: University of Oklahoma Press, 1991.

Iglehart, Charles. *International Christian University.* Tokyo: International Christian University, 1964.

Inoue, Kyoko. *MacArthur's Japanese Constitution: A Linguistic and Cultural Study of Its Making.* Chicago: University of Chicago Press, 1991.

Irokawa Daikichi. *The Age of Hirohito: In Search of Modern Japan,* trans. Mikiso Hane and John K. Urda. New York: Free Press, 1995.

Ishiguro Kazuo. *An Artist of the Floating World.* London: Faber and Faber, 1986.

Itō Hirobumi. *Commentaries on the Constitution of the Empire of Japan,* trans. Itō Miyoji. Westport, CT: Greenwood Press, 1978.

Kades, Charles L. "The American Role in Revising Japan's Constitution." *Political Science Quarterly* 104(2) (September 1989): 215–247.

Kase Toshikazu. *Journey to the Missouri.* New Haven: Yale University Press, 1950.

Kausikan, Bilahari. "Asia's Different Standard." *Foreign Policy* 92 (1993): 24–41.

Kawai Michi. *Sliding Doors.* Tokyo: Keisen Jogakuen, 1950.

Kennan, George F. *Memoirs: 1925–1950.* Boston: Little, Brown, 1967.

Koseki Shōichi. *The Birth of Japan's Postwar Constitution,* trans. Ray A. Moore. Boulder, CO: Westview Press, 1997.

Kraus, Herbert. *The Crisis of German Democracy: A Study of the Spirit of the Constitution of Weimar*, ed. William Starr Myers. Princeton, NJ: Princeton University Press, 1932.

Leahy, William D. *I Was There*. New York: Whittlesey House, 1950.

LeMay, Curtis. *Mission with LeMay*. New York: Doubleday, 1965.

Lincoln, Charles Z. *Constitutional History of New York State*. 5 vols. Rochester, NY: Lawyers Cooperative Publishing, 1906.

Linz, Juan J. and Alfred Stepan. *Problems of Democratic Transition and Consolidation: Southern Europe, South America and Post-Communist Europe*. Baltimore: Johns Hopkins University Press, 1996.

Luney, Percy R. and K. Takahashi, eds. *Japanese Constitutional Law*. Tokyo: University of Tokyo Press, 1993.

MacArthur, Douglas. *A Soldier Speaks: Public Papers and Speeches of General of the Army Douglas MacArthur*. New York: Praeger, 1965.

MacArthur, Douglas. *Reminiscences*. New York: McGraw-Hill, 1964.

Mackin, Thomas. "As Kagawa Sees Japan's Future." *Christian Century* (October 10, 1945): 1154–1155.

Maki, John M. "The Documents of Japan's Commission on the Constitution." *Journal of Asian Studies* 24(3) (1965): 475–489.

Maki, John M., trans. and ed. *Japan's Commission on the Constitution: The Final Report*. Seattle: University of Washington Press, 1980.

Masumi Junnosuke. *Postwar Politics in Japan, 1945–1955*. Berkeley: Center for Japanese Studies, University of California, 1985.

McNelly, Theodore H. "Domestic and International Influence on Constitutional Revision in Japan, 1945–1946." Ph.D. diss., Columbia University, 1952.

McNelly, Theodore H. "Herbert Norman: Security Risk or Victim of McCarthyism?" Unpublished paper, presented at Southeast Regional Seminar on Japan, George Mason University, October 7, 2000.

McNelly, Theodore H. "Induced Revolution: The Policy and Process of Constitutional Reform in Occupied Japan." In *Democratizing Japan: The Allied Occupation*, ed. Robert E. Ward and Sakamoto Yoshikazu. Honolulu: University of Hawaii Press, 1987.

McNelly, Theodore. H., ed. *Sources in Modern East Asian History and Politics*. New York: Appleton-Century-Croft, 1967.

McNelly, Theodore H. *The Origins of Japan's Democratic Constitution*. Lanham, MD: University Press of America, 2000.

Millis, Walter, ed. *The Forrestal Diaries*. New York: Viking Press, 1951.

Moore, Joe. *Japanese Workers and the Struggle for Power*. Madison: University of Wisconsin Press, 1983.

Moore, Ray A. "Japanese Government Materials on the American Occupation." In *The Occupation of Japan and Its Legacy to the Postwar World*, ed. L. H. Redman. Norfolk: MacArthur Memorial, 1976.

Moore, Ray A., and Donald L. Robinson, eds. *The Constitution of Japan: A Documentary History of Its Framing and Adoption, 1945–1947*. Princeton, NJ: Princeton University Press, 1998.

Nakamura Masanori. *The Japanese Monarchy: Ambassador Joseph Grew and the Making of the "Symbol Emperor System," 1931–1991*. New York: M.E. Sharpe, 1992.

Nishi, Toshio. *Unconditional Democracy: Education and Politics in Occupied Japan*. Stanford, CA: Hoover Institution Press, 1982.

Oppler, Alfred C. *Legal Reform in Occupied Japan: A Participant Looks Back.* Princeton, NJ: Princeton University Press, 1976.

Odawara Atsushi. "The Dawn of Constitutional Debate." *Japan Quarterly* 47(1) (January–March 2000): 17–22.

Pacific War Research Society. comp. *Japan's Longest Day.* Tokyo: Kōdansha, 1968.

Parekh, Bhikhu. "The Cultural Particularlity of Liberal Democracy." *Political Studies* [Special Issue] 40 (1992): 160–175.

Patrick, Hugh and Henry Rosovsky, eds. *Asia's New Giant: How the Japanese Economy Works.* Washington, DC: Brookings Institution Press, 1976.

Perret, Geoffrey. *Old Soldiers Never Die: The Life of Douglas MacArthur.* New York: Random House, 1996.

A Proposal for the Revision of the Text of the Constitution of Japan. Tokyo: Yomiuri Shinbunsha, 1994.

Przeworski, Adam et al. *Sustainable Democracy.* Cambridge: Cambridge University Press, 1995.

Przeworski, Adam et al. "What Makes Democracy Endure?" *Journal of Democracy* 7(1) (1996): 39–55.

Pyle, Kenneth. *The Making of Modern Japan.* Boston: D.C. Heath, 1996.

Quigley, Harold S. *Japanese Government and Politics.* New York: Century, 1932.

Quigley, Harold S. *The New Japan: Government and Politics.* Minneapolis: University of Minnesota Press, 1956.

Robinson, Donald L. *"To the Best of My Ability": The Presidency and the Constitution.* New York: W.W. Norton, 1987.

Rossiter, Clinton L. *Constitutional Dictatorship.* Princeton, NJ: Princeton University Press, 1948.

Sayle, Murray. "Letter from Japan: A Dynasty Falters." *The New Yorker* (June 12, 2000): 84–91.

Sigal, Leon V. *Fighting to a Finish: The Politics of War Termination in the U.S. and Japan, 1945.* Ithaca, NY: Cornell University Press, 1988.

Sissons, D.C.S. "Dissolution of the Japanese Lower House." In *Papers on Modern Japan* (January 1968): 106–137.

Sources of Japanese Tradition, comp. Ryusaku Tsunoda, William Theodore deBary and Donald Keene. New York: Columbia University Press, 1958.

Strategic Air Warfare. Washington, DC: Office of Air Force History, 1988.

Stockwin, J.A.A. *Governing Japan: Divided Politics in a Major Economy* (3rd ed.). Oxford, UK: Blackwell, 1999.

Sundquist, James L. *The Decline and Resurgence of Congress.* Washington, DC: Brookings Institution Press, 1981.

Supreme Commander of the Allied Powers (SCAP). Government Section. *Political Reorientation of Japan, September 1945 to September 1948.* 2 vols. Washington, DC: U.S. Government Printing Office, 1949.

Tanaka Hideo. "The Conflict between Two Legal Traditions in Making the Constitution of Japan." In *Democratizing Japan,* ed. Robert E. Ward and Sakamoto Yoshikazu. Honolulu: University of Hawaii Press, 1987.

Takemae Eiji. *GHQ [General Headquarters].* Tokyo: Iwanami Shinsho, 1983.

Titus, David. "The Making of the 'Symbol Emperor System' in Postwar Japan." *Modern Asian Studies* 14(4) (1980): 529–578.

Tōgō Shigenori. *The Cause of Japan.* New York: Simon and Schuster, 1956.

Truman, Harry S. *Memoirs.* New York: Doubleday, 1955.

Ward, Robert E. "The Commission on the Constitution and Prospects for Constitutional Change in Japan." *Journal of Asian Studies* 24(4) (1965): 401–429.

Ward, Robert E. and Sakamoto Yoshikazu, eds. *Democratizing Japan: The Allied Occupation.* Honolulu: University of Hawaii Press, 1987.

Whitney, Courtney. *MacArthur: His Rendezvous With History.* New York: Alfred A. Knopf, 1956.

Wildes, Harry E. *Typhoon Over Tokyo: The Occupation and Its Aftermath.* New York: Macmillan, 1954.

Williams, Justin, Sr. *Japan's Political Revolution under MacArthur: A Participant's Account* Athens: University of Georgia Press, 1979.

Wilson, George M. *Radical Nationalist in Japan: Kita Ikki, 1883–1937.* Cambridge, MA: Harvard University Press, 1969.

Woodward, William P. *The Allied Occupation of Japan and Japanese Religions.* Leiden: E.J. Brill, 1972.

Yoshida Shigeru. *The Yoshida Memoirs: The Story of Japan in Crisis,* trans. Kenichi Yoshida. London: Heinemann, 1961.

Japanese Language Sources

Etō Jun. *Mōhitotsu no sengoshi* [*Another Postwar History*]. Tokyo: Kōdansha, 1978.

Etō Jun. *Shūsen o toinaosu* [*Reexamining the Surrender*]. Tokyo: Hokuyōsha, 1980.

Etō Jun and Hatano Sumio, eds. *Senryō shiroku* [Occupation Period Documents], 4 vols. Tokyo: Kōdansha, 1981–1983.

Herbert Norman Zenshū [*Complete Works of E. Herbert Norman*]. 4 vols. Tokyo: Iwanami Shoten, 1977.

Hozumi Yatsuka. *Kenpō teiyō*. Tokyo: Yūhikaku, 1935.

Irie Toshio. *Kenpō seiritsu no keii to kenpōjō no shomondai* [*The Framing of the Constitution: Circumstances and Problems*]. Tokyo: Daiich Hōki Shuppan, 1976.

Kagawa Toyohiko. *Kagawa-den* [*Autobiography of Kagawa*]. Tokyo, 1956.

Kawai Michiko Bunshū [*Collected Writings of Kawai Michiko*]. Tokyo: Keisen Jogakuen Shiryōshitsu Iinkai, 1985.

Kenpō Chōsakai Jimukyoku, comp. *Kenpō Chōsakai daiyonkai sōkai gijiroku* [*Record of the Fourth Plenary Session of the Commission on the Constitution*]. Tokyo: Ōkurashō, 1961.

Kenpō Chōsakai Jimukyoku, comp. *Kenpō seitei no keika ni kansuru shōiinkai hōkokusho* [*Report of the Constitution Commission's Subcommittee on the Process of Constitutional Revision*]. Tokyo: Ōkurashō, 1961.

Kido Kōichi nikki [*The Diary of Kido Kōichi*]. Tokyo: Tokyo Daigaku Shuppankai, 1966.

Kinoshita Michio. *Sokkin nisshi* [*The Diary of an Imperial Aide*]. Tokyo: Bungei Shunjūsha, 1972.

Kojima Noboru. "Tennō to amerika to taiheiyō sensō" ["The Emperor, America and the Pacific War"]. *Bungei Shunjū* (November 1975).

Kojima Noboru. *Shiroku nihonkoku kenpō* [*The Japanese Constitution: A Historical Record*]. Tokyo: Bungei Shunjūsha, 1972.

Koseki Shōichi. *Shin kenpō no tanjō* [*The Birth of the New Constitution*]. Tokyo: Chuō Kōronsha, 1989.

Miyazawa Kiichi and Nakasone Yasuhiro. *Kaiken Goken* [*Change the Constitution, Protect the Constitution*]. Tokyo: Asahi Shinbunsha, 1997.

Moore, Ray A., ed. *Tennō ga baiburu o yonda hi* [*The Day the Emperor Read the Bible*]. Tokyo: Kōdansha, 1983.

Moore, Ray A., and Donald L. Robinson. "Yomiuri shian o kaibō suru" ["Dissecting Yomiuri's Proposal for Constitutional Reform"]. *This Is Yomiuri* (January 1995): 108–121.

Murakami Ichirō, ed. *Teikoku kenpō kaiseian gijiroku* [*Privy Council Hearings on the Bill to Revise the Japanese Imperial Constitution*]. Tokyo: Kokusho Kankōkai, 1986.

Nagai Ken'ichi and Toshitani Nobuyoshi, eds. *Shiryō nihonkoku kenpō* [A Documentary History of the Japanese Constitution]. 5 vols. Tokyo: Sanseidō, 1986.

Nishi Osamu. *Nihonkoku kenpō wa kōshite umareta* [*How the Japanese Constitution Was Born*]. Tokyo: Chuō Kōron Shinsho, 2000.

Ōkurashō zaiseishishitsu, comp. *Shōwa zaiseishi: shūsen kara kōwa made* [*Financial History of the Shōwa Period, 1945–1952*], vol. 20. Tokyo: Tōyō Keizai Shinpōsha, 1982.

Ōmori Minoru. *Makkasa no kenpō* [*MacArthur's Constitution*]. Tokyo: Kōdansha, 1975.

Sasakawa Ryōkichi. "Makkasa no kenpō seitei sakusen to Pentagon no kokuitachi [MacArthur's Strategy on Constitutional Revision and Pentagon Manipulators]." In *Kōhō no shisō to seido* [*Legal Thought and Institutions*], ed. Arata Masahiko. Tokyo: Shinsansha, 1999.

Satō Tatsuo. *Nihonkoku kenpō seiritsushi* [*Making the Japanese Constitution: A History*], vols. 1–2. Tokyo: Yūhikaku, 1962–1964.

Satō Tatsuo. "Nihonkoku kenpō seiritsushi—MacArthur sōan kara 'Nihonkoku kenpō made" ["Making the Japanese Constitution—From the 'MacArthur Draft' to the 'Japanese Constitution'"] *Juristo* 83(3) (June 1955).

Satō Tatsuo and Satō Isao. *Nihonkoku kenpō seiritsushi* [*Making the Japanese Constitution: A History*], vols. 3–4. Tokyo: Yūhikaku, 1994.

Seijika jinmei jiten [*Japanese Statesmen: A Biographical Dictionary*]. Tokyo: Nichigai Associates, 1990.

Shidehara Kijūrō. Tokyo: Shidehara heiwa zaidan [Shidehara Peace Foundation], 1955.

Shimizu Shin, ed. *Chikujō nihonkoku kenpō shingiroku* [*Record of the Debate on Each Article of the Japanese Constitution*]. 4 vols. Tokyo: Yūhikaku, 1962–1963.

Shindō Eiichi and Shimokabe Motoharu, eds. *Ashida Hitoshi nikki* [*Diary of Ashida Hitoshi*], vol. 1. Tokyo: Iwanami Shoten, 1986.

Shinobu Seizaburō. *Sengo nihon seijishi* [*A Political History of Postwar Japan*]. 2 vols. Tokyo: Kōdansha, 1965.

Shūsen shiroku [*History of Events Leading to Japan's Surrender*]. Tokyo: Japan Foreign Ministry, 1952.

Suzuki Yasuo. *Kenpō seitei zengo* [*When the Constitution Was Revised*]. Tokyo: Aoki Shoten, 1977.

Takayanagi Kenzō. *Tennō to kenpō daikyūjō* [*The Emperor and Article Nine*]. Tokyo: Yūki Shobō, 1963.

Takayanagi Kenzō, Ohtomo Ichirō, and Tanaka Hideo, eds. *Nihonkoku kenpō seitei no katei* [*The Making of the Constitution of Japan*]. 2 vols. Tokyo: Yūhikaku, 1972.

Tanaka Hideo. *Kenpō seitei katei oboegaki* [*Notes on the Framing of the Japanese Constitution*]. Tokyo: Yūhikaku, 1979.

Terasaki Hidenari and Mariko Terasaki Miller, eds. *Shōwa tennō dokuhakuroku—Terasaki Hidenari goyōgakari nikki* [*Emperor Hirohito's Monologue and the Diary of Imperial Aide Terasaki Hidenari*]. Tokyo: Bungei Shunjūsha, 1992.

Yabe Teiji. *Konoe Fumimaro*. 2 vols. Tokyo: Kōbundō, 1952.

Yoshida Shigeru. *Kaisōjūnen* [*Memories of Ten Years*]. 4 vols. Tokyo: Shinchōsha, 1957.

Index

Printed in the United States
16634LVS00001BA/44

9 780195 151169